Early Puebloan Occupations in the Chaco Region
Volume I: Excavations and Survey of Basketmaker III and Pueblo I Sites, Chaco Canyon, New Mexico, Part 1

by
Thomas C. Windes

With contributions by
Robert Crane, William Doleman, Alden Hayes, Richard Loose,
Marcia Truell (Newren), and Richard Wilshusen

National Park Service
Reports of the Chaco Center
Number 13

Arizona State Museum Archaeological Series 214

Arizona State Museum
The University of Arizona
Tucson, Arizona 85721-0026
Copyright © 2018 by the Arizona Board of Regents
All rights reserved.
Printed in the United States of America

ISBN (paper): 978-1-935565-00-0
Library of Congress Control Number: 2018944534

ARIZONA STATE MUSEUM ARCHAEOLOGICAL SERIES

General Editor: Richard C. Lange
Technical Editors: Kelly M. Alushaj, Alicia M. Vega, and Ilwad Osman

The *Archaeological Series* of the Arizona State Museum, The University of Arizona, publishes the results of research in archaeology and related disciplines conducted in the Greater Southwest. Original, monograph-length manuscripts are considered for publication, provided they deal with appropriate subject matter. Information regarding procedures on manuscript submission and review is given under Research Publications on the Arizona State Museum website: *www.statemuseum.arizona.edu/research/pubs.* Information may be also obtained from the General Editor, *Archaeological Series*, Arizona State Museum, P.O. Box 210026, The University of Arizona, Tucson, Arizona, 85721-0026; Email: langer@email.arizona.edu. Electronic publications and previous volumes in the Arizona State Museum Library or available from the University of Arizona Press are listed on the website noted above. Print-on-demand versions of the latest Arizona State Museum Archaeological Series may be obtained from several booksellers on-line.

The Arizona State Museum Archaeological Series is grateful to the many donors and supporters who continue to make this publication possible.

Front Cover: Overlooking 29SJ 423 (in the mounded sunlight in the center), an early Basketmaker III community on a prominent bench looking south-southwest. West end of West Mesa next to the Chaco River in the upper right with the Chuska Mountains along the far horizon. Mesa de Lobos and Hosta Butte along the upper left far horizon. © by Adriel Heisey (2013): NM14-7054-76.

Back Cover: Overlooking Shabik'eschee Village (29SJ 1659), a Basketmaker III community partly located on a prominent bench above the Chaco Wash; looking to the southwest. Note the great kiva excavation depression. Fajada Butte in the upper right with the Chuska Mountains along the right horizon. Mesa de Lobos and Hosta Butte along the upper left horizon. © by Adriel Heisey (2013): NM14-7054-144.

Contents

Contents	iii
List of Figures	xiii
List of Plates	xvii
List of Tables	xxi

Part 1 Contents

Chapter 1: Introduction	1
Research Strategy	4
Survey Overview	5
Excavation Overview	8
Management Goals	13
Acknowledgments	14
Chapter 2: The Natural Environment	23
Fauna	23
Flora	26
Factors Affecting Horticulture	31
Physiography and Geology	32
Soils	36
Hydrology	40
The Chaco Basin Periphery	40
The Chaco Canyon Area	42
Precipitation	42
Chaco Area Rain Gauges	45
Ground Water	50
Floodwater Events	51
Temperature	52
Wind	53
Summary	54
Chapter 3: Basketmaker III Site Excavation Reports	65
Investigations at 29SJ 299	66
Excavation Strategy	68
Site Description *by Richard Loose and Thomas C. Windes*	69
Pithouse A	69
Fill	69
Floor	69
Floor Features	69
Floor Artifacts	73
Walls	73
Pithouse A Antechamber	73
Fill	73
Floor	74
Pithouse B	74
Fill	74
Floor 1	75
Floor Features	76
Floor Artifacts	76
Walls	76
Wall Features	77
Discussion	77
Pithouse C	77
Fill	77
Floor	78

Chapter 3, cont'd.

Walls	78
Discussion	78
Pithouse D	78
Fill	81
Floor	81
Floor Features	81
Floor Artifacts	82
Walls	82
Discussion	84
Rooms/Cists	84
Room 1	84
Room 2	85
Room 3	85
Room 4	85
Room 5	85
Room 6	86
Room 7	86
Room 8	86
Room 9	87
Room 10	87
Room 11	87
Ramadas	88
Firepit	88
Site Discussion	88
Excavations at 29SJ 423 *by Thomas C. Windes*	88
Excavation Strategy	92
Pithouse A and the Shrine	93
Pit A	93
Pit B	94
Pit C	94
Other Features	95
The Shrine	95
Pithouse A Area Discussion	99
Pithouse B	100
Floor Materials	102
Area 1	102
Feature 1	102
Pithouse B Area Discussion	103
Pithouse C	103
The Great Kivas	104
Strategy	104
Structure 1	109
Great Kiva I	110
Great Kiva II	111
Walls and Benches	112
Floor and Floor Features	112
Firepit	113
Entry	113
Other Pits	113
Postholes	114
Floor Artifacts	115
Great Kiva III	115
Walls and Benches	115
Floor and Floor Features	116
Other Pits	117
Postholes	117

Chapter 3, cont'd.

The Roofing	117
Roof Engineering	118
Floor Specimens	118
Summary	119
Conclusions	119
Pithouse Y at Shabik'eschee (29SJ 1659) *by Alden C. Hayes*	120
Pithouse Y	122
Fill	122
Architectural Detail	124
Floor Materials	125
Dates	125
Pithouse Z	126
Discussion	126
Excavations at Site 29SJ 628 *by Marcia L. Truell (now M. L. Newren)*	126
Excavation Strategy	127
The Pithouses	129
Pithouse C	129
Fill in the Main Chamber	129
Fill in the Antechamber	133
Floor of the Main Chamber	133
Floor Materials	134
Floor Features	134
Walls	136
Wall Features	136
Ventilator System	136
Antechamber	137
Pithouse D	137
Fill in the Main Chamber	137
Fill in the Antechamber	140
Fill in the Ventilator	140
Floor in the Main Chamber	140
Floor Materials	141
Floor Features	141
Walls in the Main Chamber	142
Wall Features	142
Tunnel Connecting the Main Chamber and the Antechamber	142
Antechamber	142
Walls in the Antechamber	143
Ventilator System	143
Roofing	143
Pithouse G	143
Fill	146
Floor	146
Floor Materials	146
Floor Features	146
Walls	147
Wall Features	147
Ventilator System	147
Roofing	147
Pithouse E	148
Fill	148
Floor	148
Floor Materials	148
Floor Features	148
Walls	149
Wall Features	149

Chapter 3, cont'd.

Ventilator System	152
Roofing	152
Pithouse A	152
Fill	152
Floors	155
Floor Materials	156
Floor Features	156
Walls	157
Ventilator System	157
Roofing	157
Pithouse F	157
Fill	157
Floors	159
Floor Materials	159
Floor Features	159
Walls	159
Wall Features	160
Ventilator System	160
Roofing	160
Storage Cists	160
Storage Cist 1	160
Storage Cist 2	160
Storage Cist 3	160
Storage Cist 4	164
Storage Cist 5	164
Storage Cist 6	164
Storage Cist 7	164
Plaza	164
Summary and Conclusions	164
Discussion	165
Chapter 4: Pueblo I Site Excavation Reports	273
Testing at 29Mc 184	273
Further Investigations at 29SJ 299	277
Pithouse E	277
Fill	277
Floor 2	277
Floor Features	280
Floor Specimens	280
Walls	281
Wall Features	281
Discussion	281
Rooms	282
Room 12	282
Room 13	283
Room 14	283
Room 15	283
Ramada 2	283
Miscellaneous Site Features	287
Clay Basin	287
Site Conclusions	287
Excavations at 29SJ 721	288
Pithouse A	290
Fill	290
Floor	290
Floor Artifacts	292

Chapter 4, cont'd.

Floor Features	292
Fire Pit	292
Other Pits	292
Postholes	293
Walls	293
Wall Features	293
Ventilator	293
Wall Niche	294
Roof	294
Discussion	294
Pithouse B	295
Pithouse C	295
Fill	295
Floor	295
Floor Artifacts	298
Floor Features	298
Firepit	298
Walls	298
Wall Features	299
Roof	299
Discussion	299
Room 1	299
Floor	299
Walls	299
Roof	300
Cists and Isolated Features	300
Kiva 1	300
Fill	301
Floor	302
Floor Artifacts	302
Floor Features	304
Walls	304
Wall Features	304
Bench	304
Ventilator	305
Roof	305
Discussion	305
Discussion	307
Pueblo I Occupation at 29SJ 724	308
Rooms	311
Room 1	314
Fill	314
Floor	314
Floor Features	314
Firepit	314
Postholes	314
Floorpit	315
Floor Specimens	315
Walls	315
Doorways	315
Discussion	315
Room 2	315
Fill	315
Floor	315
Walls	315
Discussion	316

Chapter 4, cont'd.
- Room 3 — 316
  - Fill — 316
  - Floor — 316
  - Floor Features — 317
  - Floor Specimens — 317
  - Walls — 317
- Room 4 — 317
  - Fill — 317
  - Floor — 318
  - Floor Features — 318
  - Floor Specimens — 318
  - Walls — 318
  - Remarks — 318
- Room 5 — 318
  - Fill — 318
  - Floor — 318
  - Floor Features — 318
  - Floor Specimens — 318
  - Walls — 319
  - Discussion — 319
- Room 6 — 319
  - Fill — 319
  - Floor — 319
  - Floor Features — 319
  - Floor Specimens — 320
  - Walls — 320
  - Discussion — 320
- Room 7 — 320
  - Fill — 320
  - Floors — 320
  - Floor Features — 321
    - Floor pit — 321
  - Floor Specimens — 321
  - Walls — 321
  - Discussion — 321
- Room 8 — 321
  - Fill — 321
  - Floor — 321
  - Floor Specimens — 321
  - Walls — 321
  - Discussion — 321
- Room 9 — 322
  - Fill — 322
  - Floor — 322
  - Floor Specimens — 322
  - Floor Features — 322
    - Firepit — 322
    - Postholes — 322
    - Bins — 322
  - Walls — 323
  - Discussion — 323
- Room 10 — 323
  - Fill — 323
  - Floor — 323
  - Fill and Floor Specimens — 323
    - Surface — 323

Chapter 4, cont'd.
           Fill — 324
           Floor — 324
         Walls — 324
         Discussion — 324
       Discussion of Rooms — 324
       Ramada and Plaza Areas — 325
         Fill — 325
         Floor — 325
         Floor Features — 325
         Postholes — 325
           Firepits — 326
           Other Pits — 326
           Floor Specimens — 327
       Pithouse A — 327
         Fill — 327
         Upper bench — 332
         Upper bench features — 332
         Lower bench — 332
         Lower bench slab wall — 332
         Floor — 333
         Floor Features — 333
           Floor pits — 333
           Postholes — 333
           Floor ridge — 333
         Wing walls — 333
           Ash pit — 335
           Deflector complex — 335
           Firepit — 335
           Ventilator — 335
           Floor Specimens — 337
           Walls — 337
           Wall Cavities — 338
         Discussion — 338
       Trash Mound — 339
       Conclusions — 340
    North Roomblock (Bc 162, 29SJ 724) — 342

Chapter 5: Other Excavations and Data Recovery at Early Puebloan Sites In and Around Chaco — 387
    Pithouses and Rooms in the Vicinity of Casa Rinconada and Pueblo Bonito — 387
       Bc 50 Substructure House — 389
       Bc 50-51 Midden — 394
       Turtle Back House (Pithouse A) - Bc 51 — 396
       Structures Adjacent to Casa Rinconada Bc 64A (29SJ 1200) — 399
       Judd's Pithouse No. 1 — 402
       Under Pueblo Bonito — 403
       Judd's Pithouse 2 near Chetro Ketl — 403
       Near Peñasco Blanco — 406
       Near Fajada Butte — 408
       Shabik'eschee Village — 408
       Pithouses in the Exposed Chaco Wash Below Shabik'eschee Village — 408
         Half House — 409
         Arroyo House — 411
         Houses Noted During the 1972 Survey and Later — 414
         Summary of Shabik'eschee Village Area Features — 421
       Lake Valley — 422

Part 2 Contents

Chapter 6: Temporal Control at the Early Sites   435
- Dendrochronology   435
- Radiocarbon   441
- Archaeomagnetism   442
    - Archaeomagnetic Results from Contemporary Sites Outside of Chaco   453
    - Discussion   456
- Obsidian Hydration   456
- Ceramic Time   458
    - Brownware Ceramic Assemblage (A.D. 450-550/600)   459
    - La Plata Ceramic Assemblage (A.D. 550/600-700/750)   459
    - White Mound Ceramic Assemblage (A.D. 700/750-850/875)   459
        - Other Dated Pueblo I Houses   460
    - Kiatuthlanna Ceramic Assemblage (A.D. 850/875-925)   462
    - Red Mesa Ceramic Assemblage (A.D. 900-1040/1050)   463
- Architectural Styles   464
    - Brownware Ceramic Assemblage   464
    - La Plata Ceramic Assemblage   464
    - White Mound Ceramic Assemblage   464
    - Kiatuthlanna Ceramic Assemblage   464
    - Red Mesa Ceramic Assemblage   465
- Conclusion   465

Chapter 7: Form, Distribution, and Function of Features   491
- Feature Recording   494
    - Definitions and Abbreviations   494
- Goals   494
    - Problems with the Field Classification of Features   495
    - Feature Attributes and Classification   495
- Floor Features   496
    - Thermal Features   496
        - Firepits   499
        - Heating Pits   500
        - Hearths   504
        - Roasting Pits   504
        - Burns   505
    - Other Pits   506
        - Ladder Rests-Altars-Paho Pits   507
        - Pot Rests   508
        - Sipapus and other ritual features   508
        - Other Pits   510
        - Bell-shaped Pits   510
        - Mealing Catchment Basins   510
    - Postholes   512
    - Pithouse Work Areas and Features   514
    - Deflectors   515
- Storage Features   515
    - Storage Rooms/Cists   516
    - Pitrooms   516
- Wall Features   517
    - Wall Niches   517
    - Doorways   518
    - Ventilators   518
- Miscellaneous   519
    - Adobe Mixing Pits   519
- Major Structures   519
    - Pitstructures   519

Chapter 7, cont'd
    Unfinished Pitstructures . . . 521
  Conclusions . . . 521

Chapter 8: A Survey of Early House Settlement in the Chaco Canyon Area . . . 539
  The BM III-P I Occupation . . . 539
    Site Criteria . . . 541
    Architecture . . . 541
    Ceramics . . . 543
    Chaco Canyon Communities . . . 544
    A Brief Review of Early Sites Down Through Chaco Canyon . . . 546
    Chaco Wash . . . 546
    Pueblo Pintado Community Area: The Head of Chaco Canyon . . . 546
    Chaco East Community Area . . . 552
    Between the East Community and the Park East Boundary . . . 555
    Chacra Mesa and the Park . . . 556
    Shabik'eschee Village Community . . . 558
    Fajada Gap Community Area . . . 565
    Fajada Wash, South Fork Valley Community . . . 565
    The Canyon between Fajada Gap and South Gap . . . 580
    Werito's Rincon and Mockingbird Canyon . . . 581
    South Gap and the Pueblo Bonito Area . . . 583
    Casa Rinconada Rincon . . . 584
    South Gap . . . 585
    Escavada Wash Area . . . 585
    The Peñasco Blanco Area . . . 586
    The 29SJ 423-Peñasco Blanco/West Mesa/Padilla Wash Basketmaker III Community . . . 586
    The Southern Drainages Entering the Chaco River near the West End of the Park . . . 591
    The Padilla Wash Valley . . . 593
    Kin Klizhin Wash . . . 600
    Kim-me-ni-oli Wash . . . 603
  Abandonment and Evidence for Regional Violence . . . 605
    Human Remains . . . 605
    Burned Structures . . . 606
  Summary and Conclusions . . . 611
    The Problem of Early Sites under Pueblo II and III Sites . . . 614
  Concluding Remarks . . . 615

Chapter 9: Early Greathouse Beginnings . . . 663
  The Early Greathouses Within Chaco Canyon: A Review of Standards . . . 664
  Early Chacoan Greathouses in the Chaco Core . . . 665
    East Community . . . 666
    Una Vida . . . 669
    Kin Nahasbas . . . 672
    Pueblo Bonito . . . 672
    Peñasco Blanco . . . 677
      The Road System at Peñasco Blanco . . . 678
      The Setting at Peñasco Blanco . . . 678
  Corresponding Architectural Developments: A Northern Example . . . 680
    A Dolores Greathouse Example: McPhee Pueblo . . . 681
      The Architectural History of McPhee Pueblo . . . 682
  Early Greathouses West of Peñasco Blanco: The Arrival of a New Social Dynamic . . . 685
    Mounds as Features on the Cultural Landscape . . . 686
    The Landscape Setting . . . 687
    Early Chacoan Greathouses Outside the Chaco Core to the West . . . 689
      Casa del Rio (LA 17221) . . . 690
        Ties to the greater region: Roads and Shrines . . . 692
        The underlying Pueblo I house . . . 693
        The early Pueblo II greathouse . . . 693

Chapter 9, cont'd.

Midden 1	694
Plant indicators	695
Potential horticulture in the site area	696
Lake Valley (LA 18755)	698
Kin Bineola (LA 18705)	699
Proto-Greathouses on the Chacoan Landscape on Indian Creek	701
House of the Giant Midden	703
Casa Abajo	704
An Unusual Early Community at Willow Canyon	705
External Connections	705
The Main Community	706
Refuse	706
Unusual Mesa-Top Structures	709
House of the Weaver (LA 18235)	709
Great Bend	711
The Hogback	712
Discussion	713
The Potential for Food Surpluses	714
The Appearance of Stone Architecture	715
Possible Origins of Some Early Communities in Chaco Canyon	717
Environmental Factors	718
The Presence or Absence of Communal Structures	720
Community Settlement: A Regional Comparison	723
Early Site Histories: Contrasting Examples	724
Material Culture: Deposition and Non-local Materials	724
Conclusion	726
Chapter 10: Chaco's Beginnings: What We Know Now, And What To Do Next *Richard H. Wilshusen*	745
Archaeological Perspectives on Late Basketmaker-Early Pueblo Sites: 1969-2014	745
Southwestern Archaeology circa 1969	746
The Chaco Project's Initial Contributions	746
The Wetherill Mesa and Dolores Projects, and Follow-up Work at Crow Canyon	748
Vivian's Synthesis	749
Regional Archaeological Research Adds to the Picture	751
The Latest News: The Chaco Synthesis and This Volume	752
Tracing the Emergence of Great House Communities in the San Juan Drainage Basin	754
Late Basketmaker III: A Messy Picture (A.D. 600-750)	755
Pueblo I Patterns, Cultures, and Interaction (A.D. 750-825)	756
Late Pueblo I Villages, Hamlets, and Great Houses (A.D. 825-875)	757
Early Great Houses and the Southern San Juan Basin (A.D. 875-950)	758
How to Learn More about the Emergence of Great House Communities	758
References	763
Appendix A: Precipitation in Chaco Canyon and the Surrounding Area *by Robert K. Crane*	823
Spatial Structure of Rain	824
Conclusions	825
Appendix B: Statistical Analyses of Basketmaker III and Pueblo I Features *by William Doleman*	835
Analysis of Thermal Features	836
Correlation of Thermal Feature Function and Metric Attributes	836
Univariate Analyses	837
Multivariate Analyses	838
Summary	842
Correlation of Thermal Feature Function and Nominal Attributes	844
Correlation between Firepit Size and Pithouse Floor Area	845
Analysis of Other Pits to Identify Functional Sub types	785

Figures

Part 1 Figures

I.1.1.	Important topographic features, greathouses, and communities in Chaco Culture National Historical Park and its environs	3
I.1.2.	Surveys in and around Chaco Canyon between 1972 and 2001	7
I.1.3.	Basketmaker III and Pueblo I sites excavated by the Chaco Project in 1973 and 1974	9
I.2.1.	General location of the stands of large conifers and aspens in the Chaco East Community area	28
I.2.2.	Location of an isolated stand of aspen in the Chaco East Community area	29
I.2.3.	Location of scattered ponderosa pine and Douglas-fir along Chacra Mesa in the Chaco East Community area	30
I.2.4.	Geological structural elements of the San Juan Basin	33
I.2.5.	Soil complexes in Chaco Canyon	37
I.2.6.	Soil complexes in the Fajada Wash, South Fork Valley	38
I.2.7.	Soil complexes in the Pueblo Pintado area	39
I.2.8.	Isopluvial contours in the San Juan Basin	43
I.2.9.	Rain gauge locations within the Chaco Canyon area	48
I.3.1.	Site 29SJ 299 location among the Pueblo II and Pueblo III houses built along the ridges extending north from Fajada Butte	67
I.3.2.	Site 29SJ 299, site plan of the Basketmaker III and Pueblo I occupations	68
I.3.3.	Site 29SJ 299, Pithouses A and B plans	70
I.3.4.	Site 29SJ 299, Pithouses A and B profiles	71
I.3.5.	Site 29SJ 299, Pithouse B, post-excavation natural filling over a 40-year period	75
I.3.6.	Site 29SJ 299, Pithouse C, Rooms 8-9, and Ramada 1 plans	79
I.3.7.	Site 29SJ 299, Pithouses C and D profiles	80
I.3.8.	Site 29SJ 299, Pithouse D and Room 11, plans	83
I.3.9.	The Basketmaker III settlement in the Peñasco Blanco/29SJ 423 area	90
I.3.10.	Site 29SJ 423, an early Basketmaker III village	91
I.3.11.	Site 29SJ 423, Pithouse A and the Pueblo III Shrine, and profiles	96
I.3.12.	Site 29SJ 423. Plan views of shrine altar construction sequence	98
I.3.13.	Site 29SJ 423, Pithouse B, Areas I and II, Feature 1, plans and profiles	101
I.3.14.	Site 29SJ 423, distribution of roofing elements from the burned remains of Great Kiva III	105
I.3.15.	Site 29SJ 423, Structure 1 and Great Kiva I, plans	106
I.3.16.	Site 29SJ 423, Great Kiva II plan	107
I.3.17.	Site 29SJ 423, Great Kiva III plan	108
I.3.18.	Shabik'eschee Village, Pithouse Y, plan and profile, and Pithouse Z plan	123
I.3.19.	Site 29SJ 628, site plan	128
I.3.20.	Site 29SJ 628, Pithouses C and F plans	130
I.3.21.	Site 29SJ 628, Pithouse C, profile of fill	131
I.3.22.	Site 29SJ 628, Pithouse C architectural profiles	132
I.3.23.	Site 29SJ 628, Pithouse D plan	138
I.3.24.	Site 29SJ 628, Pithouse D architectural and fill profiles	139
I.3.25.	Site 29SJ 628, Pithouse G plan	144
I.3.26.	Site 29SJ 628, Pithouse G profiles	145
I.3.27.	Site 29SJ 628, Pithouse E plan	150
I.3.28.	Site 29SJ 628, Pithouse E profiles	151
I.3.29.	Site 29SJ 628, Pithouse A plan	153
I.3.30.	Site 29SJ 628, Pithouse A profiles	154
I.3.31.	Site 29SJ 628, Pithouse F profiles	158
I.3.32.	Site 29SJ 628, Cists 1 and 2, plans and profile	161
I.3.33.	Site 29SJ 628, Cists 3 and 4, plans and profiles	162
I.3.34.	Site 29SJ 628, Cists 5 and 6, plans and profiles	163

Part 1 Figures, cont'd

I.4.1.	Site 29Mc 184, plan of the four Pueblo I houses in the South Fork Valley, Fajada Wash	275
I.4.2.	Site 29SJ 299, Pithouse E plan	278
I.4.3.	Site 29SJ 299, Pithouse E profiles	279
I.4.4.	Site 29SJ 299, Rooms 12-15 and Ramada 2 plans	284
I.4.5.	Site 29SJ 299, Rooms 12-15 and Ramada 2 profiles	285
I.4.6.	Site 29SJ 721, site plan with contours	289
I.4.7.	Site 29SJ 721, plans of Pithouse A and Cists 1-3	291
I.4.8.	Site 29SJ 721, profiles of Pithouse A and Cist 1	291
I.4.9.	Site 29SJ 721, plans of Pithouse C, Cists 4-5, and Room 1	296
I.4.10.	Site 29SJ 721, profiles of Pithouse C, Kiva 1, and Cists 4 and 5	297
I.4.11.	Site 29SJ 721, plan of Kiva 1	303
I.4.12.	Site occupation of the 29SJ 724 ridge and its adjacent flood plain and mesa talus	310
I.4.13.	Site 29SJ 724, site overview of Roomblock I and associated pithouse	310
I.4.14.	Site 29SJ 724, Plan view of ramada and rooms showing profile lines	312
I.4.15.	Site 29SJ 724, profiles of surface rooms and ramada	312
I.4.16.	Site 29SJ 724, Pithouse A, plan view and profiles	328
I.4.17.	Site 29SJ 724, Pithouse A, profile of fill	328
I.4.18.	Site 29SJ 724, Pithouse A reoccupation	330
I.4.19.	Site 29SJ 724, Pithouse A firepit complex remodelings	336
I.5.1.	Sites in the Casa Rinconada rincon area	388
I.5.2.	Part of the late Pueblo I-early Pueblo II occupation beneath Bc 50	392
I.5.3.	Plan of the Feature 5 pithouse and ramada at Bc 50	393
I.5.4.	Basketmaker III-Pueblo I structures uncovered in the midden between Bc 50 and Bc 51	395
I.5.5.	Turtle Back House (Pithouse A) excavated in 1949 next to Bc 51	397
I.5.6.	Site 29SJ 1200, a Pueblo I component of five storage cists and probable living room	401
I.5.7.	Plan view of a small pithouse excavated by Robert Buettner in 1971	407
I.5.8.	Location of exposed pitstructures and other features in the banks of the Chaco Wash and its tributaries below the mesatop Shabik'eschee Village	409
I.5.9.	Elevation views of Basketmaker III and Pueblo I structures (29SJ 1657)	410
I.5.10.	Plan of a late unfinished greathouse (29SJ 2384) below Shabik'eschee Village	413
I.5.11.	Elevation view of Pithouse A (29SJ 1657) in the west bank of Chaco Wash below Shabik'eschee Village	415
I.5.12.	Plan view of a slab-lined trench (29SJ 1657) in the south bank of the Chaco Wash below Shabik'eschee Village	416
I.5.13.	Elevation view of Pithouse D remains (29SJ 1657) in the Chaco Wash north bank below Shabik'eschee Village	418
I.5.14.	Elevation view of a deeply buried Basketmaker III? slab-lined cist (29SJ 550)	419
I.5.15.	Elevation view of a deeply buried pitstructure (29SJ 552)	420

Part 2 Figures

I.6.1.	Date ranges for excavated Basketmaker III and Pueblo I sites in Chaco Canyon and at Lake Valley	436
I.6.2.	Probability plots of radiocarbon results from 29SJ 628, Pithouse A and Pithouse C	441
I.6.3.	Robert Dubois' Southwest Polar Curve from about A.D. 350 to about A.D. 1965	443
I.6.4.	Jeff Eighmy Southwest Polar Curve from A.D. 650 to A.D. 950	444
I.6.5.	Archaeomagnetic curve revised by Wolfman for A.D. 1000 to 1450	446
I.6.6.	Archaeomagnetic plots of samples from 29SJ 1659 (Shabik'eschee Village	447
I.6.7.	Archaeomagnetic plots of samples from 29SJ 299	448
I.6.8.	Archaeomagnetic plots of samples from 29SJ 724	450
I.6.9.	Archaeomagnetic plots of samples from 29SJ 628	451
I.6.10.	Archaeomagnetic plots of samples from 29SJ 721	452
I.6.11.	Archaeomagnetic plots of samples from Lake Valley, New Mexico	454
I.6.12.	Archaeomagnetic plots of samples from CDM-140, Canyon de Chelly, Arizona	455
I.6.13.	Archaeomagnetic plots of samples from LA 16029, Little Water, New Mexico	457

Part 2 Figures, cont'd

I.7.1.	Typical feature types found in Basketmaker and Pueblo I sites encountered during excavations of Basketmaker III and Pueblo I sites in Chaco Canyon	493
I.7.2.	Thermal feature types found in Basketmaker III and Pueblo I sites	497
I.7.3.	Histogram of other pit volumes from Basketmaker III and Pueblo I sites	511
I.8.1.	A schematic of a typical Basketmaker III pithouse of the A.D. 500s and 600s	543
I.8.2.	The Pueblo Pintado Community	548
I.8.3.	Site 29Mc 765	549
I.8.4.	Site 29Mc 784	551
I.8.5.	House orientations for the Late Pueblo I-early Pueblo II houses in the Pueblo Pintado East and West Sub-communities	553
I.8.6.	Early house midden sherd densities in the East and West sub-communities at Pueblo Pintado	553
I.8.7.	Early house midden areas in the East and West sub-communities at Pueblo Pintado	553
I.8.8.	Site 29Mc 615 plan	557
I.8.9.	Stylized settlement locations of the two large, early Basketmaker III communities	559
I.8.10.	Map of excavated features at Shabik'eschee Village in 1926-1927	560
I.8.11.	Shabik'eschee Village, a mesa-top site showing excavated pithouses	562
I.8.12.	Distribution of Basketmaker III and Pueblo I site locations in the Shabik'eschee Village	564
I.8.13.	Distribution of Pueblo I and Pueblo II houses along the South Ridge in Fajada Gap	566
I.8.14.	Site distribution in the upper Fajada Wash, upper South Fork Valley and in the upper Kin Klizhin Wash	568
I.8.15.	Distribution of Basketmaker III and Pueblo I sites in the Fajada Wash, South Fork Valley, and the upper Kin Klizhin Valley	569
I.8.16.	House sizes in the Fajada Wash, South Fork Valley. Pueblo I compared with Pueblo II houses	571
I.8.17.	Sites 29SJ 702-703	571
I.8.18.	Pueblo I house orientations in the Shabik'schee, Fajada Gap, South Fork, and Upper Kin Klizhin areas	571
I.8.19.	Pueblo I house midden sherd densities in the Shabik'schee, Fajada Gap, South Fork, and Upper Kin Klizhin areas	573
I.8.20.	Pueblo I house midden areas in the Shabik'schee, Fajada Gap, South Fork, and Upper Kin Klizhin areas	573
I.8.21.	Comparison of the Pueblo I and Pueblo II house midden densities in the South Fork Valley	574
I.8.22.	Comparison of the Pueblo I and Pueblo II house midden areas in the South Fork Valley	574
I.8.23.	Comparison of the Pueblo I and Pueblo II house orientations in the South Fork Valley	574
I.8.24.	Early prehistoric roads in and around Two Grey Hills in the Chuska Valley	577
I.8.25.	Site 29Mc 704	577
I.8.26.	Site 29SJ 1051	588
I.8.27.	Location of Basketmaker III habitation sites in the 29SJ423	589
I.8.28.	Site 29SJ 149	592
I.8.29.	Site 29SJ 110	595
I.8.30.	Pueblo I house orientations in the Padilla Wash Valley	596
I.8.31.	Pueblo I house sizes in the Padilla Wash Valley	596
I.8.32.	Pueblo I house midden areas and sherd densities in the Padilla Wash Valley	597
I.8.33.	Padilla Well Pueblo I community with the later greathouse and great kiva	598
I.8.34.	Features and landscaping in the vicinity of the Padilla Well greathouse and great kiva (29SJ 352)	598
I.8.35.	Plan of the Padilla Wash Valley greathouse (29SJ 352)	599
I.8.36.	Padilla Well, 29SJ 457, a Pueblo I house site and great kiva	601
I.8.37.	Distribution of Basketmaker III and Pueblo I sites in the Kin Klizhin park area	602

Part 2 Figures, cont'd

I.8.38.	Distribution of Basketmaker III and Pueblo I sites in the Kin Bineola park area	604
I.9.1.	The San Juan Basin showing some major southern tributaries to the Chaco River and important early greathouse areas along the Chaco River and McPhee Pueblo in Colorado	667
I.9.2.	The East Community greathouse (29Mc 560)	668
I.9.3.	Una Vida (29SJ 391) plan, Chaco Canyon	670
I.9.4.	Kin Nahasbas greathouse	673
I.9.5.	Early house plan at Pueblo Bonito	675
I.9.6.	Comparison of early greathouse big-room suites to a small Pueblo II house, 29SJ 627	676
I.9.7.	The road complex around Peñasco Blanco	679
I.9.8.	McPhee Pueblo, second construction episode, Dolores Archaeological Project	684
I.9.9.	Casa del Rio on the Chaco River, site plan	691
I.9.10.	Plan of Kin Bineola greathouse and the visible sections of early Type I masonry	702
I.9.11.	The Willow Canyon Community, near the Great Bend of the Chaco River	707
I.9.12.	Three small houses in the Willow Canyon Community built with Type I masonry	708
I.9.13.	The House of the Weaver (LA 18,235), site plan	710
I.9.14.	The Palmer Drought Severity Index from A.D. 600-1000 for Chaco Canyon	721
I.9.15.	The Palmer Drought Severity Index from A.D. 550-800 and 800-1000	722
I.9.16.	Bar graphs showing the midden areas and ceramic midden density at Pueblo I Chacoan Greathouses	725
I.A.1.	Monthly rain accumulation along Chaco Canyon	766
I.A.2.	Winter, north-south line through the Visitor's Center	767
I.A.3.	Winter, west-east line through the Visitor's Center	768
I.A.4.	Spring, north-south line through the Visitor's Center	769
I.A.5.	Spring, west-east line through the Visitor's Center	770
I.A.6.	Summer, north-south line through the Visitor's Center	771
I.A.7.	Summer, east-west line through the Visitor's Center	772
I.A.8.	Autumn, north-south line through the Visitor's Center	773
I.A.9.	Autumn, east-west line through the Visitor's Center	774

Plates

Part 1 Plates

I.2.1.	Scattered ponderosa pines across the Ojo Alamo badlands west of Chaco Canyon	27
I.2.2.	Old, lone ponderosa pine in the cliffs on Chacra Mesa in the Chaco East Community	27
I.2.3.	Storm clouds over Pueblo Pintado greathouse and community	47
I.2.4.	Flood waters in the Chaco Wash in the 1930/1940s near Visitor's Center	51
I.3.1.	Site 29SJ 299, overview of the initial excavations at the site	66
I.3.2.	Site 29SJ 299, overview of Pithouse A floor with materials left behind	69
I.3.3.	Site 29SJ 299, Pithouse A. Early archaeomagnetic sample collection	72
I.3.4.	Site 29SJ 299, antechamber of Pithouse A	74
I.3.5.	Site 29SJ 299, Pithouse B (Pueblo II kiva)	75
I.3.6.	Site 29SJ 299, Pithouse B (Pueblo II kiva) overview after completed excavation	76
I.3.7.	Site 29SJ 299, unfinished Pithouse C overview after completed excavation	78
I.3.8.	Site 29SJ 299, Pithouse D overview after completed excavation	81
I.3.9.	Site 29SJ 299, Pithouse D with main chamber floor cleared	81
I.3.10.	Site 29SJ 299, Pithouse D main chamber floor showing the firepit, adobe ridges, and the southern work area	82
I.3.11.	Site 29SJ 299, storage cists (Rooms 1-6) associated with Pithouse A	84
I.3.12.	Site 29SJ 299, storage cists (Rooms 2 and 3) associated with Pithouse A	85
I.3.13.	Site 29SJ 299, storage cist (Room 4) associated with Pithouse A	85
I.3.14.	Site 29SJ 299, storage cist (Room 5) associated with Pithouse A	86
I.3.15.	Site 29SJ 299, walk-in storage cist (Room 6) associated with Pithouse A	86
I.3.16.	Site 29SJ 299, storage cist (Room 8) between Pithouse A and unfinished Pithouse C	87
I.3.17.	Site 29SJ 299, storage cist (Room 10)	87
I.3.18.	Site 29SJ 423, site overview looking north-northeast from slickrock area south of site	89
I.3.19.	Site 29SJ 423, overview of the shrine wall and Pithouse A components	93
I.3.20.	Site 29SJ 423, closeup of Shrine Wall 1 masonry	93
I.3.21.	Site 29SJ 423, Pithouse A, Pit A	94
I.3.22.	Site 29SJ 423, Pithouse A, Pit B	94
I.3.23.	Site 29SJ 423, Features 2 and 3	95
I.3.24.	Site 29SJ 423, shrine altar with a finely-crafted sandstone	95
I.3.25.	Site 29SJ 423, shrine altar with exposed stone bowl with turquoise beads underneath	95
I.3.26.	Site 29SJ 423, Toadlena or Nava Black-on-white bowl found in the floor fill refuse of Pit B near the shrine altar	97
I.3.27.	Site 29SJ 423, overview of Pithouse B and exposed the bedrock behind it where stone removal activities may have taken place	100
I.3.28.	Site 29SJ 423, Feature 1 next to Pithouse B. Possible Navajo cist	102
I.3.29.	Site 29SJ 423, Great Kiva III showing layer of stone slabs that covered the kiva exterior walls before the last fire	104
I.3.30.	Site 29SJ 423, Structure I, arc of Postholes I-VII excavated into bedrock under south-southeast exterior side of great kiva benches	109
I.3.31.	Site 29SJ 423, main roof support Postholes A and B for Great Kiva I under the later great kiva benches	110
I.3.32.	Site 29SJ 423, Slots A-C excavated into bedrock to hold upright slabs	110
I.3.33.	Site 29SJ 423, Great Kiva III bench stones showing awl sharpening marks, presumably from work activities by the kiva occupants	112
I.3.34.	Site 29SJ 423, Other Pit 1 in the floor of Great Kiva II-III	113
I.3.35.	Site 29SJ 423, Great Kiva II postholes	114
I.3.36.	Site 29SJ 423, Great Kiva III after clearing	115
I.3.37.	Site 29SJ 423, Great Kiva III after clearing	115
I.3.38.	Site 29SJ 423, Great Kiva III upper bench top, showing the outer wall foundation slabs and the leaning interior bench-face slabs	115
I.3.39.	Site 29SJ 423, Great Kiva II-III bench with outer (GK III) bench-face slabs removed showing the vertical bench-face slabs of GK II	116

Part 1 Plates, cont'd

I.3.40.	Site 29SJ 1659, initial excavations at Pithouse Y with John Schelberg	122
I.3.41.	Site 29SJ 1659, initial excavations at Pithouse Y. Roger Huckins and John Thrift	122
I.3.42.	Site 29SJ 1659, excavations in the Pithouse Y antechamber	122
I.3.43.	Site 29SJ 1659, Pithouse Y main chamber in the firepit area	122
I.3.44.	Site 29SJ 628, initial excavations in Pithouse A. Excavation crew	127
I.3.45.	Site 29SJ 628, Pithouse C after clearing	129
I.3.46.	Site 29SJ 628, Pithouse C antechamber intentional stone fill	134
I.3.47.	Site 29SJ 628, Pithouse C, after clearing antechamber	134
I.3.48.	Site 29SJ 628, Pithouse D after clearing	139
I.3.49.	Site 29SJ 628, Pithouse D antechamber after clearing	139
I.3.50.	Site 29SJ 628, Pithouse G after clearing	143
I.3.51.	Site 29SJ 628, Pithouse E after clearing	147
I.3.52.	Site 29SJ 628, Pithouse A after clearing	155
I.3.53.	Excavations at 29SJ 628, Pithouse A, in 1973	155
I.3.54.	Site 29SJ 628 Pithouse F after clearing	157
I.3.55.	Site 29SJ 628, Storage Cist 1	163
I.3.56.	Site 29SJ 628, Storage Cist 3 after clearing	163
I.4.1.	Site 29Mc 184, House C. Peter McKenna	274
I.4.2.	Site 29SJ 299, Pithouse E floor after clearing half the structure	277
I.4.3.	Turtleback adobe wall construction	282
I.4.4.	Site 29SJ 299, storage Room 14 after clearing	283
I.4.5.	Site 29SJ 299, Ramada 2 post supports and storage Rooms 12 and 13 in background	286
I.4.6.	Site 29SJ 299, Ramada 2 post supports	287
I.4.7.	Site 29SJ 721, initial excavations at Pithouse A	288
I.4.8.	Site 29SJ 721, Pithouse A after clearing	290
I.4.9.	Site 29SJ 721, Pithouse A floor and Firepit 1	292
I.4.10.	Site 29SJ 721, Pithouse A above-floor ventilator	294
I.4.11.	Site 29SJ 721, Pithouse C with intrusive Cist 4 in the center	295
I.4.12.	Site 29SJ 721, Room 1, a slab-lined storage room	299
I.4.13.	Site 29SJ 721, Cist 1, a roasting pit	301
I.4.14.	Site 29SJ 721, Cist 2, a slab-lined storage cist reused as a firepit	301
I.4.15.	Site 29SJ 721, Cist 4, a roasting pit built in the center of Pithouse C	301
I.4.16.	Site 29SJ 721, unfinished Kiva 1 after clearing	301
I.4.17.	Site 29SJ 721, Kiva 1, pit and wall niche at north end of floor	304
I.4.18.	Site 29SJ 721, Kiva 1, west wall bench masonry	305
I.4.19.	Site 29SJ 721, Kiva 1, ventilator tunnel mouth	305
I.4.20.	Site 29SJ 724. Excavations at a classic Pueblo I house	309
I.4.21.	Overview of the Pithouse A, 29SJ 724, excavations in 1974	311
I.4.22.	Site 29SJ 724. Excavations in the surface storage rooms	313
I.4.23.	Site 29SJ 724. Excavations in the surface storage rooms	313
I.4.24.	Site 29SJ 724, Room 1 wall fall	314
I.4.25.	Site 29SJ 724, Room 2 after clearing	316
I.4.26.	Site 29SJ 724, Room 3 after clearing	316
I.4.27.	Site 29SJ 724, Room 4 before and after clearing	317
I.4.28.	Site 29SJ 724, Rooms 4 and 5 after clearing	319
I.4.29.	Site 29SJ 724, Room 6 after clearing	319
I.4.30.	Site 29SJ 724, Room 7 after clearing	320
I.4.31.	Site 29SJ 724, Rooms 7 and 8 after clearing	320
I.4.32.	Site 29SJ 724, Room 10	323
I.4.33.	Site 29SJ 724, closeup of Firepit 1 in the plaza	324
I.4.34.	Site 29SJ 724, Ramada Posthole 1, showing several shims	326
I.4.35.	Site 29SJ 724, Plaza/Ramada area	326
I.4.36.	Site 29SJ 724, Plaza Firepit 2	326
I.4.37.	Site 29SJ 724, Pithouse A, showing stone artifacts	327

Part 1 Plates, cont'd

I.4.38.	Site 29SJ 724, overview of Pithouse A	327
I.4.39.	Site 29SJ 724, Pithouse A, post-occupational fill of alluvial sands and clays	329
I.4.40.	Site 29SJ 724, Pithouse A, showing numerous large slabs in fill	329
I.4.41.	Site 29SJ 724, tiny, slab-lined firepits in the Pithouse A fill	329
I.4.42.	Site 29SJ 724, tiny, slab-lined firepits in the Pithouse A fill	329
I.4.43.	Site 29SJ 724, human footprints in the Pithouse A fill at the same level as the tiny firepits and slab wall	331
I.4.44.	Site 29SJ 724, Pithouse A fill, Feature I, matting and reeds	332
I.4.45.	Site 29SJ 724, Pithouse A floor, Other Pit 9, a long floor groove near the north wall	344
I.4.46.	Site 29SJ 724, Pithouse A floor, Other Pit 11 and the Northeast Roof Support Posthole	344
I.4.47.	Site 29SJ 724, Pithouse A floor, Other Pit 13	344
I.4.48.	Site 29SJ 724, Pithouse A floor, Other Pit 14 and the Northwest Roof Support Posthole	344
I.4.49.	Site 29SJ 724, Pithouse A floor, Other Pit 2 and the Floor Ridge	344
I.4.50.	Site 29SJ 724, Pithouse A floor fill with artifacts and other stone	337
I.5.1.	Overview looking north-northwest of the deep rincon extending south behind Bc 51	389
I.5.2.	Overview of the 1940-1941 excavations at Bc 52 just south of Bc 51	389
I.5.3.	Feature 2 (pithouse) floor at Bc 50	393
I.5.4.	Excavations next to Bc 51 at Turtle Back House, a Pueblo I pithouse	398
I.5.5.	Turtle Back House	398
I.5.6.	Pottery from the floor of Turtle Back House, (Pithouse A), Bin A	400
I.5.7.	Joe Maloney excavates a slab-lined pithouse near Casa Rinconada	401
I.5.8.	One of five slab-lined storage cists excavated at Bc 64A below Casa Rinconada	401
I.5.9.	Neil Judd's excavations at Pithouse 2, in an arroyo bank east of Chetro Ketl	404
I.5.10.	Chuskan neckbanded culinary jars recovered from Pithouse 2	405
I.5.11.	Excavations at Half House, a Pueblo I pithoue buried in the canyon bottomlands below Shabik'eschee Village, in 1947	410
I.5.12.	Arroyo House and Roberts's Small House in a side arroyo below Shabik'eschee Village	412
I.5.13.	Roberts's Small House site	413

Part 2 Plates

I.7.1	Typical pairs of ladder holes for a roof-entry access	507
I.7.2.	Typical postholes, filled with lignite coal and stone shims to wedge	513
I.7.3.	Typical adobe floor radials in a Basketmaker III pithouse	514
I.8.1.	The upright slab wall foundations of a small Pueblo I adobe house	542
I.8.2.	Looking east at Pueblo Pintado greathouse overlooking the surrounding countryside	546
I.8.3.	The big bump profile of the A.D. 900s Chaco East Community greathouse	555
I.8.4.	The 1926 proto-kiva excavations at Shabik'eschee Village, a Pueblo I pithouse	561
I.8.5.	Local topography at site 29SJ 1659 and the surrounding Basketmaker III house sites	563
I.8.6.	Overview of the Fajada Wash, South Fork Valley	567
I.8.7.	Site 29Mc 184, showing contrast between the classic A.D. 800 house and the A.D. 800 mounded proto-greathouse built with slab and Type I masonry in background (House B)	575
I.8.8.	Aerial view looking south across Mockingbird Canyon to Fajada Butte and Fajada Gap	581
I.8.9.	Overview of South Gap that separates South Mesa from West Mesa	583
I.8.10.	Overview of the broad, sandy, braided Escavada Wash north of Chaco Canyon	586
I.8.11.	Aerial photograph looking northwest above Pueblo Bonito to Pueblo Alto and the Escavada and Kimbeto washes beyond to Huerfano Mesa on the northern skyline	587
I.8.12.	Local topography at 29SJ 423 and the surrounding Basketmaker III house sites	590
I.8.13.	Overview of Peñasco Blanco and the surrounding West Mesa looking west across the Chaco River, a broad, sandy wash	591
I.8.14.	Overview of the badlands bordering the western side of Padilla Wash Valley	593
I.8.15.	Two views of Roberts' excavations in the great kiva at Shabik'eschee Village	608
I.9.1.	Classic high mounded remains of a Chacoan greathouse	663

Part 2 Plates, cont'd

I.9.2.	The high mounded roomblock of the Chaco East Community greathouse	669
I.9.3.	Type I masonry at Una Vida, Room 3, second story, north wall	669
I.9.4.	Overview of the earliest standing architecture of Type I masonry at Una Vida	669
I.9.5.	The third story section of the early southwest section of Una Vida, Room 28, constructed of Type I masonry	671
I.9.6.	Pueblo Bonito, first and second stories of the initial core of rooms	674
I.9.7.	Pueblo Bonito, showing the contrast between the early Type I masonry construction and the later Type II construction	674
I.9.8.	Early A.D. 860s construction along the west side of Pueblo Bonito	674
I.9.9.	McPhee Pueblo, the Dolores River Valley, Colorado. Room 1, Surface 2, Element 3 showing the Type I masonry construction that resembles that in Pueblo Bonito	681
I.9.10.	McPhee Pueblo, showing the large frontal room or work area	683
I.9.11.	McPhee Pueblo. Pitstructure 1, Element 4 an oversized community pithstructure constructed of Type I masonry	683
I.9.12.	Looking northwest downstream of the Chaco River near the mouth of Padilla Well Wash	692
I.9.13.	View to the west from the far western end of West Mesa overlooking the Chaco River and Padilla Well below and the Chuska Mountains in the far distance	692
I.9.14.	Huge cairns lining the edge of the West Mesa cliff overlooking the Padilla Wash Valley and Chaco River country	693
I.9.15.	Close up of the collapsed back wall of the Casa del Rio greathouse showing the use of large, tabular slabs stacked horizontally	694
I.9.16.	The massive Casa del Rio greathouse midden	695
I.9.17.	Overview of the potential horticultural area looking southeast	696
I.9.18.	Overview of the meandering Chaco River wash	696
I.9.19.	Navajo harvests from the Kim-me-ni-oli Valley, circa 1926	698
I.9.20.	Midden 2, a voluminous refuse mound fronting House 2, Lake Valley. Bob Blair	699
I.9.21.	Overview of the Kin Bineola greathouse, constructed in two building episodes in the A.D. 940s and A.D. 1110-1120s	700
I.9.22.	Kin Bineola greathouse, looking northwest into the second tier, west rooms of the main roomblock	700
I.9.23.	Closeup of Type I masonry in the western main roomblock of Kin Bineola, Room 31	700
I.9.24.	Kin Bineola greathouse showing the early Type I masonry construction in the lower room walls in Room 22	700
I.9.25.	Overview of the House of the Giant Midden, looking northeast	703
I.9.26.	Overview of the Type I stone architecture employed in the lower walls at Casa Abajo	704
I.9.27.	Small, one room structure built of Type I masonry overlooking the Willow Canyon area. Tom Windes and Eileen Bacha	709
I.9.28.	Unusual, slab-lined open area just below LA 18236 forming a plaza that overlooks the Willow Canyon Community. Eileen Bacha and Tom Windes	709
I.9.29.	The House of the Weaver, a late Pueblo I house of upright slabs and Type I masonry construction.	711
I.9.30.	The House of the Weaver, showing construction of large upright slabs and Type I masonry	711
I.9.31.	Two views of the collapsed Type I room masonry at the Great Bend greathouse A (LA 6419)	712

Tables

Part 1 Tables

I.1.1.	Chaco Project surveys in and around Chaco Canyon and the park outliers	15
I.1.2.	Various temporal classificatory schemes for the puebloan occupation of Chaco Canyon and the interior San Juan Basin	17
I.1.3.	Basketmaker III and Pueblo I sites excavated by the Chaco Center	18
I.1.4.	Volunteers that helped work on the Basketmaker III-Pueblo I project	19
I.2.1.	Dendrochronological results from Chaco Canyon	55
I.2.2.	Water samples from the Chaco Wash and the Chaco River compared with recent irrigation samples	61
I.2.3.	Precipitation data from 12 gauges in and around the Chaco Canyon region	62
I.2.4.	Variability among various rain gauge stations in the Chaco Canyon region and beyond	64
I.3.1.	List of features at site 29SJ 299 except for roofing postholes	167
I.3.2.	List of postholes in the site 29SJ 299 pithouses	173
I.3.3.	Site 29SJ 299, Pithouse A and Pithouse B distribution of Floor 1 materials	176
I.3.4.	Site 29SJ 299, Pithouse A, Stratum B and floor fill	182
I.3.5.	Site 29SJ 299, Pithouse D distribution of Floor 1 materials	188
I.3.6.	Site 29SJ 299, Room (cist) and Ramada 1 distribution of fill and floor materials	190
I.3.7.	List of ramada postholes at site 29SJ 299	192
I.3.8.	List of features at site 29SJ 423 except for postholes	193
I.3.9.	Site 29SJ 423, distribution of fill and floor materials in the Shrine and Pithouse A area	195
I.3.10.	List of postholes at site 29SJ 423	206
I.3.11.	Site 29SJ 423, distribution of materials in and around Pithouse B	209
I.3.12.	Site 29SJ 423, distribution of floor fill, floor, and construction materials for Structure 1 and Great Kivas I-III	213
I.3.13.	Site 29SJ 423, distribution of roofing elements recorded from the burned superstructure of Great Kiva III	223
I.3.14.	Data used in calculating the stresses on the superstructure of Great Kiva III, site 29SJ 423	226
I.3.15.	Results of the stresses for the Great Kiva III roof at site 29SJ 423	227
I.3.16.	List of features in and around Pithouse Y, Shabik'eschee Village except for postholes	228
I.3.17.	List of postholes in Pithouse Y at Shabik'eschee Village	229
I.3.18.	Site 29SJ 1659, Pithouses Y and Z, distribution of floor fill and Floor 1materials	230
I.3.19.	Site 29SJ 628, Pithouse C distribution of floor fill and Floor 1 materials	236
I.3.20.	List of features at site 29SJ 628 except for roofing postholes	241
I.3.21.	List of pithouse postholes at site 29SJ 628	247
I.3.22.	Site 29SJ 628, Pithouse D distribution of Floor 1 materials	253
I.3.23.	Site 29SJ 628, Pithouse G distribution of floor fill and Floor 1 materials	258
I.3.24.	Site 29SJ 628, Pithouse E distribution of floor fill and Floor 1 materials	260
I.3.25.	Site 29SJ 628, Pithouse A distribution of Floor 1 materials	266
I.3.26.	Site 29SJ 628, Pithouse F distribution of floor fill and Floor 1 materials	269
I.3.27.	Site 29SJ 628, surface storage cists and Firepit 2, distribution of materials	270
I.4.1.	Ceramic samples from site 29Mc 184	343
I.4.2.	Metrics for surface rooms exposed at 29Mc 184	347
I.4.3.	Site 29SJ 299, Pithouse E, distribution of Floor 2 materials	347
I.4.4.	Site 29SJ 299, Ramada 2, distribution of artifacts used in post support construction	349
I.4.5.	Site 29SJ 721, distribution of floor fill and floor materials	350
I.4.6.	List of features at 29SJ 721 except for postholes	355
I.4.7.	List of postholes at 29SJ 721	357
I.4.8.	List of features at 29SJ 724, except for roofing postholes	358
I.4.9.	List of postholes in Rooms 1 and 9 at 29SJ 724	361
I.4.10.	Site 29SJ 724, room and plaza distribution of Floor 1 materials	362

Part 1 Tables, cont'd

I.4.11.	List of ramada postholes in the 29SJ 724 plaza	367
I.4.12.	Site 29SJ 724, Pithouse A, distribution of materials at the same level as the fill firepits	369
I.4.13.	Site 29SJ 724, Pithouse A list and distribution of Feature I materials	370
I.4.14.	List of postholes in the 29SJ 724 pithouse	373
I.4.15.	Site 29SJ 724, Pithouse A distribution of floor fill and Floor 1 materials	375
I.4.16.	Rough sort ceramic frequencies from midden testing at 29SJ 724, Houseblock II	386
I.5.1.	Floor fill and Floor 1 materials from substructure Rooms 4 and 5 at Bc 50	424
I.5.2.	List of features at Bc 50 in the substructure Feature 5 pithouse, the associated surface ramada, and the adobe mixing basin	425
I.5.3.	Features at Turtle Back House at Bc 51	427
I.5.4.	Ceramics recovered during the 1947 excavations at Half House, from the 2003/2004 surface tallies at Bc64a, and from the Casa Rinconada refuse	428
I.5.5.	Materials from the floor fill and floor in pithouses and cists, Bc 64	430
I.5.6.	Vessels recovered from Judd's Pithouse No. 2 and Doleman's Lake Valley site	431
I.5.7.	Structures exposed between 1972 and 2003 in the Chaco and Sheep Camp Canyon washes below the mesa-top part of Shabik'eschee Village	432
I.5.8.	Collapsed bank ceramics retrieved from pithouses exposed in the Chaco Wash	433

Part 2 Tables

I.6.1.	Methods used for dating the excavated sites	466
I.6.2.	Dendrochronological results from early puebloan Chacoan sites	467
I.6.3.	List of tree-ring symbols and abbreviations	478
I.6.4.	Radiocarbon results from 29SJ 628 and 29SJ 724	480
I.6.5.	Chaco radiocarbon dates: results of paired T-tests	481
I.6.6.	Archaeomagnetic results from Basketmaker III and Pueblo I sites	485
I.6.7.	Obsidian hydration rind measurements from the UCLA Obsidian Hydration Laboratory for early puebloan sites in Chaco Canyon	489
I.6.8.	Ceramics from LA 4487, a White Mound phase pithouse village	490
I.7.1a.	Feature dimension statistics by feature type	524
I.7.1b.	Feature floor area and volume statistics by feature type	525
I.7.2.	Inventory of features from Chaco area Basketmaker III and Pueblo I sites excavated by the Chaco Project and the Lake Valley road project	526
I.7.3.	Metrics for excavated and tested Basketmaker III-Pueblo I rooms and pitstructures	528
I.7.4.	Definitions for features and use surfaces at excavated Basketmaker III and Pueblo I sites	530
I.7.5.	Feature attribute codes	532
I.7.6.	Pitstructure-heating pit correlations from Basketmaker III to early Pueblo II sites	533
I.7.7.	General statistics for Basketmaker III and Pueblo I postholes	534
I.7.8.	Pithouse data from Chaco Canyon and Lake Valley	536
I.8.1.	Material correlates for the identity of Basketmaker III, Pueblo I, and Pueblo II habitation sites	617
I.8.2.	Ceramic assemblage time in the San Juan Basin interior: Architectural trends	618
I.8.3.	Ceramic assemblage time in the San Juan Basin interior: Cibola Tradition	619
I.8.4.	House data for the initial late Pueblo I sites in the Pueblo Pintado and Chaco East communities	620
I.8.5.	Ceramic samples from sites 29Mc 765 and 29Mc 766 in the Eastern Pueblo Pintado Community	622
I.8.6.	Selected ceramic samples from the initial eastern Pueblo Pintado Community sites	625
I.8.7.	Selected ceramic samples from the initial western Pueblo Pintado Community sites	627
I.8.8.	Ceramic samples from surface deposits at site 29Mc 784, in the western group	631
I.8.9.	Ceramic samples from the earliest puebloan sites in the Chaco East Community	634
I.8.10.	Summary data from Pueblo I house sites around the periphery of Chaco Canyon	635

Part 2 Tables, cont'd

I.8.11.	Ceramic samples from surface deposits at the Basketmaker III-Pueblo I habitation sites in the Shabik'eschee Village Community	636
I.8.12.	Summary data on the Shabik'eschee Basketmaker III community sites across Chaca Mesa	641
I.8.13.	Ceramic midden samples from unexcavated sites occupied between A.D. 875 and 925 in the Fajada Gap Community	643
I.8.14.	House data for Pueblo I sites in the Fajada Wash, South Fork, and Upper Kin Klizhin valleys	645
I.8.15.	Ceramic samples from unexcavated sites occupied between A.D. 700 and 900 in the Fajada Wash, South Fork, and the Upper Kin Klizhin valleys	646
I.8.16.	Summary data on the Basketmaker III house sites in the Peñasco Blanco/West Mesa/Padilla Wash Valley Community	655
I.8.17.	Selected midden ceramic samples from Pueblo I sites from about A.D. 750 to 925 along the Padilla Wash Valley	656
I.8.18.	Ceramics from the Padilla Wash Valley greathouse and great kiva	660
I.9.1.	Households and other data from early greathouses and proto-greathouses along the Chaco Wash and the Chaco River and its tributaries, ordered from east to west	728
I.9.2.	Midden notes from selected early greathouses and proto-greathouses	729
I.9.3.	Ceramic samples from Casa del Rio, occupied between A.D. 850 and 1130	730
I.9.4.	Lithic material type groups at Padilla Well greathouse and Casa del Rio, Midden 1	734
I.9.5.	Ceramic samples from early surface deposits on Midden 1 and from the road cut in Midden 2, Lake Valley	735
I.9.6.	Ceramic samples from surface deposits at the House of the Giant Midden and Casa Abajo along the Indian Creek drainage	737
I.9.7.	Ceramic samples from early surface deposits at Willow Canyon near the Chaco River	739
I.9.8.	Ceramic samples from early surface deposits at the Great Bend and Hogback greathouses along the Chaco River	742
I.B.1.	Thermal feature metric data statistics: N, mean, standard deviation	791
I.B.2.	Analyzed thermal feature metric data and transformed variable: normality statistics	792
I.B.3.	ANOVA and pairwise T-test results for thermal feature types and metric data	793
I.B.4.	Stepwise discriminant analysis of thermal feature metric data	794
I.B.5.	Canonical discriminant analysis of thermal feature metric data	794
I.B.6.	Discriminant analysis of thermal feature measurements: reclassification results	795
I.B.7.	Contingency table of thermal feature type versus feature lining	796
I.B.8.	Contingency table of thermal feature type versus feature fill type	797
I.B.9.	Contingency table of thermal feature type versus sand versus charcoal fill	798
I.B.10.	Normality statistics for pithouse floor area and firepit volume and mouth area	799
I.B.11.	Regression analysis of firepit volume and mouth area versus pithouses floor area	799
I.B.12.	Other Pit metric data: basic statistics	799
I.B.13.	Two-stage density linkage cluster analysis of other pit dimensions: potentially significant clustering levels as indicated by CCC peaks	800
I.B.14.	Results of centroid method cluster analysis of other pit measurement data	801
I.B.15.	Results of average linkage method cluster analysis of other pit measurement data	802
I.B.16.	Average linage cluster analysis of other pits with 12 clusters	803
I.B.17.	Average linkage cluster analysis of other pits with 12 clusters	804

Chapter 1
Introduction

In 1969, the New Mexico Archeological Center (later designated the Chaco Center) was established to conduct a 15-year multidisciplinary research project in Chaco Canyon National Monument in northwestern New Mexico (see Wilshusen, Chapter 10; Mathien 2005; and Wilshusen and Hamilton 2006 for reviews). The project was a collaborative effort between the U.S. Department of the Interior National Park Service and the University of New Mexico that was housed on the university campus until 1986, when most of the staff moved to the Santa Fe regional office of the National Park Service, except for F. Joan Mathien and Thomas Windes. The collections and archives remained in Albuquerque in the hands of the Maxwell Museum at the University of New Mexico. These materials are still housed at the university but now are, again, under the auspices of Chaco Culture National Historical Park and the National Park Service.

The goals of the Chaco Center (also known as the Chaco Project) were to conduct pedestrian surveys of the national monument, record all cultural resources, and investigate the range of resources within the framework of research and park management goals (National Park Service 1970). A sample transect survey conducted by the university in 1971 under the direction of W. James Judge (1981) was followed in 1972 by a landmark inventory survey conducted by Alden Hayes (1981) of the National Park Service. These surveys quantified the cultural resources of the park for the first time. Chaco may have been the first national monument or park to be systematically and completely inventoried for cultural resources in compliance with Richard Nixon's executive order of 13 May 1971 to inventory all Federal lands (Executive Order No. 11593, 36 Federal Register 8921). This survey made possible realistic estimates of the extent of human use of the park—an important step in understanding and explaining the Chacoan and other occupations.

Chaco Canyon has received considerable attention for its archaeological remains since Lt. James Simpson (McNitt 1964; Simpson 1850) first recorded the presence of the large buildings in Chaco in 1849 and William Jackson followed with investigations in 1877 (Jackson 1878). Surveys of small houses were first conducted in Chaco by the staff of Edgar Hewett in the 1920s during excavations at Chetro Ketl and other sites. A statewide survey system was adopted in 1928 (Fisher 1930:5), which was followed by the first maps of sites in Chaco. In 1947, Lloyd Pierson of the National Park Service (1947, 1956) expanded the survey of house sites in Chaco, and sites were recorded until 1968 by the park staff, eventually tallying 398 sites throughout the canyon.

The first park-wide inventory was accomplished by the Chaco Project, although this did not cover all of the lands adjacent to the park or even the entire canyon. Later, when Congress authorized park expansion, new surveys were conducted in 1983 and 1984 of the lands to be added immediately north and south of the park and at Kin Klizhin and Kin Bineola, outlying park units to the southwest (Powers and Van Dyke 2015).

The surveys and subsequent excavations stirred interest regarding the "collapse and abandonment" of Chaco Canyon and other outlying communities during the post-Chacoan period. The Chacoan Phenomenon (Irwin-Williams 1972) apparently ceased as an organized, coherent system in Chaco Canyon between about A.D. 1100 and 1150, but continuity is seen in architecture, use of the landscape, and presumably a readapted social system that lasted for several hundred years in and beyond the Chacoan heartlands (e.g., Adler 1996; Fowler and Stein 1992; Lipe and Ortman 2000; McKenna and Toll 1992; Varien 2002). Chacoan greathouses have been the primary focus for research and interpretation of the archaeology of Chaco Canyon and the Chacoan Phenomenon since the creation of the national monument in 1907. Although the rise of greathouses and attendant modifications of the landscape were once seen as a dramatic shift in puebloan society, perhaps imposed on a simple peasant farming culture and directed or controlled by outsiders, the Basketmaker III (A.D. 500-700) and Pueblo I (A.D. 700-900) periods in Chaco and elsewhere reveal important precursors to subsequent events. Direct continuity remains to be demonstrated, but the early use of the canyon must have provided experiences and a relationship with the land that fostered later development.

The role of early settlement and population pressures, the development of agriculture, and the lack of resources in Chaco Canyon are important research topics that were integral to the interpretation of survey and excavation results. These research domains are critical for understanding the social dynamics that led to the development of Chacoan communities and the increased complexity during the Bonito phase (A.D. 860-1120; see Altschul 1978; Grebinger 1973; Judge 1979; Schelberg 1982, 1984; and Vivian 1970a). A plethora of studies have followed the early inquiries into the origin and nature of Chacoan society. Aside from a few early works, when the first Chaco Project excavations began, there was little published discussion of early Chaco social dynamics and the role of early puebloan society (for early discussions of this see Kluckhohn 1939b; Vivian and Mathews 1965).

This volume addresses the early puebloan use of Chaco Canyon and its environs (Figure I.1.1) through the results of the Chaco Project excavations, reexamination of early houses excavated prior to the Project, and surveys outside the park conducted since the 1972 inventory survey. The new information provides insights on the continuity of the Basketmaker III and Pueblo I occupations along with the seemingly sudden and dramatic rise of greathouses and communities that began in the late Pueblo I period (late A.D. 800s). The construction of greathouses has been linked to pochteca intrusions from Mesoamerica (Frisbie 1978, 1983, 1985; Kelley and Kelley 1975; Reyman 1978), the rise of political power and increased social complexity (Kantner 1996; Lekson 1999; Neitzel 2003b; Saitta 1997; Sebastian 1992; Wills 2000; Yoffee 2001), the need for turquoise (Harbottle and Weigand 1992; Weigand 1992), a changing and uncertain environment (Judge 1979), competing social systems (Kluckhohn 1939b; Vivian 1970b, 1990), and other factors (see Mathien 2005; Mills 2002 for overviews).

Much research over the past two decades has focused on "downtown Chaco," where Pueblo Bonito is prominent, but the lower canyon does not exist in isolation from the upper and central canyon and its environs. These often-ignored areas provide a more complete picture of the puebloan occupation and its later rise to prominence, part of what drove new surveys to examine the upper canyon and adjacent drainage areas. Although research effort continues on the recognition and identity of the post-Chacoan world, a renewed focus on the development and rise of the Chacoan culture is important to an understanding of Chaco in the A.D. 1000s and 1100s.

What follows in Volumes I and II brings together the work on early puebloan sites in

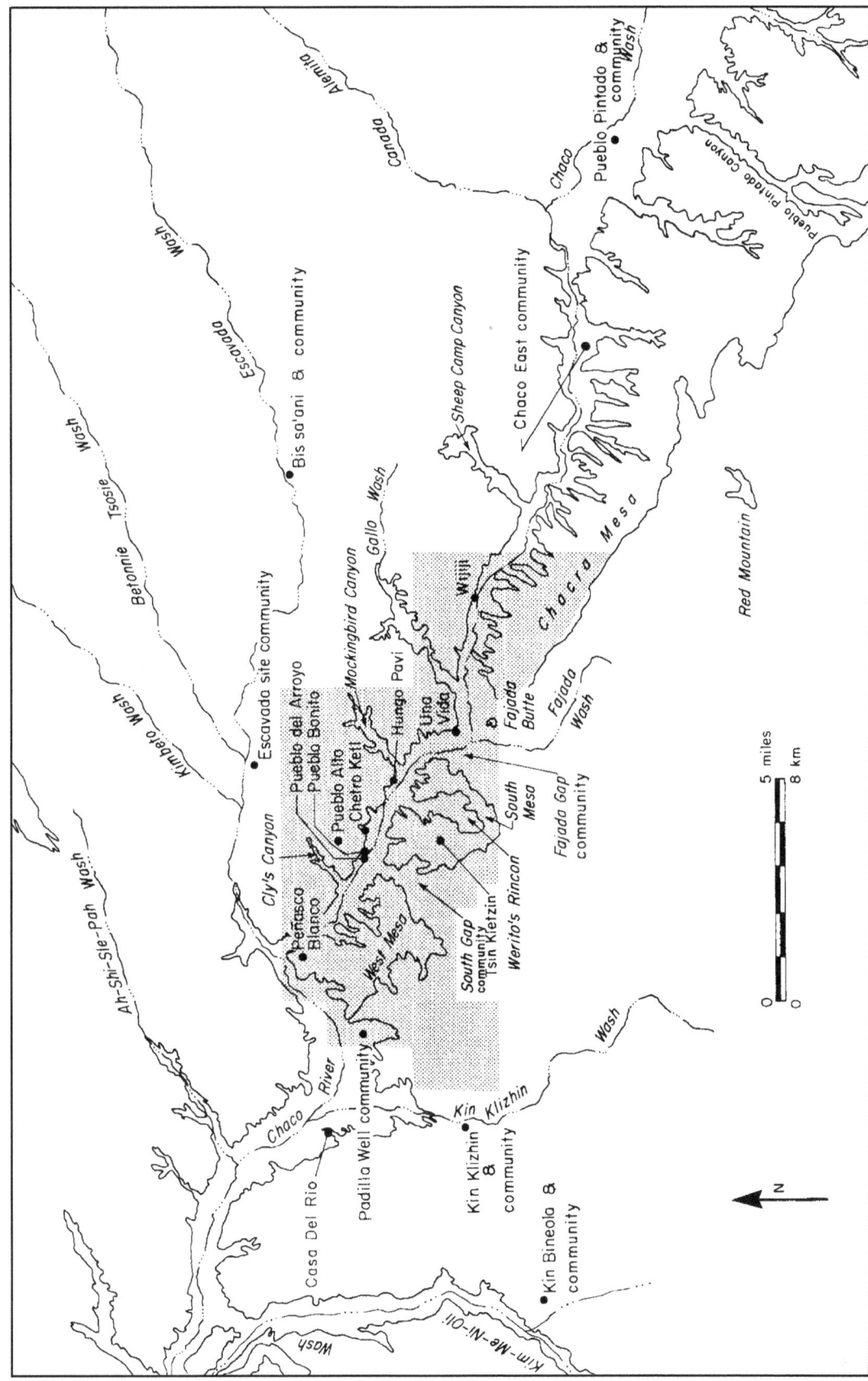

Figure 1.1.1. Important topographic features, greathouses, and communities in Chaco Culture National Historical Park and its environs (CHCU 65031).

and around Chaco and provides a mass of new information with which to interpret the early settlement and its relationship to later events. This work revises past interpretations of the early puebloan occupation and provides a new understanding of the relationship between the early occupation and the subsequent Early Bonito phase that began at the appearance of the first Chacoan greathouses and associated communities in the late A.D. 800s. The work is particularly timely given the summary of work to the west along the Arizona/New Mexico border from highway and other mitigation projects that has recently provided a new perspective on Basketmaker and Pueblo I settlement in *The Foundations of Anasazi Culture*, edited by Paul Reed (2000), the *Crucible of Pueblos* edited by Richard Wilshusen, Gregson Schachner, and James Allison (2012), and *Southwestern Pithouse Communities* edited by Lisa Young and Sarah Herr (2012).

Unfortunately, the final published results for this report have been much delayed due to work on the later Project sites first, the demise of the Chaco Center, the temporary ownership loss of the collections to the University, the dispersal of the core staff, and six years' delay then termination during the initial editing. The primary report was completed in 2006 but some additional references have been made since. Some parts of this report, mainly from Chapters 8 and 9, have been reported elsewhere (Windes 2004, 2007; Windes and Van Dyke 2012) but this version represents the latest revision and editing.

Research Strategy

The Chaco Project was guided by two plans that directed research. The master plan for Chaco emphasized strengthening the interpretative and resource management programs, with special attention given to filling in voids in the interpretative story (National Park Service 1968:1), but it provided little direction as to how this was to be accomplished. A Project-specific guide written by John Corbett, the chief archaeologist of the National Park Service, elaborated on the broad research goals but also emphasized the importance of the work for the visitor experience and to provide "authoritative up-to-date, sophisticated scientific information on the history of man and his environment in the Chaco drainage" (National Park Service 1970). The directive did not mandate an explicit expansion plan of interpretative facilities such as that which drove the Wetherill Mesa Project in the 1960s at Mesa Verde National Park (Osborne 1964). Instead, the Chaco Center focused on the reinterpretation of Chaco Canyon archaeology through survey and the excavation of a number of sites, which were chosen to represent the development of Chaco from the Archaic to the historic periods but with emphasis on the puebloan occupation.

This report covers those early puebloan sites that were excavated because they date within the Basketmaker III and Pueblo I periods (about A.D. 500 to 900). The increased emphasis on hypothesis testing in archaeology (e.g., Binford 1964; Redman 1973; Vivian 1970b; Watson et al. 1971) took hold in the middle of the project with Judge's (1975) staged approach to research: a series of problems formulated to generate hypotheses of community development in the two or three areas of Chaco where Basketmaker III and Pueblo I sites had been excavated. These areas, in turn, would serve as examples of the overall settlement within the canyon and the developing society that led to the construction of Chacoan greathouses (see Lekson 1977). But in general, the Basketmaker III and Pueblo I sites were excavated under a broad cultural historical framework that helped to document the early occupation in Chaco and served as the basis for the initial community studies later proposed by Judge.

Survey Overview

It is during the early Basketmaker III period that our first evidence of sedentary or semi-sedentary occupations is manifest in Chaco Canyon. When the 1972 survey commenced, our understanding of the Basketmaker III (A.D. 500-700) and Pueblo I (A.D. 700-900) periods was limited. Excavation in early sites had usually consisted of accidental encounters during work on later sites. The glaring exception was the large mesa-top community centered at Shabik'eschee Village, located at the eastern monument boundary midway along the canyon. Although Roberts (1929) did not fully comprehend the magnitude of Shabik'eschee Village, he con.sidered it the type site for Basketmaker III. It should not be considered typical, however, as few early sites of this magnitude have been found. The 1972 survey did, however, reveal the presence of a second large Basketmaker village centered at 29SJ 423 near the Peñasco Blanco greathouse at the west end of the canyon (see Chapters 3 and 8). Otherwise, Chaco Canyon's early puebloan occupations were probably mostly small pithouse hamlets occupied by one or two families.

The results of the 1972 survey indicated that the early occupations were widespread and increased in number through time (Hayes 1981): 135 Basketmaker III pithouse sites and 373 Pueblo I houses were identified. By early Pueblo II times (A.D. 900-1000), house sites had decreased to 353, and then to 323 by late Pueblo II/early Pueblo III (A.D. 1000-1140). It is now possible to reassess these figures and to refine their temporal placement for each period. As a result, new house estimates are much lower, particularly for the Pueblo I period. What is the basis for these discrepancies?

Before the Chaco Center excavations, research in areas well beyond Chaco Canyon provided the basic framework for understanding these early puebloan periods. Although Hayes had worked as a student in Chaco during the 1930s, his perception of the early periods was probably heavily influenced by his previous inventory survey on Wetherill Mesa (Hayes 1964) at Mesa Verde National Park and his work in Badger House (Hayes and Lancaster 1975) during the Wetherill Project. By the time the Chaco survey report was written, the few early sites that had been excavated in Chaco under his direction (Chapters 3 and 4) exhibited similarities in architecture, chronology, and ceramics with those in Mesa Verde. But the in-depth analyses of materials (Volume II), chronology (Chapter 6), and ceramic sequences (Chapter 6; see also Chapters 2 to 5 in Volume II) followed much later, some of it quite recently. These later findings provide the basis for adjustments made to the 1972 survey data that are reported here in terms of ceramic chronologies, temporal spans, house frequency and types of sites.

Work since the inventory survey has exposed some of the problems in delineating these early puebloan sites in Chaco. Classification of sites into time periods is not exact, particularly for the Basketmaker and Pueblo I eras. In part, their distinction is semantic and regional, but generations of investigators have relied on architecture and ceramics to categorize sites into the proper temporal periods using surface remains. Classification is sometimes based on survey results by field personnel with little experience in the area, and on perceptions that are unique to each archaeologist. This problem is especially acute with earlier non-habitation sites where ceramics are few in number, typically plain gray culinary ware, and the only architecture consists of scattered stones or a few upright slabs. These traits can mark sites that could date to anytime between early Basketmaker III and early Pueblo II. These problems have led to many early sites being temporally misclassified during the 1972 survey.

The intensity of the puebloan occupation of Chaco Canyon makes it difficult to segregate any early occupations from the overlying Pueblo

II and Pueblo III occupations. Although Hayes (1981) offers an overview of those occupations based on the 1972 inventory survey, it is clear that our knowledge of the Basketmaker and Pueblo I occupations remains clouded within the canyon and, in particular, within the dense communities situated along the south side of the canyon where major tributaries join the Chaco Wash and the Chaco River. An unknown number of sites are buried in the deep alluvium within the canyon; this problem primarily affects Basketmaker III and early Pueblo I sites (see Chapter 5).

The only complete site inventories of the puebloan occupations along the primary drainages that intermittently flow into the Chaco Wash and Chaco River are those within the park, but they need to be reevaluated using up-to-date standards. Events that gave rise to the aggregated settlement within Chaco Canyon are connected through time to the larger settlement system that extends outside the canyon and within the greater San Juan Basin. Although we know that some settlement occurred just outside Chaco Canyon, little systematic survey of these areas had been done.

Additional surveys of about 8,499 hectares (32.8 mi^2) have broadened our knowledge of occupation in and adjacent to Chaco Canyon beyond the 1972 monument boundaries (Figure I.1.2, Table I.1.1), which were not summarized in the Hayes (1981) survey report. Surveys were continued by the Chaco Center under a directive from Congress, Executive Order 11593, and pursuant to the 1980 amendment of the National Historic Preservation Act requiring the identification and evaluation of archaeological sites on Federal lands.

Although tracts of land outside the park were still being surveyed up through 1975, many of them were not included in the final report (Hayes 1981). Transects surveyed by Judge outside the monument boundaries in 1971 also were not included in the final survey report (although they are documented in Judge 1981).

The area from the monument's north boundary to the Escavada Wash, the largest tract not incorporated in the Hayes report (about 6 mi^2), was later summarized by McKenna (1981b). In addition, large tracts were surveyed in 1983-1984 on lands just south of the park (20.3 mi^2) that Congress had incorporated into the park (Powers and Van Dyke 2015).

Other tracts were surveyed by the author with the assistance of the Sierra Club, coordinated by Bonnie Sharpe, between 1989 and 1999, and with other volunteers. These new surveys took place in the Fajada Gap area, mainly along South Ridge (Windes 1993:360), along the South Fork valley of Fajada Wash, at the head of Kin Klizhin Wash, and at the east end of Chaco Canyon (Windes 1993: Appendix F; Windes et al. 2000). The surveys cannot be considered 100 percent inventories. The surveys in the South Fork and Kin Klizhin valleys and the East Community were conducted to inventory all puebloan house sites; Archaic, historic, Navajo, and special use sites were encountered, but only a few of them were documented. Storage facilities and isolated hearths, however, were routinely documented. Teams of five to 10 persons, walking 5-10 m apart, systematically covered these areas and marked the site locations on aerial photos. Later a recording crew documented and mapped each site. All of the house sites were mapped with alidade and plane table, yielding a level of accuracy that is seldom attained in normal pedestrian surveys. All records of these surveys are filed at the ARMS at the Laboratory of Anthropology, Museum of New Mexico in Santa Fe, at the park, and in the Chaco Collections, Albuquerque.

The Pueblo Pintado area at the east end of the canyon was resurveyed by the author with volunteers in 1999 and 2000, and the heart of the settlement area around the greathouse (29SJ 352) in Padilla Wash Valley and at the mouth of Padilla Wash was reexamined in 1999 and 2000 (Chapters 8 and 9, this volume). In addition, a large study was conducted for potential coal

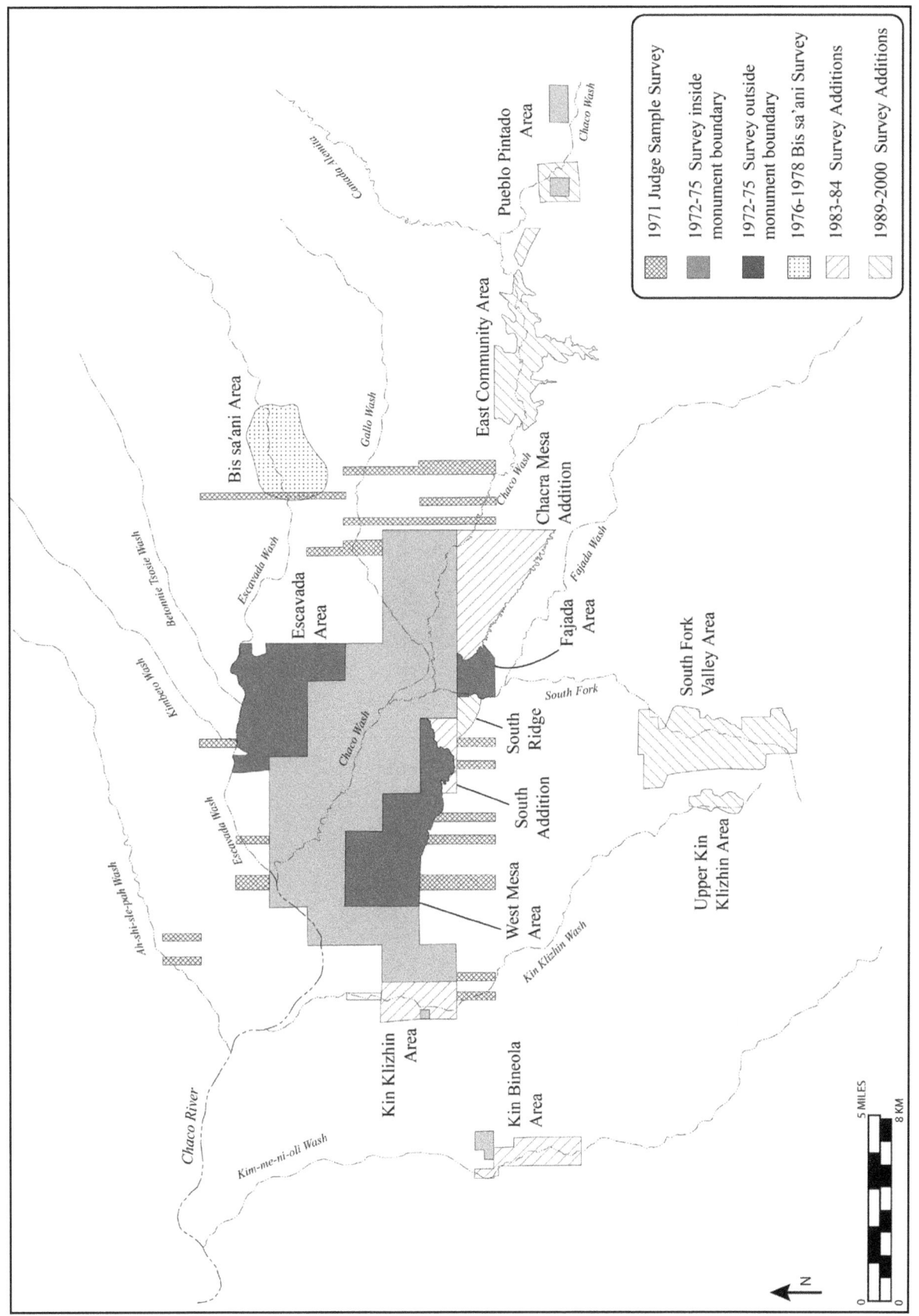

Figure I.1.2. Surveys in and around Chaco Canyon between 1972 and 2001 (small 2006-2007 survey not shown). (Original by Chris Millington, June 2005).

strip-mining along the Escavada Wash northeast of Chaco Canyon in the Bis sa'ani Community (Breternitz et al. 1982), but it failed to identify any early puebloan occupations. Finally, in 2006-2007, a survey of all sites along the north cliff face and talus was conducted up canyon from the park new east boundary to a quarter mile past Sheep Camp Canyon. Thus, much of the eastern canyon area and the areas south of Fajada Gap have now been surveyed. Records of this work are housed in the park museum collections and at the Museum of New Mexico's Laboratory of Anthropology (ARMS files).

These surveys provide new information on settlement, ceramics (Volume II, Chapter 2; Mills 2002) and chipped stone (Volume II, Chapter 7; Cameron and Young 2015). The ceramic and architectural data are summarized in Chapters 6 and 8. The 1972 survey focused more on cultural history and less on settlement studies, which were primarily seen as an adjunct goal.

Hayes's (1981) work and his archive materials provided much of the material used here as a starting point for the reexamination of the early puebloan occupation. The maps showing Hayes's site locations were redrafted in Washington, D.C., prior to publication without Hayes's review, and subsequently the published versions differ somewhat from the working copies in the Chaco archives (maps CHCU 65057-65064). In addition, the original site forms and ceramic tallies (see McKenna 1981b), also in the archives, were consulted, and many of the early sites were revisited by the author and larger ceramic tallies made. The final archaeological maps presented here were done by the author with a few exceptions.

Excavation Overview

Sites across the monument were excavated to provide a sample of early puebloan houses identified as a result of the 1972 survey. These sites were chosen to illuminate the early cultural history of the puebloan occupation, to provide new interpretative sites for the park, and to investigate their relationship to events, if any, at the later communities and greathouses that dominated the park by the A.D. 900s and 1000s (Figure I.1.3), as well as contemporary events taking place elsewhere in the San Juan Basin. In addition, they served as a precursor for later excavations at a greathouse, originally to have been Una Vida. The choice of sites was tempered by logistical constraints, including vehicle access, and the possibility that at least some were to be exhibited as park interpretive sites. An auger testing program was initiated by Alden Hayes at potential excavation sites to identify burned houses that would—hopefully—provide chronometric controls and in-situ floor artifact assemblages.

Despite the extensive research that has occurred in the canyon during the past century, large gaps remained in our understanding of events in Chaco Canyon. Even after the initial survey of the park lands in 1972, our understanding of the dynamics of the early canyon settlement remained limited. The complex nature of the archaeology within Chaco Culture National Historical Park prevented a clear examination of the early occupations and led to confusion about events, chronology, and the rise of the Early Bonito phase. This picture was complicated by the mixed artifact assemblages found on many site surfaces as a result of lengthy occupations. Some of these gaps were to be rectified by a series of excavations at early puebloan sites based on a stratification of surveyed sites from the early stages of the Pecos Classification (Table I.1.2). These stages in Chaco Canyon began at approximately A.D. 1 (Basketmaker II) and ended at approximately A.D. 1300 (late Pueblo III).

Unfortunately, we know little of the Basketmaker II use of the area except to acknowledge the presence of these sites among the myriad of "lithic" or Archaic sites recorded

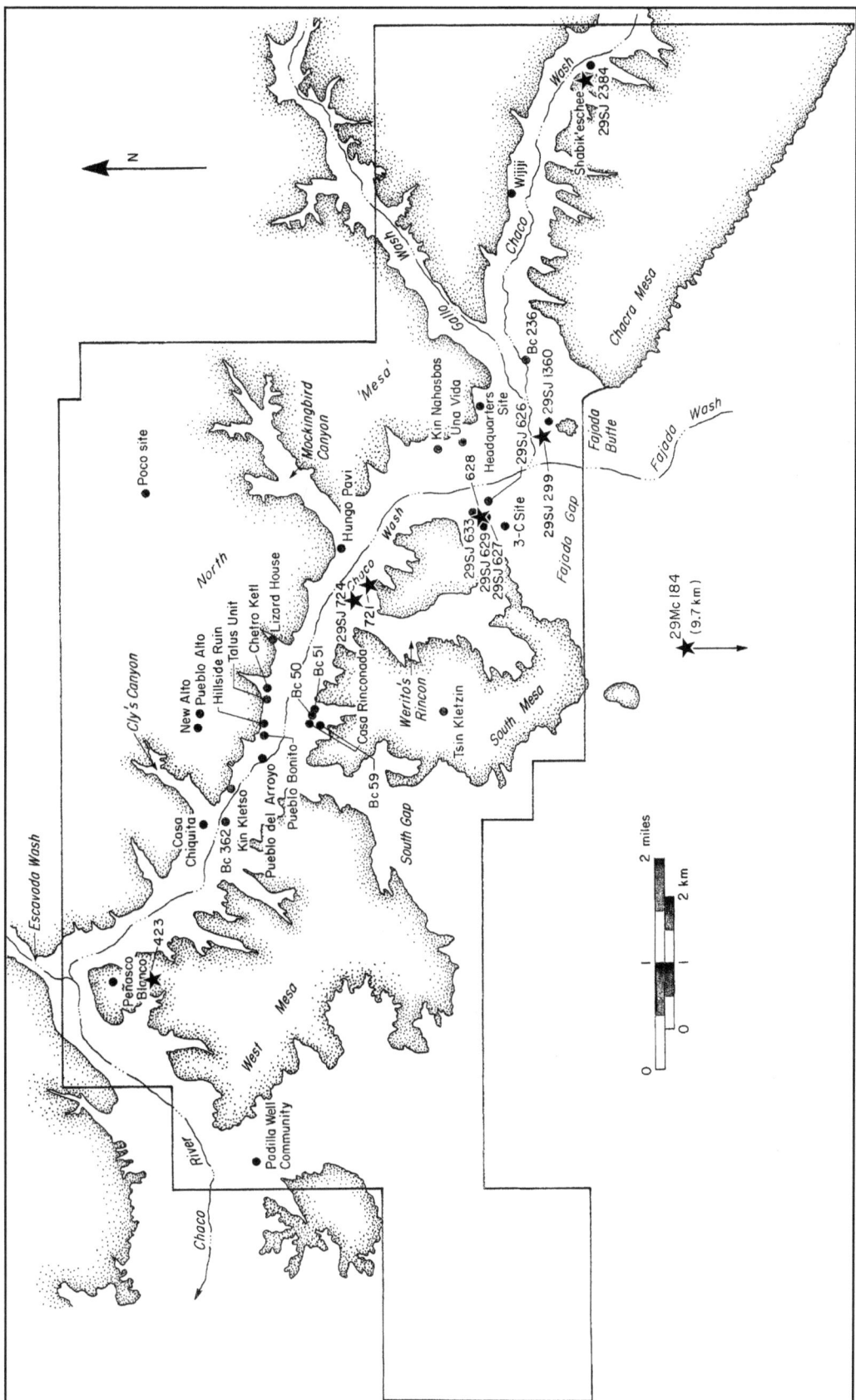

Figure 1.1.3. Basketmaker III and Pueblo I sites, marked by stars, excavated by the Chaco Project in 1973 and 1974 (CHCU 65022).

during various surveys over the past 35 years (see Elliott 1986). Excavations in rockshelters along the north side of Chaco Canyon (Mathews and Neller 1979; Simmons 1984) and west of the park have revealed ephemeral or seasonal preceramic use. A series of burned, bell-shaped pits on the top of North Mesa east of the park excavated during the Alamito Coal Mine Project (Simmons 1982) also suggested seasonal use. Recent road projects north of Pueblo Pintado, which is located near the east end of Chaco Canyon, yielded several shallow Basketmaker II pithouses near Ojo Encino (Kendrick 2000) and on Sisnathyel Mesa (Reed and Hensler 2001) near Counselors, New Mexico.

A possible Basketmaker II pit room was excavated near Star Lake, east of Pueblo Pintado, by Wait (1983:54-55). Finally, deep in the side of the Gallo Wash embankment near the Visitor's Center, four meters below the surface, a firepit (29SJ 1987) was excavated in 1973 that yielded an uncorrected radiocarbon date (195-130 B.C.: Isotope #7248; Hall 1975) that placed its use in the Basketmaker II period. No other cultural materials were found in association. Overall, our understanding of Basketmaker II in the Chaco area is poor and needs improvement. No excavation of Basketmaker II or earlier sites is covered here.

Little was known of the early puebloan Basketmaker III and Pueblo I settlements other than piecemeal information from isolated pithouses and structures partially exposed during the excavation of later architectural remains and pithouses exposed in the wash banks. The terms *pithouses* and *pitstructures* are used interchangeably in this report. In general, *pithouse* refers to the early, semi-subterranean or subterranean habitation structure common to the Basketmaker III and Pueblo I periods. In the absence of floor habitation features, such as mealing bin areas, storage pits and bins, and other signs of extensive domestic use, the pithouse is labeled a *kiva*, or rarely as a *protokiva*.

In some cases, however, the particular type of structure cannot be determined; the general term *pitstructure* covers all these structures.

Although the few sites excavated by the Chaco Project cannot be considered a representative sample of all those within the Chaco area, they do provide our first full-site glimpses of occupation in seemingly typical, small-house occupations between A.D. 500 and A.D. 900. Even though tying these early excavation results together has proved difficult after so much time has passed and the original staff has dispersed, this material provides a base for future studies of early puebloan settlement of the region.

Seven Basketmaker III and Pueblo I sites were investigated by the Chaco Center in 1973, 1974, and 1975 (Table I.1.3), and these were first summarized by McKenna and Truell (1986). Primary emphasis in this report is on the architecture (Volume I) and material remains (Volume II) collected from the seven excavations. Site descriptions and excavation notes for each site are covered in Chapters 3 and 4.

The Basketmaker III and Pueblo I excavations discussed here were conducted early in the Chaco Project years and lacked the rigorous field and recording techniques that characterized the later excavations. The subsequent excavations at several small Pueblo II houses and at Pueblo Alto shifted focus away from the early work and played a role in the results of the first excavations being relegated to the last publication. In addition, the shift in leadership from Robert Lister and Alden Hayes, who steered the early days of the Chaco Project, to a younger staff also led to a de-emphasis on the early sites and expanded efforts at the complex, artifact-rich Pueblo II sites of 29SJ 627 (Truell 1992), 29SJ 629 (Windes 1993), and 29SJ 1360 (McKenna 1984). Completion of the various site and artifact reports has taken two decades, resulting in some discontinuity in focus and aims. Excavations of Basketmaker III and Pueblo I houses by the Museum of New Mexico along the Chaco River near Lake Valley in 1976 and 1978 for improvement of State Road 371 west of Chaco (Doleman 1979; Wiseman 1982b) are also pertinent to the present study. Parts of the latter works are included here.

After Hayes tested several early sites, three were chosen in 1973 for the Basketmaker III investigation (Chapter 3): 29SJ 299, located on the ridges below Fajada Butte and south of the Visitor's Center; 29SJ 423, situated on the mesa to the south of Peñasco Blanco at the west end of the monument; and 29SJ 628, buried in the midst of an area later termed Marcia's Rincon (after Marcia Truell-Newren) across from and southwest of the Visitor's Center near the old 3-C Site (Vivian 1965). A fourth location near the mouth of Werito's Rincon, across the Chaco Wash from the Chacoan greathouse of Hungo Pavi, was investigated immediately after work at 29SJ 423 was terminated. Here, the small, multicomponent site of 29SJ 721 was excavated because the profusion of Basketmaker ceramics indicated the probable presence of several pithouses.

In addition, the survey crew conducted limited excavations and testing to obtain archaeomagnetic and tree-ring dates from previously excavated pithouses at Shabik'eschee Village (29SJ 1659) late in 1973 (Chapter 3). These attempts failed. They also excavated a new pithouse (Y) and tested another (pithouse Z) to try to obtain new chronometric information. Marcia's Rincon and the Fajada Butte sites best fulfilled management's needs (see below) for future interpretative exhibits, while the plethora of sites spanning all time periods in these two localities were well suited for longer-term research goals investigating community areas.

In 1974, work continued in Marcia's Rincon, at Fajada Butte, and at Werito's Rincon. In the former, work began at 29SJ 627, primarily occupied during the Pueblo II period (McKenna and Truell 1986; Truell 1992) but first occupied in the Pueblo I period. At Fajada Butte, the Pueblo I house at 29SJ 299 was excavated (Chapter 4). The location at the mouth of Werito's Rincon remained important because of the presence of three pristine, arc-shaped Pueblo I houses and numerous other sites of differing periods that provided a potential locale for expanded research of community areas (Judge 1975). The classic arc-shaped central house at 29SJ 724 was excavated, and the midden at the northern house was tested (Chapter 4). Finally, in early 1975, 29Mc 184 was tested as part of a search for an early Pueblo II house (Chapter 4). It, too, turned out to be a classic Pueblo I house site and was later the focus of survey investigations in the South Fork Valley (Chapter 8).

Complete excavation of the selected sites was not always accomplished. Time constraints and the difficulty of locating buried pithouses by trenching probably means that not all the Basketmaker III houses at 29SJ 299 and 29SJ 628 were located. Some pithouses at 29SJ 628 were likely within the boundaries of two later Pueblo II sites excavated just upslope (29SJ 629; Windes 1993) and downslope (29SJ 627; Truell 1992). Both these later sites had early pithouses that probably should be associated with the occupation at 29SJ 628.

Structures at 29SJ 423 on the mesa top were generally so shallow and disturbed that excavation there was terminated after only limited work, despite the similarity of the settlement to Shabik'eschee Village at the opposite end of the park. Later structures at some sites were occasionally encountered and excavated, but the suspected Mesa Verdean (Pueblo III) kiva in 29SJ 299 was left untouched. Although promising remote sensing techniques were field-tested in the park, they were not useful in determining excavation strategies until the work commenced at Pueblo Alto (Windes 1987a, b). Later, considerable success at locating pithouses through magnetometer surveys was demonstrated during the Dolores Project in southwestern Colorado (Burns et al. 1984), but these techniques were never fully realized during the Chaco Project.

A number of field problems plagued these early excavations. Collection of data was not as good as it would become in later years, both in the field (e.g., inconsistent and unstandardized note taking, cultural and language problems between the Anglo supervisors and Navajo excavation crews, lack of systematic screening, few photographs taken as a result of the use of the time-consuming 4-by-5-inch-format cameras, and failure to collect pollen and flotation samples) and in the laboratory, where most staff were relatively new to the analyses. In contrast, however, the field archaeologists were also the material culture analysts, unlike in many projects where the two groups consist of different personnel. This allowed considerable continuity between field operations and the initial laboratory analyses.

Archaeologists supervised the site excavations under the overall supervision of Alden C. Hayes. Crews were composed of Navajo laborers from the local area, including some exceptionally skilled personnel who had worked for years in archaeology as well as several teenagers and young adults with little archaeological knowledge or experience. The normal laborer-to-archeologist ratio was 4:1 or 5:1. The junior archaeologists generally took all the field notes and photographs, organized the materials for shipment, took care of the field equipment, and carried out a myriad of tasks during excavation. Cultural differences between archaeologists and laborers presented some problems, especially in communication over how to excavate, what was found, and how it was bagged. Not all laborers could speak English, and none of the archaeologists could converse in Navajo. Although this relationship worked, it did present problems at times.

Heavy equipment was not employed during work on the early sites except to remove the fill in Pithouse G at 29SJ 628 with a backhoe. All excavation was done by hand using shovels, picks, and trowels. Screening was limited to pit contents, floor fills, and fill exhibiting interesting or unusual cultural materials. The majority of screening was through 1/4" mesh; fine screening through 1/8" and 1/16" mesh was rare and limited to selected floor features and areas yielding very small artifacts. Fill was typically removed in arbitrary levels, except for control bulks that were excavated in natural stratigraphic units designated as *layers*. All structures were mapped with tape measures, a plane table on a tripod, and an alidade, with vertical control maintained from a site datum and stadia rod or line level.

Because systematic collection of flotation and pollen samples (studies then in their infancy) did not occur until 1975, botanical information from the early sites is sparse except for 29SJ 724, where samples were collected in 1975-1976. Likewise, standardized project terminologies and computerized inventories only became common by 1975. Feature designations have been standardized for this report (see Chapter 7). Although both tree-ring and archaeomagnetic samples were eagerly sought, the lack of suitable wood for tree-ring dating, and the limited availability of personnel from the Earth Sciences Laboratory at the University of Oklahoma to collect firepit samples during early excavations often led to limited chronometric dates (Chapter 6). However, W. James Judge had been trained to collect archaeomagnetic samples by 1974 and Tom Windes by 1975, making the project self-sufficient in this respect.

A number of radiocarbon samples were also collected from the early sites for dating but were not processed because of high costs, statistical imprecision, and the reliance on other methods. In 1991, a federal grant to Dr. Bruno Marino of the Applied Sciences Department at Harvard University to study carbon dioxide content in the atmosphere (Marino 1987; Marino and McElroy 1991), enabled a number of corn kernels from sites throughout Chaco Canyon to be radiocarbon dated. Almost no corn kernels were recovered from the early sites, but a floated sample from 29SJ 724 yielded enough kernels to permit dating and a CO_2 analysis. In addition, five radiocarbon samples from 29SJ 628 were processed in 2004, and obsidian hydration analyses were conducted in 1991 with mixed results. Glass cells for monitoring temperature and moisture were planted for a year in Pithouse Y at Shabik'eschee in 1989-1990 and in Pithouse A at 29SJ 299 in 1991-1992 as part of the overall obsidian hydration study (Stevenson 1993).

Each site supervisor kept daily logs of work and lists of all the specimens recovered. The latter were listed by provenience using Field Specimen (FS) numbers. Notes of the excavations and all photos were also the supervisor's task. North arrows in photographs and on excavation maps generally reflect magnetic north, although they have been changed to true north for the vast majority of the maps presented here. The invention by Julian Whittlesey of the Whittlesey bipod enabled photographs to be taken in 1974 with a 35 mm camera mounted between two tall poles directly above excavation units (e.g., room photographs at 29SJ 724; Chapter 4). This saved the supervisors from having to use the pipe bipod/ladder system designed by Alden Hayes for taking photographs, a highly risky venture that resulted in at least one fall (by Richard Loose). Later OSHA safety authorities would have been appalled.

A more systematic attempt at documenting features began in 1976 when a manual for excavation was developed (Judge et al. 1976) for 29SJ 629 and Pueblo Alto. All cultural materials recovered during the project were sent to the Chaco Center laboratory in Albuquerque, where analysis did not begin in earnest until 1976—these are stored in the Chaco Museum Collections in the Hibben Building at the University of New Mexico. The final digital data from the site inventories and analyses are kept in the Chaco Museum Collections: Chaco Project Databases are available for future research. Related materials can be found under *http://chacoarchive.org* but not the specific Project databases compiled for the excavated sites.

Management Goals

The Chaco Project was an alliance between research and management goals. Archaeological research cannot be carried out in national parks without resulting in tangible benefits to the public. One such benefit is enhancing the interpretation of the cultural remains through articles and reports, often sold in the park and made available to public, academic, and cultural resource management libraries. These articles and reports should result in changes in the interpretative programs from trail pamphlets and films to guided tours and, sometimes, with new museum or open-air exhibits of the excavations. In addition, research provides managers with a more comprehensive view and complete documentation of the cultural resources held in the public trust. Given the stature of the resources within a national park as protected national treasures, restraints must be practiced to ensure minimal or no impact to resources not specified in the research plan.

From the park and managerial perspective, the Chaco Project provided an opportunity to revise the Chacoan story. The lack of early puebloan house exhibits was to be rectified by having some of the early houses excavated close to existing roads to replicate the Ruins Road tour so popular at Mesa Verde National Park in Colorado. Furthermore, excavations close to existing roads would minimize adverse impacts to the remainder of the park. Thus, work was constrained by logistical issues, which are important factors in any research, although some sites were investigated that were not restricted by the close-to-the-road criterion. Generally, site excavations were limited to those close to roads, leaving many potential excavation sites inaccessible in the park back country. The exception was 29SJ 423 at the far west end of the park, which at the time had road access to nearby Peñasco Blanco on the mesa top.

By 1990, however, park exhibits at the newer excavated sites had not materialized and were no longer part of the interpretative planning. All the excavated sites were backfilled shortly after excavation. The changing political and financial fortunes of the National Park Service curtailed many of the long-term objectives of the Project, which cut back the ambitious community studies proposed by Judge (1975). On the other hand, federal funding allowed the Project to stay the course and to be completed after nearly four decades.

Finally, it must be remembered that the early excavated sites suffered from an inexperienced staff (the author included) and the pains of a new project, which improved greatly in later years. There was a shortage of staff until the Pueblo Alto project commenced, so that all of the material analyses from the early excavations were delayed until the larger staff arrived. This posed a problem when the laboratory work started, for the amount of the analytical backlog was formidable. Nevertheless, the Chaco Project was fortunate to have had an enduring staff that, for the most part, consisted of the same dedicated persons throughout the project who produced a wealth of new information and many new interpretations of the Chaco story. Completion of the project was provided by continuing support of both the park and regional staffs, despite several turnovers in leadership.

Acknowledgments

A tremendous amount of volunteer help was critical to the success of the project, particularly in the post-excavation years (Table I.1.4) when individuals and the Sierra Club enabled more fieldwork to be conducted outside the park to broaden our knowledge of the early puebloan settlement in and around Chaco Canyon. In addition, the curatorial staff at the Maxwell Museum and later the National Park Service's collections staff greatly assisted with the work on the maps, photographs, documents, and artifacts associated with this volume: Wendy Bustard, Greg Brown, John George, Phil LoPiccolo, Tyler Love, Brenna Lissoway, and Rita Shukla. I am indebted to Walter Waite and Clay Mathers for scanning the many over-size ink and mylar maps related to this work. Thanks to my bosses, Jim Judge, Larry Nordby, Bob Powers, and Dabney Ford, for the time and patience in allowing this work to be done, and to Navajo Nation and John Stein for work on the Navajo lands. Also my deepest respect and honor to Alden Hayes, who started me on this long journey, and to the park for its long support. I appreciate the initial editing work done by June-el Piper and layout editor Donna Carpio with regrets that it could not be completed under their guidance. The digital assistance from Beth Bagwell, Chris Millington, and Clay Mathers helped achieve many of the final figures and photographs used in this report. All the site maps and features generated for this report were completed in India ink on mylar by the author from the field maps and housed in the Chaco Archives. I especially appreciate the beautiful aerial photographs taken by Adriel Heisey and his permission for their use here. Finally, my special thanks to Richard C. Lange for accepting this report for publication and to Alicia M. Vega for the final editing and assembly through the Arizona State Museum Archaeological Series.

Table I.1.1. Chaco Project surveys in and around Chaco Canyon and the park outliers.

Where	When	Who (P.I.: crew chiefs)	Survey Type[a]	Size (mi²/ha)	Occupation Periods	No. of Sites	Comments
Chaco Monument	1972	Hayes: Bardé, Beardsley, Windes	Class III	32 / 8,291	Archaic–Historic	1,731	
Monument to Escavada Wash	1975	Hayes: McKenna	Class III	6.2 / 1,607	Archaic–Historic	163	
Western part of monument	1973–1974	Hayes: Thrift, Schelberg	Class III	11.0" / 2,850	Archaic–Historic	Unk.	Resurvey
Monument and beyond	1971	Judge: Stanford	Class III (transect)	19.8 / 5,139	Archaic–Historic	1,689	7.2 mi² (1,865 ha); Some resurveyed
South of monument boundary From South Mesa to West Mesa	1973–1975	Hayes: McKenna, Thrift, Schelberg, Windes	Class III	7.25 / 1,879 (includes a S. Addition)	Archaic–Historic	89	
South Addition	1983–1984	Powers: McKenna	Class III	0.80 / 208	Archaic? –Historic	63	
Fajada Gap: South Ridge	1988–1989	Windes	Class III	0.27 / 70	PI–PIII	21	
Fajada Wash, upper South Fork Valley	1993–1999	Windes	Class II (stratified)	6.0 / 1,546	BMIII–PIII	102	
Upper Kin Klizhin Wash	1996–1998	Windes	Class II (stratified)	0.8 / 207	PI–PII	15	
Chacra Mesa, south and east of park	1983–1984	Powers: McKenna	Class III	5.2 / 1,346	Archaic–Historic	378	

Table I.1.1. Chaco Project surveys in and around Chaco Canyon and the park outliers, cont'd

Where	When	Who (P.I.: crew chiefs)	Survey Type[a]	Size (mi²/ha)	Occupation Periods	No. of Sites	Comments
Outlier Units							
Kin Bineola	1972	Hayes: Windes	Class III	0.38 / 98	BMIII–PIII, Navajo	12	
Kin Klizhin	1972	Hayes: Bardé	Class III	0.06 / 16	late PII	1	Greathouse only
Kin Ya'a	1972	Hayes: Bardé, Beardsley, Windes	Class III	0.25 / 65	PI–PIII, Navajo	47	
Pueblo Pintado east	1972	Hayes: Windes	Class III	0.25 / 65	PI–PIII, Navajo	20	
Pueblo Pintado, isolated unit Section 12, T20N, R8W	1972	Hayes: Windes	Class III	0.5 / 130	No sites found	0	Land returned to Navajo Nation
Kin Bineola	1983–1984	Powers: McKenna	Class III	1.8 / 473	BMIII–PIII, Historic	156	
Kin Klizhin	1983–1984	Powers: McKenna	Class III	1.9 / 502	BMIII–PIII, Historic	133	
Chaco East Community	1989–1997	Windes	Class II (stratified)	4.5 / 1,172	late PI–PIII	89	Mainly house sites
Pueblo Pintado east	1998–2001	Windes	Class III	1.0 / 259	late PI–PIII, Historic	65	Partly resurveyed
Pueblo Pintado west	2000–2001	Windes	Class II (stratified)	0.27 / 70	late PI–PIII	13	Mainly house sites
North cliff face and talus east of park boundary 3.2 km	2006–2007	Windes, Kolber	Class III	0.04 / 11	PII–III, Historic	17	

Note: Site numbers cover two counties: McKinley: 29Mc 100-797 and San Juan: 29SJ 100-3034. Additional Lands survey (1983-1984) totaled 20.3 mi² (5,260 hectares). Many areas were surveyed intermittently over several years.

[a] Class II inventories are less than 100 percent pedestrian surveys and Class III inventories are 100 percent pedestrian surveys. Stratified surveys are 100 percent coverage for puebloan houses, community structures, and storage facilities only. Other sites, usually not recorded, occur in relatively low numbers. Standards for Class II and Class III cultural resource inventories set by the Bureau of Land Management are not entirely applicable here.

Table I.1.2. Various temporal classificatory schemes for the puebloan settlement of Chaco Canyon and the interior San Juan Basin.

Date A.D.	Pecos Classification Anasazi Periods	Chaco Center				Ceramic Assemblages
		Gladwin (1945) Chaco Branch Phases	Hayes (1981) Chaco Phases	Judge (1989) Chaco Phases	Windes [a] (revised, 1987a) Chaco Phases	
0	Basket Maker II					
100						
200						
300						
400					brownware	brownware
500	Basket Maker III					
600		La Plata	La Plata	Pre-system	La Plata	La Plata
700		White Mound	White Mound		White Mound	White Mound
800	Pueblo I	Kiatuthlanna	Kiatuthlanna			
900		Red Mesa	Red Mesa		Bonito / Early	Kiatuthlanna
1000	Pueblo II	Wingate	Wingate	Initialization		Red Mesa
		Hosta Butte	Hosta Butte	Formalization		
1100		Bonito	Bonito	Expansion	Classic	Gallup
	Pueblo III		McElmo	Reorganization	Late	Late Mix
1200				Collapse	McElmo	McElmo
1300		Mesa Verde	Mesa Verde	Post-system	Mesa Verde	Mesa Verde

[a] Modified from Windes (1987a): Figure 1.5

Table I.1.3. Basketmaker III and Pueblo I sites excavated by the Chaco Center.

Site	When Excavated or Tested	Site Supervisor(s)	Occupation Period(s)	No. of Excavated Pitstructures	No. of Excavated Surface Rooms	No. of Excavated Cists	No. of Middens Tested
29SJ 299	1973	Loose	BMIII, PII, PIII	4	0	9	0
29SJ 299	1974	Gillespie, Masterson, Windes	PI	1	4	0	0
29SJ 423	1973	Windes	BMIII	5	4	4	1
29SJ 628[a]	1973	Truell	late BMIII-early PI	6	0	6	0
29SJ 721	1974	Windes	BMIII, PI, early PIII	3	1	7	0
29SJ 724 Central House	1974	Windes	PI	1	10	0	1
North House	1975	Windes	PI-PII	0	0	0	1
29SJ 1659[b] (Shabik'eschee)	1973	Huckins, McLeod, Schelberg, Thrift, Windes	BMIII	1.25	0	2	0
29Mc184	1975	Windes	PI	0	0	0	3

[a] Pithouse G excavated by John Thrift's 1973 survey crew.
[b] Primarily excavated by John Thrift's 1973 survey crew.

Table I.1.4. Volunteers who helped work on the Basketmaker III-Pueblo I project.

1990 Sierra Club Service Trip
John Fries, Long Beach, CA
Elinor Large
Herb Kutchins, CA
Gina Kutchins, CA
Deborah Silverman, CNHP
Marietta Tretter, College Station, TX

1991 Sierra Club Service Trip
Leader: Bonnie Sharpe, Placentia, CA
Assistant: Jim Ilchuk, Oakland, CA
Jim Amos, El Monte, CA
Paul F. Carlton, Monrovia, CA
Lee Emery, Golden, BC Canada
John Fries, Long Beach, CA
Gretchen Lawrence, Santa Ana, CA
Donald C. Lowrie, Santa Fe, NM
Tom Meehan, Salem, OR
Ellen F. Pillard, Reno, NV
Judy Schum, Albuquerque, NM
Sylvia Simpson, Baltimore, MD
Cheryl Srnka, Alameda, CA

1992 Sierra Club Service Trip
Leader: Bonnie Sharpe, Placentia, CA
Assistant: Tom Meehan, Salem, OR
Cynthia Ames, Seattle, WA
Ann Chalson, Omaha, NE
Dan Fuller, Kansas City, KS
Judy & Marv Kieca, Castle Rock, CO
Bobbie & Tom Kocim, Lombard, IL
Ruby Layson, Frankfort, KY
Tom Moon, Haddonfield, NJ
Joe Morton, Towson, MD
Carol Pedersen, Ventura, CA
Beth Perdue, Manakin, VA
Beth Rahn, Abbottstown, PA

1992 Sierra Club Service Trip (2)
Leader: Bonnie Sharpe, Placentia, CA
Assistant: John Fries, Long Beach, CA
Amy Behrens, Ruxton, MD
Woodrow Blettel, Salem, OR
Chuck Buck, Fullerton, CA
Hilde Casserini, Potomac, MD
Jeremy Kahn, Atlanta, GA
Micheline Lessard, Ithaca, NY
Cheryl Srnka, Alameda, CA
Carol Stansfield, Monument, CO
John Stansfield, Monument, CO
Bob & Doris Sherrick, Peculiar, MO
Bette Tarrant, Omaha, NE

1993 Sierra Club Service Trip
Leader:Bonnie Sharpe,Placentia, CA
Lee Emery, Golden, BC, Canada
Cathy Evans, Oakland, CA
Nancy Follin, Culver City, CA
Nancy Jewett
Gretchen Lawrence, Santa Ana, CA
Molly McCormick, College Station, TX
Robert Meador, Yorba Linda, CA
Tom Meehan, Salem, OR
Dawn Moore, Santa Monica, CA
Barbara Reber, Newport Beach, CA
Joann Sarachman, Whittier, CA
Cheryl Srnka, Alameda, CA
Christa Shackleford, Seal Beach, CA
Anne Washburn, Pomona, CA

1994 Sierra Club Service Trip
Leader: Bonnie Sharpe, Placentia, CA
Assistant: Tom Meehan, Salem, OR
Cheryl Srnka, Alameda, CA
Jim Avila, Sacramento, CA
Woodrow Blettel, Salem, OR
John Fries, Long Beach, CA
Dan Fuller, Kansas City, KS
Claudia Ganz, New York, NY
Stephen Gewirtz, Baltimore, MD
Liz King, Sunnyvale, CA
Christine Kiefer, Avondale East, CA
Michael Kuhn, Houston, TX
Rita Locke, San Diego, CA
Molly McCormick, College Station, TX
Murray Olsen, Ogden, UT
Warren Sklar, Seattle, WA
Jim Trimbell, Green Valley, AZ
Mike Young, Westfield, MA

1995 Sierra Club Service Trip (1)
Leader: Bonnie Sharpe,Placentia, CA
Matt Earls, Venice, CA
Reid Earls III, Venice, CA
John Fries, Long Beach, CA
Terry L. Hartman, Modesto, CA
Patricia Jamison, Decatur, GA
Kathy Klingensmith, Tiburon, CA
Leslie Lihou, University City, MO
Tom Meehan, Salem, OR
Jim Mezzetta, Vallejo, CA
Edward Morente, Carson City, CA
Mike Reynolds, Tiburon, CA
Dennis Sargent, Albany, OR
Martha Sargent, Albany, OR
Chris Simon, El Cerrito, CA
Robert Suess
James Soe Nyun, San Diego, CA
 & Gaithersburg, MD
Daniel Talonn, St. Louis, MO
Jim Trimbell, Green Valley, AZ

1995 Sierra Club Service Trip (2)
Leader: Bonnie Sharpe, Placentia, CA
Valerie Banks, Hermosa Beach, CA
Alethea Brown, Kenner, LA
Dennis Charles, Camarillo, CA
Laurie Clifton, Chico,CA
Cinda & Tom Cole, Tempe, AZ
Dave Davidson, Camarillo, CA
Janet Drover, San Diego, CA
Lynn Drover, San Francisco, CA
Ron Goldwyn, Albuquerque, NM
Larry McLamore, Alexandria, VA
Paula Massouh, Alexandria, VA
Marie Sasso, Denton, TX
Diane Van Horn, McKinney, TX

1996 Sierra Club Service Trip (1)
Co-Leaders:
    Bonnie Sharpe, Placentia, CA
    Tom Meehan, Salem, OR
Cheryl Srnka, Alameda, CA
Craig Adams, San Diego, CA
Julie Arneth, Green Bay, WE
Cinda Cole, Tempe, AZ
William Dreimiller, Chagrin Falls, OH
Jan Effenberger, Boulder, CO
Alice Englebretson, Urbana, IL
Bob Hesseltine, Clements, CA
Allen Kietzke, Stockton, CA
Phillip Lucier, Los Angeles, CA
Larry McLamore, Alexandria, VA
Max Ratheal, Weatherford, TX
Barbara Rhomberg, Oakland, CA
Marilyn Riegelhuth, Concord, CA
Judy Santos, Sherman Oaks, CA
Anita Schmid, Nashville, TN
Leonard Schutz, Los Angeles, CA
Dick Sheppard, Chino Valley, AZ
Becky Van Doren, Phoenix, AZ

1996 Sierra Club Service Trip (2)
Leader: Bonnie Sharpe, Placentia, CA
Russ Bruzee, Patricia Schuh, & Max
    Bruzee/Schuh, Lake Forest, CA
Judy Cunningham, Johnstown, CO
Reid Earls, Venice, CA
John Flanigan,West Palm Beach, FL
Judy Kieca, Castle Rock, CO
Marv Kieca, Castle Rock, CO
Murray Olsen, Ogden, UT
Jamie Schubert, Lakewood, CO
Warren Sklar, Seattle, WA
Cheryl Srnka, Alameda, CA

Jim Trimbell, Green Valley, AZ
Vera Vann, Blue Diamond, NV
Anna Walker, Fenton, MI
Mike Young, Westfield, MA

1997 Sierra Club Service Trip (1)
Leader: Bonnie Sharpe, Placentia, CA
Peter Abolins, Chico, CA
Max Alin, Seattle, WA
Chuck Buck, Fullerton, CA
Cinda Cole, Tempe, AZ
Bernard Finley, Carmel, CA
John Flanigan, W. Palm Beach, FL
John Fries, Long Beach, CA
Margaret Grochocki, W. Jordan, UT
Tom Hartman, Hayward, CA
Victor Jahn, TX
Molly McCormick, College Station, TX
Nathan McIntire, Tempe, AZ
Nancey McVean, Weatherford, TX
Tom Moon, Haddonfield, NJ
Ellen Pillard, Reno, NV
Max Ratheal, Weatherford, TX
Joann Sarachman, Whittier, CA
Jamie Schubert, Lakewood, CO
Cheryl Srnka, Alameda, CA
Karen Stlip, Dauphin, PA
Jim Trimbell, Green Valley, AZ
Carol Turner, Gainesville, FL
Lynn Withey, San Francisco, CA
Jeffrey Yann, Hacienda Heights, CA

1997 Sierra Club Service Trip (2)
Leader: Bonnie Sharpe, Placentia, CA
Patricia Brantley, Las Vegas, NM
Janene Canady, Albuquerque, NM
Sylvia Castricon, Millfield, OH
Brian Cooley, Berkeley, CA
Jon Fish, Del Mar, CA
Nancy Green, Ben, OR
Jim Harsh, Espanola, NM
Correen Kaufman, Del Mar, CA
Michael MacKlin, Houston, TX
Liz Ott
Haralds Robeznieks, Chicago, IL
Maureen Schaefer, New Orleans, LA
Daniel Schmidt, Woodbury, MN
Better Tarrant, Omaha, NE
Jill Warwick, MN?
Nancy Yates, Benicia, CA

1998 Sierra Club Service Trip (1)
Leader: Bonnie Sharpe, Placentia, CA
Assistant: Cheryl Srnka, Alameda, CA
Assistant: John Fries, Long Beach, CA
Julie Arneth, Green Bay, WI
Chuck Buck, Fullerton, CA
John Flanigan, W. Palm Beach, FL

Margaret Grohocki, W. Jordan, UT
Beverly Henson
Victor Jahn, TX
Linda Lucas, Napa CA
Marie Maryhofer
Nathan McIntyre, Tempe, AZ
Tom Meehan, Salem, OR
Eric Newmark, Santa Rosa, CA
Dalfred Ross, Napa, CA
Tim Reimer, Sioux Falls, SD
Peter Ruddock, Menlo Park, CA
Nathan Saitzberg, Larchmont, NY
Jamie Schubert, Lakewood, CO
Jim Trimbell, Green Valley, AZ
Jeff Yann, Hacienda Heights, CA

1998 Sierra Club Service Trip (2)
Leader: Bonnie Sharpe, Placentia, CA
Assistant: Cheryl Srnka, Alameda, CA
JoEllen Arnold, Sacramento, CA
Eileen Bacha, Youngstown, OH
Monica Beary, Alameda, CA
Kim Chappell, Cochranville, PA
Minou Djawdan, San Diego, CA
Martha Ettinger, Palos Verdes Est., CA
Cheri Frederick, Milwaukee, WI
Samara C. Gill, Carpinteria, CA
Janie Grussing, Palm Beach Gardens, FL
Peg Kaiser, Oakland, MD
Elizabeth McGowan, Eagle, WI
Betty Mooney, Charlottesville, VA
Joseph Mooney, Charlottesville, VA
Richard Quinn, Evanston, IL
Craig Westendorf, Phoenix, AZ

1999 Sierra Club Service Trip
Deva Abela, Tucson, AZ
Jim Avila, Sacramento, CA
Rich Blackmarr
Suzanne Bucci
Calvin Calderone
Cinda Cole, Tempe, AZ
Tom Cole, Tempe, AZ
Toa Cox
Matt Earls, Tijeras, NM
Reid Earls, III, Venice, CA
Esteban Echeverria
John Fries, Long Beach, CA
Liz King, Sunnyvale, CA
Nathan McIntyre, Tempe, AZ
Joa Mondres
Ellen Pillcrop
Max Ratheal, Weatherford, TX
Joann Sarachman
Joey Schoeneck
Jamie Schubert
Cheryl Srynka, Alameda, CA
Rodney Thompson

Marietta Tretter, College Station, TX
Jim Trimbell, Green Valley, AZ
Andy Way
Al Webster, Santa Fe, NM
Jini West
Mike Young, Westfield, MA

2000 Sierra Club Service Trip
Jack Boger
Roger Cowan, Albuquerque
Mary Ann DeWitt
Diane Flynn, Minneapolis, MN
George Folsom
Paul LaQuatra
Mike Pleban
Al Skinner, TX

Four Corners School for Outdoor Education, Monticello, UT
1993 unknown
1994 Janet Ross, Monticello, UT
1996 Lee Bauer, Canada

Other volunteers
1988 - Lisa Rhode, Chaco Culture NHP

1989 - John Roney, Albuquerque

1990 - G.B. Cornucopia, Chaco
   Culture NHP
Mark Padilla
Ellen Pillard, Reno, NV
Pat Schuh
Deborah Silverman, Chaco Culture NHP

1991 - Lee Bauer, Canada
Cheryl Ford, Albuquerque
Mike Larkin, Albuquerque
Peter McKenna, Albuquerque
Willy Schuster, Kronberg, Germany
John Stein, Gallup, NM
Gwinn Vivian, Tucson, AZ

1993 - Ruth Erkkila
Heather Pringle, Canada
Sam Wainer
Nelson Weindling

1994 - Valerie Banks, Redondo
   Beach, CA
Jane Eastwood, MN
Dabney Ford, Chaco Culture NHP
Rory Gauthier, Chaco Culture NHP
Trevor Potter
Tracy Sumner
Gwinn Vivian, Tucson, AZ

1995 - Randi Gladwell, Albuquerque

Anne Goldberg, Albuquerque
Anne Hodges, Albuquerque?
Vic Holmes, Sandia Park, NM
Connor Windes, Albuquerque
Mary Jo Windes, Albuquerque

1996 - Rodd Bark
Carol Trujillo, Chaco Culture NHP

1997 - Rachel Anderson, Chaco Culture NHP
Taft Blackhorse, Shiprock, NM
Anne Goldberg, Tucson, AZ

1998 - Rachel Anderson, Chaco Culture NHP
William Doleman, Albuquerque

1999 - Rachel Anderson, Chaco Culture NHP
William Doleman, Albuquerque
"Dusty" Windes, Albuquerque
Jeremy Moss, Albuquerque

2000 - Jeremy Moss, Albuquerque

2001 - Willy Schuster, Kronberg, Germany

2001 - Eileen Bacha, Youngstown, OH
Valerie Banks, Redondo Beach, CA
Diane Flynn, Minneapolis, MN
Holly Flynn, Minneapolis, MN
Hannah Fretwell, Albuquerque
Peg Kaiser, Oakland, MD
Jamie Schubert, Lakewood, CO
Cheryl Srnka, Alameda, CA

2002-Eileen Bacha, Youngstown, OH
Valerie Banks, Redondo Beach, CA
Hannah Fretwell, Albuquerque
Peg Kaiser, Oakland, MD
Richard Moeller, Santa Fe, NM
Ursula Moeller, Santa Fe, NM
Jamie Schubert, Lakewood, CO

2003 - Eileen Bacha, Youngstown, OH
Beth Bagwell, Albuquerque
G. B. Cornucopia, Chaco Culture HP
Steve Emmons, Albuquerque
Stephanie Ford, Albuquerque
Randi Gladwell, Albuquerque
John George, Albuquerque
Peg Kaiser, Oakland, MD
Teri Orr, Albuquerque, NM

2004 - Connie Constan, Albuquerque
Diane Flynn, Albuquerque

Chapter 2
The Natural Environment

A multitude of natural, environmental, and topographic variables are critical for understanding the puebloan use and occupancy of the Chaco Canyon region. These factors change through time and require modeling of the past and present conditions if we are to understand their importance to the former inhabitants and their impacts on daily life. A later review of climate across the Southwest is nicely summarized by Kenneth Peterson (2012).

Local flora and fauna, for instance, were widely exploited by the inhabitants of Chaco Canyon. The local vegetation is dominated by members of the Compositae and Chenopodiaceae families, with the major species evident today being well-represented in archaeological deposits (Toll, Volume II, Chapter 14). Today, saltbush (*Atriplex* spp.), rabbitbrush (*Chrysothamnus* spp.), sagebrush (*Artemisia* spp.), snakeweed (*Gutierrezia* sp.), and greasewood (*Sarcobatus* spp.) provide the majority of low ground cover in the region. Grazing has greatly reduced or eliminated many of the grasses that once dominated. Many of the brush species are present today in the immediate vicinity (A. Cully 1976; Cully and Cully 1985; Mathien 1991; McKenna 1984:6-7; and Windes 1987a: Table I.2.4) and indicate an environment little changed from the past. Although hunting was an important subsistence strategy throughout the puebloan occupation of Chaco Canyon, horticulture assumed the greatest importance, particularly after the Pueblo I period.

Fauna

Game was an important source of protein and ancillary materials for the inhabitants of Chaco. We expect that the large species were most common early in the puebloan occupation before human predation impacted their numbers. By 1900, the big game animals formerly common to northwestern New Mexico whose remains are found in the archaeological deposits (mule deer, pronghorn antelope, elk, and bighorn sheep) were nearly regionally extinct as a result of hunting pressure (e.g., Bailey 1931).

The faunal remains at sites are widely reported in the works of the Chaco Center (see Volume II, Chapter 11), and present-day fauna have been covered in previous reports (e.g., Hibben 1937a; J. Cully 1985), but a number of changes have occurred in the past decades that are worthy of note. The prior couple of decades were particularly wet, but the last two decades have been of drought (through 2014). The range of some animals has been affected by these changes, which may have relevance to our understanding prehistoric conditions.

A number of animals with ranges 20-30 miles outside Chaco Canyon have been observed lately: a steady series of Rocky Mountain elk sightings has occurred yearly in Chaco since the first elk in 45 years was observed by the author and Gwinn Vivian in 1995 east of Shabik'eschee Village. Perhaps in prehistoric times routes between the continental divide east of Chaco and

Mt. Taylor to the south sometimes led elk into the main canyon. But a large increase in elk in nearby Largo Canyon to the north of Chaco may be contributing to a small but steady spillover of animals into Chaco (Peter McKenna, personal communication 2000). These animals generally prefer wooded habitat, although they will cross extensive plains (Gates 1967:35).

Prior to 1995, elk had not been seen in Chaco Canyon since three animals wintered there in 1950 (Gwinn Vivian, personal communication 1995; Vivian and Mathews 1965:3). Navajos living around Pueblo Pintado have told the author of other recent incursions of elk into the canyon in the 1990s. By the winter of 2000-2001, a herd of about 20 animals had moved into the eastern part of the park. In October 2002, 32 animals on Chacra Mesa were counted by airplane survey. The number rose to 47 animals by the spring of 2004 and more than 100 by 2012. Possibly the increased vehicular traffic and human habitation have affected traditional migratory routes across the continental divide, although evidence for elk by 1906 at Mt. Taylor and in the Zuni Mountains by 1906 was lacking (Bailey 1931:31), suggesting that these areas too were outside normal elk habitat. In prehistoric times, elk may have been more common and closer to the park area than now, although their sparse presence in the local archaeological record suggests otherwise (see Akins 1984:Table 18).

The most common artiodactyl in the prehistoric record in Chaco is the mule deer, which is the most numerous game mammal in New Mexico and one that can thrive in close proximity to humans (Stewart 1967:42, 50). Mule deer herds frequent the canyon and are often observed near seep areas. One such herd of seven animals was killed by poachers in the East Community area in the late 1980s. A herd of 17 animals was observed in the park by Rafael's Spring in West Mesa (personal observation, 1994); an October 2002 plane survey counted 34 in the park, and 33 were counted in the spring of 2004. On average, there are about six mule deer per square mile (Stewart 1967:44), although this seems likely only within Chaco Canyon. Elsewhere in Navajo country, Hill (1938:96) was told that deer were once so plentiful that four to 10 men could kill as many as 100 deer in a fortnight's hunt. Navajo informants told Judd (1954:349) that in the fall, with the approach of cold weather, many deer and antelope entered the canyon (this probably relates to conditions in the 1800s).

The wide-open country north and south of Chaco and west to the Chuska Mountains is suitable for antelope and may have been prehistorically as well (Bailey 1931:22; Russell 1964: Map 1). This animal once rivaled the western bison in numbers (Larsen 1967:61). Akins (1984: Table 18) identified antelope remains in deposits from throughout the puebloan occupation of the canyon, second to deer in terms of numbers of artiodactyl remains. In historic times, antelope and deer moved into Chaco country during the fall and were hunted there (Judd 1954:64, 349). After their demise by the late 1800s, antelope were locally extinct until they were reintroduced around Chaco in 1941 (Russell 1964: Tables 15, 22). Herds of 20 or more were observed by the author in the 1970s south of Chaco near Seven Lakes, evidently descendents of the 11 that were released on the Pitt Ranch in 1941 and the 15 released on the Westbrook Ranch in 1955. A pair of antelope was seen grazing as far north as just south of Fajada Butte and around Kin Klizhin in 1995, and three were spotted just south of the Fajada South Fork Pueblo I community in May 2002 but since then none have been sighted. In earlier times, when visitors were infrequent, a small antelope herd would occasionally wander into the Fajada Butte area from the south (Vivian and Mathews 1965:16). Like mule deer, pronghorn can live in close association with humans (Larsen 1967:66).

Antelope bands with as many as 60 to 70 animals were seen near Star Lake, east of Pueblo

Pintado, in 1975 and 1976 (Wait 1983:30). They probably derived from the 40 animals released at the Bob Ranch east of Pueblo Pintado in 1955 and the 40 more released at the nearby Farr Ranch. Prehistorically, antelope drives were probably infrequent because of the drastic reduction in numbers after such a communal pursuit (Hill 1938:n. 148; Wait 1983:31)—the only known game trap in the Chaco area is a Navajo one identified to Hill (1938:96) near the Escavada Wash.

Despite the presence of bighorn sheep remains in deposits from as early as the Basketmaker III period at Chaco—at times exceeding even those of pronghorn (Akins 1984:20)—it seems unlikely that bighorn sheep lived along the mesas of Chaco once the canyon became occupied by humans. Trapping along the peripheries of the San Juan Basin is the likely source of bighorn sheep remains in the canyon (Judd 1954:64; Windes 2008).

Finally, the brush- and shrub-covered canyon has long been the habitat of cottontails, while the grass plains to the south constitute jackrabbit habitat. In the 1980s, the latter began appearing inside the canyon around Fajada Butte, where they had not been observed in the 1970s. These observations suggest that the ebb and flow of regional game species, all of which have been found in the local prehistoric deposits, are a normal occurrence and should be considered in an attempt to explain hunting strategies.

Prairie dogs, a particularly favorite meal late in the puebloan occupation, have been absent in the park since being wiped out by the plague and subsequent poisoning campaigns in the 1930s (Findley et al. 1975:132, 134) except for a large colony observed near Fajada Butte in the 1940s (Gwinn Vivian, personal communication 2004). In very recent years, however, they have recolonized areas just outside the park boundaries. They, along with rabbits, kangaroo rats, porcupines, coyotes, foxes, dogs, ravens, bluejays, grasshoppers, and cutworms—all native to Chaco—were a constant threat to agricultural crops. They may have been dealt with in a manner described by the Navajo (Hill 1938:37-39).

Predatory mammals, except for coyotes, are rarely seen in or around the park. Occasionally, mountain lions have occupied Chacra Mesa (Vivian and Mathews 1965:16). Mark Gaede (personal communication, 2003), a photographer, observed a mountain lion on the cliffs behind Kin Bineola in 1975, which may have been the same as the one last observed west of Chaco in 1976 by Robert Powers (Windes 1987a:48). In 1996, mountain lion signs were noted around the Visitor's Center. The last mountain lion sightings were observed in the eastern canyon in 2007, 2011, and 2012. Occasionally bobcats and foxes are observed in the park; solitary badgers are more common. A lone badger was observed hunting with a pair of coyotes a few times in the residence area (1994-1995). A solitary black bear wandered into the park housing area in May 2000, the first historic sighting of a bear in the park, but a few others have been sighted since, including in 2012, usually during the winter months. In the recent months of 2014, local Navajos report sightings of wolves in the eastern canyon area.

Many species of birds are found in Chaco Canyon, including many migratory ones. Astoundingly, a pair of wild turkeys moved into Chaco Canyon near Chetro Ketl in 1997 and 1998, although the area is unfavorable turkey habitat. The only pictograph of turkeys (nine birds painted in red ochre) in Chaco known to the author occurs at site 29SJ 1699 in the same area. Turkey remains are relatively infrequent in faunal assemblages from sites in Chaco until the early A.D. 1100s, although they are quite common in Mesa Verdean deposits and puebloan sites north of the San Juan River, where they become common in Pueblo II times (Driver 2002:157). Raptors and other birds often frequent the park (J. Cully 1985). Bald eagles are extremely rare but sometimes golden eagles are present, as are peregrine falcons.

Other small mammals, reptiles, snakes,

spiders, and so on, are common to the canyon but are not economically important. Some, however, such as the kangaroo rat, have been particularly destructive of archaeological sites. Interestingly, tarantulas had never been observed in the region by the author until one was found in the south tributary to Fajada Wash on site 29Mc 659 in October 1998. Although rarely seen except during their mating season, few tarantulas have been reported from Chaco.

Flora

Modern flora, like the fauna, has been widely reported for Chaco Canyon (Cully and Cully 1985; Dunmire and Tierney 1997; Floyd-Hanna and Hanna 1995; Kelley and Potter 1974). Seeds and pollen from prehistoric sites suggest little change in the floral record from that seen today except for the introduction of exotic species. Between the 1930s and 1950s, the Soil Conservation Service and the Civilian Conservation Corps planted 700,000 cottonwoods, willows, and tamarisk to offset the effects of over-grazing and erosion (Whitefield 1998). Various other projects after 1935 resulted in reseeding the area, sometimes with non-native plant species (Cully and Cully 1985). In 1974, 100,000 ponderosa pine seedlings were planted throughout the canyon but none is known to have survived. Earl Neller, of the Chaco Project (personal communication, 2000), planted two blue spruce trees in the rincon across from Wijiji in 1972 but neither had survived by 1975.

Overall, the canyon bottomlands are dominated by greasewood, saltbush, grama grass, ricegrass, and galleta grass. The adjacent benches and broken ledges support a community of sagebrush, rabbitbush, and scattered junipers. The southern mesas (Chacra Mesa, South Mesa, and West Mesa) are dominated by rabbitbush, snakeweed, and sagebrush, while the areas further south and to the north are dominated by alkali sacaton. Today, wetlands and riparian areas are limited, but prehistoric use of cottonwood (*Populus* sp.), willows, and reeds in construction suggest that these habitats were more common at times in the past.

The extent of tree cover is of some interest considering the economic importance of trees to the inhabitants. Few trees exist within the park today, and further south, west, and north the land is practically devoid of trees. Wood, of course, was needed for building materials; for fuel used in cooking, heating, firing pottery, and cremating the dead; for providing soil nutrients; and for medicinal uses. If a scattered pygmy piñon and juniper forest once existed on South Mesa, as one now does on Chacra Mesa, then organic matter from it would have replenished the nutrient content of the soils below (e.g., Cully and Toll 2015; Gasser 1990:4.4; Nabhan 1983:162-165; Sandor et al. 2007). This would have been a compelling reason to practice silviculture in Chaco Canyon to protect Chacra's trees (Windes 1987a:213).

A number of ponderosa trees are reported in the Gallo Canyon (see Windes 1987a), where the park campground is located, whose Navajo name describes a line of (ponderosa) trees (Van Valkenbugh 1941:23). Oddly, these trees were not reported by the usually astute Simpson when he traveled through the canyon in 1849 (McNitt 1964; Simpson 1850). Navajo park workers today say that the pine stumps were pried from the ground for firewood by the early 1900s but that some of the original wood is still present in old hogan roofs. Other Navajo accounts (Judd 1954:344, 349) mention ponderosa pines in Mockingbird and Weritos canyons, probably in the 1800s, but not in the Gallo; some of these were also seen by Douglass (1935:46) in 1926. Gwinn Vivian (1972) reported two stumps on the mesa top above the 29SJ 706 staircase near Bc 53 in the Casa Rinconada area, but these were from live trees cored by Douglass in 1923 (Vivian 1972:16). Of course, the ponderosa pine growing in Pueblo Bonito during much of its occupation

(Judd 1954; cf., Wills 2012a) may be proof that some pines grew locally during puebloan times.

Ponderosa pines were also scattered over the desolate badlands at Ojo Alamo and the De-Na-Zin Wash to the west (Plate I.2.1; Reed 1968:166; Vivian 1972:16-17). Young aspen have been noted by the author in the banks of the Kimbeto Wash adjacent to San Juan County Road 7900, the park entry road to the northeast.

In the portion of Chaco Canyon east of the park, the flora exhibits subtle changes as the elevation and precipitation rise slightly. Aspen, Douglas-fir, and ponderosa pine (Figure I.2.1, Plate I.2.2) grow in pockets 10 km east of the park in the East Community area, and they are of considerable age. A grove of aspen in a seep area first noted by Gordon Vivian (Vivian and Mathews 1965:6-7) was mapped and sampled, revealing some trees that were nearly 100 years old (Figure I.2.2, Table I.2.1). There are also wide-leaf yucca and increased numbers of piñon trees.

Nearby, in the canyon, conifers grow in pockets where snow accumulates and is protected from the spring sun (Figure I.2.3). Many of the older ponderosa pines are half dead and scarred by porcupine and lightning strikes, although there are a handful of young trees. The stand was examined by Neil Judd (Judd 1954:2) and A. E. Douglass in the 1920s (Douglass 1935:46), when 25 live and dead ponderosas were noted. One fallen tree nearby, a badly weathered Douglas-fir, recently provided the first Chacoan specimen to link the historic and prehistoric periods (CHM-190: A.D. 917p-1574vv). During its early years, its size would have been useful for roofing in the East Community greathouse but was left untouched; perhaps its location directly east of the greathouse and its rarity afforded it special meaning and protection by the local inhabitants.

An inventory and sampling of the ponderosa pines in the East Community, first by Jeff Dean and Gwinn Vivian in 1968, then by Gwinn Vivian in 1970-1971, and finally by the author and Gwinn Vivian in 1995, yielded several trees over 300 years old (Plate I.2.2, Table I.2.1). Steel-tool marks on stumps and even on some live trees indicate multiple harvesting efforts;

Plate I.2.2. An old, lone ponderosa pine in the cliffs on Chacra Mesa in the Chaco East Community. Tree is Chaco 16. Photograph by Gordon Vivian ? (CHCU neg. 77913).

Plate I.2.1. Scattered ponderosa pines across the Ojo Alamo badlands west of Chaco Canyon. Photograph by Gordon Vivian? in 1951. (CHCU neg. 77883).

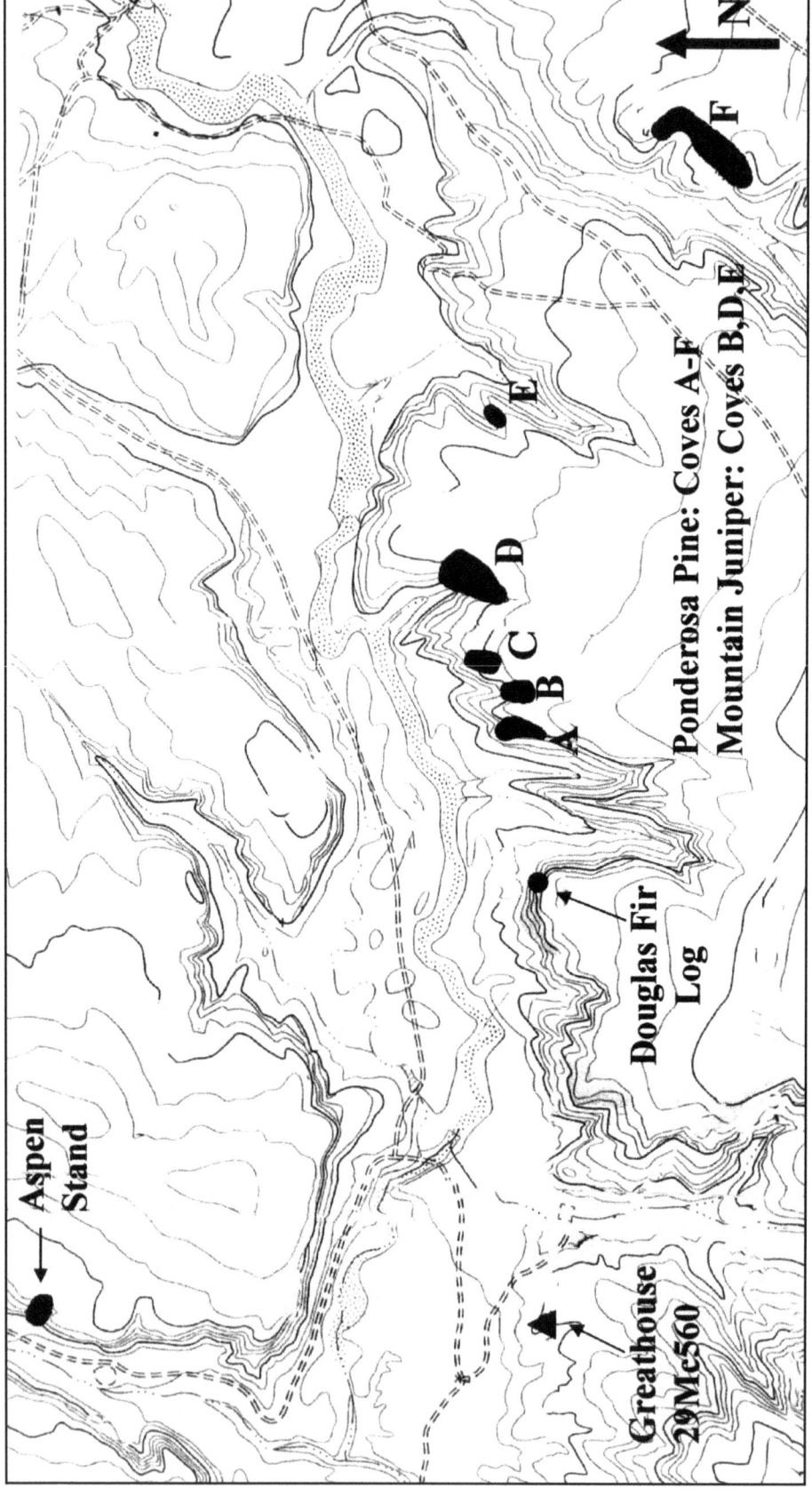

Figure I.2.1. General location of the stands of large conifers and aspens in the Chaco East Community area. North rain gauge is at the mouth of Wild Horse Canyon. Map by Beth Bagwell, October 2004.

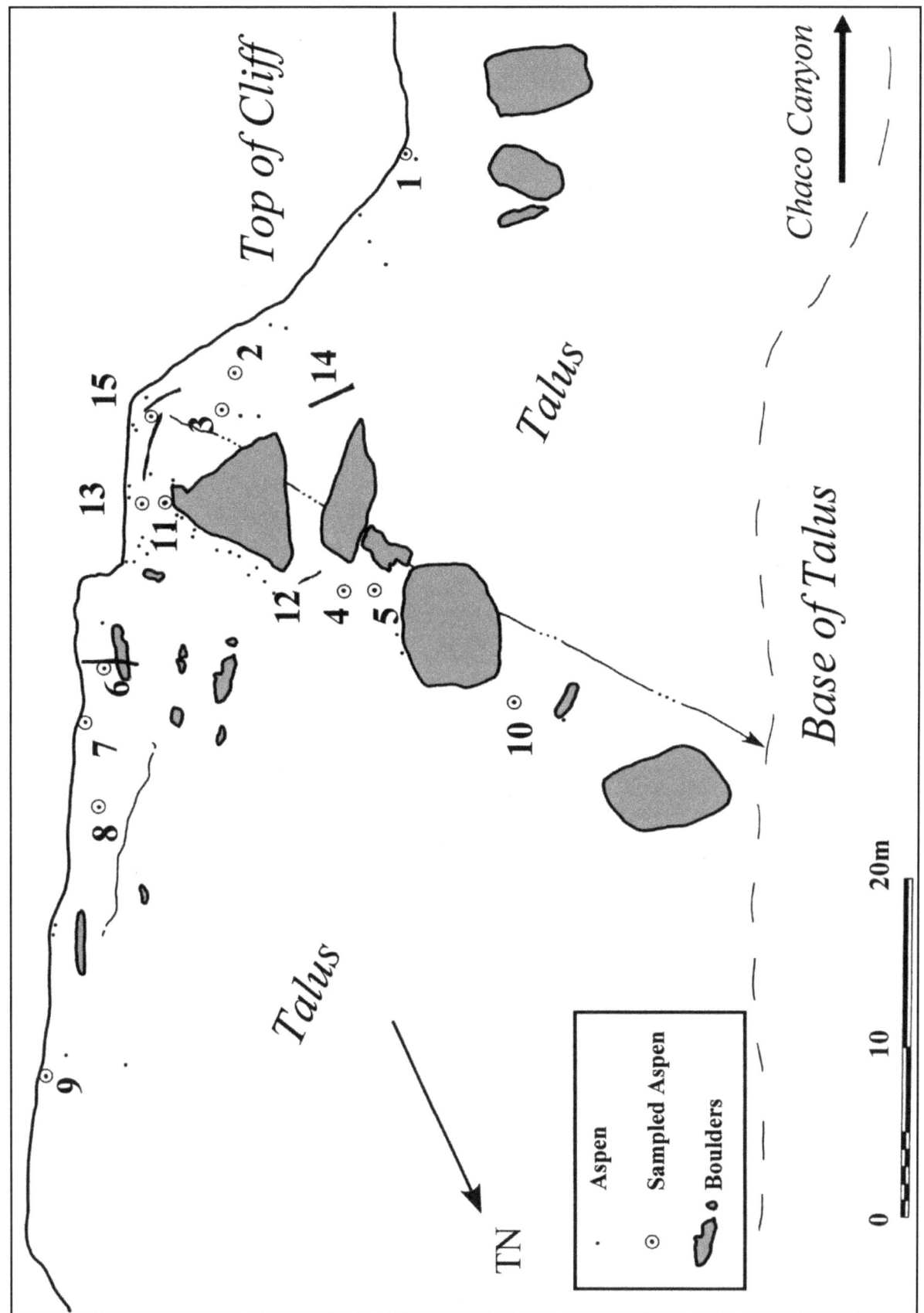

Figure I.2.2. Location of an isolated stand of aspen in the Chaco East Community area (CHCU 52622). Original by Jim Trimbell and Edward Morente, 15 June 1995. Map by Beth Bagwell, October 2004.

30   Windes

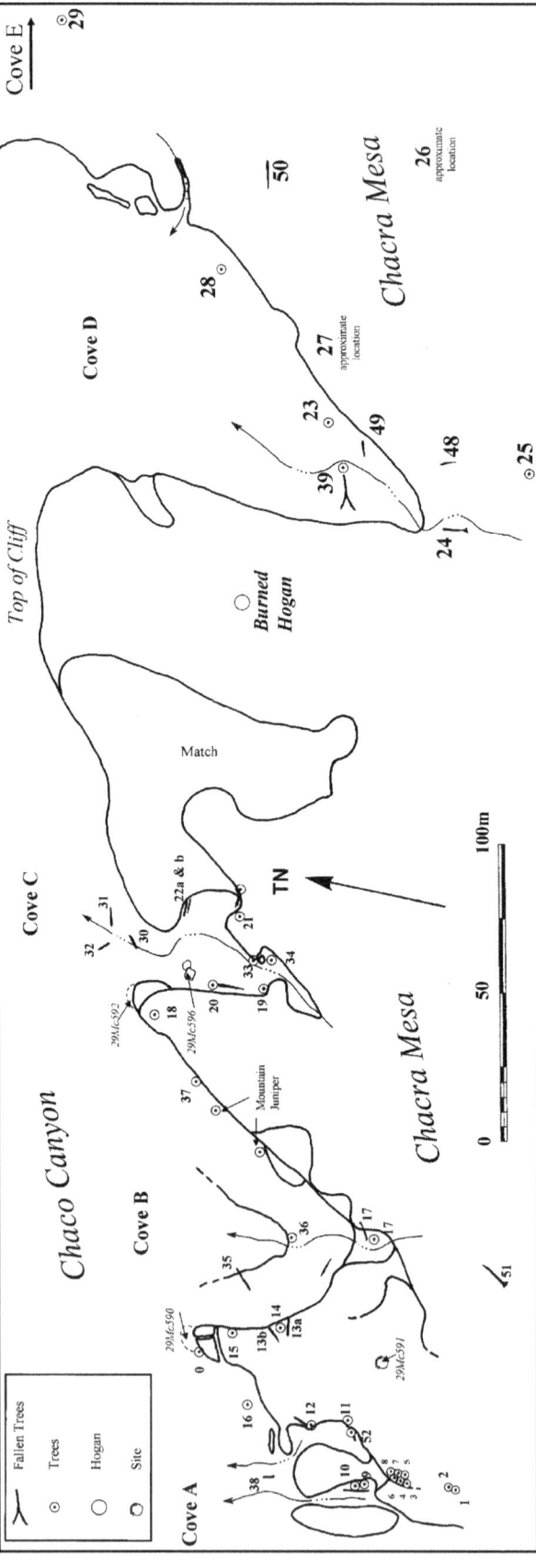

Figure I.2.3. Location of scattered ponderosa pine and Douglas-fir along Chacra Mesa in the Chaco East Community area (CHCU 52625). Original by J. Trimbell, E. Morente, R. Earls, L. Lithou, T. Hartman, C. Simon, K. Kingsensmith, M. Reynolds, and G. Vivian, June 1995. Map by Beth Bagwell, October 2004.

presumably, based on tree-ring dates of associated structures, Richard Wetherill and others after him occasionally secured the trees from this area for building. Ponderosa pines used in nearby early eighteenth-century fortified Navajo structures at 29Mc 585 (CM-35; see McKenna and Windes 2011; Vivian 1960:85-87, 156) presumably were taken from these same stands and suggest that pines existed here in small numbers back into prehistoric times. The lack of ponderosa pine in other, contemporary Navajo structures along the mesa suggests that pine was always scarce in the canyon. Ponderosa pine slowly increases east along Chacra Mesa, especially east of Pintado Pass. Few now would be worth harvesting for roofing for Chacoan houses: they are either too large or too small and often deformed. The marginal condition of these trees and their isolated presence into prehistoric times suggest that few would have been available for housing during the greathouse days.

Finally, among the large ponderosa trees is a small cluster of huge, old mountain juniper (*Juniperus scorpulorium*) trees, with the two oldest at least 440 and 508 years of age. These trees are mostly dead, but isolated parts of them continue living. Otherwise, the area is dominated by *Juniperus monosperma* (single-seed juniper), a scraggly, pygmy conifer. The advanced age of the mountain junipers suggests that a few large junipers adequate for greathouse roof beams or for court kiva pilaster bases may have been obtained locally.

Factors Affecting Horticulture

The majority of the Chacoan small sites contain evidence for the importance of horticulture; this evidence is overwhelming after Pueblo I times. Economic plant remains found in small-house excavations, food preparation areas littered with food-processing tools, and the allocation of storage space all lend credence to this supposition. What is debated, however, is the range of subsistence activities and the time allocated by households to them in and around the sites. How were they balanced given the constraints posed by the environment, and what level of cooperation, if any, did households have with one another?

This section re-examines the potential for horticulture in and around Chaco Canyon, and its role within the BMIII and PI communities, with newly collected data that can shed new light on estimates for the importance of horticulture. Environmental constraints that affect horticulture in Chaco Canyon are examined in relation to other areas of the San Juan Basin.

The dense clusters of puebloan houses found in Chaco Canyon suggest that site placement was heavily influenced by favorable horticultural conditions, especially locations where runoff farming could be practiced. Small houses are scattered throughout the entire length of Chaco Canyon and south into the valleys, but they are particularly dense within and around the gaps of the canyon along the south side. Generally, every tributary of the canyon exhibits Pueblo II and Pueblo III sites, with the mouths of the larger drainages exhibiting the densest site concentrations adjacent to the Chaco Wash. These locations also reflect some Basketmaker and early Puebloan use. Conversely, there is a notable lack of small house sites along the north side of the canyon until after A.D. 1100 (Windes 1987a:403), when they are found clustered against the cliffs near Chetro Ketl and Pueblo Bonito. Without a doubt, some sites on the north side are buried from view, but the difference between the two sides of the canyon is real. In addition, with a few exceptions, puebloan occupation was absent on top of the mesas bordering the canyon.

The physiography, soil, rainfall, runoff, and temperatures are the important variables affecting horticulture that are examined here. We are still unsure what the exact limits were for successful horticulture in Chaco Canyon (see Peterson [1987a, 2012] and Van West and Dean

[2000] for parallels in the Dolores and North Rio Grande regions), and the issue has provoked much debate (e.g., see Sebastian 1988, 1992; Toll et al. 1985 for summaries). Nevertheless, the range of different environment factors measured historically provides an estimate of the limits for successful horticulture in the canyon area.

Physiography and Geology

The topography in the Chaco Canyon area varies greatly. Overall, the canyon and its environs lie within a former Cretaceous seaway that bisected North America from the Gulf of Mexico to the Arctic Ocean, with seas advancing across the San Juan Basin in a southwest direction and receding in a northeast direction. Numerous advances and retreats across the low-lying continental platform resulted in different episodes of sedimentation: the formations of the Mesaverde Group present the classic examples of inland sea regressions and transgressions. The Point Lookout Sandstone is the shallow-water, near-shore, marine sandstone deposited as the seas withdrew. The base of the Menefee Formation represents fluvial deposits of mudstone and sandstone on a low-level coastal plain. In a few places, small and ephemeral interchannel swamps persisted, resulting in very thin, local coal beds. Finally, the advancing sea flooded the coastal areas, and littoral and shallow-water marine sands were deposited as the Cliff House Sandstone (Miller et al. 1991:39).

After the region was uplifted and tilted, Chaco Wash and adjacent streams cut courses mainly independent of the geologic strata. Chaco Wash, in particular, cuts nearly parallel to the strike of the Cliff House Sandstone, the thick, massive unit that borders the north side of Chaco Canyon. This drainage cut into the softer sandstones, shales, and clays of the Menefee Formation, although the canyon bottom is now filled with sediments up to 38 m deep (Love 1977:297).

The Chaco Wash begins its journey from the western slopes of the Continental Divide in the Star Lake region, northeast of Pueblo Pintado, where the canyon first cuts into the Cliff House Sandstone, and ends at the junction of the Chaco and Escavada washes, a canyon journey of 32 km. The Chaco Wash drains a substantial area (1,497 km^2) when measured upstream from the bridge near the park Visitor's Center. At the west end of the park, it joins the Escavada Wash to become the Chaco River, an ephemeral steam about 178 km long that empties into the San Juan River, a tributary of the Colorado River, at Waterflow, New Mexico, near the town of Shiprock.

Chaco Canyon is part of a much larger physiographic region that is crucial for understanding the prehistoric habitation. The San Juan Basin, a nearly circular depression, is rimmed on the north and northwest by the Hogback monocline, on the west by the Defiance uplift or monocline, on the east by the Nacimiento and Archuleta uplifts, and on the south by the Chaco Slope (Figure I.2.4). The monoclines and uplifts that rim the San Juan Basin on its west, north, and east sides are well defined by hogbacks that dip steeply toward the basin center, but the Chaco Slope on the south dips slightly northward 2°-5°. A number of ephemeral washes important to our discussion follow this northward dip toward Chaco Canyon and the Chaco River.

The Chaco Basin (11,500 km^2) forms the primary region of the Chacoan occupation and drains the greater part of the San Juan Basin. The drainage systems of the Chaco River/Chaco Wash help define the topography: the northern drainage basin (4,000 km^2) is characterized by aeolian dunes, unconsolidated sediments, and numerous small badlands, which flank the margins of dissected pediment surfaces (Wells 1983:121). This area is dominated by the Kirtland and Fruitland formations of Upper Cretaceous and lower Tertiary sandstones and shales; permanent Chacoan occupations in these areas were sparse.

To the west and south of the Chaco River/ Chaco Wash, drainage channels start along

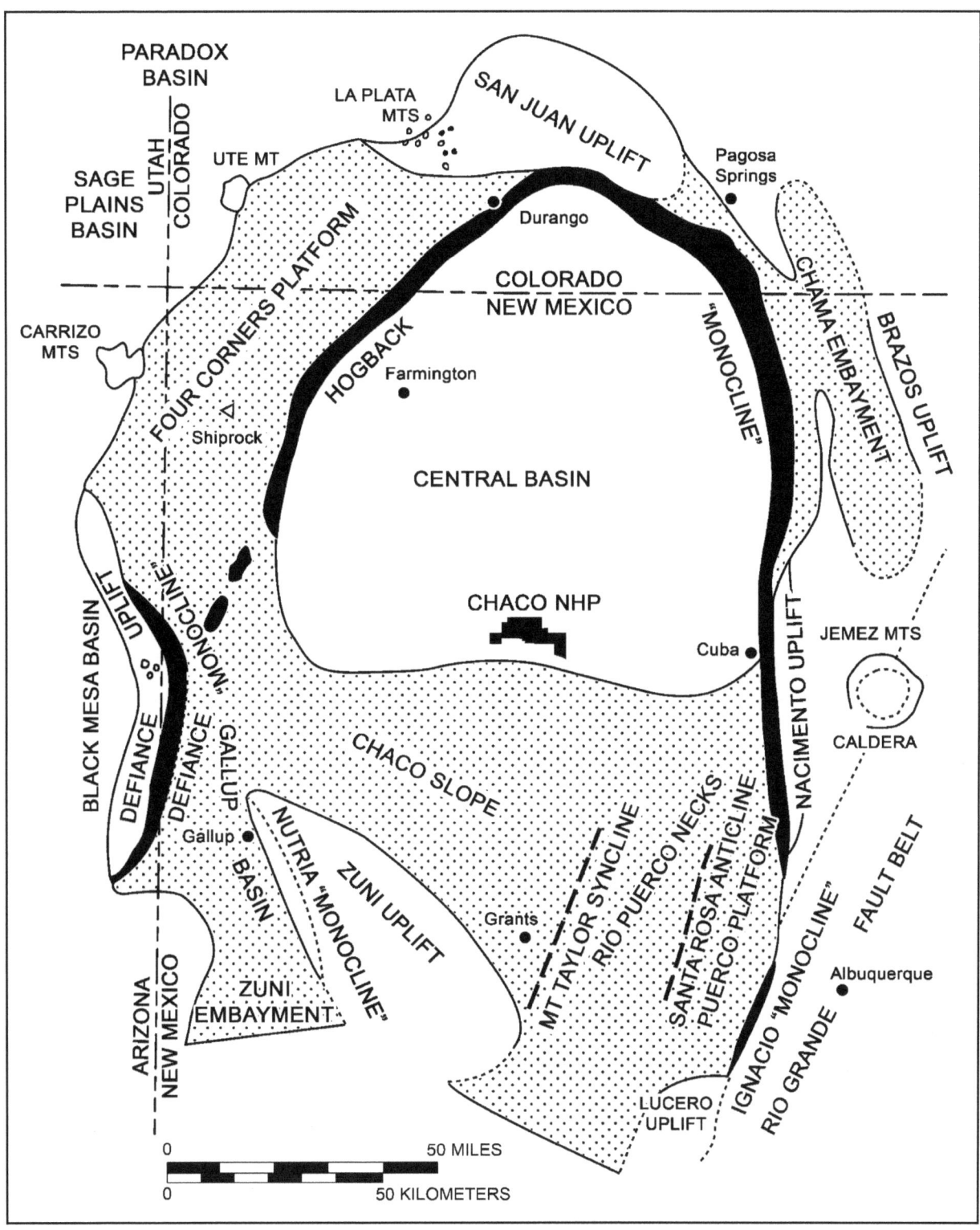

Figure I.2.4. Geological structural elements of the San Juan Basin (from Miller et al. 1991: Figure 11).

the foothills of the Chuska Mountains and the Dutton Plateau—both areas of dense prehistoric occupation. It is the southern tributaries of the Chaco Wash and the Chaco River that give life to the Chaco story from the park's perspective. From east-to-west, these are the Fajada (or Vincente), Kin Klizhin, Kim-me-ni-oli (Kin Bineola), Indian Creek, Standing Rock, and Coyote Canyon washes. The headwaters of the eastern two are in a long, east-west ridge 15 km south of Chaco Canyon. The latter four drainages sweep north from the Dutton Plateau through this ridge barrier and continue north to the Chaco River west of Chaco Canyon. These western washes are well known for their Chacoan communities and prominent greathouses: Kin Ya'a, Bluewater Spring, Bee Burrow, and Kin Bineola lie in the Kim-me-ni-oli Wash and its tributaries. In Indian Creek are found Muddy Water, Section 8, and Indian Creek ruins.

Outside the canyon, the character of the landscape changes, sometimes dramatically. A broad plain sweeps north from the canyon above the cliffs (locally known as "North Mesa"), gradually descending to the broad, sandy Escavada Wash and its tributaries, which drain from the northeast almost to U.S. Highway 550. This area is characterized by broad expanses of exposed clays and shales, part of the Fruitland Formation of late Cretaceous age. Some Anasazi occupation was concentrated immediately north of the park's main canyon along the Escavada Wash, but otherwise prehistoric settlement to the immediate north was sparse and locally clustered. A few short tributaries dissect the North Mesa, but permanent Chacoan occupation of them is practically nonexistent. Within the park, two are prominent: Gallo Wash, which drains 93.8 km^2 (36.2 mi^2) and was the beginning of a long canal system that passed by Una Vida and Hungo Pavi (Vivian 1972:3), and Mockingbird Canyon, adjacent to Hungo Pavi. Cold air draining through these channels into Chaco Canyon probably made them unfavorable areas for occupation. The exception is the two Mesa Verdean occupations in Gallo Canyon, which were situated in rockshelters that provided solar heating in winter.

To the east, the canyon gradually gains elevation as it ascends into the broad valleys east of Pueblo Pintado. Locally, the easternmost Chacoan occupation was concentrated around the Pueblo Pintado greathouse. A number of side tributaries cut into the North and Chacra mesas along the route to the east, providing access to the northern plains and rolling hill country, but only Chaco Wash itself cuts all the way through Chacra Mesa (at Pueblo Pintado, where it is utilized by the Crownpoint-Cuba highway). Two drainages do cut deeply into Chacra Mesa just west of Pueblo Pintado, where another major Chacoan settlement was located (the East Community: Windes et al. 2000).

On the south side of the canyon, a prominent remnant of Cliff House sandstone, Chacra Mesa, was left isolated by the downcutting Chaco Wash. This mesa extends from the west end of the park near the Peñasco Blanco greathouse, 75 km east to Torreon, almost reaching the Rio Puerco of the East. Within the park, Chacra Mesa has been severed by erosion into three sections known as West Mesa, South Mesa, and the long, eastern remnant of Chacra Mesa. The name "Chaco" might have drived from a phonetically corrupt use of Chacra (Van Valkenburgh 1941:19).

Just southeast of South Mesa are two lesser, but high, hills that abound in burned coal deposits, which produced clinker in bright hues of orange, red, and gray useful for ornaments and paint (see Fretwell, Volume II, Chapter 10). A small mine dug into the coal deposits near the top on the west side of Hill 6664 suggests some prehistoric use.

Along the south talus base of Chacra Mesa, the land sweeps south from Chaco Canyon at a gradual ascent until reaching a long, east-west divide 15 km south of the park boundary. This divide blocks visibility into the southern areas of the San Juan Basin around Crownpoint except through a few natural corridors. A treeless, grass-covered land gently dissected by minor, alluvium-filled drainages marks this area between Chaco Canyon and the Dutton Plateau. This region is dominated by small mesas, buttes, knolls, and ledges of the Menefee Formation—a deposit exposed over a huge area of the San Juan Basin from Chacra Mesa south to the Dutton Plateau and west to the Chuska foothills (Figure I.2.4). These formations often expose well-indurated, hard, dark brown sandstones that weather into tabular material much sought after in the region for building materials.

Despite the seemingly bland aspect of the landscape, where the subtle hills and valleys are richly defined only during sunrises and sunsets, a few features are worthy of special note. An isolated remnant of Chacra Mesa, Fajada Butte, at the entrance to this southern region, is a prominent marker for the area, both within Chaco Canyon, when arriving from the north along the route in from U.S. Highway 550, and from the divide coming south along State Highway 57 (the old south entrance to the park). It is a powerful landmark rooted in Navajo mythology (Van Valkenburgh 1941:22, 1974:37-38), as well as the locus for a well-known solstice marker known as the Sun Dagger (Sofaer et al. 1979).

Although it is shorter than the adjacent Chacra and South mesas, it is visible from as far east as Cabezon Peak—a volcanic plug rising 240 m above the surrounding Cretaceous sediments in the Rio Puerco of the East drainage, southeast of Cuba, and the locality of another Chacoan community, Guadalupe (Irwin-Williams and Baker et al. 1991; Pippin 1987). Cabezon Peak, also sacred to the Navajo (Van Valkenburgh 1941:10), is an active Puebloan shrine and exhibits prehistoric shrines on top that could be Chacoan in origin.

Fajada and Huerfano buttes are prominent markers on the landscape and are visible from many sites. Huerfano, a loaf-shaped mesa with several pinnacles on top, near the Blanco Trading Post on U.S. Highway 550, crests the north horizon from Chaco Canyon and is another important place in Navajo mythology (Van Valkenburgh 1941:55, 1974:31). It is the home of the Navajo Twin War Gods and presumably was important to puebloan peoples in prehistoric times as well (Windes 1987a:1). It can be seen as far north as Chimney Rock, Colorado; from Far View House at Mesa Verde National Park; from Chaco Canyon to the south, and from the Chuska Mountains to the west. Huerfano Mesa was an important visual communications link across the basin.

Fajada Wash (formerly the Vicente Wash), the most prominent tributary of the Chaco Wash, enters the canyon adjacent to Fajada Butte and drains an area of 515 km^2 along the south side of Chacra Mesa for about 33.5 km, with headwaters at the Continental Divide 9 km east of the Cuba/Crownpoint Highway. An auxiliary drainage, the South Fork tributary, continues nearly due south from Fajada Butte, paralleling the east side of State Road 57 (the south entrance to the park) until reaching its headwaters at the east-west divide, mentioned above. A probable prehistoric road appears to run from the Fajada Gap area south to beyond the east-west divide, directly up the South Fork Valley (Nials et al. 1987: Maps 16 and 17), and past the Greenlee and Lower Greenlee greathouses. The South Fork tributary figures prominently in the puebloan settlement of the Chaco area and in this report (Chapter 8; Van Dyke 2002).

South Gap is a second break in Chacra Mesa in the Pueblo Bonito area. It allows visibility to Hosta Butte—a shrine area south of Crownpoint—and access via a prehistoric road to Coyote Canyon in the south. Hosta Butte is yet another sacred Navajo peak (Van Valkenburgh 1941:54) and was undoubtedly sacred in the past, judging from the prehistoric shrines on top. A well-established drainage basin for South Gap, however, is surprisingly lacking. Leaving the canyon through South Gap, the moderate relief gradually ascends until cresting the highlands that divide the prominent drainages of the Fajada Wash and Kin Klizhin Wash. Puebloan settlement was also heavy within South Gap and along the adjacent drainages.

Finally, to the west, the Chaco Wash joins the broad, sandy Escavada Wash just below Peñasco Blanco, where standing water is common. At this junction, the primary drainage is inappropriately designated the Chaco "River", a broad wash that is the premier drainage for most of the southern San Juan Basin. This wash runs 119 km west from the park and then turns abruptly north another 59 km to empty into the San Juan River near Shiprock. The wash varies from 152 to 549 m wide, averaging 213 m (Miller et al. 1991:6), and is dry at most times except during spring snow melt and late summer rains.

Of local interest, a third north-flowing tributary, Kim-me-ni-oli Wash, enters the Chaco River at La Vida Mission near State Road 371, with its headwaters in the Continental Divide 48 km to the south near Crownpoint. It drains an area of 1,200 km^2 (Wells et al. 1983:177), borders the Kin Klizhin Wash on the west, and cuts through the east-west ridge where the latter drainage begins. This drainage contains the Kin Ya'a Chacoan community near its head, the Bee Burrow community about midway along a side tributary, the Kin Bineola community, and the Lake Valley sites near its mouth.

Soils

By modern standards, the soils in Chaco Canyon are inadequate for successful farming. Nevertheless, they must have sufficed for the puebloan and Navajo farming techniques practiced there (e.g., see Benson 2010; Benson et al. 2003, 2006; Judd 1954:53-59). Three primary soil deposits are recognized in the Chaco Canyon area: Blancot-Notal (BT), Huerfano-Muff-Uffens (HU), and Shepard-Huerfano-Notal (SC; Keetch 1980: Sheet 21). These soils have been renamed since a recent inventory (Figure I.2.5). All have moderate-to-high sodium content, and the Blancot-Notal deposits (now the Battlerock-Notal complex) are interpreted as unsuitable for horticulture because of high-sodium flood deposits (Scofield 1922). This unit characterizes the basic bottomlands of Chaco Canyon, as well as the major southern side drainages along the Fajada, South Gap, Padilla Well, Kin Klizhin, and Kim-me-ni-oli washes, where communities proliferated. Geologically, this unit corresponds to the Naha and Tsegi Alluvium deposits. For the purposes of identifying suitable soils for ancient farming, the soil maps (Keetch 1980; Natural Resources Conservation Service 2002; Weide et al. 1979) are too broadly defined to show the small sandy areas of arable soils that were undoubtedly favored for farming. The Blancot-Notal (Battlerock-Notal) deposits are the most heavily occupied soil zone during the puebloan period.

For all three soils, effective rooting depth ranges between 5 and 21 cm, permeability is moderately slow, runoff is medium, and the hazard of water erosion is moderate (Keetch 1980). Salt-tolerant plants, such as greasewood (*Sarcobatus vermiculatus*) and saltbush (*Atriplex* spp.), are prevalent in the flats of the Blancot-Notal deposits, while grasses dominate the elevated soils surrounding the flats. Soils of the Sheppard-Huerfano-Notal series (now designated Doak Silt Loam), primarily mapped southeast of South Mesa (Figure I.2.5), are the only ones of the three soil series now used elsewhere in the San Juan Basin for irrigated farming (Keetch 1980:7).

The two largest Basketmaker sites are located in the thin, sandy deposits in the Rock Outcrop-Persayo complex (BC) on mesa tops, associated with gravelly sands (Qgs) of Upper Pleistocene age. Pueblo I sites tend be located on adjacent floodplain deposits.

The soils were not only remapped in Chaco Canyon in the 1990s (see above) but work extended to the South Fork Valley south of Fajada Butte (Figure I.2.6) and to the Pueblo Pintado area (Figure I.2.7).

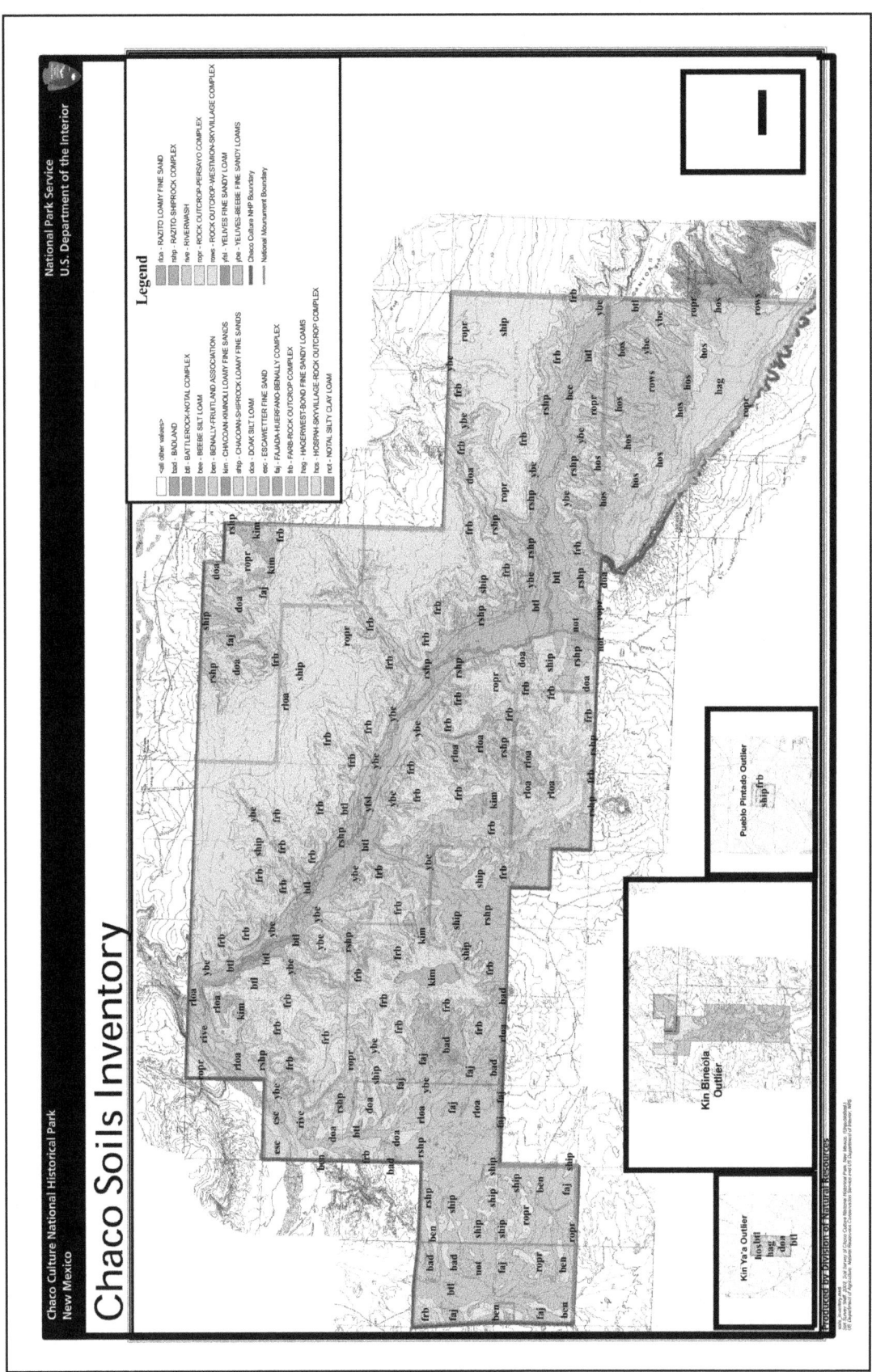

Figure 1.2.5. Soil complexes in Chaco Canyon (Soils Survey Staff 2004).

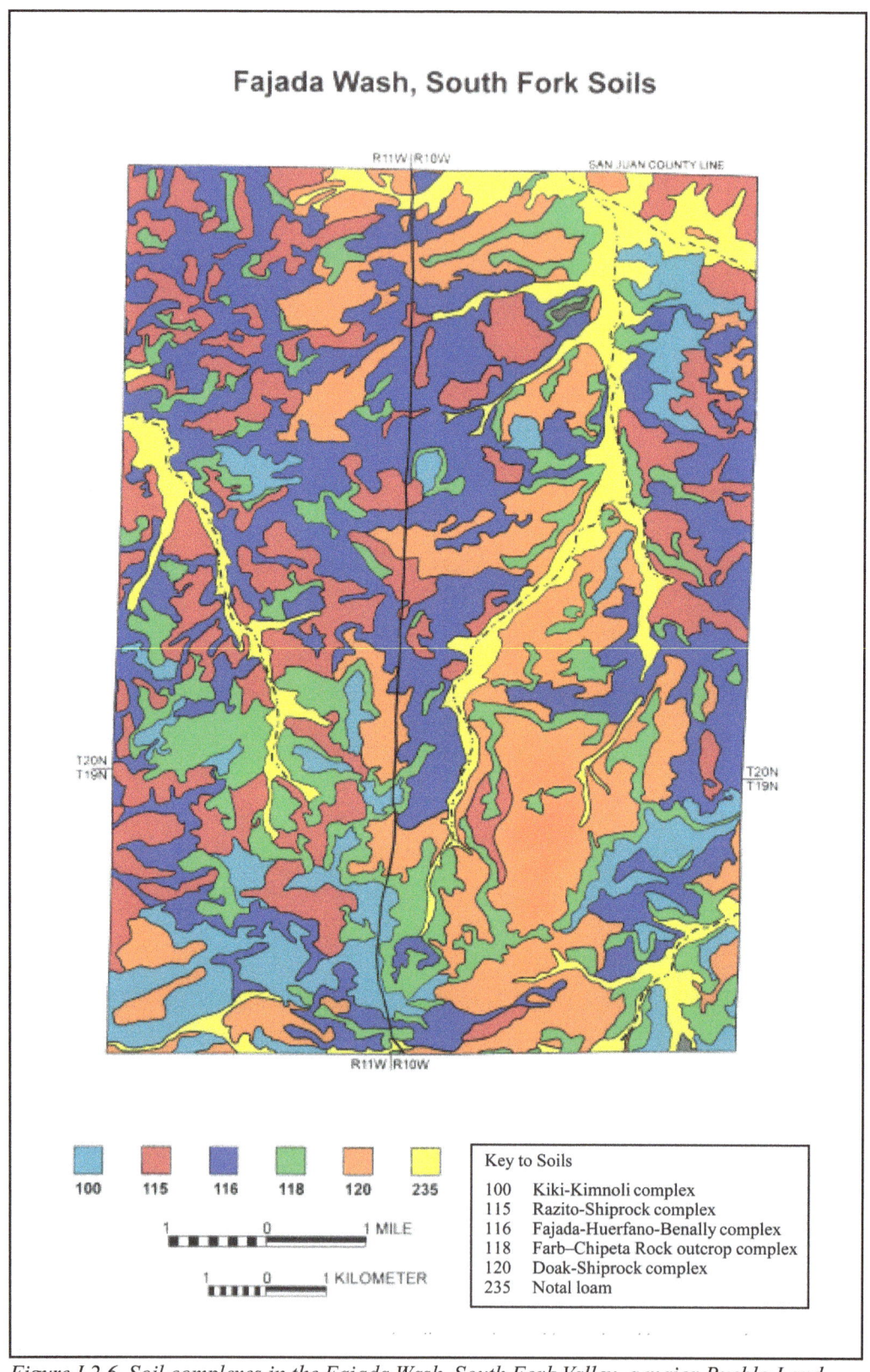

Figure I.2.6. Soil complexes in the Fajada Wash, South Fork Valley, a major Pueblo I and Pueblo II community area (Natural Resources Conservation Service 2002). Black vertical line is the park south entrance State Road 57.

Chapter 2: The Natural Environment 39

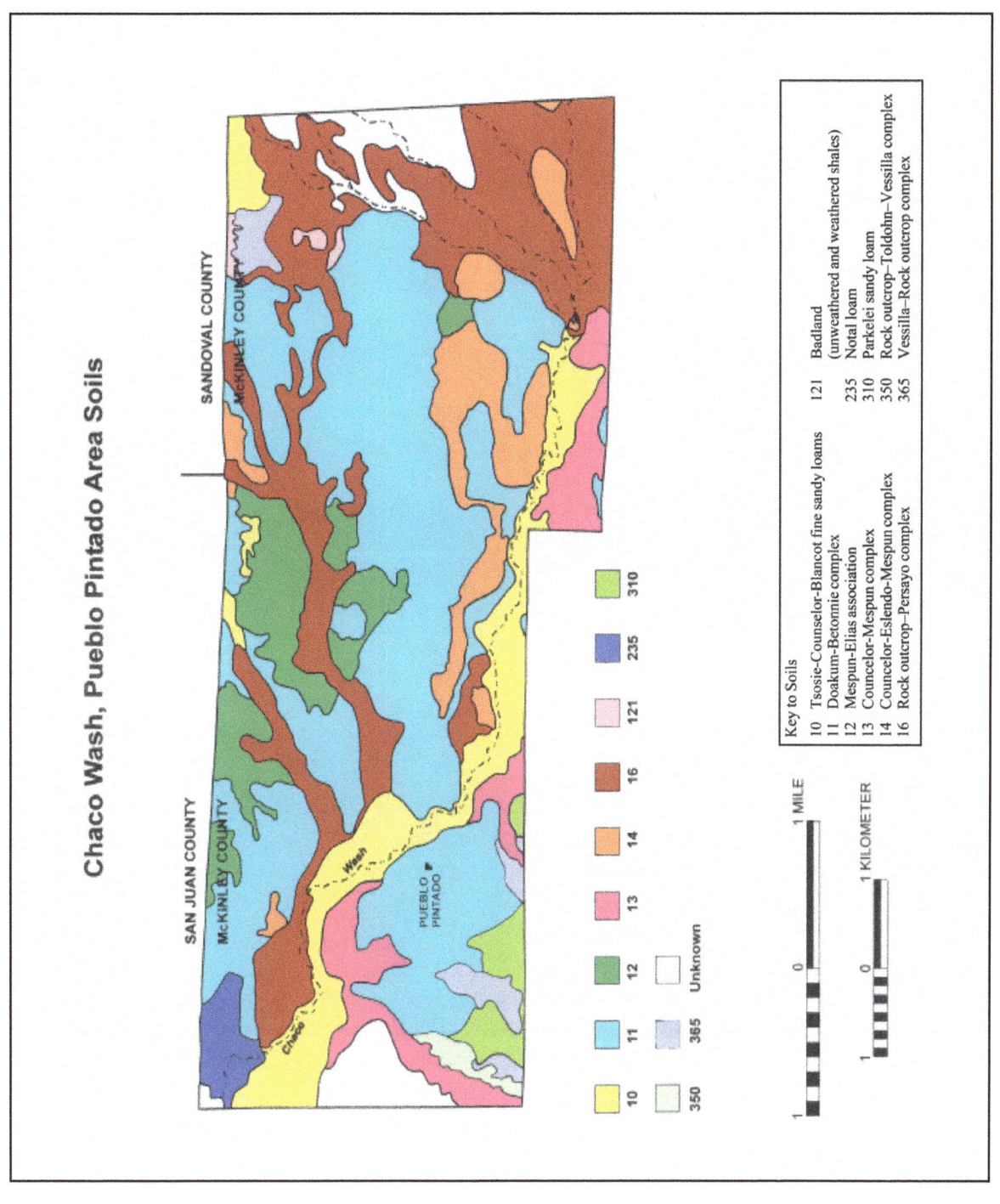

Figure I.2.7. Soil complexes in the Pueblo Pintado area (Natural Resources Conservation Service 2002).

Hydrology

Water, now and in the past, is a critical resource in the San Juan Basin that affects its occupation and use. The initial Anglo impressions of the basin were not favorable: Lt. Simpson (1850:92) found it to be "one extended, naked, barren waste;" geologist Loew (1875:103) concurred, and archaeologist A.V. Kidder described the region as

> little better than a desert; many parts of it, indeed are absolutely barren wastes of sand and rock which do not even support the usual dry flora of the Southwest. It is almost devoid of springs, has no permanent streams, is subject to severe sandstorms, is blistering hot in the summer and bitterly cold in the winter (Kidder 1924:179).

It still appears barren and devoid of water resources. Presently, wells provide most of the water for domestic and economic use. The majority of the basin interior is used for livestock grazing, with windmills and earthen stock tanks providing water. Despite its barrenness, water must have been available to the puebloan communities that once utilized the landscape. Simpson noted, however, that all the ruins he encountered during his expedition in 1849 were near water (McNitt 1964:131), although the decades just prior to his travels exhibited above-normal precipitation (Dean and Robinson 1977).

This section examines the area hydrology as a clue to potential water resources of the past. Widespread energy development of the basin has occurred since the 1920s; the first oil well was drilled near Durango in 1890 (Dugan 1977:83), while exploratory wells at Seven Lakes were sunk in 1911 (Christiansen 1989:47-51; Dugan 1977:83), 34 km south of Chaco Canyon. Dave Love (New Mexico Bureau of Mines and Mineral Resources, personal communication 1999) believes the number of shafts drilled into the basin substrata now is about 100,000, providing a good view of subsurface water resources. Drilling has impacted the deep aquifers and may have drained some of the near-surface flows, but it is cattle and sheep grazing that has probably altered the near-surface water supplies the most by affecting the runoff and erosional cycles.

The Chaco Basin Periphery

Elevated land masses form the western and southern boundaries of the basin. These water-bearing regions must have been important prehistorically given the concentration of sites and springs along their flanks.

To the west, the Chuska Mountains are capped by the Chuska Sandstone, 213 m to 550 m thick and of Oligocene or late Eocene age (Hackman and Olson 1977). The cap is locally intruded and overlain by basaltic volcanic rocks of Pliocene age (Appledorn and Wright 1957). The volcanic rocks yield unique materials found as far east as Chaco Canyon: trachyte (e.g., Mills et al. 1997; Warren 1967b) used for pottery temper and Washington Pass Chert (a.k.a. Narbona Pass Chert) used for chipped stone material (e.g., Warren 1967b:121-122).

The Chuska Mountains collect much of the moisture from storms before they cross the San Juan and Chaco basins. Since recording started in recent years, the amount of moisture measured at the top of Nabona Pass has varied considerably between 309 and 699 mm (1977-2003; mean = 467 mm, 18.4"; s.d. = 112 mm, CV = 23.9 percent, N = 21). Many of the unusually numerous lakes and swamps scattered across the mountain top (Wright 1964) are interconnected, and in wet years the runoff flows across and down off the east escarpment.

In 1941, an extraordinarily wet year that caused the fall of Threatening Rock into Pueblo Bonito in Chaco Canyon, the largest lake on top of the Chuskas (Long Lake) overflowed east down past a small Navajo farm, provoking the inhabitants to dam the lake and build irrigation structures for farming (Wright 1964:590). Likewise, runoff behind Skunk Springs is channeled into ditches by Navajos for farming—these ditches may have originally been built to serve the huge Chacoan community nearby (John Stein, personal communication 1995). In 1849, Simpson observed lush cornfields along the nearby Tunicha Wash (Kues 1992:91; Simpson 1850), further evidence for the agricultural potential along the Chuska drainages.

In addition to direct runoff from the Chuska Mountains, seepage from the lakes and swamps is discharged by springs at the base of the Chuska Sandstone along both the east and west sides of the mountain (Edmonds 1967:90; Stone et al. 1983:25; Warren 1967a:7, 9). Some water also infiltrates downward into underlying sandstones of Cretaceous age or older. Near Tocito, several small springs originate in the Gallup Sandstone, while others arise from volcanic dike ridges, like those near Bennett Peak (Warren 1967a:9). The profusion of potential water sources may be an important factor in the massive prehistoric settlement, much of it early, along the flanks and drainages of the mountain. Both present-day and prehistoric communities are often associated with existing springs, which indicates the relative permanence of these water sources (Warren 1967a:11-12).

To the south, the Dutton Plateau (Lobo Mesa) is an elevated escarpment of the Point Lookout Sandstone. Numerous springs occur along the contact zones of the Point Lookout-Menefee Formation (Cooper and John 1968:Plate 2) and the underlying Crevasse Canyon Formation (Stone et al. 1983:35). Again, present-day Navajo and prehistoric Chacoan communities (Kantner 1994) associated with these springs attest to the longevity of the water sources.

South of the Dutton Plateau, along the flanks of the Zuni Mountains, water issues from the San Andres Limestone and also northward into the San Juan Basin and southeast toward the Grants and Bluewater region (Cooper and John 1968: Plate 2; Cooper and West 1967:146). The latter areas are packed with Chacoan communities. Seeps and springs also provide water from the Gallup Sandstone and by leakage into adjacent deposits in the Gallup area (Cooper and West 1967:148), and where the Rio San Jose intercepts the water table east of the Continental Divide.

In addition, the drainages formed in the Dutton Plateau highlands dissect the basin as they flow to the Chaco River. In wet years, runoff from melting snows and from late summer storms supply these drainages with significant amounts of water—numerous Chacoan communities are located where drainages diffuse onto the basin floor. In wet years, the lower Kim-me-ni-oli Wash, far from its headwaters in the Dutton Plateau, was suitable historically for damming and irrigation, with crops of peaches, watermelons, corn, and alfalfa being grown (Miller et al. 1991:7). Evidence of prehistoric dams and ditches is also noted there, as well as in the adjacent Kin Klizhin Wash (Judd 1954:55-57).

Aside from runoff, water for prehistoric domestic purposes was limited to seeps, springs, and shallow wells. These sources were undoubtedly critical for settlement in the otherwise arid basin interior. The primary source for groundwater is shallow, Quaternary alluvial aquifers within major drainages, like the Chaco and Escavada washes, as modern well records attest (Stone et al. 1983:60, Table 1). The water is easily tapped by digging shallow wells—a knowledge Simpson used on his 1849 journey across the San Juan Basin (McNitt 1964:60, 89). In many places, valley fill still provides the sole source of potable water for inhabitants (Stone et al. 1983:24). The Chaco River, the primary drainage in the San Juan Basin, has very shallow potable groundwater, which in the drought years of 2001-2003 was a mere 50-90 cm below the surface and of good quality (Table I.2.2).

Away from these drainages, water is less certain, with modern wells necessary to reach water 15 to 30 m into the exposed Menefee Formation. Some wells in the Menefee, however, are very shallow (less than 6 m), so that holes sunk in the Menefee or in the valley alluvial deposits must have been adequate for populations living in the barrens south of Chaco, where this study is partly focused. Water resources from the Menefee are contingent on the distribution of sandstone aquifers. Recharge occurs in topographically high, broad sandstone outcrop areas, like South Mesa.

The availability of water outside the alluvial deposits depends on the bedrock geology (Scott et al. 1984). Three geologic units in the Chaco Basin provide the primary sources for seeps, and springs: the uppermost unit of the Cliff House Sandstone; the Menefee Formation, the most exposed and widespread unit in the Chaco Basin, underlying the Cliff House Sandstone; and the lower Point Lookout Sandstone. All three units belong to the Mesa Verde Group, which has a gradual rise northward of about four degrees (Bullard 1983:79; Fassett and Hinds 1970; Stone and Jackson 1980:9; Wells and Smith 1983:29). Seeps and springs generally occur at the contact zone between lenses of the carbonaceous shales and the overlying sandstones.

The Chaco Canyon Area

Within Chaco Canyon, the blocky, massive Cliff House Sandstone provides seeps and springs at the contact zone with the thin, underlying Lewis Shale that overlies the massive Menefee Formation. These water sources are exposed where erosion has dissected the Cliff House Sandstone north and south of the main canyon to form side canyons. Particularly notable are the water sources in Clys and Mockingbird canyons on the north side and that behind Kin Nahasbas (Judd 1954:344; Windes 1987a:37-41). On the south side, notable sources are found close to the premier Basketmaker III settlements at Shabik'eschee, near Wijiji (spring, 29SJ 1620),

and 29SJ 423, near Peñasco Blanco (Judd 1954:344, 350). Others exist in Werito's Rincon and near Casa Chiquita (at Rafael's Spring). Occasional hand-and-toe-hold or cut-step access into incised sandstone drainage basins attests to their importance in prehistoric times.

Moist springs and summers and the practice of floodwater farming may have ameliorated the problem of low yearly moisture. A recent example of 28 years of precipitation in Chaco (Windes 1993: Figure I.2.5) illustrates one possible scenario. A period of much wetter springs could have provided the boost needed for initial plant germination, even though the summers were dry. In contrast, dry springs often discouraged the Chaco Navajo from planting crops (e.g., Brugge 1980). May serves as a pivotal month for successful farming. Interestingly, the Chaco Wash was known as a favorable farming district (Hill 1938:51), although this may have been influenced by the above-normal period of precipitation in the decades immediately preceding Hill's fieldwork (see Dean and Robinson 1977).

Precipitation

Lack of precipitation is the major limiting factor for successful horticulture in the Chaco Basin. The mountain ranges surrounding the San Juan Basin deplete precipitation for the basin interior, as illustrated in Figure I.2.8. No matter the direction from which storms approach, much of the moisture in them is captured by the surrounding mountain peaks. Potential evapotranspiration is also relatively high in the Chaco Basin, relative to the surrounding region (Tuan et al. 1973:48-49), so that the interior basin is normally moisture deficient. It seems unlikely that the Chacoans experienced a very different climate than today, particularly given tree-ring data showing that the northwestern plateau has always been a dry place since A.D. 652 (Burns 1983).

Rose et al. (1982) modeling of precipitation in the Chaco Canyon area and the northwestern

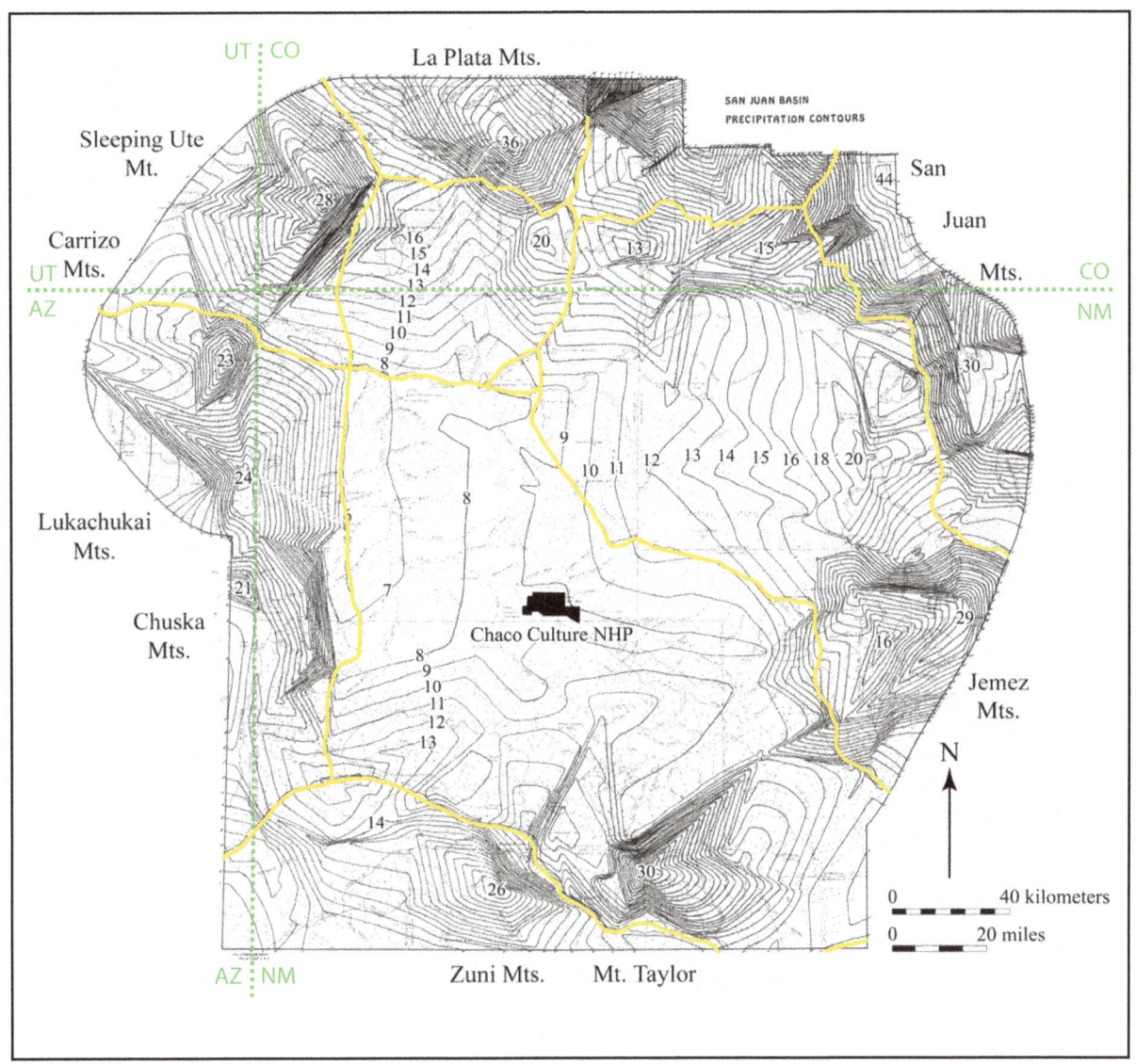

Figure I.2.8. Isopluvial contours in the San Juan Basin (in inches) (CHCU 65034).

plateau provides valuable insights into yearly conditions from A.D. 900 on. Precipitation variability by decade between A.D. 680 and A.D. 900 has been modeled by Dean and Robinson (1977) and revised by Dean (1996). Van West and Grissino-Mayer (2005) have provided a new model of past environmental conditions that combines precipitation and temperature. Although it may not be directly relevant to Chaco, it applies to the southern areas of the San Juan Basin and along the Red Rock Valley, where effects on populations had ramifications for contact and movement within the Chaco area.

Despite the lack of precise figures, a strong relationship is apparent between site frequency and rainfall (Burns 1983), or more precisely, rainfall and temperature (Van West and Grissino-Mayer 2005). During the wetter periods (e.g., in the A.D. 900s/early 1000s, early 1100s, and mid-1200s) site frequency is high, while the opposite is true for drier periods. For the Basketmaker III and Pueblo I periods, moisture was well above normal in the decades of the A.D. 730s, 850s, and 890s (>2 s.d.: Dean and Robinson 1977), but 2 s.d. below normal in the A.D. 750s (and 910s, and 990s)—the latter condition was widespread at this time throughout the San Juan Basin. During the Chaco occupation, the +3.40 s.d. for the A.D. 940s was the highest since before A.D. 680. The wettest period reached +7.90 s.d. above normal in the A.D. 1610s. In the A.D. 800s and 900s, when periods of moisture were well above normal, greathouses appeared.

In the 1950s, deficits of -2.80 s.d. for Chaco and -3.50 s.d. in the northern Rio Grande were severe enough to create the catastrophic 500-year killoff of piñon trees in many parts of the state (Betancourt et al. 1993:51-57). This was being repeated during the years of the 2000-2003 drought, when millions of piñon trees in the northern Rio Grande and the San Juan Basin were weakened and then killed by bark beetles. The killoff will force a retreat of piñons from their margin areas in many places. The droughts continue as of 2015.

The manipulation of runoff by occupants of Chaco Canyon has been the basis of various explanatory models of the Chacoan Phenomenon and the rise of the greathouses (e.g., Grebinger 1973; Judge et al. 1981; Sebastian 1988, 1992; Vivian 1970a, 1970b, 1990). Understanding runoff potential throughout the Chaco area, then, is critical for interpreting human use of Chaco and its environs, even within the smallest micro environmental niches.

One of the most crucial aspects for understanding the puebloan occupation of Chaco Canyon and its environs is farming potential. Although this topic is much discussed (see Benson 2010; Benson et al. 2003, 2006; Schelberg 1982; Sebastian 1988, 1992; Vivian 1972, 1974, 1984, 1990), no systematic studies linking soil productivity, temperature, precipitation, and other variables critical to crop success have been conducted until Benson's studies (e.g., Benson 2010). Such studies as those conducted during and after the Dolores Project (Peterson 1987b; Peterson and Clay 1987; Van West 1994; Van West and Dean 2000; Varien et al. 2000) are critical for assessing crop types, crop yields, and, ultimately, estimates of the population that might have resided here. At Chaco the farming potential is highly variable, with weather patterns, temperature, and soils greatly influenced by the canyon and cliff topography (see Windes 1993).

We can assume that a wide variety of techniques were utilized by inhabitants in and around Chaco to maximize crop yields. These survival strategies would have resulted from centuries of experience, particularly after corn and other crops became important subsistence foods. Some of these strategies have been discussed by Van West and Dean (2000), Vivian (1990), and Schelberg (1984, 1992). But corn is a notoriously thirsty plant, and dry farming alone would not have yielded substantial harvests in the Chaco area and the interior San Juan Basin.

A retrodicted estimate of precipitation by season and year for the past 1,330 years (Dean and Funkhauser 2002) reveals that the average annual precipitation in Chaco Canyon is about 8.9 inches (226 mm). This total reflects a sharp deficit for normal dry farming, meaning that on the average the area can be labeled as one of incipient drought (Palmer 1965). Overall, this model of past precipitation patterns in Chaco and the San Juan Basin is probably quite accurate, particularly as a relative indicator. The determination was based partly on results of the official weather gauge once placed next to Pueblo Bonito and now at the Visitor's Center, 8 km up canyon from Pueblo Bonito.

Rainfall measurements measured in the same summer months (Season 2) at these two locations during the past 23 years have shown significant variation (Tables I.2.3 and I.2.4), as first suggested by Gillespie (1985:18-19). In addition, weather gauges in towns distant from Chaco Canyon (e.g., Bloomfield) were used in past calculations to assess relative local precipitation, along with tree-ring data from trees that came from distant mountain ranges (English et al. 2001). Retrodicted trends for Chaco also blend the sharp contrasts found at different places within the canyon. The differences in rainfall throughout the canyon are dramatic when compared month by month and year to year. The new information summarized here provides some concrete data for determining potential rainfall in areas at Chaco in the more and less favorable areas for horticulture.

Obviously, other factors can ameliorate shortage of rainfall, such as the shallow water table within the broad, braided Chaco River and Escavada Wash channels. The effect of incised channeling of the Chaco Wash on the local farming population is much debated (e.g., Bryan 1954, Force et al. 2002; Hall 1977, 2010; Love 1980). Certainly, if farmers were utilizing the canyon floodplain for crops, a receding water table would have drastic results on production. The bottomland has always been saline and unsuitable for farming, and it might be better to view the entire strip of bottomland within Chaco Canyon as a dead zone unproductive for farming except where alluvial side deposits have replenished the soils. The numerous soil pockets and runoff areas in drainages bordering the main channel, however, were potential crop areas that Chacoan water-control devices clearly served (Vivian 1972, 1974, 1984, 1990, 2004) and these areas were also used as fields by the Navajo (i.e., Judd 1954:53-54).

As early as A.D. 850, dunes and, later, a masonry dam may have blocked the wash below Peñasco Blanco, forming a shallow intermittent lake (Force 2004; Force et al. 2002; cf. Love et al. 2011). If present in earlier times, the lake or shallow water table with standing wash water as it is now would have increased the suitability of the area for farming; it may have helped attract the first large Basketmaker III community centered on the nearby mesa top at 29SJ 423 and around Peñasco Blanco (see Chapters 3 and 8).

Upstream, an unknown number of Basketmaker III, Pueblo I, and early Pueblo II pithouses are buried deep in alluvial deposits of the canyon. Because of the high risk of flooding, it is unlikely that pithouses would have been built on the bottomlands if the wash had not been incised. In addition, if the water table had been high, dampness would have made living inside the pithouses intolerable. Thus, the Chaco Wash was deeply incised at times, and later a substantial amount of deposition buried the early pithouses (Chapter 5). Pithouses were found in the sides of the wash from near Chetro Ketl (Judd's Pithouse 2; 29SJ 1678, with a floor 3.8 m below the present valley floor) and below Shabik'eschee (the floor of Judd's easternmost of several pithouses was 4.1 m below the surface; Judd 1927:168, 1964:21). Nearly 2 m of sediment had been deposited above the roof level of Judd's (1924:404) Pithouse 2 after it was abandoned around A.D. 900. The fact that an A.D. 1000s house (29SJ 904) was built on top of the sediments nearby attests to the massive deposition that took place, probably during the period of regional aggradation of floodplains starting in the late A.D. 600s and early A.D. 700s (Dean 1992: Figure 4-1). Similar periods of rapid, deep deposition also occurred below Shabik'eschee judging from the difference between the depths of the Basketmaker III and Pueblo I structures in the wash banks.

These findings suggest that the flats were not being used for farming because they would have been too dry and too alkaline, and that other niches served for this purpose. Considering the long use of the Shabik'eschee area, particularly in the long, deep rincon on the east side of the mesa, the attraction must have been the slightly wetter microclimate, as revealed by the rain gauge data.

Chaco Area Rain Gauges

In cooperation with the Navajo Nation Water Resources Department, 12 precipitation ("rain") gauges have been installed in and around Chaco Canyon spanning an area roughly 30 miles north-to-south and 20 miles east-to-west, which provide the subtle precipitation differences that occur over the area for the former Chacoan and other inhabitants. Most were installed by the author in the early 1990s during employment with the National Park Service. Dwindling funds and personnel, however, may cause some of these gauges to be removed after 2014. Currently, the gauges are read by Navajo Nation and National Park Service personnel as well as by the author. These gauges are either static, requiring dipstick readings every month (or three times a year: 1 January, 1 May, and 1 October), or clock-driven with charts, which require periodic calibration by the author.

The average Chaco precipitation over the past 1,000 years, according to Rose et al. (1982), was about 250 mm (9.8"), whereas Dean and Funkhauser (2002) place it at 226 mm (8.9") for the past 1,330 years; either way, it was often dry. During the years of recorded yearly precipitation at Pueblo Bonito (N = 48) the average has been 218 mm (8.59"), while at the Visitor's Center (N = 54 years) it has averaged 230 mm (9.04"). For comparison, for the Dolores Archaeological Project, Colorado, Peterson (1987b:225) reported a wide range of precipitation—between 330 and 457 mm (13-18")—for successful dry farming and corn growth (also see Adams and Peterson 1999:23).

Other factors besides rainfall, however, ultimately affect success (Homburg and Sandor 2011; Van West and Dean 2000). According to Hack (1942:23) the Hopi enjoyed successful harvests when they planted in areas receiving 300 mm of annual moisture, and where the length of the growing season was about 130 days (Hack 1942:8, 20), although this period has been revised to between 155 and 193 frost-free days for the Hopi (Adams 1979:289, 291, 293). Despite these conditions, Hack considered the rainfall inadequate without other efforts to increase the amount of water in the fields, especially through floodwater farming. Dry years in Hopi lands were probably equivalent to normal years in Chaco Canyon. Still, even wet years in recent times have resulted in sporadic success for Hopi farmers (e.g., Bindell 1998, see also Dominguez and Kolm 2005:739).

The rain gauge data from the Chaco area (Tables I.2.3-I.2.4) provide important clues for farming potential in different places in and around Chaco Canyon that might be applicable to understanding the settlement of the prehistoric residents. Although there is much debate over recent climatic changes and how modern industrial societies might be contributing to them, precipitation patterns are probably little changed for storms that enter the San Juan Basin. The topography, which constitutes a major influence on storm patterns as they move across the Southwest, has been unchanged for thousands of years.

Of course, the gauges are not foolproof; mechanical and human error, vandalism, birds, cows, government shutdowns, power shortages, and other impacts have occasionally affected the accuracy of the data. In addition, given the variability in climate, very long records are desired but seldom achieved. Here, I have divided the readings into three seasons (Season 1=January-April; Season 2=May-September; Season 3=October-December) and the yearly total. The most variable season is important Season 2, the farming season, but in part because it contains the most months.

Our gauges have, as of January 2015, been in operation between 20 and 54 years in the same locations. If they can be kept in operation, the additional data will lead to more accurate interpretations in the future. As it is, they provide the first on-the-ground, lengthy records for precipitation in the Chaco area, help with current interpretations, and contribute to future modeling attempts. Table I.2.4 provides Wilcoxon two-sample tests against many of the gauge pairings in order to test for exceptional probability differences (at greater than an alpha of $\rho = .05$) among the various station seasons and yearly totals using SAS PROC NPAR1WAY for the non normally distributed precipitation data, which requires non-parametric testing.

Despite 83 years of weather records for Chaco Canyon, these data only reflect the immediate area around the recording station (Pueblo Bonito or the Visitor's Center). The first station was installed next to Pueblo Bonito during Neil Judd's work in the 1920s but not consistently monitored until 1933, where it remained with minor relocations until it was moved to the present Visitor's Center in 1960. The Visitor's Center gauge provides more realistic readings for the area near Fajada Butte, where two of our early excavated sites (29SJ 299 and 29SJ 628) are located. Other gauges measure precipitation at several areas near excavated, tested, and newly surveyed sites reported in this work.

Of the twelve local gauges (Figure I.2.9), six are located in the heart of the lower Chaco Canyon along two north-south axes centered at Pueblo Bonito and the Visitor's Center. These six monitor rainfall from storms that either come in through the eroded gaps in Chacra Mesa to the south or roll up the canyon from the west. They also cover the large community settlements at South and Fajada gaps (see Windes 1993), including the top of North Mesa. For the most part, these newer gauges have been in existence for 19 to 22 years as of February 2014.

Since 1989, the expanded number and locations of precipitation gauges have given us a more realistic picture of precipitation in the region. It is clear that elevation plays an important role in expected amounts of precipitation—higher elevations receive more than lower ones, even when the change in elevation is relatively small (see Crane, Appendix A). Higher-elevation gauges in the canyon are located at Pueblo Pintado, the Chaco East Community, near Gallo Canyon, and near Pueblo Alto at the north park boundary where State Road 57 once entered the park.

Other differences in precipitation are the result of seemingly minor changes in topography. These changes affect the storms that move across the Chaco Basin, causing changes in direction and increased moisture in certain locations. Unfortunately, the important western areas of the park and beyond it do not have rain gauges, but the ground cover suggests that it very dry.

To the east of the main canyon, the station at the windmill repair yards east of the Pueblo Pintado school indicates that this is one of the wettest areas in the canyon, but this advantage is tempered by its higher elevation (1981 m or 6500 ft vs. 1859-1890 m or 6100-6200 ft in the lower canyon) and a probable shorter growing season. The 21 full years of record reveal an annual mean of 245 mm (9.7") of precipitation, with more than half coming during the critical summer season. More water means faster crop growth, which can offset a shorter growing season. Summer storms blow in from the south through Pueblo Pintado Canyon, and often hover directly over the Chacoan community area (Plate I.2.3) before sweeping off to the northeast.

Interestingly, the Navajo have bestowed the name "Rain Mountain" to the greathouse site of Pueblo Pintado (Wozniak 1993:17). Another gauge located at the Star Lake (1953-2002) gas pumping station to the northeast of Pueblo Pintado received less precipitation than Pintado, 233 mm (9.18"), but its higher and colder elevation (2025 m; 6643 ft) precludes dependence on horticulture; puebloan houses are absent in the area and readings are no longer made there.

Just down canyon from Pueblo Pintado, the nearby Chaco East Community (Windes et

Plate I.2.3. Storm clouds over Pueblo Pintado greathouse and community. Photograph by John M. Campbell, 2004.

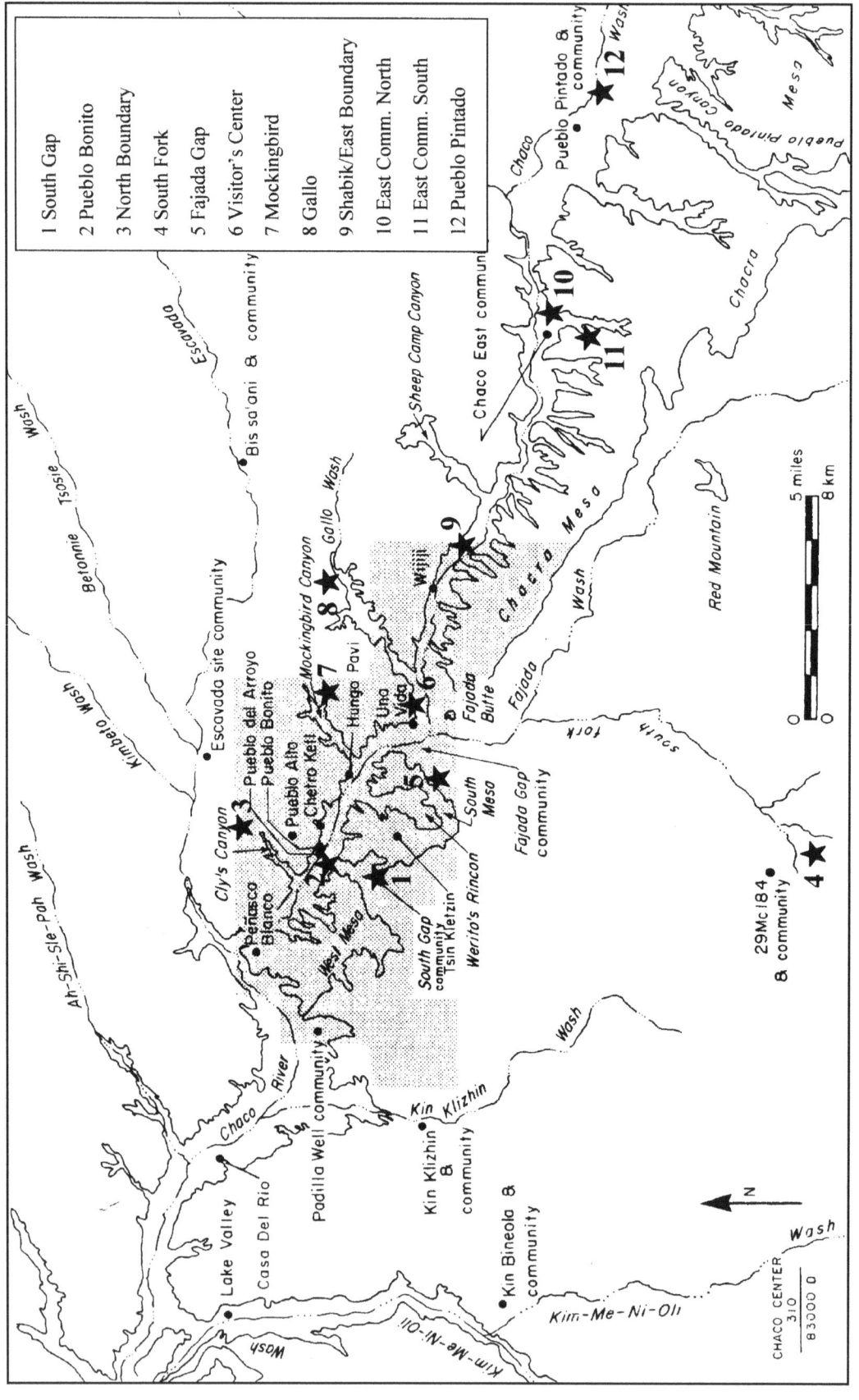

Figure I.2.9. Rain gauge locations within the Chaco Canyon area. Gauges marked by stars.

al. 2000) also receives a relatively high annual precipitation (2 gauges north and south, both with over 234 mm or 9.2"). Even further down canyon near the park's east boundary, the floodplain gauge below the Shabik'eschee community revealed amounts (205 mm or 8.1") that are similar to that at Pueblo Bonito for each of the three seasons, but always a little higher than within Fajada Gap with 197 mm (7.7"). Sites out among the ridges near Fajada Butte in Fajada Gap receive some of the poorest annual amounts within the canyon, whereas the nearby Visitor's Center against the north side of the canyon receives substantially more (230 mm; 9.0"). South from Fajada Butte 10 km along the South Fork of the Fajada Wash (see Chapters 4 and 8) is the driest recorded area (168 mm; 6.6") with 20 years of data. For most of its puebloan history, there is a lack of occupation in the South Fork. A similar placed row of north-to-south gauges, at Pueblo Bonito and in nearby South Gap, are somewhat more favorable (218 mm, 8.6" and 209 mm, 8.2", respectively). Of course, the gauges with data records recorded since 1992 are more likely to yield lower average amounts because of the recent droughts over the past 15 years.

Rather than the yearly amounts, however, it is the timing of the important late winter-spring (Season 1) and summer precipitation (Season 2) that determines the fate of farmers and their crops. The "spring" (January through April) seasonal amounts are, on the average, low, with the six canyon gauges recording amounts of 56 mm (2.2") or less, but this period of moisture is critical for the germination of the plants. During the growing season (May through September), late summer rains are crucial for maintaining crop growth and overcoming the traditionally very dry months of June and early July.

Overall, the average for all canyon gauges during the growing season is between 102 and 121 mm (4.0" and 4.8"), which is not much moisture unless runoff is trapped and diverted to the crops. The worst recorded summer growing area is along the South Fork Valley (91 mm, 3.6") of the Fajada Wash. The best areas, for comparison, were at Crownpoint (154 mm, 6.06"), which is next to the high mesa country of the Dutton Plateau and the Chacoan greathouse community at nearby Kin Ya'a nearly 48 km (30 mi.) away, and at the Seven Lakes Store (138 mm, 5.5") at the end of the park south entrance road about 35 km (22 mi.) south of Fajada Butte. Within downtown Chaco Canyon, where small houses and greathouses are clustered, the Bonito summer mean is 110 mm (4.4"), while at Pueblo Pintado, where crop surplus may have been common (see Chapter 8), it is 133 mm (5.2"). The wettest areas in Chaco Canyon are at the eastern end where the Chaco East and Pueblo Pintado communities are located.

The dry-appearing region south of Fajada Butte was monitored with a rain gauge placed in 1996. It was here that an early puebloan settlement was investigated (Chapter 8) along the South Fork drainage about 10 km south of Fajada Butte. The gauge is located in the heart of large Pueblo I and Pueblo II settlements in the South Fork Valley, and it confirms the extreme marginal setting of the area for farming. Its gauge readings are consistently the driest among the 12 in the region for each of the three seasons monitored as well as for the mean yearly total (168 mm, 6.6") for the 20 years of record. If we drop the two wettest readings for the important summer season (164 and 169 mm in 2006 and 1999, respectively), then for 18 of the 20 years, the mean precipitation is only a dry 83 mm (3.27") for the summer. The early impacts of settlement, which may have included denuding the area of wood, together with the average dry conditions may have been largely responsible for the lack of occupation after the mid A.D. 1000s, which even then may have been largely used only in the summer by canyon farmers. Historically there has been little Navajo occupation of the area.

The two gauges at Pitt Ranch and Seven Lakes south of the ridge that heads the South Fork and Kin Klizhin valleys, reflect higher amounts (yearly means of 220 mm, 8.7", and 242 mm, 9.5" respectively) than the South Fork Valley gauge. Statistically, these figures are the same as at Chaco (Table I.2.3) except that Bonito is slightly wetter during the winter months. Both Pitt Ranch and Seven Lakes border the vast drainage system of the Kim-me-ni-oli Wash and its tributaries, where several Chacoan greathouses are located (Kin Ya'a, Kin Bineola, Bee Burrow, and Lake Valley) but the Pitt Ranch station is closest to Bee Burrow, a mere 6 km to the north.

The 37-yearly record for the Pitt Ranch gauge is second to the park's in longevity within the interior San Juan Basin. It is 31 km south of Pueblo Bonito and 8 km west of Seven Lakes. It was maintained intermittently between 1943 and 1967 but was then shut down, probably at the death of the ranch owner or the sale of the property. The Navajo Nation reinstalled the gauge in 1995 and monitoring continues to the present (2015) despite the ranch house's demise from arson in about 2007. Nearby, Seven Lakes is named for the up-to seven lakes that periodically form during wet periods and would seem an ideal area for farming, such as happened in September 2013. The Seven Lakes store gauge reflects similar precipitation records compared to Pitt Ranch, although its recording life is shorter (20 years; through 2014).

Although precipitation amounts at Pitt Ranch and Seven Lakes seem adequate for puebloan farming, few sites are known in the vicinity; for instance, there is an A.D. 1200s cliff shelter site that has been looted just east behind the Seven Lakes Store. The area has not been systematically surveyed, however. A 2005 reconnaissance of the north side of the valley area south of Navajo Highway 9 about four miles east of the Seven Lakes store by Ruth Van Dyke and the author failed to reveal any puebloan house sites, much less any cultural debris.

John Stein's (personal communication 2002) survey of the South Road from Chaco to Kin Ya'a (Kincaid 1983), crossing the Kim-me-ni-oli Wash valley, also found that the area further to the west is devoid of sites. Our understanding of Chaco must include those unoccupied areas and the reasons the apparently favorable conditions failed to entice puebloan community settlement or Chacoan greathouses. It appears that a swath of uninhabited land marks the area due east and south of Chaco Canyon nearly to the Dutton Plateau.

Historically, Seven Lakes is known for the state's first oil discovery, in 1911 (Christiansen 1989:47-53), with sporadic drilling into the 1960s (Dugan and Arnold 2002). Power for the early drilling was supplied by steam boilers fueled by wood cut in the area, depleting the local piñons and junipers. The area is still marked by rusted equipment abandoned from these efforts. Thus, while local woodlands are sparse today, there were probably adequate wood resources prehistorically. This area should be studied further to assess why there was no major Chacoan use of the area. Could it form a buffer zone between other puebloan groups, or was it just too cold and unsuitable for runoff or dry farming?

Ground Water

Little is known of the level of ground water within the Chaco area, although Dean (1988, 1996) has modeled its relationship with other climatic events that can have profound effects on prehistoric populations. When the Chaco Project began fieldwork in 1971, the water table within Chaco Wash was close to the surface of the inner wash channel, but in the 1990s it inexplicably dropped. The water table is now estimated to be about 1.5 and 4.5 m below the inner channel, but its level appears highly variable (Whitefield 1998). We do know that the Chaco Wash has undergone cutting and filling events because former buried channels are evident in the present banks (Love 1977, 1980), as are deeply buried Basketmaker III and Pueblo I pithouses. Historic attempts at farming relied primarily on runoff from the side canyons (rincons) to supply water to the fields located along the sides on the canyon.

North of Chaco, in the Escavada Wash, Navajos planted crops directly within the broad, sandy wash. Escavada Wash becomes the Chaco River beyond its confluence with the Chaco Wash, just below the Chacoan greathouse of Peñasco Blanco. A number of large sites are found along the Chaco River (Chapter 9), and thus, the prehistoric potential for farming the wash seems evident. Massive amounts of refuse and discarded mealing stones for food processing are common at these sites, suggesting that an abundance of foods were produced in these areas.

In 2002 and 2003, tests were made in the channel bottom from Pueblo Pintado (in the Chaco Wash) west along the Chaco River almost to Shiprock, in order to collect water samples for quality and to determine the present ground water depth. Despite being in the midst of a several year drought, the river yielded pooled water at about 50-60 cm below the surface in every locality except at Lake Valley, where it was deeper (ca. 75 cm), but easily within the rooting depth of corn.

The quality of the samples (Table I.2.2), analyzed at New Mexico Tech, indicate that water quality would have been suitable for domesticated plants. These findings indicate that riverbed fields would have been possible even in the worst of times, a tremendous hedge against drought. Most of the sites located along the Chaco River are situated where a variety of physiographical conditions produce multiple field locations from which the drought-conscious farmer can select. Prominent side drainages, abrupt bluffs and cliffs, and dune areas are all viable alternatives for capturing water (see Hack 1942), and these seem to be locales that were favored by Chacoan farmers. But the most certain advantage would seem to be the Chaco riverbed with its high water table and broad, sandy, braided channel.

Floodwater Events

Knowledge of recent flood history in Chaco provides insights into flood patterns and runoff. For a short period of time (1976-1988), the U.S. Geological Survey had monitoring stations on the Fajada, Gallo, and Chaco washes (see Windes 1993: Table I.2.3). This was a period of generally above-average spring precipitation. Floods (Plate I.2.4) typically occurred during rapid late winter/early spring snow melt (January and February) or when huge storms crossed the upper watersheds near Pueblo Pintado during a span of several days during August and September. Neither of these two periods is particularly advantageous for agriculture. When moisture was critical for crops, the washes only ran sporadically, although in recent very wet years in the 1990s the Chaco Wash ran nearly year-round. The impounding of water at numerous earthen stock dams along nearly every side drainage has reduced downstream runoff and influenced these runoff records.

The Chaco Wash, with a watershed of 982 km^2 (379 mi^2) by the time it reaches Fajada Gap, provides the greatest amount of water, but it carries salts and minerals that prohibit floodwater farming (e.g., Judd 1964:230-231; Scofield 1922). A 12-year average for the Chaco Wash shows

Plate I.2.4. Flood waters in the Chaco Wash in the 1930/1940s? near the present-day Visitor's Center. Photograph by Myrtle or Gordon Vivian? Note windmill and well on bank (CHCU neg. 77903).

only a paltry yield of 3,380 acre/ft per year (U.S. Geological Survey 1988:331) and a peak discharge of 1,260 cfs (Mastromarchi 2002). However, larger floods have occurred which were not recorded.

The smaller side tributaries to the Chaco Wash may be more suitable for floodwater farming, although their runoff potential is considerably smaller. Gallo Wash drains 93.8 km^2 (36.2 mi^2) of land and, until recently, a large stock tank impounded runoff at the head of the canyon. When this broke (ca. 1995) the discharge resulted in an extraordinary crop of dense sunflowers along a short stretch of the Gallo suggesting its fertility for growing domestic plants. A probable prehistoric dam (Vivian 1972) indicates that the Gallo was used to store water, which was released into a ditch that ran down the north side of Chaco Canyon past Una Vida. Ceramics collected from the ditch suggest an A.D. 900s origin, if not later (Gwinn Vivian, personal communication 1991).

Nearby Fajada Wash empties an area of 515 km^2 (199 mi^2) (U.S. Geological Survey 1982:462). At least one hydraulic structure (29SJ 2044) has been found in the incised channel of the Fajada Wash in Fajada Gap, the location of a large community (Windes 1993), while potential headgate stones (29Mc 693) were found in the South Fork Valley (Chapter 8) where a large concentration of Pueblo I sites is located. Other ditches have been recorded along the south side of the canyon across from Pueblo Bonito (Judd 1954:58, 345-350), and one was tested by Gwinn Vivian in 1969 below Casa Rinconada. These finds suggest that water diversion was practiced in the past along both sides of and outside Chaco Canyon, and many water-control features are probably buried by sediment.

When it floods, the Fajada Wash does not contain the high salts and other undesirable minerals (Kim Ong, U.S. Geological Survey water quality analyst, personal communication 1988), nor the destructive torrents and heavy loads of sediment that sometimes roar down the Chaco Wash. Thus, it may have been a more reliable source of water during periods of above-normal, summer rainfall. This probably applies to the other side drainages in Chaco as well.

In addition to the likelihood of horticulture at the confluence of a number of side drainages and major washes, the runoff created from exposed masses of mesa slickrock must also have been important (Cully and Toll 2015; Vivian 1974, 1984, 1990). The abrupt topographic changes created by the mesas adjacent to Chaco Canyon create a zone of increased precipitation relative to the surrounding basin (Windes 1993). Like areas farmed at Hopi (Bradfield 1971), the ephemeral drainages had the advantages of wide, adjacent strips of bare sandstone ledges and benches that bordered the mesas, supplying needed runoff and soil nutrients to the fields below (Vivian 1970a, 1974).

Temperature

Adequate, prolonged, and warm temperatures are critical to horticultural success. At Chaco, the 82-year temperature record as of 1 January 2014 can be used to illustrate possible prehistoric conditions. The Chaco extremes show that 93 percent of the time, the lowest temperatures in Chaco are below zero, with numbing record colds of -38°F (1961), -37° (1971, 1990), -35° (1963, 1976), -26° (1989, 2011) and -24° (1937, 1947, 1978) being recorded, primarily in December or January. The average coldest day for the past 82 years is -12.3°F. The warmest days, normally in June or July, average 99.9°F for the past 81 years. The lowest warmest days reached 93°F (1993) and the hottest 106° (1942), with the years from 1938 to 1945 exceeding 100°F. Chaco is clearly a place of yearly extremes.

Within the San Juan Basin, Chaco Canyon exhibits the shortest growing season, except for Star Lake and Cuba to the east (Schelberg 1982:84; Windes 1993: Table I.2.2). Schelberg (1982:85) argues that damaging frosts will occur in Chaco Canyon 60 percent of the time within

120 or less days during the summer, 45 percent of the time within 110 or less days, and 30 percent of the time within 100 or less days—clearly making horticulture a risky venture (see also Benson 2010). These data were gathered from the official weather gauge at the Visitor's Center, which has constant recording errors and does not represent the temperature variations across and within the canyon.

For some, a frost-free period of less than 130 days was prohibitive for occupation (e.g., Adams 1979). Referring to the problems of cold-air drainage in Keams Canyon and around the Hopi Mesas, Adams (1979:293) could have been describing Chaco Canyon when he stated, "In an agriculturally marginal area with a growing season of 150 days or less, narrow valley areas would be avoided for agricultural activity areas in favor of more open or high areas" (see also Gillespie and Powers 1983:6-7). At Hopi, for instance, Hack (1942:19) mentions short, growing-season frosts that can cause considerable damage to crops. The scarcity of water compounds the danger of frost because it slows crop maturity.

The frost-free period calculated by Vivian and Mathews (1965:10) for Chaco was 150 days when the recording station was located at Pueblo Bonito. When it was moved in 1960 to the present Visitor's Center near Una Vida, there was a profound effect on the readings, revealing a dramatic drop in the frost-free period by almost a third (Gillespie 1985:18). It is likely that the longer period recorded at Pueblo Bonito, 8 km from the Visitor's Center, resulted from the passive solar temperatures provided by the architectural stone mass of Pueblo Bonito and the 30 m cliff behind it (e.g., Baxter 1982; Knowles 1974; Paul 1977; Williamson 1978) and this radiant energy probably was important prehistorically. Gillespie (1985:19), however, warns of the problems with the official weather reports because of inconsistent heights above ground for the gauge stations and changes in defining the frost-free season.

Modern pueblos are all located in better climes than Chaco, suggesting an acknowledgement of the poor conditions in the basin. Those pueblos nearest to the San Juan Basin, the pueblos of Zuni, Laguna, and Acoma, exhibit growing seasons of 143, 160, and 118-170 days, respectively (Windes 1993: Table I.2.5). Farming areas in and around Chaco were probably between the extremes exhibited by the official Chaco weather station and those at the historic pueblos. Clearly, some areas adjacent to cliffs provided extended growing seasons (e.g., Bradfield 1971:6)—such as the mouth of Werito's Rincon (Windes 1993:41), where sites 29SJ 721 and 724 (reported here) were located, and in South Gap. Anywhere outside the cold-air drainage flows down the canyon probably provided longer growing seasons than those now registered officially at the Visitor's Center.

Documented site locations indicate that the prehistoric inhabitants had knowledge of these varying temperature differences. Throughout the canyon, northern drainages and rincons were generally avoided for occupation, as were other colder areas. Most important for Chaco Canyon is that on calm, clear nights the cold air settles in the canyon bottom where temperatures are lowest and stay that way the longest—thus placing any crops directly along the canyon bottomlands at greater risk. The slightly higher elevations of slopes and ridges away from the central canyon are warmer, avoid the lack of cold-air pooling, and catch early sunrises that first warm the southern areas of the canyon—all attributes necessary for successful horticulture.

Wind

The effects of wind are little known for Chaco Canyon (cf., Brand 1937:42-43), although studies in the San Juan Basin provide some records. Westerly or southwesterly winds are common, and spring is the windiest season with winds averaging 10-12 mph (Anderson et al. 1973;

Windes 1987a:43). Summer winds average 8 mph. Aside from comfort, the wind can disrupt cold-air pooling (possibly extending the frost-free season) but drives moisture from the ground. Thus, dry periods are made worse by the incessant winds that seem to accompany them.

Summary

Overall, farming in Chaco was risky business (Schelberg 1992:62). Unfavorable as Chaco may seem, it did provide favorable locales for horticulture away from the main canyon bottom (see also Cully et al. 1982). Settlement at the mouths of long, deep rincons and breaks through the mesa along the southern side of the canyon seem ideal because of potential concentrations of runoff useful for floodwater farming and less cold-air drainage than is experienced along the northern side. The uniquely situated gaps and deep southern rincons appear to have enjoyed favorable microenvironmental conditions in the form of greater moisture, including rainfall, longer frost-free seasons, and warmer temperatures. Small house sites cluster at these locations but spill out beyond the canyon to the south in the earlier periods.

During the summer months, storms often penetrate the canyon through these openings. Intuitively, then, the southern gaps and openings into Chaco Canyon receive greater summer moisture than the northern side of the canyon, and this may explain the differential density of settlements along the two sides of Chaco Canyon. It is of note that during the summer monsoons, the South Gap/Pueblo Bonito area often experiences greater precipitation than upcanyon in the Fajada Gap area although this not borne out from the rain gauge data (but see Wills and Dorshow 2012).

Although it has been suggested that no area in the San Juan Basin was predictably better than any other (Rose et al. 1982; Schelberg 1982:93), this is simply not true. It is clear that the peripheries of the San Juan Basin always receive greater precipitation (Windes 1993:Table I.2.2) than Chaco Canyon and even within the canyon, there is great variability (Table I.2.3). Interpreting the precipitation patterns in the basin's interior poses problems due to the lack of records, but the region is now relatively barren and seemingly unfavorable for horticulture. Nevertheless, puebloan communities and isolated sites are scattered throughout the central basin in areas with potential runoff. Most important for the early puebloan occupation of the region, particularly in the late Pueblo I times, is the potential for reliable shallow water tables along the Chaco River from outside Chaco Canyon west and north across the San Juan Basin to Shiprock. Several late Pueblo I/ early Pueblo II communities were densely settled along this area (see Chapter 9).

In conclusion, microenvironments within Chaco Canyon were not as marginal as suggested by the modern historic climatic records. On a regional scale, however, Chaco Canyon ranks poorly in categories that are important for successful horticulture: precipitation, temperature, and frost-free seasons. Fuel, timber, and wildlife resources were also limited, so that any sizable population would have dramatically and rapidly reduced the local resources.

By all accounts, Chacoan settlements around the periphery of the San Juan Basin were more favorably located than those in Chaco Canyon. In spite of its environmental shortcomings, successful horticulture in Chaco Canyon was clearly possible. The impact of chronic and diachronic climatic variation on horticulture is still controversial. The two most important areas for potential food surpluses in the area, however, would have been at the head of Chaco Canyon at Pueblo Pintado and at the mouth of Chaco Canyon and slightly beyond at Peñasco Blanco, Padilla Well, and Casa del Rio (see Chapters 8 and 9). Environmental factors likely influenced populations and their periodicity of occupation in and around Chaco Canyon; understanding and modeling these factors are necessary to identify and interpret the Chacoan occupation.

Chapter 2: The Natural Environment 55

Table I.2.1. Dendrochronological Results from Chaco Canyon: Modern Aspen, Ponderosa Pine, Douglas-Fir, and Mountain Juniper Study.

Field No.	Tree-Ring Lab No.	Location	Live or Dead	Ax Marks	Species	Length (m)	Max. diameter (cm)	Wood Condition†	1971 sample	Age (yrs)	Dates‡ Inside	Dates‡ Outside
\multicolumn{13}{l}{Aspen Cove, Chaco East Community, north side canyon (sampled in 1995)[a]}
1	CHA 58	base of cliff	L		Aspen	13	28			46	1950	1995
2	CHA 59	base of cliff	L		Aspen	7	11			21	1975	1995
3	CHA 60	base of cliff	L		Aspen	8.5	12			53	1943	1995
4	CHA 61	talus slope	L		Aspen	10.1	30			42	1954	1995
5	CHA 62	talus slope	L		Aspen	8	20			44+	1952	1995
6	CHA 63	base of cliff	L		Aspen	2.8	9	internal decay		49	1947	1995
7	CHA 64	base of cliff	L		Aspen	5	14			37	1959	1995
8	CHA 65	base of cliff	L		Aspen	2.94	8			19	1977	1995
9	CHA 66	base of cliff	L		Aspen	2	7			34	1962	1995
10	CHA 67	talus slope	L		Aspen	6	20	rotten center		22+	1974	1995
11	CHA 68	base of cliff	D		Aspen					76	1920-	1995cB
12	CHA 69	talus slope	D, on ground		Aspen					47	1949-	1995cB
13	CHA 70	base of cliff	D, stump		Aspen	2.7	25			74	1922-	1995cB
14	CHA 71	talus slope	D, on ground		Aspen	2.1	8			57	1939-	1995c
15	CHA 72	base of cliff	D, stump+ on ground		Aspen	11.4	28			61	1935-	1995cB
\multicolumn{13}{l}{Large conifers in the Chaco East Community, south side of canyon (sampled in 1995)[b]}
0	CHA 18	base of cliff, next to 29Mc 590	D, stump+ on ground		PP	5.24	16.5 H 35.5			191		nd, B
00	CHA 19	base of cliff?/ talus; Tree 52?	D		PP	1.8	32			383+	1495 p	1877 ++vvB
1	CHA 20	mesa top	L, on ground		PP	3.8	55		x	154		nd, B
2	CHA 21	mesa top	L		PP	1.7	9	porcupine		29		nd, B
3	CHA 22	mesa top	L		PP	1.8	12			49		nd, B
4	CHA 23	mesa top	L, dying		PP	2	12	porcupine		20		nd, B
5	CHA 24	mesa top	L		PP	4	18	porcupine		37		nd, B
6	CHA 25	mesa top	L		PP	4	18	porcupine		48		nd, B
7	CHA 26	mesa top	L		PP	3	20			44		nd, B
8	CHA 27	mesa top	L, dying		PP	1.4	6-15	porcupine woodpecker; 8m standing	?	?		nd, B
9	CHA 27	cove A	D, stump + on ground	x	PP	19	55		x #9	372+	1538	1909 ++rB
10	CHA 28	cove A	D, stump	x	PP	0.8	31.5	scarred	x	264		nd, B
11	CHA 29	mesa top	L	x	PP	1.6	13		x	46		nd
12	CHA 30	mesa top	D, stump + on ground	x	PP	12.1	40		?	235+	1649	1883 +vv

Table I.2.1. Dendrochronological Results from Chaco Canyon: Modern Aspen, Ponderosa Pine, Douglas-Fir, and Mountain Juniper Study, cont'd.

Field No.	Tree-Ring Lab No.	Location	Live or Dead	Ax Marks	Species	Length (m)	Max. diameter (cm)	Wood Condition†	1971 sample	Age (yrs)	Dates‡ Inside	Dates‡ Outside
14	CHA 32	mesa top	L		PP	17	43	porcupine	x	51+	1945	1995
15	CHA 33	mesa top	L		PP	5.5	33	porcupine	x	51+	1945	1995
16	CHA 34	base of cliff	L	x	PP	18	70	scarring, woodpecker	x	422+	1574	1995
17	CHA 35	Cove B	D, cut, stump	x	PP	9.6	50		x #20?	171+	1345 p	1515 vv
18	CHA 36	mesa top, above 29Mc 592	L		PP	12	68	lightning, scarring		326+	1670	1995
19	CHA 37	Cove C	D, stump	x	PP	2.2	58	woodpecker		237+	1639	1875 +B
20	CHA 38	Cove C, nearest to 29Mc 596	D, stump + on ground	x	PP	96 (stump); 986 (other)	52	sawcut sawcut	x	383+	1478 np	1860 ++vv
21	CHA 39	Cove C	D, stump + on ground		PP	6.7	28.5	cut, burned, sawcut		304+	1579 p	1882 +vv
22A,B	CHA 40	Cove C	D, part on ground	x	PP	7.6	29	woodpecker		180+	1513	1692 +vv
23	CHA 41	Cove D, east talus slope	L, on ground		PP	10; 12 (in 1971)	64	porcupine	x	415+	1581 ±	1995
24	CHA 42	Cove D head; mesa top	D, on ground		PP	9.7	53	side burned out; entire stem		152		nd
25	CHA 43	Cove D head, south on mesa top	L		PP	5"	32	porcupine	x	109		nd
26	—	east of Cove D; mesa top (now gone)	L, now presumed dead		PP	0.6	1-2?	Chaco #25 (1971)				—
27	—	Cove D, head (now gone); E of 23	D, missing		PP	0.8	1-2?	porcupine				—
28	CHA 44	talus slope	D, stump	x	PP	4.5	47.3	woodpecker		317+	1372 p	1688 +vv
29	CHA 45	mesa top	D, stump + on ground		PP	2.6	36	limb sampled	x	89		nd
30	CHA 46	Cove C	D, on ground	x	PP	2.6	46			254+	1423	1676 +vv

Table I.2.1. Dendrochronological Results from Chaco Canyon: Modern Aspen, Ponderosa Pine, Douglas-Fir, and Mountain Juniper Study, cont'd

Field No.	Tree-Ring Lab No.	Location	Live or Dead	Ax Marks	Species	Length (m)	Max. diameter (cm)	Wood Condition†	1971 sample	Age (yrs)	Dates‡ Inside	Dates‡ Outside
32	CHA 48	below Cove C, talus slope	D, on ground		Pnm	4.9	20			20		nd
33	CHA 49	Cove C	D, stump	x	PP	1.1	38.7	burned		235+	1648	1882 vv
34	CHA 50	Cove C	D, stump	x	Mt. Jun	2.7	68	rotted center		508		nd, B
35	CHA 51	talus slope, Cove B	D, on ground	x	PP	9.5	38.1	burned		193		nd
36	CHA 52	Cove E, base of cliff	L/D	x	Mt. Jun	6.5"	50.9			350	1646±	1995 est. B
37	CHA 53	Cove E, base of cliff	L/D		Mt. Jun	4.5	59 H 84			440	1556±	1995 est. B
38	CHA 54	north of Cove A, talus slope	D, stump + on ground	x	PP	5.9	18			252+	1644 p	1895 ++vv
39	CHA 55	Cove E, base of cliff	L + 2 D on ground		Mt. Jun	9"	?			285	1711±	1995 est. B
40	CHA 56	Cove E, base of cliff; across from 29Mc 603	D		PP	10.3	55	porcupine, woodpecker		317+	1629 p	1945 vv B
41	CHA 57	mesa top, eastern side, deep side canyon	L/D		PP	9-10	60.8	porcupine, woodpecker		145+	1640	1785 +vv B
42	—	(see above)	L		PP	4	38	porcupine				B
43	—	(see above)	D, on ground	x	PP	8.2	65					
44	—	(see above)	D		PP	7"	33.3					B
45	—	(see above)	D, stump	x?	PP	1.1	66					
46	—	(see above)	L/D		PP	8"	62	lightning, porcupine				B
47	—	(see above)	D, on ground		PP	?	?					—
48	—	Cove D head; mesa top	D, on ground	x	PP	3.3	34.5	burned off at top				—
49	—	Cove D head	D, on ground		PP	4.1	38	bottom burned, next to #39				—
50	—	Cove D, NE on mesa top	D, stem on ground	x	DF?	4.5	27	corkscrew spiral weathered				—
51	—	Cove B, south on mesa top	D, entire tree on ground		PP	6.5	40	porcupine				B

Table I.2.1. Dendrochronological Results from Chaco Canyon: Modern Aspen, Ponderosa Pine, Douglas-Fir, and Mountain Juniper Study, cont'd

Field No.	Tree-Ring Lab No.	Location	Live or Dead	Ax Marks	Species	Length (m)	Max. diameter (cm)	Wood Condition†	1971 sample	Age (yrs)	Dates‡ Inside	Dates‡ Outside
Large conifers in the Chaco East Community collected by Gwinn Vivian (3 March 1971). Most should duplicate tree #s above.												
Chaco #10		same as Tree 50 above?			DF?	?	26-30"	15" frags				—
Chaco #12					PP	?	?	short, complacent	x			nd
Chaco #15					PP	?	?		x	159+	1587 p	1745 vv
Chaco #16					PP	?	?	short	x			nd
Chaco #20	CHA 38?		D	x	PP	?	46	burned	x	401+	1484	1884$_{inc}$
Chaco #21			?		PP	?	16	no sapwood	x	128+	1639 p	1767 vv
Chaco #22					PP	?	16+?	short				nd
Chaco #29					PP	?	20-30"	compressed, outer piece	x			nd
"Pine Cove & Pine Gulch": undoubtedly the same area and trees as above. Collected in Sept. 1926 by Judd.												
DPB-15					PP		53	burned		150"	fp	nd
MPB-3					PP		56			150-200		1880 Tent
DPB-19							?					nd
MPB-4					PP		?					
Chaco #2					PP		?				1535	1718 +vv
Chaco #2				x	PP		18+				1751	1871 +vv
Chaco #3												
Fallen tree on mesa in upper side rincon south of Shabik'eschee Village across from and southwest of 29SJ 2642 (sampled in 1995)												
— (old 50)		mesa top rincon talus slope	D, on ground	stone ax?	PP	9.7	58"			145+	1640 fp	1785 +vv
Fallen tree near (east of) 29Mc 577 (sampled in 1995)												
—	CHM190	cliff base; east of 29Mc 578	D, entire stem on ground		DF	9.5	52	burned all along side		658	917 p	1574 vv
Section of 1 of 2 stumps on mesa east of Bc 50-57 collected by Gwinn Vivian (5/1/71), Deric O'Bryan (1940), & RG Fisher (1936)												
—	GP 2436	talus	D, stump		PP	?	38	erratic, cut ca. 1905		85-90		nd

Table I.2.1. Dendrochronological Results from Chaco Canyon: Modern Aspen, Ponderosa Pine, Douglas-Fir, and Mountain Juniper Study, cont'd

Field No.	Tree-Ring Lab No.	Location	Live or Dead	Ax Marks	Species	Length (m)	Max. diameter (cm)	Wood Condition†	1971 sample	Age (yrs)	Dates‡ Inside	Dates‡ Outside
—	JPB-99	plaza	D, stump		PP		52"			250++	732 "p	981 +vvc

Wello's House, north side of canyon, Mockingbird Canyon (Emil Haury 8/30/29): Wrong location. Probably Wello's house near Peñasco Blanco described by Judd (1954)(site 29SJ 609), which was originally a cattle ranch built in 1879. Beams from Pine Cove?

Chaco #8			const		PP		22"	short; 3/4"core		60±	nd	nd
Chaco #9			constr		Pnn		30"	xs		125+	nd	nd
Chaco #10			constr		PP		30"	short?; xs		50	nd	nd
Chaco #11			constr		PP		30"	short; xs		50	nd	nd
Chaco #13			constr	x	PP		28"	complacent; v-cut		75-80	nd	nd
Chaco #14			constr		PP		24"	doubles; v-cut		85+	nd	nd
Chaco #15			const		PP		25"	3/4" core		159+	1587 p	1745 vv
Chaco #16			const		PP		7"	short; v-cut		11	nd	nd

Chacra Mesa east of Pintado Pintado near Burning Bridge Wash. Collected by Bill Robinson, Gwinn Vivian, and Jeff Dean (6-18-68) for the Southwest Paleoclimate Database (dated specimens only).

CMM-1					PP					262	1707 p	1968 B
CMM-2					PP					341	1628	1968 B
CMM-3					PP					75	1816	1890
CMM-4					PP					167	1802 p	1968 B
CMM-5					PP					125	1786	1910
CMM-6					PP					186	1745	1930

Table I.2.1. Dendrochronological Results from Chaco Canyon: Modern Aspen, Ponderosa Pine, Douglas-Fir, and Mountain Juniper Study, cont'd

Field No.	Tree-Ring Lab No.	Location	Live or Dead	Ax Marks	Species	Length (m)	Max. diameter (cm)	Wood Condition†	1971 sample	Age (yrs)	Dates‡ Inside	Dates‡ Outside
	CMM-8				DF					178	1791	1968
	CMM-9				DF					413	1556	1968
	CMM-10				DF					155	1814	1968
	CMM-14				DF					145	1736	1880
	CMM-16				PP					294	1607	1900
	CMM-17				PP					269	1700	1968 B
	CMM-18				PP					256	1675	1930
	CMM-19				PP					101	1800	1900
	CMM-20				PP					76	1865	1940
	CMM-23				PP					90	1791	1880
	CMM-24				PP					79	1822	1900
	CMM-25				PP					19	1850	1868 B

† Porcupine = scars from eating. Woodpecker = holes from eating. Lightning = scars from being struck.
‡ See Table I.6.3 for a list of tree-ring codes.

[a] Inside dates from live trees calculated by author from ring count and date of sampling. Several of the older live aspen had rotten cores and were missing many internal rings; thus the ages presented here are minimum. Many did not date and yielded only ring counts. Those trees that were alive when sampled presumably had outside dates of 1995 and inner dates approximate the number of rings. "Minus" dates for dead aspens are estimates based on ring counts and year recorded.

[b] The trees in the this area were first sampled by Gwinn Vivian and Jeff Dean in 1968, and resampled by Windes and Vivian in 1995. In 1998, Steve Durand of Eastern New Mexico University sampled some trees for trace elements analyses (Durand et al. 1999), although these data were not used in the published article. Trees 26 and 27 were tiny ponderosa pines that could not be relocated in 2005 and presumably no longer exist; the location of 00 is uncertain. Denny Boden, tree-ring laboratory analyst, reported (10-4-95) that CHM-219, a piñon stump step for nearby historical structure LA 100091 (29Mc 591), was "very similar" to Sample 00, a ponderosa pine (Tree 52?).

[c] Jeffrey Dean (personal communication, 1992) estimated that perhaps 40-70 outer rings were missing from JPB-99 based on the absence of sapwood rings. He said that the tree exhibited normal growth (responded to environmental conditions); thus, it was not artificially watered by the Bonito inhabitants. Recent work (Guiterman et al. 2012) suggests that this plaza tree did not have its basal part nor roots and was not grown there but hauled into Pueblo Bonito.

Table I.2.2. Water samples from the Chaco Wash and Chaco River compared with recent irrigation samples (in parts per million).

	Chaco Wash				Chaco River				Rio Grande
Analysis Results	Pueblo Bonito	Rafael's Well	below Pueblo Pintado	near Padilla's Well	at mouth of Kin Klizhin Wash	Stock Tank[a] near Kin Klizhin Wash	near Casa del Rio	near La Vida Mission	Hogback Community near Shiprock	Ditches outside Socorro
Lab No.	1-5	1-6	02-2806	02-2804	02-2805	02-2802	02-2803	03-1272	03-0960	5 samples[b]
pH			7.6	8.0	8.1	8.28	7.8	8.45	7.67	8.0-8.5
Hardness ($CaCO_3$)			100	101	42	47	26	100	324	225-299
Carbonate ($CO_3^=$)										
Bicarbonate (HCO_3^-)	192-336		150	325	350	330	245	360	223	225-287
Boron (B)								<0.06	<0.08	
Bromide (Br)			<0.1	<0.1	<0.1	<0.1	<0.1	<0.1	<0.1	
Calcium (Ca)	30-138		36	35	15	15	9.4	35	120	72-95
Chloride (Cl^-)	trace-72		3.7	4.7	2.9	27	4.1	10	31	38-103
Fluoride (F^-)			0.67	0.6	0.44	1.3	0.82	0.93	0.5	0.49-0.53
Iron (Fe)			<0.03	<0.01	0.41	0.13	<0.06	<0.05	<0.10	<0.05
Magnesium (Mg)	trace-6		2.5	3.2	1.1	2.4	0.54	3	6	11-15
Nitrate (NO_3^-)	trace-5		2.5	5.8	5.6	4.2	7.3	13	4.6	0.23-1.7
Phosphate (PO_4^{3-})			<0.5	<0.5	<0.5	<0.5	<0.5	<0.5	<0.5	0.42-<0.5
Potassium (K)			2.2	3.9	3.9	6	2.6	5.8	5.7	4.7-5.6
Silica (SiO_2)			10	<10	16	<10	13.6	49	12	25-34
Sodium (Na)			62	165	150	310	145	195	330	64-137
Sulfate (SO_4^{2-})	108-725		108	155	55	400	110	225	820	112-185
Zinc (Zn)			<0.01	<0.03	0.14	<0.03	<0.05	<0.02	<0.01	<0.001-0.01

Note: Samples 1-5 and 1-6 from Judd 1954:11. All other samples analyzed by Ann Brandvold of the New Mexico Bureau of Geology and Mineral Resources, Socorro, in 2002 and 2003. See Bauder et al. 2005 for water quality criteria for corn and other crops.

[a] Stock tank located near the mouth of Kin Klizhin Wash at a well 5,896 ft in elevation next to the Chaco River in Section 1 (see Kin Klizhin Ruins USGS 7.5' map).
[b] Five samples (02-1657, 1660, 1661, 1770, and 1772) collected from a series of agricultural irrigation ditches outside Socorro, NM, by NM Tech.

Table I.2.3. Precipitation Data from 12 Gauges In and Around the Chaco Canyon Region: Basic Data.[a]

Gauge Station[b]	Season[c]	No. of Sample Years	Mean (in.)	s.d.	Range (inches)	Coefficient Variant
Crownpoint 1935–1969	Season 1	33	2.09	0.89	3.37 (0.51–3.88)	42.58%
	Season 2	33	6.06	2.33	8.43 (2.62–11.05)	38.45%
	Season 3	34	1.88	0.79	3.10 (0.62–3.72)	42.02%
	Year	32	10.31	2.62	11.00 (5.32–16.32)	25.79%
Pitt Ranch (at burned-out ranch house) 1940–1967 and 1995–2013	Season 1	38	1.82	0.86	3.46 (0.53–3.99)	47.25%
	Season 2	39	5.06	2.28	10.18 (1.19–11.37)	45.05%
	Season 3	41	1.79	0.85	3.45 (0.25–3.70)	53.05%
	Year	36	8.69	2.80	13.22 (3.74–16.62)	32.22%
Seven Lakes (at old Seven Lakes Store) 1995–2013	Season 1	19	2.24	1.15	3.84 (0.85–4.69)	51.34%
	Season 2	19	5.47	2.09	7.69 (2.51–10.20)	38.21%
	Season 3	19	1.90	0.88	3.10 (0.40–3.50)	47.87%
	Year	19	9.60	2.36	8.09 (5.99–14.08)	32.23%
Stepp Ranch (now Ruby Ranch) 1969–1971	Season 1	2	1.13	0.64	0.90 (0.68–1.58)	56.63%
	Season 2	3	6.44	2.36	4.65 (4.34–8.99)	36.88%
	Season 3	3	1.65	0.67	1.19 (1.24–2.43)	40.60%
	Year	2	7.57	0.50	0.69 (7.21–7.92)	06.61%
South Boundary in South Gap (at old south fence line & cattle guard) 1992–2013	Season 1	22	2.44	1.26	4.59 (0.73–5.32)	51.64%
	Season 2	21	4.07	1.44	5.43 (1.08–7.51)	35.38%
	Season 3	22	1.79	0.74	3.16 (0.60–3.76)	41.34%
	Year	22	8.31	2.14	8.61 (5.23–13.84)	25.75%
Pueblo Bonito (SW side of ruin) 1933–1960 and 1992–2013	Season 1	50	2.20	1.19	5.60 (0.47–6.07)	54.09%
	Season 2	50	4.38	1.81	8.02 (1.46–9.48)	41.23%
	Season 3	49	2.02	1.15	4.58 (0.08–4.66)	56.93%
	Year	47	8.61	2.84	15.82 (3.35–19.27)	32.83%
North Boundary near Pueblo Alto (at north fence line & old SR57) 1992–2013	Season 1	20	2.16	1.15	4.34 (0.66–5.00)	53.24%
	Season 2	20	4.18	1.66	7.62 (1.33–8.95)	38.79%
	Season 3	21	1.71	0.74	3.40 (0.50–3.90)	45.61%
	Year	21	8.30	2.08	8.98 (5.98–14.96)	24.58%
Fajada Wash, South Fork Valley (on knoll top in valley) 1995–2013	Season 1	19	1.68	1.03	3.67 (0.35–4.02)	65.19%
	Season 2	19	3.64	1.52	5.06 (1.61–6.67)	41.76%
	Season 3	19	1.44	0.76	2.59 (0.21–2.80)	52.78%
	Year	19	6.66	1.56	6.24 (3.74–9.98)	23.42%
Fajada Gap (along old north-south NPS fence line) 1992–2013	Season 1	22	2.05	1.07	3.55 (0.63–4.18)	52.20%
	Season 2	22	4.13	1.82	7.42 (2.08–9.50)	44.07%
	Season 3	22	1.59	0.68	3.12 (0.13–3.25)	42.77%
	Year	22	7.79	2.19	10.94 (3.93–14.80)	28.11%
Visitor's Center 1961–2013	Season 1	53	2.11	1.05	4.08 (0.14–4.22)	49.76%
	Season 2	53	4.74	1.61	7.41 (1.64–9.05)	33.97%
	Season 3	53	2.17	1.38	6.59 (0.16–6.75)	63.59%
	Year	53	9.07	2.41	10.45 (4.67–15.12)	25.57%

Table I.2.3. Precipitation data from 12 gauges in and around the Chaco Canyon region: basic data, cont'd.[a]

Gauge Station[b]	Season[c]	No. of Sample Years	Mean (in.)	s.d.	Range (inches)	Coefficient Variant
Gallo–Mockingbird: North Mesa[d]	Season 1	21	2.37	1.19	4.03 (0.71–4.74)	50.22%
(former old oil-well pad)	Season 2	21	4.59	1.70	7.47 (1.51–8.98)	37.03%
1992–2013	Season 3	21	1.72	0.81	2.91 (0.58–3.49)	47.09%
	Year	21	8.63	2.19	9.47 (6.01–15.48)	25.38%
East Boundary near Shabik'eschee	Season 1	22	2.20	1.09	3.69 (0.70–4.39)	49.55%
(near old east boundary fence)	Season 2	22	4.26	1.72	6.27 (1.70–7.97)	40.38%
1992–2013	Season 3	22	1.65	0.75	3.21 (0.13–3.34)	45.45%
	Year	22	8.05	1.89	5.81 (5.71–11.52)	23.48%
Chaco East Community (South)	Season 1	26	2.74	1.15	4.16 (1.14–5.30)	41.97%
Head of Wild Horse Canyon	Season 2	26	4.88	2.09	9.74 (1.25–10.99)	44.68%
1992–2017	Season 3	26	2.19	1.16	34.42 (0.13–4.55)	52.97%
	Year	26	9.81	1.98	6.63 (7.48–14.11)	20.18%
Chaco East Community (North)	Season 1	25	2.55	1.13	3.91 (0.90–4.81)	46.67%
Mouth of Wild Horse Canyon	Season 2	26	4.92	1.83	6.21 (1.43–7.64)	37.20%
1992–2017	Season 3	26	1.89	0.91	3.09 (0.07–3.16)	48.15%
	Year	26	9.37	2.14	8.05 (7.06–15.11)	22.84%
Pueblo Pintado	Season 1	20	2.62	1.15	3.91 (1.00–4.91)	43.89%
(at windmill repair facility)	Season 2	21	5.28	1.87	7.68 (2.68–10.36)	35.92%
1992–2013	Season 3	21	1.84	1.03	3.82 (0.47–4.29)	55.98%
	Year	20	9.69	2.23	8.61 (6.04–14.65)	23.01%
Star Lake 1953 - 2002	Year	50	9.18	2.47	9.94 (3.85 -13.79	26.91%

[a] Sequence of gauges is from south to north, and from west to east. U.S.G.S. water year = 1 Oct to 1 Oct.
Some season or yearly gauge totals may be missing or incomplete (i.e., not counted).
[b] UTM locations of gauges:
Pueblo Alto, North Boundary: Zone 13E, E 233888, N 3997664
Pueblo Bonito: Zone 13E, E 233224, N 3994441
South Gap: Zone 13E, E 232302, N 3992887
Visitor's Center: Zone 13E, E 237784, N 3991051
Fajada Gap: Zone 13E, E 235933, N 3990071
Gallo (old oil pad): Zone 13E, E 241979, N 3994488
Mockingbird (head of): Zone 13, E 239326, N 3995110
Shabik'eschee: Zone 13, E 243580, N 3989310
East Community, mouth of Wild Horse Canyon: Zone 13E, E 251922, N 3985740
East Community, head of Wild Horse Canyon: Zone 13E, E 251626, N 3983450
Pueblo Pintado (windmill repair facility): Zone 13E, E 261500, N 3983020
PI Valley (South Fork, Fajada Wash): Zone 13E, E 234418, N 3979191
Seven Lakes Trading Post: Zone 13E, E 235161, N 3964183
Pitt Ranch: Zone 12E E 770082, N 3964713
[c] Season 1 = 1 January–30 April; Season 2 = 1 May–30 September; Season 3 = 1 October–31 December.
[d] Gauge established at oil pad 1992–2001 but moved by Navajo Nation in 2002 to 2009 to the head of Mockingbird Canyon inside the Park Service's fencing near the two-track road. Gauge moved from oil pad because of lack of protective fencing and cow damage. Returned to oil pad location in 2010.

Table I.2.4. Variability among various rain gauge stations in the Chaco Canyon region and to the south.

Gauge Locations	Year Span	Wilcoxon Two-Sample Tests[1]			
		Season 1	Season 2	Season 3	Yearly Total
Mouth of Wild Horse Canyon, East Community vs. Head of Wild Horse Canyon, East Community	1992-2012	0.1843	0.3278	0.2406	0.0795
Pitt Ranch vs. Seven Lakes	1995-2012	0.3634	0.0857	0.3097	0.2478
South Boundary in South Gap vs. Pueblo Bonito	1992-2012	0.3069	0.3623	0.4860	0.4613
South Boundary in South Gap vs. North Boundary near Pueblo Alto: North Mesa	1992-2012	0.2212	0.3910	0.4579	0.4248
North Boundary near Pueblo Alto vs. Pueblo Bonito	1992-2012	0.3812	0.3353	0.4813	0.4274
Fajada Gap South Boundary vs. Gallo/Mockingbird: North Mesa	1992-2012	0.1748	0.0995	0.4900	0.0549
Fajada Gap South Boundary vs. Visitor's Center	1992-2012	0.4301	0.1179	0.2124	<u>0.0423</u>
Visitor's Center vs. Gallo/Mockingbird: North Mesa	1992-2012	0.1748	0.4699	0.3161	0.3194
Pueblo Bonito vs. Visitor's Center	1992-2012	0.3110	0.1045	0.3981	0.2758
Crownpoint vs. Pueblo Bonito		can't match dates			
Crownpoint vs. Visitor's Center	1961-1969	0.1254	0.1001	0.3325	0.1803
Crownpoint vs. Pitt Ranch	1950-1967	0.1344	0.2009	0.1454	0.1019
Crownpoint vs. Pueblo Pintado		can't match dates			
Mouth of Wild Horse Canyon, East Community vs. Visitor's Center	1992-2012	0.1371	0.3069	0.3712	0.0759
Head of Wild Horse Canyon, East Community vs. Visitor's Center	1992-2012	<u>0.0264</u>	0.1650	0.1427	<u>0.0036</u>
Mouth of Wild Horse Canyon, East Community vs. Pueblo Bonito	1992-2012	0.2881	<u>0.0478</u>	0.4027	<u>0.0264</u>
Head of Wild Horse Canyon, East Community vs. Pueblo Bonito	1992-2012	0.0886	<u>0.0168</u>	0.2555	<u>0.0011</u>
Mouth of Wild Horse Canyon, East Community vs. East Boundary near Shabik'eschee	1992-2012	0.2758	0.1650	0.2334	<u>0.0444</u>
Head of Wild Horse Canyon, East Community vs. East Boundary near Shabik'eschee	1992-2012	0.0778	0.0680	0.0696	<u>0.0043</u>
Head of Wild Horse Canyon, East Community vs. North Boundary near Pueblo Alto	1992-2012	<u>0.0446</u>	<u>0.0351</u>	0.2593	<u>0.0023</u>
Fajada Wash, South Fork Valley vs. Visitor's Center	1995-2012	0.0729	<u>0.0353</u>	0.1239	<u>0.0008</u>
Fajada Wash, South Fork Valley vs. Fajada Gap South Boundary	1995-2012	0.0936	0.1476	0.2526	0.0500
Fajada Wash, South Fork Valley vs. Pueblo Bonito	1995-2012	<u>0.0409</u>	0.0983	0.1106	<u>0.0057</u>
Fajada Wash, South Fork Valley vs. North Boundary near Pueblo Alto	1995-2012	<u>0.0464</u>	0.0975	0.0787	<u>0.0056</u>
Fajada Wash, South Fork Valley vs. East Boundary near Shabik'eschee	1995-2012	<u>0.0332</u>	0.0748	0.1414	<u>0.0176</u>
Pitt Ranch vs. Pueblo Bonito	1940-1967	0.2094	0.3973	0.1647	0.4290
	1995-2012	0.2546	0.0894	0.4475	0.1894
Pintado vs. Mouth of Wild Horse Canyon, East Community	1992-2013	0.3373	0.1975	0.3487	0.3670
Pintado vs. Bonito	1992-2013	0.1870	<u>0.0081</u>	0.4325	<u>0.0384</u>

[1] One-sided Normal approximation, Pr > Z. Exceptional differences in precipitation are <u>underlined</u> for those greater than $p \leq 0.05$. For those comparisons with small samples (i.e., less than 20 years), a probability of < 0.01 may be more meaningful as a significant difference between precipitation amounts.

Chapter 3
Basketmaker III Site Excavation Reports

This chapter covers the site reports for excavations at four Basketmaker sites in Chaco Canyon by the Chaco Center in 1973. All sites exhibited later components, which are reported in part here as well. Features noted in the site descriptions follow the abbreviated feature designations discussed in Chapter 7. The original field terminology is mostly followed here to provide continuity to the site records, photographs, and other site collections. These terms may not, however, be consistent across sites.

Site 29SJ 299, a small hamlet of residential pithouses and surface storage cists dating in the A.D. 600s, also contained a Pueblo I house (see Chapter 4), and an early Pueblo II and a Pueblo III pitstructures. The Pueblo III structure was not excavated.

Two very large villages (29SJ 423 and 29SJ 1659) with more than 100 pithouses and a great kiva each were also investigated at the east and west ends of the park (see Figure I.8.9). Both revealed evidence of major occupations in the A.D. 500s and 600s and were composed of a number of spatially discrete sites settled north-south across the short axis of Chacra Mesa and to the adjacent bottomlands. This mesa and its remnants border the south side of Chaco Canyon in its entirety except for two breaks, extending roughly east-west for more than 64 km (40 mi).

The two villages are unique in the Chaco Basin and, possibly, in the San Juan Basin as well. The western one is marked by the distinct site of 29SJ 423 atop the jutting mesa south of the Chacoan greathouse of Peñasco Blanco. It also contains a few Navajo features and a Pueblo III shrine, an important link in the visual communication network that extends throughout the San Juan Basin (Hayes and Windes 1975; Windes et al. 2000). Unfortunately, the shallow and disturbed deposits at this site halted further investigations.

The eastern village is dominated by the puebloan type site for Basketmaker III: Shabik'eschee Village (29SJ 1659), first investigated by Roberts (1929) in 1926 and 1927 (see also Wills and Windes 1989) and later the key site in Steward's (1937) study of clan formation. This site was re-investigated by the Chaco Project to obtain archaeomagnetic samples from pithouse hearths. Pithouse Y was excavated in an attempt to improve the temporal resolution at the site, which had yielded aberrant tree-ring dates. The site also contains evidence of a Pueblo I occupation, and there is a Navajo occupation nearby, neither of which is covered here. Both 29SJ 423 and Shabik'eschee should be considered the centers for the overall villages, represented by numerous habitation sites, in which they are located—they are so used in this report.

A fourth site, 29SJ 628, exhibits late Basketmaker III architecture and layout, but is temporally early Pueblo I. It might be considered a late Basketmaker III or an early Pueblo I site, but it is included in this chapter.

Except for the seminal work of Roberts (1929) at Shabik'eschee, little previous work in Basketmaker sites had been done in Chaco Canyon prior to the 1973 excavations reported here. Half House (Adams 1951), a pithouse cut in half by the Chaco Wash below Shabik'eschee along with a number of other pithouses (29SJ 1657) are considered here part of the Shabik'eschee settlement group. Another pithouse, Arroyo House (29SJ 2394), probably part of the same floodplain group as Half House, was excavated by Roberts (1929:70-71). These early structures and others recorded in subsequent years are covered in Chapter 5. Lists of features and artifacts from the excavated structures are ganged at the end of the chapter; figures (maps) and plates (photographs) are interspersed with the text.

Despite years of rock art recording and thousands of rock art images in Chaco, Basketmaker rock art appears to be extremely rare in the canyon (Jane Kolber and Donna Yoder, personal communications, 2011), particularly when compared with images in other parts of the Four Corners area. This is surprising, given the two very large villages located at the east and west ends of the park. Painted images of any period are also extremely rare.

Investigations at 29SJ 299

Fajada Butte is a prominent sandstone and shale butte that is important in mythology and ritual (Stoffle et al. 1994; Wozniak 1993) and for the Sun Dagger solstice marker (Sofaer et al. 1979). North of the butte is a series of heavily occupied sandy ridges. These sites were first recorded in the 1971 and 1972 surveys (Hayes et al. 1981) but had already experienced considerable vandalism at the turn of the twentieth century. A massive Pueblo II and Pueblo III settlement covered the ridges, constituting part of the larger Fajada Gap Community (Figure I.3.1). At least 13 vessels from this area are listed in the American Museum of Natural History collections (Chaco Collections n.d. a, b), probably from sites 29SJ 1278 and 29SJ 1360 (McKenna 1984:8). Another eight vessels from below Fajada Butte are in the National Museum of the American Indian; most are Pueblo II and Pueblo III pots except for one Kiatuthlanna Black-on-white pitcher.

Earlier occupations are indicated by the presence of early ceramics in the middens of the later houses and as surface scatters, and by a few upright slabs on the crest of the northwestern ridge finger. In 1973, the Basketmaker III component of 29SJ 299 (Plate I.3.1) was excavated by Richard Loose (1979), followed in 1974 by the excavation of the Pueblo I component by Tom Windes, Kelly Masterson, and Bill Gillespie. The site sits at an elevation of 1890 m (6220 ft)—the same as 29SJ 628 (this chapter). A Pueblo II site, 29SJ 1360, was excavated on the same ridge by Randall Morrison in 1975 (McKenna 1984), but then budget and time constraints forced a cessation of activities in this area.

29SJ 299 was first numbered in 1971 by Dennis Stanford's survey crew, who observed the upright slabs of the Pueblo I rooms and recorded them as two pithouses. A resurvey in 1972 by the Windes crew recorded two to four Pueblo I rooms and a probable associated pitstructure, as well as some Basketmaker storage cists and an associated 5-m-diameter pitstructure depression. Both potential pitstructures were augered by Hayes in 1972, with the Basketmaker one (Pithouse A) yielding charcoal-impregnated sand

Plate I.3.1. Site 29SJ 299, overview of the initial excavations at the site. Fajada Butte is in the background. Photograph by Richard Loose, 1973 (CHCU neg. 5554).

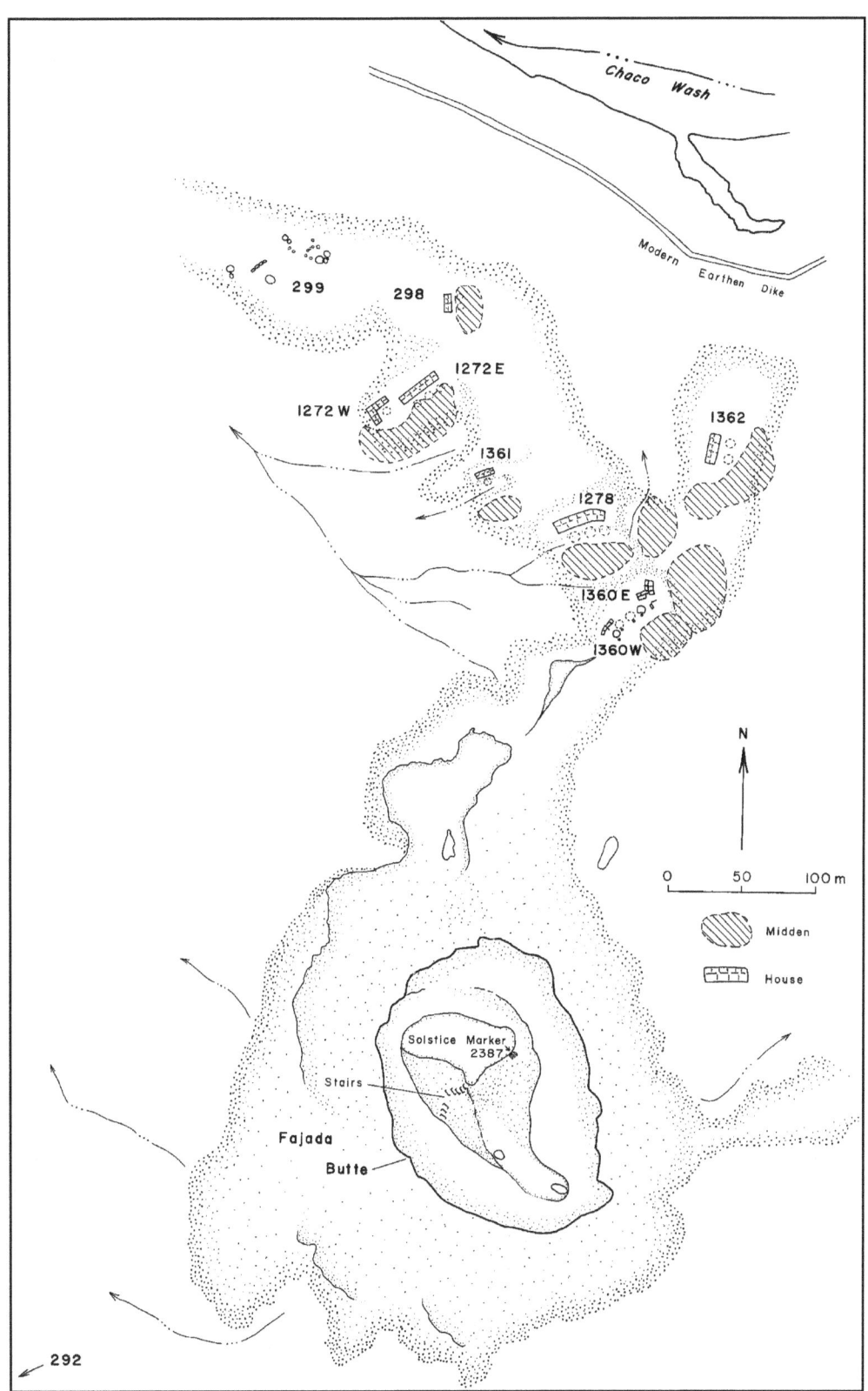

Figure I.3.1. Site 29SJ 299 location among the Pueblo II and Pueblo III houses built along the ridges extending north from Fajada Butte (revised from Windes 1993:Figure 9.9; CHCU 65102).

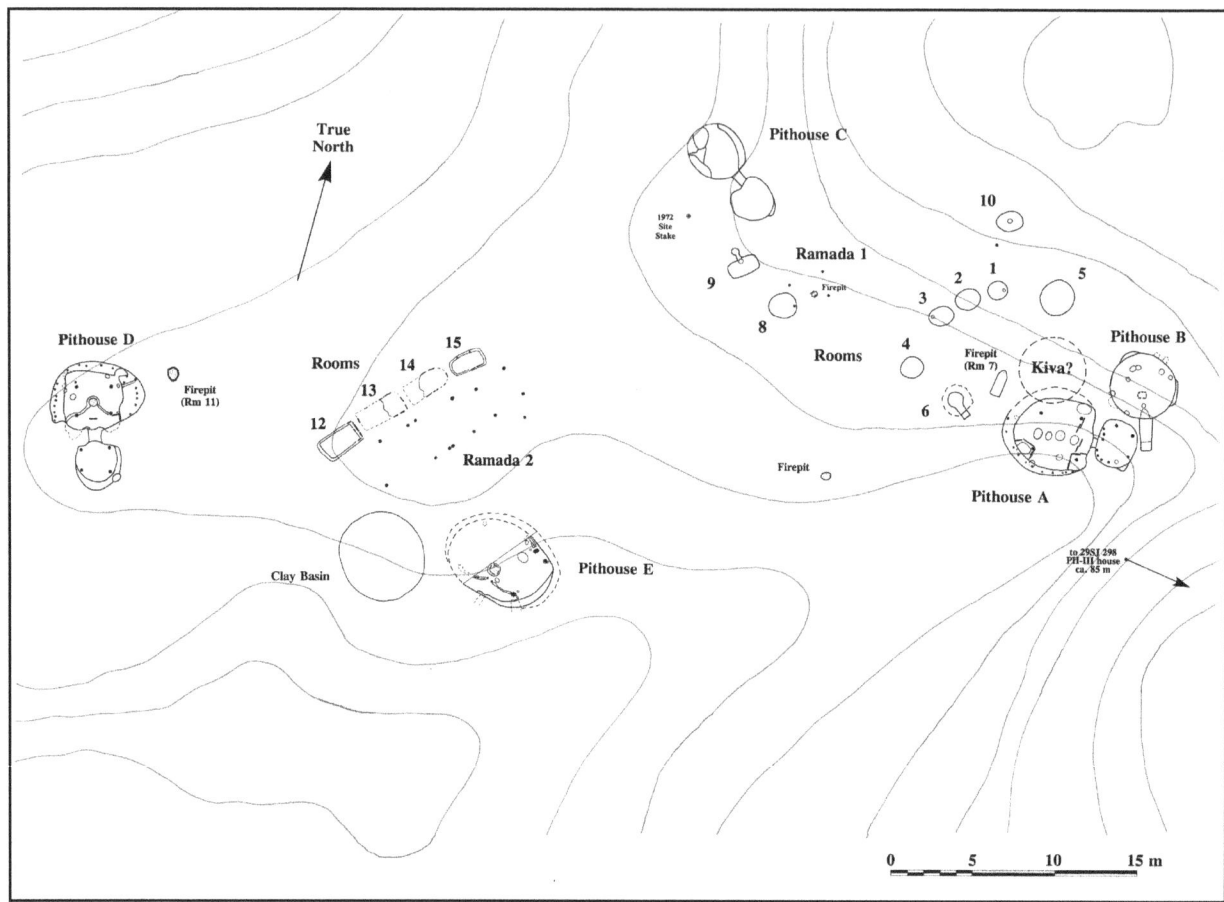

Figure I.3.2. Site 29SJ 299, site plan of the Basketmaker III and Pueblo I occupations (CHCU 95524, 65983). Contours are one foot (30.5 cm); absolute elevations are approximate. Original by Richard Loose and Tom Windes, 1973.

to a depth of 143 cm. The size of the depression suggested a possible great kiva to Hayes. The location of the site amongst a number of later sites, the convenient access from the monument's housing area as well as its potential for visitor interpretation, and the evidence of possible burning of Pithouse A were factors that led to the excavations at 29SJ 299.

Like many sites in Chaco Canyon, 29SJ 299 was more complex than the surface remains led us to believe (Figure I.3.2). The Basketmaker III occupations were represented by two burned, shallow pithouses (Pithouses A and D), an unfinished structure (Pithouse C), a ramada, and a number of storage cists and firepits scattered behind Pithouse A (Rooms 1-11). Separate from this concentration of features was Pithouse E, a ramada, and four surface rooms (Rooms 12-15) that comprised the Pueblo I occupation (Chapter 4). On the east side of Pithouse A was an early Pueblo II kiva (Pithouse B), and north of Pithouse A an unlabeled and unexcavated pitstructure filled with Mesa Verdean ceramics may have been a Pueblo III kiva.

Excavation Strategy

All work at the site was conducted by shovel and trowel, although vehicular access to the site required bulldozing a crossing over Chaco Wash. Supplies were cached in a tent set up at the bottom of the ridge to the north where vehicles were parked. In 1973, Loose was assisted by four laborers, while several laborers and archaeologists intermittently assisted in the 1974 excavations. Little screening was done except for floor contact materials; the fill in the majority of the structures was primarily aeolian sands.

Site Description
Richard Loose and Thomas C. Windes

Pithouse A (Figures I.3.3 and I.3.4, Plates I.3.2-I.3.4)

The 5-m-diameter depression noted during survey in a low saddle of the ridge was first trenched to a depth of 50 cm and then the trench (Test Trench 1) was expanded to follow the ashy contact line that delineated the pithouse walls. Subsequent surface stripping also revealed the dark, ash-stained soil filling the southern antechamber.

Fill

The main chamber's fill was removed in three natural units. The uppermost unit (Stratum A) was composed of 10-30 cm of charcoal-stained aeolian and alluvial sands. It was thickest in the center and thinned toward the pithouse walls. Underneath Stratum A was 5-10 cm of burned adobe, some with latilla impressions, charred brush, charcoal, dark sand, and charred roofing beams—Stratum B. The good condition of the beams allowed 54 samples to be taken for tree-ring dating but only 12 dated (Table I.6.2). Cutting dates were obtained at A.D. 602r, 608+r, 611r, and 612r (see Table I.6.3 for an explanation of the tree-ring date symbols). Between the beams and extending underneath them to the floor was a discontinuous deposit, 5-15 cm deep, of clean yellow-tan sand mixed with charcoal flecks (Stratum C).

Plate I.3.2. Site 29SJ 299, overview of Pithouse A floor with materials left behind when the structure burned. Looking north. 30-cm north arrow. Photograph by Richard Loose, 1973 (CHCU neg. 5572).

Floor (Plate I.3.2)

The floor was well plastered with a thin layer of clay and contained a number of features and artifacts. Parts of it had been oxidized red by contact with hot embers from the burning roof. Under the floor plaster was clean, natural, yellow-tan sand.

Floor Features (Tables I.3.1 and I.3.2)

An adobe and slab-lined circular firepit was centrally located in the main chamber. It had been well oxidized and provided a Dubois archaeomagnetic date of A.D. 615 ± 28 (Figure I.6.7, Table I.6.6), which probably dates its initial use (a revised analysis [DuBois 2008] produced a date of 560 ± 28, which is too early). Two upright slabs between OP 3 and OP 4 along with the slabs of Bin C blocked direct airflow from the antechamber and the firepit. These two slabs could be considered the deflector.

Four stone-lined postholes for the main roof

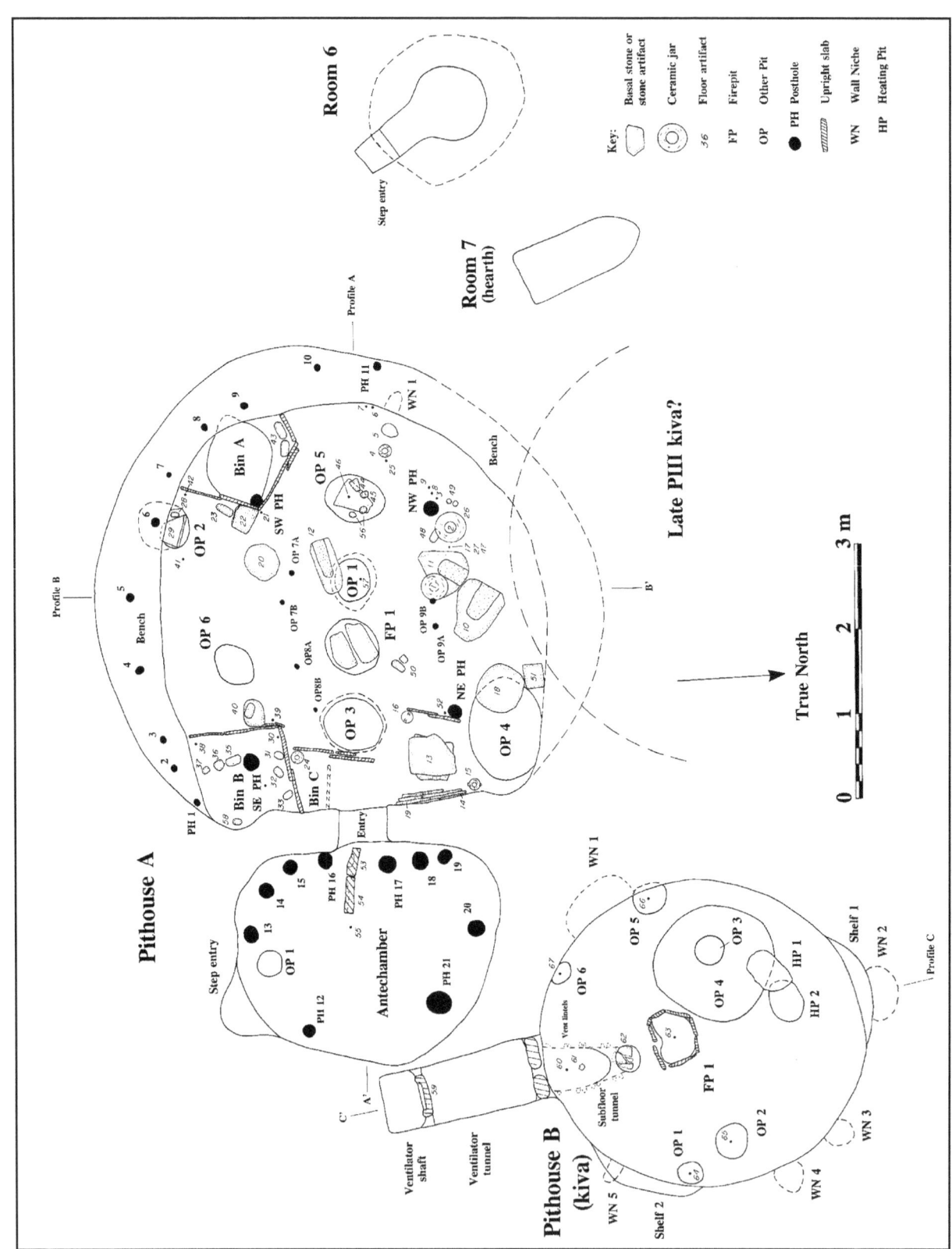

Figure I.3.3. Site 29SJ 299, Pithouses A and B (kiva) plans (CHCU 55500). See Table I.3.3 for the list of floor artifacts. Original by Richard Loose, 1973.

Chapter 3: Basketmaker III Excavation Reports 71

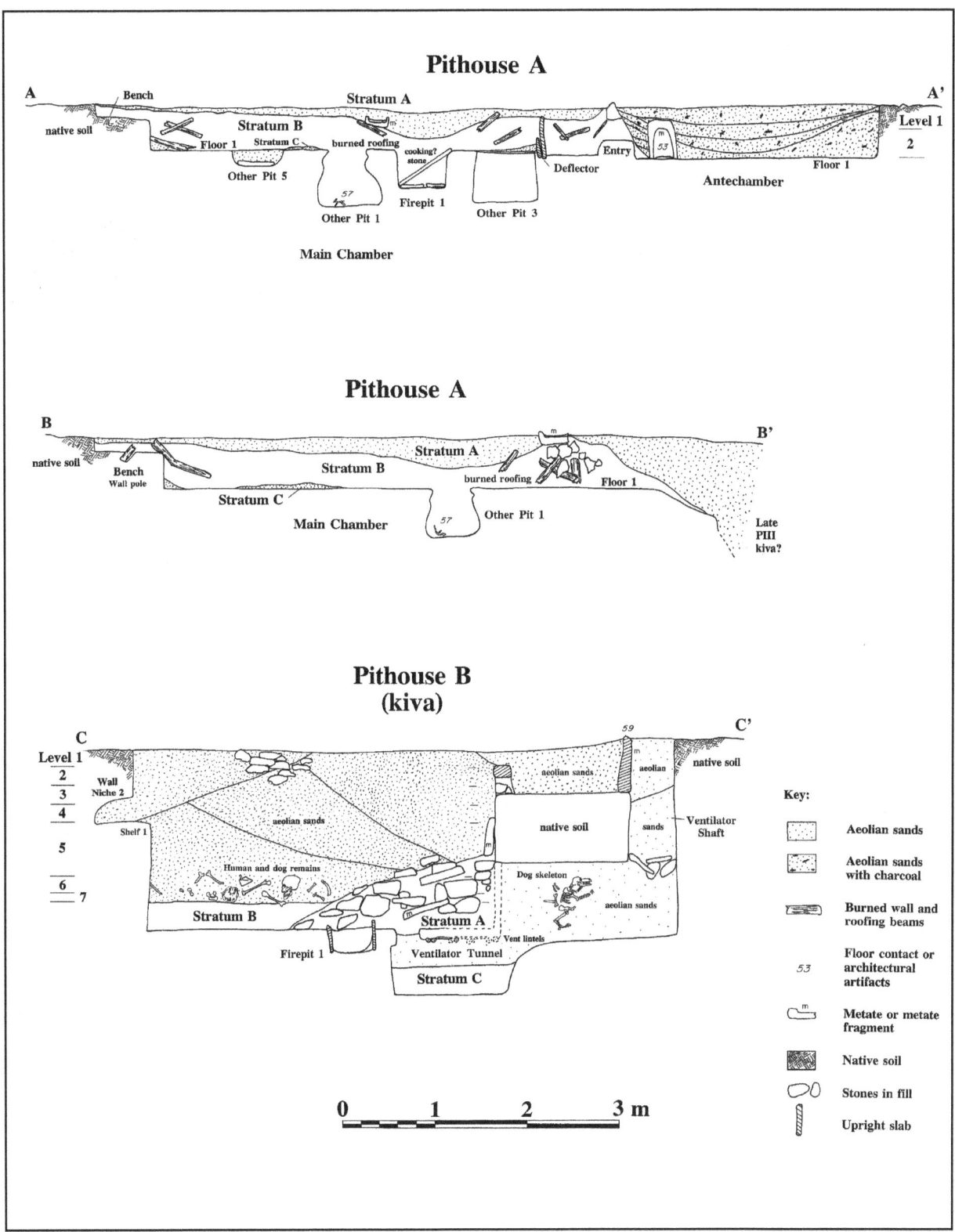

Figure I.3.4. Site 29SJ 299, Pithouses A and B profiles (CHCU 55501). Original by Richard Loose, 1973.

supports were set in the corners. They contained lignite that was probably used for packing and seating the posts. Two or three pairs of small pits are interpreted as ladder rests on the east, south, and north sides of the firepit. They ranged from 8-14 cm in diameter and 8-10 cm deep, and 23-56 cm apart. Those on the south side of the firepit were indistinct and may have resulted from rodent activity. Two circular, bowl-shaped basins filled with clean sand may have served as pot rests, although no vessels were left in them at the time of abandonment.

Three slab-lined bins were built on the floor in the corners of the pithouse. In the southwestern corner was Bin A, which contained two manos resting on a shelf. Bin B was found in the southeastern corner and also contained manos as well as quartzite polishing stones. In both cases, metates, manos, and plainware bowls found near each bin may have been used for processing foods cached in the bins. Bin C was attached to Bin B and may represent a wing wall rather than a bin. But a groove marking the presence of a former slab wall would have enclosed the space making it useful for storage. A Lino Gray olla was found on the floor in the corner. An archaeomagnetic sample taken from the oxidized eastern wall plaster in Bin C burned during the destruction of the pithouse was dated to A.D. 630 ± 18 by DuBois (Plate I.3.3, Figure I.6.7, Table I.6.6) but the revised date of 580 ± 18 (DuBois 2008) was too early.

A number of subfloor cists or storage pits were found during excavation. The central one (OP 1), contained a little burned roofing material but near the pit floor yielded small mammal bones, corncobs, several bone beads, and part of a bone pendant. The several bone beads probably belonged to a necklace (Mogollón 2004:26; see it in color on the Chaco website: *www.nps.gov*; link to Chaco Culture National Historical Park, Museum Collections, B4). The bell-shaped cist had been lined with upright sticks, 10-30 mm in diameter and spaced 5-6 cm apart, that extended 20

Plate I.3.3. Site 29SJ 299, Pithouse A. Early archaeomagnetic sample collection by pioneer Robert DuBois (right) and assistant, Henry Holasek, in Bin C. Photograph by Richard Loose, 19873 (CHCU neg. 5583).

cm above the pit floor. The remainder was unlined.

Along the southern pithouse wall just east of Bin A was another bell-shaped pit, OP 2, which contained corncobs and kernels, carrizo (*Phragmites* sp.), bone, the cist cover, a quartzite hammerstone, a quartzite floor polisher, and a possible mano fragment. Another cist (OP 3) that was found just west of the wing wall had been filled and sealed before the fire that immediately followed abandonment of the house. It was unlined and contained no cultural material. Finally, a large dished-out feature (OP 4) was located in the northeastern corner of the room. It, too, contained a stone cover lying on its floor; it had been filled prior to abandonment. A series of slabs and another stone hatch cover were found stacked against the eastern pithouse wall near the entry tunnel to the antechamber, which may have been used to line OP 4 just as Bins A and B appear to have been lined.

A sipapu (see Chapter 7) located directly west and opposite from the antechamber tunnel entry was recorded as a small bell-shaped niche at the base of the wall (WN 1). Associated with this was a small sandstone hatch cover that just covered the opening and a small, shaped chert hammerstone. No cultural material was found in the niche.

Floor Artifacts (Figure I.3.3, Tables I.3.3-I.3.4)

Three areas of the pithouse contained the majority of the floor artifacts, each associated primarily with food processing:

1. Two large trough metates, three jars, fragments of at least four other vessels, and two hammerstones were found near the northwestern roof support. In addition, three shaped sherd scoops or spoons (see Volume II, Plate 2.7A) recovered from just above these items may have been on or in the whole vessels before the roof collapsed.

2. Just outside the northeastern corner of Bin A were a metate and mano, sherds from a Lino Gray bowl, and a stone hatch cover to cover the cist.

3. Another metate and mano, with the former propped up by a broken mano, and fragments of a Lino Gray bowl were also found next to Bin B. Inside the bin were several quartzite and metamorphic polishing or pecking stones, two manos, and a bone awl.

In addition to the three concentrations, a number of whole and restorable Lino Gray vessels were recovered (see Volume II, Table II.2.11a). One was next to the deflector slab, one was under the slabs stacked against the east wall, and two others were found next to the west wall. The latter two vessels were probably on the pithouse bench until the burning roof collapsed. Fugitive red sherds from broken ollas, seed jars, and bowls were widely scattered in the pithouse.

Finally, a number of intact artifacts associated with the burned roof fall indicate that some activities were located outside on the pithouse roof. Much or all of the fill materials may have come from house activities rather than postoccupational trash deposition. These materials were not piece-plotted so a reliable interpretation of these activity loci is not possible.

The majority of materials, however, were pottery vessels and groundstone and may represent many of the same activities marked by materials on the main chamber floor, particularly food production, and tool and house maintenance. The large cobbles within the pithouse, used as floor polishers (see Jeancon 1923:21) and perhaps for other purposes, were made of materials that indicate procurement from the San Juan River vicinity to the north. In addition, the several paint ores and paint palettes suggest that activities associated with the application of fugitive red paint on the exteriors of pottery vessels and, perhaps, for painting ritual artifacts and textiles took place.

Walls

The pithouse walls were well-plastered and vertical, 30-40 cm in height. Vertical slabs of sandstone were used to line only the bins. The north wall was mostly missing because of an intrusive pit that cut below the pithouse floor. The Mesa Verde Black-on-white ceramics from this pit indicate a feature of Pueblo III age, possibly a Mesa Verde kiva occupied in the A.D. 1200s, or refuse thrown into an earlier pitstructure.

Pithouse A Antechamber (Plate I.3.4)

The D-shaped room to the east of the pithouse served as the entrance. It did not burn because neither roofing remains nor oxidized features were present; the roofing timbers must have been salvaged. The antechamber was connected to the main chamber through a raised entryway 55-60 cm wide. It was 18 cm higher than the pithouse floor and 22 cm above the antechamber floor, which prevented cold air from flowing freely into the pithouse. The antechamber floor was 2-4 cm below the pithouse floor, making it useful as a cold-air trap.

Fill. Fill was removed in 20 cm arbitrary

Plate I.3.4. Site 29SJ 299, antechamber of Pithouse A. Note the thin trough metates used in an upright slab wall. 30-cm north arrow. Photograph by Richard Loose, 1973 (CHCU neg. 5573).

levels, although there was no evidence of major stratigraphic units. Bedded and cross-bedded series of water-washed clay and aeolian sand laminae comprised the antechamber fill. Cultural material mixed with this fill included mano fragments, sherds, chipped stones, polishing stones, and paint stones.

Floor. A well-packed, smooth surface of native fill formed the floor. A series of postholes marked the former wall pole locations. These holes were 15-20 cm wide, 32-48 cm deep, and sometimes filled with lignite packing. Cultural material on the floor was scarce, but two whole trough metates rested vertically on the floor just east of the passage into the pithouse. They must have been placed to serve as a slab wall after the main chamber burned but the antechamber continued in use. A similar postoccupational slab wall was found near the floor in Pithouse A at 29SJ 724 (Chapter 4).

Pithouse B (Figures I.3.3 and I.3.4)

Northeast of Pithouse A was Pithouse B, a Pueblo II kiva or protokiva. Although it was built and occupied much later than most other structures on the site, it is reported here as part of the site excavations. Pithouse B was discovered when the stone-lined ventilator was hit while surface stripping for the Pithouse A antechamber. After excavation, it became the focus for testing new solvents for adobe preservation in hopes that the structure could be left open for exhibition (Fenn 1977; Fenn and Deck 1978), which never happened. The structure was first sprayed with acrylic emulsion resins in July 1973 by Daryll Butterbaugh and this procedure continued for at least two more years. The experiment was unsuccessful and the sides rapidly slumped. Since the pithouse was never backfilled, it has been useful for following the natural rate of deposition in the structure over the past 40 years (Figure I.3.5; see Peterson et al. 1987:159-178). The structure was last profiled by Windes in April 2013.

Fill

Pithouse B was excavated in seven arbitrary levels (10, 20, or 60 cm deep) and three natural ones. The seven levels, totaling 170 cm in depth, consisted of aeolian sands and thin layers of water-washed clays from natural in-filling. Concentrated in the lowest two levels in the northeastern quadrant of the chamber were the remains of three puebloan males and a female. The skeletons were disarticulated and scattered in the aeolian sands, along with the remains of an adult male dog. The dispersed nature of the bones suggests that the remains were reinterred from somewhere else, perhaps from one of the Pueblo II houses nearby.

Three deposits were removed as natural units. A mass of building stone and groundstone tools, designated Stratum A, is piled against the south wall and extended north past the firepit (Plate I.3.5). This material was thrown into the structure after the roof had been scavenged. Just under Stratum A, a trash deposit (Stratum B) 30 cm thick, rested on the floor. Red Mesa Black-on-white and narrow neckbanded sherds indicate its deposition in the A.D. 900s. Four partial, small, Tohatchi Banded, Tocito Gray, and Newcomb Corrugated jars and pitchers were also recovered

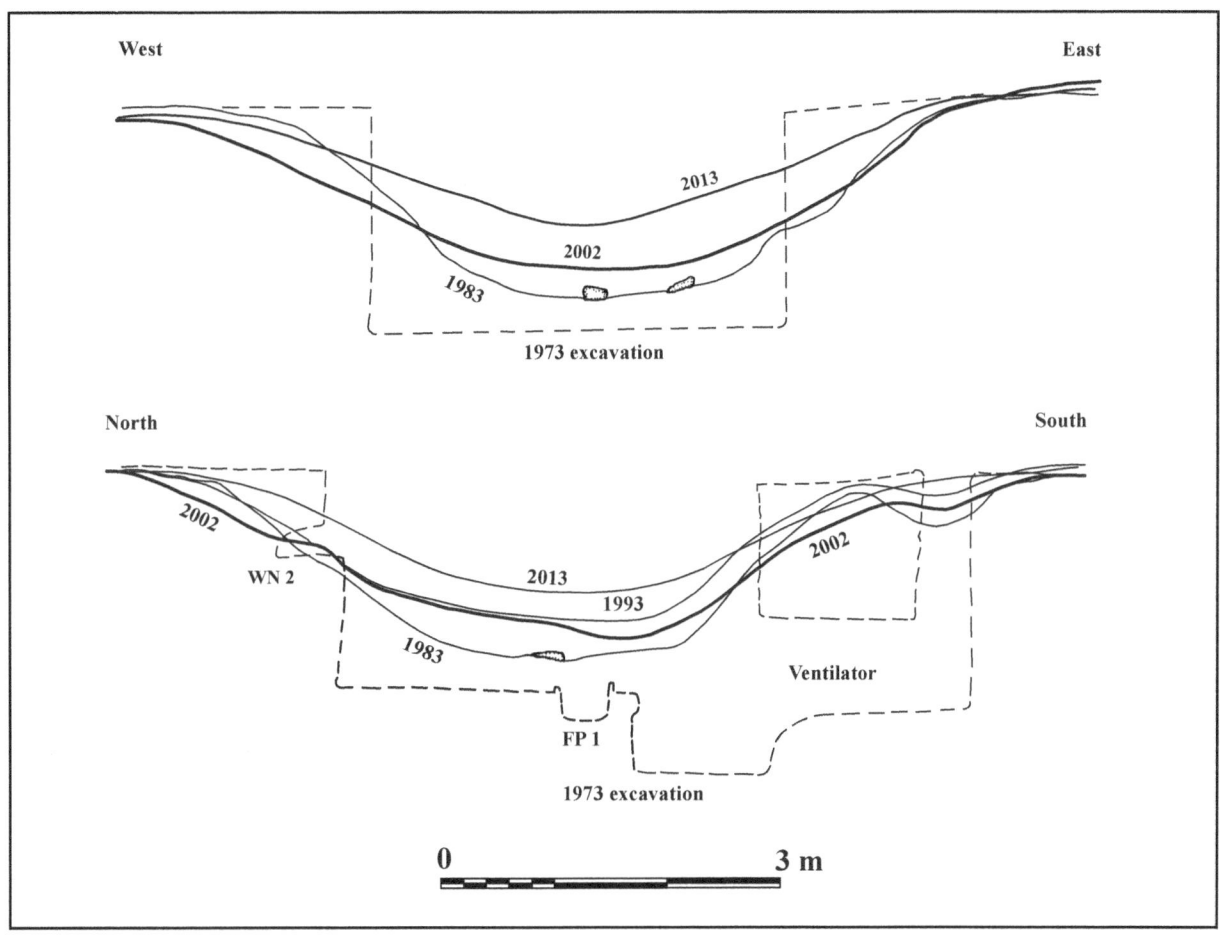

Figure I.3.5. Site 29SJ 299, Pithouse B (kiva), post-excavation natural filling over a 40-year period. Structure originally excavated in 1973 (see CHCU 65998). Profiles by Tom Windes, Mary Claffey, Jamie Schubert, Eileen Bacha, and Jill Mulholland.

Plate I.3.5. Site 29SJ 299, Pithouse B (Pueblo II kiva). Pile of stones in the lower fill over the firepit and the subfloor ventilator tunnel. Looking south. Photograph by Richard Loose, 1973 (CHCU neg. 5588).

from Stratum B and the rock fall (see Volume II, Table II.2.11A).

At the bottom of the ventilator shaft was Stratum C, a 31-cm-thick layer of alluvial clays that probably formed from water pouring down the shaft and settling at the bottom. A possible vent cover was found underneath these clays, along with four sherds of plain gray culinary wares and Red Mesa Black-on-white. Over this deposit were cross-bedded aeolian and pluvial sands containing some stones and refuse.

Floor 1 (Plate I.3.6)

The uppermost floor, about 200 cm below the surface, was flat and covered with gray clay plaster 1-3 cm thick. It was nearly circular, 360

Plate I.3.6. *Site 29SJ 299, Pithouse B (Pueblo II kiva) overview after completed excavation. Pithouse A is in the upper background. Looking south. Photograph by Richard Loose, 1973 (CHCU neg. 5589)*

cm across. Aside from a few sherds (FS 320) stuck in the floor plaster, most floor sherds were erroneously bagged with those from the floor fill. Other artifacts were conspicuously absent. There were few floor features but a number of niches in the walls.

Floor Features (Table I.3.1)

A D-shaped firepit lined with upright slabs was the sole open floor feature. Clean sand that was oxidized red filled the bottom of the firepit and was overlain by a light gray ash, which contained some burned sherds of Escavada Black-on-white (FS 232). An archaeomagnetic sample from the firepit plots too late (Figure I.6.8), but it can clearly be adjusted to the earlier part of the curve. This would produce a realistic date between approximately A.D. 950 and 1025. When DuBois (2008) revised his curve, the result fell in line (but at the late end) with other archaeological evidence at A.D. 1030 ± 17.

Six subfloor cists and two heating pits were found sealed under the Floor 1 plaster, but they were not thoroughly investigated. They had been placed in the sterile sand deposits underlying the structure. The six subfloor cists (OP 1-6) were unlined and filled with ashy deposits, similar to those in the firepit, and some refuse. Although none was noted as burned, the size, shape, location, and contents of Other Pits 1 and 2, suggest that they may have been constructed as heating pits, an interpretation confirmed by Loose (personal communication 1993). The others seem to have served as receptacles for firepit ashes. The two heating pits, located at the north end of the floor, were filled with clean sand (Loose, personal communication 1993). HP 1 overlies both OP 4 and HP 2 and may have been the last heating pit used. The spatial arrangement of these features suggests their association with Pithouse B prior to the final application of floor plaster.

Floor Artifacts (Figure I.3.3, Table I.3.3)

Twenty-four sherds were found directly on the floor of the structure and in various floor features. The sample is too small to determine a conclusive date of last use, but it is relatively consistent with the ceramics found in the fill directly above. The structure was probably abandoned in the late 900s/early 1000s and used shortly thereafter as a burial pit. Gallup Black-on-white (a single sherd) and a few indented corrugated sherds (e.g., A.D. 1000s ceramics) are limited mostly to the upper deposits; although neck indented corrugated sherds are relatively common and suggest that much of the filling took place by at least the very late A.D. 900s.

Walls

Walls of the structure slightly overhung the floor by as much as 8 cm. They had been cut into the natural ridge deposits and plastered with clay up to 1 cm thick. Five large wall niches had been carved into the walls to serve as storage cists. In addition, the ventilator in the south wall entered the structure under the floor to open next to the firepit.

Wall Features

Four of the five niches had flat bottoms with curved tops and backs. The fifth, WN 5, was cylindrical. All were located between 66 and 114 cm above the floor, contained no cultural materials, and were filled with aeolian sands. WN 3 had a small ridge or lip running across the bottom of the mouth, presumably to hold any contents securely. All but one were unlined; WN 1, had been plastered with white clay up to 5 mm thick.

The ventilator was probably initially started as a trench 50 cm deep, 70-75 cm wide, and 195 cm long, which was then covered. A vertical shaft was then sunk at the extreme southeastern end of the trench, 45-x-69-cm and 208 cm deep. A hole was punched through the pitstructure wall to enable excavation of a subfloor trench. This trench extended for 99 cm at a depth of 64 cm below the floor, which connected an opening, 25-x-30-cm, next to the firepit. The hole in the wall used to dig the tunnel was then sealed with sticks, adobe, and a large slab. The lack of a deflector suggests that the ventilation system was constructed in a single episode and that an above-floor ventilator was never used. Neither the tunnel nor the shaft was lined.

The uppermost portion of the initial trench was blocked with stones and clay at one end to form the structure wall and at the shaft end it was blocked with a large trough metate (FS 269). The space in between was filled with clean sand. The subfloor trench was roofed with 6-cm-diameter poles, 55-70 cm long, spaced in pairs 10 cm apart. Small twigs, possibly willow branches, were set at right angles to the poles and then covered with the floor plaster. A shaped sandstone slab found in the trench (FS 319) may have covered the opening when the ventilator was not in use. After abandonment, the ventilator filled with natural sands. An adult male dog, which may have been thrown down the shaft, exhibited teeth with considerable wear like those of the humans found in the main chamber, possibly indicating a similar diet of grit and corn.

Discussion

Pithouse B was built and used in the A.D. 900s or early 1000s, long after abandonment of the Basketmaker III structures on the site. It was the only structure of the period at the site but may have been associated with several houses nearby to the east (Figure I.3.1). The floor pits, heating pits, and storage niches suggest that the structure could have been used initially as a habitation. The floor, however, which lacks evidence of numerous episodes of patching, is indicative of minimal use of the structure. The final appearance of the floor, with only the firepit in use at abandonment, suggests limited activities and the transition from pithouse to kiva activities also observed for a pithouse at nearby 29SJ 629 (Windes 1993:207-208). These changes follow regional trends of more specialized use of pitstructures in the A.D. 900s (e.g., Gillespie 1976; Gilman 1983).

The architectural form indicates late A.D. 900s or early A.D. 1000s construction (Truell 1986), which is supported by the adjusted archaeomagnetic plot. Its circular shape follows those for kivas, although overhanging walls suggest architectural continuity with pithouse construction design.

Pithouse C (Figures I.3.6 and I.3.7, Plate I.3.7)

Another Basketmaker III pithouse located north-northwest of Pithouse A had been left unfinished. Thus, it reveals a stage of pithouse construction that is seldom encountered.

Fill

The main structure was excavated in five arbitrary 20-cm levels until the floor was encountered. The fill was homogenous and consisted of dark, sandy fill with some charcoal and other refuse. A skeleton of an immature dog, with

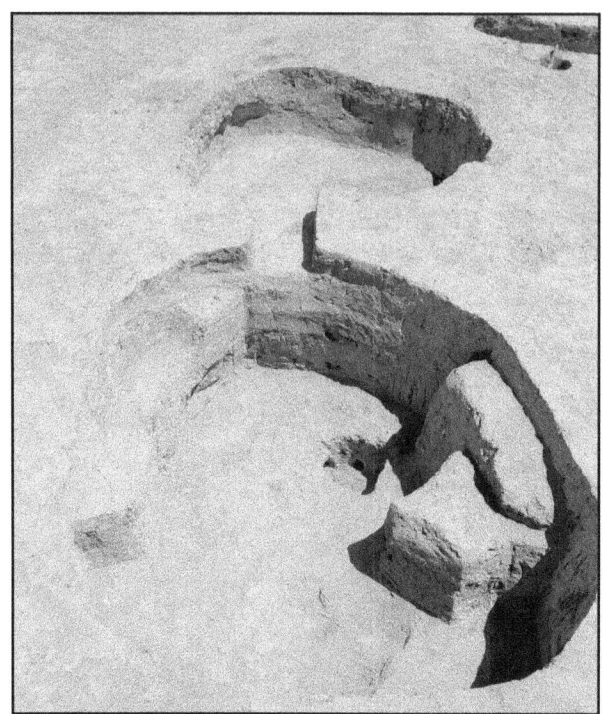

Plate I.3.7. *Site 29SJ 299, unfinished Pithouse C overview after completed excavation. Storage Room 9 cist in upper right background. Looking southeast. Photograph by Richard Loose, 1973 (CHCU neg. 5610).*

secondary dentition just erupting and epiphysial surfaces, was recovered on the floor in Level 5. It was slightly flexed and probably was an intentional burial. Cultural material in the fill was Basketmaker III and probably was deposited during occupation of nearby Pithouses A and D.

The antechamber was excavated as a single homogenous unit; the fill consisted of gray clay. A tongue of this deposit, 20 cm thick, had flowed into the main chamber to overlie the trash fill. Right after the antechamber was first built it was used as an adobe mixing pit while the main chamber filled with trash.

Floor

The floors of both the antechamber and main chamber were uneven, unplastered, and contained no features except for a large ovoid depression in the west half of the pithouse. This depression was 200-x-100-cm and up to 20 cm deep and seems to represent a continuation of initial excavation of the pithouse. The main room was 320 cm (north-south) by 369 cm long. The antechamber was 270 cm (north-south) by 254 cm and 68 cm deep. The narrow entryway connecting the antechamber and main chamber was 55 cm wide, 80 cm long, and 30 cm deep.

Walls

Walls were nearly vertical and unplastered. Benches had been formed of the native fill on the north and south sides of the structure. The benches were stepped in places and appeared unfinished. These stepped benches proved ideal for getting in and out of the structure during our excavation and may have been used the same way during the initial construction. The benches varied from 30-45 cm wide and stood up to 85 cm high. Loose, the excavator, believes that the antechamber was enlarged first and then the benches in the main chamber were cut back and down to the floor until the room was the desired size.

Discussion

Pithouse C was abandoned after partial construction for reasons that are not evident. It is similar in plan to Pithouses A and D and must have been constructed during the occupation of at least one of those houses because of the trash deposited in it. The use of the antechamber for a mortar pit also attests to some work ongoing at the site immediately after Pithouse C was abandoned, perhaps for the construction of the adjacent storage cists (Rooms 8 and 9).

Pithouse D (Figures I.3.7-I.3.9)

This pithouse was located in a slight saddle in the ridge that sloped to the northwest. Continued erosion of the slope had considerably reduced

Chapter 3: Basketmaker III Excavation Reports 79

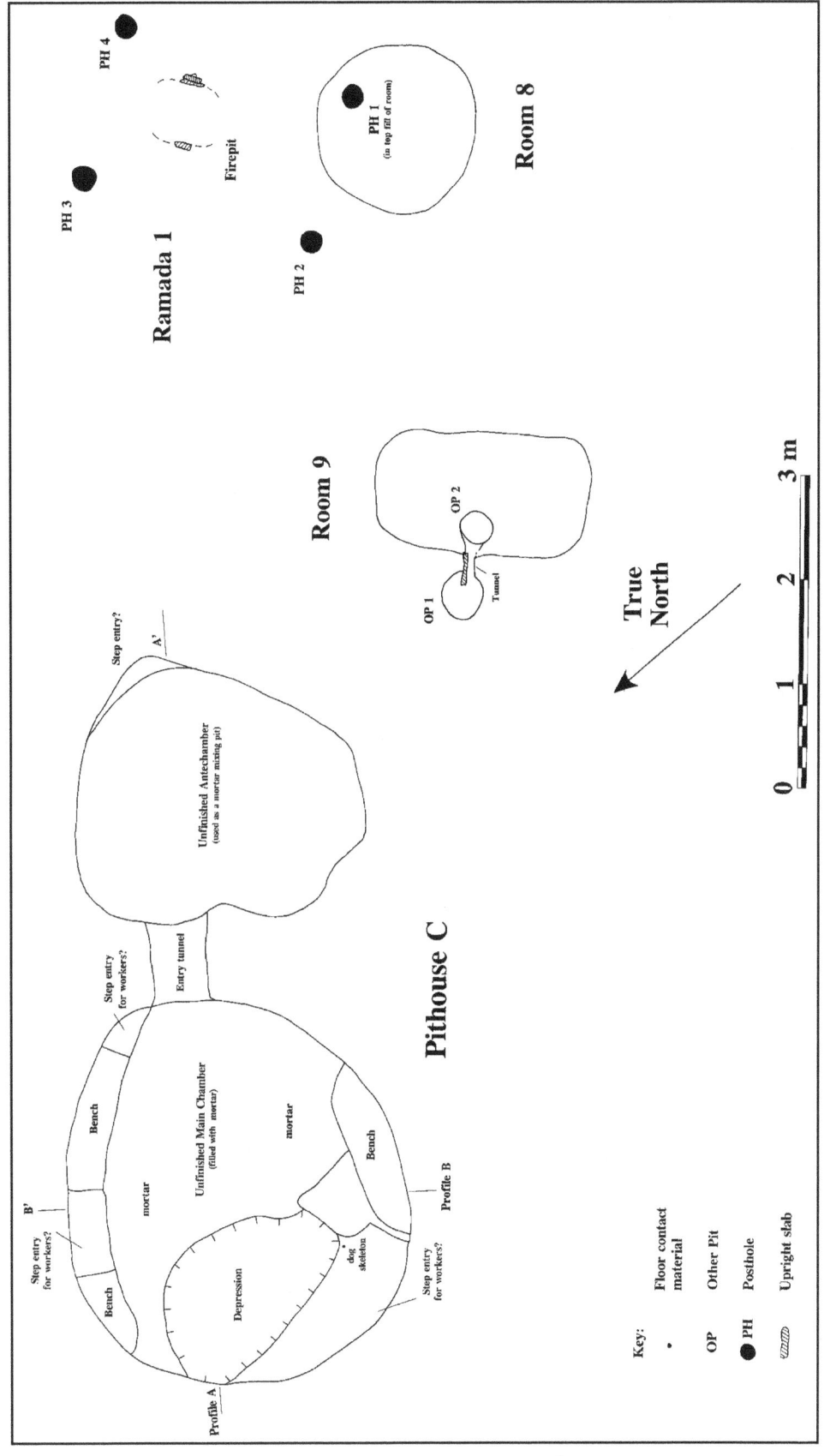

Figure I.3.6. Site 29SJ 299, Pithouse C (unfinished), Rooms 8-9, and Ramada 1 plans (CHCU 55502). Original by Richard Loose, 1973.

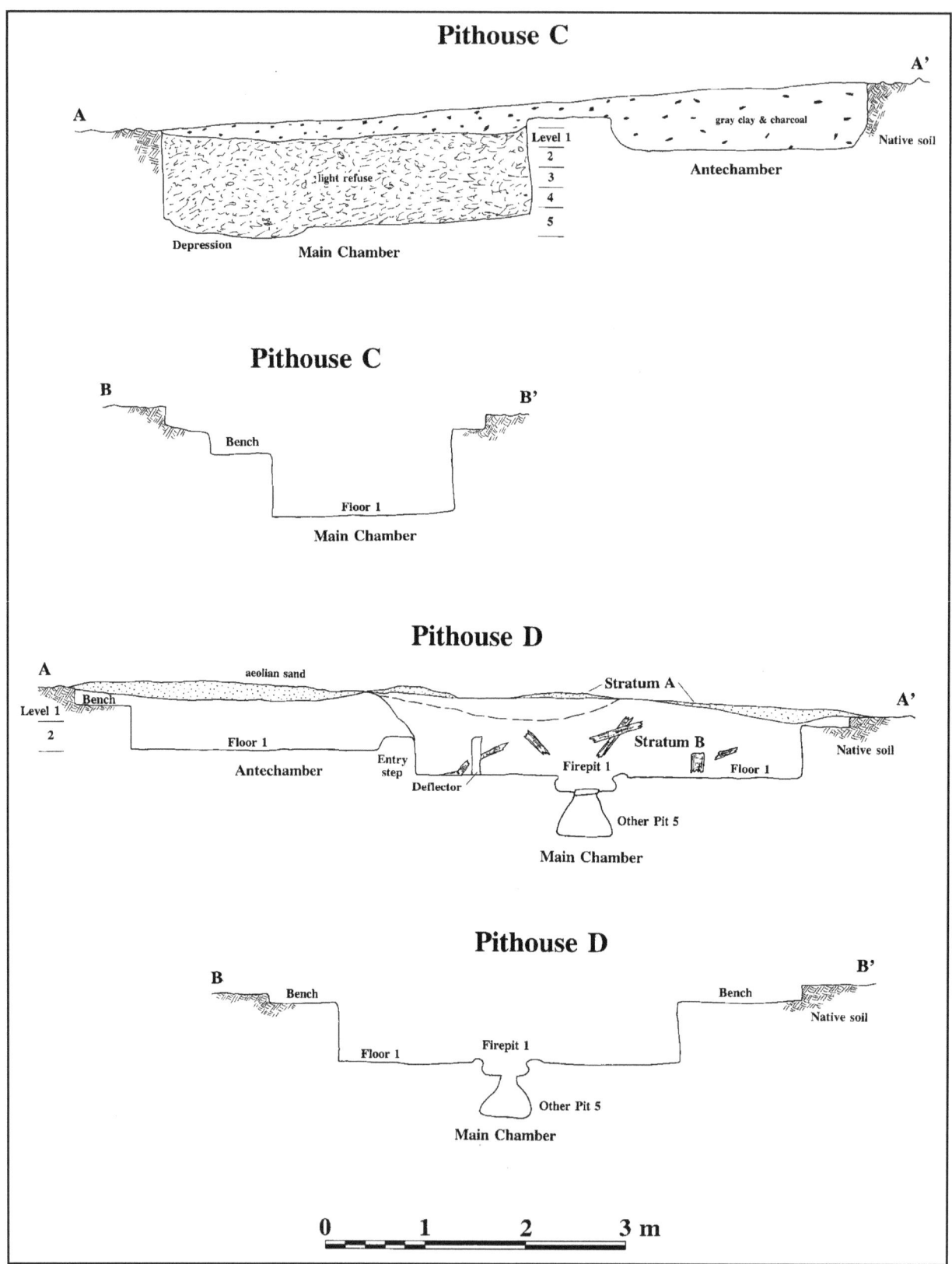

Figure I.3.7. Site 29SJ 299, Pithouses C and D profiles (CHCU 55503). Original by Richard Loose, 1973

the northwestern side of the pithouse. An antechamber was oriented southeast of the main room and connected to it by a narrow entryway. The main chamber had burned.

Fill

In the antechamber, fill was removed in two levels, 0-20 cm and 20 cm to the floor. No roofing material was encountered in the antechamber fill; that material had apparently been salvaged and the pit used for Basketmaker trash.

Fill in the main chamber consisted of two definable natural deposits, which were removed as such. The uppermost, 0-15 cm in depth, consisted of tan aeolian sand and a little refuse (Stratum A). The remainder, Stratum B, continued to the floor and consisted of burned and unburned roofing material and refuse that measured up to 75 cm thick. The burned roofing yielded only three tree-ring cutting dates, at A.D. 600rB and 607r (2) (Table I.6.2).

Floor (Plates I.3.8 and I.3.9)

The D-shaped antechamber floor, 49-51 cm below the surface, was flat and plastered. The main floor, 75-82 cm deep, was flat and well-plastered. In outline, the floor was almost square with rounded corners, 370 cm north-south by 342 cm east-west.

Floor Features (Tables I.3.1 and I.3.2)

The central firepit was nearly round and well-plastered, exhibiting fingerprints on the inner edge. It was filled with light gray ash and three unburned manos and an unburned metate. Underneath the firepit was an unlined, bell-shaped pit filled with sand stained with charcoal and ash. At Tsama, a Pueblo IV site in the Chama Valley, subfloor pits under the firepits were considered sipapus because of their shape, contents, hidden location, and ethnographic identity (Windes

Plate I.3.8. Site 29SJ 299, Pithouse D overview after completed excavation. Looking south. Photograph by Richard Loose, 1973 (CHCU neg. 5619).

Plate I.3.9. Site 29SJ 299, Pithouse D with main chamber floor cleared. Looking northwest. Photograph by Richard Loose, 1973 (CHCU neg. 5636).

1970, Windes and McKenna 2006).

A ridge of plaster ran east-to-west across the floor and partly encircled the northern side of the firepit (Plate I.3.10). The southeast and southwest main roof support holes were seated through this ridge. An area southwest of the ridge was designated Bin A; its counterpart to the southeast was Bin B. The floors of these bins were partly plastered and were 10-15 cm below than the main floor. Numerous Lino Gray sherds, a hammerstone, and a polishing stone were found

Plate I.3.10. Site 29SJ 299, Pithouse D main chamber floor showing the firepit, adobe ridges ("speed bumps"), and the southern work area. Looking southeast. Photograph by Richard Loose, 1973 (CHCU neg. 5635).

on the Bin A floor. Its fill was main chamber roof fill and several adobe turtlebacks that may have fallen from the bench. Bin B was similar to Bin A in fill and contents, yielding a stone knife, some polishing stones, and a worked deer rib on the floor. Both bins undercut the pithouse walls.

Between the two bins and 65 cm in front of the doorway into the antechamber was a sandstone deflector 36 cm high, 49 cm wide, and 5-8 cm thick, securely planted in the floor. The four main roof support postholes all contained lignite packing and had sandstone slabs in the bottom. Two were in the plaster ridge, and the others were set against the northern pithouse walls to form a rectangular support system.

Four subfloor storage pits found in the main chamber were similar to those in Pithouse A. OP 1 was located next to the eastern bench and contained on its floor a sandstone cover for the cist, a polishing/pecking stone, a possible cooking slab fragment (*comal*), and a few sherds and pieces of chipped stone. OP 2 was located next to the northern pithouse wall and contained a potlid and four polishing/pecking stones on its floor. Both cists contained roof fall, were bell-shaped and well plastered. An unlined bell-shaped pit, OP 3, extended under the west wall and contained only roof remains and refuse. Just 24 cm from OP 3 was another unlined, cylindrical pit, OP 4, that may have been filled intentionally with ashy sand and then sealed with plaster. The sipapu, OP 5, was 48 cm north of the firepit, round, and filled with clean sand.

Four postholes in the antechamber once supported the antechamber roof supports. No wood was found in them, and presumably the posts were salvaged for a nearby building before the fire. The pits were filled with ashy sand and very little lignite.

Floor Artifacts (Figure I.3.8, Table I.3.5)

Both the nature of the abandonment as a result of catastrophic fire and the condition of many of the artifacts, indicate that much of the floor artifacts are *in situ* materials. Along with pieces of chipped stone and sherds, a bone needle, a mano, and a double-sided metate were found on the floor. Numerous polishers for pottery production and for floor upkeep were also left behind. One polishing stone had previously been burned and then used afterwards for pecking—perhaps this tool was salvaged from the burned contents of Pithouse A. The antechamber floor yielded a small chopper. All other artifacts were found in the features.

Walls

The walls of the house were cut vertically from the native earth or cut with a slight overhang and then sealed with adobe plaster. Their maximum height was about 72 cm above the floor, and they were heavily burned in places. The antechamber was finished in similar fashion, with vertical walls reaching 51 cm in height. A sample from the burned main pithouse wall yielded a DuBois archaeomagnetic date of A.D. 685 ± 39 (Figure I.6.7), marking the destruction of the pithouse by fire. This was later revised (DuBois 2008) to A.D. 570 ± 39, which is too early based on the dated

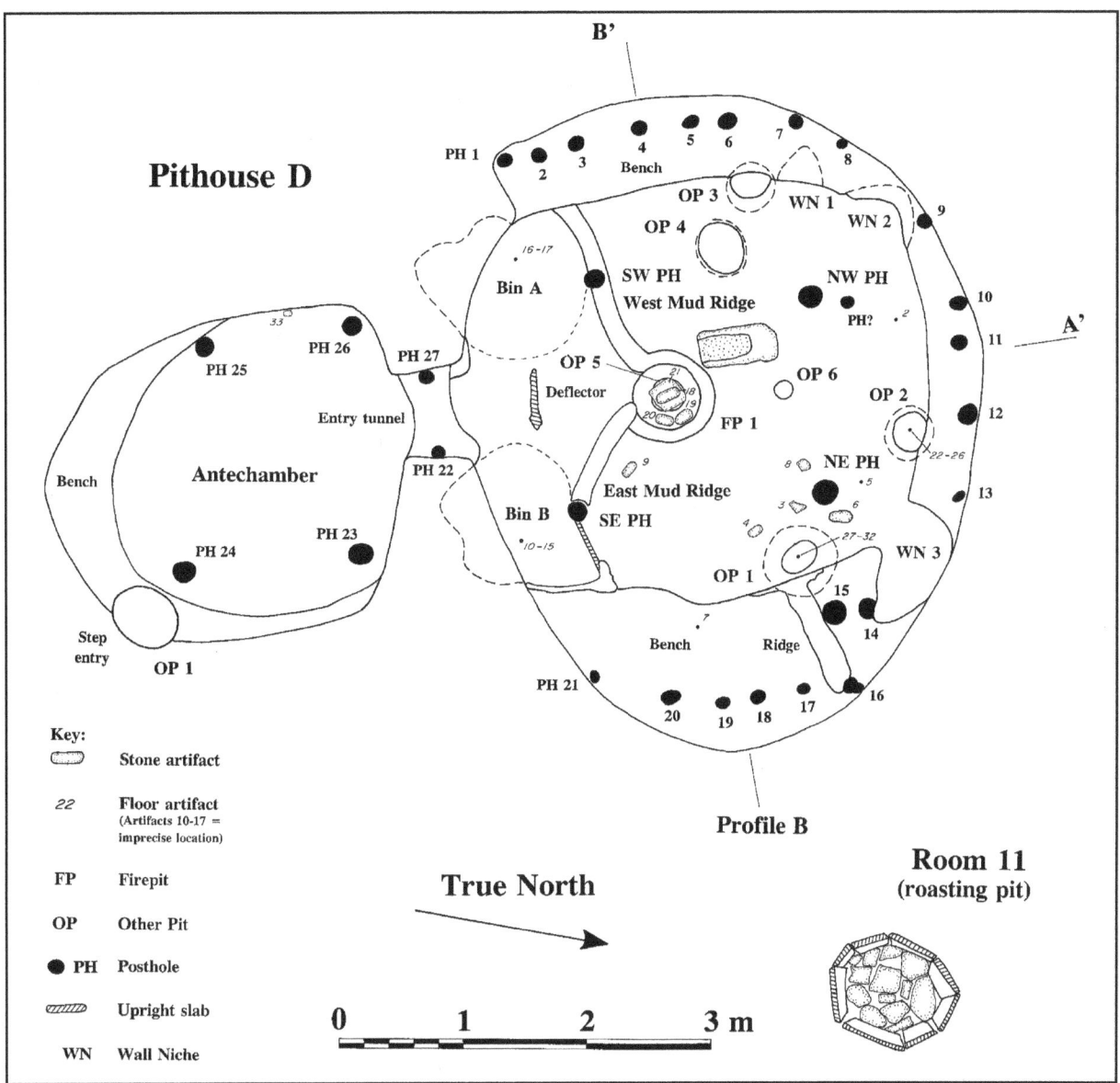

Figure I.3.8. Site 29SJ 299, Pithouse D and Room 11 (roasting pit), plans (CHCU 95522). See Table I.3.5 for the list of floor artifacts. Original by Richard Loose, 1973.

roofing remains, although possibly it is a typo and should be A.D. 670 ± 39.

The crescent-shaped main chamber bench was (15-19 cm) below the tops of the walls and up to (60 cm high). It was unusually wide along the eastern side of the house, measuring up to 125 cm. Along the north side it narrowed to between 45 and 50 cm width, and then widened along the western side to 70 cm. The bench was plastered and contained shallow pits along the edge for poles that leaned against the main superstructure to form the remaining side walls. An adobe ridge, 18-20 cm wide and 100 cm long, had been built perpendicular across the eastern bench.

The antechamber bench was a similar crescent shape, 15 cm below the ground surface and 43 cm above the floor and a maximum of 54 cm wide. At its southern end, the eastern bench was cut by a plastered, bowl-shaped feature, 42-x-50-cm wide, which probably was used as a ventilator. A ridge of adobe across the front of it would have prevented water from flowing into the main chamber. Although labeled as a "step entry" on the map, the roof support post directly in front of the feature would have blocked entry. Between the main chamber and antechamber was an elevated passage, 40 cm long and 70 cm wide, with a single posthole along each side lined with numerous small shims. This saddle-shaped passage was 14 cm above the antechamber floor and 38 cm above the main chamber floor and allowed fresh air from the antechamber to flow into the main chamber.

Three large-capacity, unplastered wall niches cut into the main chamber bench. All were filled with post-occupation fill of sand and charcoal. WN 1 and WN 2 contained no artifacts, but corn cobs and stalks, a few sherds, and a polishing pebble were found in WN 3. WN 3 was open at the bench top but once may have been roofed with small poles. One pole selected for tree-ring dating was juniper but it failed to date.

Discussion

Fill in the house indicates that the main structure burned but not the antechamber. The antechamber was stripped of roofing materials and then filled with refuse by inhabitants of a nearby house. The few in situ artifacts suggest deliberate burning and abandonment of the house. The unburned manos and metate found in the firepit are curious and may indicate ritual closing of the structure before its fiery demise.

Rooms/Cists
(Figure I.3.2, Plate I.3.11, Tables I.3.1, I.3.6)

A number of large pits and small surface rooms were associated with the pithouses at the site. Rooms 1-10 were mostly large storage pits spatially associated with Pithouse A; Rooms 12-15, a contiguous series of four shallow, rectangular rooms, were located upslope from

Plate I.3.11. Site 29SJ 299, storage cists (Rooms 1-6) associated with Pithouse A. Work tent in background. Looking north. Photograph by Richard Loose, 1973 (CHCU neg. 5593).

Pithouse E (see Chapter 4). Room 11 was a slab-lined firepit next to Pithouse D, and Room 7 might have been a kiln. The pits were used during the Basketmaker III occupation, whereas the contiguous rooms date to the Pueblo I period. Similar, large, circular, straight-walled pits arranged in a row next to a pithouse were also found at Little Water, a Basketmaker III site in the Chuska Valley (Condon 1991: Figure 17), in a pattern very reminiscent of that shown here.

Room 1

A tub-shaped storage cist, 130-x-125-cm, had been dug into the natural deposits of Menefee Shale and left unlined. Walls slanted slightly inward toward the unplastered floor. The floor was 49-50 cm below the surface but contained no artifacts. A subfloor cist 25 cm in diameter and 18 cm deep was located 15 cm from the eastern wall. The pit was filled with dark, charcoal-flecked sand, small lumps of clay, natural pebbles, a few sherds, and some bone fragments. There was no evidence of roofing.

Room 2 (Plate I.3.12)

A circular, tub-shaped storage cist, 140-x-150-cm, was found just west of Room 1. It also was an unlined pit with no evidence of roofing or aboveground walls. Walls sloped slightly inward, and the unplastered floor was 35 cm below the present, and probably the original, surface. It had filled with unstratified dark sand, bits of charcoal, and a few Lino Gray sherds. The scattered remains of an Obelisk Gray tecomaté were found on the floor.

Room 3 (Plate I.3.12)

One meter southwest of Room 2 was another tub-shaped storage room, 134-x-152-cm and 30 cm deep. Both the walls and floor were unlined, but there was no evidence of a roof. The floor was flat and of well-packed native sand with a small subfloor cist, 25 cm in diameter and 18 cm deep, near the western wall. The lower half of the fill was similar to Room 1's: dark sand, charcoal flecks, and bits of clay. From the surface to a depth of 15 cm, however, the fill yielded oxidized sandstone, sand, and clay, although the pit walls were not reddened. This burned material was deposited after the storage room had filled and then been partly cleaned out for use as a hearth. A few Lino Gray sherds were found in the unburned fill.

Room 4 (Plate I.3.13)

About 3 m south of Room 3 was a similar tub-shaped cist, 140-x-130-cm and 45 cm deep, cut into the natural stratigraphy of the ridge. Walls sloped slightly inward toward the flat, well-packed floor but were not plastered. Sherds from a La Plata Black-on-white bowl were scattered on the floor. The pit had filled with dark sand and charcoal flecks except for the uppermost 10 cm, which was burned sand and stone. The cist walls were not burned, so probably the cist had been reused as a hearth long after abandonment.

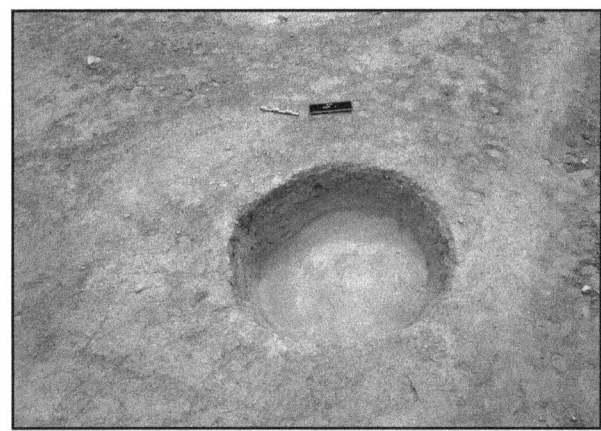

Plate I.3.13. Site 29SJ 299, storage cist (Room 4) associated with Pithouse A. 30-cm north arrow. Photograph by Richard Loose, 1973 (CHCU neg. 5601).

Plate I.3.12. Site 29SJ 299, storage cists (Rooms 2 and 3 [the right cist; with a floor pit]) associated with Pithouse A. 30-cm north arrow is next to a test trench. Photograph by Richard Loose, 1973 (CHCU neg. 5600).

Room 5 (Plate I.3.14)

East of Room 1, 181 cm, was an ovoid, tub-shaped cist, 235-x-203-cm and 65 cm deep. This cist was about 5 m due north of Pithouse A. Straight walls cut into the native ridge soils and a flat, hard-packed floor characterize the cist—none of it was plastered. It had filled with dark sand and charcoal and some refuse. Just 8 cm above the floor were the neck of a large Lino Gray olla and a quartzite pecking stone.

Plate I.3.14. Site 29SJ 299, storage cist (Room 5) associated with Pithouse A. Southeast side removed by subsequent prehistoric excavations for a late (Pueblo III?) pitstructure. Looking northwest. 30-cm north arrow. Photograph by Richard Loose, 1973 (CHCU neg. 5598).

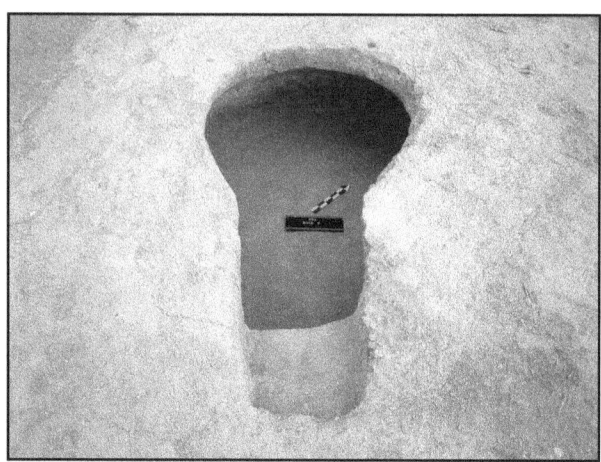

Plate I.3.15. Site 29SJ 299, walk-in storage cist (Room 6) associated with Pithouse A. Lower walls are undercut to form a bell-shaped structure. Looking northwest. 30-cm long north arrow. Photograph by Richard Loose, 1973 (CHCU neg. 5596).

Room 6 (Figure I.3.3, Plate I.3.15)

Between Room 4 and Pithouse A was an unusual bell-shaped, walk-in storage cist. It exhibited a keyhole-shaped entry with a small step, similar in design to another Basketmaker one found in the Northern Rio Grande area (Chapman and Shepard 2012:32, 38, Figure 11.12). The cist was 75 cm deep. Dark lines may be the remains of decayed sticks bent against the curving walls, although they may have been merely digging stick impressions. They were 30-50 cm long, 3 cm in diameter, and 7 cm apart. Evidence of clay plaster up to 3 cm thick, with charcoal in it, was found on the walls. A 3-5 cm layer of plaster covered the flat floor, which measured 174-x-193-cm. Sand deposited by wind and water and darkened with ash and charcoal flecks had filled the cist. Some Lino Gray sherds and small quartzite polishing stones were found in the fill.

Room 7 (Figure I.3.3)

A shallow, boat-shaped depression 151 cm long, 60-68 cm wide, and 8-10 cm deep was found just northwest of Pithouse A. The walls and uneven floor were not plastered, but the floor was burned at the northern end. Some burned sand and stones were found in the sandy fill, which was darkened by ash and charcoal. Mano and metate fragments, chipped stone, and sherds (late indented corrugated with sharply flared rims and a Gallup Black-on-white) found in the fill (Volume II, Table II.2.26) indicate a Pueblo II or Pueblo III use of the pit, perhaps as a kiln, rather than an early Basketmaker use.

Room 8 (Figure I.3.6, Plate I.3.16)

Near unfinished Pithouse C was a 165-x-175-cm cist, 40 cm deep that had slightly bell-shaped, unplastered walls and an unplastered floor. The north wall was burned but not the adjacent fill. Burned spots on the floor and up to 12 cm of the floor fill indicated use of the pit as a hearth. The uppermost 24-28 cm of fill was composed of dark sandy fill, charcoal flecks, and Lino Gray sherds. A mano was also recovered from this deposit. A posthole for a four-post ramada was found in the upper fill.

Plate I.3.16. Site 29SJ 299, storage cist (Room 8) between Pithouse A and unfinished Pithouse C. Note later Ramada 1 postholes and firepit; one ramada posthole was in the upper cist fill. Looking east. 30-cm north arrow. Photograph by Richard Loose, 1973 (CHCU neg. 5621).

Room 9 (Figure I.3.6)

Between unfinished Pithouse C and Room 8 was a rectangular cist with rounded corners, 212-x-117-cm and 30-40 cm deep, with vertical, unplastered walls and an unplastered flat, compacted floor. A plastered subfloor cist, 32-x-28-x-9-cm, placed 10 cm from the northwestern wall connected to a narrow air shaft, 20-x-12-cm, which continued to the surface outside the cist walls. This shaft was 51 cm long, 31 cm wide and 20 cm deep but had been plugged with adobe. The cist had filled with ash- and charcoal-stained sand that contained a few Lino Gray sherds.

Plate I.3.17. Site 29SJ 299, storage cist (Room 10). Note large pit in the center of the cist floor. Looking north. 30-cm north arrow. Photograph by Richard Loose, 1973 (CHCU neg. 5622).

Room 10 (Plate I.3.17)

North of Pithouse A and the majority of Basketmaker III cists was an ovoid cist, 115-x-165-cm and 20-24 cm deep. Walls sloped slightly inward and were unplastered. The flat floor exhibited revealed a thin coating of plaster. A subfloor cist, 44-x-36-cm and 11 cm deep, was centrally placed. A large sandstone slab had been left leaning against the east wall. The fill was clean, with little evidence of charcoal and no refuse.

Room 11

A circular pit, 53 cm in diameter and 44 cm deep, lined with sandstone slabs had been built 174 cm northeast of Pithouse D. The walls slanted inward and the wall slabs and the mortar between them were well oxidized. The tops of the slabs extended a maximum of 17 cm above the ground surface, which may indicate 15-20 cm of erosion since the feature was used. The floor consisted of burned, flat sandstone slabs, while the fill consisted of burned stones and sand and charcoal. Clearly the pit served as an outdoor hearth.

Ramadas
(Figures I.3.2 and I.3.6, Tables I.3.1 and I.3.7)

Two ramadas were found at the site, one with the Pueblo I house (Ramada 2) and one with the Basketmaker storage cists (Ramada 1). The latter was marked by four postholes in and around the Room 8 storage cist near unfinished Pithouse C. One posthole in the fill of the cist indicates that the ramada postdates cist abandonment. A few upright slabs, two of them metate fragments, in the center of the ramada area were burned, which suggests a firepit, but no charcoal was in association. All postholes were packed with lignite and contained a stone slab at the bottom. It is not known which of the site's inhabitants used this ramada because it is located closest to the unfinished pithouse. Since it postdates the storage cists, it may postdate Pithouse C; perhaps an undiscovered pithouse is buried nearby. Given the subsequent occupations at 29SJ 299, however, it could have been built in Pueblo I or later times.

Firepit

A firepit was mapped (Figure I.3.2) between Pithouses A and E but no cultural affiliation could be determined nor was it dated. There are no notes for the feature.

Site Discussion

29SJ 299 experienced a number of different occupations, not all of which were investigated. Pitstructures and surface storage facilities from the Basketmaker III and Pueblo I periods were excavated along with a Pueblo II pitstructure, but the possible Mesa Verdean Pueblo III kiva was left for future research. The Basketmaker III occupation of the site follows artifactual and architectural trends seen in the central Mesa Verde region and the western San Juan Basin for the A.D. 600s (see Kearns et al. 2000; Shelley 1990, 1991; Young and Herr 2012), which are substantiated by tree-ring dates from the burned roofing and earlier archaeomagnetic results (a later revision by DuBois [2008] produced dates a few decades earlier).

Pithouse occupations appear relatively brief at 29SJ 299 and by only one or two families, perhaps shifting residence from one pithouse to the other. Although both completed pithouses eventually burned, neither event appears to have been from hostilities (see Volume II, Chapter 2 for a discussion of the burned vessels from Pithouse A). They were probably burned when the residents left. The shift in residence could have been as close as the main ridge slightly to the east, where a substantial community of structures was located that may overlap 29SJ 299 in time. Only a small part of the ridge housing has been investigated through excavation (see McKenna 1984).

Pithouse A provided the richest artifact assemblage of any of the project's pithouses, which portrays the remains of much of the day-to-day activities expected for the period but the first of its kind excavated in Chaco Canyon. Unfortunately, there is little to compare with it within Chaco Canyon. The large vessel assemblage dominated by Obelisk Gray jars seemed unusual at the time when it was expected that a Lino Grayware assemblage would dominate the local pottery production. The numerous groundstone artifacts attest to the emphasis on food preparation in the house, while the semi-circle of storage cists behind it provided much storage capacity. The number of ornaments and the emphasis on paint equipment, however, may indicate that the role of ritual at the site was richer than found in pitstructures outside of Chaco Canyon.

EXCAVATIONS AT 29SJ 423
Thomas C. Windes

The vicinity around Peñasco Blanco and to the south across West Mesa yielded a number of

Basketmaker sites, and two of them were augered to examine pithouse fill and evidence of fire. One of the more promising sites, 29SJ 248, near the western end of West Mesa, revealed surface remains of 13 to 15 cists and 4 to 6 pithouses. Testing with the soil auger revealed pithouses of moderate depth and at least one possible burned pithouse. Difficulty of access and distance to the site, however, forced consideration of the second choice, 29SJ 423, a similar Basketmaker site nearby. This choice was eventually abandoned after limited work because of its shallow and disturbed deposits, and the time traveled by winding road up the mesa past Peñasco Blanco to get to the site.

One of the largest Basketmaker sites recorded during the 1972 park inventory survey was located on a mesa point (Plate I.3.18) overlooking much of the surrounding country. The center of the village, at 29SJ 423 (Figure I.3.9), was located on a long promontory of eroded Cliffhouse Sandstone overlooking Peñasco Blanco, a Chacoan greathouse, 450 m to the north. This point, at an elevation of 1945 m (6380 ft), commands an easterly view up Chaco Canyon about 8 km (5 miles) to just beyond Hungo Pavi (across from 29SJ 721 and 29SJ 724; Chapter 4), as well as down the Chaco River past the Padilla Wash Valley Community near Padilla Well (Chapter 8) to the southwest. The Chuska and La Plata mountains are visible on clear days to the west and north, respectively. The site is situated close to the confluence of the Chaco and Escavada washes, an ideal setting for valley farming. In addition, a shallow lake may have existed intermittently just below the bluff at the mouth of the Chaco Wash (Force 2003; Force et al. 2002; cf. Love et al. 2011); intermittent ponding waters from the shallow water table exists below the mesa in the Chaco Wash today.

The bench on which the site is located is has extensive exposed bedrock, particularly along the cliff edges. The bench extends north-south for about 250 m and east-west for about 150 m, being separated from the main mesa by a naturally eroded saddle. Tan, windblown sand, up to 40 cm deep, has accumulated over most of the central areas of the bench. Vegetation is Upper Sonoran with wolfberry, saltbush, sorrel, prickly pear, cliff rose, Indian rice grass, Galleta, and Grama grasses. A few stunted juniper trees grow along the west side of the bench, but moderate stands first occur about 10 km (6.2 mi) east on Chacra Mesa.

Survey of the area revealed 25 Basketmaker sites clustered along a north-south strip that resembles a similar development at Shabik'eschee Village at the east end of the park (see Figure I.8.9). Both settlements had great kivas, the only Basketmaker structures of this type known in the area, which suggest early trends that later culminated in the clusters of Chacoan communities incorporating great kivas and greathouses.

Although 29SJ 423 was located on top of the promontory, three other Basketmaker sites (29SJ 424, 29SJ 425, and 29SJ 426) were clearly part of the same settlement just below and to the east and south of the site (Figure I.3.10). These sites were found scattered along a 250 m linear stretch in the deep aeolian deposits covering much of the narrow, 35- 50-m-wide

Plate I.3.18. Site 29SJ 423, site overview looking north-northeast from slickrock area south of site. Photograph by Tom Windes, 1973 (CHCU neg. 5756).

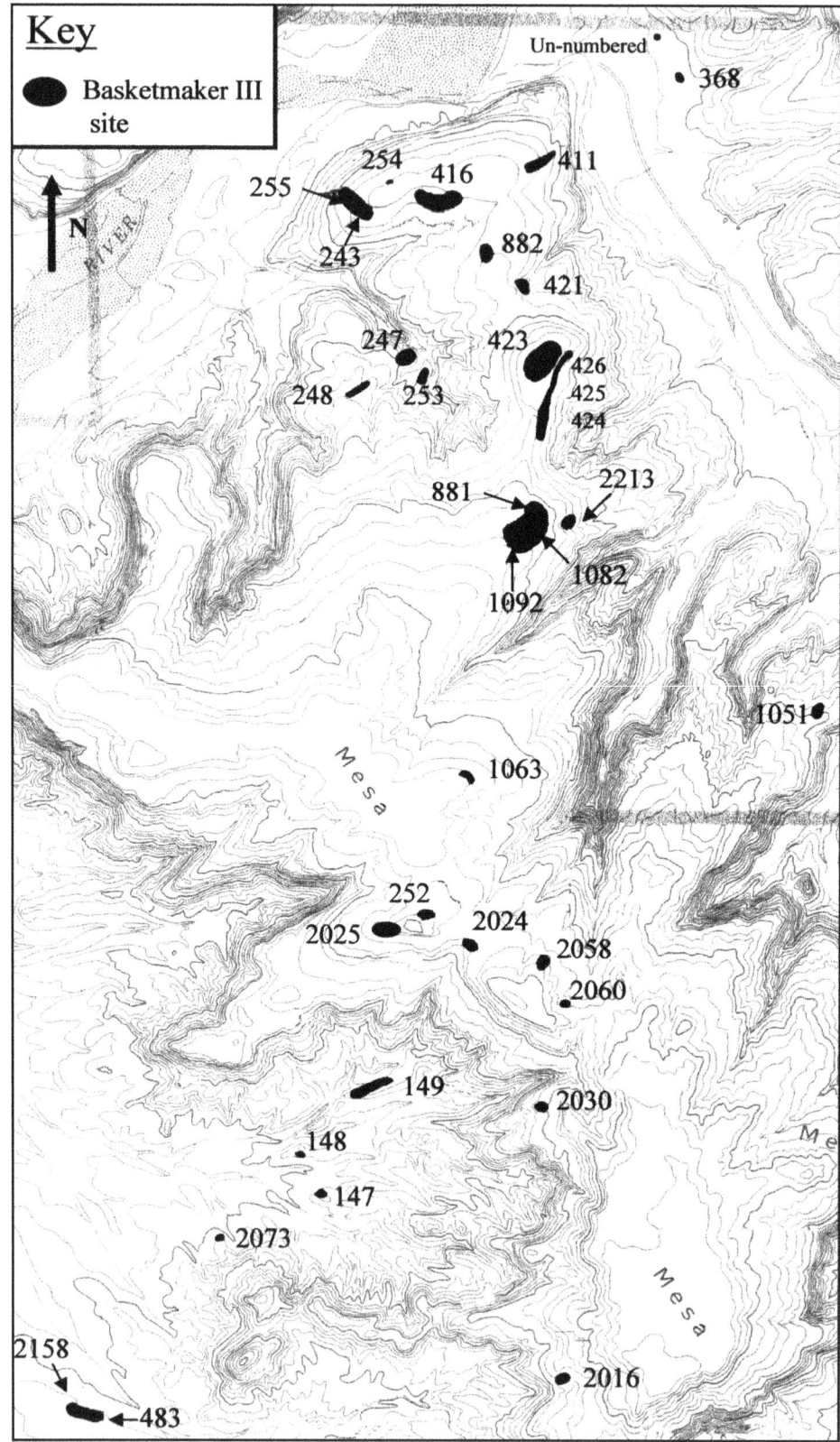

Figure I.3.9. The Basketmaker III settlement in the Peñasco Blanco/29SJ 423 area that extends in a band across West Mesa.

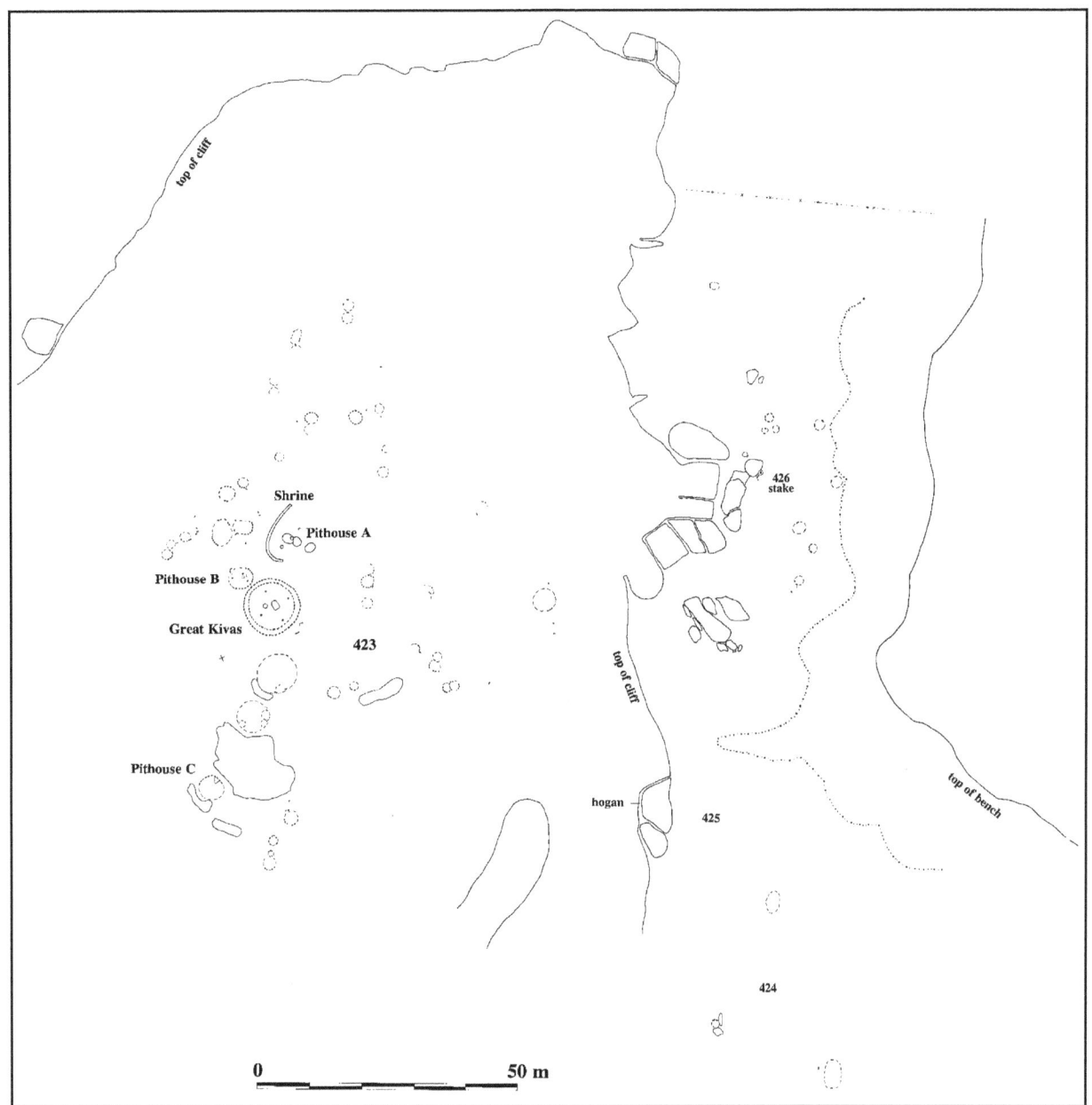

Figure I.3.10. Site 29SJ 423, an early Basketmaker III village. Incorporates sites 29SJ 423, 424, 425, and 426. Sand and refuse deposit boundaries are approximate. Mapped with alidade and plane table and GPS. North is at the top. Combined originals by Tom Windes, Gwinn Vivian, A. Behrens, C. Srnka, J. Newmark, D. Lindsay, C. Beckman, and J. Gora, ca. 2001 (CHCU 65980).

bench below 29SJ 423. Overall, the three sites encompassed approximately 3,700 m² of refuse and visible slab-lined features, in contrast to the 8,800 m² of cultural material on the mesa top. Notwithstanding the short vertical distance between 29SJ 423 and these others, all are considered a single archaeological and cultural entity encompassing the point and its surrounding benches.

Several rock art panels dispersed along the bench utilized the mesa-top cliff face, which forms the western periphery of the lower Basketmaker occupation. Most of the figures are Puebloan and probably relate to the early occupation, but there are also a number of Navajo or historical etchings that are presumably associated with Navajo use of the area. Three hogans located on the same bench about 200 m south of 29SJ 424 at 29SJ 1083 are probably the focus of a Navajo homestead. A few Navajo structures on the mesa top in 29SJ 423 and in 29SJ 425 (cists and a hogan?) were presumably associated with the 29SJ 1083 occupation. More Navajo structural remains are found directly against the north end of the mesa (29SJ 422) and along the benches to the west.

Another Basketmaker site (29SJ 421) located 300 m northwest of the mesa top might also be related to the main Basketmaker occupation. This site yields at least six surface storage cists and a pithouse exposed in a deeply cut gully. Clearly the Basketmaker sites are clustered so close together around 29SJ 423 and Peñasco Blanco that they might all be considered part of a contemporary village settlement.

Excavation Strategy

Excavation was conducted at the site between May 30 and July 12, 1973, with the assistance of five Navajo crewmen (Ken Augustine, Alvin Dennison, Gilbert Etcitty, Ben Noberto, and Bruce Yazzie), who rotated to make a daily crew of three at the site. The focus of excavations was the highest part of the site, where a number of slab-lined features were located, including a great kiva and an odd, hook-shaped masonry wall. A map of the site was made first. Surface artifacts were collected from around each feature and the vegetation cover of grasses and brush was removed by hand.

Generally, the fill was removed in arbitrary levels with only selective (eighth-inch) screening. Fill was removed using shovels and wheelbarrows and dumped on the west side of the point, creating a large backdirt pile. Loose structural stone was collected and stacked at the north end of the point to enable volume measurements. This cairn was later toppled by park personnel. Radiocarbon and tree-ring samples were collected at the site, but only the latter were analyzed. Unfortunately, archaeomagnetic sampling was in its infancy, we were unable to have samples collected from the site.

Two layers of deposition characterized the majority of fill at the site. The uppermost deposit consisted of a mantle of windblown sand that had accumulated over the past 1,400 years since abandonment. This layer was 5-10 cm deep except where it had banked deeper against slabs or walls. Below the top of the point, sand had collected to a much greater depth, particularly along the east slope and below on the eastern bench, obscuring many slab features. Underneath the sand were the unstratified, ash-stained deposits of sand mixed with cultural debris that overlay the mesa point and filled its various features. This material overlies the entire site, extending down to sterile soil or bedrock. Much of the mesa has been scoured by the winds sweeping across the point exposing much cultural material.

In addition to the wealth of undifferentiated cultural material at the site, the underlying bedrock was often modified by the inhabitants, although neither the deposits nor the bedrock features provided good stratigraphic control. The uppermost stratum of bedrock consisted of soft, decomposed, white and tan sandstone and lenses of compact gray clay. This unit, 30-35 cm thick, was commonly removed during prehistoric construction activities. Underneath was a 10-20 cm thick stratum of hard, rippled, reddish brown sandstone formed from shallow wave action in Cretaceous times. This rested on soft, crumbly white sandstone that extended several meters in depth, constituting the vast bulk of the mesa on which the site was located.

Pithouse A and the Shrine
(Figures I.3.11 and I.3.12, Table I.3.8)

Initial work began in area marked by a long, J-shaped masonry wall (Plate I.3.19). This wall, about 30 cm high and 15 m long, seemed out of place for the type of masonry construction, although the deposits in association were Basketmaker. The masonry was composed of thin flat slabs set horizontally to form a low wall 50 cm wide (Plate I.3.20). A few meters to the east was a low mound of trash and rubble that appeared to complement the wall. Between the mound and wall were a few isolated upright slabs. The previous year, an auger hole by Alden Hayes in the center of the area yielded abundant ash and charcoal that suggested a burned structure. This, along with signs that the great kiva just to the south had burned, was additional evidence that the site was worth investigating.

The area was first cleared of loose sand and the few artifacts encountered were combined with those collected from the surface. A 3-7 cm thick layer of Basketmaker trash (Level 1) was removed from the western half of the area just inside the masonry wall; below the trash was bedrock. As excavation progressed eastward and slightly downslope, the outlines of three pits (A-C) became evident. These were aligned southeast to northwest (149° to 329° relative to true north). North of the pits were the remains of three or four slab-lined features. This group of features and pits was originally designated "Pithouse 1" (subsequently Pithouse A).

Plate I.3.19. Site 29SJ 423, overview of the shrine wall and Pithouse A components (Pits A-C). Note the Escavada Wash in the upper right background. Looking north-northwest. Photograph by Tom Windes, 1973 (CHCU neg. 5700).

Plate I.3.20. Site 29SJ 423, closeup of Shrine Wall 1 masonry. Looking north-northwest. 30-cm scale. Photograph by Tom Windes, 1973 (CHCU neg. 5701).

Pit A (Plate I.3.21)

By chance, the 1972 auger hole struck Pit A, missing the surrounding bedrock. The nearly circular, 210-x-254-cm pit had been dug through the rippled sandstone into the softer white stone below. The dark-stained, trashy fill overlying the pit also constituted the 12-26 cm of fill within the pit. This trash continued to the pit bottom except on the north side where a centimeter of fine white sand separated it from the bedrock floor. All of the Pit A fill was screened through eighth-inch mesh, which yielded the usual refuse along with two pieces of turquoise.

Plate I.3.21. Site 29SJ 423, Pithouse A, Pit A (the Central pit). Note firepit with slab cover over it in the upper right corner. Looking north-northeast. 30-cm north arrow. Photograph by Tom Windes, 1973 (CHCU neg. 5707).

Plate I.3.22. Site 29SJ 423, Pithouse A, Pit B. Remains of a possible antechamber for Pit A (left background). Note the slab cover over the Pit A firepit. Looking north. 30-cm north arrow. Photograph by Tom Windes, 1973 (CHCU neg. 5706).

The south half of the floor was covered with gray-white clay that tapered in thickness from a few millimeters at the pit center to 10 cm along the south margins. A plaster of brown adobe covered this natural clay and the remainder of the bedrock floor. At the east end of the pit the adobe was built up to form a circular firepit, partly covered by an unworked slab. A collar of the same gray-white clay was fashioned along the southeastern edge of the pit and contained two small holes, 12 cm apart, at one end. The configuration of one of the holes suggests use as a support for an upright slab; the other for a post. Above the firepit at the north end of the collar were five small slabs stabilized with brown adobe.

Pit B (Plate I.3.22)

Contiguous with Pit A was a shallow chamber to the southeast, designated Pit B. It, too, was covered with the same cultural material as Pit A. The 141-x-191-cm, bean-shaped pit was 5-14 cm deep, with a rippled sandstone floor. The strip of decomposed bedrock left as the perimeter had been plastered with adobe. A small slab less than 10 cm high set along the east pit side was the only indication of a slab wall, which had probably been dismantled.

Two 3-cm-thick slabs, 13 and 30 cm high and forming a 90-cm-long wall, had been placed across the northern corner of the pit. They were affixed to the bedrock with mortar but rested on 1-2 cm of refuse. They were fragile and were supported by the refuse that had accumulated within the pit.

Pit C

A meter downslope and to the southeast of Pit B was Pit C, measuring 227-x-294-cm, and up to 34 cm deep, Refuse filled the oval pit except for a large mass of stone on the south side that was covered with adobe. Turquoise was recovered from the fill. On the downhill side the floor was exposed at the surface, but it continued into the slope on the uphill side reaching a depth of 34 cm. Its irregular white bedrock floor was patched with gray-white clay. Three or four slabs less than 25 cm high were spaced at irregular intervals around the upper perimeter of decomposed bedrock formed the partial cist walls.

Other Features

Several smaller features were found around the three pits. Less than 50 cm east of Pit B were the remains of Features 2 and 3 (Plate I.3.23). Feature 2 consisted of an oval pavement of flagstones, 96-x-73-cm, set in mortar over 1-2 cm of ashy fill. It appears to be the base of a slab-lined cist. To the north 50 cm were three vertical slabs constituting Feature 3, the probable remains of another cist. It, too, had been affixed to the unaltered bedrock with mortar, although pockets of refuse remained underneath.

A trash-filled, circular adobe firepit was found 113 cm southwest of Pit A, sunk into the soft bedrock. A possible chipped-edge sandstone slab firepit cover, 51-x-47.5-x-2.5-cm, was found lying next to Pit A. Arranged in an arc to one side of the firepit and Pit A was a series of four small bedrock pits (Figure I.3.11). The holes were irregularly shaped (Tables I.3.9-I.3.10) and could have supported only a light pole framework. No post molds were evident in the overlying deposits, nor was any wood found. Most of the bedrock surrounding the features and pits was covered with a thin layer of plaster.

The Shrine

The mound of refuse overlying Pit B, part of Pit C, and Features 1 and 2 provided the biggest surprise at the site. The mound, about 4-x-4-m and 20 cm deep, was screened for materials. The western part was characterized by abundant Basketmaker III trash, charcoal, and 0.45 m^3 of tabular stones and slab fragments. About 30 turquoise beads and scrap were also recovered. The eastern half, characterized by sand and adobe with few stones and little trash, yielded a few specimens of shell and nearly 200 pieces of turquoise. Finally, near the south end of an axis bisecting the mound north-south was a beautifully shaped sandstone cover with an inset stone lid in the center (Plates I.3.24 and I.3.25), and both overlaying a massive

Plate I.3.23. Site 29SJ 423, Features 2 and 3 (probable cist remains). Looking north-northwest. 30-cm north arrow. Photograph by Tom Windes, 1973 (CHCU neg. 5729).

Plate I.3.24. Site 29SJ 423, shrine altar with a finely-crafted sandstone cover partly hidden by a stack of stones. Looking west. 30-cm north arrow. Photograph by Tom Windes, 1973 (CHCU neg. 5699).

Plate I.3.25. Site 29SJ 423, shrine altar with lid removed to expose stone bowl with turquoise beads underneath. Toadlena or Nava Black-on-white bowl in upper right. Looking west 30-cm north arrow. Photograph by Tom Windes (CHCU neg. 5767).

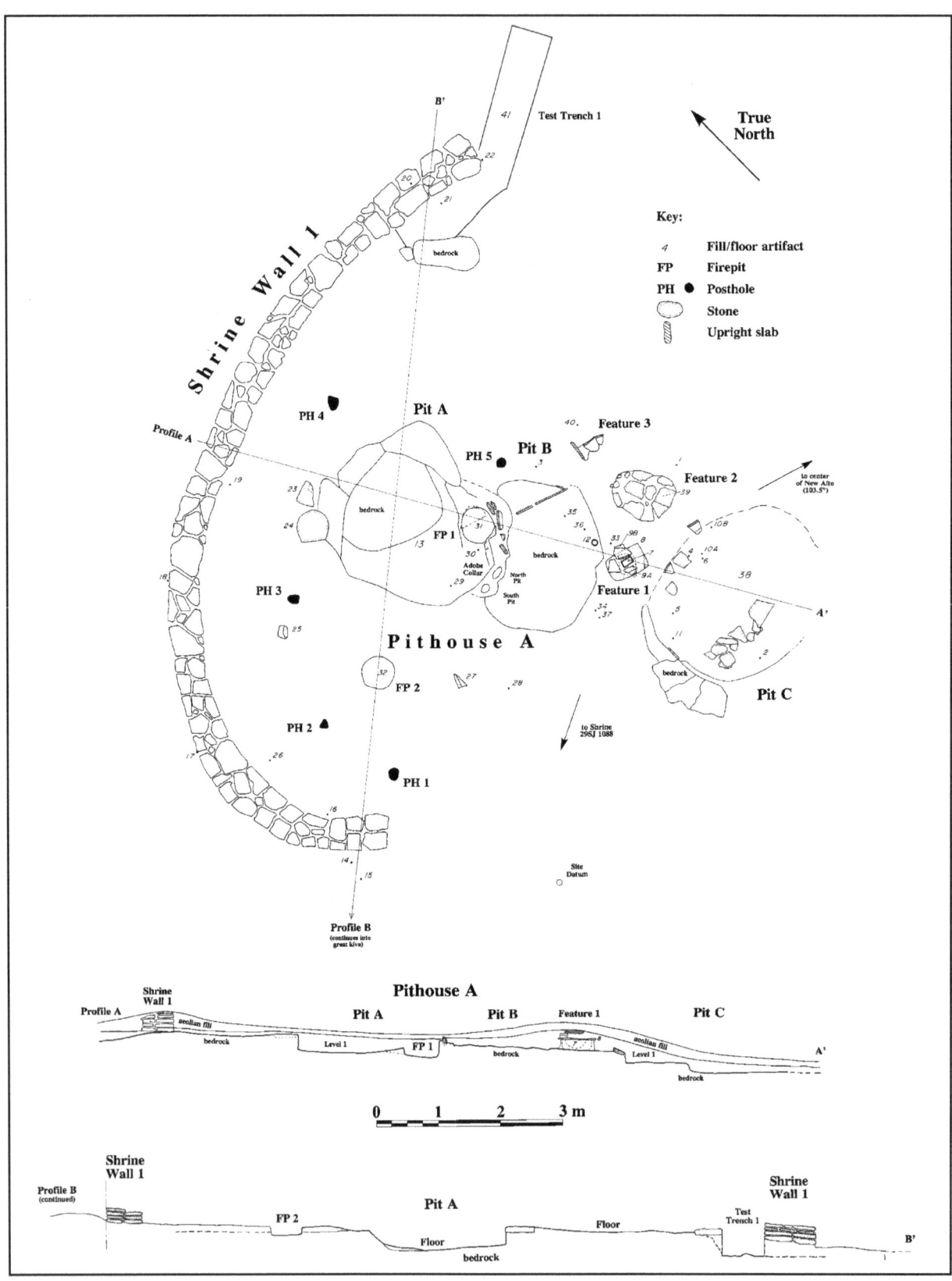

Figure I.3.11. Site 29SJ 423, Pithouse A and the Pueblo III Shrine, and profiles (CHCU 55511). See Table I.3.9 for the list of fill and floor materials. Original by Tom Windes, 1973.

stone bowl containing 146 pieces of turquoise, mostly beads (Feature 1). The discovery of the stone container and turquoise now gave new meaning to the long, arched masonry wall as part of a shrine. Three indented corrugated sherds in the surrounding trash and a small Chuskan bowl of Toadlena or Nava Black-on-white (Plate I.3.26) buried in the mound within Pit B suggest use of the shrine in the late A.D. 1000s or early 1100s. The fortuitous find of the shrine led to the discovery of a Chacoan visual communications network, which bound the Chacoan system together (Drager 1976a; Hayes 1981:42; Hayes and Windes 1975; Robinson et al. 2007; Windes et al. 2000:43, Figure I.4.2).

A curvilinear compound masonry wall (Wall 1) built of thin, tabular slabs set horizontally dominated the above-ground architecture at the site. It was originally thought to be the remains of an early great kiva, although the masonry construction clearly marked the feature as dating to a much later time than the surrounding Basketmaker deposits. The mound of refuse east of Wall 1 (the East Mound) appeared to hide more of the structure wall, but this suggestion later proved to be erroneous. Wall 1 turned out to be 15 m long, between 43 and 67 cm wide, with a maximum remaining height of 30 cm. The lack of wall rubble suggested that its original height was probably about 50 cm.

The altar (Plates I.3.24 and I.3.25) was set in the Basketmaker refuse deposits in front of Wall 1. The sequence of construction for the altar is shown in Figure I.3.12. Although most of the altar was buried in the refuse, a covering had been fashioned of natural stones that allowed access to the stone bowl hidden below the altar cover. When we found this feature (see Table I.3.8 for feature measurements), it was completely hidden by the earlier Basketmaker refuse; we suspect that it always remained so except when articles were placed in or removed from the stone bowl.

A rectangular hole cut through a slab cover (38-42-x-63-cm and 1.5 cm thick) allowed access to the bowl, and it had a finely fashioned recessed lip that would hold a thin, rectangular lid, 11-x-18.5-cm. This arrangement indicates that materials could be added to or retrieved from the stone bowl as dictated by the specific rituals involved in the shrine's use. The cover was cracked when unearthed, but the lid was perfect until it was dropped and broken after recovery. Two paint stones were used in the altar construction, seemingly scavenged from the earlier Basketmaker refuse.

The plethora of ornaments and rare minerals around the shrine and the turquoise within the altar bowl provide strong evidence that much of the rare materials were associated with shrine activities (for an example of the turquoise bead craftsmanship, see the color photo in Western National Parks Association 2004:38). Some of the minerals, such as pieces of turquoise, were found in undisputable Basketmaker contexts, but almost everything on the surface, in aeolian surface sands, and around the shrine is probably the result of ritual activities associated with the late Pueblo II-early Pueblo III shrine. Based on this assumption, the list (Table I.3.9) and distribution (Figure I.3.11) of rare minerals and ornaments at

Plate I.3.26. Site 29SJ 423, Toadlena or Nava Black-on-white bowl found in the floor fill refuse of Pit B near the shrine altar. A black shale bead was inside the bowl. Photograph by Karl Klappert, 1975? (CHCU neg. 13993).

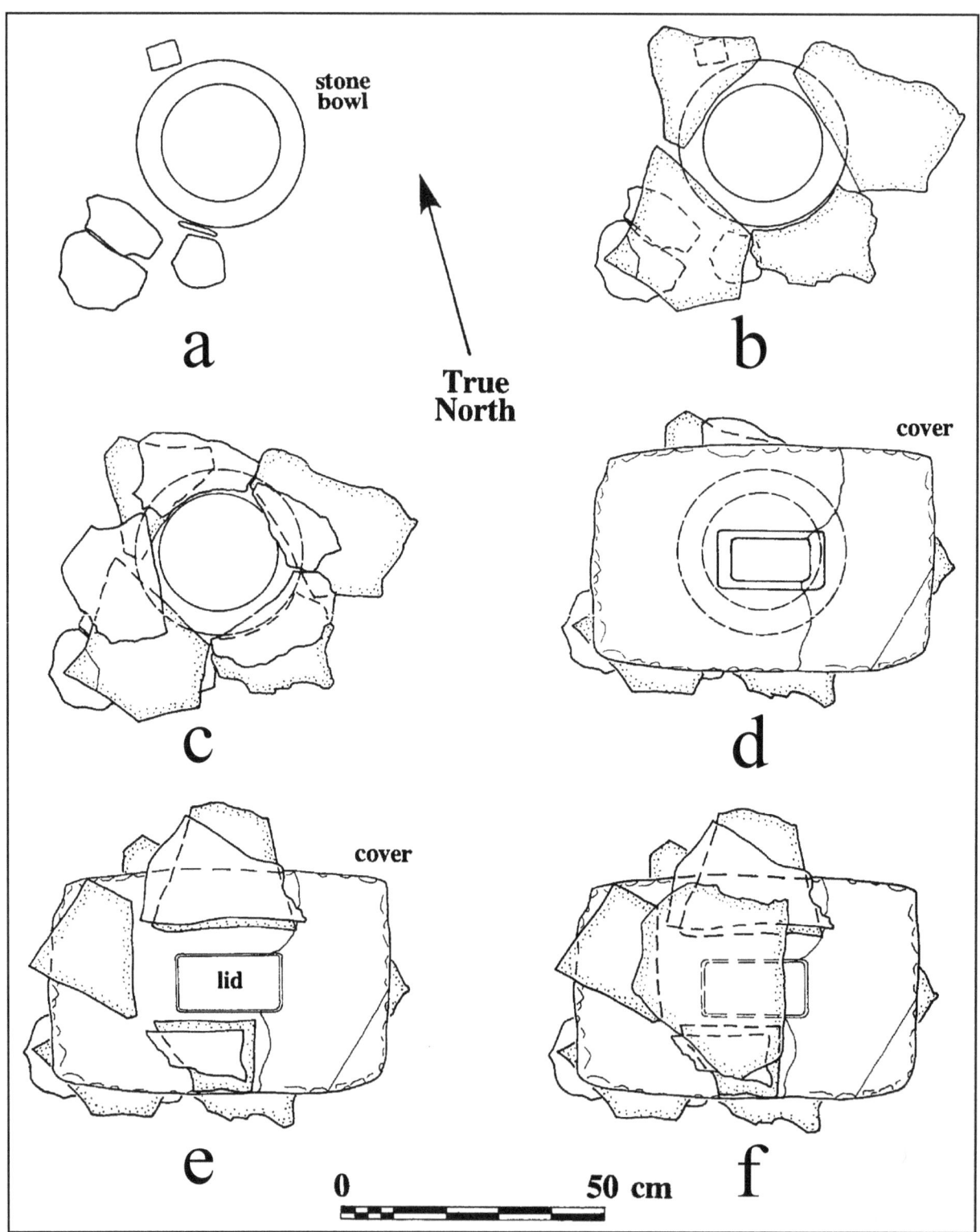

Figure I.3.12. Site 29SJ 423. Plan views of shrine altar construction sequence starting with the stone bowl set in refuse deposits (a), then stones added to support cover (b-c), then the cover is added (d), and finally more stones are added on cover top (e-f) to form a protective housing over lid access into the interior of stone bowl (CHCU 65978). Two stones are paint palettes used in the construction (see Table I.3.10). Original by Tom Windes, 1973.

the site mostly reflect activities associated with the shrine.

The area of Pithouse B, immediately adjacent to the shrine, was completely devoid of rare minerals, which also supports the likelihood that the vast majority of rare material is not of Basketmaker age. Two unusual, fetish-like natural sandstone concretions recovered during the excavations were also assigned to the shrine material list.

Interestingly, one turquoise-colored glass bead was recovered from the surface just northeast of the altar, but whether this constitutes continued use of the shrine or is a fortuitous historical discard or loss cannot be discerned. We know that the cist next to Pithouse B is historic and that the LC Cattle Ranch (29SJ 609) below the mesa bluffs to the northwest yielded much historical materials, including beads. There are also historic Navajo dwellings within the site immediately below the cliff to the east. Given the viewshed from the site location, it is not unexpected that some historic artifacts have found their way here. Still, the ornament type, color, and location suggest a recent offering at the shrine.

Just to the west below the cliff is another unusual shrine-like feature designated a stone circle (29SJ 866; Windes 1978). It is not known if there is connection between the use of this structure and the shrine (see Van Dyke 2003b, 2004, 2007b), although both are late Pueblo II. This is the only known occurrence in the San Juan Basin of the shrine communication system (Hayes and Windes 1975) where a signaling shrine and a stone circle are in close proximity to one another. Recent aerial photography interpretation reveals a possible road segment leading to the shrine from the same side of the mesa in which the stone circle is located (Figure I.9.7).

Pithouse A Area Discussion

The Basketmaker components in the Pithouse A area are difficult to interpret. The size and alignment of the three cists (Pits A-C) suggests use for storage. Each revealed the use of gray-white plaster in the initial construction and probably served as a storage unit for a pithouse family unit nearby. Other clusters of 2 or 3 cists on the site are probably associated with nearby pithouses. These three cists, measuring 2.7-6.5 m^2, were slightly larger than the norm (2.5 m^2) for the 43 cists measured at Shabik'eschee (Roberts 1929), a site similar to 29SJ 423. Only three cists at Shabik'eschee exceeded 4.7 m^2.

After the addition of the firepit and the replastering of the floor, Pit A likely functioned other than for storage. The slabs set along the pit edge above the firepit may have served as a deflector. Pit B, then, might have become an antechamber, with the collar between Pits A and B marking the entry into Pit A. On the other hand, the shallow depth of Pit B could indicate that it was built later, specifically as an auxiliary chamber to Pit A. We can assume that initially Pits A and C served for storage, but then Pit A was converted into a small pitstructure with the addition of a hearth and a small antechamber (Pit B).

Little roofing was recovered for the three pits. The absence of postholes suggests that the roofs were constructed of poles slanted around the pit perimeter to meet over the floor center. The difficulty of placing a smokehole in this kind of roof may have necessitated placement of the firepit next to the entry, as in Pit A. Bullard (1962:128) surmised that conical roofs were common for small and temporary structures.

A second firepit was added next to Pit A at about the same time Pit A was remodeled. The arc of holes would have been useful for construction of a pole and brush windscreen to protect the second firepit. The adobe-covered bedrock around the features indicates formal use of the outdoor space, which would have been protected by the windscreen from the southwesterly summer winds. After abandonment, all wood must have been salvaged and the pits then used for trash.

Subsequent Basketmaker activities around the pits are indicated by the slabs set across Pit B and the additions of Features 1 and 2. Missing slabs from around the three pits also indicate ongoing activities at the site. Although the builders of the shrine used Basketmaker metate fragments in the shrine wall, they did not use the thin wall slabs exposed in the great kiva a few meters away. Overall, few artifacts were directly associated with feature use.

Six centuries after the Basketmaker occupation, the promontory became the focus for a Pueblo III shrine, resulting in considerable disturbance of earlier material. Much of the mound overlying the pits and other features probably resulted from building the masonry shrine wall and altar, and then subsequent digging to place of offerings east of the altar. Apparently, the cultural deposits from earlier periods served as the surface for shrine activities. Except for the quantities of turquoise and shell, there were few recognizable artifacts left from the Puebloan period.

Pithouse B
(Figure I.3.13, Tables I.3.8, I.3.10-I.3.11)

Immediately north of the great kiva was a semicircular row of slabs that seemed to mark a small pithouse or a pithouse antechamber. After removal of 5-7 cm of windblown sand, an unconsolidated deposit of ash-stained sand, 2-4 cm thick, was encountered. This represented the contact zone between the surface aeolian sand and the underlying refuse and burned material. The remaining 20-30 cm of fill was designated Level 1. The upper 9 cm of this unit was dense with charcoal and ash, whereas the lower part had little burned material, consisting primarily of adobe and stone, particularly in the south half of the structure. Level 1 continued westward without a break beyond the hypothesized pithouse perimeter.

Pithouse B was partly enclosed by large, upright slabs (40-100 cm long, 25-40 cm high,

Plate I.3.27. Site 29SJ 423, overview of Pithouse B and exposed the bedrock behind it where stone removal activities may have taken place. Great kiva is in the lower left corner. Looking west. 30-cm north arrow. Photograph by Tom Windes, 1973 (CHCU neg. 5754).

and 5-10 cm thick) set on bedrock (Plate I.3.27). No wall was evident along the west side. A floor had been fashioned by removing of much of the soft bedrock, and then the irregular spots were plastered over. Decomposed bedrock also formed a mound, 10 cm high, that extended west from the center of the floor to beyond the probable wall perimeter. This mound was nearly sterile and designated Level 2; its removal left a trough in the floor 28 cm deep.

Southeast of center was an irregular bedrock firepit. Although it exhibited burning, no ash and little charcoal remained. Like the other floor features, it was filled with a soft brown material, possibly from decayed organic matter, and small charcoal pieces, including one piece of carbonized juniper, which failed to yield a date. A narrow deflector slot was cut into the bedrock 40 cm east of the firepit. Only a 14-x-4-x-8-cm piece of disintegrated and burned sandstone remained in the slot, which probably represents the remains of an upright slab deflector. On a southeast axis of 138° through the firepit and deflector was the ventilator. Two rotted, 4-cm-diameter posts (OP 4A-B), set 70 cm apart, were embedded just outside the wall slabs at the end of the ventilator

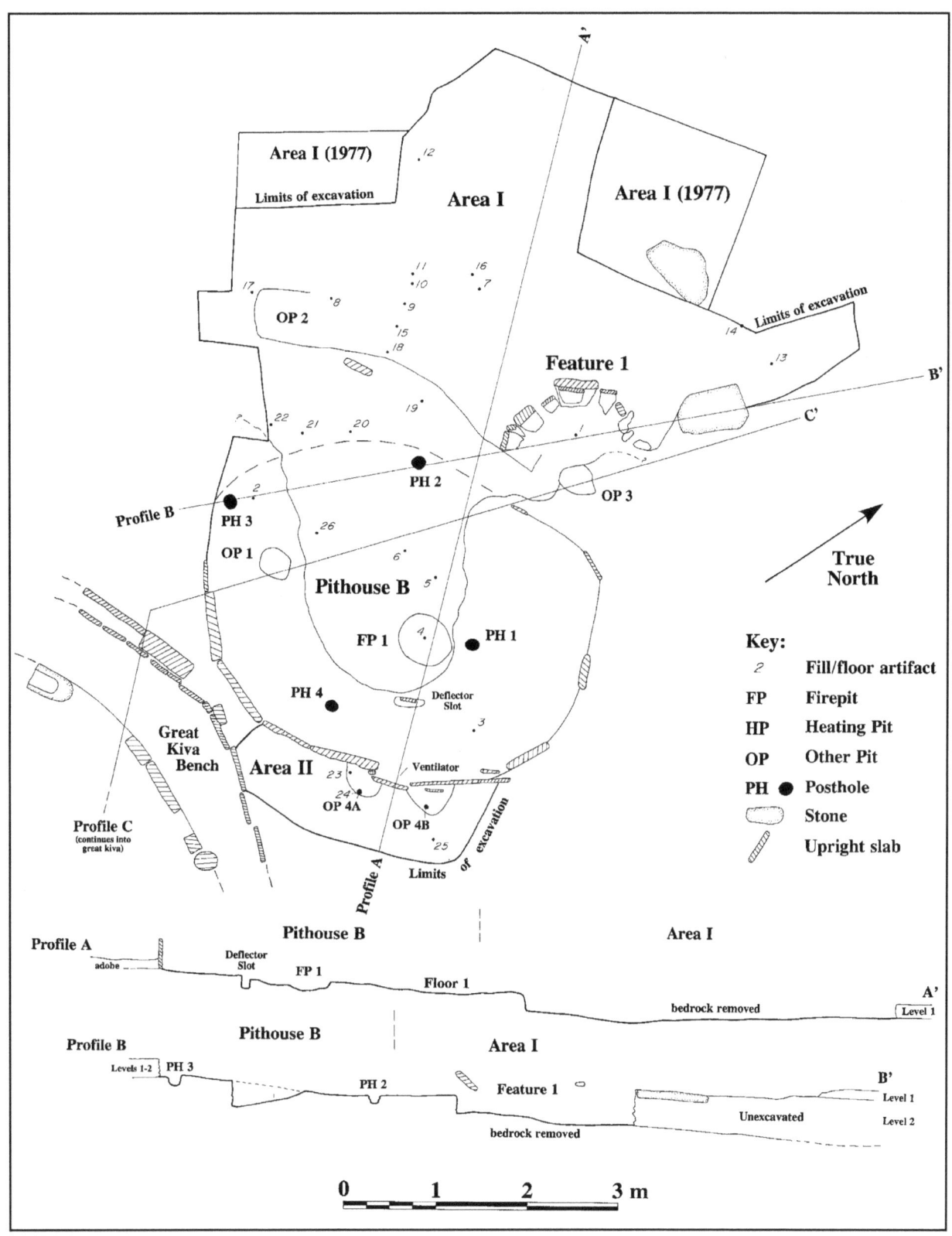

Figure I.3.13. Site 29SJ 423, Pithouse B, Areas I and II, Feature 1, plans and profiles (CHCU 55513). Profile C is found in Figure I.3.16. See Table I.3.11 for the distribution of fill and floor materials. Original by Tom Windes, 1973.

ramp. Both posts were held in place by a low, semicircular mound of adobe, 30-x-40-cm. The 15-cm-long ramp approached the pithouse wall but was blocked by an offset slab that prevented access into the main chamber.

Five pits were found in the bedrock floor. Four of them were set in a rectangle (PH 1-4) and seem to have been for the primary roof supports, although their alignment is offset from the anticipated perimeter of the structure. The fifth (OP 1) was an irregular pit, 31-x-33-cm and 4 cm deep, which may have been natural.

Floor materials (Figure I.3.13, Table I.3.11)

Overall, it was difficult to distinguish occupational materials left in situ from the dense refuse deposits covering the area. It is clear that cultural material was dense just west beyond the anticipated perimeter of Pithouse B in Area I. An odd, linear deposition of rare materials was plotted for several artifacts in that area, but few materials were actually found near or on the Pithouse B floor. The ventilator area (Area II) between Pithouse B and the great kivas also yielded little cultural material.

Area I

Because the wall slabs were missing along the west side of the structure, we thought Pithouse B may have been the antechamber of a larger structure to the west. Work proceeded west through the wall gap into an area designated Area I, and 50-150 cm outside the slab walls the fill composition changed, accompanied by a sharp, 20 cm dropoff in the bedrock. Level 1 continued down into the dropoff but yielded a higher density of cultural material, which was confirmed by selective screening. The dropoff reached a maximum of 35 cm in depth and then became shallower toward the west. From the point of initial dropoff until it reached the surface was a distance of 4 m.

Rather than an expected pithouse main chamber to the west, the area of the dropoff to the west was the result of decomposed bedrock being purposely removed down to the hard, rippled sandstone stratum, presumably for building material. At the north end of Area I, just beyond Feature 1 (not to be confused with the shrine Feature 1), a 40-cm-thick unit of the original soft sandstone remained undisturbed. The southern limits of this trough were not found. The few artifacts found mixed in with the decomposed bedrock unit lying under Level 1 were collected as Level 2.

Feature 1 (Plate I.3.28)

Just outside the Pithouse B wall slabs a semicircle of stones formed a storage cist. The stones were irregular and leaned outward, unlike at the majority of cists at the site; the feature had an estimated diameter of 130-140 cm and was 18 cm deep. No floor could be found. Fill inside the feature was identical to the surrounding fill (i.e., Level 1). On the side where the cist stones were missing, the underlying bedrock was level with the feature bottom but had been deepened 10 cm to form a step-like shelf, 32-x-44-cm. Because the

Plate I.3.28. Site 29SJ 423, Feature 1 next to Pithouse B. Possible Navajo cist. Looking southwest. 30-cm north arrow. Photograph by Tom Windes, 1973 (CHCU neg. 5743).

cist is clearly intrusive into Level 1, however, the shelf and cist may not be related.

An isolated slab similar to those in Feature 1 was set in Level 1 fill 155 cm to the southwest. Between the two features, several Navajo Polychrome sherds were found in the fill and another came from inside Feature 1. These were the only such sherds recovered from the site, and their association with features dissimilar to others at the site suggests a Navajo origin. The closest Navajo hogans are on the bench below 29SJ 423 within 100 m to the east, southeast, and northwest at 29SJ 426, 29SJ 425, and 29SJ 422, respectively.

Pithouse B Area Discussion

Although Pithouse B resembles a pithouse, it lacks many of the features common to larger pithouses. We cannot be certain that Pithouse B was part of a larger structure given the disturbance of the bedrock to the west. Nevertheless, small Basketmaker pithouses abound in Chaco Canyon with three excavated examples at Shabik'eschee and one at 29SJ 721 (Chapter 4). At this site, Pithouse A might also be viewed as some sort of habitation structure, despite its diminutive size. The small ventilator, instead of an antechamber, is unusual for the period but might also relate to the small structure size and might be an indicator of short-term use.

There is no evidence of a roof. The four offset postholes could not have held a roof centered over the structure. Perhaps the postholes mark an earlier structure no longer discernible. If a common truncated roof were employed, then the four roof supports must have rested directly on the bedrock floor. Aside from the mass of adobe on the floor, no roofing remains were observed.

Pithouse B predates construction of Great Kiva III, a few centimeters away. The exterior mortar used to affix the pithouse wall slabs was overlain by refuse that supported the secondary exterior wall slabs of Great Kiva III (Figure I.3.13). Burned material recovered from the upper pithouse fill probably derived from the last burned superstructure of the great kiva. A piece of piñon charcoal from this pithouse deposit tree-ring dated at A.D. 530vv (Table I.6.2), which is within the span of dates marking construction of Great Kiva III. It is possible that the disturbed bedrock in Area I resulted from quarrying activities by the builders of Great Kiva III as they searched for stone to cover the kiva walls. This activity could also account for the absence of the pithouse's western wall and the trough cut through its floor. The resulting pit was then used for trash.

It is uncertain how early Pithouse B was constructed. The close proximity of the great kiva(s), 35 cm away, would be unlikely unless use was not simultaneous. Generally, early structures are scattered although later houses can be built over them, as several at Shabik'eschee had been (Roberts 1929). Proximity and the possible kiva deposits found overlying the pithouse suggest that Pithouse B was occupied and abandoned prior to the initial construction of the great kivas between A.D. 520 and 540. Two charcoal fragments recovered from the pithouse floor dated to A.D. 355vv and 367vv, but considering the possible outer ring loss, Pithouse B more likely dates to the fifth or early sixth century.

Pithouse C (Figure I.3.10)

Along the top of the promontory at the south end of the cultural deposits was an arc of slabs next to exposed bedrock. The estimated diameter of this possible pithouse was 470 cm. A test pit 75-x-76-cm placed next to the north wall slabs encountered the bedrock floor at 25 cm depth. Besides the wall slabs, no other features were evident. The sandy loam fill yielded a mere five sherds and one piece of debitage. Thus, little information was expected from the structure and the work was terminated.

The Great Kivas (Figures I.3.14-I.3.17)

One of the prominent features of the site was a large, 10-m-diameter circle of slabs partly exposed on the surface. A thin mantle of aeolian sand covered it and the surrounding fill. Beyond the wall exterior, undifferentiated dark, organically stained refuse deposits up to 50 cm deep extended to bedrock. On the east and northeast sides, the cultural materials were only 5-10 cm deep, contained few artifacts, and were underlain by hard, compacted, sterile deposits.

Contrary to expectations, the structure was found to be much deeper than anticipated from work in the surrounding pithouses. Three or four superimposed structures, three of them great kivas, had been dug into the bedrock 70 cm deep, resulting in a confusing array of bedrock features. The building sequence of the four structures follows from the earliest to the latest: Structure 1, and Great Kivas I, II, and III. During the project, numbering features and structures with Roman numerals only occurred at 29SJ 423; these have not been converted to another system in order to maintain continuity with the field notes and other documents. The confusing array of features encountered during the great kiva excavations led to a mixed system of Roman numerals, Arabic, and alphabetic designations in an effort to keep construction phases separate. This did not always follow the final interpreted construction sequence.

Strategy

Artifacts and vegetation were removed from the surface within and around the slab wall and then the loose sand was removed. Sand was banked deepest (12-15 cm) against the west and southwest wall slabs, the direction of the prevailing winds. Artifacts were numerous and bagged as surface material ("loess fill"-aeolian sand), which includes the surface materials and those within the thin mantle of aeolian sand. The darker, underlying deposits, Level 1, consisted of wind- and water-deposited sand stained with ash and refuse. The kiva bench for Great Kiva III was exposed during removal of Level 1, and artifacts from it were bagged separately. Starting at the top edge of the bench and sloping down into the kiva was a saucer-shaped deposit of relatively little ash and cultural materials designated as Level 2. Although only a few centimeters thick at the bench, this deposit grew to 30 cm thick in the center of the kiva. The upper 13 cm consisted of matrix similar to Level 1 but lighter in color and with little cultural material. The lower 17 cm of matrix contained a massive sheet of large, irregular slabs that once constituted the kiva outer covering, which had toppled into the interior (Plate I.3.29). The stones averaged 22-x-38-cm and 22 cm thick and extended 120-150 cm into the kiva from the edge of the bench. This pattern of slabs indicates that the kiva adobe and pole walls were mostly stone covered. In association was a mixture of hard tan sand and adobe, which constituted the former adobe wall covering under the slabs. Despite selective screening of Level 2, few specimens were recovered, suggesting abandonment of the mesa top when Great Kiva III burned.

Plate I.3.29. Site 29SJ 423, Great Kiva III showing layer of stone slabs that covered the kiva exterior walls before the last fire. Cleared area is the latest bench top. Cairns in background are from stone recovered during excavations of the shrine/Pithouse A area. Tom Windes excavating while Lou Love looks on. Looking north. Photograph by Dave Love, 1973 (CHCU neg. 11841).

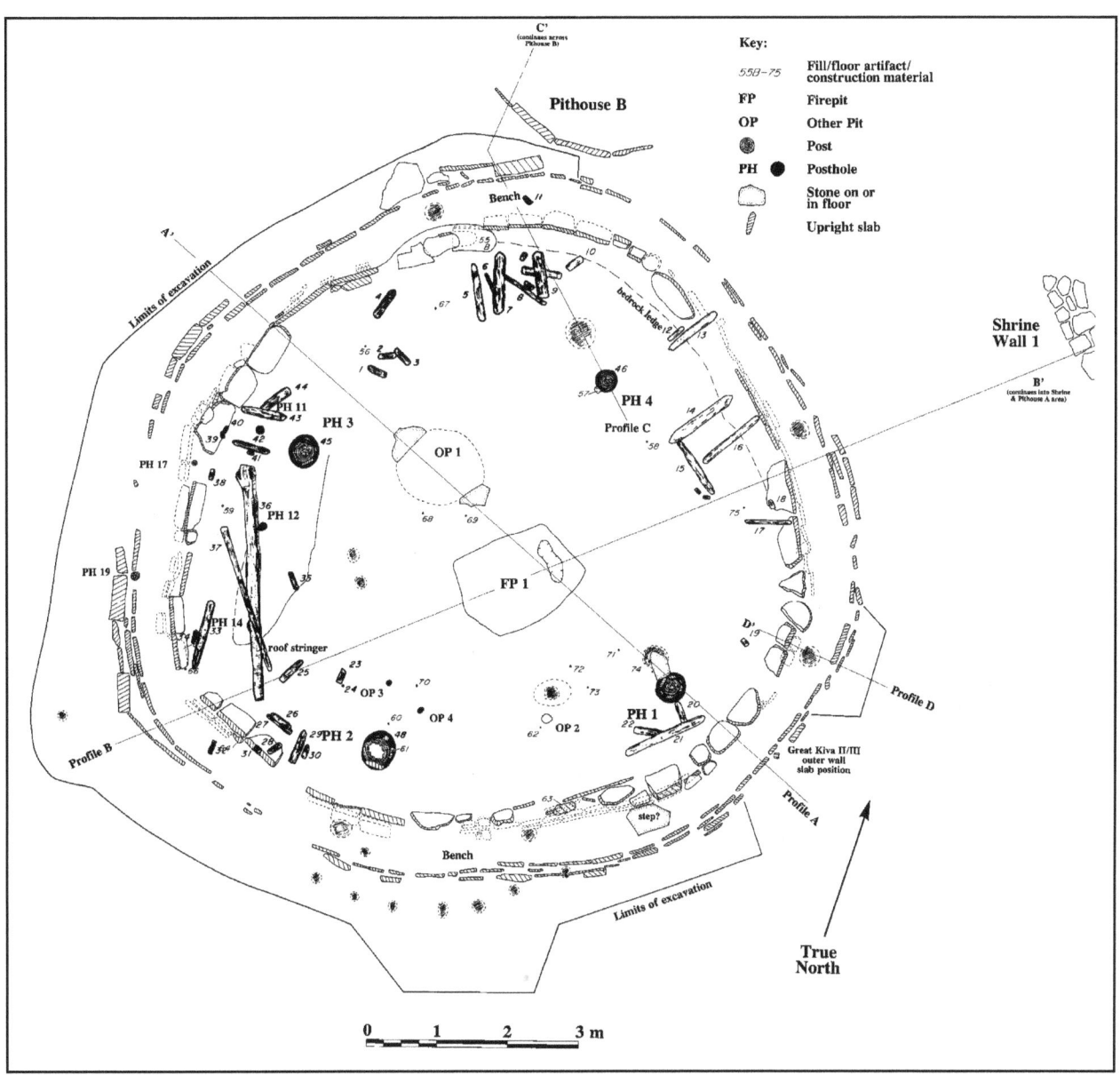

Figure I.3.14. Site 29SJ 423, distribution of roofing elements from the burned remains of Great Kiva III (CHCU 65984). Overlies CHCU 55516. See Figure I.3.16 for profiles and Table I.3.13 for data on the roofing elements. Original by Tom Windes, 1973.

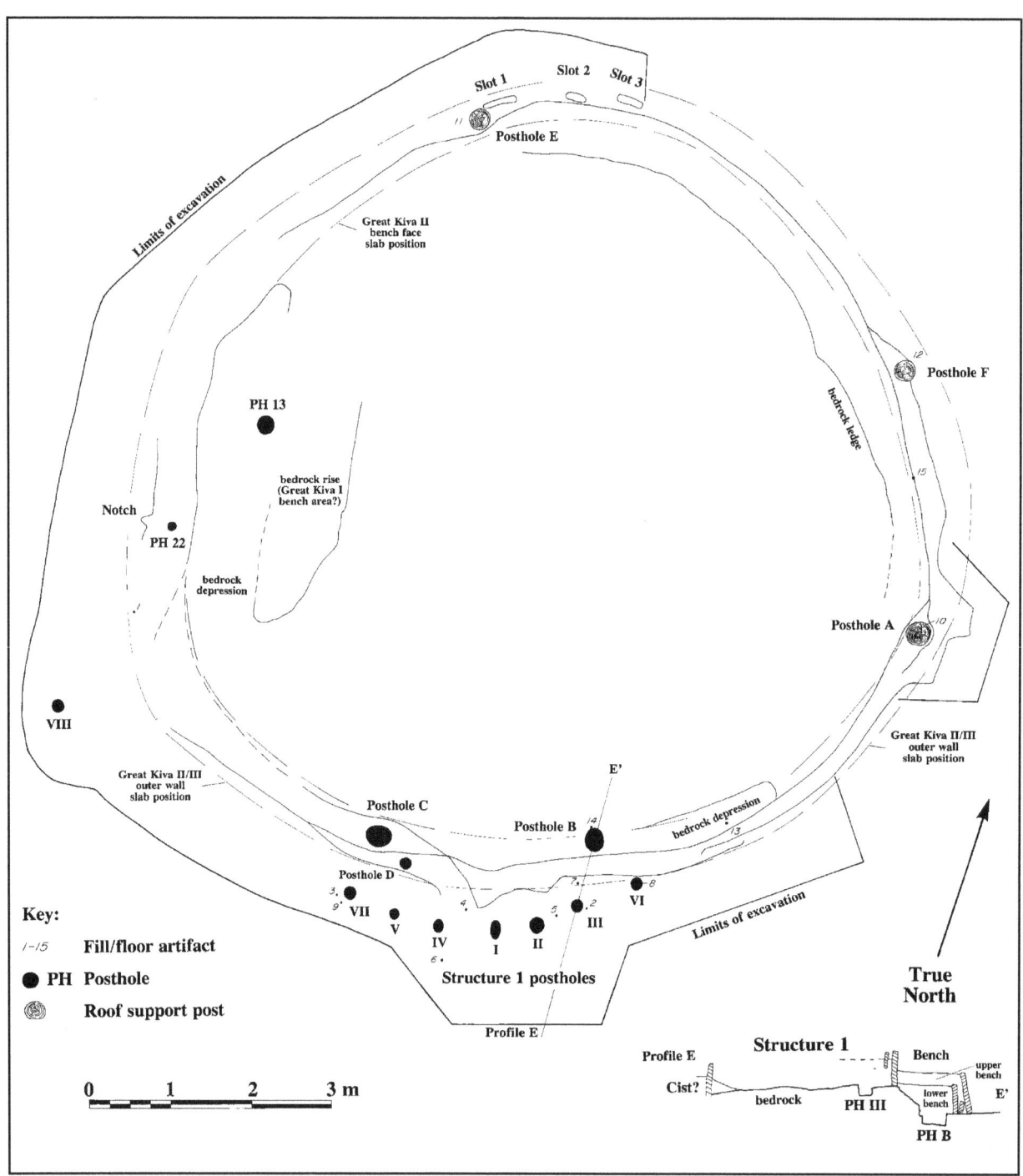

Figure I.3.15. Stie 29SJ 423, Structure 1 and Great Kiva I, plans (CHCU 55519). See Table I.3.12 for the distribution of fill and floor materials. Original by Tom Windes, 1973.

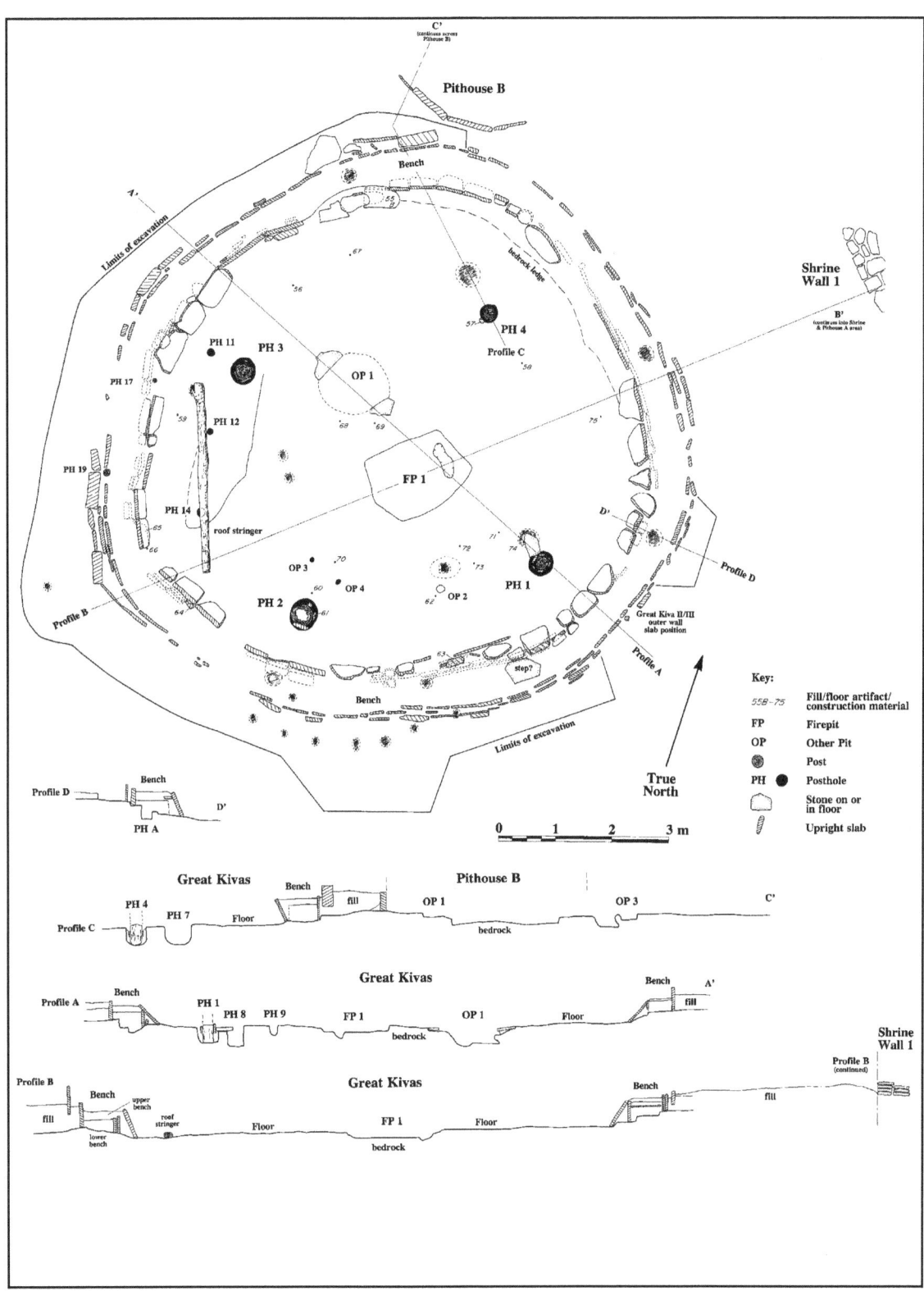

Figure I.3.16. Site 29SJ 423, Great Kiva II plan (CHCU 55517). See Table I.3.12 for the distribution of fill, floor, and construction materials. Original by Tom Windes, 1973.

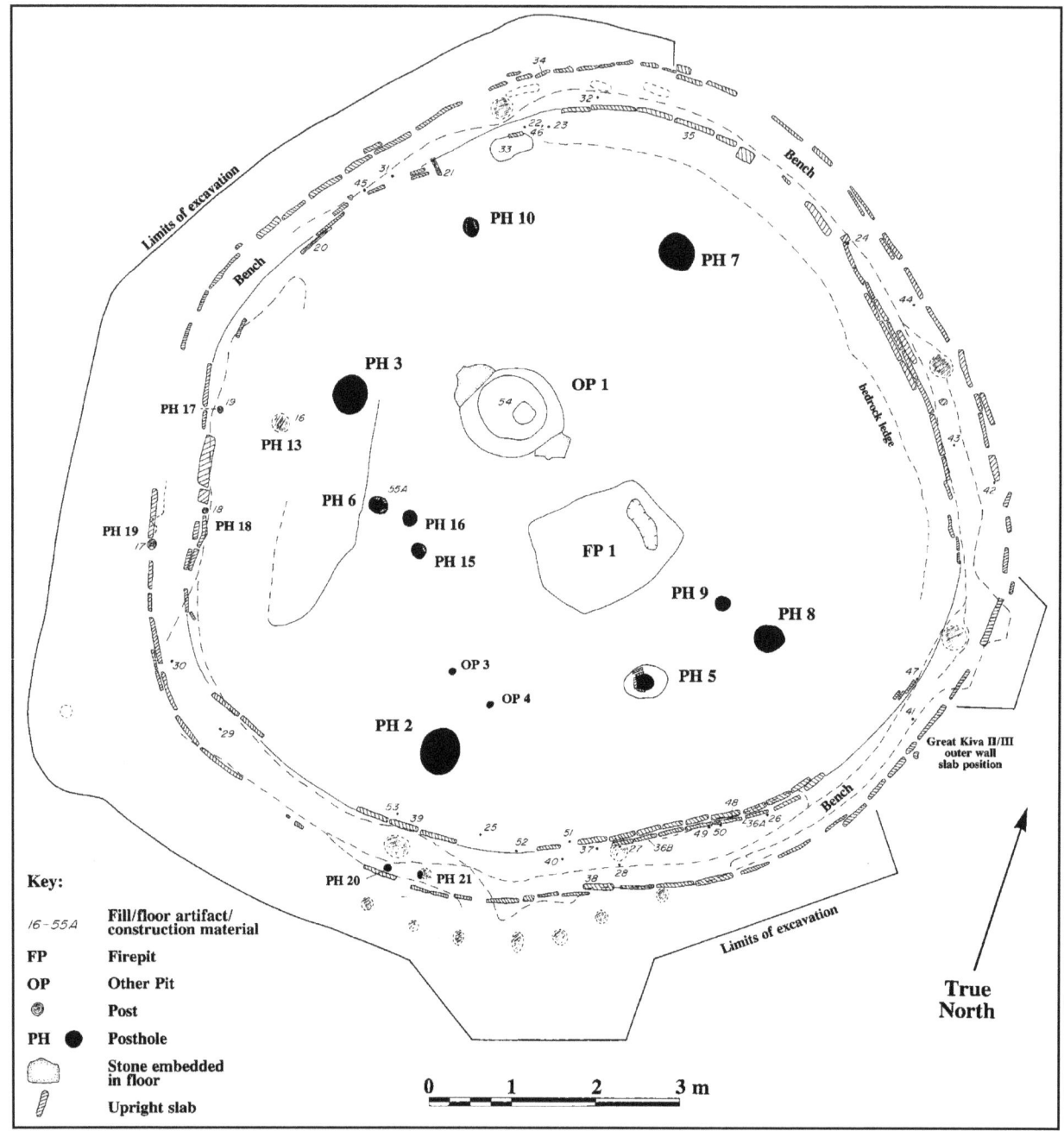

Figure I.3.17. Site 29SJ 423, Great Kiva III plan (CHCU 55516). See Table I.3.13 for the distribution of fill, floor, and construction materials (except roofing elements). Original by Tom Windes, 1973.

Level 3 extended from under Level 2 to the bedrock floor. It was about 10 cm thick in the kiva center and grew to 50 cm deep at the edge of the bench. For the most part the deposit consisted of fire-reddened sand and ash in the center of the kiva and a mass of charred, broken timbers around the kiva inner periphery (Figure I.3.14). Thirty-two of the 38 timbers, ranging from 5-17 cm in diameter (75 percent were between 8 and 14 cm diameter) were collected for dendrochronology, but only five could be dated. Rare pieces of shredded juniper bark and brush were found resting perpendicularly over the timbers, which, in turn, were overlain by the layer of wall rock. Otherwise, cultural mateial was scarce.

Structure 1 (Figure I.3.15, Tables I.3.10, I.3.12)

The arc and other outside holes (I-IX) in the ripple-marked sandstone represent the earliest, or part of the earliest, construction (Plate I.3.30). The position under the wall slabs of Holes IV-VIII indicate that they antedate Great Kivas II and III. The later of the two tree-ring dates from charcoal recovered from the bedrock near the arc of holes, A.D. 490vv, is in accordance with dates from the roof supports of Great Kiva I. Fill removed from that kiva's roof support holes was essentially the same as that in Holes I-IX, indicating deposition under similar or contemporary conditions. There is also an unusual modification of the bedrock ledges under the benches centered in front of the arc of holes that suggests a correlation between the arc and Great Kiva I.

Finally, just beyond the southeastern wall slabs was an arc of holes (I-VII) that continued under the kiva wall. These were consistent in shape and size, and spaced 36-60 cm apart. A similar hole (VIII) occurred 50 cm inside the arc under the kiva wall. A ninth (IX) was found west 410 cm from the others and 70 cm outside the wall slabs. All occurred in the rippled hard sandstone strata even with the base of the main exterior wall

Plate I.3.30. Site 29SJ 423, Structure I, arc of Postholes I-VII excavated into bedrock under south-southeast exterior side of great kiva benches. Main roof support (Posthole C) in right foreground. Looking southwest. 30-cm north arrow. Photograph by Tom Windes, 1973 (CHCU neg. 5777).

slabs but considerably above the interior main floor. Burned and unburned juniper bark, wood, twigs, charcoal, and small pieces of sandstone surrounded the arc of holes. Two of these pieces of wood were tree-ring dated to A.D. 221vv and 490vv (Table I.6.2) but indicate only that they were harvested sometime after A.D. 490. Inside the holes were fragments of charcoal, unburned wood, and decomposed organic matter (wood?).

The alignment of the arc and the presence of wood mark a row of small posts, perhaps an entry into Great Kiva I. Hole VIII may have held an auxiliary post but Hole IX is too far away to be part of this post arrangement. Alternatively, the arc might predate Great Kiva I. A projection of the arc yields a diameter of 6 m, well within the range for Basketmaker pithouses. Rows of small postholes were common to pithouse benches (e.g., at 29SJ 628 and 724, this volume). Pithouses built in the A.D. 600s in Broken Flute Cave all revealed an arc of side poles set around the perimeter (Morris 1980), although more closely spaced than those documented here. Similarly, great kiva-size Pithouses B, E, and M on Alkali Ridge also revealed side pole holes set 18-56 cm apart (Brew 1946:163, 187, Figures 30 and 33). Although we can be sure the holes mark a structure, it is uncertain how they related to the earliest great kiva, if at all.

Great Kiva I
(Figure I.3.15, Tables I.3.8, I.3.10, I.3.12)

The large floor areas and lack of domestic features common to pithouses clearly mark the next three constructions as great kivas or community structures. The earliest great kiva was evident from five postholes (A-E) placed in the soft white sandstone bedrock ledge in a circle under the later benches (Plates I.3.31 and I.3.32). The rotted remains of posts were found in Postholes A-E, but only three posts were intact enough to yield tree-ring dates: A.D. 480vv, 515vv, and 516vv (Table I.6.2). There was relatively little ring loss to the two latest dated specimens, and it is presumed that they were harvested by A.D. 516 or shortly afterwards. A sixth hole (PH 13), filled with sand, flecks of gypsum, and charcoal, and plastered over by the floors of the later kivas, completed the ring of six posts. The post butts were charred on the datable timbers indicating either harvesting by setting fires around the base of the tree or an effort to lessen in-situ damage from rot. This technique has also been noted for a roof support post in a Pueblo I great kiva (Hayes and Lancaster 1975:60). Shims were not employed in these five postholes, which ranged from 20-27 cm across and 10-27 cm deep. The position of the three slots under the benches (Plate I.3.32) along the same alignment as the early roof support postholes places them in Great Kiva I, but their purpose is unknown.

Plate I.3.31. Site 29SJ 423, main roof support Postholes A and B (foreground) for Great Kiva I under the later great kiva benches (removed). Note altered bedrock. Looking northeast. 30-cm north arrow. Photograph by Tom Windes, 1973 (CHCU neg. 5772).

Plate I.3.32. Site 29SJ 423, Slots A-C excavated into bedrock to hold upright slabs. Found under great kiva benches (removed) on northwest side. At far end of slots is main roof support Posthole E. Looking southwest. 30-cm north arrow. Photograph by Tom Windes, 1973 (CHCU neg. 5778)

Construction of the kiva started with removal of the soft overburden and the hard layer of rippled sandstone until the soft white sandstone underneath was reached. A slight, 10-15 cm rise or ledge was left behind the circle of roof supports, possibly to act as a low bench for side poles. The estimated size of this kiva, using the postholes as the outer limit, was 8.8-x-10.2-m, covering approximately 74 m^2. It was impossible to separate floor features, if any remained, from those of the following great kivas except for PH 13 and those under the benches. Because the bedrock floor deepened just inside the ring of most roof support postholes, it is assumed that the Great Kiva I floor was relatively flat and then was removed during construction of Great Kiva II. This premise is based partly on the location of post support PH 13 within the larger floor area utilized by the later kivas, its presence within the deeper later floor area, and that it had been sealed with plaster. If the floor had been deepened later, then any shallow features associated with Great Kiva I would have been removed.

Although there was no direct evidence for burning of Great Kiva I, the burned material used for fill in the Great Kiva II bench suggests the former remains of a burned structure that predated Great Kiva II. The relatively short interval between constructions suggests that the Great Kiva I roof supports were burned off rather than left to rot. There was no evidence for the post supports extending above the floor.

The roof arrangement of six posts set along the perimeter is unlike that of other pitstructures, large or small, in Chaco Canyon. The circular arrangement of posts and the low rock shelf or bench may have closer antecedents with the variable Mogollon great kivas, from which their Anasazi counterparts may have derived (Wheat 1955:213). The early dating of this kiva in the early A.D. 500s overlaps those of a similar type in the Mogollon country (Vivian and Reiter 1960:98) and suggests stronger continuity with the Mogollon than later structures at the site. Ceramics from the site also include a significant amount of early brownwares that link the occupation with ceramic traditions to the south. But multiple roof posts (more than four) set around the perimeter persisted in puebloan pitstructures into the Pueblo I and Pueblo II times (e.g., Gillespie 1976: Figures 6, 10, 36; Lightfoot 1988: Figure 2).

Floor Artifacts. Because of subsequent constructions, few cultural materials were left directly associated with the initial great kiva remained aside from the rotted posts and the posthole contents. Offerings had been placed under the east and southeast posts. Posthole A yielded three pieces of turquoise, three gray sherds, a rodent bone, and a stone chip. Posthole B, the southeastern pit, contained a solitary turquoise bead. The association of these offerings with the dated supports indicates placement at about A.D. 516 or shortly afterwards and marks some of the earliest dated turquoise in the puebloan Southwest.

Turquoise has been recovered from postholes in other early Chacoan pithouses at 29SJ 628 and 29SJ 724 (this report). Similar customs continued through the Pueblo III period for Chacoan kivas (e.g., Judd 1959:60-61; 1964:181, 192; Mathien 2003:131; Windes 1987b:404), with offerings in niches and pilaster logs, but, surprisingly, offerings were not found under the later posts of Great Kivas II and III.

Great Kiva II
(Figure I.3.16, Tables I.3.8, I.3.10, and I.3.12)

After destruction of the first great kiva, a second one was built that resembles others of the Basketmaker and Pueblo I style. Architecturally, this kiva was most evident in the construction of the outer slab wall base and the bench (see below), which was later modified by the construction of Great Kiva III. Slabs were missing from many of the structures around the great kiva, which suggests that they may have been salvaged for use in construction of the great kiva (s).

Walls and Benches (Table I.3.8). The features most crucial to understanding the building sequences of Great Kivas II and III are the two superimposed benches (Figure I.3.16). The bench face of the earlier bench of Great Kiva II was fronted by a non-continuous row of thin vertical slabs, 30-40 cm high, set along the bedrock. In places, these were supported by shorter stones less than 15 cm high set parallel and in front. Along one part, these stones and the adjoining floor were fire-reddened. Four of the stones set in the bench facing the interior and one in the outside wall had been used for sharpening tools (Plate I.3.33). Another row of vertical slabs, 30-45 cm high and placed on bedrock, formed the base of the wall exterior. In places, refuse that had built up to 35 cm thick over a long number of years helped buttress the outside slabs. The bedrock under the benches had been altered to a series of irregular steps or ledges descending from under the wall slabs to the interior kiva floor. This resulted in the exterior wall slabs being placed considerably higher than their counterparts in the bench face.

The 30-50 cm space between the bench and wall slabs was filled with refuse and sterile soil and covered with adobe plaster, concealing the post supports of the previous structure (GK II). The plastered top of the bench was even with the tops of the interior slabs or, where higher, beveled along the interior edge to join the slabs. Occasionally, small tabular stones were found lying flat about 6 cm below the top of the bench, as if for a surface, but a second lower previous bench surface could not be discerned. The bench fill yielded some ash, charred and uncharred wood fragments, and twigs and shredded juniper bark, which must have come from an earlier burned structure, but artifacts were rare.

A charred side pole (FS 312) from the collapsed wall of Great Kiva II, 14 cm in diameter and 56 cm long, was recovered from the top of

Plate I.3.33. Site 29SJ 423, Great Kiva III bench stones showing awl sharpening marks, presumably from work activities by the kiva occupants. 30-cm scale. Photograph by Tom Windes, 1973 (CHCU neg. 5780).

the bench but did not date. Only two shallow post-like impressions (9.5-x-9-cm and 7 cm deep, and 8.5-x-5-cm and 4 cm deep) (PHs 20 and 21) were found on the bench top, otherwise there was no indication that the wall side poles were seated along the bench top, although this is assumed.

Two poles (FS 255 and 256; 3 and 3.5 cm in diameter), 115 cm apart, were placed against the earlier bench face on the west-southwest side. A small pecked hole was found in bedrock for support beneath each one (PHs 17 and 18). Nearby, a third post (FS 277) next to the bench extended from Posthole 19 through both bench tops. It was 10 cm in diameter and served no apparent purpose. Fragments of three other poles (3 cm in diameter or less) found immediately in front of the earlier bench, and the two small poles listed above may have reinforced the bench slabs in a similar fashion to those found in the Shabik'eschee great kiva (Roberts 1929:Figure 25).

Floor and Floor Features. The earlier floor was slightly enlarged, creating an area 9.2-9.3 m across between the bench faces (about 61 m2 of floor space). This enlargement was accomplished by removal of an additional strip of bedrock, 1.5 m wide, along the west-southwestern side. A slight rise in the floor along the previous perimeter appeared to mark where this enlargement began. The kiva diameter was 10.2-10.3 m between the outer walls.

Because of the common use of the same bedrock floor surface for Great Kiva II and Great Kiva III, it is difficult to assign floor features to a specific use in either kiva or whether they were common to both. If pits had been left open at abandonment, then use with Great Kiva III is ensured but does not negate use initially with Great Kiva II. An attempt here has been made to assign sealed pits, clearly not in use at the time of Great Kiva's III destruction, to Great Kiva II and open pits to Great Kiva III. In some cases, paired pits conflict with this separation when one was sealed and the other was not. In other cases, the positions of some pits clearly depict common use for either one or both Great Kivas II and III (e.g., the firepit and some roof supports). Obviously, some error must be assumed in these tentative separations.

Firepit. Southeast from the center of the floor, a shallow, roughly rectangular firepit had been dug into the bedrock. A small irregular pit, 28-x-56-cm and 16 cm deep, was situated at the north end. The blackened firepit, 118-x-160-cm and 4-10 cm deep, contained burned roofing, indicating that it had been cleaned out when the last kiva burned. No deflector or ventilator could be found. The large firepit probably served for Great Kivas II and III in succession but it was not possible to discern remodeling or whether an earlier, smaller firepit(s) had been present.

The firepit in the bedrock floor was probably made first for Great Kiva II because the removal of bedrock would have destroyed any firepit for Great Kiva I. The shallow depth of the newer firepit would have been insufficient to prevent a scattering of ashes from the slightest breeze. Conceivably, the pit was made shallower by subsequent floor remodeling during the construction of Great Kiva III. Nevertheless, there was little evidence of a firepit-rim coping or sides of adobe or stone that would have deepened the firepit (but see under Great Kiva III roof) nor for a deflector to impede ashes scattering from ventilator drafts.

Entry. Evidence of an antechamber or ventilator was lacking. A set of posts (PHs 17 and 18), 115 cm apart, was set against the bench face on the southwestern side of Great Kiva II. Wall slabs behind these posts were absent, which suggests a possible entryway into the chamber. This location may have marked entries into both great kivas. The Shabik'eschee great kiva also revealed two small posts, 117 cm apart, along the southeastern side of the chamber, which Roberts (1929:80) interpreted as the ventilator opening. Morris (1980:55, 58) gave no explanation for a similar arrangement of paired posts set on pithouse benches in Broken Flute Cave, but those posts were not related to entry or ventilation.

Other Pits. A large circular pit (OP 1) just west of the firepit resembled a firepit but was unburned. It was plastered over and had two tabular stones set horizontally in the floor on opposite sides (Plate I.3.34). At its mouth, the pit was 100-x-107-cm but formed only a small cavity 33-x-39-cm at the bottom with sloping walls. Overall, the pit was 29 cm deep. The

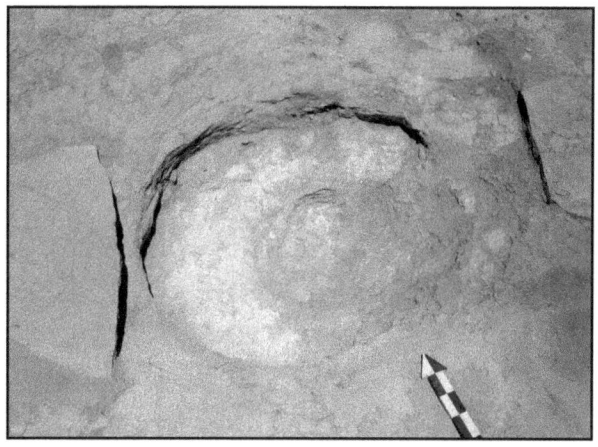

Plate I.3.34. Site 29SJ 423, Other Pit 1 in the floor of Great Kiva II-III. Looking north-northeast. 30-cm north arrow. Photograph by Tom Windes, 1973 (CHCU neg. 5733).

pit fill consisted of sparse cultural material in an unburned sandy matrix. The pit has been tentatively assigned to Great Kiva II use but could have been in use with Great Kiva III and then sealed.

Postholes (Table I.3.10). Roof post supports (PH 2, 3, 7, and 8) were set in a quadrilateral arrangement at the four principal directions. Posts in PH 7 and 8 were replaced as supports for Great Kiva III but PHs 2 and 3 were used in common for both roofs. PH 7, revealed no evidence of shims nor burning. PH 8, 12 cm west of the east main posthole (PH 1) for Great Kiva III, contained ash at the bottom and had been burned down one side as if the former post had been burned out. A large flat stone had been set over it before it was plastered shut. We can presume that the wood posts left in the supports when Great Kiva III burned were not those used for Great Kiva II, which presumably were consumed by earlier fires.

Along the alignment of the four-post arrangement were two other sealed pits, PH 5 and PH 6, which may have been secondary additions to prop sagging roof stringers for the Great Kiva II roof. Each of the pits contained sterile yellowish brown sand, identical in appearance to the surrounding crumbling bedrock, but contained no wood. PH 5 is a large hole with four shims that fits the dimensions of the other main roof support holes. It was filled with tan sterile sand underlain by ash. The position of PH 6 in line with the south and west post holes, its depth, and the four possible shims found inside it also indicate that it too held a post used to support a sagging stringer. But PH 6 is much smaller and is in close proximity to two others of like size, set 25 cm apart (PH 15 and PH 16; Plate I.3.35). Although PH 6 was not plastered over, the absence of wood suggests its use with Great Kiva II.

These three, and a smaller pair (OP3 and OP 4, set 59 cm apart), might be supports for small altar posts (Wilshusen 1988d, 1989b) or, less likely, ladder supports for a roof entry. Small

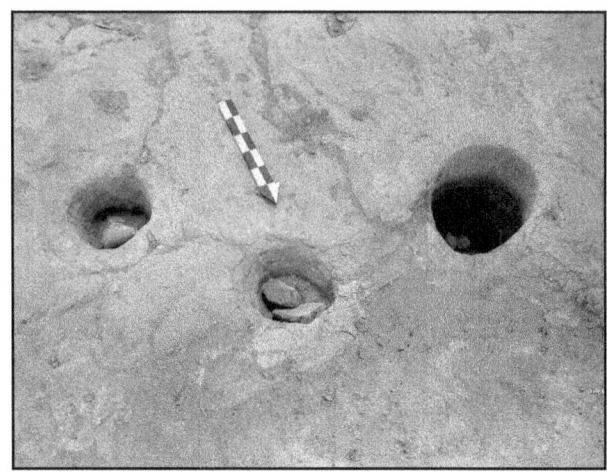

Plate I.3.35. Site 29SJ 423, Great Kiva II postholes. PH 15 (left) and 16 (center) are possible entry ladder supports; PH 2 (right) is an auxiliary roof support. Looking south-southwest. 30-cm north arrow. Photograph by Tom Windes, 1973 (CHCU neg. 5736).

stones recovered from the fill of PHs 15 and 16 and OP 3 suggest the use of post shims. OP 4 had been sealed but OP 3 was empty until filled with burned deposits from the destruction of Great Kiva III, indicating that it was last used during activities in Great Kiva III. OP 3 and OP 4 might have held an altar screen during the use of either or both great kivas, but it was removed before the terminal use of Great Kiva III. Finally, there are two isolated posthole-like pits (PH 9 and PH 10) that can be assigned no specific function except to have held posts of some sort. Sand resembling the surrounding crumbly bedrock sandstone was found in all the sealed holes except PH 15, which contained brown sand and decayed organic matter. PH 10 also contained chunks of gray clay and pieces of charcoal. Most floor pits lacked refuse or charcoal flecks suggesting synchronous filling. They may have been filled when the floor was deepened during the construction of Great Kiva III. Although the plaster used to seal the many pits differed in color and texture, suggesting that the seals were non-coeval, all seals revealed a light ash content.

Fire caused the destruction of the second great kiva. Besides signs of burning in PH 7, other indicators were manifest around the bench. The two previously mentioned posts set on the floor next to the bench were burned. A charred pole was recovered from the top of the bench covered by the Great Kiva III additions. Parts of the floor and bench were fire-reddened. Finally, masses of burned twigs, vegetal matter, and ash, probably from wall or roofing remains, were found sealed over by the final construction. This material was similar to that found from the destruction of Great Kiva III and attests to walls or roof of similar materials that burned.

Floor Artifacts. Relatively little trash and the presence of several complete artifacts on the floor between the Great Kiva II and Great Kiva III bench faces and on top of the Great Kiva II bench suggests an accidental burning that left articles in situ. A few artifacts were found on top of the early bench and on the floor along the low ledge directly in front of the bench (Table I.3.12). Two awls found on the ledge next to the earlier bench face may mark hide-working areas. Tools like these may have made the sharpening marks found on some of the bench stones. A usable mano, some bone beads, an abrader, two projectile points, and a scraper were also found associated with the bench. OP 2 contained a polishing stone and a piece of debitage came from the plaster seal over PH 13. This assemblage was larger than all the complete artifacts recovered from the much greater area of Great Kiva III.

Great Kiva III
(Figure I.3.17, Tables I.3.8, I.3.10, and I.3.12)

For a third time, the great kiva was rebuilt (Plates I.3.36-I.3.38). The lack of natural deposition over any of the Great Kiva II features suggests that Great Kiva III construction was immediate or that the kiva had been cleaned out later for reuse.

Walls and Benches. The previous bench had weakened from the earlier fire; it had slumped in several places and slabs were displaced. The last builders sought to prevent further deterioration

Plate I.3.36. Site 29SJ 423, Great Kiva III after clearing. Looking south. 30-cm north arrow. Photograph by Tom Windes (CHCU neg. 5725).

Plate I.3.37. Site 29SJ 423, Great Kiva III after clearing. Note slanting bench-face slabs placed against earlier Great Kiva II bench slabs. Burned roof stringer on kiva floor (FS 175; tree-ring dated at A.D. 550v). Background: Bruce Yazzie (left) and Ken Augustine. Looking north-northeast. 30-cm north arrow. Photograph by Tom Windes, 1973 (CHCU neg. 5728).

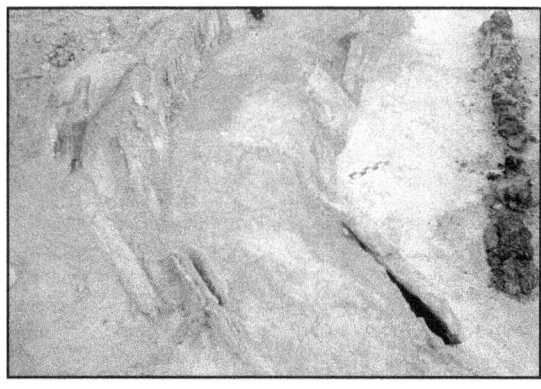

Plate I.3.38. Site 29SJ 423, Great Kiva III upper bench top, showing the outer wall foundation slabs and the leaning interior bench-face slabs. Looking northwest. 30-cm north arrow. Photograph by Tom Windes, 1973 (CHCU neg. 5717).

Plate I.3.39. Site 29SJ 423, Great Kiva II-III bench with outer (GK III) bench-face slabs removed showing the vertical bench-face slabs of GK II. Top of bench is Great Kiva III construction. Looking north-northeast. 30-cm north arrow. Photograph by Tom Windes, 1973 (CHCU neg. 5719).

by leaning large slabs and blocks, anchored in trash and set 5-20 cm outside and parallel to the previous bench, against the earlier bench face (Plates I.3.37-I.3.39). Small tabular stones were occasionally placed along the top edge of the bench to act as rests for the leaner slabs (Figure I.3.18). Along the northwest side several of these slabs had either slumped (Figure I.3.17) or fallen after the final fire. As with the previous construction, metates or metate fragments sometimes were used as slabs.

Trash and burned material were used to fill the space between the two sets of bench face slabs and to increase the previous bench height 6-13 cm. The top of the latest bench had also been plastered with adobe. On the southeastern side (at 140°), a flat stone had been set flush in the bench top as if it were a step marking an entryway. It was without noticeable wear from prolonged foot use, however. The slab additions widened the bench to 50-60 cm, lessening the floor area to about 58 m². If the bench had been used for seating spectators or participants, however, the additions would have made sitting difficult.

In addition, a series of short slabs were set outside the existing exterior wall slabs above the bedrock. These secondary slabs may have served to support the additional weight of the stone-covered side walls. The mass of stones recovered from the kiva was calculated to have covered the exterior walls to a height of at least 134 cm of height, but probably it was closer to 150 cm. The stones were similar to the local bedrock and many had ripple marks, indicating local procurement, perhaps from the building excavation or, more likely, the nearby Pithouse B/Area I bedrock source. The function of the stones is not clear but they may have served to lessen deterioration of the walls from weathering or to make up for a lack of available adobe.

Parts of the kiva superstructure uncovered during excavation revealed that the layer of stones covered a sandy wall of adobe about 15 cm thick (see above, Plate I.3.29). This, in turn, covered a layer of shredded juniper bark and brush set perpendicular to and over the side poles of the wall. No post impressions were evident along the upper bench top, but the numerous pole remains found slanting toward the floor leave little doubt that side poles rested upon the bench and the quadrilateral framework of stringers in the traditional manner.

<u>Floor and Floor Features.</u> There was a decided dip in the floor between the previous and subsequent bench faces. Along some sections, the last bench face slabs had been set along this dip. Therefore, it is conjectured that the floor had been deepened during the last construction, which removed evidence of any previous shallow features. This might explain the shallowness of the firepit. There is no significant difference between the depths of the holes of Great Kivas II and III, indicating that only parts of the floor were removed. The soft bedrock deteriorates rapidly under normal (present-day) foot traffic and could have prompted removal of the more decomposed parts, particularly if they were badly burned. Several rough spots in the final floor were covered with gray clay.

Other Pits. The holes not covered with plaster are presumed to have been in use until the very end and, thus, are mapped belonging to Great Kiva III (Figure I.3.17). The lone exception is PH 2, which probably previously held a Great Kiva II post. Yet, it is possible that some holes fell into disuse and were sealed during the tenure of Great Kiva III, and that they were wrongly assigned to Great Kiva II. Six holes were open when Great Kiva III burned. OP 3 (paired with OP 4), PH 11, and PH 15 (paired with PH 16 in GK II) were empty until filled with burned deposits. The upper part of PH 14 was tan sterile sand underlain by the same sand mixed with ash. Conical-shaped PH 12 was filled with a cream-white sterile sand, which might have been intentionally powdered from the bedrock surrounding the hole.

Postholes. At the time of discovery, the floor was littered with cylindrical holes with slightly concave bottoms except for conical-shaped PH 11 and PH 12. Little speculation is needed to assign the majority of holes as anchors for posts, although not necessarily for roof supports. Many held fragments of decaying wood or post stubs and had small tabular fragments of sandstone (i.e., OPs 2-3 and PHs 9-10) that probably served as post shims.

The only holes in evident use at the end contained the charred stubs of the four main roof supports in Postholes 1-4. Three of these piñon posts ranged in diameter from 23-27 cm; the fourth was about 41 cm in diameter, all resting in pits 33-55 cm across and 31-45 cm deep. All the stubs had been wedged in their bedrock holes with multiple sandstone shims. These four and a roof stringer were tree-ring dated to A.D. 435vv, 519vv, 550vv, 554vv, and 557r (Table I.6.2). Along with dates from the posts, the four charred side poles found on or just above the floor that dated to A.D. 510vv, 523vv, 535v, and 550r indicate probable construction of Great Kiva III at about A.D. 557. Given the circumstances, the A.D. 535v and 550r dates might represent salvageable timbers from Great Kiva II and the possible temporal range for the latter's construction.

Placement of the main east and north roof supports (PHs 1 and 4) had changed position slightly from the Great Kiva II roof construction. There was no indication why a shift in the roof supports was necessary, although it could not have been for a stronger central roof support. This could only be accomplished by moving the supports closer together to relieve the burden on the stringers, the beams most likely to fail. Perhaps the added weight of the stone on the side walls necessitated shifts designed to lessen the weight load on the side poles.

The Roofing. When the kiva burned, it left a mass of timbers around the inner periphery of the chamber (Figure I.3.14, Table I.3.13) but none within the rectangle bounded by the four stringers and posts. The fire-reddened sand and ash within the central rectangle suggested that the fire was hottest toward the center as a result of the draft through the smoke hole. Thus, if any roof had been present in the center it would have been reduced to ash close to an opening. The unburned chunks of adobe and several stones found resting on the ashy floor next to the firepit might have bordered the roof opening or have been firepit liner remains. Once the side walls collapsed, aided by the weight of the stone covering, they smothered the fire and preserved many of the timbers in charcoal form. The lack of burned adobe beyond a few pieces suggests a light outer covering of sandy adobe. The main supports apparently remained standing until burned to ash because no large pieces of charcoal, which might have derived from carbonized posts, were recovered. On the other hand, Lightfoot (1988:267) suggests that the remaining roof supports may have been salvaged, but there is no evidence for it considering the stubs were still left in situ, and they would have been much too large for use in any other structures nearby.

If the central area of the roof between the primary posts was left unroofed, this also could explain the absence of burned timbers. Antecedents for unroofed or partially roofed great kivas are common (Martin and Rinaldo 1939:350, 356; Truell 1975:216; Morris 1980:81). Hewett considered the nearby upper great kiva at Chetro Ketl to lack a central roof (in Vivian and Reiter 1960:42) in the same manner argued here for Great Kiva III.

Roof Engineering. The probability that the central part of Great Kiva III was unroofed is supported by the large differences between the actual, calculated stress of a full roof and allowable safety tolerances. Roof strength is dependent on two crucial factors: the degree of compression of the vertical posts and the resistance to bending failure of the horizontal stringers set across the posts. Failure of either, of course, would result in massive collapse of the roof. By today's standards, piñon is considered unsuitable for construction because it is crooked and has many knots; therefore, it lacks published stress specifications. The woods closest to piñon in terms of strength are lodgepole and ponderosa pines (Barney Etzkorn, Engineering Section, US Forest Service, Albuquerque, personal communication 1975).

The weight and stresses of the roof and walls of Great Kiva III were calculated from data presented in Table I.3.14. The resultant figures (Table I.3.15) revealed that the four posts were capable of safely supporting eight times the weight of a full roof. But wood is much weaker when set horizontal, and this is reflected in the dangerous overloads supported by the four stringers based on the diameter and length of the one (FS 175) found on the floor.

The disparity between the probable roof load and safety tolerances becomes clearer when several unmeasured factors are considered. The calculated weights for Great Kiva III probably are too low. Although the strength of poorer grades of wood (No. 1) has been used in the calculations, they are probably superior to those in prehistoric buildings. Often wood appears sound but fails for no observable reason; thus, a safety factor of five or ten times the normal strength becomes the allowable stress preference (Thurston 1890:636, 648, 658). Prolonged stress above these recommended tolerances can eventually lead to failure (Thurston 1890:658). In addition, the point of rupture has been determined in wood without visible flaws (i.e., knots, shakes, and checks). Flaws, however, are extremely common in piñon—the material used in Great Kiva III. Finally, the increase in strength from seasoning is usually largely offset by development of checks in and around knots, and of shakes and checks along the neutral axis (Luxford and Trayer 1940:49). Thus, the point of rupture of wood is normally closer to the "green" rather than the "air-dried" value (Table I.3.15).

Stress on the stringers was calculated as if equal weight rested on four stringers spanning the distance between each post. Only two parallel roof stringers may have supported a series of beams set perpendicular across them in conventional construction (e.g., Haury 1940:Figure 20; Wheat 1954: Figures 26-27). If this were the case, then the two stringers may have supported nearly double the weight presented in Table I.3.14. The stress on stringers is perhaps the main reason why auxiliary posts are common additions in pitstructures and why PH 5 and PH 6 were needed to assist the roofing support in Great Kiva II (see Figure I.3.16).

Given the great disparity between loads for a full Great Kiva III roof and the lack of a safety margin as well as the lack of burned roofing in the center of the structure, it is surmised that the area between the main posts in Great Kiva III was left open to the skies. The importance of the night skies, both the moon and the constellations, is well known for agrarian peoples in general and for the puebloans in particular (Gullett 2012; Sofaer et al. 1979); thus, including them in ritual and ceremony in great kivas is likely.

Floor Specimens (Table I.3.12). Few artifacts from the final abandonment were found. All of the usable tools left were of chipped stone, including a cluster of three between OP

1 and OP 8. The empty firepit and the paucity of artifacts in Great Kiva III suggest that the kiva was intentionally cleaned and burned. The concentration of debitage, a drill or punch, and the hammerstone recovered from the exterior stone wall layer likely represent a specific post-abandonment activity.

Summary

The earliest construction, Structure 1, appears to be the remains of a pithouse or part of the entry into the earliest great kiva. Because the only features were postholes, little can be discerned for Structure 1. The two dated pieces of charcoal (A.D. 221vv and 490vv) found in association, however, suggest that the features were in use about the time of construction of Great Kiva I. Likewise, little remained of Great Kiva I aside from the circle of primary roof support holes (and some posts), but these, at least, indicate the shape and minimal size of this unusual structure. The close dating of two of the three roof posts and their condition suggest that the structure was built after about A.D. 516 but before A.D. 535, and probably closer to A.D. 520.

After Great Kiva I burned, it was replaced by Great Kiva II and constructed in the traditional manner of many Basketmaker III and Pueblo I (and later) great kivas. This construction lacks in situ dates but is bracketed between A.D. 516 and 557. If the earlier near-cutting dates recovered from the last construction represent salvaged wood, then the latter could date between A.D. 535 and 550. Materials recovered from Great Kiva II suggest that it may have burned accidentally. The third great kiva was a close copy of the second, which basically utilized many of its existing features, and was built by A.D. 557 or slightly later. Unfortunately, the length of last use could not be determined, but it too was destroyed by fire after it had been cleaned out. There appeared to have been no effort to disturb the remains once Great Kiva III burned.

Conclusions

Clearly the occupation at 29SJ 423 was a major one covering an extensive period of time (at least from the late A.D. 400s to the late 500s and perhaps into the 600s). The density of early houses in a strip running north-south across West Mesa, like the one on Chacra Mesa that includes Shabik'eschee Village (Wills and Windes 1989), marks the two settlements as important communities in the occupation of Chaco Canyon (see Figure I.8.9; cf. Wills et al. 2012). The continual efforts to keep a viable great kiva in use at 29SJ 423 points to the importance of the site and of the large community in which it was located. Both settlements, with great kivas in their midst, suggest a cultural continuity with later events in the San Juan Basin that herald the development of the Chacoan Phenomenon and Bonito phase communities by the A.D. late 800s and 900s.

Pithouse B, at least, appears to have predated the construction of the great kivas. Unfortunately, the long use of the mesa top and its shallow deposits led to much disturbance of the deposits with few cultural materials left in situ. Aside from the constructions of the great kivas, the archaeology of 29SJ 423 was beset with confusion and difficulty of interpretation which led to our eventual relocation to another site (29SJ 721; Chapter 4). Yet, the site and community hold considerable promise for future research, particularly considering the unusual setting of this and the Shabik'eschee community within the canyon occupation.

The problem of building on bedrock did not deter occupation, although it may have altered the method of construction and left the pithouses shallower and smaller than normal. There is a trend in the northern San Juan Region for habitation dwellings to become progressively deeper during the Basketmaker II and through the Pueblo I periods (e.g., Bullard 1962:125; Eddy 1961; Morris and Burgh 1954). The shallow floors at 29SJ 423 are reminiscent of early Basketmaker II dish-shaped floors. The small structures at the site may also reflect intermittent or seasonal occupation (e.g., Wills and Windes 1989) rather than constraints imposed by building on bedrock.

The length of Basketmaker occupation at 29SJ 423 is unknown without more extensive excavation. The main occupation took place in the A.D. 500s, if the construction efforts of the great kivas are an indication of population size and societal complexity. This period coincides with an unusually long, wet, warm period that began in A.D. 509 and extended through A.D. 525 (Van West and Grissino-Mayer 2005; based on reconstructions from the El Malpais preciptiation chronology and the San Francisco Peaks temperature chronology) that would make marginal areas, such as Chaco, particularly attractive for horticulturists (but only if this chronology is applicable to the Chaco area). Even with the following environmental downturns in precipitation or temperature, the efforts to rebuild the great kivas suggested an enduring cycle of habitation and ritual within the community for at least another 30 or 40 years.

These great kivas apparently served as the focal point for the entire community of sites spread across the mesa, although they may not have been used continuously throughout the entire life of the community. Other great kivas may exist in the community, which are not apparent on the surface, although this is unlikely. Hayes (1981:24) suggests that a number of Basketmaker III house clusters existed within Chaco Canyon—none as large as the 29SJ 423 and Shabik'eschee communities—but only these two largest ones exhibited great kivas. Although a more thorough re-survey is needed to establish reasonable limits for a contemporaneous canyon-wide settlement, it appears that these two very large early Basketmaker III communities probably contained the majority of inhabitants at the time. The 29SJ 423 great kivas may be the earliest for which there are tree-ring dates. It is not known when these large community structures first appear, but the unusual construction of Great Kiva I, the tree-ring dates, and the amount of brownware at the site postulates that it happened early in the sixth century or earlier. Wheat (1955:213) has argued that the great kiva was a trait borrowed from the Mogollon—and the evidence at 29SJ 423 adds credence to this proposed connection.

Besides the importance of the Basketmaker community and the relationship of great kivas to it, the discovery of the Pueblo III shrine on top of the Basketmaker remains was an unexpected piece of luck. The elevation and visibility at the promontory were crucial aspects for positioning the shrine as part of a visual communication system, verified by extensive line-of-sight fieldwork. This shrine was the keystone for the discovery of the widespread Chacoan communications network. The shrine is evidence that the visual communication network, which was evident from the construction of the early greathouses in the canyon (Mathien and Windes 1989:32), may have expanded regionally beyond the canyon in late Pueblo II or early Pueblo III times.

A case might be made for placement of the shrine in conjunction with earlier sacred ground and ties to the past; no other shrines in the region share locations with earlier puebloan sites. The shrine and Basketmaker location at 29SJ 423 is probably a fortuitous circumstance or it tied a specific group identity together with nearby Peñasco Blanco and the early occupation of the 29SJ 423 settlement (see Van Dyke 2003b).

PITHOUSE Y AT SHABIK'ESCHEE (29SJ 1659)
Alden C. Hayes

Shabik'eschee Village (Figure I.8.10), on the south side of Chaco Canyon, is situated on the lowest bench of Chacra Mesa 30 m above the canyon floor at an elevation of 1,945 m (6,380 ft)—identical to 29SJ 423 in layout and location. Unlike most of the bare, northeast-running points of Chacra, this one is covered with 1-2 m of soil—a tight, stabilized sandy loess. The cover is scattered saltbush and wolfberry interspersed with annual forbs, although perennial grasses are becoming reestablished.

The site was discovered in 1926 by Frank H. H. Roberts of the National Geographic Society's Pueblo Bonito Expedition, who excavated three pitstructures and several slab-lined storage pits that summer. He returned the following season under the auspices of the Smithsonian Institution and uncovered another 18 pithouses, a great kiva, and numerous storage cists (Roberts 1929). Roberts's report of his discoveries to his colleagues at the first Southwestern Archeological conference, held at Pecos late in the same summer of 1927, contributed greatly to the concept of the Pecos Classification of Anasazi evolution, and Shabik'eschee became, and has long remained, erroneously, the type site of the Basketmaker III period.

Charcoal specimens collected by Roberts were not dated, but Deric O'Bryan revisited the site in 1940 and collected more charcoal for Gila Pueblo. There was no publication of a complete list of the 13 tree-ring dated specimens until after Gila Pueblo's entire collection became the property of the University of Arizona's Laboratory of Tree-Ring Research, and Bryant Bannister (1965) listed O'Bryan's dates as ranging from A.D. 734+ to 757. A cutting date of A.D. 753 was attributed to the great kiva, and one of A.D. 757 to House H.

These dates posed a problem. The houses at Shabik'eschee were shallow pithouses, most of them with antechambers, whereas buildings on the surface were confined to small, scattered storage cists. The pottery was Lino Gray and La Plata Black-on-white—typical of Basketmaker III. However, by the mid-700s on Alkali Ridge in Utah (Brew 1946), and on Mesa Verde in Colorado (Hayes and Lancaster 1975), houses were long arcs of contiguous surface rooms, pithouses had undergone the change to deep protokivas with constricted ventilator shafts, and banded-neck utility pottery had appeared. If the dates were to be taken as accurate the inference was that Chaco was a marginal area in that period and the "type site" was 50-75 years behind the times. After the excavations of Pithouses Y and Z were completed, the Arizona laboratory revised these dates, rejecting the A.D. 700s placement for the Gila Pueblo samples (Robinson et al. 1974) for an earlier period. Several new tree-ring dates were later obtained from the great kiva bench construction small poles (the latest dating at A.D. 554+vv; Table I.6.2) when Windes took archaeomagnetic samples from the burned bench. The latter yielded poor results (A.D. 450 ± 60; Table I.6.6), which seems too early.

The old excavation pits at the site had not been backfilled and the Chaco Center was determined to reexpose firepits on the floors of the pithouses to get archaeomagnetic samples for dating. The project was started in early August 1973 under the immediate supervision of John B. Thrift, who, with a four-person crew (Roger Huckins, Milo McLeod, John Schelberg, and Bruce Yazzie) (Plates I.3.40-I.3.43) and one volunteer (SuSu Knight), recleared the floors of Houses A, F-1, and H (see Figure I.8.10). The firepits of all three were found to be either lined with stone slabs or were left unlined after being cut down into the caprock. There was not enough burned adobe for sampling.

Scattered light trash and upright slabs protruding from the ground in an area from 65-120 m northwest of the great kiva—in the vicinity of Roberts's "Protokiva house" and House X—were an indication that there were still unexcavated structures at the site. We decided to explore for dendrochronological specimens in this area.

Test Trenches 1 and 2 (not shown on map) were laid out 1 m wide and approximately two meters long, and each encountered sterile soil at about 15 cm. In the process of clearing vegetation

Plate I.3.40. Site 29SJ 1659 (Shabik'eschee), initial excavations (Test Trench 1) at Pithouse Y with John Schelberg. Looking southeast. Photograph by Roger Huckins, 1973 (CHCU neg. 5880).

Plate I.3.41. Site 29SJ 1659 (Shabik'eschee), initial excavations (Test Trench 3) at Pithouse Y. Roger Huckins (left) and John Thrift. Photograph by Milo McLeod, 1973 (CHCU neg. 5884).

Plate I.3.42. Site 29SJ 1659 (Shabik'eschee), excavations in the Pithouse Y antechamber. Note slab-lined cist deep in the fill next to the shovel. Tom Windes (left) and Bruce Yazzie. Looking east. Photograph by Milo McLeod, 1973 (CHCU neg. 5890).

Plate I.3.43. Site 29SJ 1659 (Shabik'eschee), Pithouse Y main chamber in the firepit area. Note antechamber in background to left center. Looking southeast. 30-cm north arrow. Photograph by Tom Windes, 1973 (CHCU neg. 5892).

around the trenches, seven round, slab-lined cists were encountered. The cists were from 1-1.2 m wide with floors at, or slightly below, the original ground surface. A third, 6-m-long trench (TT 3) was started about 7 m north of the first area, and near its center the top of a pithouse wall was reached at a depth of 90 cm. Labeled "Pithouse Y," it was completely excavated with the exception of a large balk in the northwest quarter of the main chamber. This chamber was excavated primarily by the 1973 survey crew, consisting of Roger Huckins, Earl Neller, Milo McLeod, John Schelberg, and John Thrift with help from Tom Windes, Bruce Yazzie, and volunteer SuSu Knight.

Pithouse Y (Figure I.3.18)

Fill

Two distinct strata were identified in the fill. The upper, from 90-120 cm thick, was loose, organically stained sand and thin trash consisting of charcoal, burned bone, sherds, and lithic chips. The lower stratum was from 20-40 cm of compacted aeolian sand on the floor. Some

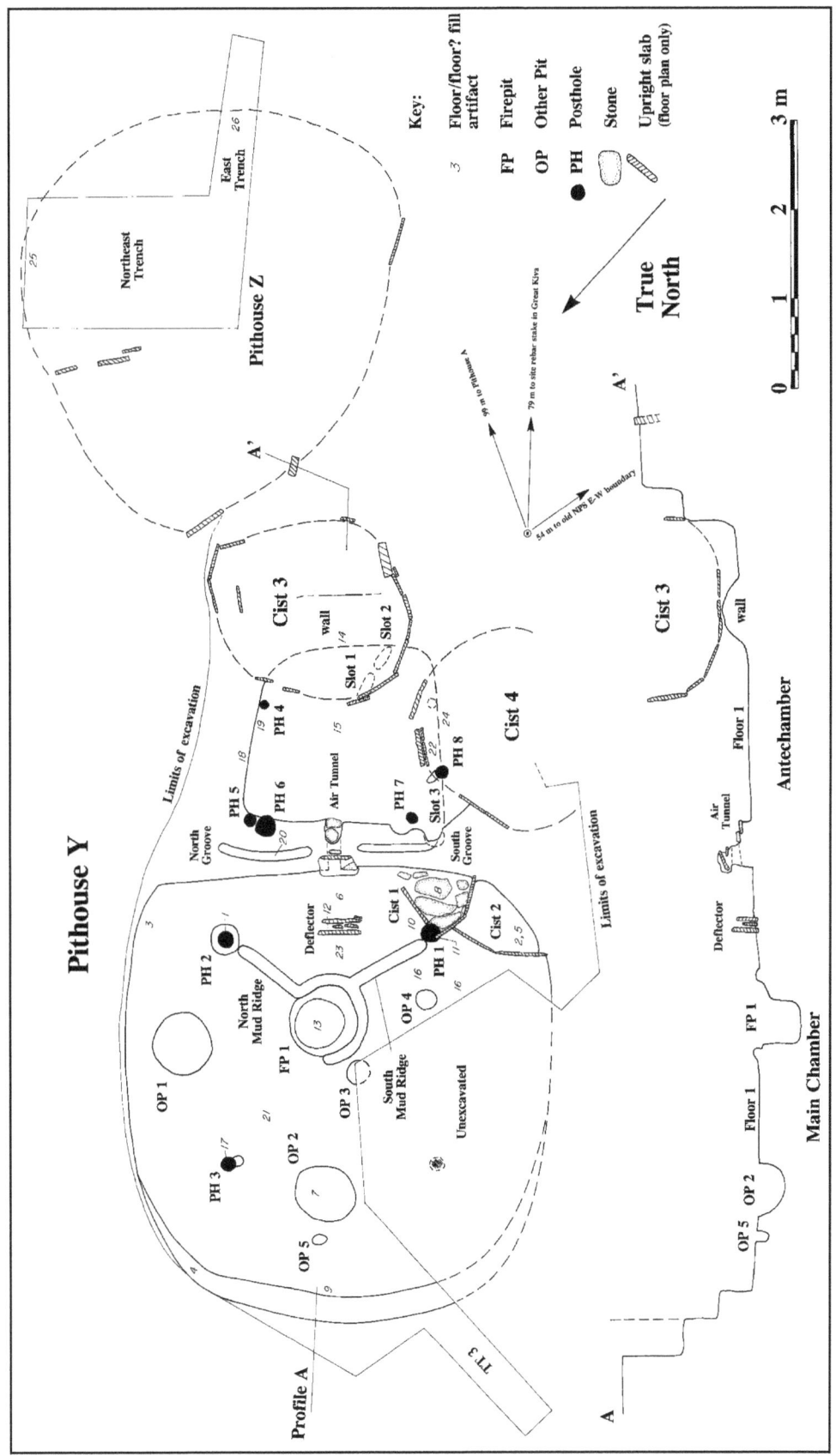

Figure I.3.18. Shabikeschee Village, Pithouse Y, plan and profile, and Pithouse Z plan (CHCU 65960). See Table I.3.18 for the list of floor fill and floor artifacts. Original by John Thrift and Tom Windes, 1973.

artifacts in the lower fill, or on the bench or floor, were catalogued by provenience, but generally there was no attempt to separate the two strata. Eight sandstone slabs in the upper fill over the north quarter of the pithouse were probably the remains of a collapsed, postoccupational storage cist.

Architectural Detail
(Plate I.3.43, Tables I.3.16 and I.3.17)

Pithouse Y was a somewhat D-shaped pit extending 83 cm below the original ground surface, and measuring about 4.75 m in diameter. Orientation was 140.5°—or roughly southeast. The outline was subcircular with a nearly straight southeast wall. A bench 32 cm wide stood 39 cm above the floor along the rear wall and was presumed to line the two side walls as well. There was no bench along the front, southeastern wall, and there was no evidence of timber on the excavated part of the bench. Three walls were unplastered cuts into the compacted sandy native soil, but the southeast wall, dividing the main chamber from the anteroom, was built up of adobe from the floor to a height of 39 cm— the same height as the bench at the northwest wall. This low partition, from 40-70 cm thick, was breached in the middle by a passageway 40 cm wide. The opening was partly plugged with stones and bridged to reduce it to a small vent over which a worn step provided passage between the two rooms. Long, shallow grooves on top of the wall and flanking the step may have held slabs or matting.

The floor, a thin layer of packed clay, was slightly dished, dropping 7 cm from the wall to the room's center. A round firepit, the dominant feature of the floor, was located 60 cm southeast of center on the northwest-southeast axis. The pit, 55 cm in diameter and 50 cm deep, had straight sides and a flat bottom and was filled with ash and charcoal. A rounded adobe rim, 6 cm high by 15 wide, ringed three quarters of the circumference of the pit, leaving it open on the northeast quarter. Extensions of the rim running to the east and south for 80 and 93 cm respectively, formed rudimentary wing walls which terminated at postholes for roof supports. A third posthole was found on the north quarter of the floor. A fourth undoubtedly lay in a corresponding position under the unexcavated bulk. Postholes were from 20-32 cm wide and from 61-87 cm deep. The two at the ends of the wing wall contained rotted wood. Another hole, 25 cm wide and 50 cm deep, located 25 cm west of the firepit, was filled with clean sand. It may have held an auxiliary support post for a sagging roof which was removed after repairs were made.

Other pits or holes in the floor were a 15-cm-deep sipapu placed on the main axis of the house, 60 cm from the rear wall; a pot rest or heating pit, 18 cm deep, southwest of the firepit; and two basin-shaped pits of unknown function near the northeast wall and immediately in front of the sipapu. These last were 69 cm wide and 30 deep.

A deflector made of standing slabs (one a trough metate), shimmed with smaller spalls of sandstone, stood 30 cm high at a point midway between the firepit and the vent. The low slabs may have served as a core for an adobe deflector, but if so, no trace of the adobe remained.

An extension of the adobe wing wall, in the form of standing slabs running from the south posthole to the south corner, made a partition between slab-walled bins on either side. The one to the east side had a flagstone floor.

A subrectangular antechamber was 1.9 m from back to front and narrowed from 2.2 m wide at the northwest partition to about 1.9 m. The floor was 8 cm higher than that of the main room. The chamber was only about 24 cm high and, like the partition, appeared to have been built of adobe. The soil outside the walls was explored at two points—outside the north corner and at the middle of the southeast wall, where sterile soil was reached at the approximate level of the floor inside. The two sections were 47 and 76 cm thick, respectively. A possible explanation for this unusual situation is that the builders may have dug a large oblong pit, placing the main room back against the initial cutbank at the northwest end and then crossing the pit with an adobe partition. This would have put the walls for a restricted antechamber well within the original pit at the southeast end and, finally, required backfilling of the area between the outside of the antechamber wall and the wall of the initial pit, which shows at the right of Section A to A' (Figure I.3.18). Our excavations were not carried far enough to verify this.

Two intrusive slab-lined cists lay over the southeast and southwest walls of the antechamber. The first, the only one nearly completely excavated, was basin-shaped in cross-section and floored with adobe, under which was an earlier floor of flagstones.

Floor Materials (Figure I.3.18, Table I.3.18)

The pithouse was rich with cultural materials, much of it trash. A number of whole items and concentrations of materials, however, suggest viable contexts that probably were associated with the pithouse occupation. Unfortunately, recording of many items was not closely controlled by recording and thus their association with the pithouse use is tentative. Nevertheless, a number of items worth discussing reveal the diversity of materials and the activities that took place in or around the pithouse. Worked bone (n = 16) was relatively common, with numerous awls and beads in various stages of manufacture. Most of the chipped stone was concentrated between the firepit and Posthole 3, marking a possible flintknapper's work area. Two fragments of turquoise and a turquoise pendant were recovered as well as a rare sandstone file that may have been used for ornament production (for others see Judd 1954:123-124; Windes 1993: Table 4.13). In addition, burned selenite was found, which may be used for polishing ornaments (see Windes 1993:168). Turquoise was found scattered throughout the village by Roberts (1929:142), although it is usually rare in early puebloan sites.

Surprisingly, the usual ubiquitous tools associated with food production—manos, metates, and hammerstones—were rare. Manos, common in all the Pueblo II house excavations, were notably absent from our floor excavations. Only two hammerstones and a worn-out metate found in the antechamber attest to possible mealing activities, although the metate last served as a paint palette. Minerals for paint production were recovered from the pithouse as well as palettes exhibiting red and blue paints. The red paint may be related to pottery production; this color (fugitive red) is commonly smeared over the exterior of vessels. Fragments from Lino Fugitive Red vessels were common in the excavations. The yellow and blue paints may indicate use for ritual activities. Two clay pipes were also recovered, from the base of the bench and in Cist 1, which may have had ritual use (e.g., Heitman 2011:187) as well as some unfired clay tables and a pebble pottery polisher. Cist 1 also yielded a projectile point and a blade, apparently items cached along with the pipe.

Other ground stones include a large river cobble that presumably served as a floor polisher—an object common to other early house excavations in this report. Three potlids for small and large vessels suggest that storage jars may have been used in the pithouse. Overall, however, the frequency of ground stone tools was low when compared with the vast numbers recovered from sites in the Pueblo II period.

Dates

Eleven pieces of charcoal from the firepit in Pithouse Y were sent to the Laboratory of Tree-Ring Research. Four pieces (two from the same stick) were dated at A.D. 242vv, 275vv, and 537v (Table I.6.2). It is probable that the "vv" specimens lacked many of the outside rings, but 7v could reflect either structure use or, more likely, deadwood. An archaeomagnetic sample from the firepit, however, yielded a date of A.D. 640 ± 21 (Figure I.6.6, Table I.6.6), which is more in line with the pithouse architectural style (later revised to A.D. 600 ± 21 by DuBois 2008). The house architecture and form closely resemble Pithouses A and D from 29SJ 299 (above), which also date in the A.D. 600s.

Pithouse Z (Figure I.3.18)

An L-shaped test pit dug from 3-6 m east of the Pithouse Y antechamber discovered another structure, Pithouse Z. A floor of the native compacted sand was found 35-40 cm below the old ground surface. An arc of standing slabs outside the test pit probably followed the perimeter of a pitstructure up to 6 m in diameter. The soil within it had been disturbed by earlier digging—probably an unrecorded test by either Roberts or O'Bryan—but the earlier excavation was limited. In following the floor into undisturbed soil we found two nearly complete Lino Gray jars covered in a fugitive red wash. Limited time prevented our extending the test farther.

Discussion

The evidence in the vicinity of Pithouses Y and Z indicates that Pithouse Y was built and occupied first—probably in the late A.D. 500s/early 600s. Some remodeling was done when the passageway to the antechamber was converted to a small vent and step, but the house was abandoned and elements of the superstructure removed for use elsewhere. A period elapsed sufficient for the accumulation of 20 cm of windblown sand before Pithouse Z was built nearby, but a depression in the old pit about 65 cm deep became a trash deposit for the people in the later house. Some of this trash had already accumulated before the two cists were built over Pithouse Y's antechamber. They, and the seven cists plotted around Test Trenches 1 and 2, probably related to the Pithouse Z occupation. The later house was abandoned sometime before the introduction of banded-neck utility ware.

After our revisit to Shabik'eschee, the Laboratory of Tree-Ring Research published the results of a reexamination of charcoal from the site (Robinson et al. 1974). Two of the Gila Pueblo dates were found to be from 172-198 years too late. The cutting date of A.D. 753 from the great kiva now reads 327vv, and the A.D. 750+ date is corrected to 352vv (Table I.6.2). Other wood dates were obtained by Windes after clearing the great kiva bench for archaeomagnetic sampling (see Chapter 6). Two undated specimens collected by Gila Pueblo were dated at 428++vv, and one of Roberts's previously undated pieces rendered a date of 557++vv. No new dates were published for the wood from House H, from which came the Gila Pueblo cutting date of A.D. 757, but if they have the same discrepancy as that of the great kiva charcoal, they, too, may date in the late A.D. 500s. Robinson and his colleagues are confident that the new information dates Shabik'eschee to the sixth century.

The dates from Pithouse Y are consistent with the new readings of the older collections and point to an occupation between about A.D. 550 and A.D. 700. Shabik'eschee's trait assemblage would fit nicely into that span in any district in the Anasazi area, and the site's circumstances are no longer thought to be anomalous.

EXCAVATIONS AT SITE 29SJ 628
Marcia L. Truell (now M. L. Newren)

In 1973, excavations at 29SJ 628 were carried out under the overall field direction of Alden C. Hayes near the juncture of the Fajada and Chaco washes in an area later known as Marcia's Rincon, northwest of Fajada Butte (Plate I.3.44).

Plate I.3.44. Site 29SJ 628, initial excavations in Pithouse A. Fajada Butte and Chacra Mesa in background; Gene Begay, Chee Beyale, and Jimmy Lopez in trench. Looking southeast. Photograph by Marcia Truell, 1973 (CHCU neg. 5912).

The initial intention was to strip the overburden from the entire site surface; however, this deposit proved to be so thick, averaging 40-60 cm, that the entire area could not be cleared to the original ground surface by hand. The majority of the site features could not be detected from surface indications, a factor which led the 1972 survey crew to estimate only a single pithouse in association with six storage cists. Since pithouses similar to those excavated at 29SJ 628 were also found later at nearby 29SJ 627 (McKenna and Truell 1986), 60 m downslope, it appears that there may be other late Basketmaker III and early Pueblo I houses in the intervening and surrounding areas. From evidence recovered in other nearby excavated houses (Truell 1992:13-14; Windes 1993:208), it can be suggested that the entire rincon was intensively settled in late Basketmaker III and early Pueblo I times. The site was located between two later Pueblo II houses (29SJ 627 and 29SJ 629), also excavated during the Chaco Project, at an elevation of 1,896 m (6,220 ft).

Six pithouses and six storage cists were excavated at 29SJ 628 (Figure I.3.19 although others probably remain unidentified. The amount of overburden and the density of occupation made it difficult to directly associate individual pithouses with the six slab-lined storage cists. The excavations were carried out primarily with the help of a Navajo labor crew of Gene Begay, Chee Beyale, and Jimmy Lopez, but sometimes was augmented with laborers from the other site excavations. James Kee later joined the regular crew. Sharon Sullivan and Kellie Masterson provided much-needed volunteer help at the site.

Because of heavy precipitation received during the previous winter, a dense cover of tansy mustard (*Descurania pinnata*) had accumulated throughout the rincon. Where this growth overlays sites, it is a particularly bright green until it turns a dark yellow-brown as it dies. Other prominent cover removed during site clearing included shadscale (*Atriplex confertifolis*), fourwing saltbush (*Atriplex canescens*), snakeweed (*Gutierrezia* spp.), mallow (*Malva* spp.), wild Heliotrope (*Phacelia sericea*), galleta grass (*Hilaria jamesii*), and canaigre/sorrel/dock/wild rhubarb (*Rumex hymenosepalus*). Overlying the sandy overburden, a thin horizon soil had begun to form. The overall diversity of plants and animals found in the greater 29SJ 628 vicinity can be found in A. Cully (1985), J. Cully (1985), and McKenna (1984:6-8).

Excavation Strategy

Generally, the pithouses at 29SJ 628 were excavated in arbitrary 30 cm increments, or levels, with a pie-shaped segment of the house fill being retained for stratigraphic control until the remaining fill had been removed. Half of the fill in each surface storage cist was removed and the remaining fill profiled and then removed.

Only floor contact materials and selected soils were screened. Floor contact materials were dry-screened through eighth-inch mesh whereas fill containing interesting cultural material such as seeds and beads was put through sixteenth-inch screens. In the case of Pithouse C, however,

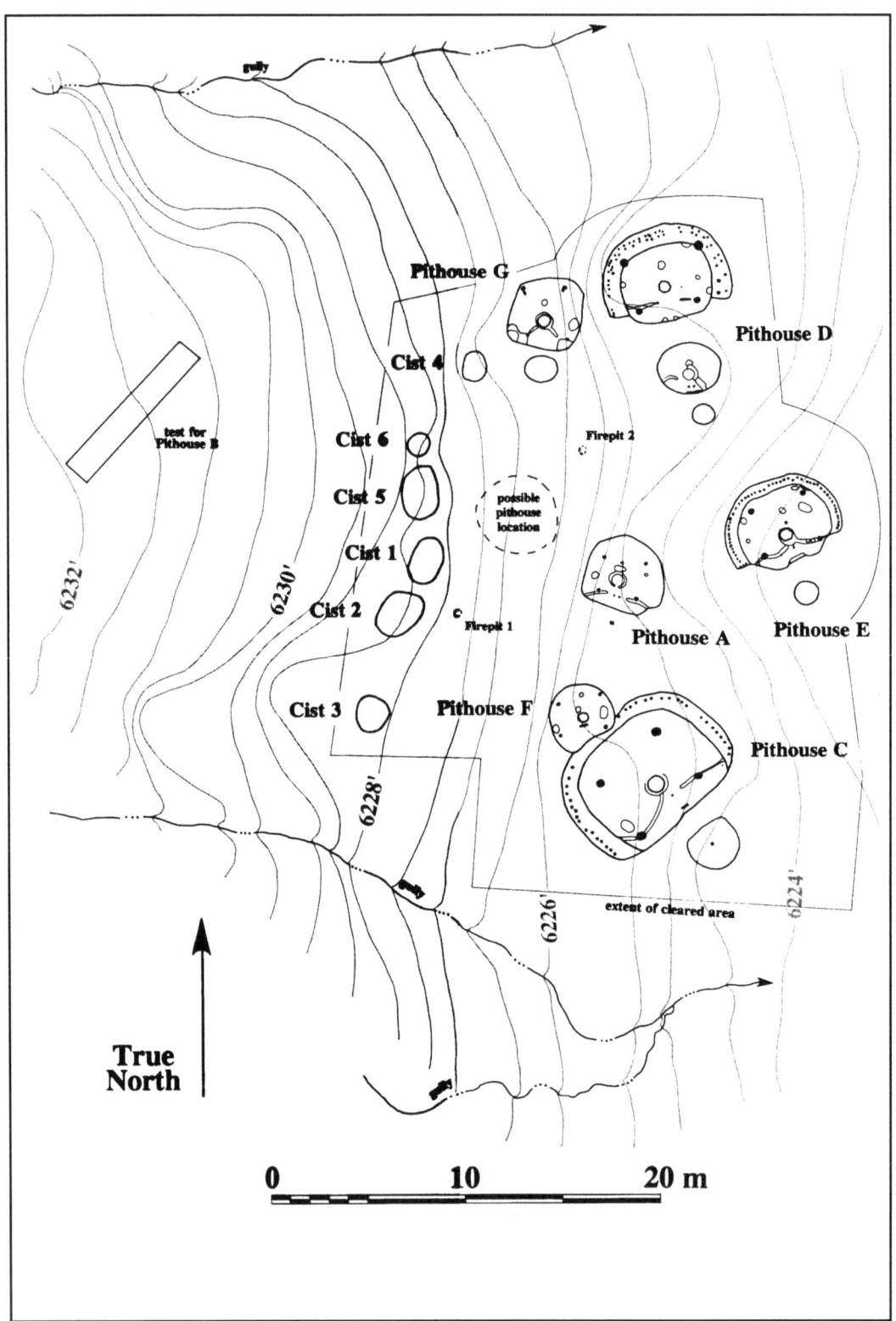

Figure I.3.19. Site 29SJ 628, site plan (CHCU 52664). Contour interval is six inches (15 cm); absolute elevation is approximate. Some pitstructures may remain undiscovered. Originals by Marcia Truell, Tom Windes, and Richard Loose, 1973 (modified from McKenna 1986:Figure 1.11).

only about one fourth of the floor material was screened. Often lower floors were encountered during the excavations, but these were left unexcavated because the site was destined for open viewing and interpretation—an event that has yet to have happened.

The Pithouses

In the examination of the architecture and stratigraphy of the six specific pithouses, each structure discussed below will be presented in the order in which they were interpreted as being constructed, from earliest to latest. The earliest house to be considered is Pithouse C, the largest and most southerly of the excavated group.

Pithouse C
(Figures I.3.20-I.3.21, Plate I.3.45)

Fill in the Main Chamber (Figure I.3.21)

From 58-87 cm of yellow-tan sandy soil resulting from downslope soil movement covered the remaining upper parts of the pithouse walls with the greatest depth above the antechamber. This was removed as one arbitrary excavation unit above the walls, leaving a part that dipped deeper in the center of the structure to be included in the second excavation unit. The thickness of this alluvial deposit diminished steadily across the site to the north as one follows the occupation surface. It appears that Pithouse C lay in a slight depression subsequently concealed by aggradation.

At present, a drainage lies just south of Pithouse C and may have had a prehistoric counterpart in the same vicinity that caused the depression in the southern part of the site before construction of Pithouse C. Although cross-bedding was not noted in native soil forming the Pithouse C walls, downslope excavations at nearby 29SJ 627 in 1974 and 1975 revealed waterlain deposits in the lower room walls at

Plate I.3.45. Site 29SJ 628, Pithouse C after clearing. Looking south. Photograph by Marcia Truell, 1973 (CHCU neg. 5979).

the southern end of the roomblock in Rooms 1, 6, and 11 (Truell 1992). These rooms lie in the same relative position to the present drainage as Pithouse C at 29SJ 628, suggesting that an old drainage caused the depression where Pithouse C was built.

The greatest depth of the Pithouse C overburden lay above the west walls of the antechamber. Beneath the alluvial layer in the main chamber was a thick, rich, gooey deposit of trash interfingered with lenses of washed, cross-bedded sands. The second excavation unit, 40-45 cm thick, removed this deposit from the top of the walls to the bench top. The trash was composed of brown, sandy soil with flecks and small chunks of charcoal scattered throughout. Many pieces of adobe construction material, often retaining their turtleback construction-block shape, were found in this layer. Roughly 1,500 sherds and 1,900 pieces of bone were recovered along with numerous other materials from the trash, which constituted the majority of the house fill. This trash layer is estimated to have comprised 22 m^3 of the 29-30 m^3 space within the house if the original ground surface is considered the top of the walls. Based on this calculation, the average artifact density for all artifacts is approximately 270 artifacts/m^3 of trash.

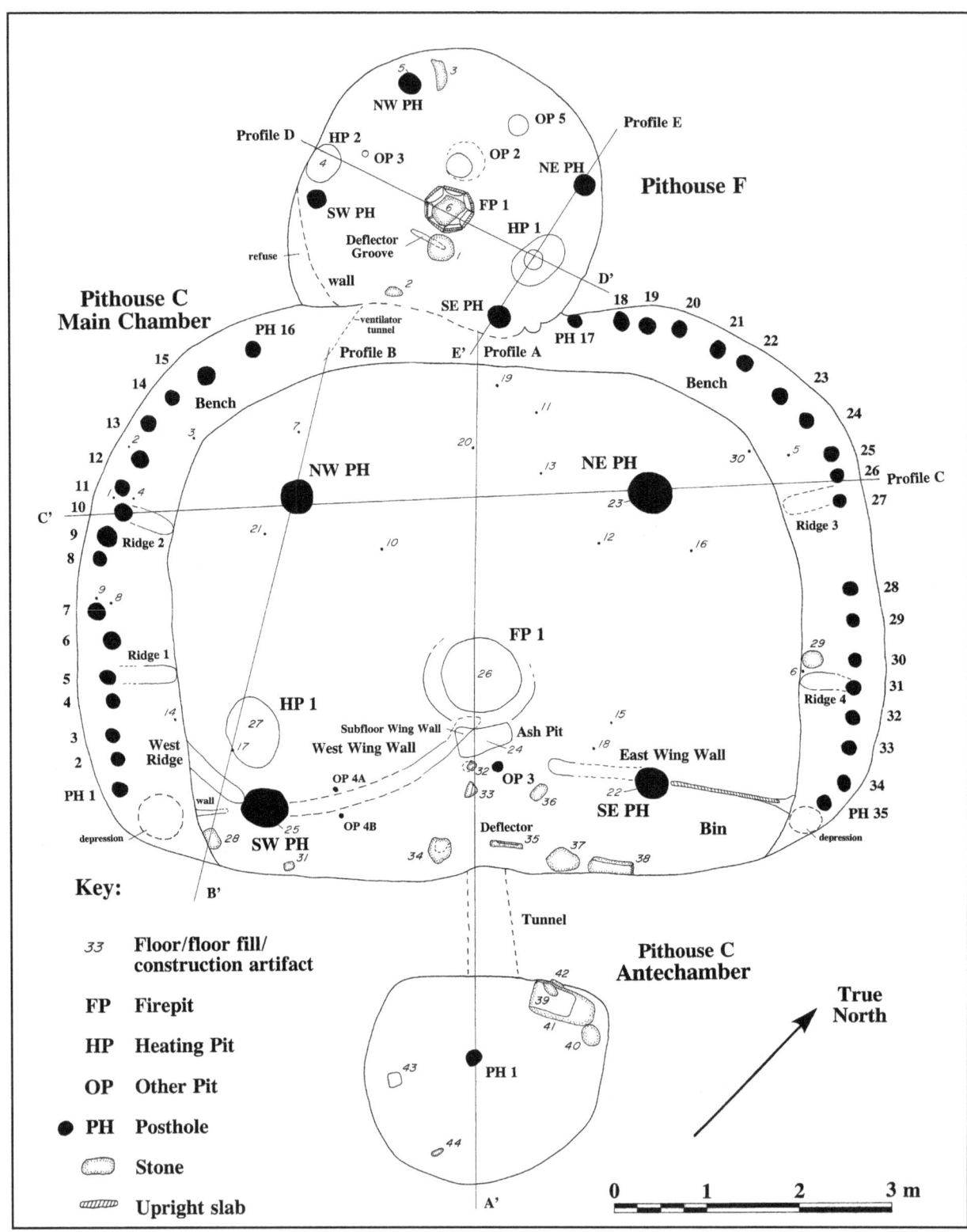

Figure I.3.20. Site 29SJ 628, Pithouses C and F plans and distribution of floor fill and floor materials (CHCU 55542). See Tables I.3.19, I.3.21, I.3.26 for the lists of specimens. Original by Marcia Truell and Richard Loose, 1973.

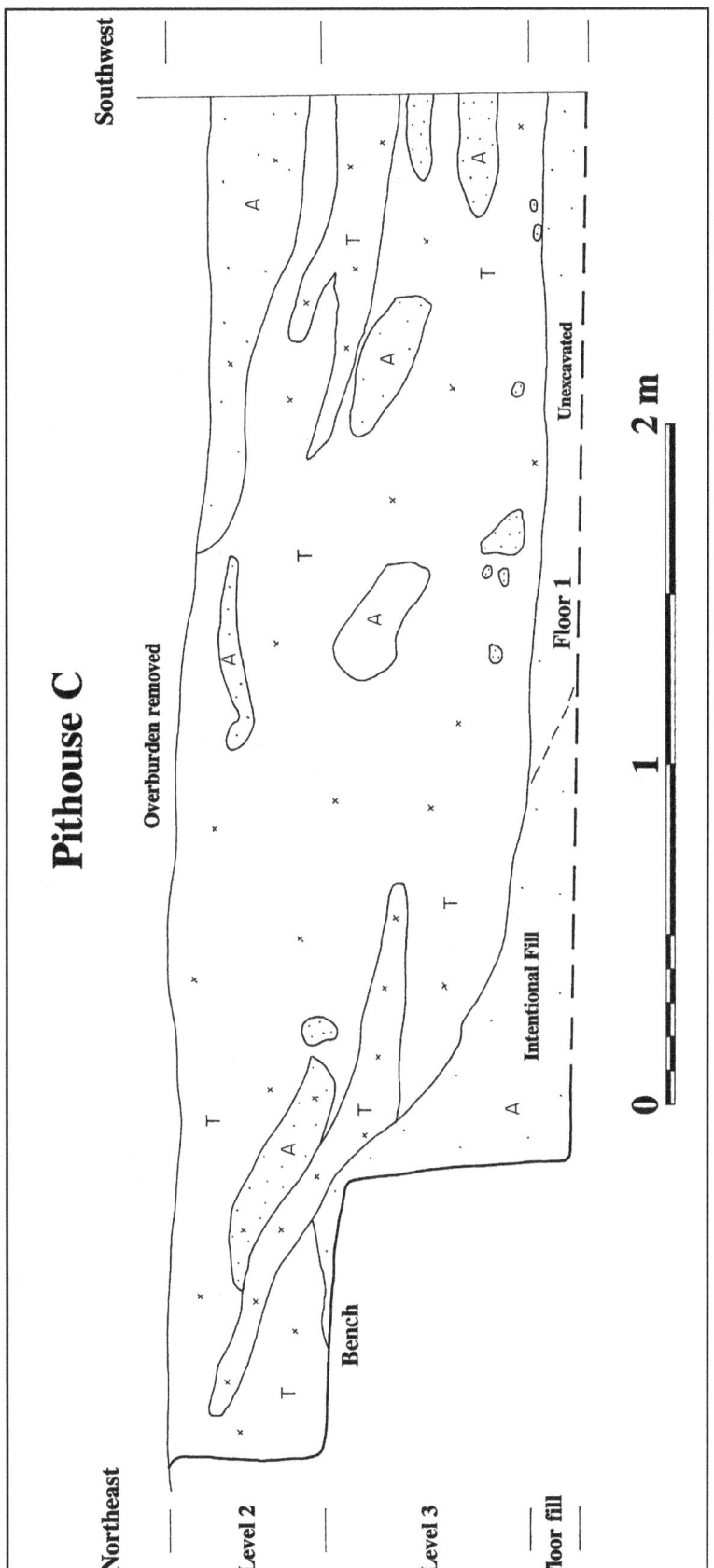

Figure I.3.21. Site 29SJ 628, Pithouse C, profile of fill (CHCU 65969). Location of this profile not marked in Figure I.3.20; see Figure I.3.22 for marked profiles. Original by Marcia Truell, 1973.

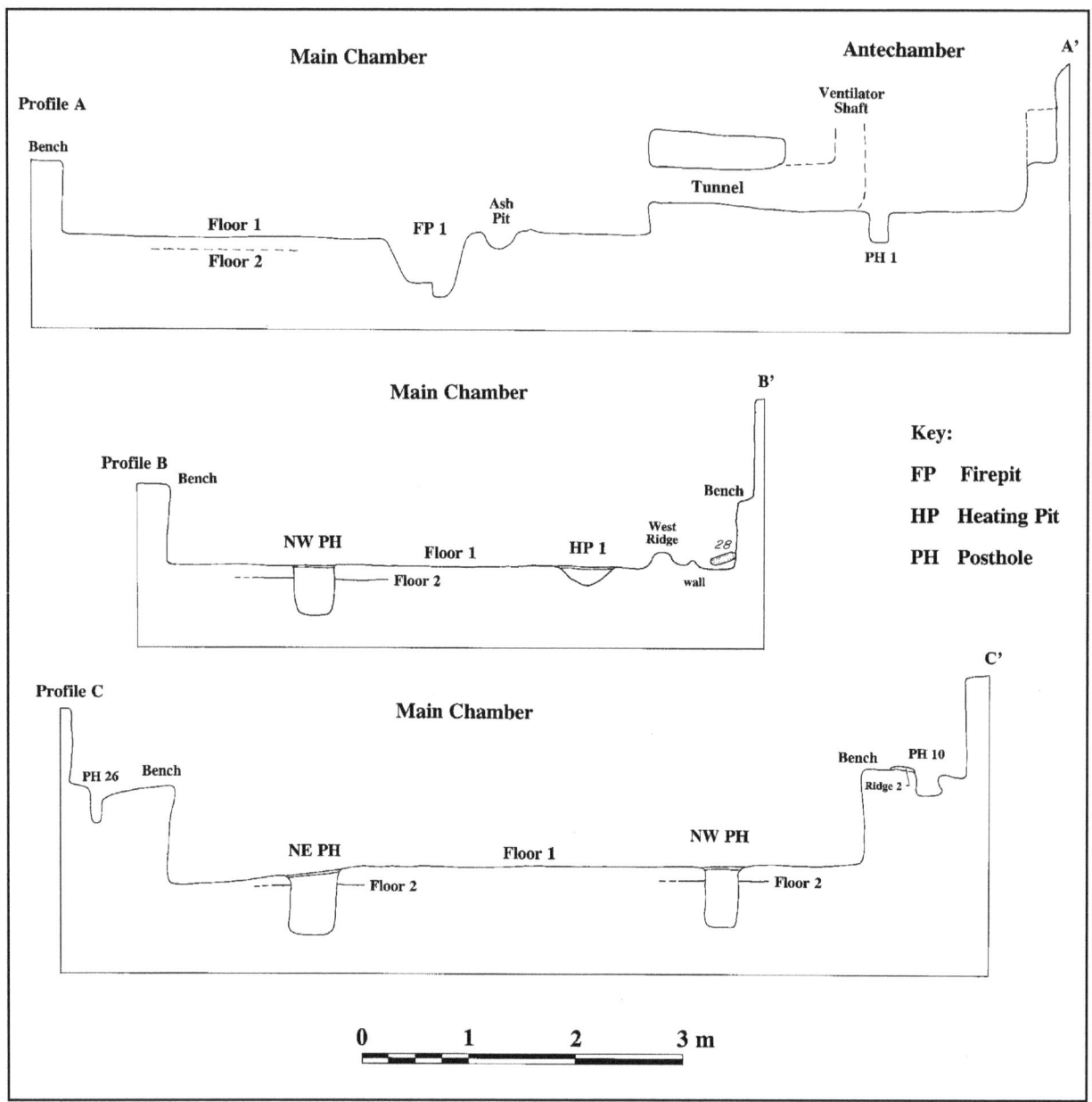

Figure I.3.22. Site 29SJ 628, Pithouse C architectural profiles (CHCU 55544). Original by Marcia Truell, 1973.

Despite areas of complexity in this trash layer, the deposit had a consistent organic content throughout the fill, and possibly represented a short period of accumulation. The majority of pottery recorded was Lino Gray and largely Pueblo I whitewares.

Beneath this trash was a stratum of yellow-tan fill that resembled the overburden material and had accumulated in mounds against the bench along the north and west walls—the upslope sides of the structure—and extended out onto the floor about 140 cm. This deposit varied in thickness from 65 cm-100 cm with an estimated volume of between 7 and 8 m^3. This stratum was removed as the third excavation unit along with the remaining trash layer described above. Artifact density within this tan sand layer was very low but was not calculated. Occasional cross-bedded lenses were evident, suggesting accumulation of waterlain material which filled the structure after removal of the roof. A large part of this layer showed no sign of being alluvial material and may have been intentional fill derived from excavation of another pithouse in the vicinity.

A fourth deposit of bright orange-yellow sand, generally only a couple of centimeters in depth, covered the upper floor in a continuous layer. Its distinctive bright yellow color and even distribution over the floor contrasts with the tan alluvial sand that had washed into the house. This medium- to fine-grained yellow sand was found repeatedly on the floors of Basketmaker pithouses excavated in Chaco in 1973 and is a common occurrence in puebloan pithouses of the period (e.g., Adams 1951:277; Allen and McNutt 1955:246; Kidder and Guersey 1919:72); Morris 1959:29). Alden Hayes (personal communication 1973) reported finding similar deposits on pithouse floors at Badger House, Mesa Verde, in Pithouses A, B, and G (see Hayes and Lancaster 1975:7).

No evident function has been attached to this apparently intentionally spread layer of material. It is possible that this material was used in the floor plastering process or that it may have been spread on floors like sawdust in a butcher's shop. The floor contact material, treated as a discrete unit, consisted of the 15 cm of material overlying the floor, including trash in the center of the house and along the southern wall, blown sand along the northern wall, and the bright yellow sand which covered the entire floor.

Fill in the Antechamber

The antechamber was dug in three levels: the upper two were each 40 cm thick while the lowest—the floor fill—was 13-15 cm thick. The deepest deposits of overburden for the entire site, 46-87 cm thick, overlay the antechamber. The majority of this was removed as Level 1, which began 46 cm below the ground surface on the southeast side. Material above this had been removed during testing for the antechamber. The second level consisted of hard clay matrix and stone artifacts which had filled the antechamber when it had been remodeled into a ventilator shaft. The stone had been thrown into the antechamber in a haphazard fashion and filled the chamber all the way from the floor to the top of the walls, level with the original ground surface (Plate I.3.46). The remaining fill of stone and clay went to the floor and was removed as Level 3. There was no evidence of the bright yellow sand that was seen in the main chamber.

Floor of the Main Chamber

The uppermost floor was a gray, shale-derived clay plaster about 3 cm in thickness. Beneath it was a second floor 15-19 cm below the first, composed of the same clay. The second floor was not cleared and was only observed in a small test pit. A light, sandy trash formed the fill between these surfaces, and a thin layer of bright yellow sand also overlay the lower floor.

The structure was large by contemporary standards, measuring 872 cm (east-west) by 610 cm (north-south) in the main chamber (38 m^2)

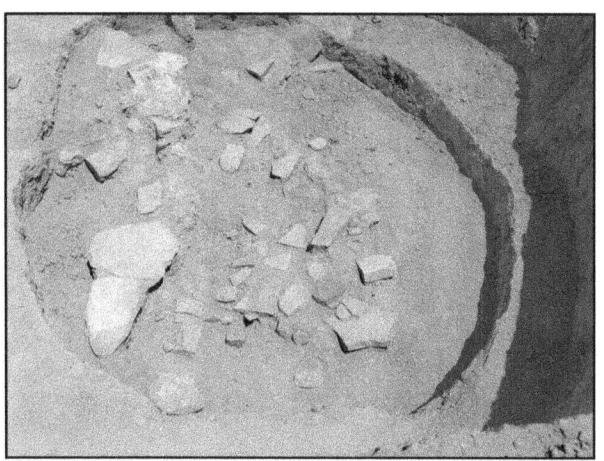

Plate I.3.46. Site 29SJ 628, Pithouse C antechamber intentional stone fill. Secondary ventilator shaft (unexcavated) in approximate center of the stone concentration. Looking east. 30-cm north arrow. Photograph by Marcia Truell, 1973 (CHCU neg. 5964).

Plate I.3.47. Site 29SJ 628, Pithouse C, after clearing antechamber. Note posthole in center of floor, the metate and floor polishers in the corner, and the floor mano. Looking northwest. Photograph by Marcia Truell, 1973 (CHCU neg. 5971).

and 255 cm (east-west) by 230 cm (north-south) in the antechamber (5.1 m²) before remodeling.

Floor Materials (Figure I.3.20, Table I.3.19)

A number of artifacts were found scattered across the floor and bench-top surfaces. Although some may be attributable to postoccupational refuse, the ground stone and bone tools were probably left behind at abandonment as tools of low value that could be easily replaced. Fifteen bone tools, including 13 awls, were left concentrated in the north half of the main structure, including several on the bench. None were left in the antechamber or behind the wing wall area. Conversely, ground stone was left exclusively in the southern part of the main chamber, behind the wing wall, and in the antechamber (Plate I.3.47). These distinctions in tool distribution suggest specific work areas and a continuity of widely established norms throughout the Anasazi region where similar tool locations have been noted in other contemporary structures.

Floor Features (Tables I.3.20-I.3.21)

Despite the size of the floor, there were few floor features. A large central adobe-lined firepit was found filled with yellow and burned purple sand containing very little charcoal. It had an indistinct base where excavation ceased, and the highly burned rim was flush with the floor, unlike others at the site that coped up above the floor. The upper 35 cm of the pit's interior walls were also heavily oxidized.

Archaeomagnetic samples taken from the rim yielded a DuBois date of A.D. 760 ± 40 (Figure I.6.12, Table I.6.6), later revised to A.D. 720 ± 40 (DuBois 2008). A radiocarbon corrected age (A.D. 730 ± 60; Table I.6.4) from the burned brush contents temporally supports the archaeomagnetic date. About 10 cm below the rim was another highly burned fire pit rim that probably went with a lower floor, although it was not sampled.

An upright metate remained in place about 25 cm from the ventilator tunnel opening in the main room, offset slightly to the northeast of center of the opening, and may have served as the deflector. The trough metate was set in the floor and reinforced by a slight plaster coping on the tunnel side, with the metate's grinding surface facing the room interior.

The efficiency of the possible deflector slab is subject to question. Its location 142 cm from the fire pit and offset enough to prevent blocking the draft from the ventilator tunnel makes it inefficient. Perhaps there had originally been another slab adjacent to the first, or perhaps a jacal or wood framework constituted the west end of the feature, despite the lack of evidence. The area between the slab and the fire pit had been disturbed by rodent burrowing, but 55 cm from the fire pit was a small hole (11 cm in diameter and 9 cm deep) that could have been part of a deflector. When the antechamber was converted into a ventilator, roof entry was necessary. Often ladder access through the fire pit smoke hole is evident by ladder pits that in this area had been disturbed by rodents, but except for the single pit, these ladder marks were not evident.

Just southeast of the fire pit was an irregularly shaped trough ash pit filled with burned sand, a small amount of charcoal, and quantities of white/gray ash. The brush charcoal yielded a corrected radiocarbon age of A.D. 420 ± 70 (Table I.6.4), which is archaeologically much too early. The pit bottom was formed by the lower floor, and a piece of the lower floor wing wall, roughly 9 cm wide and 5 cm high, ran across one corner. Despite its distinctive outline, the pit was neither plastered nor burned. Alden Hayes (personal communication 1973) says it is unusual to find ash pits in houses this early and notes that the burned fill may have been a secondary utilization of the pit. He suggests that the deflector slab was originally seated in this hole but had been pulled out and the hole subsequently used as an ash pit.

Just north of the southwest wing wall segment was an oval, plaster-lined heating pit. It was burned, although not intensively, to a depth of about 11 cm below the rim. An intentional plug of gray plaster like that used for the floor sealed the pit, which remained filled almost to its rim with burned sand. Burned brush from the pit contents yielded a corrected radiocarbon age of A.D. 620 ± 50 (Table I.6.4), which seems a century too early based on other chronometric dates from the site.

The four main postholes that seated the principal roof supports were large and deep (Table I.3.21). All lacked shims but had quantities of shale packing, which presumably held the posts in place. Except for the southwest hole, the shale packing extended between the two floors and, in all cases, three-quarters of the way around each postmold. The packing also extended for some distance out under the uppermost floor. An advantage of using shale packing, in addition to its local availability, is that it is fairly resistant to shrinkage.

All four postholes had been plastered over flush with the uppermost floor. This plaster was an intentional cap placed over these holes, not merely a sheet of washed clay which might have naturally formed after abandonment. No identifiable offerings were found within these postholes, although ceramics were common (see Table I.3.19). It appears that trash was thrown into the holes just before they were plugged.

Wing walls extended to the firepit from the pithouse walls, but both were in poor condition. An upright slab, 34 cm high, 93 cm long, and 3-5 cm thick, had been plastered into the floor and constituted the primary remains of the east wing wall. The western extent of the former wall was marked by a small pinnacle of plaster 33 cm high and 12-13 cm wide. A small indentation in it may have marked a former secondary post support. Most of the wall's original position could be traced from a break in the floor plaster, which indicated an original wall length of about 265 cm. The west wing wall remains consisted of gray, clay plaster 15 cm wide, 13-20 cm high, and 89 cm long that was progressively shorter as it extended toward the posthole. It ran to the northwestern edge of the southwest post seat from the southwestern part of the bench but was not parallel to the south room wall as the east wing wall had been.

To the south of the west wing wall was a very small, short, thin wall about 28 cm long and 16 cm high where it joined the bench. About 28 cm from the bench, this gray plaster merged with the floor. The function of this small partition is unknown. Another low plaster ridge about 3 cm high and 12 cm wide radiated out a short distance from the west side of the ash-filled pit, south of the firepit, and may at one time have extended to the east edge of the southwest post seat as part of the wing wall. Despite the disturbed nature of the floor, two small holes a few centimeters deep seem to indicate where this eastern segment had been. A similar ridge found below in the ash-filled pit for the lower floor suggests that the feature position and morphology were replicated when the structure floor was resurfaced.

Walls. Pithouse C was dug into native soil but apparently the antechamber walls and much of the walls behind the bench were never plastered. Occasionally, these surfaces were stained by the trash that had been thrown into the abandoned house. Because of the large mass of consolidated adobe which spilled down over the central section of the south wall, it was difficult to determine whether the south wall had been plastered while the structure was in use.

Wall Features (Table I.3.20)

There was little modification of the house walls except for those relating to bench and roof support and the entry/ventilating system.

The upper part of the pithouse walls had been cut back 90 cm into the native soil leaving a shelf 90 cm above the floor. The vertical face of this feature is relatively perpendicular to the house floor, but the roughly horizontal bench top slopes downward as it approaches the pithouse walls. Both the top and bench face were covered with two coats of gray clay plaster.

Three, and probably four, low, loaf-shaped, plaster ridges about 50+cm long, 20 cm wide, and 6 cm high ran from the front partly across the bench top. These appeared to have been paired; the eastern two being approximately 180 cm apart and the western ones 143 cm apart. All of them were adjacent to leaner holes and did not continue beyond the holes to the house walls. The function of these unique features is unknown.

Thirty-five postholes in the bench, which would have accommodated the leaning members of the roof framework, were set in a line 45-65 cm back from the bench face. Several more holes were removed along the northwestern side when Pithouse F was constructed. In addition, a small gap in the line of holes along the eastern side may be attributed to rodent disturbance. If the existing spacing of leaner holes was maintained through the disturbed areas, then 45 or 46 holes would have been originally present. On the average, the holes were 14-20 cm in diameter and 11 cm deep. An inward pitch of about 45° from the vertical was noted in several of the holes. The remainder were vertical; possibly the poles were set in sand or packed in some fashion which did not affect the vertical edges of the holes.

Ventilator System

The ventilator tunnel extended through the southeast wall for 120 cm before entering the antechamber. It was 35 cm wide and 33 cm high at the opening into the main structure and flush with the wall but widened to 55 cm at entry into the antechamber. The base of the tunnel was about 30 cm above the main floor but was even with the antechamber floor. There was no noticeable slope to the tunnel floor, which was surfaced with a thick coat of gray-shale-derived plaster. The antechamber was eventually filled in with rubble, leaving a secondary ventilator shaft that extended to the surface from the antechamber center (Plate I.3.46).

A large slab which had been used as a lintel was found in a slightly slumped position in the roof of the tunnel opening, although there were no signs of beam holes or other supports along the interior. It is possible that other slabs that once formed the floor of the passageway between the main chamber and the antechamber were left to roof the tunnel, but they are no longer evident. Nevertheless, some structural support for the tunnel roof would have been necessary during remodeling because of the prior existence of the passageway.

Antechamber (Plate I.3.47)

The elevation of the antechamber floor prior to remodeling indicates that it was associated with the upper floor of the main chamber. Thus, a second, lower, floor may have existed in the antechamber which we did not excavate. The upper floor was plastered, like the main room, with gray, shale-clay plaster covered with a layer of yellow sand, although only small areas of it were cleared during our excavation.

A single, vertical, plaster-lined hole (PH 1; 15 cm in diameter) was found in the antechamber just north of the room's center. A post impression was visible along one side of the hole interior. Since there was no sign of a lateral entrance, the posthole may have been for a single-pole entry ladder but also may have served as a central roof support for a pitched antechamber roof, which would have resembled that postulated by Roberts (1929:12, Figure 2) with an access through the side of the leaning roof members. It may also have served as a rack and for other multiple functions.

Roofing. No roof material was recovered from the structure, suggesting that the roof had been stripped for use elsewhere after abandonment. The postholes, however, indicate a roofing scheme like that postulated by Roberts (1929:12, Figure 2). An adobe wall along and above the south wall of the main chamber would have accommodated the leaning members of the roof above where the bench was absent. No indications for a superstructure over the entryway at the top of the walls could be discerned, but a single posthole centered in the antechamber suggests use of a conical roof resembling that illustrated by Roberts (1929: Figure 2).

Pithouse D
(Figures I.3.23-I.3.24, Plates I.3.48-I.3.49)

Pithouse D had a number of features that distinguished it from other houses at the site. It is unique in that it had both an antechamber and ventilator system which functioned simultaneously. In addition, a large, dish-shaped clay surface lay over the trash-filled structure just below the original ground surface.

Fill in the Main Chamber

The top of the main room walls lay directly beneath the clay surface a few centimeters below the present ground surface. This very shallow, 15-cm-deep, overburden contrasted sharply with the correspondingly thick deposit which overlay Pithouse C. The clay surface consisted of gray clay similar to that used for the bench and floors at the site. This deposit ranged from 5-15 cm thick and precisely covered the 4.8-m-diameter main chamber, ceasing at the edge of the walls underneath. Whether this feature was cultural or a natural phenomenon formed from ponded clays could not be determined, although its symmetrical nature and correspondence with the house walls suggests the former. It may have been a clay mixing pit, although it seems too large and shallow for such use. It may have functioned as a surface for drying vegetal material. A similar cap was found over Pithouse D at 29SJ 299 (this chapter), overlaying parts of a burned roof. Loose felt that this feature was formed from roofing material that had eventually ponded. There was also a similar cap next to Pithouse E at 29SJ 299 (Chapter 4).

About 140-160 cm of fill existed between the 29SJ 628 cap and the pithouse floor. Directly beneath the clay surface was a series of alternating

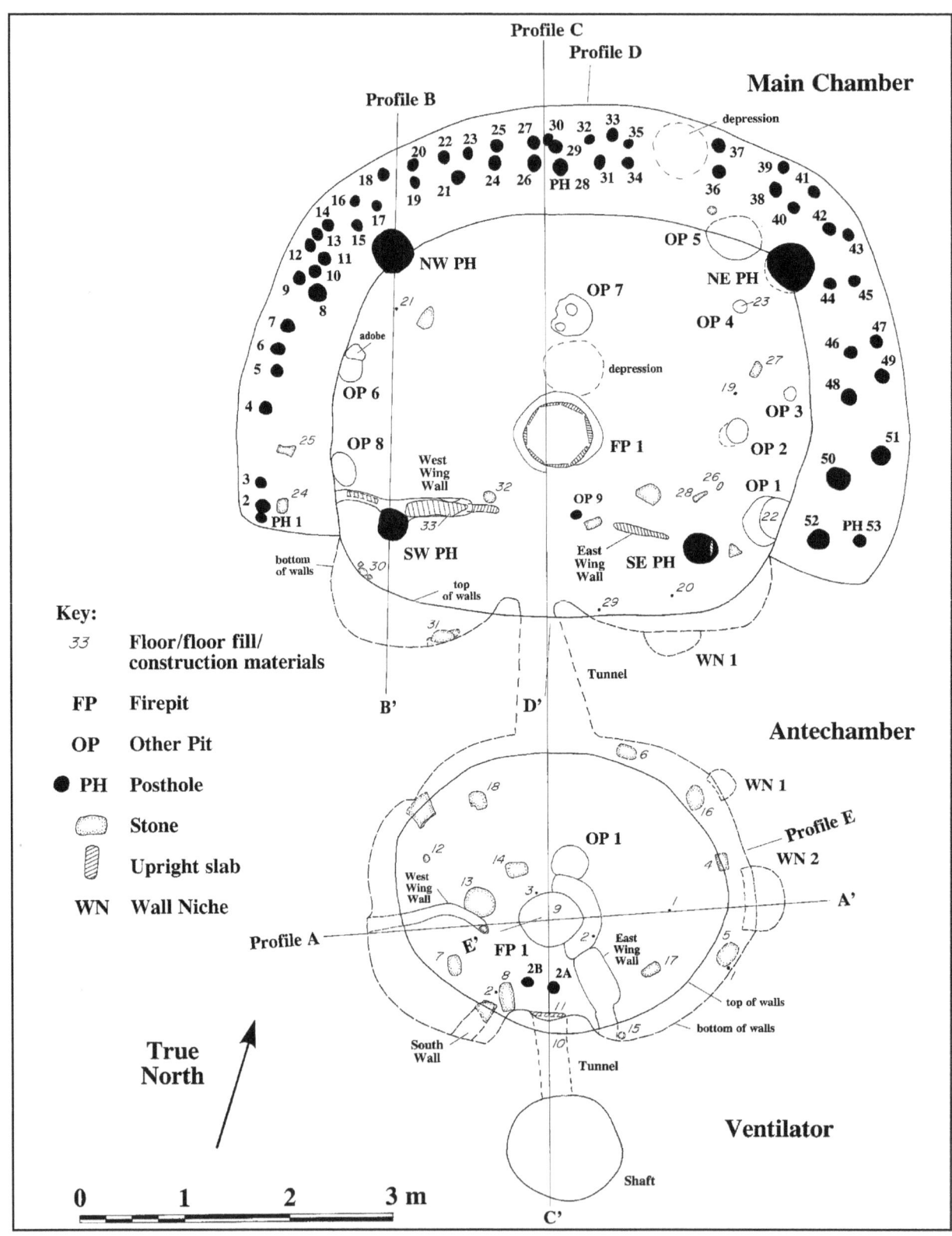

Figure I.3.23. Site 29SJ 628, Pithouse D plan and distribution of floor fill, floor, and construction specimens (see Table I.3.22 for the list of specimens) (CHCU 55548). Original by Marcia Truell, 1973.

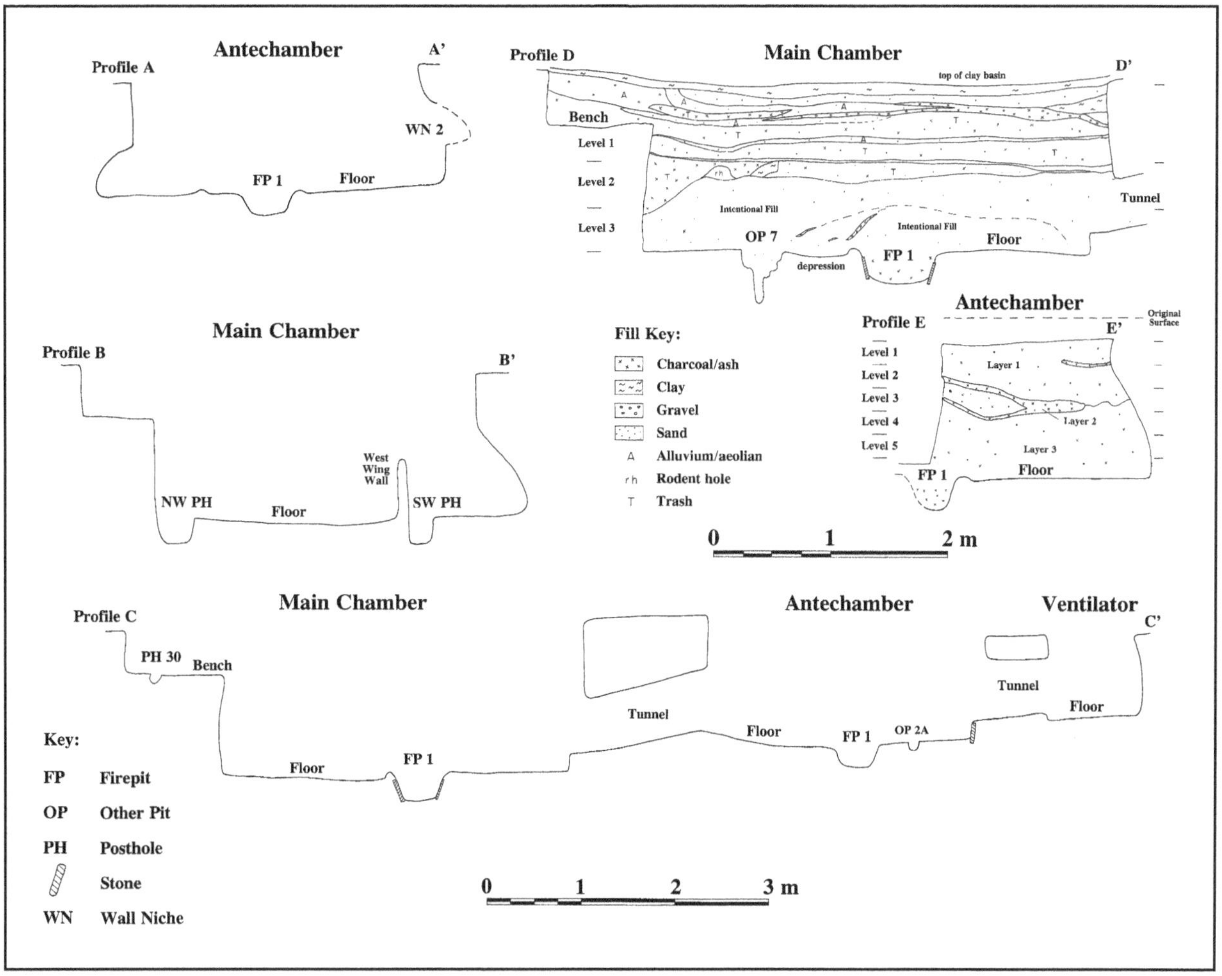

Figure I.3.24. Site 29SJ 628, Pithouse D architectural and fill profiles (CHCU 55550). Original by Marcia Truell, 1973.

Plate I.3.48. Site 29SJ 628, Pithouse D after clearing. Looking southwest. Photograph by Marcia Truell, 1973 (CHCU neg. 6026).

Plate I.3.49. Site 29SJ 628, Pithouse D antechamber after clearing. Note firepit in antechamber and ventilator opening to the upper right. Looking southeast. Photograph by Marcia Truell, 1973 (CHCU neg. 5996).

layers of washed sand and clay that continued for about 60-80 cm and 25 cm below the bench top. Some layers of very fine sands may have been wind-transported materials, but the majority of clay and sand contained a good deal of medium-grained sand and charcoal and appeared to have been water-deposited. Within this unit, directly beneath the clay cap, was part of a human cranium. Perhaps this cranium was associated with the placement of the clay cap, although given the natural appearance of the deposit, it seems unlikely.

A layer of dark, charcoal-stained soil was present beneath these natural strata, which probably represented the last cultural use of the abandoned house. This trash deposit was located directly adjacent to the bench along the north side of the house and did not appear to have been burned in place.

A less concentrated deposit of trash was encountered beneath the one above and characterized the remainder of the structure fill, 55-60 cm deep. This trash contained less organic material than the lens above it, and the upper part was surprisingly flat. The lower part of the layer contained two distinctive, centrally located mounds of trash, which, although similar to the upper parts in content and appearance, were segregated by a series of thin, dark-brown, concentrated charcoal lenses that outlined the two episodes. Again, the lenses do not appear to have been burned in place but rather were basal deposits from a basket load that was thrown in. The house floor was covered with a thin layer of yellow sand identical to that in Pithouse C.

The deposits described above were removed in four arbitrary units (see Figure I.3.24). Levels 1 and 2 were 60-cm-deep units, the first corresponding with the beginning of natural deposits directly under the clay cap. Level 2 included the concentrated trash along the north bench face and the upper part of the lighter trash within the lower part of the structure. This level yielded the only datable tree-ring specimen from the site (A.D. 674 vv; Table I.6.2). Level 3 was 20-25 cm deep and contained light trash, including the two mounded dumps. Finally, the floor fill resting directly on the floor was removed as a 10-15 cm thick unit that included the yellow sand and some light trash. The overall depth of the main chamber was 160-165 cm deep.

Fill in the Antechamber (Figure I.3.24)

Naturally deposited, yellow-tan, sandy soil with scattered charcoal flecks constituted the majority of the fill in the antechamber, which was excavated in five arbitrary, 20-cm-deep levels with the 15 cm of floor fill as a sixth level. Overall, the antechamber was 118-122 cm deep. The only exceptions to natural deposition found in the fill were a thin lens of pure yellow sand at the base of Level 1 and a dark, branching trash lens in Levels 3 and 4. Overall, a slight increase in charcoal density coincided with increasing depth starting at the base of Level 3 at about 60 cm below the original ground surface. The latter was a mere 5-10 cm below the present site surface. Indented corrugated sherds recovered from Levels 2 and 3 attest to the slow in-filling of the antechamber.

Fill in the Ventilator

The ventilator tunnel, which was connected to the antechamber, and the ventilator shaft were filled with yellow sandy soil flecked with charcoal similar to that in the other two chambers. The shaft was about 85 cm deep. There was little cultural debris in the fill.

Floor in the Main Chamber

The floor area of Pithouse D was approximately 15.4 m² (excluding the bench) and measured 490 cm (north-south) by 630 cm (east-west), including the bench. The floor was plastered with gray clay, 10-20 cm thick, and covered with fine yellow sand that was probably an intentional deposit.

The overall floor was in good condition, and no lower floors were discovered.

Floor Materials (Figure I.3.23, Table I.3.22)

Few items were recovered off the floor: an antler tip with a drilled base, a turquoise fragment, two bone awls, three polishing stones, two sandstone slabs, and the bottom of a vessel. These were widely scattered and do not suggest specific activity areas.

Floor Features (Tables I.3.20 and I.3.21)

Features similar to those encountered in Pithouse C were also present in Pithouse D. Overall, 14 features in the main chamber floor took up 0.9 m² of the floor area. The circular firepit was rimmed by an adobe collar 10 cm wide and 4 cm high, extending above the surrounding floor. Eight upright stone slabs constituted the firepit walls but its floor was unlined. The pit was highly oxidized and filled nearly to the rim with yellow and burned-purple sand similar to many other hearths at the site. The burned color of the sand has been attributed to a high iron content. Charcoal and carbonized corncobs were found in the fill, generally in higher quantities than from other site hearths. An archaeomagnetic sample from the hearth was dated by DuBois at A.D. 770 ± 33 (Figure I.6.13, Table I.6.6), but later revised to 740 ± 33 (DuBois 2008). No deflector was found.

Obvious pits for ladder seats in the main chamber were not found, although the small depression between the firepit and ventilator might have served this purpose. This shallow pit, 40 cm south of the firepit, however, is more likely the west end of the west wing wall (see below). Besides, the ladder rests in the antechamber attest to the entry route via the ventilator shaft.

Five large other pits were set around the margins of the main floor. These were all filled with clean yellow-tan sand, probably postoccupational, and were unplastered except for OP 1. Three small pits were clustered on the east side of the floor, but one of these, OP 4, contained some lignite and may have been an auxiliary posthole. OP 7, north of the firepit, was possibly the sipapu. A shallow depression on the bench may have served as a pot rest. It is difficult to assign a function to the majority of pits. The larger ones, generally set against the walls and out of the way, probably served for storage. The shape of OP 5 suggests that it once held a jar.

Four large postholes—two in the wing walls and two set into the edge of the northern part of the bench—served as the primary roof support holes (Table I.3.21). None of the poles set in the bench (see below) or posts remained when excavated. Except for the southeast primary post support, all were filled with crushed lignite, a typical Chacoan pattern. OP 4, may have been for an auxiliary post set under the eastern stringer because it, too, contained lignite and was cylindrical in shape.

Originally, two thin wing walls of adobe and thin stone slabs snaked out from the southeastern and southwestern corners toward each other, each incorporating a primary roof support. Only an upright slab, 50 cm long, 8 cm wide, 43 cm high, and still held in place by a bit of plaster coping, marked the eastern wing wall. A small floor pit west of the slab may mark the end post for the missing jacal remains at the western end.

The western wing wall remained intact and was composed of three large, upright slabs—one a complete trough metate—set into the floor and covered with a thick coat of gray plaster. A wide fillet of clay, shaped like a sausage, ran along the top of the wall to finish the upper surface. The wing wall was 44-57 cm high, with the shorter end at the east. It was 7-14 cm wide and 138 cm long, although the appearance of the eastern end suggests it might have been longer. An odd, circular depression, about 20 cm across, was noted in the upper part of the wall on the north side about 40 cm from the eastern end.

Walls in the Main Chamber

Walls were formed of native soil into which the structure had been dug. Where the bench was absent along the south side of the main room, the wall bellied out as it neared the floor on either side of the antechamber passageway. The same plaster material used for the bench covered the wall in this area up to a height of 100-110 cm above the floor, or equivalent with the top of the bench. Otherwise, the walls above the bench level were left unplastered.

Wall Features

A bench 102-160 cm high, 90-100 cm wide, and covering 10 m² encircled three-quarters of the main chamber. Along the back part of the bench top was an arc of small postholes used to seat poles that leaned against the main roof stringers. The majority of the 53 holes formed a double arc that suggest partial rebuilding of the roof with the leaners offset from their original positions. The northern main roof supports were partly set into the bench face, but the bench was not plastered behind where the roof posts had been set. A mano and a sandstone slab covered in red paint were found on the bench.

A single niche was built into the wall at floor level in the southeastern corner. Postoccupational sands filled the cavity. Although it was not lined, its walls were distinguished by small red-brown spots. It could have been used for a limited amount of storage.

Tunnel Connecting the Main Chamber and the Antechamber

An oval tunnel, 30-50 cm wide, 60 cm high, and about 125 cm long, connected the two chambers but would have forced occupants to crawl or shuffle stooped over between them. The floor of the passage was flush with the main chamber but was elevated about 20 cm above the antechamber, where it widened to 70 cm and became more arched as it progressed. The entire tunnel interior was plastered with gray plaster. There were no signs of internal wall or roof supports.

Antechamber (Plate I.3.49)

The antechamber floor was plastered with the usual gray-shale plaster and was in good condition with little evidence of wear and repair. A number of manos, hammerstones, and an ax fragment, lap anvil, metate fragment, and half of a red shale pendant on the floor attest to storage or a diverse set of activities in the room.

The firepit was shallow and circular with an adobe collar and located south of the room center. It was not slab-lined and only burned along the top and 10 cm below the rim. Charcoal and burned corncobs were recovered throughout the fill, but generally it consisted of a marbled mixture of yellow and oxidized-to-purple sand. Part of the 20-cm wide rim collar was replastered on the east side, while the west side exhibited no collar and was flush with the floor. An archaeomagnetic sample taken from the firepit rim did not date (Figure I.6.13, Table I.6.6).

Two pits, presumably to support a ladder, were found 18 cm north of the connecting tunnel and 34 cm south of the firepit. They were only 15 cm apart, seemingly not far enough apart for a ladder, and filled with clean, postoccupational sand. A single basin-shaped pit on the north side of the firepit could have been a pot rest. It was filled with postoccupational sands and was analogous in position to one in Pithouse A.

Dissimilar, low clay ridge wing walls extended from the walls toward the firepit. The southeastern one connected to the firepit rim and was 5 cm high, 30 cm wide, and more than 76 cm long. The part where it once joined the wall was missing. The southwestern one did not extend to the firepit and was approximately 10 cm wide, 6 cm high and more than 115 cm long. Its position relative to the other clay ridge and to the ventilator is considerably offset. No mention in the notes is made of another feature that more closely mirrors the southeastern wing wall in shape and position. The southwestern ridge extends out from the wall only a short distance before terminating, although it might once have also connected to the firepit.

Walls in the Antechamber

The antechamber walls were not vertical but flared outward as they reached the floor. None appeared to have been plastered, although the walls were highly compacted. Two cavities were located in the northern part of the antechamber. The lower one, Niche A, was a mere 15 cm above the floor and was a questionable feature. The other, Niche B, was larger and sat 45 cm above the floor. Its walls were compacted and easily defined, unlike those in Niche A. Both were filled with postoccupational sands.

Ventilator System

A ventilator system extended south from the antechamber, making the house a string of three separate chambers. The oval tunnel, 32-56 cm wide, 59-62 cm high, and 76 cm long, entered the antechamber where the wall bulged inward 16-17 cm towards the firepit. The edge of the opening, like the passageway entry into the main chamber, was ringed with gray plaster. The tunnel floor entered 31 cm above the antechamber floor and was elevated 5-6 cm above the bottom of the shaft. An upright metate fragment was set flush in the wall in plaster between the tunnel floor and the antechamber floor, similar to one in Pithouse A at 29SJ 721. Only the tunnel floor was plastered. There was no evidence of internal tunnel supports.

The vent shaft was circular, 100-108 cm in diameter, and about 85 cm deep. It, like the connecting shaft, was filled with postoccupational deposits of charcoal-flecked yellow-tan sand washed into the structure after abandonment.

Roofing

Few roofing remains were found in the chambers, although the main chamber revealed the traditional four-main-post arrangement with leaner poles set along three-quarters of the bench. The double placement of the leaners suggests at least partial rebuilding of the roof. No evidence for roofing posts was found on the surface around the other two chambers; they may have been covered by a flat superstructure. A ponderosa pine roofing fragment found in the Level 2 fill, however, provided a tree-ring date of A.D. 674vv (Table I.6.2), suggesting only that construction occurred after 674.

Pithouse G
(Figures I.3.25-I.3.26, Plate I.3.50)

Late in the summer, Pithouse G was excavated by the survey crew led by John Thrift. The similarity of the shape and features of the chamber to the Pithouse D antechamber suggested that the structure was merely the antechamber for a

Plate I.3.50. Site 29SJ 628, Pithouse G after clearing. Mapping tape over Other Pit 1 (a bell-shaped cist). Ventilator shaft in upper right of photograph; edge of Pithouse D in upper left. Looking southeast. 30-cm north arrow. Photograph by Milo McLeod, 1973 (CHCU neg. 6003)

144 Windes et al.

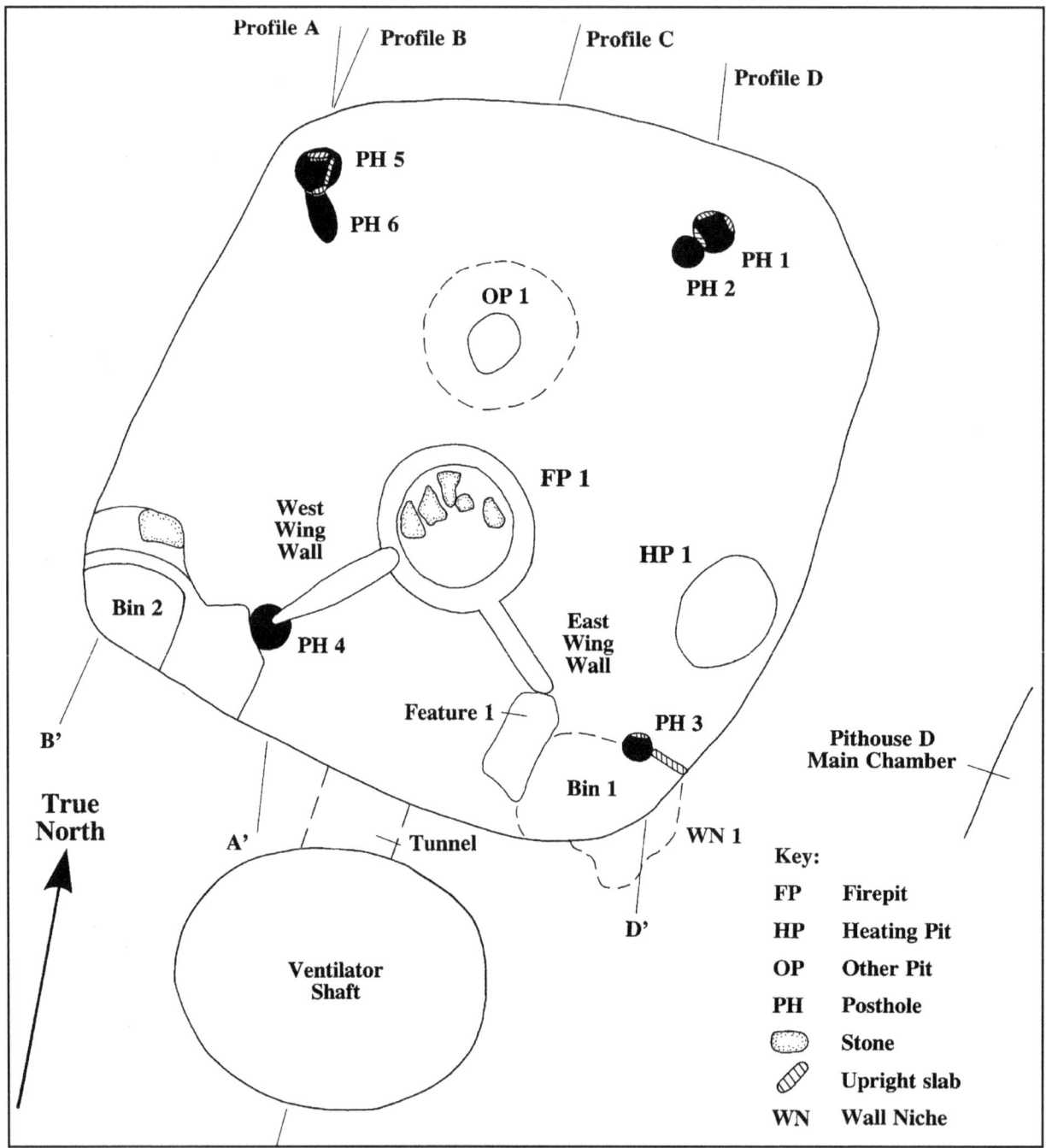

Figure I.3.25. Site 29SJ 628, Pithouse G plan (CHCU 65962). Floor artifacts not plotted (see Table I.3.23 for specimen list). Original by John Thrift and Milo McLeod, 1973. See Figure I.3.26 for profiles.

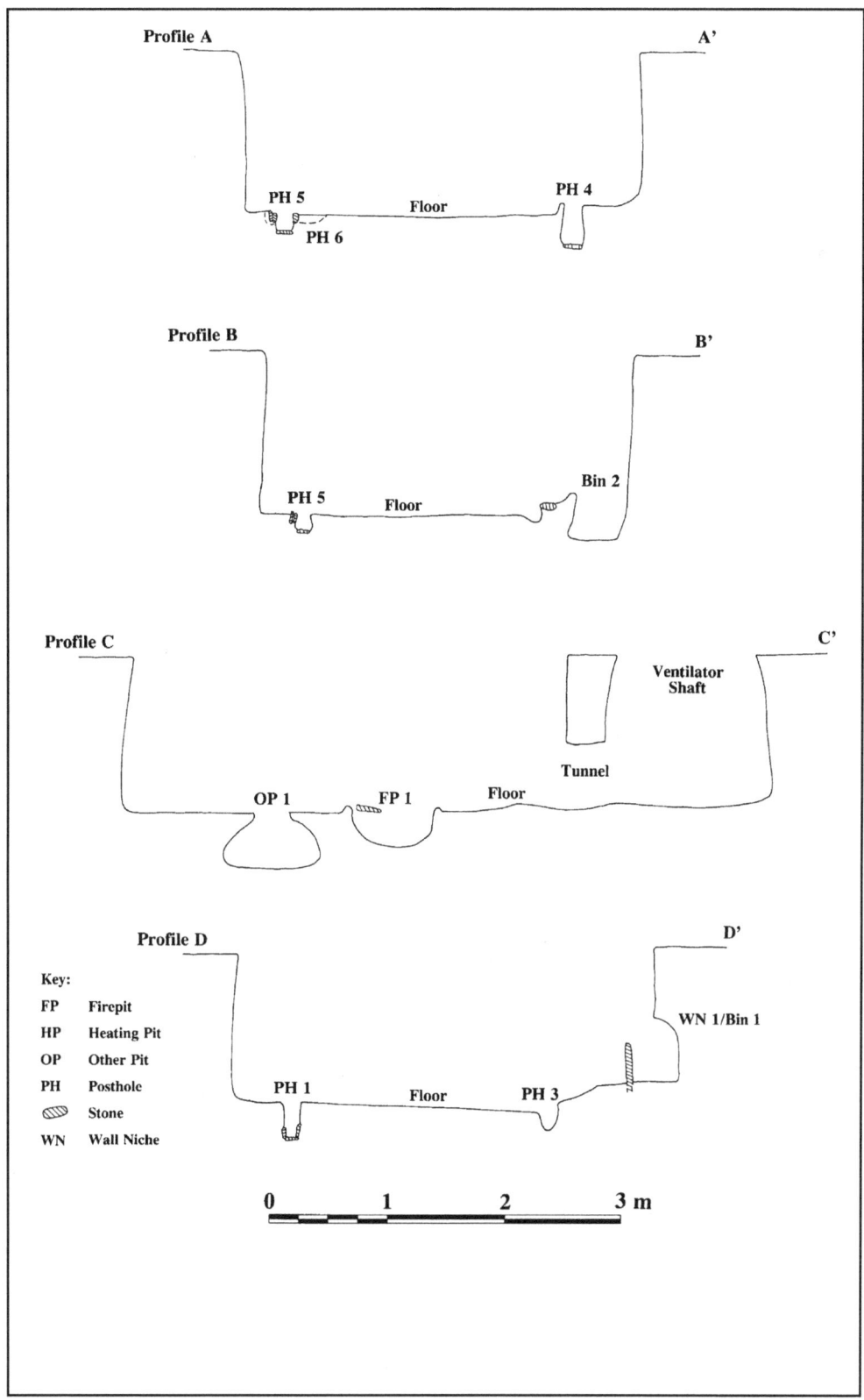

Figure I.3.26. Site 29SJ 628, Pithouse G profiles (CHCU 65963). Originals by John Thrift and Milo McLeod, 1973.

larger house, but this was not substantiated upon reinvestigation in 1976.

Fill

Alluvial deposits of sand constituted the majority of the 16.6 m³ of structure fill. After 10 cm of loose sand was removed and the wall tops identified, this fill was removed in four arbitrary units, totaling 150 cm in depth. Except for the upper 16 cm and the lower 35 cm that were relatively clean sand, the fill was darkened by decomposed organic material, although, overall, cultural materials were sparse. A roasting pit (RP 1) was found in the fill 80 cm above the floor, which indicates reuse of the structure. Late ceramics (Volume II, Table I.2.20) and other refuse in the fill suggest that reuse occurred while the site was still occupied.

A row of sandstone slabs set at a slant was found in the southwestern corner of the house in the first 50-cm-deep level. These slabs probably represented a slab-lined cist or a roasting pit, although no mention is made of burned deposits. Incorporated into the row of slabs were a mano and a metate fragment, while underneath were two small slabs that may have been part of the feature floor. Underneath this feature and to the northwest were three burned slabs that covered some charcoal and burned bird bone. Otherwise, little was noted in the pithouse fill.

Floor

A gray clay plaster covered the 12.2 m² floor without evidence of burning.

Floor Materials (Figure I.3.25, Table I.3.23)

Little had been left behind when the structure was abandoned. Just two unmodified slabs of sandstone rested on the floor, one by the northeast post seat and the other next to the firepit and north of the eastern wing wall.

South of the eastern wing wall in an area often found with food-processing materials was a large lump of clay 41-45 cm long, 28-37 wide, and 3 cm high (Feature 1) underlain by a thin layer of sand and clay. The size and location of the material suggests a metate rest, although its lack of continuity with the floor may indicate that it was postoccupational. Thrift suggests that it was part of the entry liner coping that fell into the structure when the roof was removed.

Floor Features (Tables I.3.20-I.3.21)

South of the room center was a straight-sided, flat-bottomed, slab-lined firepit (FP 1) filled with ash and sand suggesting two or three episodes of use. A 10-cm-wide adobe collar encircled the firepit in the typical style. Pollen and flotation samples were taken from the firepit but only the latter were processed. In 1976 the house was reexcavated, and an archaeomagnetic sample taken from the firepit provided a date, reassessed in 1996, between A.D. 650 and 725 (Figure I.6.12, Table I.6.6), which fits the archaeological evidence. DuBois' (2008) final reanalysis after slight curve modification placed the sample at A.D. 700 ± 40. The firepit, however, had been replastered and, after it had been filled with clean sand, had been re-dug and used to dump ash. Five burned stones found on top of the firepit may have marked use of another firepit. One of the stones was a concretion used as a grinding stone. About 70 cm east of the firepit was a burned oval basin (HP 1) filled with clean sand that served as a heating pit.

Signs for ladder rests were absent. No deflector was found. John Thrift's notes suggested that a deflector may have been composed of clay, but he did not elaborate on this issue.

The traditional four pits used to support the rectangular arrangement of posts for the roof were evident (Table I.3.21). The southern pair was incorporated into the adobe ridges radiating from the firepit while the northern pair had been placed just out from the bench. An impression in the adobe ridge wing wall suggested that the southwestern post had been 15-17 cm in diameter. Except for the southeastern pit, which was in poor condition, perhaps damaged when the post was salvaged, a basal stone had been placed in each primary posthole. Shims were found in three of the pits and lignite in the northern two. PH 2, a cylindrical pit near the northeastern posthole, might have served for an auxiliary roof support or was an earlier posthole. The early posthole (PH 6), next to Posthole 5, and PH 2 suggest that the roof may have been renovated and the northern roof supports moved slightly outward.

OP 1, just 40 cm north of the firepit, may have been the sipapu, although it was larger than normal (about 122 liters capacity), was bell-shaped, and contained clean sand. In the southeastern corner were located the poorly-preserved remains of a slab-and-adobe storage bin or food preparation area (Bin 1). Bin 2 was a storage bin in the southwestern corner against the south and west house walls. It was an above-floor feature with north and west walls formed of thick gray clay, 28 and 44 cm thick and 28 and 8 cm high, respectively. It had filled with 102 liters of post occupational deposits.

The eastern portion of the wing wall is only partly present. An upright sandstone slab set into the floor extended 64 cm from the east wall to the southeastern posthole. There was a gap in the wing wall between the posthole and the low adobe ridge extending southeast from the firepit where another slab might have been present. Another low adobe ridge ran southwest from the fire pit and enclosed the southwestern posthole before terminating at the storage bin.

Walls

Little is known of the walls. Presumably they were of plastered native earth. They were slightly flared outward as they approached the floor except along the north side.

Wall Features

In the southeastern corner was a niche (WN 1) of moderate capacity (33 liters) placed in the wall just above the floor. It was filled with post occupational fill.

Ventilator System

A narrow 56-cm-wide and 48-cm-high tunnel extended 50 cm through the pithouse wall south of the fire pit and connected a large, circular ventilator shaft that narrowed slightly as it reached 131 cm to the original ground surface. The shaft was 189 cm in diameter at the floor and 154 cm at the surface. Access to the main chamber may have been through the ventilator, but it would have been a tight passage. Several pieces of ground stone, three concretions, a sherd, a piece of chipped stone, a chopper, and 12 faunal bones (Table I.3.23) were recovered from the floor of the shaft. These had been tossed down the ventilator shaft after house abandonment.

Roofing

There was no evidence of roofing in the fill. The main post supports, however, attest to a traditional

Plate I.3.51. Site 29SJ 628, Pithouse E after clearing. Looking south. Photograph by Marcia Truell, 1973 (CHCU 5985).

framework, although the nature of the closing material is unknown because none was found.

Pithouse E
(Figures I.3.27-I.3.28, Plate I.3.51)

Pithouse E was probably constructed after Pithouse D because it did not have an antechamber, although it retained the large, circular ventilator shaft. Its location 3 m downslope from Pithouse A probably prevented substantial accumulation of overburden, which collected into the Pithouse A depression instead. The greatest thickness of alluvial material, 25 cm, was found above the main chamber wall tops. The least amount of overburden, 5 cm, overlay the ventilator shaft. This overburden consisted of alluvial deposits of laminated, yellow-tan sands sprinkled with a few charcoal flecks and sherds from upslope.

Fill

Under the overburden and filling the main chamber were deposits of trash reaching nearly to the floor. These deposits were removed in five levels totaling 135 cm in depth. Each level corresponded approximately with episodes of trash filling, with the upper three each separated by a 3-5 cm thick layer of gray clay that probably washed into the depression during intervals when trash was not accumulating. Unfortunately, the control balk that was to be used for mapping and describing the fill by natural unit collapsed before recording had started. Trash continued into the lowest 15-cm unit removed as floor fill. The lowest few centimeters of fill consisted of bright yellow sand that resembled the floor deposits in Pithouses C and D. Overall, the deposits reached the floor 135 cm below the original ground surface.

Floor

A coat of gray plaster covered the house floor but this was a replastering of the original floor located about 5 cm lower. Only parts of the lower floor were examined. The floor was 675 cm north-to-south and 595 cm east-west, covering 15.1 m^2.

Floor Materials (Figure I.3.27, Table I.3.24)

Although the structure had been filled with trash, there was a notable concentration of stone artifacts (manos, sandstone slabs, an anvil, and a polishing stone) behind the wing walls. Since this area often contains stored food-preparation tools (e.g., Morris 1939:25), the assemblage seems to coincide with abandonment behavior rather than postoccupational trash.

Floor Features (Tables I.3.20 and I.3.21)

The floor was covered by numerous pits, taking up 2.1 m^2 of area. The firepit was located about 50 cm south of the room center. It was lined with eight stone slabs with a basal stone in the bottom. The slabs were capped by 6 cm of gray clay plaster that extended 6 cm above the surrounding floor. The lower third of fill was tan sand, although the entire firepit from the basal slab up was well oxidized. An archaeomagnetic sample collected from the clay collar yielded a DuBois date of A.D. 780 ± 28 but later revised (DuBois 2008) to 740 ± 28 (Figure I.6.11, Table I.6.6). An oval heating pit sealed with gray plaster but unsuitable for archaeomagnetism occupied the northwestern quadrant of the house. Burned sand filled the lower half of the pit, while unburned tan sand containing a few charcoal flecks occupied the remainder. The pit walls were well burned only above the point where the sand layers met. The pit was flush with the floor.

Although no deflector remained, the place it had occupied was evident. A slightly curving trench cut into the floor 37 cm long and 10 cm deep, about 20 cm south of the firepit and 75 cm north of the ventilator, probably held a large stone slab, possibly a discarded metate. Inexplicably, the interior trench walls were highly burned. Yellow sand similar to that covering the floor filled the groove.

Between the deflector groove and ventilator were two small pits aligned north-south. Their location suggests that each was part of a pair for supporting a double-pole ladder that had shifted location. Extensive rodent burrowing just west of these two pits seems to have obliterated the companion pits. The pit closest to the deflector suggests that the angle of the ladder would have allowed it to rest against the deflector. Both pits were filled with yellow floor sand, although if one set had been replaced by another it seems odd that the original pair was left unsealed.

Four main roof supports set in a rectangular pattern in the floor marked the final roof placement (Table I.3.21). Two were part of the wing walls but the others were set slightly out from the bench along the north side of the house. All contained small stone shims set in the bottom of the holes. The posts had been removed. Two other large postholes, not recognized in the field, were set partly into the face of the bench for the initial northeastern and northwestern roof posts. These were recorded as plastered wall niches (see below) but bulges in the bench above the niches were undoubtedly created by the pressure of the roof posts. In addition, these niches are directly behind the existing main supports and are a consistent size with the existing postholes.

In line with the firepit, deflector, and the ventilator tunnel was a small pit filled with sand located 30 cm northeast of the firepit. The walls were plastered and presumably it was the sipapu, although normally it might have been located closer to the north wall. Five remaining other pits were of unknown function. OP 1 and OP 4 may have been auxiliary roof supports or post supports of some sort. A small piece of turquoise and clean sand filled OP 1. An oblong basin (OP 2), possibly a pot rest, was located next to the northeastern side of the bench. A bell-shaped pit (OP 3) next to the bench and the northwestern posthole could have served for limited storage. Next to the sipapu was another basin-shaped pit that looked like a pot rest (OP 7) but the area was rodent disturbed and the pit's cultural origin uncertain. All the pits had limited capacity (9 liters) except for OP 3 (17 liters).

Little remained of the wing walls except for broken lines of plaster that marked their former positions. The eastern one had bowed outward toward the south wall and included the southeastern posthole and two other holes (OPs 5 and 6). These latter ones may have held additional post reinforcements for the wing wall, although they are relatively shallow. Overall, the eastern wing wall was 165 cm long and 25 cm wide at the maximum. Where it attached to the house wall, at the end of the bench, the wing wall was even with the bench top, 85 cm high, but appears to have descended to a height even with the fire pit where it attached.

The western wing wall also attached to the fire pit but was not symmetrical with its companion. It curved south to attach to the house wall beyond the end of the bench. It was about 180 cm and 25 cm wide. The southwestern posthole was incorporated within the wing wall as well as with a smaller unnumbered posthole, 6 cm in diameter and 6 cm deep. The latter probably held a post to reinforce the wing wall. Two broken upright slabs were embedded in the floor plaster that marked the former position of the wing wall.

Walls

Tan, sandy native deposits characterized the pithouse walls and bench, which were then covered with 3-6 cm of thick, gray plaster. Areas of the wall above the bench that would have been hidden by the leaning roof poles were not plastered. Unlike in Pithouses A and D, the south wall exhibited only a slight bulge inward at the floor and the bench face did not recede noticeably.

Wall Features

A bench encircled all but the south side of the pithouse interior. It tapered and disappeared into the south wall where the two wing walls emerged. Carved out of the yellow-tan native soil when the

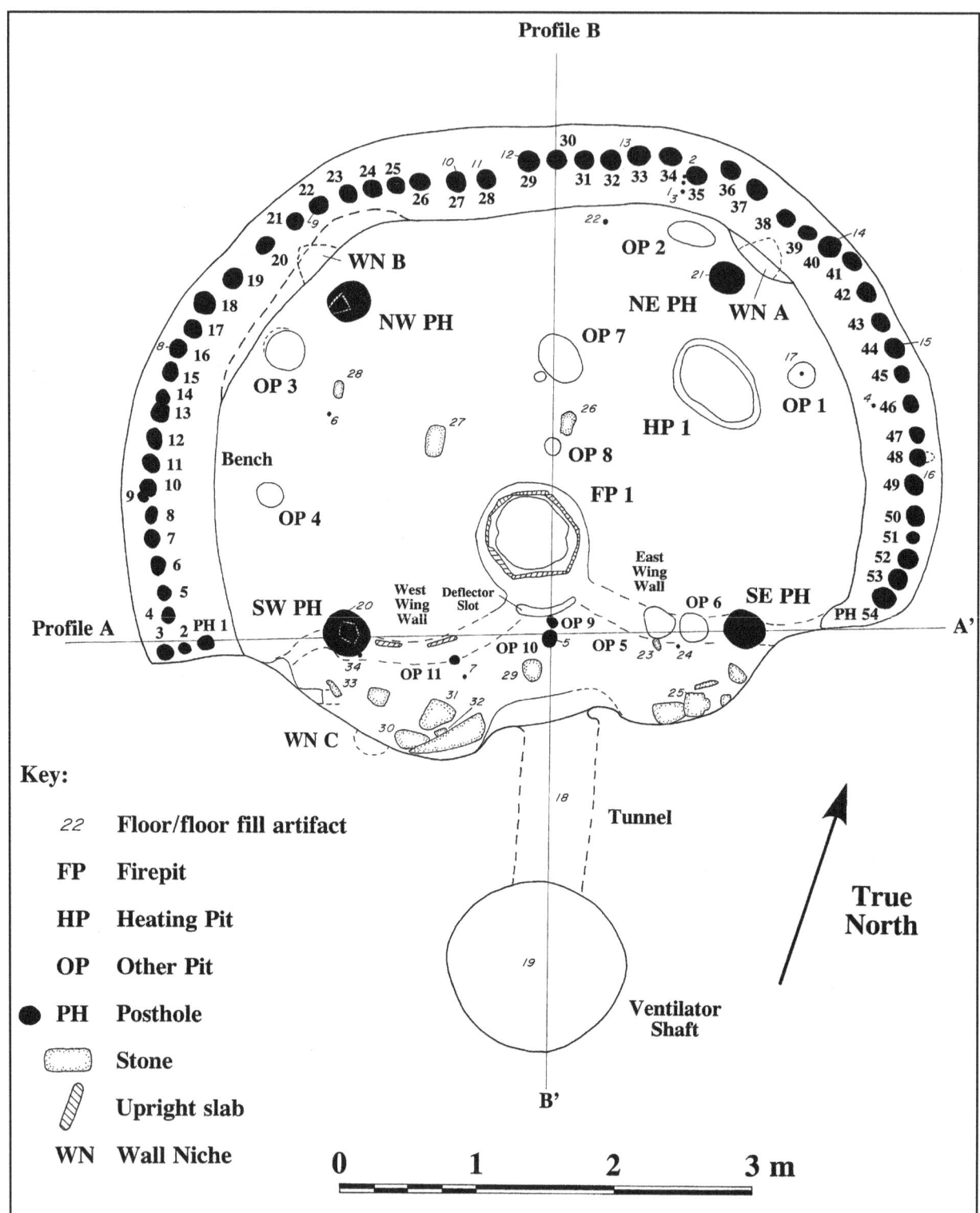

Figure I.3.27. Site 29SJ 628, Pithouse E plan and distribution of floor fill and floor materials (see Table I.3.24 for list of specimens) (CHCU 55555). Original by Marcia Truell, 1973. See Figure I.3.28 for profiles.

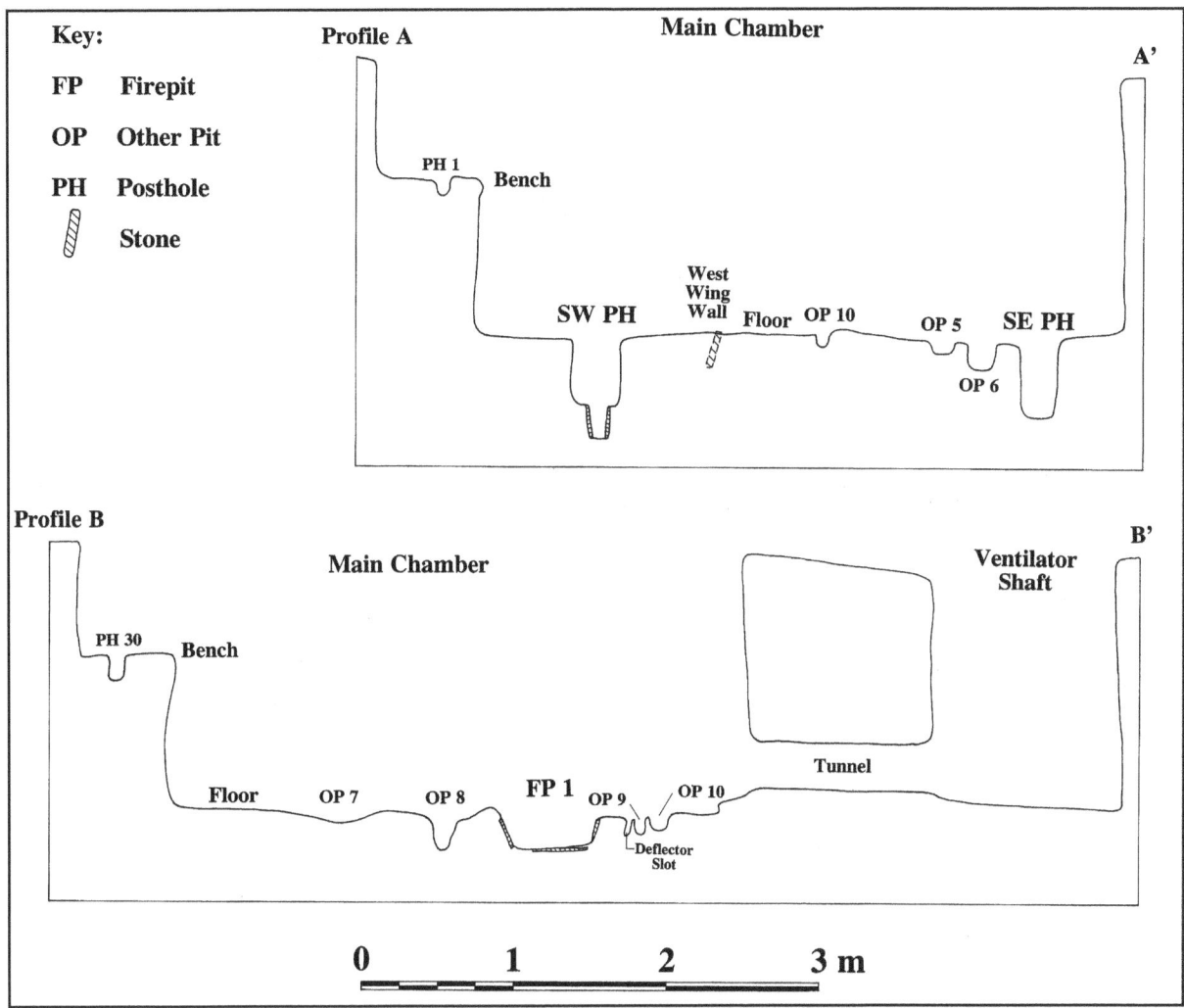

Figure I.3.28. Site 29SJ 628, Pithouse E profiles (CHUC 55557). Original by Marcia Truell, 1973.

house was first constructed, the bench was 93 cm high and 63 cm wide, and the vertical face was plastered.

Fifty-four postholes extended the length of the bench top, set 10-30 cm out from the house wall. All the holes were set at an angle into the bench so that the roof poles leaned over the house floor except for the last one in the southeastern corner, which was set vertical, had the largest diameter, and was deepest. In some cases the holes were close to one another or overlapped, suggesting that the roof had been rebuilt and new leaner poles added.

Found in these postholes (Table I.3.24) were several artifacts, which were uncommon relative to the trash deposit artifacts. Generally, the posthole artifacts are of an ornamental or ceremonial nature and appear to have been intentionally placed. Two cloud blowers of unfired clay, a piece of turquoise, a piece of a quartzite river cobble, an obsidian chip, a selenite pendant, two pieces of debitage, a bone awl, and an unworked piece of bone were recovered from these postholes.

Two storage wall niches found in the north wall were probably renovated post sockets for the initial roof supports (see above). Another was located behind the wing wall in the southeastern wall, although extensive rodent activity made its identification tenuous. It and the adjacent burrows were filled with the same trash deposits filling the main chamber.

Ventilator System

The ventilator tunnel extended through the south wall 120 cm before intersecting the ventilator shaft. The tunnel opening was arched, 46 cm wide at its base and about 40 cm high, and bulged out into the main chamber 26 cm. Thick coats of gray plaster applied around the mouth created this inward bulge; the tunnel and shaft floors were also plastered. A small step projected 20 cm from the opening and stood 7 cm above the main floor but 7 cm below the tunnel floor. No sign of reinforcing of the tunnel roof or walls was encountered, and it was probably excavated as a tunnel rather than constructed through trenching.

A large, circular shaft, 165 cm deep and 125-130 cm in diameter, connected the ventilator tunnel. The large size of the shaft was probably necessary to facilitate its construction and linkage to the tunnel. It would have provided difficult entry; presumably access was through the main chamber roof.

Roofing

As in the other houses, little physical evidence of the roofing remained. A traditional four-post main support system with poles set on the bench to lean against horizontal stringers set across the four posts is envisioned. Closing material of small poles, brush, or willows sealed over with thick adobe was normal, although no evidence of it remained in the structure. The arrangement of the bench postholes and the shift of the northern post supports indicate an episode of roof reconstruction.

Pithouse A
(Figures I.3.29-I.3.30, Plates I.3.52-I.3.53)

The latest pithouse in the excavated group was located 3 m upslope from Pithouse E and about 4 m north of Pithouse C.

Fill

The fill was removed in four arbitrary levels that cross-cut the natural units (see Figure I.3.29). The first three were each 35 cm deep; the last removed the remaining 25 cm of fill above the floor. Approximately 15.7 m3 of fill was removed from the pithouse. A pollen column was removed by Stephen Hall from the pie-shaped control block left temporarily in the northern part of the house. These 15 samples have not been analyzed, although most contained pollen (Stephen Hall, personal communication 2013).

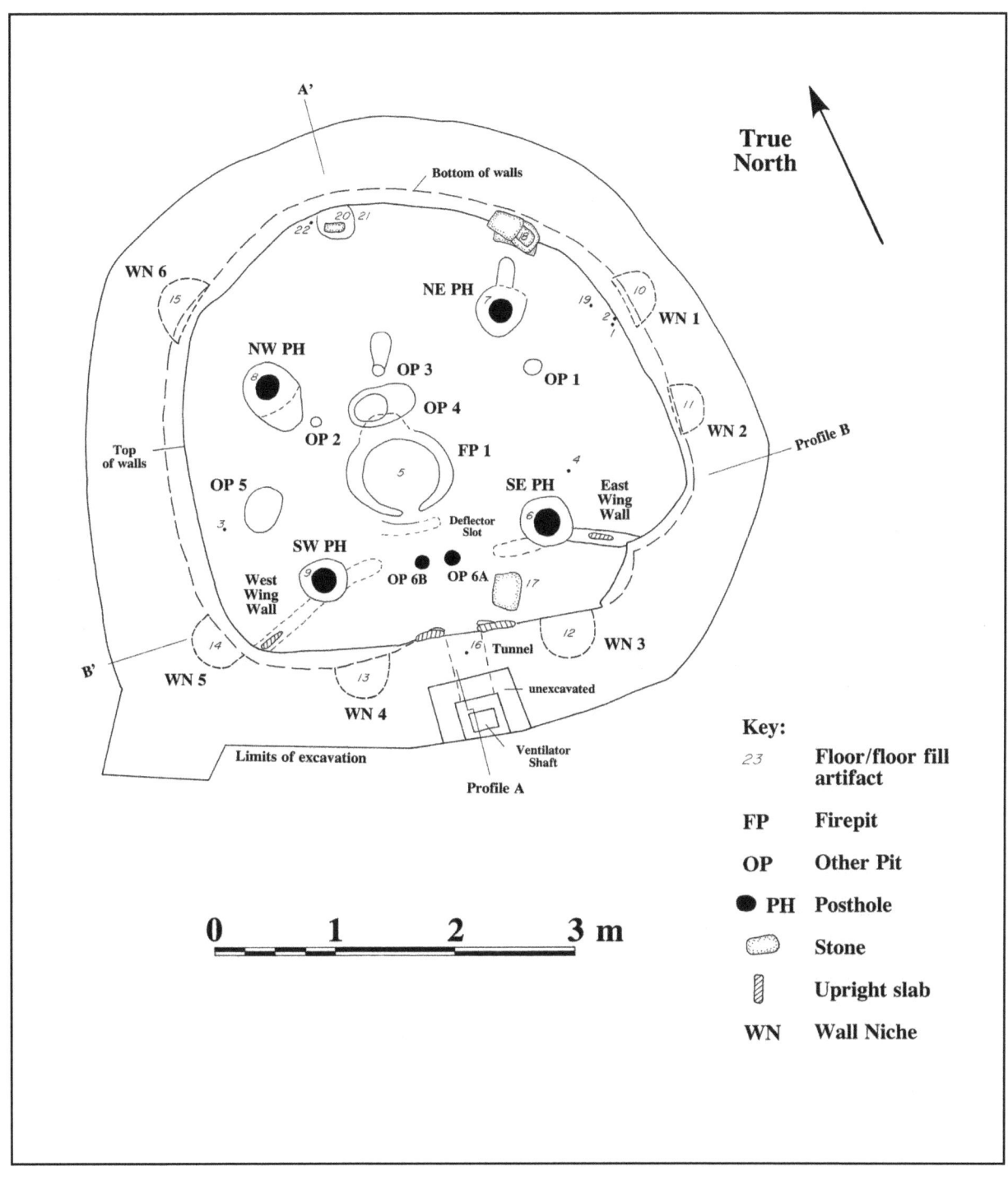

Figure I.3.29. Site 29SJ 628, Pithouse A plan and distribution of floor fill and floor materials (see Table I.3.25 for specimen list)(CHCU 55553). Scale is approximate. Some features may be distorted. Floor postholes in black are correct size but placed within the originally mapped posthole of incorrect size. Original by Marcia Truell, 1973. See Figure I.3.30 for profiles.

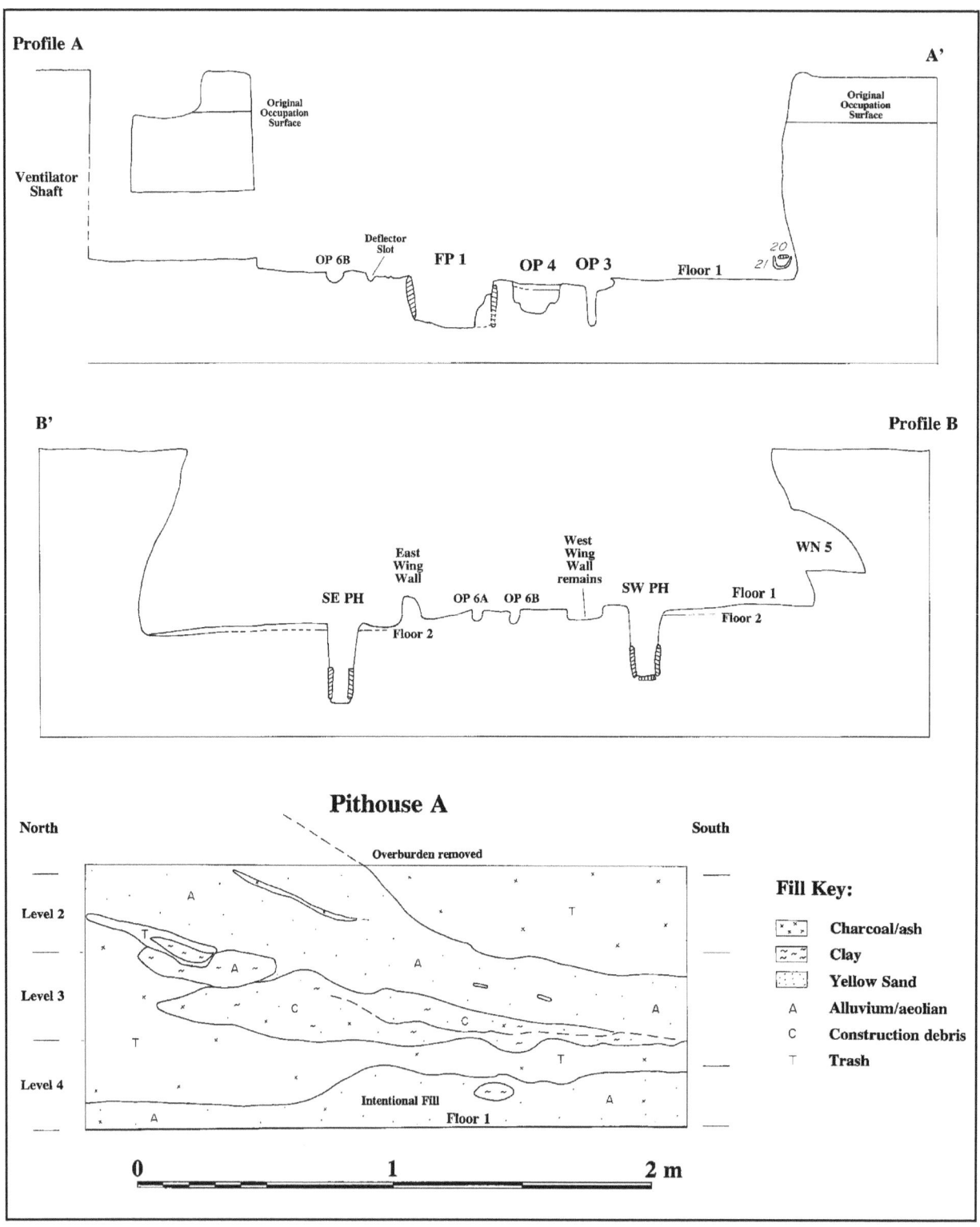

Figure I.3.30. Site 29SJ 628, Pithouse A profiles (CHCU 55537). Fill profile at bottom of this figure not indicated on plan view (Figure I.3.29). No scale (map distorted). Original by Marcia Truell, 1973.

Plate I.3.52. Site 29SJ 628, Pithouse A after clearing. Note Pithouse F in upper background. Looking south. Photograph by Marcia Truell, 1973 (CHCU neg. 5949).

Plate I.3.53. Site Excavations at 29SJ 628, Pithouse A, in 1973. Marcia Truell stands on the pithouse floor. Photographed by Alden Hayes, 1973 (CHCU park 76-136-106 slide).

A 35-cm-thick deposit of yellow-tan alluvial sands overlay the pithouse walls and extended to little over a meter deep in the house center. It increased even more in depth along the southern side. Because of its intermediate location, Pithouse A collected less overburden than Pithouse C but more than Pithouses D, G, and E. Beneath this deposit was a layer rich in burned wood and shale but with little cultural material. The trash dipped downward in the house center 70 cm before encountering another layer of natural sands underlain by laminated clays and sands.

Another episode of trash consisted of lenses of gray clay, sands, adobe, and black organic material underlay the natural deposit and extended to a mere 10 cm above the house floor. An exceptionally large amount of small animal bone, including bird, rabbit, mice and other rodents, as well as deer bone came from this layer. In addition, numerous bone awls were recovered, primarily from the northeastern part of the house. Lino Gray sherds covered with fugitive red paint, polished black sherds, La Plata Black-on-white, and a few neckbanded sherds also came from the deposit. The remaining 10 cm of fill consisted of nearly clean yellow-tan sand with scattered charcoal flecks and a paucity of cultural material.

The lack of laminations suggests that the sand represented native fill from excavations of an undiscovered house nearby. Finally, a thin layer of yellow sand covered the floor as it did in the other houses. The sand was noticeably coarser than the overlying material and the fine-grained material found on site. The distinctive yellow sand has not been found outcropping locally.

Floors

As with every other house, a thick coat of gray plaster, 2-3 cm thick, covered the uppermost floor. The floor measured 390-x-425-cm with a floor area of 14.2 m². A test in the southeastern corner revealed the original floor 3 cm below the first. The lower floor was also covered by coarse yellow sand, but the subfloor was not investigated elsewhere. In several spots along the floor edges the upper plaster had flaked off, revealing the lower one merging with the walls.

There was little floor area behind the wing walls, a mere space of 1.6 m², or 11 percent of the total usable space. It is the second smallest site pithouse, but the presence of two large wall niches above the area may have partly compensated for the relative lack of work and storage space.

Floor Materials (Figure I.3.29, Table I.3.25)

Few artifacts were found on the floor, but it cannot be certain if these were left at abandonment or thrown in shortly afterwards. Most were concentrated near the north wall, including a partial Lino Gray seed jar, a mano, and a bone spatula found together just west of a grinding stone covered with red paint. The latter lay on top of two sandstone slabs, which may have held a passive abrader on which the paint stone had been used.

A concentration of brush charcoal on the floor yielded a corrected radiocarbon age of A.D. 710 ± 60 (Table I.6.4), which is a reasonable age for the occupation.

One of the very few metate fragments recovered from the site came from behind the wing walls. Its presence may be indicative of the work area function commonly assigned to these locations.

Floor Features (Tables I.3.20 and I.3.21)

The relatively few features on the upper floor took up only 1.1 m² of the total floor space. The firepit was offset slightly south of the room center. It was lined with slabs affixed with adobe mortar and capped with a collar of adobe extending 20 cm above the floor. On the north side, it covered an earlier pot rest. This rim was only slightly burned and covered another rim, probably associated with the lower floor firepit, from which an archaeomagnetic sample was taken that DuBois dated to A.D. 830 ± 31 (Figure I.6.11, Table I.6.6) but later corrected to A.D. 790 ± 31 (DuBois 2008). Brush from the firepit provided a corrected radiocarbon age of A.D. 700 ± 50, but when pooled with the floor sample, yielded an age of A.D. 705 ± 38 (Tables I.6.4 and I.6.5) for the structure's last use. This is much earlier than the archaeomagnetic dates, which appear more reasonable. No deflector slab remained between the firepit and ventilator, but the floor plaster was disturbed about 6 cm from the firepit, where it once probably stood.

About 13 cm south of the proposed deflector location were two small holes set about 15 cm apart that probably held a roof-entry, two-pole ladder. Both pits were filled with the same coarse yellow sand that covered the floor. Four post seats set in a rectangular pattern held the main roof supports (Table I.3.21). These were shimmed with small pieces of sandstone set in the bottom of the pits. Only the southeastern posthole still contained the badly rotted remains of a post unsuitable for tree-ring dating. This particular post had been held in place by a long, cylindrical concretion in addition to the bottom shims. Three of the postholes also contained a packing of lignite.

The five remaining floor other pits consisted of two pot rests, a sipapu, and two others of unknown function. All were filled with relatively clean sand: the sipapu with a coarse, yellow sand that also covered the floor and the remainder with a post occupational fine, yellow-tan sand common to the site. The upper part of the 26-cm-deep sipapu, just north of the fire pit, was plastered like the floor, as was the pot rest near the fire pit rim. A small sump about 10 cm in diameter and 3-4 cm deep on the northeastern side of the sipapu may have resulted from rodent activity or may be cultural. Although both pot rests were morphologically similar to heating pits, neither revealed evidence of burning. The one under the fire pit rim extension probably went with the lower floor. A secondary pit in the bottom extended an additional 10 cm deep.

Only a single pinnacle of gray clay 42 cm high in the southwestern corner and two lines of clay on the floor and walls mark the former wing wall positions. Both southern post seats were incorporated within the wing walls, but neither wall was connected to the fire pit or to one another. The 92 cm between them was where the ladder rests were located. The house walls bulged slightly inward where the wing walls once attached.

Walls

The walls were unplastered native soil marked by more compacted deposits and a veneer of rootlets and calcium carbonate that distinguished them from the house fill. They sloped gradually downward to about 30 cm above the wall niches and then bulged outward until they were below the level of the niches, where they became vertical. In the wing wall area, they had a pronounced flare at the floor. The house was without a bench.

Six arched wall niches had been placed around the house walls, 9-30 cm above the upper floor. All were large storage receptacles with volumes of about 15-43 liters. All had plastered interiors and were filled with the same post occupational trash filling the pithouse. Niche C had a flat slab lying on the bottom, while unfired gray clay was on the floors of Niches C and F. An obsidian blade came from Niche F.

Ventilator System

The slight bulge in the southern wall marked entry of the ventilator tunnel, where it was lined with two upright slabs and a thick layer of plaster. The room floor coped up 5-6 cm to meet the tunnel floor, which then dropped 8-10 cm inside the tunnel. The tunnel was 109 cm long, where it intersected the shaft, and was plastered for its entire length. Dimensions of the tunnel were 27.5 cm wide and 43 cm high. No internal wall or roof supports were evident aside from the entrance slabs. The mouth of the shaft was rectangular but originally it was probably round or oval, approximately 26 cm across and 125 cm deep as measured from the original ground surface. Both shaft and tunnel were filled with dark, charcoal-laden trash.

Roofing

No roofing remained, although the superstructure was carried by the traditional four-post arrangement. Because it lacked a bench, side poles must have been set on the ground surface but no evidence of them remained. All material from the framework had been removed except for the lone post left in its socket.

Pithouse F
(Figures I.3.20, I.3.31, Plate I.3.54)

The smallest pithouse excavated at the site was encountered when the walls of Pithouse C were defined. From the surface this house appeared to have been an auxiliary chamber to Pithouse C, but it was discovered that the northwestern part of the bench and associated wall of the latter were gone. Thus, Pithouse F had been cut into the side of Pithouse C subsequent to its abandonment and filling.

Fill

Pithouse F, like Pithouse C, was filled with trash. This trash was less rich in organic and cultural material, however, and the sandy fill was considerably moister. The trash seemed to continue behind the southwestern part of Pithouse F, as if it had once been larger. Although this possibility

Plate I.3.54. Site 29SJ 628 Pithouse F after clearing. This pithouse cut into the earlier Pithouse C at top of photo. Looking south. 30-cm north arrow. Photograph by Milo McLeod, 1973 (CHCU neg. 6005).

158 *Windes et al.*

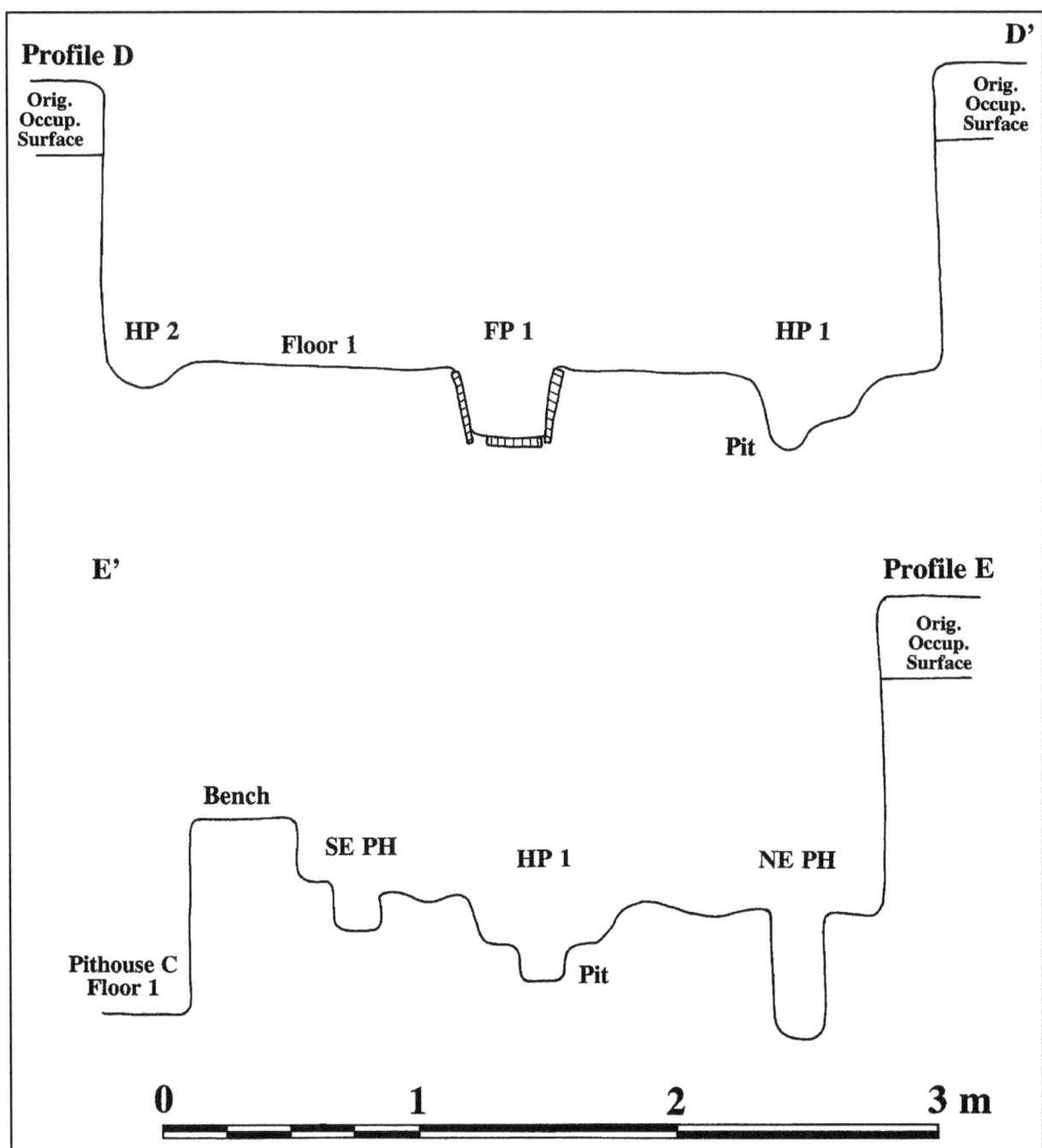

Figure I.3.31. Site 29SJ 628, Pithouse F profiles (CHCU 65961); see Figure I.3.20 for plan view and profile locations. Originals by Kellie Masterson, 1973.

was not investigated, there was no evidence of an earlier room under F that would have joined with Pithouse C. The mystery was left unresolved.

About 30-36 cm of overburden, removed during clearing of Pithouse C, covered Pithouse F. The material was primarily yellow-tan sand with charcoal flecks and little cultural material. Below this, the 9.1 m^3 of trash filling the structure was removed in two levels each of 30-32 cm in depth and a floor-fill level of 5 cm, including the thin deposit of coarse yellow sand spread over the floor. A roasting pit (RP 1) found high in the fill marks reuse of the structure late in the site occupation.

Floor

The tiny pithouse measured 320-x-330-cm at floor level, an area of 8.0 m^2. A layer of gray clay plaster covered the floor, overlain with the coarse, yellow sand brought in during the occupation. A slight reddish tinge marked the floor (and walls) in spots as if from oxidation or an usual clay mixture used in preparation of the plaster.

Floor Materials (Figure I.3.20, Table I.3.26)

Very little was found on the floor. A sandstone slab lay over the deflector slab groove and another was found embedded in the floor near the ventilator.

Floor Features (Tables I.3.20-I.3.21)

Despite its small size, the traditional complex of features was evident along with several other pits. These all totaled 1.1 m^2 of area, reducing the usable floor space to 6.9 m^2. The fire pit was highly burned, lined with seven or eight upright and closely spaced slabs, and had a single flat slab at its base. Only a slight indication of a narrow, plastered rim existed along the eastern side. Unfortunately, the paucity of mortar prevented archaeomagnetic sampling. Yellow and burned purple, fine-grained sand filled the fire pit. A groove just southeast of the fire pit marked the former deflector slab. A small, upright slab at one end was probably a shim. The lining on the south side was very sandy.

An oval heating pit (HP 1) filled with burned sand (but no charcoal), like those in Pithouses C and E, was located on the eastern side. The pit rim was highly burned but too sandy for archaeomagnetic sampling. A small pit was found in the bottom, with a semicircular series of indentations marking the pit walls too regularly spaced to have been made by a digging stick. Their function is unknown. Another oval pit (HP 2, formerly OP 4) located against the west wall and filled with slightly burned yellow sand, but little charcoal, may have been another heating pit.

No ladder rests holes were found. Four lignite-packed postholes supported the main roof supports, which were missing (Table I.3.21). A sandstone slab stuck in the northeastern hole was the only evidence of shims to hold the posts in place.

There were few other pits. A bell-shaped storage pit (OP 2) filled with yellow sand was located just north of the firepit. OP 3 was found northwest of the firepit and was excavated to a depth of 9 cm but no bottom could be found. It was 7 cm in diameter and may have been a soil auger hole made by Alden Hayes before the house was excavated. OP 5 was a small, sand-filled pit of unknown use. There was no evidence for wing walls.

Walls

The existing walls were a reddish color and of native soil covered by a thin coating of adobe plaster. Walls were nearly vertical; the south side was missing where it had been removed during our Pithouse C excavation. Walls were only 75 cm high.

Wall Features

No wall features were encountered, and there was no bench.

Ventilator System

The Pithouse F ventilator system had been built into the upper fill of Pithouse C and was not identified during the excavation of Pithouse C. Neither a stone lining nor walls to stabilize the soft Pithouse C fill for ventilator construction were encountered, and therefore its construction remains problematical.

Roofing

A four-post roof support system held the roof, although the post arrangement was more trapezoid than rectangular (Table I.3.21). No roofing materials were recovered from the fill, and presumably, it was all removed. Without a bench, the side wall poles must have rested on the ground surface, although no evidence remains.

Storage Cists
(Figures I.3.32-I.3.34, Tables I.3.20, I.3.27)

Six above-ground storage cists were found slightly upslope from the excavated pithouses. It is uncertain if the cists were contemporaneous and with which pithouses they were associated.

Storage Cist 1 (Figure I.3.32, Plate I.3.55)

About 6 m due west of Pithouse A were four upright slabs that marked the south end of a semi-subterranean cist 157-x-238-cm. These slabs, the tallest at 25 cm above the surface, and those adjacent in Cist 2 helped pinpoint the location of the site when it was first recorded in 1972. The remaining wall slabs were missing. Postoccupational deposits of alluvial sands mixed with a scattering of charcoal flecks filled the cist.

Two floors were found in the cist. The flat upper floor, 33 cm below the surface, was plastered with gray clay, and there was a small subfloor pit at its south end, which was also plastered with gray clay. The bottom of the pit was formed by the lower cist floor. Several cobbles and a polishing stone were recovered from the pit. A second cist floor, 23-25 cm below the uppermost, was also plastered with gray clay and contained several floor artifacts: a partial Lino Gray seed jar filled with yellowish clay, a polishing stone, a bone awl, and a cobble polisher. The fill between the two floors was similar to the postoccupational fill above the first floor except for the greater density of charcoal.

Storage Cist 2 (Figure I.3.32)

Adjacent to Storage Cist 1 on the south side and probably part of a set of two cists built together was another semi-subterranean cist, 200-x-260-cm. Upright slabs also marked the presence of this cist. It was somewhat rounder than Cist 1 and filled with similar postoccupational deposits of sandy alluvium and charcoal flecks. The upper part of the fill was hardened yellow-tan laminated sand containing a few indented corrugated sherds that washed in from upslope (probably from 29SJ 629).

The uppermost floor varied in depth below the original surface from 10 cm at the south end to 50 cm at the north end, and it was dish-shaped with the floor shallower around the edges. A well-preserved gray plaster covered the floor. Within the floor, the tops of wall slabs associated with a second, lower, floor could be seen, but was not excavated. Little was recovered from the floor: a few sherds and bones and a mano fragment.

Storage Cist 3 (Figure I.3.33, Plate I.3.56)

This small, 160-x-172-cm cist was located 3 m south of the paired unit discussed above. It was filled almost to the top of its remaining wall slabs

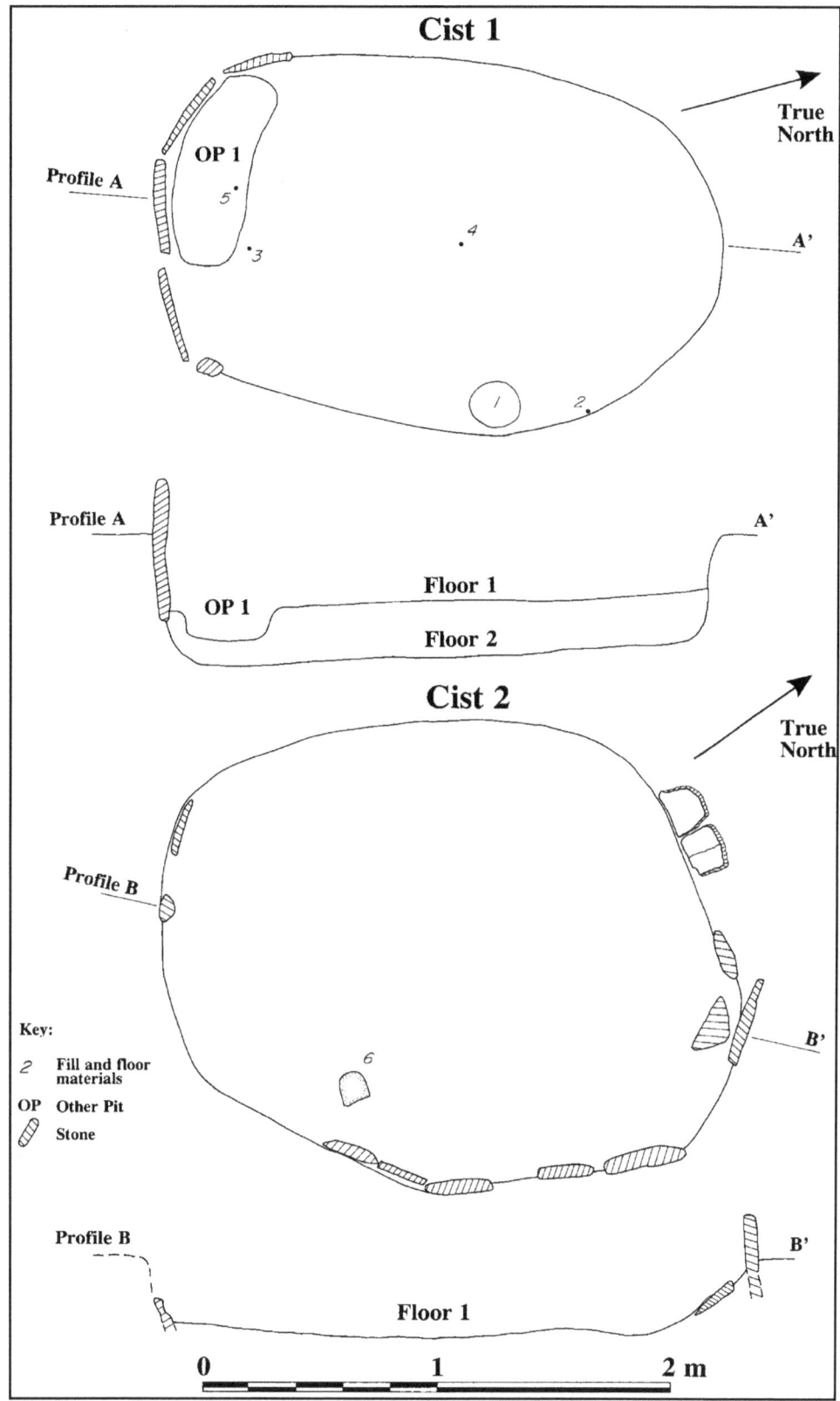

Figure I.3.32. Site 29SJ 628, Cists 1 and 2, plans and profiles (see Table I.3.27 for specimen list)(CHCU 65964). Originals by Marcia Truell and Sharon Sullivan, 1973.

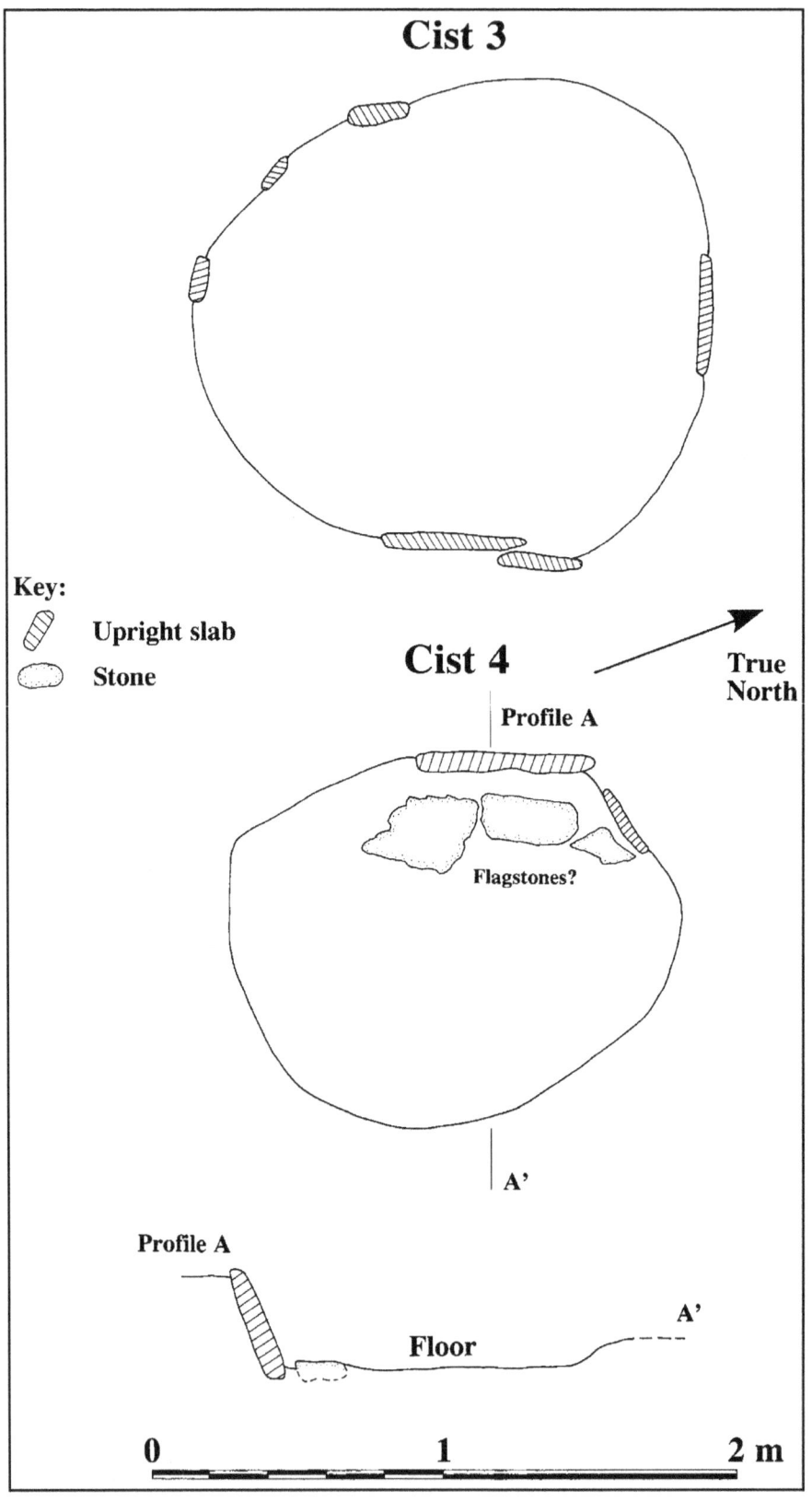

Figure I.3.33. Site 29SJ 628, Cists 3 and 4, plans and profile (CHCU 65965). Originals by Marcia Truell and Sharon Sullivan, 1973.

Plate I.3.55. Site 29SJ 628, Storage Cist 1. Crushed Lino Gray jar on lower floor in top center of cist. Looking east. Photograph by Marcia Truell, 1973 (CHCU neg. 5923).

Plate I.3.56. Site 29SJ 628, Storage Cist 3 after clearing. Note stones protruding through upper floor. Lower floor not exposed. Looking southeast. Photograph by Marcia Truell, 1973 (CHCU neg. 5930).

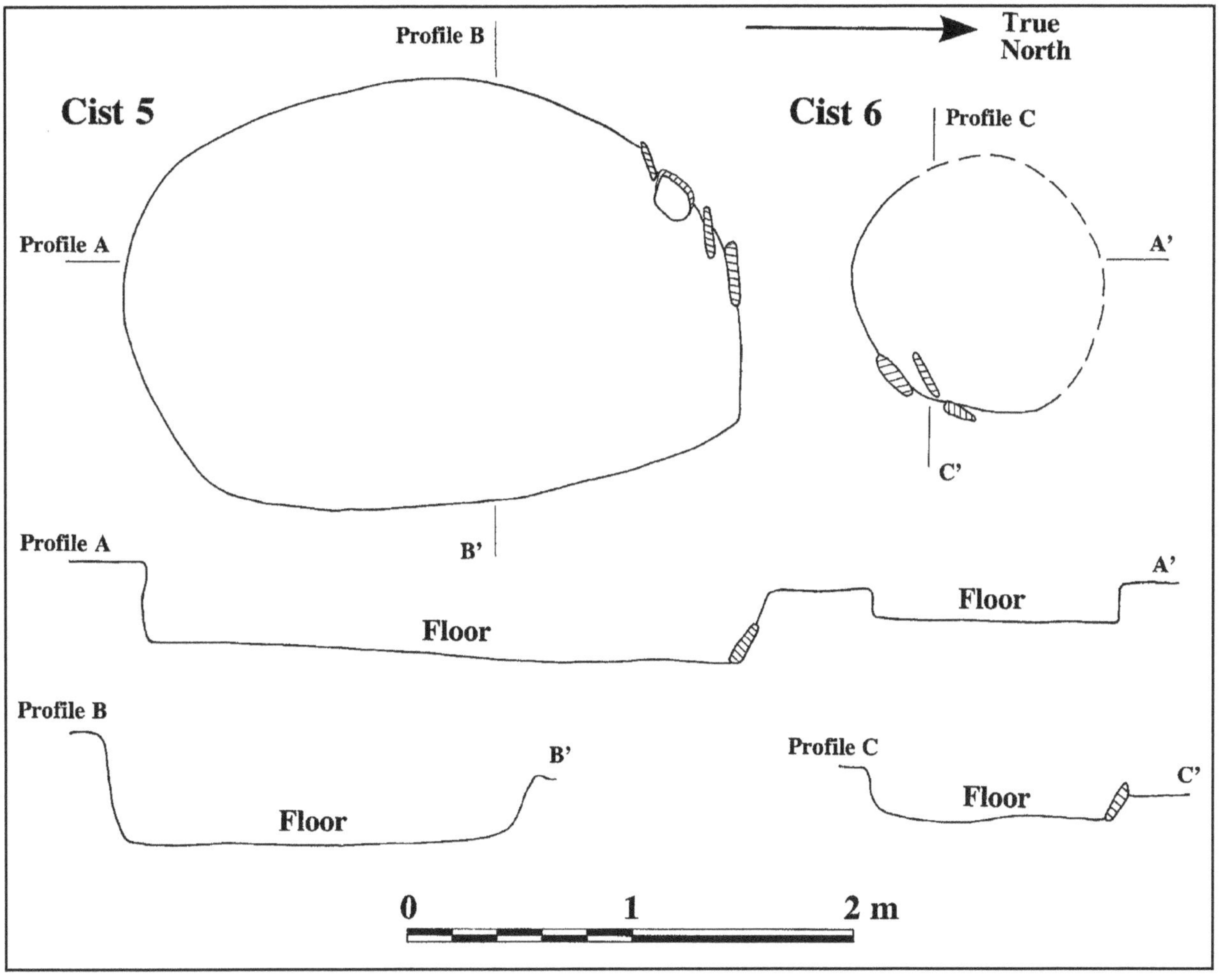

Figure I.3.34. Site 29SJ 628, Cists 5 and 6, plans and profiles (CHCU 65966). Originals by Marcia Truell, 1973.

with gray shale-derived clay and small sandstone slabs that appeared to have been haphazardly thrown into the once-wet clay. A test pit revealed that the clay was 21 cm thick and the cist about 26 cm deep. Apparently, this small storage cist had been reused as a clay mixing pit.

Storage Cist 4 (Figure I.3.33)

Another small isolated 125-x-160-cm cist was located just west of Pithouse G. Only two of its wall slabs remained; the rest apparently had been robbed. It was only 10 cm deep and filled with sandy alluvial deposits, a few sherds, and two abrader fragments. The floor was plastered with a gray clay and had three flagstones embedded in it.

Storage Cist 5 (Figure I.3.34)

Just northwest of Cist 1 was in a large cist, 192-x-270-cm, that had only four upright slabs, which marked its northern end. Since slabs were missing for most of its periphery, the dimensions were defined by the extent of the gray floor plaster. Exposure, however, may have reduced the original size of the floor. The floor was flat and slightly burned in several places. It was about 32 cm deep at the southern end and 35 cm deep at the northern end. There was no cultural material on the floor, although some sherds, bones, a mano, and a paint stone came from the sandy alluvium mixed with scattered charcoal flecks.

Storage Cist 6 (Figure I.3.34)

A smaller cist, about 105 cm in diameter and a mere 8 cm deep, was located just north of Storage Cist 5 as if they had been paired. It was poorly preserved and contained only three of its wall slabs and a small amount of gray plaster at its base that may have been the remnants of floor. Two of the upright "slabs" were chunks of shale. No cultural material was recovered from the cist, although the fill consisted of sandy alluvium spotted with charcoal.

Storage Cist 7

An upright slab was found northwest of Pithouse G that might have marked another storage cist. It was not investigated, however.

Plaza

The original ground surface between the pithouses and the storage cists was difficult to follow. Where the tops of pithouse walls were visible, the surface was followed out as far as possible but these surfaces were always suspect. The general lack of features marking a use-surface made the definition of a plaza work area tentative. No clear, hard packed surfaces were found, although two plaza outdoor firepits were located (Figure I.3.19, Table I.3.20). Firepit 1 was located directly in front of Storage Cist 2, while Firepit 2 was found between Pithouses A and G. No other features or clues of activity areas were noted for the outside surfaces.

Summary and Conclusions

Archaeomagnetic and radiocarbon dates were obtained from five of the six excavated pithouses at 29SJ 628 that were generally supportive of the relative architectural chronology derived previously. These dates were highly variable but roughly support a site occupation from about the late A.D. 600s into the early 700s (Chapter 6). Pithouses C, D, and E, in particular, suggest a short, consecutive construction sequence. The large upper floor of Pithouse C is D-shaped with a flat south wall, a bench, and an antechamber converted into a ventilator. The latter conversion probably took place in a relatively short time period.

Pithouse D, possibly built while Pithouse C was still in use, had a smaller main chamber than C but continued to have a flattish south wall and a bench. The interesting thing about Pithouse D is that it had both a ventilator and an antechamber—a set-up of questionable functional advantage appearing as if the builder were not quite certain what the vogue of the day was. The ventilator shaft was a relatively large, circular feature with dirt walls.

Compensation for the reduced floor area can be seen in the storage niches that occurred in both the antechamber and the south wall of the main chamber. In addition, these walls containing niches flare as they approach the floor, lessening the area to be roofed but increasing the floor space, and the northern roof support posts were incorporated into the bench face instead of the floor.

Pithouse E, probably constructed after Pithouse D, no longer retained the antechamber but kept the circular ventilator shaft, albeit of a slightly larger diameter than that of Pithouse D. The trend in the reduction of floor area continued. Pithouse E, with only 15.1 m^2 of floor area, had its northern main roof supports set into the bench as at Pithouse D, but later they were moved out into the main floor. The shape of its south wall had also changed from that in Pithouse D: at the ventilator opening, the wall curved sharply inward and then back outward on either side. This form became accentuated in the subsequent Pithouse A.

Pithouse A, although it differed greatly from Pithouse E and, according to the archaeomagnetic date, was built about 50 years after Pithouse E, had features that appeared to have been outgrowths of architectural trends in the three earlier houses. The floor area was further reduced, the walls flared outward, and the bench was absent. Niches encircle the chamber walls. The same undulation in the south wall at the ventilator opening in Pithouse E was present, and the house was more circular than the previous structures. Although the original shape of the ventilator shaft was is unknown, it was smaller and probably square. The apparent architectural hiatus between Pithouses E and A may indicate a break in occupation span or bias from incomplete excavation of all the site houses.

Two additional houses, Pithouses F and G, could not be initially chronometrically placed in the construction sequence. No dates were obtained from Pithouse F, and the archaeomagnetic sample from Pithouse G dated much too late. Recent reanalysis of the sample, however, places Pithouse G as one of the earliest at the site. Architecturally, Pithouse G shares some attributes with Pithouse D. The Pithouse G ventilator was slightly larger in diameter and the walls, which had wall niches, flared outward as they approached the floor except on the north side. No bench was present.

It is possible that Pithouse G was contemporaneous with Pithouse A, despite the similarities to Pithouse D, but then our assumptions about large circular ventilators being intermediate in time between antechambers and small, narrow, rectangular ventilator openings could be wrong or could have exceptions. An abrader fragment recovered from the upper fill of Pithouse G that fit the remaining fragment from the Pithouse D floor suggests that Pithouse G was abandoned before Pithouse D. Nevertheless, the proximity and similarity of the latter two houses suggests both were built by a single family or group over a short span of time.

The latest house at the site may have been Pithouse F. It was the smallest, was circular, and the walls were relatively vertical. Clearly, Pithouse C had long been abandoned and filled before Pithouse F was built. Morphologically, there seems a larger gap between the styles of Pithouses F and A then between Pithouses A and E. Pithouse F appears less utilitarian than the other pithouses at the site and similar to other proto-kivas or kivas dug in the rincon. Floor features, however, indicate that it was a living room.

Discussion

It seems that a single group may have been responsible for construction at the site. Since some house construction is a male-linked activity (Gillespie 1976), and males marry into matrilineal families, we would expect some diversity in construction styles. There are probably features, however, mainly floor features, that would reflect the woman's wishes and show less diversity if the same matrilineal group occupied the site.

Although the proximity of the pithouses, chronometric dates, and architecture suggest a sequential occupation of the houses, particularly Pithouses C, D, and E, it is difficult to assess this from the few cultural remains on the floors and the features. Any potential continuity among houses has been broken by not investigating the lower floors found in several of the houses and the unknown extent of the site settlement. Undoubtedly more contemporary site houses exist, probably including Pithouse A (left unexcavated) and Pithouse C at nearby 29SJ 627 (Truell 1992). The few floor artifacts did little to aid identification of specific work areas or tool kits, which could have reflected aspects of residential continuity. Considerably more work in the rincon addressing long-term residence and continuity was planned (Judge 1975), and much more was accomplished, but a systematic program to address this issue with follow-up publications did not materialize.

An examination of the floor features as a possible link to residential continuity was attempted. Hearth areas, considered the prominent domain of females (e.g., Gillespie 1976), might reflect attributes that uniquely distinguish individual or closely affiliated social groups. All structures exhibited firepits offset to the south from center of the main chamber, a location favored throughout the Anasazi region. Construction standards can vary (see McKenna 1986:32-37), however, but those at 29SJ 628 were all slab-lined, except in Pithouse C, and partly filled with a basal layer of burned sand, except in Pithouse G, which revealed several thin basal layers attributed to reuse.

In all cases but Pithouse E, which was burned down to the basal slab, the burning on the sides of the pit ceased at the top of the sand. There was little uniformity in the presence and size of the clay collar that occasionally capped the top of the firepit slabs. It was absent in Pithouse C, and it varied from 4-20 cm in height in Pithouse A where it had been replastered. Remains of carbonized fuel (brush) were found in each firepit except in Pithouse E. There, the firepit apparently had been cleaned out just prior to abandonment. Thus, if there was social continuity in the pithouse community, it is not apparent in the firepit construction, use, or abandonment.

Table I.3.1. List of Features at Site 29SJ 299 Except for Roofing Postholes.[a]

Feature	Length (cm)	Width (cm)	Height/ Depth (cm)	Volume (liters)	Fill Type	Fill Period	Lining	Open/Sealed	Comments
Pithouse A: Firepit 1	69	66	29/40	118.±	27?	Occ	L-P	O	Mouth = 3245 cm². Slab bottom. Without traditional collar rim.
Other Pit 1 top bottom	37 56	35 53	62	120.0	32,42	PO	L	O	Bell-shaped. Lined with sticks. Formerly central subfloor cist.
Other Pit 2 top bottom	32 48	31 36	53	100.8±	30	Int	U	S	Bell-shaped. Sealed with hatch cover. Formerly southern cist.
Other Pit 3	78	52	45-54	187.1	12	Int	U	S	Formerly eastern subfloor cist.
Other Pit 4	124	85	22	166.2	12	Int	L-S?	S	Assoc. with hatch cover. Formerly NE cist.
Other Pit 5	69	60	16	48.6	10,30	Occ?	U?	O	Pot Rest with slab bottom.
Other Pit 6	63	48	15	25.4	10	Occ?	U?	O	Pot Rest.
Other Pit 7A 7B	5 4	5 4	8-10 8-10	0.2 0.1	10? 10?	? ?	U? U?	O O	Ladder rests 36 cm apart.
Other Pit 8A 8B	6 5	6 5	8-10 8-10	0.3 0.2	10? 10?	? ?	U? U?	O O	Ladder rests 56 cm apart.
Other Pit 9A 9B	7± 5±	7± 5±	8-10 8-10	0.3± 0.2±	10? 10?	? ?	U? U?	O O	Ladder rests 23 cm apart north of FP1. Map location approximate.
Bin A pit in bottom	143 90	100 80	30-60 26	262.0 124.8±	42 42?	PO PO	L-S U?	O O	Manos on shelves in corners. Undercuts pithouse wall.
Bin B	110	105	40-48	443.9	42?	PO	L-S	O	Contains manos & polishing stones.
Bin C	70	40±	30±	79.0±	42?	PO	L-S	O	Part of Bin B?
Wall Niche 1	17	12	25	7.7±	32?	PO	U?	O	At floor level. Sipapu? Assoc. with small cover.

Chapter 3: Basketmaker III Excavation Reports 167

168   Windes et al.

Table I.3.1. List of Features at Site 29SJ 299 Except for Roofing Postholes, cont'd.[a]

Feature	Length (cm)	Width (cm)	Height/ Depth (cm)	Volume (liters)	Fill Type	Fill Period	Lining	Open/Sealed	Comments
Deflector	50	3-5	40	-	-	-	-	-	Consists of 2 upright slabs.
Tunnel	40	50-60	36+	-	?	PO	U?	O	18 cm above the main floor & 22 cm above ante chamber floor.
Pithouse A antechamber:									
Other Pit 1	30	30	13	9.0	?	PO?	U?	O	
Step entry	40-100	47	-	-	-	-	U?	O	7 cm above floor in SE wall.
Pithouse B (kiva):									
Firepit 1	56	42	21	59.1	25,28	Occ	L-SP	O	D-shaped; slab bottom.
Heating Pit 1	52	35	?	?	20/21	Occ	U	S-FP	Mouth = 1692 cm². Cuts HP 2.
Heating Pit 2	50	37	?	?	20/21	Occ	U	S-FP	Mouth = 1486 cm². Cut by HP 1.
Other Pit 1	36	33	24	13.7	26	Occ	U	S	Ash pit. Bowl-shaped.
Other Pit 2	40	40	17	15.7	26	Occ	U	S	Ash pit. Bowl-shaped.
Other Pit 3	35	34	25	23.3	26	Occ	U	S	Burned ash pit cut by OP 4.
Other Pit 4	137	133	26	379.3	20,26	Occ	U	S	
Other Pit 5	41	39	14	13.2	26,33	Occ	U	S	Bowl-shaped.
Other Pit 6	24	18	10	4.1	26	Occ	U	S	
Wall Niche 1 mouth base	96 117	38	56	120.6	10	PO	L-P	O	83 cm above floor.
Wall Niche 2 mouth base	58 66	28	44	40.1	10	PO	U	O	114 cm above floor. 18 cm wide Shelf 1 in front.
Wall Niche 3 mouth base	19 37	20 22	27	12.4	10	PO	U	O	72 cm above floor.
Wall Niche 4 mouth base	26 31	24 26	33	18.2	10	PO	U	O	60 cm above floor.
Wall Niche 5	21	20	27	8.9	10	PO	U	O	76 cm above floor.
Shelf 1	135	18	-	-	-	-	?	-	114 cm above floor.
Shelf 2	140	20	-	-	-	-	?	-	137 cm above floor.

Table I.3.1. List of Features at Site 29SJ 299 Except for Roofing Postholes, cont'd.[a]

Feature	Length (cm)	Width (cm)	Height/Depth (cm)	Volume (liters)	Fill Type	Fill Period	Lining	Open/Sealed	Comments
Ventilator tunnel subfloor	99	45	64	-	11,31	PO	L-S	O	Pole, twig, & adobe roofing. Assoc. with vent. cover.
Ventilator tunnel floor level	204	51	79-99	-	31	PO	U	O	
Ventilator shaft	30	25	208	-	11	PO	U	O	Plastered top edge.
Pithouse C:									
Tunnel	78	54	35+	-	-	PO	U	O	Unfinished. 95 cm above main floor & 31 cm above antechamber floor.
Pithouse D:									
Firepit 1	58	53	18	34.2	26	Occ	L-P	O	Mouth = 2219 cm². Manos in fill. Adobe collar 18 cm wide & 2-3 cm high.
Other Pit 1 top bottom	27 62	23 58	56	90.7	43	PO	L-P	O	Assoc. with cist cover. Bell-shaped pit. Formerly eastern subfloor cist.
Other Pit 2 top bottom	32 42	26 40	54	53.8	42	PO	L-P	O	Bell-shaped pit. Formerly northern subfloor cist.
Other Pit 3 top bottom	30 40	22 38	43	36.3	43	PO	U	O	Bell-shaped pit. Formerly western subfloor cist.
Other Pit 4 top bottom	40 42	31 40	43	60.0	22	Int	U	S	Formerly west-central subfloor cist.
Other Pit 5 top bottom	30 52	25 55	54?	39.4	22	PO?	U	S?	Under FP 1; bell-shaped pit with fill burned on top. Assoc. with cist cover.
Other Pit 6	13	13	4	0.5	10	Occ?	U?	O	Sipapu.
Bin A	140	128	15-40±	619.6	43	PO	L-P	O	10-15 cm lower than main floor. Undercuts pithouse wall 50 cm. Floor area = 1549 cm².

Table I.3.1. List of Features at Site 29SJ 299 Except for Roofing Postholes, cont'd.[a]

Feature	Length (cm)	Width (cm)	Height/ Depth (cm)	Volume (liters)	Fill Type	Fill Period	Lining	Open/Sealed	Comments
Bin B	130	95	15-40±	520.4	43?	PO	L-P	O	10-15 cm lower than main floor. Undercuts pithouse wall 36cm. Floor area = 1301 cm^2.
Wall Niche 1	39	28	32	27.4	43	PO	U	O	14 cm above floor. ½-moon shaped.
Wall Niche 2	70	40	33	72.6±	22	PO	U	O	Floor level. ½-moon shaped.
Wall Niche 3 mouth base	52 95	45	60	110.8±	31	PO	U	O	Floor level. Roofed with sticks at bench top?
Tunnel	40	70	32+	-	?	PO	U	O	Connects antechamber & main room. 38 cm above main floor & 14 cm above antechamber floor.
Deflector	49	3-5	36	-	-	-	-	-	Upright slab. 64 cm from tunnel.
East Wing Wall	155	18-20	5-10	-	-	-	L-P	-	Adobe ridge. Contains 1 slab at east end.
West Wing Wall	150	18-20	5-10	-	-	-	L-P	-	Adobe ridge.
Pithouse D antechamber:									
Other Pit 1	50	42	51	91.±	?	PO	L-P	O	Bowl-shaped entry through wall.
Pithouse E:									
Firepit 1	60	53	42	106.4	27	Occ	L-SP	O	Mouth = 2549 cm^2. 5 slab liner (inc. 1 metate).
Heating Pit 1	73	53	20	61.7	26,28	Occ	L-P	S	Mouth = 3084 cm^2. Sealed with red-brown adobe.
Other Pit 1 top bottom	15 23	15 23	48	13.6±	11	PO	L-P	S	Sealed with red-brown adobe. Bell-shaped.
Other Pit 2A 2B	79+ 38	14 22	5 11	4.1+ 3.6±	11 11	PO PO	L-P L-P	S?	Sealed with red-brown adobe. Filled with red sand. Cuts OP 7A.
Other Pit 3A 3B	12+ 21	13 16	3 10	0.4+ 2.5±	11 11	PO PO	L-P L-P	S S	Sealed with red-brown adobe. Sealed with red-brown adobe. Lined with white plaster.

Table I.3.1. List of Features at Site 29SJ 299 Except for Roofing Postholes, cont'd.[a]

Feature	Length (cm)	Width (cm)	Height/ Depth (cm)	Volume (liters)	Fill Type	Fill Period	Lining	Open/Sealed	Comments
Other Pit 4	33	20	12	7.4	11	PO	L-P	S	Sealed with red-brown plaster. Lined with white plaster.
Other Pit 5	13	11	10	1.5	11	PO	L-P	S	Sealed with red-brown plaster. Posthole?
Other Pit 6A	8	8	5	0.3	-	PO	?	O	Deflector posthole?
6B	8	8	5	0.3	-	PO	?	O	Deflector posthole?
Ventilator tunnel	?	33	35	-	-	PO	U	S	Sealed with adobe & whitish plaster. Floor, 10-15 cm above room floor, repaired with red-brown adobe.
Ventilator slot	25	1	1	-	11	PO	?	?	For slab 38-x-35-x-cm found nearby?
Deflector groove	33	5	4	0.4	-	PO	?	O	Groove for stone slab.
East Wing Wall	185	6-20		-	-	-	L-SP	-	Groove for stone slab.
Groove A	26	9	?	-	11?	PO	?	O	Groove for stones lab.
Groove B	41	8-12	?	-	11?	PO	?	O	Groove for stone slab.
Groove C	38	20	?	-	11?	PO	?	O	Groove for stone slab.
Groove D	29	3	?	-	11?	PO	?	O	Groove for stone slab.
West Wing Wall	100+	12	?	-	-	-	L-SP	-	Part left unexcavated.
Surface Features:									
Room 1	130	125	50	6256.2	30	PO	U	O	
pit in floor	25	25	18	8.3	30	PO	U	O	
Room 2	150	140	35	5614.4	30	PO	U	O	Lino Gray seed jar on floor.
Room 3	152	134	30	4657.6	11,20	PO	U	O	PO roasting pit in top fill.
pit in floor	25	25	18	8.3	11	PO	U	O	
Room 4	141	130	45	6344.9	11,20	PO	U	O	PO hearth in top fill.
Room 5	235	203	58-65	2316.6	30	PO	U	O	Cut by Mesa Verde kiva?
Room 6 top	170	90	72-75	1100±	10,11	PO	L-P/ sticks	O	Bell-shaped with entry. Entry step = 40-x-33-x-16-cm.
bottom	190	174							
Room 7 (hearth)	151	68	8-10	92.4	11,21?	Occ/PO	U	O	Late hearth? Burned floor-N. end.
Room 8	175	165	31-40	805.8	27,30	Occ/PO	U	O	PO roasting pit in fill.

Table I.3.1. List of Features at Site 29SJ 299 Except for Roofing Postholes, cont'd.[a]

Feature	Length (cm)	Width (cm)	Height/ Depth (cm)	Volume (liters)	Fill Type	Fill Period	Lining	Open/Sealed	Comments
Room 9	212	117	30-40	743.9	22	PO	U	O	Contains small ventilator; form resembles Hohokam pithouse.
pit in floor	32	28	9	5.7	22	PO	U	O	
Room 10	165	115	24	369.5	10	PO	U	O	Floor covered with plaster.
pit in floor	44	36	11	13.8	10	PO	U	O	
Room 11 top	90	86	44	174.2	27,30	Occ	L-S	O	Roasting Pit mouth = 6307 cm². Slab floor. Next to Pithouse D.
bottom	55	53							
Room 12	220	111-126	24	?	43	PO	L-P	O	Floor = 2.66 m².
Room 13	279	134	9	?	43	PO	L-S	O	Floor = 3.70 m².
Room 14	265	118	10-15	?	43	PO	L-S	O	Floor = 3.10 m².
Room 15	182	80-95	31	?	43	PO	L-SP	O	Floor = 1.66 m².
Ramada 1	240	165	0	-	10	PO	-	O	Floor = 6.36 m². Partly over Rm 8. Only scattered remains.
firepit	56	?	?	?	?	?	L-S	O	
Ramada 2	2400	1000	0	-	10	PO	-	O	Area = 24.0 m². Assoc. with Pithouse E.

[a] See Tables I.7.4-I.7.5 for an explanation of the feature and attribute codes.
[b] Wall niche measurements are ordered here by mouth width, mouth height, and depth.

Table I.3.2. List of Postholes in the Site 29SJ 299 Pithouses.[a]

Posthole No.	Length (cm)	Width (cm)	Depth (cm)	Volume (liters)	Fill Type	Fill Period	Shims	Base Stone	Est. post size (cm)	Lining	Comments
Pithouse A:											
NE Posthole	17	17	58	13.2	52	Occ	0	0		L-S	
NW Posthole	18	18	42	10.7	52	Occ	0	0		L-S	
SW Posthole	16	16	60	12.1	52	Occ	0	0		L-S	In Bin A.
SE Posthole	17	17	42	9.5	52	Occ	0	0		L-S	In Bin B.
Pithouse A bench:											
Posthole 1	7	7	?	?	?	?				U	
Posthole 2	7	7	?	?	?	?				U	
Posthole 3	8	8	?	?	?	?				U	
Posthole 4	10	10	?	?	?	?				U	
Posthole 5	10	10	?	?	?	?				U	
Posthole 6	11	11	5	0.4	?	?				U	
Posthole 7	6	6	?	?	?	?				U	
Posthole 8	7	7	?	?	?	?				U	
Posthole 9	8	8	?	?	?	?				U	
Posthole 10	9	9	?	?	?	?				U	
Posthole 11	9	9	?	?	?	?				U	
Pithouse A antechamber:											
Posthole 12	15	15	46	7.8	52?	Occ	0	0		U	
Posthole 13	20	20	36	9.7	52?	Occ	0	0		U	
Posthole 14	16	16	36	8.0	52?	Occ	0	0		U	
Posthole 15	17	17	32	6.9	52	Occ	0	0		U	
Posthole 16	18	18	44	12.2	52?	Occ	0	0		U	
Posthole 17	20	20	34	10.2	52?	Occ	0	0		U	
Posthole 18	21	21	34	11.4	52?	Occ	0	0		U	
Posthole 19	17	15	?	?	52	Occ	0	0		U	

Table I.3.2. List of Postholes in the Site 29SJ 299 Pithouses, cont'd.[a]

Posthole No.	Length (cm)	Width (cm)	Depth (cm)	Volume (liters)	Fill Type	Fill Period	Shims	Base Stone	Est. post size (cm)	Lining	Comments
Posthole 20	21	21	48	15.5	52?	Occ	0	0		U	
Posthole 21	28	28	44	27.0	52?	Occ	0	0		U	
Pithouse D:											
NE posthole	18	18	43	14.0	52	Occ	0	1		U	
NW Posthole	18	18	67	18.7	52	Occ	0	1		U	
SW Posthole	16	16	50	8.8	52	Occ	0	1		U	
SE Posthole	15	15	60	11.3	52	Occ	0	1		U	
Pithouse D bench:											
Posthole 1	14	14	8±	1.1	?	?	0	0		U	
Posthole 2	13	13	8±	1.1	?	?	0	0		U	
Posthole 3	13	13	8±	1.1	?	?	0	0		U	
Posthole 4	13	13	10	1.3	?	?	0	0		U	
Posthole 5	15	10	10±	1.1	?	?	0	0		U	
Posthole 6	15	15	10±	1.7	?	?	0	0		U	
Posthole 7	12	12	10±	1.1	?	?	0	0		U	
Posthole 8	8	8	10±	0.5	?	?	0	0		U	
Posthole 9	12	12	8-10	1.0	?	?	0	0		U	
Posthole 10	15	15	10±	1.6	?	?	0	0		U	
Posthole 11	13	13	9±	1.2	?	?	0	0		U	
Posthole 12	15	15	8±	1.4	?	?	0	0		U	
Posthole 13	11	6	8±	1.8	?	?	0	0		U	
Posthole 14	17	17	8±	1.6	?	?	0	0		U	
Posthole 15	20	20	52	16.3	12,13	?	0	0		U	
Posthole 16	16	12	10	1.5	?	?	0	0		U	
Posthole 17	11	8	5±	0.4	?	?	0	0		U	
Posthole 18	12	12	5±	0.6	?	?	0	0		U	

Table I.3.2. List of Postholes in the Site 29SJ 299 Pithouses, cont'd.[a]

Posthole No.	Length (cm)	Width (cm)	Depth (cm)	Volume (liters)	Fill Type	Fill Period	Shims	Base Stone	Est. post size (cm)	Lining	Comments
Posthole 19	12	10	5±	0.5	?	?	0	0		U	
Posthole 20	16	11	8±	1.1	?	?	0	0		U	
Posthole 21	10	7	8-10	0.5	?	?	0	0		U	
Pithouse D antechamber:											
Posthole 22	12	12	18	2.0	?	?	0	0		U	In entry between chambers.
Posthole 23	18	18	34	8.7	11,13	?	0	0		U	
Posthole 24	19	19	41	11.6	11,13	?	0	0		U	
Posthole 25	16	16	40	8.0	11,13	?	0	0		U	
Posthole 26	19	19	41	11.6	11,13	?	0	0		U	
Posthole 27	13	13	13	1.8	?	?	0	0		U	In entry between chambers.
Pithouse E:											
Posthole 1	41	25	63	46.3	52	Occ	6	1		U	Hole is burned. Hole leans towards house center.
Posthole 2	37	29	90	73.4	52	Occ	5	1		U	Hole is burned.
Posthole 3	35	21	65	45.6	52	Occ	0	0		U	Auxiliary PH. Hole leans towards house center.

[a] See Tables I.7.4–I.7.5 for an explanation of the feature and attribute codes.

Table I.3.3. Site 29SJ 299, Pithouse A and Pithouse B Distribution of Floor 1 Materials.[a]

Artifact Number	Artifact Class	Lithic Material, Ceramic Ware, or Faunal Species	FS No.
Pithouse A			
1	Obelisk Gray olla (21.1 cm diameter-x-19.0 cm high)	Cibola Grayware. Restored, with pieces missing. Calculated volume = 19,439 ml (see Volume II, Plate II.2.2c,d).	104
2	Obelisk Gray tecomaté jar (33.5 cm in diameter-x-27.0 cm high) with Lino Gray olla neck in mouth	Cibola Graywares. Restored, with pieces missing. Calculated volume = 15,902 ml (see Volume II, Plate II.2.2c,d).	105
3	Lino Gray jar	Cibola Grayware (65 body sherds).	106
4	Obelisk Gray tecomaté jar (19.2 cm diameter-x-16.3 cm high) jar with bone spoon [scraper?] inside	Cibola Grayware. Restored, with pieces missing. Tecomaté jar has a calculated volume of 2,770 ml (see Volume II, Plate II.2.2c,d).	107
4	Obelisk Gray tecomaté jar (ca. 26 cm diameter-x-24 cm high)	Cibola Grayware. 1/6 vessel (12 sherds).	107
5	Cover for jar or nearby sipapu (23-x-20-x-2-cm; 1295 g)	2000 (sandstone). Edge chipped to shape. 1 surface 50 percent burned and blackened.	108
6	Obelisk Gray tecomaté fragment (ca. 20 cm diameter-x-18 cm high)	Cibola Grayware. 1/3 vessel. Sooted. North of Bin A, against bench wall. FS bag includes 2 narrow clapboard jar sherds (?).	109
7	Lino Gray jar with bulging neck collar (17 cm diameter-x-13 cm high)	Cibola Grayware. Calculated volume = 1,912± ml. 1/3 of a jar. North of Bin A, against bench wall.	110
8	Lino Gray pinch ware jar (7.5 cm in diameter-x-7.5+ cm high)	Cibola Grayware. Crude; partly restorable; top missing (see Volume II, Plate II.2.3a).	111
9	Concretion (12.7-x-11.7-x-6.8-cm; 847.5 g)	2000 (sandstone). Half sphere with cup in center. Ground & burned.	112
10	Trough metate (69-x-55-x-5-cm; 27.7 kg)	2000 (sandstone). Whole, in 2 pieces (recent?). Trough = 41.5-x-22.5-x-2.5cm.	113
11	Trough metate (62-x-53-x-4-cm; 21.8 kg)	2000 (sandstone). Trough = 35-x-20-x-2-cm.	114
12	Trough metate (67-x-39-x-4-cm; 19.3 kg)	2000 (sandstone). Trough = 48-x-20-x-2-cm.	115
13	Trough metate (43-x-36-x-7-cm; 18.6 kg)(whole;new)	2000 (sandstone). Trough = 24-x-19-x-1-cm. Found upside down; circle (8.5-x-9.5-cm) of red paint on bottom (Munsell 1975: 10YR 4/8).	116

Table I.3.3. Site 29SJ 299, Pithouse A and Pithouse B Distribution of Floor 1 Materials, cont'd.[a]

Artifact Number	Artifact Class	Lithic Material, Ceramic Ware, or Faunal Species	FS No.
14	Trough metate fragment (42.5-+-x-44-x-5.5-cm; 12.5+ kg)	2000 (sandstone). Trough = ?-x-22-x-3.2-cm. Worn out. Found leaning against wall with front of trough missing.	117
15	Lino Gray canteen (14 cm diameter-x-14 cm high)	Cibola Grayware. Partly restorable. 2 lugs (see Volume II, Plate II.2.2a). Near NE corner.	118
15	Obelisk Gray jar (ca. 19 cm diameter-x-21 cm high)	Cibola Grayware. 4/5 vessel (37 sherds). Bottom burned out. Near NE corner.	118C
16	La Plata B/w bowl (medium)	Cibola Whiteware (see Volume II, Plate II.2.5a, II.2.7).	119
17	Obelisk Gray tecomaté jar (part of #6?) (ca. 17-cm diameter-x-14-cm high)	Cibola Grayware. 1/3 vessel (30 sherds).	122
18	Cist hatch cover (57-x-53-x-3-cm)	2000 (sandstone). Left on site.	123
19	Cist hatch cover (60-x-56-x-3-cm)	2000 (sandstone). Left on site.	124
20	Cist hatch cover (43-x-40-x-2.5-cm)	2000 (sandstone). Left on site.	125
21	Obelisk Gray tecomaté (ca. 20 cm diameter-x-17 cm high)	Cibola Grayware. 1/3 vessel (72 sherds). Outside of Bin A.	126
21	La Plata B/w bowl (16 cm diameter-x-8.5 cm high)	Cibola Whiteware. 1/3+ vessel (17 sherds). Heavily blackened and burned. Outside eastern corner of Bin A.	126
22	Anvil-abrader (32-x-28-x-7-cm; 9850 g)	2000 (sandstone). Reworked metate fragment with 2-3 flat grinding surfaces for both sides. Burned. Much new grinding and pecking.	127
23	Floor polisher (17-x-10-x-6.8-cm; 1950 g)	2000 (sandstone). Loaf-shaped with a few peck marks. Burned.	128
24	Obelisk Gray olla (21.1 cm diameter-x-19.0 cm high)	Cibola Grayware. Sooted. In Bin C. Restored, with pieces missing. Calculated volume = 3,780 ml (see Volume II, Plate II.2.2e).	129[b]
25	Hammerstone (7.6-x-6.2-x-5.8-cm; 289.5 g)	1053 (High Surface Chert with black inclusions).	130
26	Raw clay (15+ pieces; 5 g)	Natural clay.	133
27	Pottery scraping sherds associated with artifacts 1, 2, and 3 (whole vessels) + misc. sherds (FS 134)	Cibola Grayware (see Volume II, Plate II.2.13 and Table II.2.11b).	93

178 Windes et al.

Table I.3.3. Site 29SJ 299, Pithouse A and Pithouse B Distribution of Floor 1 Materials, cont'd.[a]

Artifact Number	Artifact Class	Lithic Material, Ceramic Ware, or Faunal Species	FS No.
27	Misc. sherds (256)	Scattered with restorable vessels (see Volume II, Table II.2.26).	134
28a	Floor polisher (12.9-x-9.7-x-5-cm; 954.4 g)	4000 (quartzite). 100 percent burned cobble. Has minor scattered pecking marks. In OP 2.	138A1
28b	Mano? fragment (6.5-+-x-10.8-x-3.3-cm; 318.6 g)	2000 (sandstone). Burned. In OP 2.	138A2
28c	Hammerstone (7.5-x-6.3-x-4.7-cm; 327.7 g)	4000 (black quartzite). In OP 2.	138B
29	Cist hatch-cover (29-x-21.5-x-2-cm; 1903 g)	2000 (sandstone). Edge chipped to shape. Both surfaces burned, 60 percent and 100 percent, respectively. In OP 2.	139
30	Bone awl (13.4-x-1.7-x-0.7-cm; 14.6 g)	Unidentified large mammal (artiodactyl).	140, 169
31	Floor polisher (14-x-10-x-6-cm; 1198 g)	4000 (banded quartzite). 100 percent burned cobble. In Bin B.	141
32	Floor polisher (16-x-9-x-7-cm; 1723 g)	3100 (granite). Cobble; some pecking on 1 side & ends. In Bin B.	142
33	Floor polisher (17-x-11-x-9-cm; 2322 g)	3242 (diorite; San Juan River cobble?). Cobble, with minor burning. Pecking marks on 1 side. In Bin B.	143
34	Floor polisher (12-x-8-x-6-cm; 1023 g)	3300 (porphyritic andesite; San Juan River cobble?). Cobble. Pecking on ends. In Bin B.	144
35	Mano (19.2-x-11.4-x-3.2-cm; 1330 g)	2000 (sandstone). Large pecking marks on 1 flat surface–used as an abrader on 1 surface? In Bin B.	145
36	Mano (10-x-8-x-5-cm; 708 g)	2000 (sandstone). In Bin B.	146
37	Polishing stone (9-x-8-x-4-cm; 392 g)	4000 (quartzite). Cobble; heavily battered on both ends. Red stain or burn on 1 side. In Bin B.	147
38	Floor polisher (12-x-10-x-5-cm; 893 g)	4000 (quartzite). Cobble; scattered minor pecking marks. Bin B.	148
39	Sherds (6) from Obelisk Gray jar	Cibola Grayware. Outside NW corner of Bin B. Missing.	149
40	Anvil-abrader (25-x-22-x-3.6-cm; 2767 g)	2000 (sandstone). Reworked metate fragment. Ground flat on opposite sides. Rectangular tabular shape. Burned spot. In Bin B.	150

Table I.3.3. Site 29SJ 299, Pithouse A and Pithouse B Distribution of Floor 1 Materials, cont'd.[a]

Artifact Number	Artifact Class	Lithic Material, Ceramic Ware, or Faunal Species	FS No.
40	Mano (19.2-x-13.0-x-3.8-cm; 1610.6 g)	2000 (sandstone). Burned black on the only use surface. In Bin B.	150
40	Mano fragment (8.3+-x-11.3-x-3.3-cm; 416.5 g)	2000 (sandstone). Airfoil shape. Minor burned spot. In Bin B.	150
41	Floor polisher (11-x-10-x-6-cm; 944 g)	4000 (quartzite). Cobble. Fire-cracked and 100 percent burned. Next to OP 2.	152
42	Floor polisher (11.7-x-10.3-x-2-cm; 499 g)	4515 (metamorphic amphibolite?; dark green). Flattish, discoid shape. Highly polished.	153
43a	Mano (21-x-11.7-x-3.8-cm; 1655 g)	2000 (sandstone). Tabular stone. In Bin A..	154.1
43b	Mano/abrader/palette (17.5-x-12.7-x-2.6-cm; 1122 g)	2000 (sandstone). Finely ground on side opposite metate-use side. Fine side reveals perhaps paint residue in a few pits: yellow-brown Munsell 10YR 5/8. Mano worn out? In Bin A.	154.2
44	Trough metate fragments	2000 (sandstone). In OP 5. Left at site.	156
45	Abrader-anvil (16-x-10-x-8-cm; 1814 g)	2000 (sandstone). In OP 5. Burned. Ground and pecked into loaf shape.	157
46a	Chipped stone (3: 0.1, 0.2, 1.4 g)	1112 (cherty silicified wood).	158C
46b	Unmodified minerals (5): Selenite (3; 3.8 g) Calcite (2; 5.0 g)	All burned. 5040 (gypsum). 2770 (calcite).	158D
46c	Side-notched projectile point (2.0-x-1.2-x-0.4-cm; 0.7 g)	3500 (obsidian). In OP 5, "Tourist" point: unifacially flaked. Sourced as Valle Grande, Jemez, by Shackley and Dillian (2000).	159
47a	Sherds (2): Obleisk Gray	Cibola Grayware.	161
47a	Polishing/hammerstone (6.9-x-5.9-x-4.8-cm; 285.8 g)	4000 (quartzite). Cobble with lightly battered ends. Burned?	161.2
47a	Flake (2.3-x-1.4-x-0.4-cm; 1.4 g)	1112 (cherty silicified wood).	161.1
47b	Flake (1.9-x-1.4-x-0.1-cm; 0.5 g)	1142 (undifferentiated chalcedonic silicified wood).	162
48	Active abrader (7.3-x-5.8-x-3.3-cm; 142 g)	2000 (coarse yellow sandstone). Ground flat on 1 side. Loaf-shaped.	163
49a	Hammerstone (7.1-x-6-x-5.5-cm; 316.5 g)	1142 (chalcedonic silicified wood).	164.1
49b	Hammerstone (9.1-x-7.8-x-5.8-cm; 493 g)	2202 (silicified brown/gray concretion/chert).	164.2

Table I.3.3. Site 29SJ 299, Pithouse A and Pithouse B Distribution of Floor 1 Materials, cont'd.[a]

Artifact Number	Artifact Class	Lithic Material, Ceramic Ware, or Faunal Species	FS No.
50a	Mano (17-x-9.8-x-2.8-cm; 755 g)	2000 (sandstone). 20 percent burned. Minor paint?? deposits on ground side opposite metate-use surface: red (Munsell 10R 4/6?), yellow brown (Munsell 10YR 5/6?). Next to hearth	165.1
50b	Mano fragment (8.3+-x-9.7-x-2.9-cm; 351.0+ g)	2000 (sandstone). 100 percent burned; 1 end & 1 side exhibits percussion spall removal. 1/3-1/4 mano. Next to hearth	165.2
51	Mortar	2000 (sandstone). Missing	166
52	Sherds (plain gray = 9; indented corrugated = 1)	Cibola Graywares	167
53	Trough metate fragment (54+-x-39-x-8-cm; 19.4 kg+)	2000 (sandstone). Used upright in slab wall, mortared to floor. Trough = 30+-x-25-x-5-cm. Trough end missing; 4/5 metate. Kill hole through trough.	190
54	Trough metate (53.5-x-54-x-10-cm; 34.5 kg)	2000 (sandstone). Used upright in slab wall, mortared to floor. Trough = 35-x-21-x-6-cm. Whole.	191
55	Human bone (1)	Male, right tibula fragment	192
56	Hammerstones (2)?	4000 (quartzite)? Not analyzed	no #
57a	Tubular bead necklace (10 beads; range 3-4-x-16-34-mm; 0.1-0.8 g)	Indeterminant medium-size bird shaft (see on the Chaco Website, image B4 and Western National Parks Association 2004:26 for color photographs). In OP 1. See Plate II.10.1a	173A
57b	Gaming piece (2.3-x-0.5-x-0.1-cm; 0.2 g)	Bone from medium/large mammal. In OP 1	173B
58	Firedog/abrader? (14.2-x-10.0-x-5.7-cm; 1209 g)	2000 (sandstone). Irregular chunk flaked to shape and well-ground flat on two opposing surfaces. Parallel cutting? marks across 1 surface. 100 percent burned and partly blackened. In Bin C	193
Pithouse B			
59	Trough metate (58-x-48-x-12-cm; 39.0 kg)	2000 (sandstone). Used in construction of ventilator shaft. Trough = 43-x-22-x-9-cm	269

Table I.3.3. Site 29SJ 299, Pithouse A and Pithouse B Distribution of Floor 1 Materials, cont'd.[a]

Artifact Number	Artifact Class	Lithic Material, Ceramic Ware, or Faunal Species	FS No.
60	Sherds (plain gray = 2; Red Mesa B/w = 2)	Cibola Grayware and Whiteware. In ventilator tunnel floor.	230
61	Active abrader (7.3-x-6.3-x-2.4-cm; 106 g)	2000 (coarse yellow sandstone). Mano-like fragment.	229
62	Ventilator tunnel cover (38.5-x-30.5-x-2.0-cm; est. 4635 g)	2000 (sandstone) Chipped edge; rectangular. 6 fragments, plus 1 missing. Ventilator tunnel opening cover?	319; 288
63	Sherds (plain gray = 3; PII-PIII whiteware = 2)	Cibola Grayware and Whiteware. In Firepit.	232
64	Sherds (Escavada/Puerco B/w = 2)	Cibola Whiteware. In OP 1.	321
65	Sherds (Partial Kiatuthlanna B/w bowl)	Cibola Whiteware. In OP 2.	323
66	Chipped stone (10 flakes from the same 2 cores)	1011 (fossiliferous chert): 2 whole & 1 unutilized flakes (5.6-17.6 g) 1140 (chalcedonic silicified wood): 2 unutilized & 5 utilized flakes (1.9-10.9 g).	324
67	Sherds (plain gray = 5)	Cibola Grayware. In OP 6.	325
--	Sherds in floor (plain gray = 4; BMIII-PI whiteware = 2; PII-PIII whiteware = 2)	Cibola Grayware and Whiteware. No specific location.	320

[a] See distribution in Figure I.3.3 and whole and restorable vessel information in Volume II, Table 2.11.
[b] FS 129 has other catalogued items but these are in error.

Table I.3.4. Site 29SJ 299, Pithouse A, Stratum B (Associated Roof Fall Materials) and Floor Fill.[a]

Pithouse A Antechamber (fill above floor)

Artifact Number	Artifact Class	Lithic Material, Ceramic Ware, or Faunal Species	FS No.
-	Azurite (2):	5310 (azurite).	
	13-x-13-x-8-cm; 2.5 g	Natural, ball-like shape. Some grinding. Munsell 5B 5.5/4±.	176
	5-x-5-x-4-cm; 0.1 g	Irregular piece, ground flat on 3 sides. Munsell 5B 5.5/4±.	176
-	Turquoise	5300 (turquoise). Modified. Missing.	177
-	Stones	Missing.	
-	Bones (37)	Cottontail (3; 2 burned), jackrabbit (2; 1 burned), Gunnison's prairie dog (1), *Peromyscus* sp. mouse (1), small/medium mammal (18; 1 burned), medium/large mammal (3; all burned), unknown bird (2), unknown bird or mammal (7).	178
-	Worked bone (38.7-x-4.5-x-2.4-mm; 0.6 g)	Indeterminant medium/large-size mammal, shaft fragment.	178-1
-	Bone bead fragment (15.6-x-5.7-x-1.6-mm; 1.6 g)	Indeterminant medium-size mammal, shaft fragment.	178-2
-	Sherds (300):	Multiple ceramic traditions.	
	Lino Gray (10)		
	plain gray (207)		
	Lino Fugitive Red (68)		
	Obelisk Gray (4)		
	Woodruff Smudged (1)		
	La Plata B/w (5)		
	Lino B/g (1)		
	PII-III indented corrugated rim (2)		
-	Palette/abrader (12.2-x-10.8-x-2.2-cm; 452.3 g)	2000 (sandstone). Irregular, tabular stone. 1 surface moderately ground; opposite side, lightly ground. All surfaces and edges covered in red paint (Munsell 2.5YR 4/8). Sooted and burned? Former firepit liner?	179
-	Abrader (7.7-x-7.5-x-2.4-cm; 267.2 g)	2000 (sandstone). Tabular shape, finely ground on 1 surface and poorly ground on opposite surface. 1 edge=some grinding. May have some faint paint residue on 1 surface.	180
-	Abrader fragment (8.7+-x-8.6+-x 5.7-cm; 608+g)	2000 (sandstone). Cobble-like shape; former mano fragment? 90 percent burned. 2 opposite surfaces well ground, + 1 edge.	180
-	Abrader fragment (5.7+?-x-6.8-x-3.0-cm;221.6+g)	2000 (sandstone). 2 opposite surface well ground. Faint paint smears on both surfaces?–yellow-brown Munsell 2.5Y 6/4, yellow-red Munsell 5YR 5/8?	180
-	Chopper (10.2-x-9.1-x-1.9-cm; 259.9 g)	2000 (sandstone). Former mano fragment reused by bifacial flaking 2 edges and unifacial flaking a 3rd edge.	180

Table I.3.4. Site 29SJ 299, Pithouse A, Stratum B (Associated Roof Fall Materials) and Floor Fill, cont'd.[a]

Artifact Number	Artifact Class	Lithic Material, Ceramic Ware, or Faunal Species	FS No.
-	Manuport (7.1-x-6.0-x-3.0-cm; 202.6 g)	4000 (quartzite). Natural pebble.	180
-	Concretion (10.3-x-7.6-x-2.8-cm; 242.7 g)	2000 (sandstone). Roughly a hemisphere, bowl-like. Broken edges where cracked in half are intermittently ground, as is bottom.	181
-	Chipped stones (24)		
	Core (max. size, 5.4 cm; 31.4 g)	1010 (fossiliferous chert).	
	Utilized flake (0.6 g)	1050 (High Surface Chert).	
	Whole flake (1.0 g)	1052 (High Surface Chert).	
	Whole flakes (2; 8.9 g)	1053 (High Surface Chert).	
	Angular debris (2.6 g)	1053 (High Surface Chert).	
	Angular debris (0.4 g)	1060 (red jasper).	
	Utilized flakes (3; 12.4 g)	1112 (cherty silicified wood).	
	Utilized flake (1.0 g)	1113 (cherty silicified wood).	
	Angular debris (2; 1.0 g)	1113 (cherty silicified wood).	
	Utilized flake (1.0 g)	1140 (chalcedonic silicified wood).	
	Retouched flake (0.4 g)	1140 (chalcedonic silicified wood).	
	Whole flake (0.9 g)	1140 (chalcedonic silicified wood).	
	Angular debris (2; 2.5 g)	1142 (chalcedonic silicified wood).	
	Utilized flake (1.3 g)	1145 (chalcedonic silicified wood).	
	Retouched flake (6.7 g)	1230 (chalcedony with red inclusions).	
	Angular debris (0.9 g)	3520 (Jemez obsidian). Not analyzed to source.	
	Utilized flake (0.6 g)	4005 (quartzite).	
	Whole flake (0.8 g)	Missing. Probably natural pebbles of quartzite.	182
-	Polishing stones	2000 (sandstone). Left on site.	183
-	Shaped stone (16-x-13-x-5-cm)	2000 (sandstone). Left on site.	184
-	Trough metate fragment	2000 (soft yellowish sandstone). Irregular chunk with ca. 15 sharpening grooves all over, plus 2 ground notches. Much grinding on bottom and some edges ground off. Two largest grooves (by awls?): 125-x-5 mm and 105-x-4 mm.	185
-	Sharpening stone (24-x-19-x-9.8 cm; 3870 g)		186
-	Palette (19-x-16.2-x-7.2 cm; 2328 g)	2000 (sandstone). Former metate fragment? Ground trough area (9-x-10 cm) used for yellow paint mixing (Munsell 10YR 6/8).	187
-	Mano (17.2-x-11.1-x-4.3 cm; 1432 g)	2000 (sandstone). Blocky, tabular shape. 100 percent burned.	188
-	Pestle	Missing.	189

184 Windes et al.

Table I.3.4. Site 29SJ 299, Pithouse A, Stratum B (Associated Roof Fall Materials) and Floor Fill, cont'd.[a]

Artifact Number	Artifact Class	Lithic Material, Ceramic Ware, or Faunal Species	FS No.
Pithouse A Main Chamber (Stratum B)			
-	Dendrochronological and C-14 samples (53)	From burned structural wood roof elements.	25-77
-	Roofing impressions (8): largest= 11.2-x-11.1-x-6.7 cm; 397 g 13.3-x-8.6-x-5.8 cm; 536 g	From the pithouse roof adobe. 100 percent oxidized. Stratum A+. Brush impressions, + 1 beam impression, est. at 6 cm diameter. Brush & corn leaf? impressions, + 1 beam impression, est. at 8 cm diameter.	79
-	Obelisk Gray fugitive red jar fragments (10 sherds)	Cibola Grayware. Maybe 1/15 of a jar. Stratum A.	80
-	Bone awl (4 fragments)(109.1-x-5.2-x-3.0 mm; 1.4 g)	*Lepus* sp. (jackrabbit) radius. 100 percent burned black. Stratum A.	81
-	Obelisk Gray jar fragments (19 sherds)	Cibola Grayware. Maybe 1/10 of a jar. Stratum A.	82
-	Charred roofing brush? (6.5- g)	Carbonized brush (unidentified).	83
-	Bone awl (95.2-x-5.2-x-3.0 mm; 4.1 g)	*Lepus* sp. (jackrabbit) distal end. 2 pieces.	84
-	Bone bead fragment (28.6-x-8.5-x-2.0 mm; 0.6 g)	Indeterminant bird/mammal long bone.	85
-	Groundstone (26.8-x-12.9-x-5.7 cm; 4020± g)	2000 (sandstone). Pecked to a loaf shape; mano-blank like. 1 concave ground surface; opposite side ground flat.	86
-	Bone (1)	Small/medium-size mammal long bone, burned.	86
-	Bones (3)	Cottontail innominate (1), jackrabbit rib and radius (2); 1 slightly burned).	87
-	Chipped stones (7) Utilized flake (2.0 g) Utilized flake (0.8 g) Whole flake (1.1 g) Angular debris (7.8 g)	1052 (High Surface Chert). 1120 (red silicified wood). 1140 (chalcedonic silicified wood). 1140 (chalcedonic silicified wood).	88
-	Sherds (100) Lino Gray (2) Plain gray (54) Lino Fugitive Red (8) Obelisk Gray (34) La Plata B/s (1) Wingate B/r (1)	Mixed ceramic traditions. Redware is out of context.	89

Table I.3.4. Site 29SJ 299, Pithouse A, Stratum B (Associated Roof Fall Materials) and Floor Fill, cont'd.[a]

Artifact Number	Artifact Class	Lithic Material, Ceramic Ware, or Faunal Species	FS No.
-	Sherds (8): Obleisk Gray	Cibola Grayware.	90
-	Pecking stone? (7.6-x-6.5-x-5.9-cm; 421.1 g)	4000 (quartzite). Natural pyramidal cobble with some pecking on 1 edge.	91
-	Obelisk Gray jar fragment (18-x-20-cm)	Cibola Grayware. Freshly broken into 5 pieces.	92
-	Pottery scrapers (3) 1) Obeisk Gray jar sherd (8.6-x-6.8±-x-0.5-cm; 44.6+ g) 2) Plain gray sooted jar sherd (9.3-x-5.8-0.4; 42.4 g) 3) La Plata B/w bowl sherd (9.5-x-7.2±-x-0.4-cm; 35.3+g)	Associated with vessels in NW quadrant. See Vol. I, Plate 2.7. Beveled around all edges, but missing 1 side (CHCU 10257). Beveled around all edges (CHCU 10256). Beveled around all edges, but missing 1 side (CHCU 10255).	93
-	Pottery scrapers (2) 1) Plain gray jar sherd (7.9-x-5.6-x-0.5-cm; 40.3 g) 2) BMIII whiteware jar sherd (12.0-x-6.7-x-0.5-cm; 71.2 g)	Outside of Bin B. See Vol. I, Plate 2.7. Beveled around all edges (CHCU 10249). Beveled around all edges (CHCU 10250).	94
-	Groundstone (28-x-15-x-4.7-cm; 2305.7 g)	2000 (sandstone). Irregular, tabular shape, 100 percent burned. Ground smooth on 1 surface and burned black. Firepit liner stone? 19 cm above floor.	95
-	Sherds (7) Lino Gray (2) Plain gray (2) Lino Fugitive Red (1) Obelisk Gray (1) La Plata B/w (1)	Cibola Tradition. Fill in Bin A.	96
-	Chipped stone (5) Whole flake (0.9 g) Angular debris (0.7 g) Utilized flake (6.4 g) Utilized flake (0.1 g)	Fill in Bin A. 1052 (High Surface Chert). 1053 (High Surface Chert). 1145 (chalcedonic silicified wood). 3510 (Grants Ridge obsidian). Sourced to Mt. Taylor, Shackley and Dillian (2000).	96, 96C
-	Selenite (3.5-x-1.9-x-0.9-cm; 9.6 g)	5040 (natural selenite). Irregular, tabular. Unmodified.	96B
-	Worked bone (115.0-x-11.4-x-1.9-mm; 5.6 g)	*Lepus* sp. (jackrabbit) tibia. Ground and beveled.	96D
-	Bones (4)	Cottontail femur (1), jackrabbit humerus, metatarsal, tibia (3; 1 boiled). Fill in Bin A.	96

Table I.3.4. Site 29SJ 299, Pithouse A, Stratum B (Associated Roof Fall Materials) and Floor Fill, cont'd.[a]

Artifact Number	Artifact Class	Lithic Material, Ceramic Ware, or Faunal Species	FS No.
-	Sherds (13) Plain gray (4) Obelisk Gray (9)	Cibola Grayware. Inside Bin B	97
-	Mano (18.0-x-12.2-x-5.0-cm; 2157.6 g)	2000 (sandstone). 1 metate grinding surface. Top concave and ground smooth with faint red paint?-Munsell 2.5YR 5/6? Inside Bin B	97A
-	Mano (19.8-x-12.4-x-4.5-cm; 1739.7 g)	2000 (sandstone). 1 metate grinding surface. Top moderately ground to accommodate hand comfort. Inside Bin B	97
-	Floor polisher? (16.4-x-9.0-x-8.5-cm; 2131.8 g)	3300? (porphyritic andesite; San Juan River cobble?). Natural cobble with some pecking marks on 1 end. Inside Bin B	97A
-	Minerals (3) Selenite (7.6-x-3.3-x-0.6-cm; 19.9 g) Limonite (3.7-x-2.2-x-1.8-cm; 4.3 g) Hematite (1.6-x-1.3-x-0.7-cm; 2.0 g)	Natural flat piece Natural?, irregular shape. Some wear, natural?. Munsell 10YR 7/8 Natural but 1 surface ground. Munsell 2.5YR 4/6	98A
-	Manuport (4.8-x-3.2-x-1.6-g; 37.2 g)	4000 (quartzite)	98
-	Manuport (6.2-x-5.1-x-1.3-cm; 61.1 g)	3300? (porphyritic andesite; San Juan River cobble). Minor pecking on 1 end	98 100
-	Metate fragment (?-x-46-cm wide-x-?)	Near center of room. Left at site	101
-	Trough metate	2000 (sandstone). 40 cm long trough. Left on site. Just outside Bin B.	102
-	Mano (16.0-x-10.5-x-3.0-cm; 735 g)	2000 (sandstone). 1 surface used in metate; opposite side highly ground smooth but not pecked. 1 burned edge. Worn out tool? Under FS 101	102
-	Groundstone (16.5-x-12.3-x-4.0-cm; 1541.9 g)	2000 (sandstone). Tabular shape. 1 side moderately ground; opposite side ground and pecked. 70 percent burned and blackened. Firepit liner or firedog? Orignally called a mano. Under FS 101	102
-	Floor polisher? (13.2-x-9.5-x-6.5-cm; 1282.9 g)	3300? (porphyritic andesite; San Juan River cobble). Large, biscuit-mano style, pecked and ground to shape; riddled with natural pits. 2 surfaces ground (1 well ground). Under FS 101	102
-	Floor polisher? (17.0-x-13.4-x-3.1-cm; 1196.1 g)	4000 (quartzite). Natural cobble. Discoid shape. 100 percent burned	103

Table I.3.4. Site 29SJ 299, Pithouse A, Stratum B (Associated Roof Fall Materials) and Floor Fill, cont'd.[a]

Artifact Number	Artifact Class	Lithic Material, Ceramic Ware, or Faunal Species	FS No.
-	Polishing stone (10.5-x-9.5-x-5.0-cm; 738.1 g)	4000 (quartzite). Orangish natural cobble. Highly polished on 2 opposing surfaces.	103
-	Pecking stone? (10.0-x-8.2-x-4.1-cm; 517.7 g)	4000 (quartzite). Natural pebble. Pecked on 1 edge and near 1 end.	103
-	Manuport (11.5-x-8.1-x-3.5-cm; 538 g)	3242? (diorite; San Juan River pebble?). Discoid, natural pebble. Peck marks around edges.	
-	Manuport (11.5-x-4.7-x-1.9-cm; 156 g)	4000 (quartzite). Elliptical, flattish pebble. 30 percent burned.	
-	Sherds (18) Plain gray (1) Lino Fugitive Red (10) Obelisk Gray (7)	Cibola Grayware. In Bin C.	168
-	Chipped stone (1): Retouched flake (5.3 g)	1113 (cherty silicified wood). In Bin C	168
-	Minerals (5): 5.7-x-3.2-x-0.6-cm, 16.7 g (in 3 pieces); 5.0-x-2.5-x-0.5-cm, 9.9 g; 4.8-x-1.6-x-0.5-cm, 5.6 g	5040 (natural selenite). All a flat, tabular but irregular shape. Natural; unmodified. In Bin C.	168C
-	Manuport (4.3-x-1.9-x-0.9-cm; 6.3 g)	1112 (cherty silicified wood). Natural. In Bin C.	168C
-	Unhafted blade (3.5-x-1.9-x-0.7-cm; 6.1 g)	1113 (cherty silicified wood). In Bin C.	168E
-	Chopper (8.5-x-6.0-x-3.8-cm; 275 g)	4000 (quartzite). Fractured cobble, bifacially flaked along 1 edge. Flaked edge dulled by pounding.	168
-	Bones (3)	Cottontail innominate and femur (2; 1 boiled), jackrabbit scapula (1). In Bin C.	168

[a] See distribution in Figure I.3.3 and whole and restorable vessel information in Volume II, Table II.2.11. All bones noted that revealed burning or cooking brown.

Table I.3.5. Site 29SJ 299, Pithouse D Distribution of Floor 1 Materials.[a]

Artifact Species	Artifact Class	Lithic Material, Ceramic Ware, or Faunal Species	FS No.
1	Trough metate, double sided (64-x-35-x-8-cm, 27.0 kg)	2000 (sandstone). Has trough grinding surfaces on opposite sides.	349
2	Needle (10.7-x-5-x-2.7-cm; 1.3 g)	Fibula of a medium/large mammal.	350
3	Shaped slab (11.0 g)	2000 (sandstone). Discarded?	352
4	Floor polisher (12.2-x-8-x-3.3-cm; 522 g)	4000 (quartzite). 100 percent burned and blackened. Natural cobble with 1 edge broken off. Polished? smooth on 2 opposing surfaces.	353
5	Selenite (3-x-1.4-x-0.3-cm; 2.0 g)	5041 (gypsum). Partly rectangular.	356
6	Mano (12-x-7-x-5-cm; 620 g)	2000 (sandstone).	357
7	La Plata B/w bowl fragment (CHCU 10258)	Cibola Whiteware with human figure design. On east bench top (see Volume II, Plate II.2.5d and II.2.7).	358
8	Reshaped metate fragment (13-x-12.7-x-4-cm; 1110 g)	2000 (sandstone). Chipped edge, dulled by pounding, burned.	359
9	Abrader/firedog (16.0-x-8.3-x-5.9-cm; 761.5 g)	2000 (sandstone). Blockish shape. 100 percent burned. 1 surface well-ground. Reused as a firedog. In firepit.	360
-	Plain gray sherds (2)	Cibola Tradition. In Wall Niche 3 fill.	368
10	Knife (5.3-x-1.8-x-1-cm; 10.4 g)	1112 (cherty silicified wood). In bottom of Bin B.	370
11	Pot polisher (6-x-4-x-1.3-cm; 45.6 g)	4000 (yellow quartzite). Many hammer marks on 2 edges. In Bin B.	371.1
12	Pot polisher (5-x-4-x-2-cm; 66 g)	4000 (purple quartzite). Minor hammer marks on 1 end. In Bin B.	371.2
13	Pot polisher (5.3-x-4-x-1.3-cm; 52 g)	4000 (tan quartzite). Minor hammer marks on 1 end. In Bin B.	371.3
14	Undiff. polisher (1.7-x-1.3-x-1-cm; 3 g)	4000 (white quartzite). In Bin B.	371.4
-	Sherds (21): plain gray (10), Lino Fugitive Red (2), Obelisk Gray (3), La Plata B/w (2), unclassified whiteware (1), mudware (3)	Cibola Tradition. In Bin B fill and on floor.	373
15	Awl (11.7-x-2-x-5-cm; 8.6 g)	Rib of a large mammal. In Bin B.	374
-	Sherds (13): plain gray (6), Lino Gray (1), Obelisk Gray (3), La Plata B/w (3)	Cibola Tradition. On Bin A floor.	375
16	Hammerstone (5.6-x-4.4-x-3.7-cm; 130 g)	1051 (High Surface Chert; moss agate). Bin A.	376
17	Polishing/pecking stone (7.4-x-4.8-x-4.1-cm; 244 g)	4000 (brown quartzite). 100 percent burned and blackened. 1 end hammered before & after burning, plus 2 narrow (2-5 mm) grooves pecked longitudinally across oblong-shaped natural pebble. Bin A.	377

Table I.3.5. Site 29SJ 299, Pithouse D Distribution of Floor 1 Materials, cont'd.[a]

Artifact Species	Artifact Class	Lithic Material, Ceramic Ware, or Faunal Species	FS No.
18	Mano (20-x-12-x-4-cm; 1508 g)	2000 (sandstone). In firepit.	380.1
19	Mano (19-x-12-x-4-cm; 1547 g)	2000 (sandstone). In firepit.	380.2
20	Mano (16-x-9-x-5-cm; 1135 g)	2000 (sandstone). In firepit.	380.3
21	Undiff. passive abrader (21-x-17-x-5-cm; 2721 g)	2000 (sandstone). On firepit floor, plugging Other Pit 5 cist.	381
22	Floor polisher/pecking stone #1? (10.6-x-9.1-x-4.2-cm; 642 g)	4515 (metamorphic amphibolite; green). Natural cobble, polished flat on 2 opposing surfaces. Unburned. In OP 2.	383.1
23	Polishing/pecking stone #4 (9.3-x-6.4-x-3.7-cm; 328 g)	4000 (quartzite). Natural cobble, polished on 1 surface; opposite ends pecked but blackened over. 100 percent burned and blackened. In OP 2.	383.2
24	Floor polisher #2 (9.7-x-7.3-x-4.8-cm; 511 g)	4000 (quartzite). Natural cobble, pecked on 1 end but blackened over. 100 percent burned and blackened. In OP 2.	383.3
25	Floor polisher #3 (13.3-x-9.0-x-4.0-cm; 707 g)	4000 (quartzite). Natural cobble, 2 surfaces possibly polished. 100 percent burned and blackened. In OP 2.	383.4
26	Pot lid (2 pieces; 12.9-x-12.0-x-1.3-cm; 252 g)	2000 (sandstone). Natural disc from concretion sphere. Edges partly ground. 3 spots along edges burned and blackened. In OP 2.	384
–	Sherds (2): plain gray (1), unclassified whiteware (1)	Cibola Tradition. In OP 4 fill.	386
27	Pecking stone (8.2-x-6.9-x-4.8-cm; 420 g)	4000 (quartzite). Natural cobble pecked on both ends. Fire-blackened spot? Analyzed as a "floor polisher". In OP 1.	388.1
28	Chopper (6.3-x-3.9-x-2.4 cm; 84 g)	1112 (cherty silicified wood). In OP 1.	388.2
29	Shaped stone (lid?, 28-x-20-x-4-cm; 3061 g)	2000 (sandstone). Edge chipped to form. 1 surface 40 percent burned. Natural yellow residue on bottom, Munsell 10YR 6/6. In OP 1.	389
30	Cooking stone? fragment (306 g)	2000 (sandstone). Fire-blackened. Discarded. In OP 1.	390
31	Shaped stone (18-x-11.5-x-3.5-cm; 1381 g)	2000 (sandstone). Reshaped metate trough fragment; possible firedog. In OP 1.	391
32	Sherds (10): plain gray (3), Obelisk Gray (4), Lino Gray (1), La Plata B/w bowl (1), unclassified whiteware bowl (1)	Cibola Grayware. In OP 1 (see Volume II, Table II.2.26).	392
33	Chopper (5.8-x-5.1-x-2.1-cm; 95 g)	2912 (black ironstone). Worked meteor fragment? In antechamber.	402
–	Sherds (9): Lino Fugitive Red (1), Obelisk Gray (6), La Plata B/w (2)	Cibola Tradition. Scattered over main chamber floor.	354

[a] See distribution in Figure I.3.8.

Table I.3.6. Site 29SJ 299, Room (cist) and Ramada 1 Distribution of Fill and Floor Materials.

Artifact Number	Artifact Class	Lithic Material, Ceramic Ware, or Faunal Species	FS No.
Room 1			
-	Sherds (7): plain gray (3), culinary jar rim fillet (1), Gallup B/w (1), Black Mesa B/w (1)	Mixed ceramic traditions. See Volume II, Table II.2.26.	199
-	Bones (3)	*Lepus californicus* (jack rabbit) femurs (2); *Sylvilagus* sp. (cottontail rabbit) innominate (1).	199
Room 2			
-	Obelisk Gray jar (ca. 37 pieces)(19.6 dia.-x-19.0 cm high)	Cibola Grayware. Restorable jar (burned?) dispersed on floor.	200
Room 3			
-	Sherds (2): plain gray, Lino Fugitive Red	Cibola Grayware. See Volume II, Table II.2.26.	201
Room 4			
-	Sherds (19): plain gray (2), Lino Fugitive Red (16), La Plata B/w (1)	Cibola Tradition. Dispersed on floor. See Volume II, Table II.2.26..	202
Room 5			
-	Sherds (93): plain gray (83), Lino Fugitive Red (3), Obelisk Gray (4), La Plata B/w (3)	Cibola Tradition. See Volume II, Table II.2.26.	203
-	Lino Gray olla neck (7 cm high)	Cibola Grayware. 8 cm above floor, NW quad.	204
Room 6			
-	Sherds (13): Lino Gray (1), plain gray (9), Lino Fugitive Red (1), Obelisk Gray (1), La Plata B/w (1)	Cibola Tradition. See Volume II, Table II.2.26.	206
-	Pendant blank (1.7-x-1.2-x-0.1-cm; 0.6 g)	5050 (calcite). Rectangular piece rounded at corners.	206D
-	Misc. stones	Information unknown.	206
Room 7 (hearth)			
-	Sherds (45): unclassified indented corrugated (37), culinary jar rim fillet (1), Red Mesa B/w (3), Gallup B/w (1), unclassified PII-PIII M/w (1), unclassified whiteware (1), La Plata B/r (1)	Mixed ceramic traditions. See Volume II, Table II.2.26.	207

Table I.3.6. Site 29SJ 299, Room (cist) and Ramada 1 Distribution of Fill and Floor Materials, cont'd.

Artifact Number	Artifact Class	Lithic Material, Ceramic Ware, or Faunal Species	FS No.
-	Mano (16.0±-x-9.7-x-3.1-cm; 729.5 g)	2000 (sandstone). Wedge-shaped; ground on 1 surface. Corner missing.	207A
-	Mano fragment (8.8+-x-11.6-x-3.0-cm; 489.7 g)	2000 (sandstone). About 2/5s size. Ground on 1 surface.	207B
-	Mano fragment (6.5+-x-10.4-x-2.0-cm; 161.2 g)	2000 (sandstone). About 1/3-1/4 size. Ground on 1 wedge-shaped surface.	207C
-	Metate? fragment (15.7+-x-20.2-x-5.9-cm; 2356 g)	2000 (sandstone). Ground on 2 opposite concave surfaces. Burned.	207-04
-	Chipped stone (2): 8.0 and 46.6 g	1113 (cherty silicified wood). From same core.	207F
Room 8			
-	Sherds (7): plain gray	Cibola Grayware. See Volume II, Table II.2.26.	326
-	Mano (14.8-x-10.5-x-1.9-cm; 517.0 g)	2000 (sandstone). Wedge-shaped.	327
Room 9			
-	Sherds (3): plain gray	See Volume II, Table II.2.26.	328
Room 11 (Roasting Pit)			
-	Sherds (7): Lino Gray (1), plain gray (4), Obelisk Gray (1), Sanostee B/o (1)	Mixed ceramic traditions. See Volume II, Table II.2.26.	329
-	Bones(3)	*Ovis aries* (adult domestic sheep metatarsals).	330
Ramada 1			
-	Metate fragment (39-x-24-x-7-cm; 6.1 kg)	2000 (sandstone). Burned. Firepit liner?	318
-	Metate fragment	2000 (sandstone). Missing. Firepit liner?	318

Note: All ground stone measured in order by length by width by thickness.

Table I.3.7. List of Ramada Postholes at Site 29SJ299.[a]

Posthole No.	Length (cm)	Width (cm)	Depth (cm)	Volume[b] (liters)	Fill Type	Fill Period	Shims	Base Stone	Est. postsize (cm)	Lining	Comments
Ramada in fill above Room 8:											
Posthole 1	25	20	25	9.9	52	Occ	0	1	-	U	
Posthole 2	20	20	20	6.3	52	Occ	0	1	-	U	
Posthole 3	26	26	12	6.4	52	Occ	0	1	-	U	
Posthole 4	20	20	15	4.7	52	Occ	0	1	-	U	
Ramada associated with Pithouse E:[c]											
Posthole 1	26	26	10	10.7	16,52	Occ	1-5	1	15-x-8	U	
Posthole 2E	17	17	22	9.5	52	Occ	3-4	1	17	U	4 burned shims.
Posthole 2W	18	14	26	13.2	52	Occ	5	1	18-x-14	U	2 burned shims.
Posthole 3	16	16	24	9.5	13	Occ	6-13	1	16	U	4 burned shims.
Posthole 4	22	18	28	15.2	13	Occ	5	1	22-x-18	U	Post burned out. 3 burned shims.
Posthole 5	20	20	40	22.5	52	Occ	5-8	1	15	U	3 burned shims.
Posthole 6 upper	24	23	34	14.9	16,52	Occ	2-3	1	-	U	1 burned shim.
Posthole 6 lower	26	26	30	8.7	13	Occ	0	0	22	U	
Posthole 7	22	22	24	15.1	13	Occ	4	1	-	U	
Posthole 8	16	16	20+	8.0	13	Occ	2-3	1	-	U	2 burned shims.
Posthole 9	13	13	17	11.0	13,28	Occ	5	1	-	U	Sealed. 3 burned shims.
Posthole 10	32	28	15	16.8	13,15	Occ	2	1	-	U	Truncated. 1 burned shim.
Posthole 11	20	20	10+	2.8	52	Occ	0-1	1	-	U	
Posthole 12	18	18	9	1.7	11	PO	0	0	-	L-P	Basin-shaped. Isolated from others.

[a] See Tables I.7.4-I.7.5 for an explanation of the feature and attribute codes.
[b] Volumes for features are approximate.
[c] Holes classified in field as post supports.

Table I.3.8. List of Features at Site 29SJ 423 Except for Postholes.[a]

Feature	Length (cm)	Width (cm)	Height/Depth (cm)	Volume[b] (liters)	Fill Type	Fill Period	Lining	Open/Sealed	Comments
Pithouse A area:									
Pit A	254	210	12-26	1159.5	32	PO	L-P	O	Storage cist or small pithouse (Plate 3.21).
Firepit 1	57	53	10	34.5	32	PO	L-P	O	Mouth = 2347 cm². Replastered once with 7 cm of adobe.
Pit B	191	141	5-14	192.0	32	PO	L-P	O	McElmo B/w minature bowl just above floor–related to Feature 1 (Plate 3.22).
N. Pit in collar	20	10	6	0.9	?	PO	L-P	O	Deflector slab groove?
S. Pit in collar	15	12	6?	0.7?	?	PO	L-P	O	Deflector slab groove?
Pit C	294	227	0-34	1505.8	26,32,42	PO	L-S	O	
Wall 1	1460	52-65	24-36	-	-	Occ	L-M	-	Enclosing shrine wall (Plate 3.20).
Feature 1	65	43	29	-	33?	Occ	L-S	O	Shrine of stone bowl & cover (see Figure I.3.12, Plates 3.24–3.25).
Feature 2	96	73	0	-	32	PO	L-S	O	Flagstone & adobe floor cist. Sides dismantled (Plate 3.23).
Feature 3	50+	30+	?	-	?	PO	L-S	O	Dismantled cist? (Plate 3.23).
Firepit 2	56	53	12-18	33.8	32	PO	L-P	O	Surface feature.
Pithouse B									Figure I.3.13, Plate 3.27
Firepit 1	51	44	7	16.1	20	?	?	O	Mouth = 2442 cm².
Other Pit 1	35	31	4	5.2	32	PO	U	O	Formerly Pit 5.
Other Pit 2	81	61	4-13	39.5±	32	PO	U	O	Pecked out bedrock hole. Not a feature? Formerly Pit 6.
Other Pit 3	34	31	11	8.3	32	PO	U	O	Step? in bedrock. Formerly Pit 7.
Other Pit 4A	3-4	3-4	6±6	0.08	16	?	?	O	North deflector post support.
Other Pit 4B	4	4		0.08	16	?	?	O	South deflector post support.
Deflector slot	28	9	8-14	3.0	?	?	L-P?	O	1 shim.
Great Kivas:									
Firepit 1	160	118	4-10	82.1	47	PO	U	O	Little burn evident. Cleaned out: used with GK II and GK III.
pit in bottom	56	28	16		?	PO	U	O	Natural pit in bottom?

Table I.3.8. List of Features at Site 29SJ 423 Except for Postholes, cont'd.[a]

Feature	Length (cm)	Width (cm)	Height/ Depth (cm)	Volume[b] (liters)	Fill Type	Fill Period	Lining	Open/ Sealed	Comments
Other Pit 1	107	100	29	225.7	30	PO	U	S	Fill mostly sterile. Band of natural clay crosses through pit. Associated with Great Kiva II?
inner hole	81	76	13-15						
pit in bottom	8	6.5	6.5						
Other Pit 2	15	15	4	0.7	11	PO	U	O	Natural feature? Formerly Pit 15.
Other Pit 3	8	8	8	0.4	47	PO	U	O	Altar screen or ladder rest? 53 cm from OP 4. 1 shim. Associated with Great Kiva II-III.
Other Pit 4	8	6.5	6.5	0.3	18	PO	U	S	Altar screen or ladder rest? Part of Great Kiva II-III.
Slot A	42	8	5-7	1.8	?	PO	U	O	Assoc. with Posthole E & Great Kiva I. Groove for slab.
Slot B	25	8	5-7	1.3	?	PO	U	O	Assoc. with Posthole E & Great Kiva I. Groove for slab.
Slot C	30	8	5-11	1.7	?	PO	U	O	Assoc. with Posthole E & Great Kiva I. Groove for slab.
Notch	14	9	7	-	?	PO	U	O	Post support?
Extramural									
Feature 1	130	80+	30±	-	?	O/PO	L-S	O	In Level 1 fill next to Pithouse B. Possible Navajo roasting pit (Plate I.3.28).

[a] See Tables I.7.4-I.7.5 for an explanation of the feature and attribute codes.
[b] Volumes for features are approximate.

Table I.3.9. Site 29SJ 423, Distribution of Fill and Floor Materials in the Shrine and Pithouse A Area.[a]

Artifact Number	Artifact Class	Lithic Material[b], Ceramic Ware or Faunal Species	FS No.
Shrine materials (Wall 1 and Feature 1)			
-	Mineral (2-x-2-x-1 mm; 0.0 g)	5300 (turquoise). Natural chip with 1 surface ground. Matrix. Rock Color 5BG 6/6. Site surface.	8
1	Minerals (34)	Site surface.	9
	Beads (6; 3-5 diameter-x-1-3 mm thick)	5300 (turquoise). Rock Color (10G 8/2 [5], 5G 6/6 [1]).	
	Mosaic inlays (2; 10-x-9-x-2 mm; 8-x-6-x-3 mm)	5300 (turquoise). Matrix & varigated colors: Rock Color 5BG 6/6.	
	Worked & unworked chips (23; 8-x-4-x-3 to 3-x-2-x-2 mm)	5300 (turquoise). Rock Colors 5G 5/2, 10G 8/2, 5BG 6/6, 5BG 7/2, 5B 7/6..	
	Natural nodules (2; 5-x-4-x-1 mm; 5-x-3-x-2 mm)	5310 (azurite). Rock Color 5PB 3/2.	
	Bead (3 mm diameter-x-1.5 mm thick)	2770 (calcite). Center hole 1.5 mm diameter.	
1	Chipped stone (12-x-8-x-2 mm; 0.3 g)	1040 (Brushy Basin chert). Rock color 10GY 5/2. Site surface.	9
-	Mineral crystal (15-x-12-x-10 mm; 2.2 g)	5000 (quartz). Natural. Site surface.	12
2	Bracelet (complete; 7.0-x-6.7 diameter-x-0.4 cm thick; 7.8 g)	*Glycymeris gigantea*. Rock Color 10YR 8/2. Site surface.	15
3	Beads (2; 3 & 4 mm diameter-x-1 & 1.5 mm thick)	5300 (turquoise). 1 mm center holes. Rock Color 10G 8/2. Floor fill.	19
4	Pendant (33-x-17-x-4 mm; 4.0 g)	*Haliotis cracherodii*. Inner curve reveals iridescent shell color; exterior & edges. Ground . No hole–incomplete? Floor fill (4 cm above floor).	56
5	Mosaic inlays (2; 9-x-7-x-1 mm; 9-x-5-x-1 mm)Mosaic inlay fragments (2)	*Haliotis cracherodii*. Floor fill (recovered from backdirt screening).	57
5	Bead (13 mm long-x-7 mm diameter; 0.4 g)	*Olivella dama*. Natural shell with tip ground off for string hole. Floor fill (recovered from backdirt screening)	57
5	Beads (2; both 4mm long-x-5 mm diameter)	*Olivella dama*. Both beads are natural shells cut into smaller sections. Floor fill (recovered from backdirt screening).	57
6	Minerals (70)	Concentration in floor fill.	58
	Beads (49; range from 3-5 mm diameter-x-1.5-3 mm thick)	5300 (turquoise). Rock Colors 10G 8/2 (ca. 38), 5BG 6/6 (ca.11).	
	Mosaic inlays (3; 8-x-6-x-2, 5-x-4-x-1mm [2])	5300 (turquoise). 2 opposite surfaces ground. Rock Colors 10G 8/2, 5BG 6/6 [2].	
	Worked & unworked chips (18; 10-x-6-x-3 to 4-x-2-x-1mm)	5300 (turquoise). Rock Color 10G 8/2 [5], 5BG 6/6 [13].	
7	Minerals (128)	Feature 1; found in bottom of stone bowl (FS 248).	59
	Beads (127; 4-5 mm diameter-x-2 mm thick) (plus 24-33 beads missing?)	5300 (turquoise). Holes 1 mm diameter. Rock Color 5G 7/4, 10G 6/2 (majority), 5 BG 6/6. Probable necklace. See detailed color photograph in Western National Parks Association 2004:38.	
	Unworked chip (4-x-4-x-2 mm)	5300 (turquoise). 5BG 6/6.	

Table I.3.9. Site 29SJ 423, Distribution of Fill and Floor Materials in the Shrine and Pithouse A Area, cont'd.[a]

Artifact Number	Artifact Class	Lithic Material[b], Ceramic Ware or Faunal Species	FS No.
7	Stone bowl (33 diameter-x-13.2 cm high; inner: 23 diameter-x-8.5 cm deep; 17.7 kg)	2000 (tan sandstone; Munsell 5Y 7/3). Bowl pecked & ground to shape; flat top & bottom, vertical inner & outer sides. Contained 127+ turquoise beads (necklace?). Floor. See Figure I.3.12.	248
7	Altar lid for shrine cover (18.6-x-10.8-x-0.7 cm; 348.6 g)	2000 (sandstone). Rectangular piece ground flat on 2 sides & on all 4 sides. Crafted to fit seating hole in altar cover. See Figure I.3.12.	247
8	Altar cover (63.5-x-43.3-x-2.0 cm; 9.2 kg)	2000 (sandstone). Edge-chipped, rectangular shape with 2 opposing surfaces ground flat. Some minor grinding on edges. Rectangular hole cut through center with 1.5-2.5 cm wide ground recessed ledge to hold lid. See Figure I.3.12.	247
9A	Palette (18.2-x-14-x-5.1 cm; 1482.5 g)	2000 (sandstone). Part of altar construction (stone #5). Natural tabular stone caked with red (Munsell 10R 4/6) paint on one surface & small area of yellow (Munsell 10YR 6/8) paint. 100 percent burned.	247B
9B	Palette? (31-x-20-x-5.3 cm; 3.5 kg)	2000 (sandstone). Part of altar construction (stone # 4). Natural tabular stone with minor light smears of pink (Munsell 5YR 8/3) paint? on bottom.	247
10A/B	Minerals (31) Beads (11; 4 mm diameter-x-1 mm thick) Worked & unworked chips (20; 6-x-3-x-3 to 1-x-1-x-1 mm)	Floor fill. All Rock Colors 10G 6/2 & 5BG 6/6 5300 (turquoise). Disc-shape. 1 mm diameter holes.	79
11	Worked mineral (11-x-6-x-3 mm)	5300 (turquoise). Ground flat on 1surface. Rock Color 5G 7/4. Associated with dog jaw. Floor fill.	90
11	Minerals (4) Worked & unworked chips (3; 6-x-4-x-3; 4-x-4-x-1; 5-x-1-x-1 mm)	Pit C floor fill. 5300 (turquoise). Rock Colors 10G 8/2 (2), 5BG 6/65310.	91
	Natural nodule (9-x-6-x-5 mm; 0.3 g)	5320 (azurite/malachite). Rock Colors 5PB 5/2 & 5G 5/2.	91
12	Toadlena/Nava B/w bowl (9.1 cm diameter-x-4.9 cm high)	Chuskan Whiteware. Associated with FS 246. Pit B floor fill. In repatriation process. See Plate I.2.26.	245
12	Bead (3.5 mm diameter-x-1.5 mm thick)	2650 (black shale). Inside bowl (FS 245). In repatriation process.	246
13	Bead (8 mm diameter-x-2 mm thick)	5300 (turquoise). Rock Color 10G 8/2. 2 mm center hole. Pit A5300 (turquoise). Rock Color 10GY 4/4.	74
13	Unworked chip (6-x-4-x-2 mm)		
14	Mano (17.4-x-11.5-x-3.1 cm; 1009.1g)	2000 (sandstone). Tabular with edges pecked & ground. One surface finely ground; other just high spots. Wall 1 construction? (Top of Level 3).	28B
15	Unworked mineral chip (6-x-4-x-2 mm; 0.2 g)	5300 (turquoise). Rock Color 5G 5/2. Top of Level 3 under Wall 1 fall.	29
16	Worked mineral (5-x-3-x-2 mm)	5300 (turquoise). Ground on 2 opposite surfaces + some edges. Rock Color 5G 7/4. Level 1 next to Wall 1.	38
-	Minerals (58) Beads (14; 2.5-5 mm diameter-x-1-2 mm thick) Mosaic inlay chunks (8; 12-x-11-x-4 to 2-x-2-x-1 mm) Worked & unworked chips (34; 10-x-8-x-5 to 2-x-2-x-1mm) Beads (2; 3 mm diameter-x-1 mm thick)	Floor fill–East Rubble Mound in & around Feature 1: Rock Colors 5G 7/2, 10G 8/2, 5BG 6/6, 5B 7/6. 5300 (turquoise).5300 (turquoise). 5300 (turquoise). Matrix common. 2650 (shale). Rock Colors 5Y 3/2, 5Y 5/2.	60

Table I.3.9. Site 29SJ 423, Distribution of Fill and Floor Materials in the Shrine and Pithouse A Area, cont'd.[a]

Artifact Number	Artifact Class	Lithic Material[b], Ceramic Ware or Faunal Species	FS No.
17	Chipped stones (3): Core (4.8-x-3.3-x-3.0 cm; 30.5 g) San Jose projectile point (3.2-x-2.0-x-0.3 cm; 3.4 g) Core (5.1-x-3.9-x-1.7 cm; 41.0 g)	In Wall 1. 1112 (cherty silicified wood). Variegated colors. 1113 (cherty silicified wood). 1130 (palmwood with vascular rays).	25
18	Biscuit mano/hammerstone (9.0-x-6.8-x-3.1 cm; 352.2 g)	2000 (sandstone). Some pecking on 1 face and both ends. Used in Wall 1 construction?	23
18	Minerals (4): Bead fragment (3.5 mm diameter-x-1 mm thick) Unworked chip (4-x-3-x-2 mm) Natural nodules (2; 4-x-2-x-2 mm, 1-x-1-x-1 mm)	Surface, contact with Wall 1. 2770 (calcite)? 2 mm center hole. Might be shell. 5300 (turquoise). Rock Color 5G 6/6/320 (azurite). Rock color 5PB 3/2.	24
19	Worked mineral (5-x-3-x-1 mm)	5300 (turquoise). Ground on 2 opposite surfaces. Rock Color 5BG 6/6. Level 2 next to Wall 1.	37
20	Minerals (3): Unmodified chips (2; 4-x-3-x-3mm, 2-x-2-x-1 mm) Unmodified nodule (4-x-3-x-2 mm)	In ant nest on Wall 1. 5300 (turquoise). Rock Colors 5G 6/6?, 10G 8/2. 5320 (azurite). Rock Color indeterminant (dark purplish blue).	63A
-	Hammerstone (6.2-x-4.9-x-3.4 cm; 152.7 g)	4000 (quartzite). Natural pebble slightly battered on 1 end. Used in Wall 1 construction (inside in middle).	7
-	Metate fragment (28+-x-17+-x-6.5 cm)	2000 (sandstone). Trough depth: 5.5 cm. Used in Wall 1 construction. Left on site.	13
-	Manuport (6.2-x-5.0-x-2.5 cm; 107.8 g)	4000 (quartzite). Natural discoid pebble with minor pecking on opposite faces. Used in Wall 1 construction.	20
-	Metate fragment (53+-x-34-x-10 cm)	2000 (sandstone). Trough: 34+-x-17.5-x-7.5 cm deep. Part of Wall 1 construction. Left on site.	33
-	Metate fragment (48.5-x-33.5-x-7.5 cm)	2000 (sandstone). Trough: 28+-x-21-x-4.0 cm deep. Part of Wall 1 construction. Left on site.	34
-	Stone (fetish?; 4.8-x-1.9-x-1.3 cm; 16.1 g)	1110 (splintery silicified wood). Sub cylindrical; possibly ground to shape. Top of Wall 1.	49
-	Minerals; unworked chips (3; 9x 4-x-3; 5-x-4-x-3; 5-x-5-x-4 mm)	5300 (turquoise). Some matrix. Rock Colors 10G 8/2 [2], 5B 7/6. Surface of Great Kiva III.	105
-	Bead (4.5 mm diameter-x-0.75 mm thick)	2770 (calcite)? 2 mm center hole. Level 1 of Great Kiva III.	116
-	Unworked chip (2-x-2-x-1 mm)	5300 (turquoise). Rock Color 5BG 4/6? Level 2 of Great Kiva III.	116
-	Fetish? (5.7-x-1.9-x-0.9 cm; 14.3 g)	2000 (sandstone). Ground flat, file-like object notched in center of 1 end. All surfaces ground to shape. Level 2 of Great Kiva II.	134A

Table I.3.9. Site 29SJ 423, Distribution of Fill and Floor Materials in the Shrine and Pithouse A Area, cont'd.[a]

Artifact Class	Lithic Material[b], Ceramic Ware or Faunal Species	FS No.
Minerals (12) Mosaic inlay (8-x-6-x-1 mm)	Site surface west of Wall 1. 5300 (turquoise). Ground rectangular with slight curving of 1 surface. Back is flat. Rock Color 10G 8/2.	-
Bead blank (9-x-7-x-3 mm)	5300 (turquoise). Roughly squared with drill hole started in center. Rock Color 10G 8/2.	-
Bead blank (9-x-3-x-2 mm)	5300 (turquoise). Broken during drilling. Rock Color 10G 8/2.	-
Unworked chips (9; 10-x-8-x-3 to 4-x-3-x-2 mm)	5300 (turquoise). Rock Colors 10G 8/2 [8], 5BG 6/6.	243
Minerals (10) Worked & unworked chips (7; largest 5-x-4-x-2 mm) Natural nodules (3; largest 2-x-1-x-1 mm)	Site surface east & north of Feature 1. 5300 (turquoise). Rock Colors 10G 8/2 through 5BG 6/6. 5310 (azurite). Rock Color 5BG 4/6.	244
Bead (9-x-5-x-3 mm; 0.1 g)	Glass. Drilled longitudinally through side of disc bead. Rock Color 5B 6/3. Site surface east & north of Feature 1.	244
Mineral (4-x-4-x-1 mm)	5320 (malachite)? Rock Color 5G 6/2. Site backdirt.	390
Bead (12 mm long-x-5 mm diameter; 0.1 g)	*Olivella dama*. Tip ground off for string hole. Surface southeast of Great Kiva III.	419
Charcoal (29.8 g)	Floor.	17
Corncob fragment	*Zea mays*. Carbonized. Floor.	18
Bone	Jackrabbit (*Lepus californicus*) tibia. Burned. Floor fill.	21
Bones (2)	*Canis familiarus* (dog) skull fragment, small/medium long bone. Floor fill.	90
Bones (260)	Cottontail (64; 31 boiled, 3 burned), jackrabbit (11; 9 boiled, 1 burned), prairie dog (5; 1 boiled), mt. sheep (2), canid (2), gray fox (1), artiodactyl (1; boiled), small/medium mammal (153; 106 boiled, 13 burned), medium mammal (6; 1 boiled), medium/large mammal (6; 6 boiled), quail (1; boiled), teal (1; boiled), unknown (7; 7 boiled). Pit A fill.	71B
Beads (3 tubular) Bead fragment (2.5-x-0.7-x-0.2 cm; 0.9 g) Bead fragment (1.4-x-0.5-x-0.1 cm; 0.1 g) Bead fragment (1.6-x-0.7-x-0.3 cm; 0.4 g)	Pit A fill. *Lepus californicus* proximal femur shaft fragment. Indeterminant medium bird shaft fragment. Indeterminant medium mammal shaft fragment.	71, 71B
Knife fragment (30-x-27-x-6 mm; 5.0+ g)	1140 (chalcedonic silicified wood). Squarish end. Pit A fill. See Plate II.6.3i.	72
Corncob fragment (0.1 g)	*Zea mays*. Carbonized. Pit A fill.	73
Retouched flake (1.1-x-0.6-x-0.1 cm; not weighed)	1020 (red and white chert), with unifacial & bifacial flaking.	73
Sherds (41) Plain gray jars (27) Plain gray jars with Fugitive Red (2) Plain gray polished jars (9) Woodruff Red jars (3)	Pit A fill. Cibola Grayware. Cibola Grayware. Obelisk Gray tradition. Mogollon tradition.	75

Chapter 3: Basketmaker III Excavation Reports   199

Table I.3.9. Site 29SJ 423, Distribution of Fill and Floor Materials in the Shrine and Pithouse A Area, cont'd.[a]

Artifact Number	Artifact Class	Lithic Material[b], Ceramic Ware or Faunal Species	FS No.
13	Chipped stones (33)	Pit A fill.	
	Utilized flake (3.1 g)	1053 (High Surface Chert).	
	Angular debris (2; total 2.7 g)	1053 (High Surface Chert).	
	Core (2.8-x-2.5-x-2.4 cm; 23.5 g)	1053 (High Surface Chert).	
	Whole flake (0.4 g)	1055 (High Surface Chert).	
	Angular debris (1.8 g)	1110 (splintery silicified wood).	
	Utilized flake (2.4 g)	1112 (cherty silicified wood).	
	Angular debris (4; total 4.7 g)	1112 (cherty silicified wood).	
	Core (3.3-x-2.9-x-1.5 cm; 10.8 g)	1112 (cherty silicified wood).	
	Angular debris (2.2 g)	1120 (red silicified wood).	
	Whole flake (6.7 g)	1130 (palm wood).	
	Utilized flakes (2; total 2.5 g)	1140 (cherty silicified wood).	
	Angular debris (5.8 g)	1140 (cherty silicified wood).	
	Utilized flake (5.2 g)	1142 (cherty silicified wood).	
	Retouched flake (1.4 g)	1142 (cherty silicified wood).	
	Whole flake (0.5 g)	1142 (cherty silicified wood).	
	Whole flakes (6; total 6.2 g)	1145 (cherty silicified wood).	
	Utilized flake (6.9 g)	1213 (banded chalcedony).	
	Utilized flake (0.2 g)	3510 (Grants obsidian). Sourced to Mt. Taylor.	
	Utilized flake (0.1 g)	3520 (Jemez obsidian). Sourced to Valle Grande.	
	Utilized flake (11.3 g)	5200 (hematite concretion).	
	Angular debris (0.4 g)	5200 (hematite).	76
13	Abrader fragment (7.0+-x-6.4-x-3.4 cm; 249.9+ g)	2000 (sandstone). Rectangular, tabular piece moderately ground on opposite surfaces. Burned 100 percent. Spotty red (Munsell 2.5YR 4/6) paint on 1 surface. Pit A fill.	77
13	Dendrochronological specimen (est. 7.0+ diameter)	*Juniperus* sp. Pit A fill.	391
21	Retouched flake (0.7 g)	1140 (chalcedonic silicified wood). Level 2.	26
22	Retouched flake (11.8 g)	1053 (High Surface Chert). Level 2.	27
23	Metate fragment (37+-x-31-x-7 cm)	2000 (sandstone). Trough: 17+-x-17+-x-6 cm deep. Floor. Left on site.	89
-	Sherds (56) Lino Gray jars (4) Plain gray jars (45) Plain gray polished jars (7)	Level 2 (N & NW of Pit A). Cibola Grayware. Obelisk Gray tradition.	39

200 Windes et al.

Table I.3.9. Site 29SJ 423, Distribution of Fill and Floor Materials in the Shrine and Pithouse A Area, cont'd.[a]

Artifact Number	Artifact Class	Lithic Material[b], Ceramic Ware or Faunal Species	FS No.
–	Chipped stones (55)	Level 2 (N & NW of Pit A).	
	Whole flake (1.3 g)	1010 (fossiliferous chert).	
	Utilized flake (4.5 g)	1050 (High Surface Chert).	
	Retouched flake (0.3 g)	1050 (High Surface Chert).	
	Whole flake (0.1 g)	1050 (High Surface Chert).	
	Angular debris (0.1 g)	1051 (High Surface Chert).	
	Angular debris (0.9 g)	1052 (High Surface Chert).	
	Utilized flakes (3; total 3.7 g)	1052 (High Surface Chert).	
	Whole flakes (3; total 3.8 g)	1052 (High Surface Chert).	
	Utilized flakes (3; 5.4 g)	1053 (High Surface Chert).	
	Whole flakes (2; total 2.4 g)	1053 (High Surface Chert).	
	Angular debris (3; 6.6 g)	1053 (High Surface Chert).	
	Utilized flake (3.2 g)	1060 (dark red jasper).	
	Utilized flakes (2; total 7.8 g)	1072 (Zuni yellow spotted chert).	
	Utilized flake (2.7 g)	1112 (cherty silicified wood).	
	Retouched flake (1.8 g)	1112 (cherty silicified wood).	
	Angular debris (3; total 8.7 g)	1112 (cherty silicified wood).	
	Cores (4.0-x-2.3-x-2.8 cm; 41.4 g)(3.2-x-3.0-x-2.3 cm; 26.1 g)	1112 (cherty silicified wood).	
	Utilized flakes (2; total 2.0 g)	1140 (chalcedonic silicified wood).	
	Whole flakes (3; total 5.1 g)	1140 (chalcedonic silicified wood).	
	Utilized flakes (4; total 6.3 g)	1142 (chalcedonic silicified wood).	
	Whole flake (0.1 g)	1142 (chalcedonic silicified wood).	
	Angular debris (2; 0.1 & 6.8g)	1142 (chalcedonic silicified wood).	
	Utilized flake (0.7 g)	1145 (chalcedonic silicified wood).	
	Angular debris (0.9 g)	1145 (chalcedonic silicified wood).	
	Core (3.1-x-2.7-x-1.3 cm; 10.5 g)	1145 (chalcedonic silicified wood).	
	Angular debris (0.5 g)	1610 (dark gray chert).	
	Angular debris (0.2 g)	3520 (Jemez obsidian). Sourced from Bland Canyon(?).	
	Whole flakes (5; total 237.3 g)	4005 (quartzite).	
	Core (5.0-x-4.0-x-2.0 cm; 45.3 g)	4005 (quartzite).	
	Angular debris (1.8 g)	4005 (quartzite).	
		5111 (limonite).	40
–	Manuports? (2; 0.1 g)	1140 (chalcedonic silicified wood). Tiny rounded pebbles; turkey gizzard stones?	40
–	Mineral? (1.1-x-1.1-x-0.4 cm; 1.2 g)	Unknown mineral. Possible hard charcoal fragment.	40
–	Mineral (1.9-x-1.6-x-1.0 cm; 3.3 g)	5200 (hematite). Unmodified.	40
–	Chipped stones (2)	Level 2 (N & NW of Pit A).	
	Retouched flake (1.0 g)	1052 (High Surface Chert).	
	Utilized flake (6.2 g)	1060 (dark red jasper).	41

Table I.3.9. Site 29SJ 423, Distribution of Fill and Floor Materials in the Shrine and Pithouse A Area, cont'd.[a]

Artifact Number	Artifact Class	Lithic Material[b], Ceramic Ware or Faunal Species	FS No.
-	Manuport (3.7-x-2.9-x-1.2 cm; 19.5 g)	4000 (quartzite). Flattish, discoid natural pebble. Level 2 (N & NW portion of structure inside).	42
-	Bone	Cottontail (*Sylvilagus* sp.) patella. Level 2.	43
24	Hatch cover ? (51-x-47.5-x-2.5 cm)	Cottontail (sandstone). Associated with FS 89. Floor. Left on site.	112
25	Metate Fragment (22.5 +-x-23 +-x-5.5 cm)	2000 (sandstone). Trough: 20+-x-9+-x-4.5 cm deep. Top of Level 2. Left on site.	35
26	Bones (4)	Cottontail (1), bushy-tailed woodrat (1), small/medium mammal (4).	61
26	Human bones (5)	Cranium fragments.	61
27	Metate fragment (12 +-x-12 +-x-7 cm)	2000 (sandstone). Floor. Left on site.	88
28	Charcoal (58.8 g)	Floor fill.	54
29	Stone (11.0-x-10.0-x-2.7 cm; 322.2 g) Abrader (15.8-x-12.1-x-4.3 cm; 878.8 g)	2000 (sandstone). Irregular-shaped with no obvious grinding except for bagware. 2000 (sandstone). Floor fill Pit A. Tabular, wedge-shaped. Opposite surfaces ground.	86
30	Charcoal (44.8 g)	Floor fill.	51
30	Dendrochronological specimen (3.8+ cm diameter)	*Pinus edulis*. No date (CNM-78)(carbonized). Part of FS 51. 10-20 cm above floor.	393
30	Dendrochronological speciman (2.6+ cm diameter)	*Pinus edulis*. No date (CNM-79)(carbonized). Part of FS 51. 10-20 cm to floor.	394
30	Dendrochronological specimen (3.8+ cm diameter)	*Pinus edulis*. No date (CNM-80)(carbonized). Part of FS 51. 10-20 cm to floor.	395
31	Charcoal (104. 1 g)	FP 1 fill.	82
32	Lino gray sherd	Cibola Grayware. In FP 2 fill.	78
32	Whole flake (8.9 g)	1020 (chert) or possibly 1072 (Zuni chert). In FP 2 fill.	78
32	Bones (2)	Jackrabbit (*Lepus californicus*) metacarpel (boiled) & small/medium size mammal long bone fragment. FP 2.	78
32	Charcoal (36.3 g)	FP 2 fill.	80
-	Groundstones (3): Groundstone (18-x-10.0-x-4.7 cm; 1075.6 g) Mano fragment (9.5+-x-11.6-x-2.0 cm; 327.7+ g) Mano fragment (10.8+-x-11.5-x-2.9 cm; 486.5+ g)	2000 (sandstone). Floor fill. Irreg. shape, moderate pecking & minor grinding on 1 surface. 1 surface ground. Burned orange. Tabular with edge grinding & 1 ground surface. Burned dark gray.	87
33	Charcoal (28.1 g)	Floor fill.	50

Table I.3.9. Site 29SJ 423, Distribution of Fill and Floor Materials in the Shrine and Pithouse A Area, cont'd.[a]

Artifact Number	Artifact Class	Lithic Material[b], Ceramic Ware or Faunal Species	FS No.
34	Charcoal (62.7 g) and Unidentified human remains	Floor fill. Underwent preparation process (unidentified remains).	52
35	Charcoal (55.0 g)	Floor fill.	53
36	Bone	Cottontail (*Sylvilagus* sp.) femur epiphysis. Floor fill.	62
36	Adult human remains (possibly male)	Floor fill. Underwent NAGPRA repatriation process. Consist of skull fragment, 5 long bone fragments, a carpel, metacrapel fragment, 5 hand & 3 foot phalangies, a tarsal, & a foot middle phalanx. Disinterred or disturbed burial?	62,66
-	Chipped tools (6) Utilized flake (16.7 g) Retouched flake (2.4 g) Retouched flake (2.0 g) Retouched flake (3.4 g) Retouched flake (0.3 g) Retouched flake (0.2 g)	Floor fill (East Rubble Mound over Feature 1). 1053 (High Surface Chert). 1140 (chalcedonic silicified wood). 1142 (chalcedonic silicified wood). 1142 (chalcedonic silicified wood). 3520 (Jemez obsidian). Sourced to Bland Canyon (?). 3530 (Polvadera Peak obsidian). Sourced to El Rechuelos. Possible point fragment.	64
-	Mineral (1.2-x-0.8-x-0.4 cm; 2.7 g)	Unknown mineral; calcite? Heavy tiny tabular block. Natural?, with 1 surface ground flat?	65
-	Punch/awl (6.2-x-1.9-x-1.3 cm; 21.5 g)	2000 (sandstone). Unusual tapered stone, slightly ground to a point at 1 end. Shaped like a giant incisor. Level 1 (East Rubble Mound over Feature 1).	65A
-	Bones (526)	Cottontail (157; 77 boiled, 7 burned), jackrabbit (19; 10 boiled, 1 burned), mule deer (1), artiodactyl (2), woodrat (1), small/medium mammal (307; 116 boiled, 22 burned), medium/large mammal (29; 1 burned), falcon (1), collared lizard (1), mice (4), & rodent (4). Floor fill (East Rubble Mound over Feature 1).	66
-	Sherds (185) Lino Gray jars (12) Plain gray jars (122) Plain Gray jars with Fugitive Red (2) Plain Gray polished jars (46) Unclassified whiteware (2) Unclassified painted redware (1)	Floor fill (East Rubble Mound over Feature 1). Cibola Grayware. Cibola Grayware. Cibola Grayware. Obelisk Gray tradition. Cibola Whiteware. Unknown redware.	67

Chapter 3: Basketmaker III Excavation Reports   203

Table I.3.9. Site 29SJ 423, Distribution of Fill and Floor Materials in the Shrine and Pithouse A Area, cont'd.[a]

Artifact Number	Artifact Class	Lithic Material[b], Ceramic Ware or Faunal Species	FS No.
-	Whole flake (3.7 g)	1050 (High Surface Chert). Not in Cameron analysis.	67B
-	Chipped stones (256)	Floor fill (East Rubble Mound over Feature 1).	68
	Whole flakes (6; total 23.5 g)	1011 (fossiliferous chert).	
	Angular debris (5; total 4.9 g)	1011 (fossiliferous chert).	
	Cores (3; total 97.5 g)	1011 (fossiliferous chert).	
	Angular debris (1.3 g)	1040 (Morrison formation chert).	
	Utilized flake (2; total 1.4 g)	1070 (yellow chert).	
	Utilized flake (1.3 g)	1072 (Zuni yellow spotted chert).	
	Core (12.7 g)	1072 (Zuni yellow spotted chert).	
	Utilized flakes (9; total 60.1 g)	1050-1053 (High Surface Chert).	
	Whole flakes (23; total 44.2 g)	1050-1053 (High Surface Chert).	
	Angular debris (27; total 85.8 g)	1050-1053 (High Surface Chert).	
	Cores (7; total 183.0 g)	1050-1053 (High Surface Chert).	
	Manuport (1; 92.9 g)	1050-1053 (High Surface Chert.	
	Angular debris (11; total 87.3 g)	1110 (splintery silicified wood).	
	Utilized flakes (2; total 25.6 g)	1111 (Nacimiento formation silicified wood).	
	Whole flakes (6; total 11.1 g)	1112 (cherty silicified wood).	
	Angular debris (3; 18.3 g)	1112 (cherty silicified wood).	
	Cores (4; total 117.8 g)	1112 (cherty silicified wood).	
	Utilized flake (2.2 g)	1120 (red silicified wood).	
	Whole flake (0.5 g)	1120 (red silicified wood).	
	Angular debris (0.1 g)	1120 (red silicified wood).	
	Angular debris (10.8)	1130 (palm wood).	
	Utilized flakes (24; total 110.3 g)	1140-1145 (chalcedonic silicified wood).	
	Retouched flake (2.6 g)	1140-1145 (chalcedonic silicified wood).	
	Whole flakes (40; total 62.4 g)	1140-1145 (chalcedonic silicified wood).	
	Angular debris (44; total 70.1 g)	1140-1145 (chalcedonic silicified wood).	
	Cores (4; 7.6 g)	1140-1145 (chalcedonic silicified wood).	
	Angular debris (3.5 g)	1150 (jasperized wood).	
	Whole flake (0.1 g)	1230 (chalcedony with red inclusions).	
	Angular debris (4; total 30.8 g)	1230 (chalcedony with red inclusions).	
	Utilized flake (4.5 g)	1320 (red chalcedony).	
	Whole flake (0.1 g)	1320 (red chalcedony).	
	Utilized flake (1.7 g)	1650 (olive chert).	
	Whole flake (1.3 g)	2200 (silicified quartzose sandstone).	
	Core (181.8 g)	2221 (Pintado chert).	
	Utilized flake (1.7 g)	2700 (limestone).	
	Utilized flakes (3; 3.1 g)	3510 (Grants obsidian). 1 sourced to Mt. Taylor.	
	Whole flake (0.1 g)	3510 (Grants obsidian). Sourced to Mt. Taylor (?)	
	Angular debris (0.1 g)	3510 (Grants obsidian). Not sourced.	
	Whole flakes (2; 0.1 g)	3520 (Grants obsidian). 2 sourced to Mt. Taylor (?)	
	Core (2.5-x-2.2-x-1.4 cm; 6.4 g).	3520 (Jemez obsidian). Sourced to Cow Canyon, AZ.	
	Tested core Utilized flakes (3; total 6.0 g)	4000, 4005 (quartzite).	
	Whole flakes (3; total 50.6 g)	4000 (quartzite).	
	Angular debris (3.4 g)	4005 (quartzite).	

204 Windes et al.

Table I.3.9. Site 29SJ 423, Distribution of Fill and Floor Materials in the Shrine and Pithouse A Area, cont'd.[a]

Artifact Number	Artifact Class	Lithic Material[b], Ceramic Ware or Faunal Species	FS No.
-	Mineral (1.4-x-1.3-x-0.6 cm; 1.2 g)	Limonite (5110). Natural, covered in caliche. East Rubble Mound.	68D
-	Manuport (1.4-x-1.2-x-0.6 cm; 0.7 g)	1650 (olive chert). Natural, 1 edge broken off. 1 surface ground flat? Rock color 10Y 5/4 (light olive green).	68C
-	Manuport? (0.8-x-0.7-x-0.2 cm; 0.0 g)	1140 (chalcedonic silicified wood). Rounded & polished former flake? Turkey gizzard stone?	68C
-	Manuport (6.8+-x-5.6-x-3.9 cm; 215.4+ g)	4000 (quartzite). Natural pebble with end missing. Flakes off both ends. Floor fill (East Rubble Mound over Feature 1).	69
-	Manuports (15; largest 7.9-x-4.7-x-2.2 cm; total 830 g)	Natural pebbles of quartzite & chert. East Rubble Mound.	70A
-	Manuport fragment (4.3+-x-3.7-x-2.2 cm; 57.4+ g)Manuport (7.0-x-5.4-x-3.5 cm; 190 g)	4000 (quartzite). Natural pebbles. Floor fill (East Rubble Mound over Feature 1).	70B
37	Dendrochronological specimen (3.4+ cm diameter)	*Pinus edulis*. No date (CNM-77). Level 1 (0-18 cm above floor in area 53-x-45 cm).	392
Pit C			
38	Bones (36)	Cottontail (14), jackrabbit (3), prairie dog (1), woodrat (1), wolf (2), mule deer (2), pronghorn antelope (2), small/medium mammal (10; 1 burned), medium/large mammal (1). Pit C floor fill.	95
36	Shark tooth (21-x-1.3-x-0.4 cm; 0.9 g)	Cretaceous era fossilized tooth, unmodified.	95B
38	Chipped stones (10)	Pit C floor fill.	
	Whole flake (1.5 g)	1051 (High Surface chert).	
	Angular debris (0.7 g)	1051 (High Surface chert).	
	Core (4.9-x-3.4-x-1.7 cm; 29.5 g)	1053 (High Surface chert).	
	Core (4.5-x-3.5-x-2.2 cm; 32.6 g)	1053 (High Surface chert).	
	Core (3.0-x-3.0-x-1.7 cm; 15.7 g)	1112 (cherty silicified wood). Not analyzed in analysis.	
	Utilized flake (3.4 g)	1112 (cherty silicified wood).	
	Core (6.7-x-3.5-x-2.5 cm; 71.1 g)	1112 (cherty silicified wood).	
	Utilized flake (4.9 g)	1142 (chalcedonic silicified wood).	
	Whole flake (4.5 g)	4000 (quartzite).	
	Angular debris (4.7 g)	4005 (quartzite).	96
38	Sherds (47)	Pit C floor fill.	
	Lino Gray jar rims (2)	Cibola Grayware.	
	Plain gray jars (43)	Cibola Grayware.	
	Plain gray polished jars (1)	Obelisk Gray tradition.	
	Woodruff Red (1)	Mogollon tradition.	97

Table I.3.9. Site 29SJ 423, Distribution of Fill and Floor Materials in the Shrine and Pithouse A Area, cont'd.[a]

Artifact Number	Artifact Class	Lithic Material[b], Ceramic Ware or Faunal Species	FS No.
38	Palette (5.7-x-4.3-x-0.9 cm; 37.5 g)	4000 (quartzite). Red (Munsell 2.5YR 4/6) paint smeared across 1 surface of natural flat, discoid-shaped pebble. Pit C floor fill.	98
38	Hammerstone (12-x-8.9-x-6.8 cm; 926 g)	4000 (quartzite). Possible red (Munsell 10R 5/3?) paint residue in small area. End & edge battered. Pit C floor fill.	99
38	Groundstone (19.0-x-15.0-x-4.0 cm; 1814 g)	2000 (sandstone). Natural tabular, sub-wedge shaped stone with grinding of 1 surface. Pit C floor fill.	100
39	Bones (6)	Cottontail (1), small/medium size mammal (5). Fill under Feature 2.	304
39	Lino Gray jar sherd	Cibola Grayware. Fill under Feature 2.	305
40	Metate fragment (30+-x-19+-x-6 cm)	2000 (sandstone). Trough: 12+-x-10+-x-4 cm deep. Left on site. Level 1 ash fill.	36
41	Sherds (13)	Test Trench 1 floor fill.	92
	Plain gray jars (8)	Cibola Grayware.	
	Plain gray jars with Fugitive Red (2)	Cibola Grayware.	
	Plain gray polished jars (3)	Obelisk Gray tradition.	
41	Chipped stones (14)	Test Trench 1 floor fill.	93
	Whole flake (10.0 g)	1030 (black chert).	
	Utilized flake (0.1 g)	1070 (yellow chert).	
	Utilized flake (18.3 g)	1112 (cherty silicified wood).	
	Whole flake (1.6 g)	1112 (cherty silicified wood).	
	Angular debris (0.3 g)	1112 (cherty silicified wood).	
	Whole flake (2.2 g)	1120 (red silicified wood).	
	Utilized flakes (2; total 1.9)	1140-1145 (chalcedonic silicified wood).	
	Whole flake (1.5 g)	1140-1145 (chalcedonic silicified wood).	
	Angular flakes (4; total 2.4 g)	1140-1145 (chalcedonic silicified wood).	
	Whole flake (0.6 g)	2202 (silicified fine-grain brown concretion).	
41	Bones (58)	Cottontail (22), jackrabbit (6), small/medium mammal (21; 2 burned), medium/large mammal (9). Test Trench 1 floor fill.	94

[a] See distribution in Figure I.3.11. All shell, turquoise, and unusual minerals here assumed to be associated with late Pueblo II shrine rather than Basketmaker activities. All bones examined for cooking brown and burning (Akins; analysis data base).
[b] Obsidian sourcing from Shackely and Dillian (2000).

Table I.3.10. List of Postholes at Site 29SJ 423.[a]

Posthole No.	Length (cm)	Width (cm)	Depth (cm)	Volume[b] (liters)	Fill Type	Fill Period	Shims	Base Stone	Post size (cm)	Lining	Comments
Pithouse A area:											
Posthole 1	20	14	14	3.7	?	PO	0	0	-	?	Comprises arc.
Posthole 2	15	13	7	1.0	?	PO	0	0	-	?	Comprises arc.
Posthole 3	17	15	8	1.8	?	PO	0	0	-	?	Comprises arc.
Posthole 4	23	15	13	4.3	?	PO	0	0	-	?	Comprises arc.
Posthole 5	14	14	3	0.6	?	PO	0	0	-	?	Natural feature?
Pithouse B:											
Posthole 1	14.5	12	19	2.7	15	Occ	0	0	-	U	
Posthole 2	16	13	7.5	1.1	11,15	Occ	0	0	-	U	
Posthole 3	17	16	8	1.7	11,15	Occ	0	0	-	U	
Posthole 4	14	12	20	2.5	11,15	Occ	0	0	-	U	
Structure 1											
Posthole I	22	14	8	1.9	15	Occ	0	0	-	U	Sidepole hole?
Posthole II	19	19	15	4.2	15	Occ	0	0	-	U	Sidepole hole?
Posthole III	15	14	9-13	1.9	30	PO	0	0	-	U	Sidepole hole?
Posthole IV	18	18	8.5	2.2	11,14	PO	0	0	-	U	Sidepole hole?
Posthole V	13	12	10-14	1.5	30?	PO	0	0	-	U	Sidepole hole?
Posthole VI	18	15	20	4.3	47	PO	0	0	-	U	Sidepole hole?
Posthole VII	16.5	15	14.5	2.8	11,14	PO	0	0	-	U	Sidepole hole?
Posthole VIII	14.5	12.5	12	1.7	15	Occ	0	0	-	U	
Posthole D	15	14	8	1.3	?	?	0	0	-	U	Roof support?
Great Kiva I											
Posthole A	30	27	10-18	10.4	15,17	Occ	0	0	21 x 15	U	A.D 516 vv. Post burned on bottom. FS313.

Table I.3.10. List of Postholes at Site 29SJ 423, cont'd.[a]

Posthole No.	Length (cm)	Width (cm)	Depth (cm)	Volume[b] (liters)	Fill Type	Fill Period	Shims	Base Stone	Post size (cm)	Lining	Comments
Posthole B	24	20	11/18	8.7	15	Occ	0	0	-	U	
Posthole C	29	24	11-13	7.6	15	Occ	0	0	-	U	
Posthole E	25	23	23-26	13.0	16	Occ	0	0	18 x 14	U	A.D 480vv. Post burned on bottom. FS363.
Posthole F	25	23	27	13.4	15,16	Occ	0	0	19 x 17	U	A.D 515vv. Post burned on bottom. FS362.
Posthole 13	23	20	18	6.9	11,50	PO	1?	0	-	U	Sealed with plaster.
Great Kiva II											
Posthole 5	54	43	33	51.9	47	PO	9	0	25 x 23	U	Sealed with plaster. Auxiliary support.
Posthole 6	22	21	29	11.4	47	PO	4	0	-	U	Auxiliary support.
Posthole 7	41	40	33	48.3	10	PO	0	0		U	Plastered over.
Posthole 8	36	33	32-38	33.8	10/18	PO	0	0	-	U	Plastered over. 1 side burned.
Posthole 9	18	17	15	3.5	?	?	3	0	-	U	Plastered over.
Posthole 10	22	19	15	4.3	11,18	PO	2	0	-	U	Plastered over.
Posthole 15	18	16.5	12	2.8	10,18	PO	1	0	-	U	Ladder rest? 22 cm from PH 16. Plastered over. Formerly Hole 5.
Posthole 16	18	17	11	2.9	11	PO	2	0	-	U	Ladder rest? Plastered over. Formerly Hole 6.
Posthole 17	7	7	?	?	17	Occ	0	0	3 x 3	U	Fronts bench slabs. FS 256.
Posthole 18	9	8	4	0.2	17	Occ	0	0	3.5 x 3.5	U	Fronts bench slabs. FS 255.
Posthole 19	12	12	5±	0.6	17	Occ	0	0	10 x 10	U	In top of upper bench. FS 277.
Posthole 20	9.5	9	7	0.5	?	?	0	0	-	U	In top of lower bench.
Posthole 21	8.5	5	4	0.14	?	?	0	0	-	U	In top of lower bench–overlies Posthole D.
Great Kiva III											
Posthole 1	45	38	32	37.9	17	Occ	8	0	25 x 24	U	A.D 519vv, FS 229.

208   Windes et al.

Table I.3.10. List of Postholes at Site 29SJ 423, cont'd.[a]

Posthole No.	Length (cm)	Width (cm)	Depth (cm)	Volume[b] (liters)	Fill Type	Fill Period	Shims	Base Stone	Post size (cm)	Lining	Comments
Posthole 2	51	50	36	75.5	17	Occ	3	0	41 x 41	U	A.D 554 vv. Also used in GK II. FS 221.
Posthole 3	50	45	45	70.5	17	Occ	6	0	28 x 26	U	A.D. 557r, FS 228.
Posthole 4	36	33	31	22.5	17	Occ	7	0	23 x 22	U	A.D 435vv, FS 230.
Posthole 11	12	12	8	1.1	26,47	PO	0	0	-	U	
Posthole 12	10	10	13.5	1.1	10/18	PO	0	0	-	U	Cone-shaped.
Posthole 14	18	16	13	2.0	10/18/11	PO	0	0	-	U	

[a] See Tables I.7.4-I.7.5 for an explanation of the feature and attribute codes.
[b] Volumes for features are approximate.

Table I.3.11. Site 29SJ 423, distribution of materials in and around Pithouse B.[a]

Artifact Number	Artifact Class	Lithic Material, Ceramic Ware, or Faunal Species	FS No.
Feature I (Historic cist)			
1	Sherds (17)	Level 1	
	Lino Gray (1)	Cibola Grayware.	
	Plain gray jar (7)	Cibola Grayware.	
	Plain gray polished jar (7)	Obelisk Gray tradition.	
	Woodruff Red bowl (1)	Mogollon tradition.	
	Woodruff Red jar (1)	Mogollon tradition.	294
1	Bones (3)	Cottontail (32; 28 boiled), small/medium mammal (21; 21 boiled), medium mammal (1; boiled), unknown (1; boiled). Level 1.	295, 355
1	Chipped stones (5)	Level 1	
	Whole flake (2.0 g)	1050 (High Surface Chert).	
	Whole flake (4.3 g)	1053 (High Surface Chert).	
	Retouched flake (3.1 g)	1113 (cherty silicified wood).	
	Utitized flake (2.7 g)	1140 (chalcedonic silicified wood).	
	Whole flake (0.1 g)	1140 (chalcedonic silicified wood).	296
Feature II (Pithouse B)			
2	Mineral (4.9 x 3.4 x 1.1 cm; 20 g)	5041 (selenite gypsum). Natural, irregular shaped piece. Level 1 (4 cm above floor).	241
3	Bones (9)	Canid sp. (1), medium mammal (2), medium/large mammal (6). Level 1 (5 cm down).	249
4	Dendrochronological specimen	Juniperus sp. (CNM-51). Carbonized. Too few rings to date. FP 1 fill.	274
5	Dendrochronological specimen	Piñon (Pinus edulis). Carbonized. CNM-55; AD 307fp-367vv). Floor.	278
6	Dendrochronological specimen	Piñon (pinus edulis). Carbonized. CNM-56, 57; AD 277fp-355vv). Floor.	279
26	Beamer? fragment (12.0 x 2.3 x 0.4 cm; 21.8 g)	Indeterminant large mammal. Split edges & 1 end ground. Floor.	240
-	Knife (18 x 16 x 2 mm; 0.5 g)	1140 (chalcedonic silicified wood). Triangular-shaped. Level 1.	283
-	Sherds (130)	Level 1	
	Lino Gray jar rims (4)	Cibola Grayware.	
	Plain gray jar (85)	Cibola Grayware.	
	Plain gray polished jar (2)	Obelisk Gray tradition.	
	Unclassified redware (39)	Unknown redware.	285

210 *Windes et al.*

Table I.3.11. Site 29SJ 423, distribution of materials in and around Pithouse B, cont'd.[a]

Artifact Number	Artifact Class	Lithic Material, Ceramic Ware, or Faunal Species	FS No.
-	Sherds (43)	Floor	286
	Lino Gray jar rims (4)	Cibola Grayware.	
	Plain gray jar (23)	Cibola Grayware.	
	Plain gray polished jar (8)	Obelisk Gray tradition.	
	Polished smudged (2)	Mogollon tradition.	
	Woodruff Red jars (6)	Mogollon tradition.	
-	Chipped stones (16)	Level 1	287
	Angular debris (5.8 g)	1010 (fossiliferous chert).	
	Whole flake (3.7 g)	1053 (High Surface Chert).	
	Core (4.5 x 2.8 x 2.3 cm; 34.5 g)	1053 (High Surface Chert).	
	Whole flakes (2; total 1.0 g)	1072 (Zuni yellow-spotted chert).	
	Utilized flake (1.8 g)	1075 (dark brown chert).	
	Whole flake (6.4 g)	1112 (cherty silicified wood).	
	Utilized flake (2; 4.1 g)	1140 (chalcedonic silicified wood).	
	Angular debris (8.0 g)	1140 (chalcedonic silicified wood).	
	Utilized flake (1.7 g)	1142 (chalcedonic silicified wood).	
	Core (5.3 x 3.5 x 2.3 cm; 42.0 g)	1142 (chalcedonic silicified wood).	
	Whole flake (1.2 g)	1145 (chalcedonic silicified wood).	
	Angular debris (0.3 g)	1145 (chalcedonic silicified wood).	
	Core (6.0 x 5.9 x 4.1 cm; 179.2 g)	1145 (chalcedonic silicified wood).	
	Angular debris (4.3 g)	4000 (quartzite).	
-	Mineral (1.8 x 0.9 x 0.4 cm; 1.1 g)	5041 (selenite gypsum). Irregular, natural piece.	287B
-	Chipped stones (6)	Floor	288
	Whole flake (3.0 g)	1052 (High Surface Chert).	
	Whole flake (0.5 g)	1053 (High Surface Chert).	
	Utilized flake (11.8 g)	1140 (chalcedonic silicified wood).	
	Utilized flake (7.3 g)	1142 (chalcedonic silicified wood).	
	Whole flake (0.5 g)	1142 (chalcedonic silicified wood).	
	Whole flake (10.2 g)	1145 (chalcedonic silicified wood).	
-	Bones (234)	Cottontail (50; 33 boiled), jackrabbit (6; 3 boiled), coyote (1; 1 boiled), artiodactyl (9; 4 boiled, 1 burned), mt. sheep (1; boiled), wood rat (2, 1 boiled), small/medium mammal (125; 108 boiled, 1 burned, medium mammal (2), medium/large mammal (38). Level 1.	289
-	Bones (12)	*Canid* sp. (1), cottontail (3), coyote (1), small/medium mammal (7). Floor.	290
-	Limonite (4.5 x 2.3 x 2.1 cm; 23.9 g)	5110 (limonite). Natural chunk ground on 1 side (Munsell 10YR 6/8). Level 1.	291

Table I.3.11. Site 29SJ 423, distribution of materials in and around Pithouse B, cont'd.[a]

Artifact Number	Artifact Class	Lithic Material, Ceramic Ware, or Faunal Species	FS No.
-	Hammerstone (8.1 x 6.4 x 3.6 cm; 208.5 g)	1120 (red cherty silicified wood). 1 end battered to pieces. Level 1.	292
	Hammerstone (5.5 x 4.5 x 4.4 cm; 147.8 g)	4000 (quartzite). Edge battered. Level 1.	
-	Chipped stones (3)	Level 1	293
	Angular debris (29.1 g)	1011 (fossiliferous chert).	
	Angular debris (90.5 g)	1110 (splintery silicified wood).	
	Angular debris (134.1 g)	1112 (cherty silicified wood).	
-	Manuports (2; largest 8.3 x 5.2 x 2.7 cm; total 208.7 g)	4000 (quartzite). Natural pebbles.	293
-	Concretion fragment (formerly 8.2 cm diameter; 125 g)	2000 (sandstone, in part). Natural, partial sphere. Level 1.	297
-	Awl (5.7 x 1.6 x 0.5 cm; 4.3 g)	Indeterminant large mammal shaft splinter. Level 2.	418
Area I (midden)			
7	Knife (33 x 13 x 16 mm; 0.7 g)	1120 (red cherty silicified wood). Rod-like shape. Level 1 (above burned area).	242
8	Dendrochronological specimen (4.4+ cm diameter)	Piñon (*Pinus edulis*). Carbonized. CNM-46. Dated AD 450fp-530vv. Level 1.	251
9	Mano fragment? (7.4+ x 9.3 x 3.5 cm; 225+ g)	2000 (soft sandstone). Level 1 (on top of Level 2).	259
10	Concretion (5.5 long x 4.7 cm diameter bowl; 49.8 g)	2000 (sandstone). Shaped like a pipe bowl or ladle with broken stem. Burned red. Level 1 (5 cm above Level 2).	260
11	Projectile point (30 x 12 x 3 mm; 0.7 g)	1080 (Washington Pass chert). Stem missing; burned red. Level 1 (top of Level 2).	262
12	Projectile point (31 x 15 x 3 mm; 1.1 g)	1070 (yellowish-brown chert). Corner notched; ears missing. Level 1 (15 cm above Level 2).	263
13	Knife fragment (24+ x 30 x 7 mm; 2.7+ g)	1042 (slate gray argilliceous chert). Rounded end. Level 1.	265
14	Bead (19 x 4 x 1 mm; 0.4 g)	Indeterminant medium-size bird shaft fragment. Level 1 (18 cm down).	268
15	Knife (47 x 27 x 11 mm; 16.2 g)	1140 (chalcedonic silicified wood). Level 1 (14 cm down).	266
16	Mineral (2.9 x 2.5 x 1.1 cm; 5.6 g)	2821 (jet). Natural chunk ground on edges & 1 surface. Top of Level 2.	281
17	Tooth	Medium-size mammal, incisor. Level 1 (20 cm down).	282
18	Sherds (2)	Polished red jar (Tallohogan Red?).Level 1 (25 cm down; top of Level 2).	298
19	Mineral crystals (12 x 11 x 7 mm; 2.5 g)	2770 (calcite). Natural. Level 1.	299

212 Windes et al.

Table I.3.11. Site 29SJ 423, distribution of materials in and around Pithouse B, cont'd.[a]

	Artifact Class	Lithic Material, Ceramic Ware, or Faunal Species.	FS No.
20	Non-hafted, bifacially-flaked blade (30 x 11 x 0.4 mm; 1.0 g)	1070 (yellowish-brown chert). Level 1 (6 cm above bedrock).	307
21	Bones (19)	*Canid* sp. (1, boiled), cottontail (4: 4 boiled), jackrabbit (1; boiled), artiodactyl (1), small/medium mammal (2), medium/large mammal (9), unknown (1). Level 1 (Top of Level 2).	308
-	Pendant? fragment (2.8+ x 2.3 x 0.4 cm; 3.7+ g)	2251 (red dog shale). Ground flat on 2 opposite faces + 2 edges. Yellow & red coloration. Level 1 (10 cm above bedrock).	309
-	Groundstone fragment (12+ x 14.5 x 2.3 cm; 652.0 g)	2000 (sandstone). Tabular, irregular shape. 100% burned; firepit liner? Ground flat on 2 opposite faces. Level 1.	320
-	Mano fragment (4.7+ x 9.2± x 2.1 cm; 120+ g)	2000 (sandstone). Tabular, flat stone. Highly ground on 2 opposite faces.	
-	Hammerstone (8.5 x 6.9 x 5.9 cm; 403 g)	1011 (fossiliferous chert). Some edge battering. Level 1.	321
-	Hammerstone/chopper (9 x 8.5 x 4.9 cm; 519.7 g)	1011 (fossiliferous chert)? Flaked & battered along 1 edge. Level 1.	322
-	Manuports (3; largest 5.5 x 3.4 x 2.2 cm; total 123.1 g)	Natural pebbles of quartzite and chert. Level 1.	
-	Concretions (3) Natural shallow dish (13.2 x 10.2 x 2.4 cm; 330.8 g) Natural tiny sphere (8 mm diameter; 0.5 g) Fossilized shrimp burrow (4.7 x 3 x 1.8 cm; 18.4 g)	Level 1 Iron mineral. 2000 (sandstone). Iron mineral.	323
-	Whole flake (2.9 g)	1112 (cherty silicified wood). Level 1.	325
	Sherds (265) Lino Gray jar rims (15) Plain gray jars (170) Plain gray polished jars (70) Polished smudged (2) La Plata B/w bowls (4) Lino B/g bowl (1) Unclassified redware (3)	Level 1 Cibola Grayware. Cibola Grayware. Obelisk Gray tradition. Mogollon tradition. Cibola Whiteware. Tusayan Whiteware. Unknown redware.	325
-	Sherds (42) Lino Gray jar rims (4) Plain Gray jars (17) Plain gray polished (21)	Level 2 Cibola Grayware. Cibola Grayware. Obelisk Gray tradition.	326

[a] See distribution in **Figure 3.13**. Bones listed as boiled were analyzed as exhibiting "cooking" brown (Akins: analysis data base).

Table I.3.12. Site 29SJ 423, Distribution of Floor Fill, Floor, and Construction Materials for Structure I and Great Kivas I–III.[a]

Artifact Number	Artifact Class	Lithic Material, Ceramic Ware, or Faunal Species	FS No.
Structure 1			
1	Dendrochrological specimen (3.2+ cm diameter)	*Pinus edulis* (piñon). No date (CNM-69). Between inner and outer slabs.	364
2	Bead (13 long x 7 mm diameter; 0.1 g)	*Olivella dama*. Broken hole in side; ground hole in top. Near top of Hole III.	370
3	Side scraper (31 x 20 x 5 mm; 4.3 g)	1140 (chalcedonic silicified wood). Outside of Hole VII on bedrock.	371
4	Dendrochronological specimen (0.8+ cm diameter)	*Pinus edulis*. Dated AD 113np-221vv (CNM-70). On bedrock in roof burn material outside kiva between Posthole I and IV.	372
5	Dendrochronological specimens (3) (unburned)(est. diameter 4.8+ cm)	*Juniperus* sp. No date (CNM-71). Roof fall on bedrock between Holes II & III.	373
6	Unburned twigs (0.8 cm diameter)	*Pinus edulis*. No date (CNM-72). In roof fall.	374
7	Dendrochronological specimen (1.8± cm diameter)	*Populus* sp. (Cottonwood?) No date (CNM-73). In roof burn material.	375
8	Dendrochronolgical specimen (2.6+ cm est. diameter)	*Pinus edulis*. No date (CNM-74). In Hole VI (burned roofing?).	376
9	Dendrochronological specimen (3.2+ cm est. diameter)	*Pinus edulis*. Dated 458fp - 490vv (CNM-75). In fill near Hole VII. Roofing?	377
Great Kiva I construction			
10	Roof support post (15 x 21 cm diameter x 12 cm long)	*Pinus edulis*. Dated at AD 365fp-516vv (CNM-61). Unburned except for burned spots on sides below floor. Tree burned down? Posthole A.	313
10	Sherds (4) Lino Gray jar (1) Obelisk Gray jars (3)	Cibola Grayware. In Posthole A.	330
10	Chipped stones (2) Whole flake (3.3 g) Retouched flake (6.6 g)	Posthole A. 1053 (High Surface chert). 1113 (cherty silicified wood).	335
10	Bone	Small/medium mammal long bone fragment (burned). Posthole A.	340
10	Turquoise inlays (3; 7 x 4 x 1 mm; 6 x 4 x 2 mm; 6 x 5 x 1 mm; each 0.1 g)	5300 (turquoise). Rock Color 5G 7/4 & 10G 8/2. Each piece ground flat on 2 opposite sides. Some edge grinding. Posthole A.	351
11	Roof support post (14 x 18 cm diameter x 19 cm long)	*Pinus edulis*. Dated AD 326fp-515vv (CNM-67). Unburned except burned on bottom. Tree burned down? Posthole E.	362
12	Roof support post (17 x 19 cm diameter x 16 cm long)	*Pinus edulis*. Dated AD 329±p-480vv (CNM-68). Unburned except burned on bottom. Tree burned down? Posthole F.	363

Table I.3.12. Site 29SJ 423, Distribution of Floor Fill, Floor, and Construction Materials for Structure I and Great Kivas I–III, cont'd.[a]

Artifact Number	Artifact Class	Lithic Material, Ceramic Ware, or Faunal Species	FS No.
13	Dendrochronological specimens (3.0+ cm est. diameter)	*Pinus edulis*. Dated AD 354fp-449vv (CNM-62). In fill of lower (Great Kiva II) bench.	314
14	Dendrochronological specimens (10 cm est. diameter)	Non-coniferous. No date (CNM-65). In fill of lower (Great Kiva II) bench.	317
15	Roofing element? (4.8± cm diameter)	*Juniperus* sp. No date (CNM-66). In fill of lower (Great Kiva II) bench.	318
Great Kiva II construction			
16	Dendrochronological specimen (3.8+ cm diameter)	*Juniperus* sp. No date (CNM-47). Under plaster seal of PH 13.	252
16	Chipped stone (angular debris? 2.5 g)	1050 (High Surface Chert). In plaster over PH 13.	267
17	Upright post (10 cm diameter x 24 cm long)	*Pinus edulis*. No date (CNM-54). Burned roofing? Upright on bench and in bench against inner wall slabs.	277
18	Upright post (3.5 cm diameter x 7 cm long)	*Juniperus* sp. No date (CNM-49). Against primary bench face slabs behind secondary bench face slabs.	255
19	Upright post (3.0 cm diameter x 14 cm long)	*Pinus edulis*. No date (CNM-50). Against primary bench face slabs behind secondary bench face slabs.	256
20	Dendrochronological specimen (3 x 14 cm size x 56 cm long)	*Pinus ponderosa*. No date (CNM-60). Burned roofing? On top of lower bench behind primary slab facing.	312
21	Bench construction element (4.5 cm diameter x 8 cm long)	*Pinus edulis*. No date (CNM-52). Behind secondary bench face slab. Extends into lower bench.	275
22	Roofing impression (4.7 x 4.0 x 2.8 cm; 30 g)	Adobe. Burned; with vegetal impressions. Associated with FS 197-199. Between bench slab outer walls.	200
23	Dendrochronological specimen (5.4± cm diameter)	*Pinus edulis*. No date (CNM-53). Burned roofing? In bench fill behind step? or bench face.	276
24	Dendrochronological specimen (1.8+ cm est. diameter)	*Pinus edulis*. No date (CNM-59). Burned roofing? On top of lower bench.	311
25	Roofing element (11 cm diameter)	*Pinus edulis*. No date (CNM-48). Between secondary and primary bench face slabs on bedrock ledge.	253
In fill of lower (Great Kiva II) bench			
-	Sherds: Plain gray (4), Obelisk Gray (1)	Cibola Grayware.	301

Table 1.3.12. Site 29SJ 423, Distribution of Floor Fill, Floor, and Construction Materials for Structure 1 and Great Kivas 1–III, cont'd.[a]

Artifact Number	Artifact Class	Lithic Material, Ceramic Ware, or Faunal Species	FS No.
–	Chipped stones (10) Whole flakes (2; 14.2 g) Core (4.2 x 3.1 x 1.4 cm; 17.5 g) Utilized flake (0.4 g) Angular debris (0.2 g) Whole flake (3.0 g) Utilized flakes (2; 4.5 g) Utilized flake (9.2 g) Utilized flake (1.9 g)	1051 (High Surface Chert). 1053 (High Surface Chert). 1112 (cherty silicified wood). 1113 (cherty silicified wood). 1120 (red silicified wood). 1140 (chalcedonic silicified wood). 1145 (chalcedonic silicified wood). 3510 (Grants Ridge obsidian).	302
–	Manuport (4.5 x 3.0 x 1.4 cm; 28.0 g)	4000 (quartzite). Natural pebble.	302D
–	Bone	Pronghorn (*Antilocarpa americana*) mandible fragment. Burned.	303
26	Corncob fragments (8)	*Zea mays*. Carbonized.	342
27	Bead fragment (ca. 12 diameter x 4 mm thick; 0.1 g)	Unknown shell type. Disc shape. 4mm hole in center. Rock Color N9 (white). Location is approximate.	350
28	Bead fragment (9 diameter x 2 mm thick).	5300 (turquoise). Rock color 10G 8/2. Broken in half. 2.5 mm hole. Lower bench against bedrock.	360
29	Mosaic inlay (5 x 3 x 2 mm; 0.0 g)	5300 (turquoise). Rock color 5BG 6/6. Opposite 2 surfaces & 2 edges ground.	352
30	Mosaic inlay (13 x 6 x 3 mm; 0.2 g)	5300 (turquoise). Rock color 10G 8/2. In pieces. 2 opposite surfaces ground flat; 1 edge ground.	353
30	Manuport (5.6 x 4.5 x 1.2 cm; 48.2 g)	4000 (tan quartzite). Natural flat, discoid pebble.	365
31	Polishing stone? (3.7 x 2.1 x 1.0 cm; 10.2 g)	1030 (black chert). Natural, tear-shaped pebble.	356
32	Corncob fragments (20)	*Zea mays*. Carbonized.	354
32	Bone	*Sylvilagus* (cottontail) sp. tibia.	361
–	Sherds (5) Plain gray jar (1) Plain gray polished jar (3) Woodruff Red (1)	Cibola Grayware. Obelisk Gray tradition. Mogollon tradition.	366
–	Chipped stones (7) Core (5.3 x 4.0 x 3.4 cm; 60.8 g) Utilized flake (2.6 g) Whole flakes (3; total 31.0 g) Retouched flake (0.1 g) Core (2.7 x 2.0 x 1.4 cm; 7.8 g)	1053 (High Surface Chert). 1145 (chalcedonic silicified wood). 1140, 1142 (chalcedonic silicified wood). 3503 (unidentified obsidian). Sourced to Mt. Taylor. 3510 (Grants obsidian). Not sourced.	367

Table I.3.12. Site 29SJ 423, Distribution of Floor Fill, Floor, and Construction Materials for Structure I and Great Kivas I–III, cont'd.[a]

Artifact Number	Artifact Class	Lithic Material, Ceramic Ware, or Faunal Species	FS No.
-	Mineral (1.3 x 1.2 x 0.7 cm; 1.3 g)	5110 (limonite concretion). Unworked.	367
-	Bones (21)	Cottontail (5), jackrabbit (7; 1 boiled). small/medium mammal (5), medium/large mammal (1), plains pocket mouse (1), unknown (2).	368
-	Concretion (4.5 x 2.9 cm diameter; 11.6 g) Concretion (1.1 x 1.5 cm diameter; 6.3 g)	Iron mineral. 2 rod-like concretions, largest pointed at one end. 5110 (limonitie). Munsell color 7.5YR 6/6. V-cut from trowel?	369
Part of primary (Great Kiva II) bench face and outer wall construction			
33	Miniature metate? (27 x 18.7 x 4.6 cm; 2748.7 g)	2000 (sandstone). Irregular shape, with very shallow trough without defined sides. Part of primary bench face construction.	378
34	Sharpening stone (38 x 22 x 22 cm)	2000 (sandstone). 22 grooves (12-45 mm long x 3-7 mm wide x 2-5 mm deep). Upright slab of outer wall. Left in field.	381
35	Sharpening stone (31 x 19 x 9 cm)	2000 (sandstone). 4 grooves (35-50 mm long x 4 mm wide x 5 mm deep). Part of primary bench face construction. Left in field.	379
36A	Groundstone (27.8 x 18.4 x 3.8 cm; 1978.0 g)	2000 (sandstone). Irregular natural shape with shallow 16-cm-wide trough without defined edges. Part of primary bench face.	383
36B	Sharpening stone (29 x 13 x 9 cm)	2000 (sandstone). 2 grooves (30 mm long x 3 mm wide x 2 mm deep). Part of primary bench face. Left in field.	382
37	Lap anvil (21.1 x 19.2 x 6.0 cm; 3.5 kg)	2000 (sandstone). Subrectagular shape; 2 opposite surfaces highly ground & slightly pecked; some edge grinding. 100% burned? Behind secondary bench face; stuck horizontally into lower bench 20 cm below top.	300
38	Sharpening stone (42 x 21 x 10 cm)	2000 (sandstone). 2 grooves (70 & 110 mm long x 7 & 5 mm wide x 5 & 4 mm deep, respectively). Upright slab, inner circle, outer wall. Left in field.	380
39	Sharpening stone (45 x 30 x 14 cm)	2000 (sandstone). Three grooves (22, 35 & 200 mm long x 6, 7, & 3 mm wide, respectively; 2-6 mm deep). Part of primary? bench face. Left in field.	357
On top of lower bench: Great Kiva II abandonment material			
40	Bead (4 diameter x 1 mm thick)	Unknown shell type. Disc shape. Hole in bead = 1.5 mm diameter.	348
41	Projectile point fragment (1.2+ x 1.8 x 0.3 cm; 0.7 g)	1052 (High Surface Chert). Corner notched; stem, tip, & side are missing.	344
42	Side scraper (3.4 x 1.8 x 0.6 cm; 3.7 g)	1112 (cherty silicified wood).	345
43	Grooved abrader (8.2 x 6.3 x 2.5 cm; 132.9 g)	2000 (soft sandstone). Irregular shape. Groove 2.7 cm wide.	324
44	Bead (5.5 diameter x 2 mm thick)	*Olivella dama*. Disc shape. Hole in bead = 2 mm. Bead follows curvature of shell, thus appearing warped.	349

Table I.3.12. Site 29SJ 423, Distribution of Floor Fill, Floor, and Construction Materials for Structure I and Great Kivas I–III, cont'd.[a]

Artifact Number	Artifact Class	Lithic Material, Ceramic Ware, or Faunal Species	FS No.
45	Bone	*Lepus californicus* (jackrabbit) radius (burned).	341
-	Sherds (20) Plain gray jar (17) Plain gray polished jar (3)	Cibola Grayware. Obelisk Gray tradition.	329
-	Chipped stones (7) Angular debris (2.2 g) Whole flake (1.0 g) Angular debris (10.6 g) Whole flake (0.3 g) Core (3.5 x 2.7 x 1.6 cm; 13.0 g) Utilized flake (3.0 g) Whole flake (5.5 g)	1050 (High Surface chert). 1053 (High Surface chert). 1070 (yellowish-brown chert). 1113 (cherty silicified wood). 1142 (chalcedonic silicified wood). 1145 (chalcedonic silicified wood). 4000 (quartzite).	334
-	Bones (7)	Cottontail (4; 2 boiled); jackrabbit (2; 1 boiled); medium/large mammal (1; burned).	339
Between Outer and Inner Bench Slabs: Great Kiva II abandonment material?			
46	Lino Gray jar sherd "tray"	Between bench slabs outer wall (associated with FS 199).	197
46	Bones (9)	Cottontail (1; burned), jackrabbit (7; 5 burned), small/medium mammal (1; burned). Between bench slabs outer wall (associated with FS 199; found on FS 197).	198
46	Bead (16 x 7 x 4+ mm; 0.0 g)	*Lepus californicus* femur shaft fragment. Tubular; cut & ground on ends. Between bench slabs outer wall (associated with FS 199; found on FS 197).	198
46	Misc. chipped stone (2) Core (6.3 x 5.4 x 3.0 cm; 81.2 g) Utilized flake (4.5 g)	Between bench slab outer walls (associated with FS 197-198). 1053 (High Surface Chert). 1113 (cherty silicified wood).	199
47	Polishing stone? (7.2 x 4.1 x 3.2 cm; 135.6 g)	4000 (black quartzite). Natural pebble. Between outer wall slabs.	343
48	Non-hafted? bifacially-flaked blade (22 x 11 x 3 mm; 0.3 g)	1052 (High Surface Chert). Corner notched. Between secondary and primary bench face slabs (1st & 2nd) on bed rock ledge.	264
49	Awl (11.9 x 1.6 x 0.8 cm; 12.8 g)	Indeterminant large mammal shaft splinter fragment tip. Between secondary and primary bench face slab (1st & 2nd) on bedrock ledge.	271
50	Awl (8.7 x 1.0 x 0.6 cm; 4.7 g)	Indeterminant medium/large mammal shaft fragment tip. Between secondary and primary bench face slab (1st & 2nd) on rock ledge.	272
50	Bone	*Sylvilagus* (cottontail) sp. metatarsal. Between secondary and primary bench face slab (1st & 2nd) on rock ledge.	272

Table I.3.12. Site 29SJ 423, Distribution of Floor Fill, Floor, and Construction Materials for Structure I and Great Kivas I–III, cont'd.[a]

Artifact Number	Artifact Class	Lithic Material, Ceramic Ware, or Faunal Species	FS No.
51	Concretion (fetish?)(10.2 x 2.7 x 2.3 cm; 73.6 g)	2000 (sandstone). Tapered cylinder, pointed at both ends. Between secondary and primary bench face slabs (1st & 2nd) 5 cm above bedrock ledge.	284
52	Mineral (8 x 7 x 5 mm; 0.2 g)	5300 (turquoise). Modified nodule. Rock Color 10G 8/2. Near FS 270. Between secondary and primary bench face slabs (1st & 2nd) on bedrock ledge.	261
52	Worked bone (5.5 x 0.7 x 0.1 cm; 1.2 g)	*Sylvilagus* (cottontail) sp. tibia medial shaft fragment. Between secondary and primary bench face slab (1st & 2nd) on bed rock ledge. Near FS 261.	270
53	Biscuit mano (9.3 x 8.5 x 4.3 cm; 493.5 g)	2000 (sandstone). Broken? 100% burned. Between secondary and primary bench face slabs.	257
–	Hammerstone (8.7 x 6.2 x 4.0 cm; 321.3 g)	4000 (quartzite). Natural pebble battered on 1 end. Between slabs of outer wall.	399
Great Kiva II floor features: Other Pit 1 fill			
54	Manuport (1.8 x 1.5 x 1.1 cm; 4.0 g)	4000 (yellow quartzite). Natural pebble.	232
54	Chipped stones (2) Retouched flake (7.9 g) Whole flake (5.2 g)	1050 (High Surface Chert). 4005 (quartzite).	233
54	Sherds: Obelisk Gray (5)	Cibola Grayware.	234
54	Hammerstone (7.2 x 6.9 x 4.2 cm; 259.0 g)	4000 (quartzite). Natural pebble with some edge & end battering.	397
55A	Mineral specimen (54 x 30 x 14 mm; 7.4 g)	Calcium carbonate? Irregular, lumpy piece. Rock Color 5YR 8.1. PH 6 fill.	224
55A	Manuport (5.3 x 4.4 x 1.9 cm; 64.3 g)	4000 (dark quartzite). Natural pebble. PH 6 fill.	226
Great Kiva III construction			
55B	Metate (53 x 31 x 5 cm)	2000 (sandstone). Trough: 34 x 19 x 3 cm deep. Bench face wall fall (secondary). Left on site.	273
56	Metate fragment (31+ x 31+ x 4.5 cm)	2000 (sandstone). Trough: 28+ x 22+ x 2 cm deep. Level 3 (20 cm above floor). Outer wall covering stone. Left in field.	138
57	Shim/mano (16 x 9.4 x 6.6 cm; 1747.1 g)	2000 (sandstone). Former metate fragment reshaped by pecking into a blocky possible mano blank. Burned. North PH, south side.	258

Table I.3.12. Site 29SJ 423, Distribution of Floor Fill, Floor, and Construction Materials for Structure 1 and Great Kivas I–III, cont'd.[a]

Artifact Number	Artifact Class	Lithic Material, Ceramic Ware, or Faunal Species	FS No.
58	Metate fragment (55+ x 26+ x 6.5cm)	2000 (sandstone). Trough: 39 long x 6 cm deep (width unknown). Part of FS 193. Outer wall covering stone. Level 3 (14 cm above floor). Left in field.	168
59	Sharpening stone (24 x 19 x 9.5 cm; 3060± g)	2000 (soft sandstone). Block with deep ax-like sharpening groove, 8.5 cm wide & 5 cm deep. Burned. Some edge grinding. Outer wall covering stone. Level 3 (on top of roof fall; 36 cm above floor).	181
60	Metate fragment (26+ x 12+ x 7cm)	2000 (sandstone). Trough: 12+ x 11+ x 3 cm deep. Outer wall covering stone. Level 3 (5 cm above floor). Left in field.	182
61	Metate fragment (40+ x 36 x 9 cm)	2000 (sandstone). Trough: 17+ x 14+ x 1 cm deep. Outer wall covering stone. Level 3 (5-35 cm above floor). Left in field.	185
62	Metate fragment (66 x 42 x 6.5 cm)	2000 (sandstone). Trough: 15+ x 12+ x 5.5 cm deep. Part of FS 168 (thus, trough = 20 cm wide). Outer wall covering stone. Level 3 (11 cm above floor). Left in field.	193
63	Groundstone (20.0+ x 30.7 x 5.4 cm; 25.9 kg)	2000 (sandstone). Trapezoid, tabular block lightly but finely ground on 1 surface and 1 side. Slightly burned. Part of secondary bench face.	306
64	Metate fragment (? x 16+ x 7 cm thick)	2000 (sandstone). Part of bench face. Left in field.	238
65	Metate (53 x 42 x 6 cm)	2000 (sandstone). Trough: 35 x 19.5 x 6 cm deep (hole thru bottom). Secondary bench face slab.	254
	Great Kiva III		
66	Pot cover (10.1 x 8.7 x 0.6 cm; 82.9 g)	2000 (sandstone). 100% burned; in pieces. Above bench 2 cm.	237
67	Mosaic inlay piece (8 x 6 x 1 mm; 0.1 g)	5300 (turquoise). Rectangular, flat piece; ground on both surfaces & all edges. Rock Color 10GY 7/2. Floor.	154
68	Drill (formal) (20 x 13 x 2 mm; 0.5 g)	1140 (chalcedonic silicified wood). Tourist-point like. Floor.	161
69	Worked bone (1.4 x 0.9 x 0.2 cm; 0.23 g)	Indeterminant medium/large mammal fragment (toothed). Floor.	213
70	Corncob fragment (not weighed)	*Zea mays*. Carbonized. Floor.	180
71	End scraper (22 x 16 x 3 mm; 1.6 g)	1113 (cherty silicified chert). Squarish. Associated with FS 207. Floor.	210
72	Non-hafted bifacially-flaked blade (23 x 14 x 5 mm; 0.8 g)	1140 (chalcedonic silicified wood). Triangular shaped. Floor.	211
73	Projectile point fragment (18 x 19 x 2 mm; 0.2+ g)	1113 (cherty silicified chert). Corner notched; side & 1 tang missing. Floor.	212

Table I.3.12. Site 29SJ 423, Distribution of Floor Fill, Floor, and Construction Materials for Structure I and Great Kivas I–III, cont'd.[a]

Artifact Number	Artifact Class	Lithic Material, Ceramic Ware, or Faunal Species	FS No.
74	Bifacially-flaked blade (32 x 10 x 2 mm; 0.7 g)	1054 (High Surface Chert). Point? Stem missing; serrated edges. Next to rock cover in PH 8.	236
75	Non-hafted, bifacially-flaked blade (24 x 12 x 4 mm; 0.9 g)	1150 (yellow-brown jasper silicified wood). Level 3 (13 cm above floor).	169
-	Sherds (70)	Level 3	202
	Plain gray unpolished jar (34)	Cibola Grayware.	
	Plain gray polished jar (33)	Obelisk Gray tradition.	
	La Plata B/w (3)	Cibola Whiteware.	
-	Sherd (Plain gray polished jar)	Obelisk Gray tradition. Level 3.	
-	Chipped stones (108)	Level 3	203
	Angular debris (2; total 5.6 g)	1010 (fossiliferous chert).	
	Utilized flakes (3; total 15.2 g)	1050, 1053 (High Surface cherts).	
	Whole flakes (10; total 21.4 g)	1050, 1053 (High Surface cherts).	
	Angular debris (10; total 55.7 g)	1050, 1053 (High Surface cherts).	
	Cores (5; total 153.1 g)	1050, 1053 (High Surface cherts).	
	Utilized flake (0.8 g)	1060 (dark red jasper).	
	Whole flake (0.1 g)	1060 (dark red jasper).	
	Angular debris (2; total 4.7 g)	1060 (dark red jasper).	
	Angular debris (0.5 g)	1070 (yellowish-brown chert).	
	Utilized flakes (5; total 28.3 g)	1112-1113 (cherty silicified wood).	
	Retouched flake (7.5 g)	1112-1113 (cherty silicified wood).	
	Whole flakes (3; total 22.6 g)	1112-1113 (cherty silicified wood).	
	Angular debris (10; 24.5 g)	1112-1113 (cherty silicified wood).	
	Cores (2; 29.6 g)	1112-1113 (cherty silicified wood).	
	Utilized flakes (2; total 4.5 g)	1140, 1142 (chalcedonic silicified wood).	
	Retouched flake (2.9 g)	1140 (chalcedonic silicified wood).	
	Whole flakes (4; total 1.9 g)	1140, 1142 (chalcedonic silicified wood).	
	Angular debris (28; total 34.2 g)	1140, 1142 (chalcedonic silicified wood).	
	Whole flakes (4; total 4.0 g)	2651 (Lower Mancos shale).	
	Angular debris (6; total 42.8 g)	2651 (Lower Mancos shale).	
	Utilized flakes (3; total 3.6 g)	3510 (Grants Ridge obsidian). Not sourced.	
	Whole flake (0.6 g)	3510 (Grants Ridge obsidian). Not sourced.	
	Angular debris (1.3 g)	3520 (Jemez obsidian). Not sourced. Missing.	
	Utilized flake (14.0 g)	4005 (quartzite).	
	Whole flake (2.2 g)	4005 (quartzite).	

Table I.3.12. Site 29SJ 423, Distribution of Floor Fill, Floor, and Construction Materials for Structure 1 and Great Kivas I–III, cont'd.[a]

Artifact Number	Artifact Class	Lithic Material, Ceramic Ware, or Faunal Species	FS No.
-	Minerals (1.7 x 1.0 x 0.5 cm; 1.0 g) (1.5 x 0.8 x 0.7 cm; 0.6 g)	5221 (hematite). Munsell color red 2.5YR 4/6. Unmodified. 5221 (hematite). Unmodified.	203 203
-	Unclassified whiteware sherd	Cibola Whiteware.	204
-	Manuports (7; largest 8.9 x 6.3 x 3.1 cm; total 441.2 g) Includes a flattish, discoid petrified wood (3.5 x 2.3 x 1.8 cm; 10 g)	Quartzite & cherts (some broken). Level 3.	204
-	Hammerstone (9.4 x 6.3 x 4.4 cm; 354.8 g)	4000 (quartzite). Burned. Both ends battered. Level 3.	205
-	Bones (40)	Cottontail (7; 5 burned), jackrabbit (4; 1 burned), grizzly bear metatarsal (1; burned), small/medium mammal (21; 16 burned), medium/large mammal (7; 4 burned). Level 3.	206
-	Sherds (63) Plain gray unpolished jar (15) Plain gray polished jar (36) La Plata B/w bowl (1) Unclassified polished BMIII-PI whiteware (3) Tallahogan Red (3)	Floor Cibola Grayware. Obelisk Gray tradition. Cibola Whiteware. Cibola Whiteware. Redware tradition.	214
-	Chipped stones (71) Whole flake (1.0 g) Core (3.9 x 2.5 x 2.0 cm; 21.2 g) Whole flake (5.3 g) Utilized flakes (2; total 2.7 g) Retouched flake (0.4 g) Whole flakes (2; total 4.2 g) Angular debris (14; total 63.4 g) Utilized flake (1.3 g) Angular debris (2; total 3.9) Angular debris (4; total 21.7 g) Utilized flakes (4; total 38.9 g) Whole flakes (2; total 2.1 g) Angular debris (7; total 22.3 g) Utilized flakes (7; total 25.0 g) Whole flake (5.1 g) Angular debris (11; total 21.4 g) Utilized flakes (3; total 26.4 g) Retouched flake (4.8 g) Whole flakes (2; total 0.7 g) Angular debris (0.9 g) Utilized flake (0.3 g) Retouched flake (25.0 g) Angular debris (2.9 g)	Floor 1010 (fossiliferous chert). 1010 (fossiliferous chert). 1030 (black chert). 1050-1053 (High Surface Cherts). 1050-1053 (High Surface Cherts). 1050-1053 (High Surface Cherts). 1050-1053 (High Surface Cherts). 1080 (Washington Pass/Nabona Chert). 1080 (Washington Pass/Nabona Chert). 1110 (splintery silicified wood). 1112-1113 (cherty silicified wood). 1112-1113 (cherty silicified wood). 1112-1113 (cherty silicified wood). 1140, 1142 (chalcedonic silicified wood). 1140, 1142 (chalcedonic silicified wood). 1140, 1142 (chalcedonic silicified wood). 1234 (chalcedony with red & black inclusions). 1234 (chalcedony with red & black inclusions). 3510 (Grants Ridge obsidian). Not sourced. 3510 (Grants Ridge obsidian). Sourced to Mt. Taylor. 3520 (Jemez obsidian). Not sourced. 4000 (quartzite). 4005 (quartzite).	215

222 Windes et al.

Table I.3.12. Site 29SJ 423, Distribution of Floor Fill, Floor, and Construction Materials for Structure I and Great Kivas I–III, cont'd.[a]

Artifact Number	Artifact Class	Lithic Material, Ceramic Ware, or Faunal Species	FS No.
	Minerals (4; largest 2.4 x 1.1 x 0.2 cm; all = 1.7 g)	5040 (gypsum). Irregular, flat natural pieces.	215B
	Mineral (2.3 x 2.1 x 1.1 cm; 6.3 g)	5221 (hematite). Angular, irregular natural piece.	215B
–	Worked bone (2.3 x 1.3 x 0.4 cm; 0.9 g) Bones (9)	Indeterminant medium/large mammal fragment. Floor. Cottontail (2; burned), jackrabbit (2; burned), small/medium mammal (3; burned).	216
–	Manuports (8; largest 6.3 x 5.7 x 2.9 cm; total 349.7 g)	Quartzites and cherts. Natural pebbles. Largest is burned. Floor.	217
–	Non-hafted, bifacially-flaked blade fragment (20 x 12 x 3 mm; 0.6 g)	1112 (cherty silicified wood). Triangular shaped. Floor.	218
–	Chopper (6.1 x 4.9 x 1.3 cm; 54.0 g)	4000 (quartzite). Natural pebble flaked along 1 end. Floor.	219
–	Crystal (9 x 8 x 3 mm; 0.6 g)	Natural chip. Floor.	220
–	Retouched flake (23 x 23 x 4 mm; 0.5 g)	1145 (chalcedonic silicified wood). Level 3.	400
–	Drill (formal)(17 x 12 x 3 mm; 0.5 g)	1140 (chalcedonic silicified chert). Triangular shape. Similar to a fortuitous perforator. Level 3.	401
–	Bead (10 mm long-x-7 mm diameter)	*Olivella dama*. Tip ground off for string hole. Level 2 of Great Kiva III.	417
–	Bead (12 mm long-x-5 mm diameter; 0.1 g)	*Olivella dama*. Tip ground off for string hole. Surface southeast of Great Kiva III.	419

[a] See distribution in Figures 3.15–3.17. All bones examined for cooking brown and burning (Akins; analysis data base).
[b] Obsidian pieces sourced by Shackley and Dillian (2000).

Table I.3.13. Site 29SJ 423, Distribution of Roofing Elements Recorded from the Burned Superstructure of Great Kiva III.[a]

Artifact Number	Artifact Class	Wood Species	FS No.
1	Roofing element (13 cm diameter x 36 cm)	Floor. Not collected.	-
2	Roofing element (11 cm diameter x 37 cm)	Floor. Not collected.	-
3	Roofing element (9 cm diameter x 35 cm)	Floor. Not collected.	-
4	Roofing element (13 cm diameter x 27 cm long)	*Populus* sp. No date (CNM-2). Floor (roof fall).	137
5	Roofing element (10 cm diameter x 81 cm long)	*Juniperus* sp. No date (CNM-1). Floor (roof fall).	135
6	Roofing element (4.6+ cm estimated diameter)	*Juniperus* sp. No date (CNM-5). Level 3 (on top of FS 145).	142
7	Roofing element (8 x 17 cm diameter x 98 cm long)	*Juniperus* sp. No date (CNM-8). Level 3 (on floor).	145
8	Roofing element (5 cm diameter x 76 cm long)	*Pinus edulis* (piñon). No date (CNM-6). Level 3 (contact with FS 145 & 149; 4 cm above floor).	143
9	Roofing element (14 cm diameter x 66 cm long)	*Juniperus* sp. No date (CNM-10). Level 3 (on floor; contact with FS 143 & 147).	149
10	Roofing element (9 cm diameter x 25 cm long)	*Pinus edulis.* No date (CNM-9). Level 3 (10 cm above floor).	147
11	Roofing element (8.5 cm diameter x 30 cm)	On upper bench. Not collected.	-
12	Roofing element (8 cm diameter x 24 cm)	Level 3 (10cm above floor). Not collected.	-
13	Roofing element (9 cm diameter x 67 cm long)	*Juniperus* sp. No date (CNM-11). Level 3 (from top bench to 10 cm above floor).	150
14	Roofing element (15 cm diameter x 105 cm long)	*Juniperus* sp. No date (CNM-16, 17). Floor (contact with FS 159).	158
15	Roofing element (8.5 cm diameter x 75 cm long)	*Juniperus* sp. No date (CNM-18). Floor (contact with FS 158).	159
16	Roofing element (14 cm diameter x 98 cm long)	*Juniperus* sp. No date (CNM-19). Floor to bench face (lower).	163
17	Roofing element (9 cm diameter x 54 cm long)	Level 3 (just above floor). Not collected.	--
18	Roofing element (5.5 cm diameter x 13 cm long)	*Populus* sp. No date (CNM-25). Floor.	173
19	Roofing element (6 cm diameter x 9 cm long)	*Pinus edulis.* No date (CNM-26). Level 3 (10 cm above floor).	174
20	Roofing element (9 cm diameter x 34 cm long)	*Populus* sp. No date (CNM-27). Floor (associated with FS 177).	176
21	Roofing element (12 cm diameter x 119 cm long)	*Pinus edulis.* No date (CNM-29). Level 3 (5 cm above floor; contact with FS 176 & 178).	177
22	Roofing element (10 cm diameter x 30 cm long)	*Pinus edulis.* Dated AD 340p-523vv (CNM-30). Level 3 (3 cm above floor; contact with FS 177).	178
23	Roofing elements (8; largest 5.4+ cm estimated diameter)	*Populus* sp. No date (CNM-3). Level 3 (8 cm above floor).	139

Table I.3.13. Site 29SJ 423, Distribution of Roofing Elements Recorded from the Burned Superstructure of Great Kiva III, cont'd.[a]

Artifact Number	Artifact Class	Wood Species	FS No.
24	Roofing closure material (13; largest 0.8 cm diameter)	*Populus* sp. No date (CNM-4). Level 3 (on floor).	141
25	Roofing element (10 cm diameter x 41 cm long)	*Pinus edulis*. Dated A.D. 480p-550r (CNM-31). Floor (associated with FS 175).	179
26	Roofing element (13 cm diameter x 32 cm long)	*Populus* sp. No date (CNM-32). Level 3 (14 cm above floor; on top of FS 184).	183
27	Roofing element (7 cm diameter x 40 cm long)	*Juniperus* sp. No date (CNM-33). Floor.	184
28	Roofing element (10 cm diameter x 23 cm long)	Non-coniferous tree. No date (CNM-35; same as FS 227). Level 3 (33 cm above floor).	187
29	Roofing element (12 cm diameter x 44 cm long)	*Juniperus* sp. No date (CNM-36). Level 3 (7cm above floor).	188
30	Roofing element (11+ cm diameter x 18 cm long)	*Juniperus* sp. No date (CNM-37). Level 3 (2 cm above floor; under FS 188).	191
-	Roofing fragments (9; unknown sizes)	*Juniperus* sp., *Populus* sp., & non-coniferous. CNM-38. Level 3, Floor.	192
31	Roofing element (8 cm diameter x 8 cm long)	Non-coniferous tree. No date (CNM-42; same as FS 187). Level 3.	227
32	Roofing element (6.2+ cm estimated diameter)	*Juniperus* sp. No date (CNM-12). Level 3 (on bench).	151
33	Roofing element (8.5 cm diameter x 95 cm long)	*Populus* sp. No date (CNM-39). Level 3 (8 cm above floor).	195
34	Roofing element (8 cm diameter x 15 cm long)	*Juniperus* sp. No date (CNM-40). Level 3 (9 cm above floor; contact with FS 195).	196
35	Roofing element (6.0+ cm estimated diameter)	*Populus* sp. No date; 2 rings (CNM-13). Level 3 (8 cm above floor).	152
36	Roof primary (main southern E-W stringer; 12-15 cm diameter x 330 cm long)	*Pinus edulis*. Dated AD 473p-550v (CNM-28). Floor.	175
37	Roofing element (11 cm diameter x 215 cm)	*Populus* sp. No date (CNM-34). Level 3 (12 cm above floor; on top of FS 175).	186
38	Roofing element (9 cm diameter x 17 cm long)	*Pinus edulis*. Dated AD 425p-535v (CNM-24). Level 3 (4 cm. above floor).	172
39	Roofing element (11 cm estimated diameter)	*Juniperus* sp. No date (CNM-23). Level 3 against lower bench face (associated with FS 167).	170
40	Roofing element (7 cm diameter x 9 cm long)	*Juniperus* sp. No date (CNM-22). Level 3 against lower bench face (10cm above floor; associated with FS 170).	167

Table I.3.13. Site 29SJ 423, Distribution of Roofing Elements Recorded from the Burned Superstructure of Great Kiva III, cont'd.[a]

Artifact Number	Artifact Class	Wood Species	FS No.
41	Roofing element (6 cm diameter x 8 cm long)	*Pinus edulis*. Dated A.D. 391np-510vv (CNM-21). Floor (associated with FS 165).	166
42	Roofing element (8 cm diameter x 52 cm long)	*Populus* sp. No date (CNM-20). Floor.	165
43	Roofing element (14 cm diameter x 57 cm long)	*Pinus ponderosa*. No date; 26 rings (CNM-14). Floor.	156
44	Roofing element (12 cm diameter x 47 cm long)	*Juniperus* sp. No date (CNM-15). Floor (contact with FS 156).	157
45	Roof support post (26-28 cm diameter x 9 cm long)	*Pinus edulis*. Dated AD 289np-557r (CNM-43). West PH.	228
46	Roof support post (22-23 cm diameter x 8 cm long)	*Pinus edulis*. Dated AD 297±np-435vv (CNM-44). North PH.	230
47	Roof support post (24-25 cm diameter x 11 cm long)	*Pinus edulis*. Dated AD 426fp-519vv (CNM-45). East PH.	229
48	Roof support post (41 cm diameter x 12 cm long)	*Pinus edulis*. Dated AD 347p-554vv (CNM-41). South PH.	221

[a] See distribution in Figure I.3.17.

Table I.3.14. Data Used in Calculating the Stresses on the Superstructure of Great Kiva III, Site 29SJ 423.

Known:		
	Diameter of roof support posts	25 cm (mean of 3 posts)
	Length of stringers	440+ cm
	Diameter of stringers	15-20 cm
	Diameter of side poles	10-15 cm
	Height & thickness of rock wall covering	10+ x 150 cm
Estimated		
	Height of roof support posts	185 cm
	Height & angle of walls	244 cm at 35°
	Thickness of adobe wall covering	10 cm walls 15 cm for roof top
Weight of materials[a]		
	Douglas fir (data not used)	30 lb/ft^3
	Lodgepole pine (data not used)	28 lb/f^3
	Ponderosa pine	29 lb/ft^3
	Sandstone	145 lb/ft^3
	Adobe (data not used)	111 lb/ft^3
	Packed earth	100 lb/ft^3
Resultant weights		
	Great Kiva III roof	12,500 lbs (27558 kg)
	Great Kiva III walls	9,256 lbs (20406 kg) stress on each of 4 stringers

[a] After Carmichael 1950:Table 1-9, and Luxford and Trayer 1940:Table 6.

Table I.3.15. Results of the allowable, absolute, and calculated stresses for the Great Kiva III roof at Site 29SJ 423 (in lbs/in^2).[a]

	Allowable[b]		Absolute point of rupture[c]			
			Green wood		Air dry wood	
	Posts	Stringers	Posts	Stringers	Posts	Stringers
Ponderosa pine	700	925	2450	5100	5320	9400
Lodgepole pine	725	975	2610	5500	5370	9400
Douglas-fir	245-385	850-1000	3870	7700	7440	12600

Calculated for a superstructure 185 cm high, walls at 35°

Full roof:	Posts	Stringers	Diameter	Open roof:	Posts	Stringers	Diameter
		53077	15 cm			19824	15 cm
		22376	20 cm			8364	20 cm
	162.7	11456	25 cm		121.7	4282	25 cm
		6630	30 cm			2478	30 cm

Calculated for a superstructure 235 cm high, walls at 45°

Full roof:	Posts	Stringers	Diameter	Open roof:	Posts	Stringers	Diameter
		28169	15 cm			14744	15 cm
		11883	20 cm			6220	20 cm
	86.4	6085	25 cm		45.2	3185	25 cm
		3521	30 cm			1843	30 cm

[a] Compare with Lightfoot 1988; see also Syngg and Windes 1998.
[b] After National Forest Products Association 1971.
[c] After Forest Products Laboratory 1974:Table 8.

Table I.3.16. List of Features In and Around Pithouse Y, Shabik'eschee Village (Site 29SJ 1659) Except for Postholes.[a]

Feature	Length (cm)	Width (cm)	Height/ Depth (cm)	Volume[b] (liters)	Fill Type	Fill Period	Lining	Open/ Sealed	Comments
29SJ 1659 Pithouse Y									
Firepit 1	79	72	50	157.7	25	Occ	L-P	O	Mouth = 4656 cm². Adobe rimmed. Inner pit = 56 x 51 cm.
Other Pit 1	71	67	30	84.3±	11,30	?	U?	O	
Other Pit 2	68	60	31	71.7±	11,30	?	U	O	
Other Pit 3	26	24	50	22.3	10	?	?	O	20 cm north of FP 1.
Other Pit 4	23	21	18	5.6	?	?	?	O	
Other Pit 5	17	11	15	1.7	?	?	?	O	Sipapu. 2 m WNW of FP 1.
Cist 1	70	70	65	243.8	32	PO	L-S	O	Slab floor, inc. a mano.
Cist 2	100	60	45±	201.9	32	PO	L-S	O	Earth floor.
Cist 3	213	200	90±	2496.6	32	PO	L-S	O	Intrusive feature, ca. 50 cm above antechamber floor. Upper cist floor = clay; lower floor = slabs.
Cist 4	200±	200±	70±	2400±	32	PO	L-S	O	Intrusive feature, 18-24 cm above antechamber floor. Floor = 2-3 layers of slabs.
Slot 1	33	11	11	4.1	30	PO	U	O	Bin wall slab support?
Slot 2	31	11	7	1.6	30	PO	?	O	Bin wall slab support?
Slot 3	22	8	8	1.3	30	PO	?	O	Bin wall slab support?
Air tunnel	25	17	20-21	-	31,41	-	?	O	Through main chamber-antechamber wall.
Deflector	48	17	30	-	-	-	L-S	-	Consists of 2 upright slabs.
North groove	105	9-12	5-11	8.0	?	PO	L-P	O	In top of adobe wall between antechamber and main chamber. For upright slabs?
South groove	90	8-10	8-12	7.8	?	PO	L-P	O	Same, above.
East Wing Wall	80	13	6?	-	-	-	L-P	-	Rounded mud ridge.
South Wing Wall	92	13	6	-	-	-	L-P	-	Rounded mud ridge.

[a] See Tables I.7.4-I.7.5 for an explanation of the feature and attribute codes.
[b] Volumes for features are approximate.

Table I.3.17. List of postholes in Pithouse Y at Shabik'eschee Village (Site 29SJ 1659).[a]

Posthole No.	Length (cm)	Width (cm)	Depth (cm)	Volume[b] (liters)	Fill Type	Fill Period	Shims	Base Stone	Est. post size (cm)	Lining	Comments
29SJ 1659 Pithouse Y											
Posthole 1	20	20	70	20.5	15	Occ	0	0	-	?	Main support.
Posthole 2	35	32	61	14.2	15	Occ	0	0	18 x 15	?	Main support.
Posthole 3	26	15	87	17.4	?	PO	0	0	15 x 15	?	Main support.
Posthole 4	11	10	45	3.7	30?	PO	0	0	-	?	Antechamber.
Posthole 5	15	13	8	1.3	?	PO	0	0	-	?	Antechamber.
Posthole 6	24	23	27	11.1	?	PO	0	0	-	?	Antechamber.
Posthole 7	13	10	26	3.3	?	PO	0	0	-	?	Antechamber.
Posthole 8	12	11	34	5.9	?	PO	0	0	-	?	Antechamber.

[a] See Tables I.7.4-I.7.5 for an explanation of the feature and attribute codes.
[b] Volumes for features are approximate.

Table I.3.18. Site 29SJ 1659, Pithouses Y and Z, Distribution of Floor Fill and Floor 1 Materials.[a]

Artifact Number	Artifact Class	Lithic Material, Ceramic Ware, or Faunal Species	FS No.
Pithouse Y			
1	Wood, rotted fragments	*Juniperus* sp. (Tree-Ring Lab sample: SHV-6: no date) In PH 2.	1
1	Wood (unburned)	Not analyzed. In PH 2.	7
2	Lino Gray jar body sherd Obelisk Gray jar body sherds (4)	Cibola Grayware. In Cist 2 fill. 3 sooted.	3
2	Wood for species identification	Not analyzed. In Cist 2.	49
3	Awl (8.7 x 1.0 x 0.4 cm; 3.7 g)	Large mammal, indeterminate splinter. NE intersection of fill and wall.	4
3	Worked bone (max. 3.7 x 1.4 x 0.4 cm; 7 g)	Medium-to-large mammal, indeterminate element. Long, tapering piece with beveled tip (6 pieces). NE intersection of fill and wall.	10
3	Lino Gray body jar sherd with basket-impressed exterior Lino Gray body jar sherd Lino Fugitive Red jar sherd Obelisk Gray jar body sherds (7) La Plata B/w jar sherd	Cibola Ware. Fill, NE intersection of fill and wall.	57
3	Scraper (4.7 x 2.3 x 0.5 cm; 3.9 g)	Indeterminate large mammal shaft fragment, rounded. Next to NE wall.	139
-	Hematite (2.4 x 2.2 x 0.7 cm; 4.4 g)	5221 (red ocher). Natural discoid shape. Minor grinding; bag wear? Munsell 2.5YR 4/6.	5
-	Limonite (1.8 x 1.2 x 0.5 cm; 1.3 g) Limonite (5.3 x 2.4 x 0.5 cm; 7.3 g)	5110 (yellow ocher). Natural; some grinding on 2 surfaces. 5110 (yellow ocher). Natural; some grinding on 1 surface. Munsell 10YR 6/8.	5
4	File? (5.2+ x 2.7 x 1.4 cm; 48+ g)	2790? (ironstone). Flat rectangular shape, highly ground & polished on 2 surfaces and edges (beveled). Both ends broken. North area on bench top. Similar to historic file from Chaco Carlisle Ranch, 29SJ 612 (9.1 x 2.6 x 0.9 cm; 52.5 g).	11
4	Bead (1.3 x 0.4 x 0.1 cm; 0.2 g)	Medium size mammal, indeterminate shaft end. On bench.	50
5	Projectile point (11.2 g) Misc. blade (11.0 g)	4000 (quartzite) Resting on slab-lined floor in Cist 1. 2205 (quartzose silicified sandstone).	12
6	Pendant (14 x 13 x 1.3 mm; 0.4 g)	5300 (turquoise, green) All 2 surfaces and 4 edges ground. Squarish shape. Biconical hole (1.5 mm) in center. Rock Color 5 GY 5/2 - 5 G 7/2.	18
7	Sherd palette? (12.6 x 12.5 x 0.5 cm; 97 g)	Lino Gray olla sherd. Inside spotted & streaked with azurite blue (Rock Color 5 B 5/6) paint. 10 cm above floor. See Volume II, Figure 5.2.	30
7	Plain Gray jar sherd Lino Fugitive Red jar sherd	Cibola Grayware. 10 cm above floor.	30

Chapter 3: Basketmaker III Excavation Reports 231

Table I.3.18. Site 29SJ 1659, Pithouses Y and Z, Distribution of Floor Fill and Floor 1 Materials, cont'd.[a]

Artifact Number	Artifact Class	Lithic Material, Ceramic Ware, or Faunal Species	FS No.
8	Gray clay tablet (4.3 x 3.8 x 0.8 cm; 21.1 g) Gray clay fragments (largest 2.3 x 2.3 x 0.4 cm; 7.0 g)	Lite natural clay modeled into a square tablet; smooth on the 2 surfaces. 4 other natural pieces. In Cist 1.	31
8	Pipe (4.2+ x 1.7-2.2 cm dia; 21.7+ g) (estimated length, 5 cm)	Black clay, conical tubular pipe with hole through center. Stem is broken off. In Cist 1. See Volume II, Plate 2.9A.	33
8	Pot cover (18.0 x 15.2 x 1.7 cm; 724 g)	2000 (sandstone) Natural faces but edge chipped to a discoid shape. 100% burned. Slightly blackened on 1 surface. In Cist 1.	44
8	Manuport (3.5 x 3.2 x 1.4 cm; 26.2 g)	4000 (quartzite). Natural pebble. In Cist 1.	45
8	Bone	*Sylvilagus* (cottontail) sp. scapula. In Cist 1.	46
9	Chopper (10.6 x 7.0 x 2.4 cm; 236.8 g)	1072 (yellow spotted chert). Flaked to shape with sharp edge. Base of bench.	32
9	Pipe (6.1 x 2.7 max./1.4 min. cm; 29.4 g)	Lino polished black. Corner broken off. Conical/tubular with hole through center. Base of bench. See Volume II, Plate 2.9C.	34
10	Mano? fragment (6.1+ x 8.5 x 2.3 cm; 185.8+ g)	2000 (sandstone). Natural?	38
11	Wood	Not analyzed. In PH 1.	39
11	Wood	*Juniperus* sp. (Tree-Ring Lab sample SHV-7; no date). In PH 1.	61
11	Charcoal	Not analyzed. In PH 1.	40
11	Obelisk Gray jar sherd Fugitive Red jar sherd	Cibola Grayware. In PH 1.	41
11	Manuport (2.5 x 2.3 x 1.1 cm; 11.7 g)	4000 (quartzite). Natural pebble. In PH 1.	42
12	Bead (1.8 x 1.3 x 0.2 cm; 1.8 g)	Indeterminate large bird shaft fragment; ends rounded.	43
13	Charcoal	Not analyzed. In FP 1.	47
13	Wood for fuel (6)	Piñon (*Pinus edulis*). Dated at 242vv, 275vv, & 537v (SHV-8 through 13). In FP 1.	118
14	Pipe (3.2+ x 1.7 cm dia; 12.2 g+; est length 5 cm)	Gray pottery with 4 evenly-spaced rows of double punctate marks running up sides. Conical with hole through center. Cup-end missing. See Volume II, Plate 2.9B.	51
15	Gray clay (largest: 4.3 x 3.1 x 1.0 cm; 20.1 g)	Unfired, modeled by hand with a rounded rim–fragment of a pot? Antechamber fill.	37
15	Worked bone	Artiodactyl sp. femur/tibia fragment. Antechamber fill (floor fill?). Missing.	52
15	Worked bone (8.9 x 3.4 x 2.2 cm; 24.6 g)	Bighorn sheep (*Ovis canadensis*) radius, distal 1/3. Shaft beveled. Antechamber fill.	53

232 Windes et al.

Table I.3.18. Site 29SJ 1659, Pithouses Y and Z, Distribution of Floor Fill and Floor 1 Materials. cont'd.[a]

Artifact Number	Artifact Class	Lithic Material, Ceramic Ware, or Faunal Species	FS No.
15	Awl (8.6 x 1.1x 0.5 cm; 6.0 g)	Indeterminate large mammal shaft splinter. Antechamber fill.	54
15	Worked? bone	Indeterminate medium/large mammal rib fragment. Boiled. Antechamber fill. Not catalogued.	55
15	Worked bone disc (1.6 x 1.0 x 0.1 cm; 0.3 g)	Indeterminate medium/large mammal fragment. Antechamber fill.	56
15	Selenite chunks (15+)(total 692 g) (largest 14.1 x 6.9 x 3.3 cm; 178 g)	5041 (gypsum). A collection of natural pieces. Antechamber fill.	84A
15	Pot cover (7.0 x 6.2 x 0.6 cm; 41.2 g)	2000 (sandstone) Edge-chipped to ovoid shape. Slightly ground on 1 surface. Antechamber fill.	84B
15	Polishing stone (6.4 x 3.8 x 1.4 cm; 50.4 g) Polishing stone (7.3 x 4.3 x 1.2 cm; 56.8 g)	4000 (white quartzite). Highly polished natural pebble. 4000 (gray quartzite). Natural pebble with clay? ground into 1 surface.	84B
15	Lino Gray body jar sherd	Cibola Grayware. Antechamber fill.	84C
15	Pot cover (6.2 x 6.1 x 0.7 cm; 46 g)	2000 (sandstone). Edge-chipped to discoid shape. Natural surfaces, 1 smoke blackened. Antechamber fill (floor fill?).	94
15	Manuport (19.3 x 12.8 x 8.2 cm; 1740.0 g)	2000 (soft, yellow sandstone). Burned at both ends (35%); no modification. Natural lumpy piece (field designated as a shaft straightener). Antechamber fill (floor fill?). Burned.	95
15	Awl (11.1 x 1.5 x 0.7 cm; 9.9 g)	Indeterminate large mammal shaft splinter. Antechamber fill.	138
16	Lino Gray body jar sherds (2) Lino Fugitive Red jar sherds (26) Obelisk Gray (3)	Cibola Grayware. Floor contact, mostly from same Fugitive red olla.	58
16	La Plata B/w partial bowl (est 23± dia x 12.5 cm high)	Cibola Whiteware. 1/4 vessel.	59, 63
16	Manuport (9.3 x 4.0 x 3.1 cm; 175.4 g)	4000 (quartzite). Natural pebble. Very minor peck marks.	62A
16	Worked bone (2.1 x 0.4 x 0.07 cm; 0.3 g)	Indeterminate medium-size mammal shaft fragment. Ends rounded. Floor.	70
16	Worked sherd die? (2.6 x 1.9 x 0.4 cm; 3.0 g)	Tallahogan Red jar sherd ground & broken into a discoid shape. Floor.	71
16	Projectile point (3.1 x 1.7 x 0.2 cm; 0.9 g)	1113 (chert silicified wood). Corner notched. 1 tang missing.	72
16	Utilized flake (1.2 g)	1052 (chalcedonic High Surface Chert).	73
16	Awl (14.3 x 2.2 x 1.1 cm; 21 g)	Artiodactyl tibia. On floor.	74

Table I.3.18. Site 29SJ 1659, Pithouses Y and Z, Distribution of Floor Fill and Floor 1 Materials. cont'd.[a]

Artifact Number	Artifact Class	Lithic Material, Ceramic Ware, or Faunal Species	FS No.
16	Lino Fugitive Red partial olla (10 large fragments) Lino Gray bowl sherd with Fugitive Red? on inside La Plata B/w bowl sherds (2)	Cibola ware. Floor contact between FP 1 and Cist 2.	75
17	Lino Fugitive Red jar sherd Obelisk Gray jar sherd	In PH 3.	76
17	Bones (2)	*Sylvilagus* (cottontail) sp. mandible and ulna fragments. In PH 3.	77
17	Manuports (2) (3.5 x 1.1 x 0.8 cm; 3.7 g)(1.2 x 0.7 x 0.3 cm; 0.6 g)	1110 (splintery silicified wood). In PH 3.	78
17	Selenite (2.0 x 1.5 x 0.5 cm; 1.7 g)	5041 (gypsum). Natural or ground? on 1 surface. Irreg. In PH 3.	78A
18	Lino Fugitive Red olla (partial)	Cibola Grayware. On bench top.	82
19	Metate/palette (56 x 40 x 6.7 cm; 17.3 kg). Thin-style with shallow trough of 3.3 cm depth, 19.5 wide x 36 cm long.	2000 (sandstone). Whole metate with small kill? hole. A smear of red paint on top and extensive heavily-caked hematite (2.5 YR 4/8) and limonite (7.5 YR 6/6 Munsell) on 2 ground surfaces on bottom. Metate reused as a paint palette. Spot of green paint from truck bed? In antechamber, fallen? from SE wall top, 1.4 m from wall.	85
20	Turquoise (9 x 6 x 6 mm; 1.0 g)	5300 (turquoise, green). Squarish cylinder; ground on all 4 sides. North wall slot. Rock Color 5 BG 6/6.	87
21	Worked bone (10.2 x 1.2 x 0.9 cm; 4.5 g)	Jackrabbit (*Lepus* sp.) tibia (ground). Between FP 1 & PH 3.	89A
21	Worked bone (5.3 x 1.4 x 2.2 cm; 6.9 g)	Antelope (*Antilocapra americana*) metapodial distal 1/4. Between FP 1 & PH 3.	89B
21	Plain gray jar sherds (45) Lino Gray jar rim sherds (4) Fugitive Red jar sherds (7) Obelisk Gray jar sherds (9)	Cibola Grayware. 2+ sooted. Fill between FP 1 and PH 3.	90

Table I.3.18. Site 29SJ 1659, Pithouses Y and Z, Distribution of Floor Fill and Floor 1 Materials. cont'd.[a]

Artifact Number	Artifact Class	Lithic Material, Ceramic Ware, or Faunal Species	FS No.
21	Chipped and natural stones (70)		
	Angular debris (11.3 g)	1010 (fossiliferous chert). Between FP 1 and PH 3.	
	Angular debris (3.2 g)	1011 (fossiliferous chert).	
	Core (3.2 x 2.8 x 1.3 cm; 17.3 g)	1052 (chalcedonic High Surface Chert with white cortex).	
	Core (7.7 x 5.7 x 3.0 cm; 107.6 g)	1052 (chalcedonic High Surface Chert with yellowish cortex).	
	Retouched flake (0.3 g)	1053 (chalcedonic High Surface Chert).	
	Whole flakes (2)(total 7.4 g)	1053 (chalcedonic High Surface Chert).	
	Angular debris (5)(total 92.3 g)	1110 (splintery silicified wood).	
	Angular debris (9.3 g)	1112 (cherty silicified wood).	
	Angular debris (2)(total 12.1 g)	1140 (chalcedonic silicified wood).	
	Whole flakes (2)(1.0 & 1.5 g)	1142 (chalcedonic silicified wood).	
	Angular debris (2)(total 12.1 g)	1142 (chalcedonic silicified wood).	
	Whole flake (0.1 g)	1150 (jasperized silicified wood).	
	Manuports (42)(total 893 g)	4000 (quartzite) Natural pebbles.	91
21	Manuport (3.8 x 2.0+ x 1.0 cm; 12.3+ g)	4000 (quartzite). Natural pebble broken in half.	91A
21	Limonite (2.6 x 2.0 x 0.9 cm; 3.1 g)	5110 (yellow ocher). Natural piece. Rock Color 7.5 YR 6/6.	
	Limonite (2.9 x 2.9 x 1.5 g; 10.4 g)	Natural piece, burned. 1 surface ground flat. Rock Color 2.5 YR 6/8.	
	Limonite (4.0 x 2.1 x 0.9 cm; 4.8 g)	Natural piece, 1 surface & 1 edge ground. Rock Color 7.5 YR 6/6.	
	Limonite (4.1 x 2.8 x 1.0 cm; 11.0 g)	Natural piece, 1 edge ground. Rock Color 7.5 YR 7/8.	
	Selenite (4.4 x 2.1 x 1.3 cm; 10.2 g)	5041 (gypsum). Burned white (Rock Color N 9). Natural piece.	91A
21	Pottery polisher (3.6 x 2.2 x 1.7 cm; 18.3 g)	4000 (quartzite). 1 highly polished faceted surface. Natural pebble. Between FP 1 & PH 3.	91B
21	Hammerstone (8.3 x 6.9 x 4.8 cm; 402.3 g)	1112 (cherty silicified wood). Pounded on 2 ends. Discoid shape.	92
21	Hammerstone (6.7 x 6.0 x 5.0 cm; 264 g)	2221 (quartzitic sandstone; Pintado chert). Pounded all over. Between FP 1 & PH 3.	93
21	Awl (8.1 x 1.5 x 0.8 cm; 7.7 g)	Indeterminate large mammal shaft splinter. In fill between FP 1 &PH3.	141
21	Awl (5.1 x 0.8 x 0.4 cm; 1.6 g)	Indeterminate mammal shaft splinter. In fill between FP 1 & PH 3.	142
21	Bead (1.2 x 0.6 x 0.1 cm; 0.2 g)	Indeterminate large bird shaft fragment. In fill between FP 1 & PH 3.	143
21	Retouched flake (5.0 x 2.6 x 1.1 cm; 16.1 g)	1053 (chalcedonic High Surface Chert). In fill between FP 1 & PH 3.	144
21	Groundstone	In fill between FP 1 & PH 3. Missing.	145
-	Bones (7)	*Sylvilagus* sp. (cottontail) sp. tibia, humerus, & radius; small/medium mammal long bones (2), skull, & phalanx fragments. Floor.	96
22	Azurite ball (10 mm dia; 1.8 g)	5320 (azurite). Natural? Spot of green adhering. Rock-Color 5 PB 5/2 (grayish blue). In Cist 4 fill in pithouse fill.	97

Table I.3.18. Site 29SJ 1659, Pithouses Y and Z, Distribution of Floor Fill and Floor 1 Materials. cont'd.[a]

Artifact Number	Artifact Class	Lithic Material, Ceramic Ware, or Faunal Species	FS No.
23	Turquoise (6 x 5 x 3 cm; 0.1 g)	5300 (turquoise, green). Ground on 1 surface. Rock Color 10 G 8/2. Between FP 1 & deflector.	98
24	Projectile point (2.0 x 1.1 x 0.2 cm; 0.8 g)	1113 (cherty silicified wood). Corner notched. 5 cm above bench level but item located in Cist 4. Cameron analysis shows two projectile points of 1080 material (Washington Pass chert)—missing.	66
-	Plain gray jar sherds (2) Plain gray with Fugitive Red (1) Obelisk Gary (1)	Cibola Grayware. 1 sooted. Antechamber floor. Cibola Grayware?	99
-	Charcoal	Juniper (*Juniperus* sp.) & piñon (*Pinus edulis*). Sub-floor firepit. Location unknown.	103
-	Polisher? (12.1 x 2.6 x 0.9 cm; 14.3 g)	Indeterminate large mammal shaft fragment 6" off TT 3 floor.	132
Pithouse Y fill paintstones			
-	Cobble (18.0 x 11.3 x 6.8 cm; 2218.0 g)	4000 (quartzite). Natural, mano loaf-like shape. Some pecking (anvil use?) & grinding on 1 flat surface. Red paint (Munsell 10R/2.5YR 4/8) on flat surface, covering 2.7 x 7.2 cm area. Slightly smoked and burned?	105
-	Abrader/mano fragment (13.9+? X 13.1 x 3.9 cm; 1359.9 g)	2000 (sandstone). Well ground on 1 surface & pecked on other (tabular shape). Yellow? and red/burned? (Munsell 10YR 6/8?) paint traces?	106
-	Mano (18.8 x 13.1 x 2.9 cm; 1243.6 g)	2000 (sandstone). Tabular with 1 well-ground surface with yellow paint? traces, with opposite side highly pecked with red paint smear (4 x 10 cm)(Munsell 2.5YR 4/6).	111
-	Polishing stone? (9.2 x 6.9 x 4.1 cm; 405.7 g)	4000 (white quartzite). Natural ovoid cobble, designated a "mano" in field. Minor pecking marks on ends. Washed out red paint smear (3.9 x 4.4 cm) on 1 surface (Munsell light red 2.5YR 6/6).	115
Pithouse Z			
25	Lino Fugitive Red olla (ca. 44 cm high x 36 cm dia)	Cibola Grayware. Partially restorable jar with tall neck. NE Trench floor;55 cm below surface (see Volume II, Plate 2.3B).	146/ 147
26	Lino Gray pitcher (23 cm high x 21 cm dia)	Cibola Grayware. Has handle. East Trench floor (see Volume II, Plate 2.2B).	148
26	Plain gray jar sherds (5) Lino Smudged bowl sherd	Cibola Grayware. East Trench floor.	148

[a] See distribution in Figure I.3.18. Locations for cultural materials not in features are approximate.

Note: Uncertain which materials were within 10 cm of floor (e.g., floor fill). Sherd counts may be undercounted because of difficulty of assembling numbers from dispersed collections. In addition, inconsistency in assigning separating Lino Gray from Obelisk Gray sherds.

Table I.3.19. Site 29SJ 628, Pithouse C Distribution of Floor Fill and Floor 1 Materials.[a]

Artifact Number	Artifact Class	Lithic Material, Ceramic Ware, or Faunal Species	FS No.
Main Chamber floor fill and floor			
1	Spatula (18.9 x 1.7 x 0.3cm; 29.5 g)	Indeterminate large mammal shaft fragment. Bench fill.	158
2	Awl (10.1 x 1.1 x 0.7 cm; 8.8 g)	Indeterminate large mammal shaft fragment. Bench fill.	159
3	Awl (9.1 x 0.6 x 0.4 cm; 1.7 g)	Jackrabbit (*Lepus* sp.) ulna medial shaft. Bench.	160
4	Awl (9.8 x 1.8 x 0.4 cm; 6.1 g)	Jackrabbit (*Lepus* sp.) tibia. On bench. Just N of FS 158.	161
5	Awl (29.8 x 2.2 x 1.0 cm; 50.8 g)	Indeterminate large mammal shaft splinter. Bench.	188
6	Awl (15.2 x 1.0 x 0.3 cm; 8.4 g)	Indeterminate large mammal shaft splinter. Bench.	189
7	Pipe (6.1 x 1.0 to 1.9 cm diameter; 18.5 g)	Dark gray clay, tube type with 2.5 mm center hole. Floor.	192
8	Worked bone (7.7 x 1.5 x 0.9 cm; 11.7 g)	Artiodactyl metapodial.	205
9	Biface blade (5.9 x 3.7 x 0.9 cm; 23.4 g)	1022 (misc. chert; variegated pastel colors; coarse grain). Bench. Bifacially flaked.	207
10	Awl (15.6 x 1.8 x 0.8 cm; 18.2 g)	Indeterminate large mammal shaft splinter. Floor.	208
11	Awl (13.2 x 1.0 x 0.6 cm; 5.9 g)	Indeterminate medium-to-large mammal shaft splinter. Floor.	209
12	Awl (14.7 x 1.3 x 0.4 cm; 7.3 g)	Indeterminate large mammal shaft splinter. Floor.	210
13	Projectile point (1.9 x 1.3 x 0.2 cm; 0.7 g)	3520 (Jemez obsidian). Corner notched; 1 tang missing. Obsidian Hydration Lab #7686 (UCLA). Sourced to the Valle Grande by Shackley and Dillian (2000). Tourist point. Floor.	211
14	Awl (15.5 x 2.6 x 0.7 cm; 15.0 g)	Indeterminate large mammal shaft splinter. Floor.	212
15	Utilized flakes (2)(3.6 g & 4.4 g)	3520 (Jemez obsidian). OHL (UCLA) #7687-7688. Sourced to the Valle Grande by Shackley and Dillian (2000). Floor.	213
16	Awl (10.1 x 1.2 x 0.7 cm; 4.9 g)	Jackrabbit (*Lepus* sp.) tibia. Floor.	214
17	Awl (6.7 x 0.8 x 0.2 cm; 1.7 g)	Jackrabbit (*Lepus* sp.) tibia medial shaft. Floor.	215
18	Awl (6.9 x 1.1 x 0.3 cm; 1.4 g)	Dog/coyote/wolf (*Canis* sp.) radius medial shaft splinter. Floor.	216
19	Awl (8.7 x 2.1 x 1.5 cm; 8.8 g)	Bobcat (*Lynx rufus*) ulna. Burned. Floor.	217
20	Awl (14.1 x 1.4 x 1.7 cm; 6.7 g)	Dog/coyote/wolf (*Canis* sp.) ulna. Floor.	218
21	Bone	Pronghorn antelope (*Antilocapra americana*) metatarsal.	233
-	Bones (30)	Jackrabbit (9; 1 boiled), cottontail rabbit (18; 10 boiled), & artiodactyl (3).	236
-	Sherds (44)	Floor (see Table 2.30, Volume II).	237
-	Adobe (4)(total 911 g)		238
-	Concretions (3): (9.8 diameter; 533.6 g) (9.2 x 2.5 x 1.7 cm; 54.2 g) (7.2 x 1.3 x 1.0 cm; 16.0 g)	2000 (sandstone) Hemi-spherical shape with lip at 1 end; 10 percent burned, slightly ground on top. Fossilized shrimp burrow tube; with light grinding. Fossilized shrimp burrow rod. Unmodified.	239

Table I.3.19. Site 29SJ 628, Pithouse C Distribution of Floor Fill and Floor 1 Materials, cont'd.[a]

Artifact Number	Artifact Class	Lithic Material, Ceramic Ware, or Faunal Species	FS No.
-	Chipped stone (10):		
	Whole flake (3.9 g)	1053 (chalcedonic High Surface Chert).	
	Core (52.6 g)	1072 (yellow-spotted Zuni chert).	
	Utilized flake (8.6 g)	1140 (chalcedonic silicified wood).	
	Retouched flakes (2) (total 4.1 g)	1140 (chalcedonic silicified wood).	
	Angular debris (2)(total 1.9)	1140 (chalcedonic silicified wood).	
	Utilized flake (5.2 g)	1142 (chalcedonic silicified wood).	
	Utilized flake (4.2 g)	1234 (translucent chalcedony with red & black inclusions).	
	Whole flake (5.1 g)	2202 (silicified fine-grained brown concretion).	240
-	Hammerstone (12.2 x 9.0 x 7.3 cm; 814.7 g)	2126 (Cliff House sandstone, very hard). Irregular shape, battered along natural edges.	
	Hammerstone rejuvenation flake (3.5 x 3.3 x 2.4 cm; 29.0 g)	1140 (chalcedonic silicified wood).	240B
-	Manuport (5.5 x 4.4 x 1.0 cm; 39.5 g)	4000 (quartzite). Natural, discoid flattish pebble. Analyzed as a polishing stone.	240B
-	Abrader? (12.8 x 6.6 x 4.2 cm; 638.0 g)	2000 (sandstone). Tabular stone ground flat on 1 side; edge battered. 85% burned and blackened. Firedog or FP liner.	240B
-	Minerals (5.4 x 1.7 x 0.8 cm, 7.1 g; 5.4 x 2.6 x 0.4 cm, 8.4 g)	5041 (gypsum selenite). Natural, tabular, irregular pieces.	240C
-	Metate fragment (15+ x 20.3+ x 3.2 cm; 1210.0 g)	2000 (sandstone). 1/6± metate. 100% burned and blackened. FP liner?	241
-	Charcoal (24.2-g)	*Rhus trilobata* (tentative) and other vegetal material.	242
-	Corncobs fragments (14)(total 2.2 g)	*Zea mays*. Carbonized. Floor.	243
22	Sherds (2) Lino Gray jar sherd La Plata B/w bowl sherd	SE Posthole.	505
22	Bones (8)	Jackrabbit (3; 2 burned), cottontail rabbit (4), & unidentified small-to-medium mammal (1). SE Posthole.	506
22	Charcoal (9.8-g)	Species not identified. SE Posthole.	507
22	Concretion (11.0 x 6.6 x 3.6 cm)	2000 (sandstone). SE Posthole.	508
22	Lignite chunk (4.5 x 3.2 x 1.9 cm; 16.0 g)	2822 (lignite). SE Posthole.	509
23	Sherds (31)	NE Posthole (see Table II.2.30, Volume II).	510
23	Bones (15)	Jackrabbit (7; 1 burned), cottontail rabbit (4; 1 burned), prairie dog (3), & unidentified medium-to-large mammal (1). NE Posthole.	511
23	Charcoal (5.6-g)	Species not identified. NE Posthole.	512
23	Corncob fragment (0.7-g)	*Zea mays*. Carbonized. NE Posthole.	513
24	Bones (43)	Jackrabbit (5; 1 burned), cottontail rabbit (30), woodrat (2), kangaroo rat (2), Mexican vole (1), & unidentified rodent (3; 1 burned). Mostly post-occupational? Ash Pit (OP 1).	527
24	Chipped stone	Ash Pit (OP 1). Missing.	528
24	Charcoal (42.4 g)	Pine (*Pinus* sp.), *Juniperus* sp., greasewood (*Sarcobatus vermiculatus*). Ash Pit (OP 1).	529
24	Radiocarbon date (13.7 g)	Greasewood (*Sarcobatus vermiculatus*). Calibrated A.D. 420±70 (see Table I.6.4).	529

Table I.3.19. Site 29SJ 628, Pithouse C Distribution of Floor Fill and Floor 1 Materials, cont'd.[a]

Artifact Number	Artifact Class	Lithic Material, Ceramic Ware, or Faunal Species	FS No.
24	Pecking stone (5.0 x 3.6 x 3.1 cm; 80.2 g)	4000 (quartzite). Pebble battered on opposite ends. Ash Pit (OP1). NW Posthole.	835
25	Woodruff Smudged bowl sherd		530
25	Lignite flakes (70)(30 g)	2822 (lignite). NW Posthole.	531
25	Bone (0.7 x 0.6 x 0.2 cm; 0.0 g)	Unidentified & unanalyzed. NW Posthole.	531
25	Flake (1.0 x 0.8 x 0.3 cm; 0.3 g)	1140 (chalcedonic silicified wood) NW Posthole.	531
25	Bone	Cottontail rabbit (*Sylvilagus* sp.) skull. NW Posthole.	532
25	Corncob fragments (24)(total 0.6 g)	*Zea mays*. Carbonized. SW Posthole.	538
25	Charcoal (4.9-g)	SW Posthole.	539
25	Sherds (6)	SW Posthole (see Volume II, Table II.2.30).	540
25	Hammerstone fragment (4.6+ x 3.9 x 2.7 cm; 53.3+ g)	4000 (quartzite). Pebble battered along 1 edge. In SW Posthole.	541
25	Minerals (2) (3.0 x 2.1 x 1.9 cm; 7.3 g; 3.6 x 2.2 x 0.5 cm; 4.1 g)	5041 (gypsum selenite). Natural, tabular pieces.	541
25	Bones (6)	Jackrabbit (2), cottontail rabbit (3), & unidentified small-to-medium mammal (1). In SW Posthole.	542
26	Charcoal (54.1 g)	Pine (*Pinus* sp.), *Juniperus* sp., greasewood (*Sarcobatus vermiculatus*) & rabbitbush (*Chrysothamnus*?). FP 1.	543
26	Radiocarbon date (17.5 g)	Greasewood (*Sarcobatus vermiculatus*). Calibrated AD 730±60 (see Table 6.4).	543
26	Corn cob fragment (0.3 g)	*Zea mays*. Carbonized. FP 1.	684
26	Ash	FP 1. Missing.	685
26	Utilized flake (2)(total 4.6 g)	1140 (chalcedonic silicified wood). FP 1.	686
26	Bones (7)	Cottontail rabbit (7). None burned. FP 1.	687
-	Corncob fragments (3; total 1.5 g)	*Zea mays*. Carbonized. In bench postholes.	544
-	Charcoal (12.4-g)	In bench postholes.	545
-	Utilized flake (7.9 g) Utilized flake (19.3 g)	1112 (cherty silicified wood). In bench posthole. 1142 (chalcedonic silicified wood).	546
-	Sherds	In bench postholes.	547
-	Bones (13)	Jackrabbit (9; 1 burned), cottontail rabbit (3; 1 burned), & prairie dog (1). In bench postholes.	548

Table I.3.19. Site 29SJ 628, Pithouse C Distribution of Floor Fill and Floor 1 Materials, cont'd.[a]

Artifact Number	Artifact Class	Lithic Material, Ceramic Ware, or Faunal Species	FS No.
-	Chipped stone (10): Angular debris (3.6 g) Core (66.3 g) Utilized flake (0.1 g) Angular debris (2)(total 18.6 g) Core (14.9 g) Utilized flake (3.3 g) Whole flake (2.8 g) Tested natural nodule (3.0 x 2.1 x 1.7 cm; 11.0 g) Tested natural nodule (3.0 x 2.2 x 1.7 cm; 9.6 g)	Bench 1011 (fossiliferous chert). 1011 (fossiliferous chert). 1140 (chalcedonic silicified wood). 1140 (chalcedonic silicified wood). 1140 (chalcedonic silicified wood). 1142 (chalcedonic silicified wood). 1142 (chalcedonic silicified wood). 3510 (Grants obsidian) #178. Horace Mesa, Mt. Taylor (sourcing by Shackley and Dillian 2000). 3510 (Grants obsidian) #177. Horace Mesa, Mt. Taylor (sourcing by Shackley and Dillian 2000).	549
-	Mineral (2.1 x 1.7 x 1.2 cm; 1.7 g)	5110 (limonite). Natural chunk broken to expose soft yellow (Munsell 10YR 7/7) residue; slightly ground?	549C
-	Minerals (3; largest 4.8 x 2.5 x 1.0 cm; all 19.2 g)	5041 (gypsum selenite). Natural, tabular, irregular pieces.	549C
-	Sherds (15)	Bench (see Volume II, Table II. 2.30,).	550
-	Bones (45)	Jackrabbit (23), cottontail rabbit (20), & unidentified small-to-medium mammal (2). Bench.	551
-	Corn cob fragments (2)(1.8 g)	*Zea mays*. Carbonized. Bench.	552
-	Charcoal (17.3 g)	Bench.	553
-	Calcium carbonate (1.8 x 1.2 x 1.4 cm; 1.2 g)	5040 (soft white gypsum). Natural oval chunk, abraded on 1 side–cultural? Rock color N9. Bench.	554
27	Charcoal (144.8 g)	Pine (*Pinus* sp.), *Juniperus* sp., greasewood (*Sarcobatus vermiculatus*), misc. shrubs. HP 1.	558, 504
27	Radiocarbon date (29.2 g)	Greasewood (*Sarcobatus vermiculatus*). Calibrated A.D. 620±50 (see Table 6.4).	558, 504
28	Mano (19.4 x 11.8 x 2.4 cm; 1343.0 g)	2000 (sandstone). Bifacially ground. 10 cm above floor.	624
29	Concretion fragment (24.6+ x 19.0 x 3.5 cm; 1920+ g)	2000 (sandstone). Lightly burned on 1 surface. Oval shape but natural. Bench.	625
30	Hammerstone (5.7 x 5.7 x 5.2 cm; 209. 7 g)	2221 (quartzitic sandstone, Pintado chert). Spherical, lightly battered all over. Floor.	626
31	Hammerstone/pestle? (7.1 x 7.1 x 7.1 cm; 693 g)	4000 (quartzite). Natural squarish white cobble, hammered all around end edge. Washed? faint red paint (Munsell 2.5YR6/6?) on sides. Floor.	627
32	Firepit liner stone? (14.9 x 12.9 x 1.8 cm; 570 g)	2000 (sandstone). Ground on 1 surface. Highly burned; blackened on edges. Floor.	628
33	Metate fragment (20+ x 11+ x 6 cm; 1446 g)	2000 (sandstone). Floor.	629
34	Metate fragment (25.5+ x 23.1 x 4.5 cm; 4+ kg)	2000 (sandstone). Highly ground flat on bottom. Faint splotches of red paint (Munsell 2.5YR4/6?) around edges of trough. Floor.	630
35	Metate (58 x 34 x 5 cm)	2000 (sandstone). Thin trough metate used as the deflector slab. Set in floor 10 cm with trough open at top. Left in situ.	none

Table I.3.19. Site 29SJ 628, Pithouse C Distribution of Floor Fill and Floor 1 Materials, cont'd.[a]

Artifact Number	Artifact Class	Lithic Material, Ceramic Ware, or Faunal Species	FS No.
36	Groundstone (21.5 x 12.3 x 10.7 cm; 3020± g)	2000 (sandstone). Natural block ground flat on 1 surface. Highly burned with some spalling. Floor.	631
37	Lap Anvil? (36.4 x 28.1 x 9.4 cm; 14 kg)	2000 (sandstone). Finely ground on 2 surfaces and lightly pecked on one. Floor.	632
38	Metate (56 x 28 x 15 cm; 32 kg)	2000 (sandstone). Floor, leaning against wall. Whole trough metate. Trough = 36 x 17 x 6 cm.	633
-	Manuport?	4000 (quartzite). Natural pebble. Bench posthole. Missing.	681
-	Awl (8.8+ x 2.2 x 1.5 cm; 12.5+ g)	Indeterminate large mammal splinter. Tip missing (estimated length 9.3 cm). Bench.	682
-	Chopper (8.8 x 7.2 x 4.0 cm; 350.2 g)	2221 (quartzitic sandstone, Pintado chert). Cobble edges flaked. Floor.	818
-	Utilized flake (38.5 g)	1142 (chalcedonic silicified wood). Floor.	819
-	Biface (8.0 x 6.2 x 1.0 cm; 54.8 g)	1110/1113 (splintery/cherty silicified wood). Ovoid, flat shaped with corner missing. 100% edge chipped with some retouch. Bench posthole.	834
Antechamber floor fill and floor			
39	Floor polisher (18.5 x 13.5 x 6.0 cm; 2365 g)	2000 (sandstone). Oval-shaped cobble with opposing faces ground flat. 12 cm above floor (4cm above FS 650).	648
40	Lap anvil (24.0 x 20.2 x 5.0 cm; 4000± g)	2126 (Cliff House sandstone). Ovoid, flattish stone with 2 opposing slightly concave ground surfaces. Shaped by hammer and grinding. 17 cm above floor.	649
40	Charcoal (5.5-g)	Species unknown. Under FS 649.	671
41	Metate (69 x 34 x 9 cm; 31.8 kg)	2000 (sandstone). 10.5 cm above floor. Whole trough metate. Trough = 47 x 26 x 1 cm.	650
42	Floor polisher (18.1 x 17.6 x 5.4 cm; 2292.2 g)	4000 (banded quartzite). River cobble, oval with 2 gently rounded polished surfaces. Burn ring on 1 surface. 16 cm above floor.	651
43	Mano (17.6 x 13.3 x 2.5 cm; 861 g)	2000 (sandstone). Flattish shape. 1 trough metate use surface, with reddish color (paint??) around surface edges. Opposite side slightly abraded for hand comfort? Analyzed as an abrader.	652
44	Concretion (14.7 x 5.6 x 3.7 cm; 374. 4 g)	2000 (sandstone). Natural, oblong shape, slightly burned? on 1 side.	653

[a] See distribution in Figure I.3.20. All bones examined for cooking brown and burning (Akins: analysis data base).

Chapter 3: Basketmaker III Excavation Reports 241

Table I.3.20. List of Features at Site 29SJ 628 Except for Roofing Postholes.[a]

Feature	Length (cm)	Width (cm)	Height/ Depth (cm)	Volume[b] (liters)	Fill Type	Fill Period	Lining	Open/ Sealed	Comments
Pithouse A:									
Firepit 1	64	57	36	84.6	20	Occ/Int	L-S	O	Mouth = 3149 cm2. C14 date
Other Pit 1	11	11	15	2.2	10	PO	L-P	O	
Other Pit 2	7.5	7.5	6	0.2	10	PO	?	O	
Other Pit 3	6	6	26	1.1	10	Occ?	L-P	O	Sipapu
Other Pit 4	49	29	26	32.3	10	Occ?	U	O	Formerly Pot Rest.
Pit in bottom	24	24	36	16.3	10	Occ?	U	O	
Other Pit 5	20	11.5	26	±18.3	10	Occ?	U	O	Formerly Pot Rest 2
Other Pit 6A	11-12	11-12	7	1.1	10	PO?	U	O	East ladder rest (15 cm from OP 6B)
Other Pit 6B	10-11	10-11	7	0.7	10	PO?	U	O	West ladder rest.
Wall Niche 1 (A)	57	33	27	22.5	10/30	PO	L-P	O	30 cm above floor
Wall Niche 2 (B)	40	38	22.5	15.1	10/30	PO	L-P	O	22 cm above floor
Wall Niche 3 (C)	47.5	37	37.5	43.2	10/30	PO	L-P	O	9 cm above floor
Wall Niche 4 (D)	7.5	38	30	29.2	10/30	PO	L-P	O	23 cm above floor
Wall Niche 5 (E)	40	37.5	35	32.1	10/30	PO	L-P	O	22 cm above floor
Wall Niche 6 (F)	55	48	30	31.7	10/30	PO	L-P	O	20 cm above floor
Ventilator tunnel	109	27.5	43	71.0	32	PO	U/L-P	O	Floor plastered
Ventilator shaft	26	26	112	-	32	PO	U	O	
Deflector	55±	8-11	?	-	56	Occ	-	-	Deflector slab missing
East Wing Wall	150±	?	42+	-	56	Occ	L-SP	-	Wall mostly missing
West Wing Wall	160±	?	?	-	56	Occ	L-SP	-	Wall mostly missing
Pithouse C:									
Firepit 1	85	80	43±	±181.3	28	Occ	L-P	O	Definite bottom not found

Table I.3.20. List of Features at Site 29SJ 628 Except for Roofing Postholes, cont'd.[a]

Feature	Length (cm)	Width (cm)	Height/ Depth (cm)	Volume[b] (liters)	Fill Type	Fill Period	Lining	Open/ Sealed	Comments
Firepit 2	?	?	?	?	?	?	?	?	Earlier FP 1 (Floor 2?)
Heating Pit 1	80	55	16	36.2	21	Occ	L-P	S	Formerly OP 2
Other Pit 1	61	30	15	16.3	21/22	Occ	U?	O	Ash pit
Other Pit 3	10	10	9	0.7	?	?	U?	O	Ladder rest?
Other Pits 4A-B	4	4	3-5±	0.05	?	?	U	O	Postholes assoc. with FP 1 wingwall ridge
Bench Ridge 1	63	20	3	-	-	-	L-P	-	Unknown function
Bench Ridge 2	46	19	2-3	-	-	-	L-P	-	Unknown function
Bench Ridge 3	50?	20	6	-	-	-	L-P	-	Unknown function
Bench Ridge 4	50+	20	5	-	-	-	L-P	-	Unknown function
Ventilator tunnel	120	35-55	33	-	30?	PO	L-P	O	Floor plastered; slab ceiling. 30 cm above main floor, flush with antechamber floor. Modified entry
Ventilator shaft	30±?	30±?	65±	-	-	PO	L-S	O?	Placed in abandoned antechamber
Deflector	58	34	5	-	-	Occ	-	-	An upright metate 25 cm from ventilator tunnel
East Wing Wall	265	15	34+	-	-	Occ	L-SP	-	A slab between bench & SE Posthole. Bin area?
West Wing Wall	89	15	20+	-	-	Occ	L-P	-	Connects bench to SW Posthole
West Ridge	28	5	0-16	-	-	-	L-P	-	Just south of West Wingwall
Wingwall at FP 1	240±	12	2-3	-	-	-	L-P	-	Mostly missing
Pithouse C antechamber:									
Posthole 1	15	15	30	6.7	?	?	?	-	Central roof support or ladder rest
Pithouse D:									
Firepit 1	65	60	34	106.6	27	Occ	L-SP	O	Mouth = 3136 cm²
Other Pit 1	36	26	20	16.0e	10	PO	U/L-P	O	Plaster rim 17 cm high, 8 cm wide
Other Pit 2	23	17	20	7.7	10	PO	U?	O	Expands under floor plaster

Table I.3.20. List of Features at Site 29SJ 628 Except for Roofing Postholes, cont'd.[a]

Feature	Length (cm)	Width (cm)	Height/ Depth (cm)	Volume[b] (liters)	Fill Type	Fill Period	Lining	Open/ Sealed	Comments
Other Pit 3	12	10	17	2.0	10	PO	U?	O	Expands under floor plaster
Other Pit 4	13	13	25	3.5	13	PO	U?	O	Posthole?
Other Pit 5	52	43	33	55.6	10	PO	U?	O	Expands under bench
Other Pit 6	25	20	20	12.6	10	PO	U?	O	
Other Pit 7	40	30	14-26	24.0e	10?	PO	U	O	Unfinished pit? Sipapu?
Pit in bottom	10	10	±3	0.2	10?	PO	U	O	
Pit in bottom	7	9	±3	0.2	10?	PO	U	O	
Other Pit 8	33	22	23	12.3	10	PO	U?	O	Pot Rest?
Other Pit 9	9	9	3	0.2		PO	U	O	40 cm south of FP 1. Ladder or deflector posthole?
Wall Niche 1	53	25	36	19.1e	11	PO	?	O	At floor level in SE corner
Entry tunnel	126	30-50	60-70	-	?	PO	U/L-P	O	20 cm above main floor, level with antechamber floor. Floor was plastered
East Wing Wall	50	8	43	-	-	-	L-SP	-	A single upright slab
West Wing Wall	138	7-14	44-57	-	-	-	L-SP	-	3 upright slabs (1 is a metate) covered with plaster
Pithouse D antechamber:									
Firepit 1	60	50	20	46.5	27	Occ	L-P	O	Replastered rim on east half, 4 cm high and 18 cm wide. Mouth = 2324 cm[2]
Other Pit 1	33	30	25	22.1	11	PO	?	O	Pot rest.
Other Pit 2A	10	10	10	0.9	10	PO?	?	O	15 cm from OP 2B, 18 cm from ventilator tunnel. Ladder rest
Other Pit 2B	10	8	9	0.7	10	PO?	?	O	Same, above. Ladder rest
Wall Niche 1 (A)	33	27	16	±14.3	11?	PO	?	O	Feature? 16 cm above floor
Wall Niche 2 (B)	55	40	47	88.4	11?	PO	?	O	45 cm above floor
Ventilator tunnel	76	30	59	-	11	PO	U/L-P	O	Protrudes into chamber 16-17 cm; metate frag. at base of opening. Tunnel 32 cm above antechamber floor. Floor plastered

Table I.3.20. List of Features at Site 29SJ 628 Except for Roofing Postholes, cont'd.[a]

Feature	Length (cm)	Width (cm)	Height/Depth (cm)	Volume[b] (liters)	Fill Type	Fill Period	Lining	Open/Sealed	Comments
Ventilator shaft	108	100	85	-	11	PO	U	O	
East Wing Wall	76	30	5	-	-	-	L-P	-	Piece missing. Adobe ridge
West Wing Wall	115+	10	6	-	-	-	L-P	-	Incomplete? Adobe ridge
South Wall	45	18	25	-	-	-	L-P/S	-	Incomplete? Not in analysis
Pithouse E:									
Firepit 1	67	61	21.5	56.9	11?	PO	L-SP	-	Mouth = 2529 cm². Slab botto.
Heating Pit 1	75	50	14	46.9	10,28	Occ	?	S	Mouth = 3909 cm2.
Other Pit 1	18	18	11-14	4.0	10	PO	?	O	Roof support? Turquoise chip
Other Pit 2	32	19	18.2	9.0	10	PO	?	O	Pot rest?
Other Pit 3	27	23	28	17.3	10	PO	?	O	Bell-shaped
Other Pit 4	15.5	15.5	15-16	4.2	10?	PO	?	O	Roof support?
Other Pit 5	29	21	10	2.5	10?	PO	?	O	Wingwall posthole?
Other Pit 6	19	17	20	5.0	10?	PO	?	O	Wingwall posthole?
Other Pit 7	35	30	7	2.8	10?	PO	?	O	Feature?
Other Pit 8	11	11	23	2.0	10	PO	L-P	O	Sipapu
Other Pit 9	6	6	8	0.4	10	PO?	U	O	Ladder rest. Paired hole missing
Other Pit 10	10	10	5	0.9	10	PO?	U	O	Ladder rest. Paired hole missing
Other Pit 11	6	6	6	0.3	10	PO?	?	O	West Wing Wall Posthole
Wall Niche 1 (A)	33	26	18	8.7	11?	PO	L-P	S	At floor level. Old post mold?
Wall Niche 2 (B)	33	21	18.5	8.1	11?	PO	L-P	S	At floor level. Old post mold?
Wall Niche 3 (C)	13	23	28	-	11?	PO?	U	O	At floor level? Rodent hole?
Ventilator tunnel	120	46	40	-	?	PO	U/L-P	O	14 cm above chamber floor. Projects 27 cm into chamber. Tunnel floor was plastered

Table I.3.20. List of Features at Site 29SJ 628 Except for Roofing Postholes, cont'd.[a]

Feature	Length (cm)	Width (cm)	Height/ Depth (cm)	Volume[b] (liters)	Fill Type	Fill Period	Lining	Open/ Sealed	Comments
Ventilator shaft	130	125	165	-	?	PO	U	O	
Deflector groove	37	8	10	2.7	10?	PO	U	O	Former slab seat
East Wing Wall	165	25	85	-	-	-	L-P?	-	Mostly missing
West Wing Wall	180	20	101	-	-	-	L-PS	-	Mostly missing
Pithouse F:									
Roasting Pit 1	45	35	30e	37.7e	27?	Occ	L-SP	O	In fill far above floor. No fieldnotes
Firepit 1	50	50	28	40.8	27	Occ	L-SP	O	Mouth = 1801 cm². Slab in bottom, 7-8 upright slabs
Heating Pit 1	65	40	14	36.1	28	Occ	U	O	Mouth = 2329 cm². No charcoal present.
Pit in bottom	22	20	15	9.2e	?	?	U	O	Lined with upright sticks? Pit = posthole?
Heating Pit 2	41	31	10	9.2	11,28	Occ?	U	O	Mouth = 1096 cm². Uncertain heating pit. Also possible pot rest. Formerly OP 4
Other Pit 1									See NW Posthole
Other Pit 2 top bottom	23 25	21 23	34	32.2	10	PO	U	O	Bell-shaped pit
Other Pit 3	7	7	9?	0.3	11	PO	U	O	Recent auger hole?
Other Pit 4									See HP 2.
Other Pit 5	22	21	10	3.7	11	PO	U	O	Posthole?
Deflector groove	32.5	5	8.5	13.8	11?	PO	U	O	Former slab seat. One shim. Slab nearby might be deflector
Pithouse G:									
Roasting Pit 2	115?	40?	?	?	?	?	?	?	In fill 80 cm above floor
Firepit 1	65	56	25	75.2	27	Occ	L-P	O	Mouth = 2507 cm². Rim= 10 cm wide, 5 cm high. Ash fill = 21 cm deep. Formerly Feature 1
Heating Pit 1	66	45.5	15	44.3	11?	PO	U	O	Mouth = 2953 cm². Burned sides. Formerly Feature 3
Other Pit 1 top bottom	32 80	31 80	47	122e	10	PO	U	O	Bell-shaped. Formerly Feature 2

246 Windes et al.

Table I.3.20. List of Features at Site 29SJ 628 Except for Roofing Postholes, cont'd.[a]

Feature	Length (cm)	Width (cm)	Height/ Depth (cm)	Volume[b] (liters)	Fill Type	Fill Period	Lining	Open/ Sealed	Comments
Feature 1	45	37	28	-	-	PO	-	-	Postoccupational feature (adobe block) that contains roof adobe & hatch liner? Metate rest?
Wall Niche 1/ Bin1	75±	25	55	51.6	45?	PO	U/L-PS	O	Formerly Feature 4. At floor level
Bin 2 top bottom	41 46	41 32	28	101.7	11	PO	L-P	O	Storage Bin. Formerly Feature 5
East Wing Wall	64	12	?	-	-	-	L-S	-	Adobe ridge
West Wing Wall	75	14	10	-	-	-	?	-	Adobe ridge
Ventilator tunnel	50	56	48	-	?	PO	?	O	
Ventilator shaft bottom	154 182	153 189	131	-	30	PO	U/L-S?	O	Feature 10
Surface features:									
Cist 1	238	157	33	2021	11	PO	L-S	O	2 floors
OP 1	85	32	25	54	11	PO	L-P	O	In lower floor
Cist 2	260	200	50	1841	11	PO	L-S	O	2 floors?
Cist 3	172	160	26	581	12	Occ	L-S	O	Coverted to a clay mixing pit
Cist 4	160	125	29	649	10	PO	L-S	O	Robbed of stone
Cist 5	270	192	32-35	1210	11	PO	L-S	O	Burn spots on the clay floor
Cist 6	105	105	8	163	11	PO	L-S	O	Cist?
Firepit 1	47	43	14	2.8	-	-	L-S	O	Mouth = 2021 cm2. 189 cm east of Cist 2
Firepit 2	32	18	6	2+	-	-	L-S	O	Mouth = 491 cm2. Just south of Pithouse G antechamber near surface
Other Pit 2	550	523	35-40	-	-	-	L-P	O	Adobe mixing pit? In fill above Pithouse D. Contained Burial 1

[a] See Tables I.7.4-I.7.5 for an explanation of the feature and attribute codes.
[b] Volumes for features are approximate.

Table I.3.21. List of Pithouse Postholes at Site 29SJ 628.[a]

Posthole No.	Length (cm)	Width (cm)	Depth (cm)	Volume[b] (liters)	Fill Type	Fill Period	Shims	Base Stone	Est. post size (cm)	Lining	Comments
Pithouse A:											
NE Posthole	43	40	49	.	52	Occ	+	1	8	U?	
SE Posthole	43	41	48	.	16,52	Occ	+	0	9	U?	
SW Posthole	40	37	56	.	52	Occ	+	1	11	U?	
NW Posthole	44	43	53	.	52	Occ	+	1	10	U?	
Pithouse C:											
NE Posthole	44	39	62	100.2	52	Occ	0	1	-	U?	Plaster seal.
SE Posthole	36	31	57	52.0	52	Occ	0	0	-	U?	Plaster seal.
SW Posthole	52	40	38	63.9	52	Occ	0	0	-	U?	Plaster seal.
NW Posthole	35	35	60	64.4	52	Occ	0	1	-	U?	Plaster seal.
Pithouse C bench:											
Posthole 1	17	17	10	2.3	?	?	0	0	-	U	
Posthole 2	16	16	9	1.8	?	?	0	0	-	U	
Posthole 3	15	15	11	1.9	?	?	0	0	-	U	
Posthole 4	15	15	12	2.1	?	?	0	0	-	U	
Posthole 5	17	17	10	2.7	?	?	0	0	-	U	
Posthole 6	20	20	10	3.1	?	?	0	0	-	U	
Posthole 7	18	18	15	3.8	?	?	0	0	-	U	
Posthole 8	15	15	9	1.6	?	?	0	0	-	U	
Posthole 9	22	22	16	6.1	?	?	0	0	-	U	
Posthole 10	20	20	12	3.8/6.4	?	?	0	0	-	U	
Posthole 11	16	16	11	2.2	?	?	0	0	-	U	
Posthole 12	19	19	14	4.0	?	?	0	0	-	U	
Posthole 13	18	18	13	3.3	?	?	0	0	-	U	
Posthole 14	16	16	11	2.2	?	?	0	0	-	U	
Posthole 15	19	19	12	3.4	?	?	0	0	-	U	
Posthole 16	18	18	11	2.8	?	?	0	0	-	U	
Posthole 17	13	13	11	1.5	?	?	0	0	-	U	
Posthole 18	21	21	10	3.5	?	?	0	0	-	U	
Posthole 19	17	17	11	2.5	?	?	0	0	-	U	
Posthole 20	17	17	15	3.4	?	?	0	0	-	U	
Posthole 21	18	18	14	3.6	?	?	0	0	-	U	
Posthole 22	18	18	11	2.8	?	?	0	0	-	U	

Table I.3.21. List of Pithouse Postholes at Site 29SJ 628, cont'd.[a]

Posthole No.	Length (cm)	Width (cm)	Depth (cm)	Volume[b] (liters)	Fill Type	Fill Period	Shims	Base Stone	Est. post size (cm)	Lining	Comments
Posthole 23	16	16	12	2.4	?	?	0	0	-	U	
Posthole 24	17	17	11	2.5	?	?	0	0	-	U	
Posthole 25	17	17	12/26?	2.7/5.9	?	?	0	0	-	U	
Posthole 26	16	16	12	2.4/2.8	?	?	0	0	-	U	
Posthole 27	14	14	12	1.8	?	?	0	0	-	U	
Posthole 28	16	16	10	2.0	?	?	0	0	-	U	
Posthole 29	14	14	11	1.7	?	?	0	0	-	U	
Posthole 30	14	14	12	1.8	?	?	0	0	-	U	
Posthole 31	16	16	10	2.0	?	?	0	0	-	U	
Posthole 32	17	17	14	3.2	?	?	0	0	-	U	
Posthole 33	16	16	7	1.4	?	?	0	0	-	U	
Posthole 34	14	14	9	1.4	?	?	0	0	-	U	
Posthole 35	15	15	9	1.6	?	?	0	0	-	U	
Pithouse D:											
NE Posthole	45	45	29	47.7	52	Occ	0	0	-	U	
SE Posthole	31	28	56	42.2	52	Occ	1	0	-	U	
SW Posthole	30	30	28	19.6.	11?	PO	0	0	-	U	
NW Posthole	40	35	33	41.4	52	Occ	0	0	-	U	
Pithouse D bench:											
Posthole 1	10	8	10	0.8	?	?	0	0	-	U	
Posthole 2	13	12	12	1.4	?	?	0	0	-	U	
Posthole 3	11	10	8	0.7	?	?	0	0	-	U	
Posthole 4	12	12	9	1.1	?	?	0	0	-	U	
Posthole 5	12	12	8	0.8	?	?	0	0	-	U	
Posthole 6	13	12	11	1.3	?	?	0	0	-	U	
Posthole 7	15	13	11	1.5	?	?	0	0	-	U	
Posthole 8	18	17	13	3.2	?	?	0	0	-	U	Inner row.
Posthole 9	13	13	6	0.8	?	?	0	0	-	U	Outer row.
Posthole 10	13	11	5	0.6	?	?	0	0	-	U	
Posthole 11	12	12	9	1.1	?	?	0	0	-	U	Inner row.
Posthole 12	13	11	7	0.8	?	?	0	0	-	U	Outer row.
Posthole 13	12	10	10	0.9	?	?	0	0	-	U	
Posthole 14	12	11	7	0.7	?	?	0	0	-	U	

Table I.3.21. List of Pithouse Postholes at Site 29SJ 628, cont'd.[a]

Posthole No.	Length (cm)	Width (cm)	Depth (cm)	Volume[b] (liters)	Fill Type	Fill Period	Shims	Base Stone	Est. post size (cm)	Lining	Comments
Posthole 15	12	10	9	0.8	?	?	0	0	-	U	
Posthole 16	11	10	5	0.4	?	?	0	0	-	U	
Posthole 17	10	9	11	0.9	?	?	0	0	-	U	
Posthole 18	12	11	13	1.3	?	?	0	0	-	U	
Posthole 19	11	8	10	0.8	?	?	0	0	-	U	Inner row.
Posthole 20	12	10	8	0.7	?	?	0	0	-	U	Outer row.
Posthole 21	12	12	3	0.4	?	?	0	0	-	U	Outer row.
Posthole 22	12	11	6	0.6	?	?	0	0	-	U	Inner row.
Posthole 23	11	10	3	0.3	?	?	0	0	-	U	
Posthole 24	13	11	8	1.0	?	?	0	0	-	U	Inner row.
Posthole 25	12	11	3	0.3	?	?	0	0	-	U	Outer row.
Posthole 26	15	13	11	1.8	?	?	0	0	-	U	Inner row.
Posthole 27	12	11	4	0.4	?	?	0	0	-	U	Outer row.
Posthole 28	14	13	10	1.6	?	?	0	0	-	U	Inner row.
Posthole 29	13	13	6	0.7	?	?	0	0	-	U	Outer row.
Posthole 30	11	10	10?	0.8	?	?	0	0	-	U	Outer row.
Posthole 31	14	11	16.5	1.8	?	?	0	0	-	U	Inner row.
Posthole 32	10	8	4	0.2	?	?	0	0	-	U	Outer row.
Posthole 33	13	12	8	0.9	?	?	0	0	-	U	Outer row.
Posthole 34	12	11	8	0.8	?	?	0	0	-	U	Inner row.
Posthole 35	8	8	7	0.3	?	?	0	0	-	U	Outer row.
Posthole 36	12	11	6	0.6	?	?	0	0	-	U	Inner row.
Posthole 37	12	12	6	0.7	?	?	0	0	-	U	Outer row.
Posthole 38	14	12	6	0.8	?	?	0	0	-	U	Inner row.
Posthole 39	11	11	6.5	0.6	?	?	0	0	-	U	Outer row.
Posthole 40	12	11	4	0.4	?	?	0	0	-	U	Inner row.
Posthole 41	11	11	5	0.5	?	?	0	0	-	U	Outer row.
Posthole 42	12	11	3	0.3	?	?	0	0	-	U	Inner row.
Posthole 43	11	10	4	0.3	?	?	0	0	-	U	Outer row.
Posthole 44	12	10	6	0.5	?	?	0	0	-	U	Inner row.
Posthole 45	12	10	7	0.7	?	?	0	0	-	U	Outer row.
Posthole 46	12	11	7	0.7	?	?	0	0	-	U	Inner row.
Posthole 47	12	12	7	0.7	?	?	0	0	-	U	Outer row.
Posthole 48	15	15	6	1.1	?	?	0	0	-	U	Inner row.
Posthole 49	13	12	7	0.9	?	?	0	0	-	U	Outer row.

Table I.3.21. List of Pithouse Postholes at Site 29SJ 628, cont'd.[a]

Posthole No.	Length (cm)	Width (cm)	Depth (cm)	Volume[b] (liters)	Fill Type	Fill Period	Shims	Base Stone	Est. post size (cm)	Lining	Comments
Posthole 50	24	21	32	12.7	?	?	0	0	-	U	Inner row.
Posthole 51	18	18	10	2.6	?	?	0	0	-	U	Outer row.
Posthole 52	20	18	20	5.6	?	?	0	0	-	U	Inner row.
Posthole 53	13	11	5	0.6	?	?	0	0	-	U	Outer row.
Pithouse E:											
NE Posthole	23	23	59	31.2	52	Occ	2+	0?	12	U	
SE Posthole	30	20	52	26.9	52	Occ	2+	0?	-	U	
SW Posthole	32	31	70	41.4	52	Occ	5	0?	11	U	
NW Posthole	30	30	60	40.1	52	Occ	3	0?	13	U	
Pithouse E bench:											
Posthole 1	12	10	8	0.8	?	?	0	0	-	U	
Posthole 2	9	8	6	0.3	?	?	0	0	-	U	
Posthole 3	11	11	9	0.8	?	?	0	0	-	U	
Posthole 4	11	10	9	0.8	?	?	0	0	-	U	
Posthole 5	11	10	10	1.0	?	?	0	0	-	U	
Posthole 6	13	10	12	1.4	?	?	0	0	-	U	
Posthole 7	14	12	6	0.5	?	?	0	0	-	U	
Posthole 8	13	8	13	2.0	?	?	0	0	-	U	
Posthole 9	8	8	8	0.9	?	?	0	0	-	U	
Posthole 10	12	11	9	0.4	?	?	0	0	-	U	
Posthole 11	13	12	12	1.4	?	?	0	0	-	U	
Posthole 12	14	12	12	1.6	?	?	0	0	-	U	
Posthole 13	12	12	6	0.6	?	?	0	0	-	U	
Posthole 14	12	10	11	0.9	?	?	0	0	-	U	
Posthole 15	14	11	17	1.7	?	?	0	0	-	U	
Posthole 16	12	12	13	1.6	?	?	0	0	-	U	Turquoise chip.
Posthole 17	13	12	14	2.0	?	?	0	0	-	U	
Posthole 18	16	16	12	2.5	?	?	0	0	-	U	
Posthole 19	16	14	12	2.1	?	?	0	0	-	U	
Posthole 20	14	12	12	1.6	?	?	0	0	-	U	
Posthole 21	13	12	12	1.5	?	?	0	0	-	U	
Posthole 22	14	12	12	1.7	?	?	0	0	-	U	Cobble in fill.
Posthole 23	12	12	12	1.1	?	?	0	0	-	U	

Table I.3.21. List of Pithouse Postholes at Site 29SJ 628, cont'd.[a]

Posthole No.	Length (cm)	Width (cm)	Depth (cm)	Volume[b] (liters)	Fill Type	Fill Period	Shims	Base Stone	Est. post size (cm)	Lining	Comments
Posthole 24	13	12	15	2.2	?	?	0	0	-	U	
Posthole 25	13	12	15	1.8	?	?	0	0	-	U	
Posthole 26	14	11	16	2.1	?	?	0	0	-	U	
Posthole 27	13	13	12	1.8	?	?	0	0	-	U	Bone awl.
Posthole 28	14	13	11	1.5	?	?	0	0	-	U	Pipe.
Posthole 29	15	15	11	1.9	?	?	0	0	-	U	Obsidian flake.
Posthole 30	13	12	11	1.5	?	?	0	0	-	U	
Posthole 31	14	12	13	1.7	?	?	0	0	-	U	
Posthole 32	14	13	10	1.5	?	?	0	0	-	U	
Posthole 33	16	14	14	2.5	?	?	0	0	-	U	
Posthole 34	16	12	10	1.6	?	?	0	0	-	U	
Posthole 35	16	13	13	1.9	?	?	0	0	-	U	
Posthole 36	14	13	19	2.6	?	?	0	0	-	U	
Posthole 37	16	13	12	2.0	?	?	0	0	-	U	
Posthole 38	13	11	10	1.2	?	?	0	0	-	U	
Posthole 39	12	10	9	0.8	?	?	0	0	-	U	
Posthole 40	15	15	11	2.2	?	?	0	0	-	U	Pipe.
Posthole 41	15	11	9	1.2	?	?	0	0	-	U	
Posthole 42	15	12	10	1.5	?	?	0	0	-	U	
Posthole 43	15	11	11	1.4	?	?	0	0	-	U	
Posthole 44	15	14	11	1.8	?	?	0	0	-	U	Chipped stone.
Posthole 45	11	11	10	0.8	?	?	0	0	-	U	
Posthole 46	13	11	10	1.1	?	?	0	0	-	U	
Posthole 47	12	11	9	0.9	?	?	0	0	-	U	
Posthole 48	12	12	18	2.2	?	?	0	0	-	U	
Posthole 49	15	13	11	1.6	?	?	0	0	-	U	Selenite pendant. Flake.
Posthole 50	14	13	8	1.3	?	?	0	0	-	U	
Posthole 51	10	8	10	0.5	?	?	0	0	-	U	
Posthole 52	15	13	9	1.3	?	?	0	0	-	U	
Posthole 53	15	14	22	3.5	?	?	0	0	-	U	
Posthole 54	16	15	45	9.3	?	?	0	0	-	U	

Table I.3.21. List of Pithouse Postholes at Site 29SJ 628, cont'd.[a]

Posthole No.	Length (cm)	Width (cm)	Depth (cm)	Volume[b] (liters)	Fill Type	Fill Period	Shims	Base Stone	Est. post size (cm)	Lining	Comments
Pithouse F:											
NE Posthole	20	20	51	17.1	52	Occ	1	0	-	U	
SE Posthole	23	23	25	7.2	52	Occ	0	0	-	U	
SW Posthole	21	21	20	6.7	52	Occ	0	0	-	U	
NW Posthole	24	20	40	15.5	52	Occ	0	0	-	U	Bone awl.
Pithouse G:											
Posthole 1	24	22	34.5	14.3	52	Occ	3	1	-	U	Feature 6A.
Posthole 2	20	20	25	+7.9	?	?	0	0	-	U	Feature 6B. Older PH.
Posthole 3	15	15	15	+2.7	52?	Occ?	1	0	-		Feature 9. Disturbed.
Posthole 4	24	23	38	16.5	52	Occ	0	1	15 x 17	U	Feature 8.
Posthole 5	32	17.5	16	15.4	52?	Occ?	4	1	15 x 14	U	Feature 7A.
Posthole 6	25	15	8+	+2.5	?	?	0	0	-	U	Feature 7B. Older PH.

[a] See Tables I.7.4-I.7.5 for an explanation of the feature and attribute codes.
[b] For the most part, bench posthole dimensions (length and width) taken from field maps. Posthole areas calculated from field maps with digital planimeter.

Table I.3.22. Site 29SJ 628, Pithouse D Distribution of Floor 1 Materials.[a]

	Artifact Class	Lithic Material, Ceramic Ware, or Faunal Species	FS No.
Antechamber			
1	Pendant fragment (3.8 x 3.1 x 0.4 cm; 8.1 g)	2551 (red dog shale). 2 separated pieces; elliptical shape with 2 surfaces ground & all edges beveled. Biconical hole 2 mm diameter. 1 piece in fill above floor.	308, 339
2	Mano (22.6 x 11.8 x 2.4 cm; 1122 g)	2000 (sandstone). 2 separated pieces. Floor.	309
-	Axe (14.2 x 8.1 x 3.3 cm; 557 g)	3040 (gabbro). Location uncertain. Floor.	310
3	Pot polisher? (5.6 x 4.0 x 4.0 cm; 112 g)	4000 (quartzite). Natural pebble with 2 small pecked areas. Floor.	311
-	Sherds (79)	Antechamber Floor (see Volume II, Table II.3.20).	326
-	Minerals (6; largest 8.5 x 4.3 x 0.7 cm; all = 63.0 g)	5041 (gypsum selenite). Natural, unmodified, tabular, irregular pieces.	326C
-	Worked bone (4.2 x 1.8 x 0.6 cm; 4.7 g)	Indeterminate large mammal medial shaft. Floor.	328
-	Bones (79)	Jackrabbit (6), cottontail (9), coyote (2), badger (23), dog (5), pocket gopher (1), mountain sheep (1), artiodactyl (9; 5 boiled), mule deer (1), prairie dog (5; 5 boiled), mammal (6), pronghorn (11). Floor.	328
4	Axe fragment (13.0+ x 9.1 x 4.7 cm; 731+ g)	4525 (greenstone). Poll missing. Bit sharpened by flake removal. Floor.	334
5	Abrader (21.0 x 14.3 x 3.0 cm; 931.5 g)	2000 (sandstone). Light grinding on 2 opposite flat surfaces. Floor.	335
6	Mano	2000 (sandstone). Floor. Missing.	336
7	Mano (19.1 x 11.6 x 2.2 cm; 994.0 g)	2000 (sandstone). Floor.	337
8	Mano (21.4 x 11.0 x 2.6 cm; 1103 g)	2000 (sandstone). Floor.	338
9	Sherds (2): La Plata B/w Unclassified BMIII-PI B/w	FP 1 Cibola Whiteware. Cibola Whiteware.	347
9	Utilized flake (12. 0 g)	1140 (chalcedonic silicified wood). FP 1.	348
9	Charcoal (23.6 g)	Includes *Sarcobatus vermiculatus* and *Zea mays*. FP 1 in antechamber.	349, 676
9	Corn cob frag (0.9- g)	*Zea mays* (carbonized). FP 1 in antechamber.	677
10	Sharpening abrader (8.6 x 6.7 x 4.8 cm; 284 g)	2000 (sandstone). Sooted & 100% burned. 4 grooves across top (2-5 mm wide); some bottom grinding. Ventilator tunnel. Approximate location.	350
10	Bone	Coyote (*Canis latrans*) radius. Ventilator tunnel. Approximate location.	351

Table I.3.22. Site 29SJ 628, Pithouse D Distribution of Floor 1 Materials, cont'd.[a]

Antechamber	Artifact Class	Lithic Material, Ceramic Ware, or Faunal Species	FS No.
11	Metate fragment (21+ x 33 x 8 cm)	2000 (sandstone). Upright stone used for ventilator mouth construction. Left in situ.	-
-	Concretions (8)	2000 (sandstone). Floor.	
	(6.8 x 7.3 cm; 309 g)	Sub-spherical; natural.	
	(3.9 x 3.2 cm; 51 g)	Spherical; natural.	
	(4.2 x 2.8 cm; 47 g)	Sub-spherical; natural.	
	(3.3 x 2.7cm; 26.7 g)	Spherical; some minor grinding on exterior?	
	(8.8 x 5.3 cm; 180.8 g)	Bowl-shaped; natural.	
	(3.4 x 4.2 x 4.5 cm; 63.3 g)	Unmodified shrimp burrow cast.	
	(4.2 x 4.1 cm; 57.8 g)	Unmodified shrimp burrow cast.	
	(8.4 x 4.6 x 4.6 cm; 196.2 g)	Unmodified sandstone chunk pocketed with concretion mineral shells.	361
-	Limonite (6.3 x 5.1 x 2.9 cm; 68 g)	5110 (soft yellow ocher). Natural chunk (Munsell 10YR 7/8). Bag ware?	361
-	Groundstone (14.2 x 11.5 x 2.5 cm; 117.7 g)	2000 (sandstone). Burned; high spots on 1 surface ground. Floor.	
-	Lapidary abrader fragment (11.4+ x 9.0 x 1.7 cm; 301+ g)	2000 (sandstone). 1 finely ground surface of tabular stone. 100% burned with sooting. Final use as firepit liner. Red paint? residue (Munsell 2.5 YR 5/6?).	
-	Abrader fragment (10.4+ x 6.7 x 3.2 cm; 219.5+ g)	2000 (sandstone). Lightly ground on 1 surface.	362
-	Chipped stone (6)	Floor	
	Angular debris (2.0 g)	1052 (chalcedonic High Surface Chert).	
	Utilized flake (4.8 g)	1140 (chalcedonic silicified wood).	
	Whole flakes (2)(8.8 g)	1140 (chalcedonic silicified wood).	
	Whole flake (1.4 g)	1142 (chalcedonic silicified wood).	
	Utilized flake (25.4 g)	2202 (silicified fine-grained brown concretion).	363
-	Adobe impressions (8.5+ x 7.3+ x 5.1 cm; 11.2+ x 7.3+ x 4.8 cm thick; total 525 g)	Roofing impressions. Estimated 6 cm diameter beam & other secondary material. Floor.	364
-	Sandstones (3)(largest 4.5 x 3.8 x 2.6 cm; total 81.4 g)	2000 (sandstone). Highly friable chunk, 100% burned–for paint? Munsell 10R 4/6 - 4/8. Floor.	365
-	Limonite (6.2 x 5.5 x 3.9 cm; 19.1 g)	5110 (yellow ocher). Natural? friable lump (Munsell 5Y 8/4). Floor.	366
12	Hammerstone/polishing stone? (9.0 x 7.0 x 5.0 cm; 448 g)	4000 (quartzite). Ends battered. Antechamber floor.	713
13	Concretion (28.0 x 24.7 x 5.0 cm; 4500 g)	2000 (sandstone). Natural, partial crude sphere with red paint (Munsell 2.5YR 5/6?) on sole flat, minor ground surface. Antechamber floor.	714
14	Mano (17.6 x 11.9 x 1.9 cm; 796 g)	2000 (sandstone). 1 surface ground. Antechamber floor.	715
15	Manuport (7.8 x 5.9 x 4.0 cm; 272.1 g)	4000 (quartzite). Burned spot. A few peck marks + flakes removed. Antechamber floor.	716
16	Groundstone (20.0 x 16.5 x 4.1 cm; 1800 g)	2000 (sandstone). Slight grinding on 2 surfaces, plus 1 surface pecked. Burned. Antechamber floor.	717

Table I.3.22. Site 29SJ 628, Pithouse D Distribution of Floor 1 Materials, cont'd.[a]

Antechamber	Artifact Class	Lithic Material, Ceramic Ware, or Faunal Species	FS No.
17	Lapidary abrader & mano (15.3 x 11.5 x 2.9 cm; 981 g)	2000 (hard, gray well indurated sandstone). Finely ground on 2 surfaces, mano side pecked. Antechamber floor.	718
18	Metate fragment (18+ x 16+ x 8 cm; 3.2+ kg)	2000 (sandstone). Antechamber floor.	719

Main Chamber

	Artifact Class	Lithic Material, Ceramic Ware, or Faunal Species	FS No.
19	Needle?	Unknown bird or mammal fragment. Floor fill. Missing.	598
20	Awl (4.4 x 0.6 x 0.2 cm; 0.7 g)	Jackrabbit (*Lepus* sp.) tibia. Floor fill.	599
21	Bone	Antler tip, base drilled. Floor. Missing.	604
-	Sherds (23)	Mixed temporal periods. Bench top (see Volume II, Table II.2.30).	
	Lino Gray (2)	Cibola Grayware.	
	Plain gray (13)	Cibola Grayware.	
	Lino Gray with fugitive red (2)	Cibola Grayware.	
	Wide neckbanded (1)	Cibola Grayware.	
	Narrow neckbanded (1)	Cibola Grayware.	
	Red Mesa B/w (2)	Cibola Whiteware.	
	Unclassified PII-PIII whiteware (1)	Cibola Whiteware.	
	Lino B/g (1)	Tusayan Whiteware.	657
-	Concretion fragment (10.8 diameter x 4.9 cm hi; 179.7 g)	2000 (sandstone). Natural bowl-shaped. Bench.	
-	Concretion fragment (3.5 diameter x 3.1+ cm hi; 13.5 g)	Hard shell mineral nodule.	658
-	Concretion (5.5 x 4.7 x 1.1 cm; 29.6 g)	Natural mineral chunk with hematite (Munsell 2.5YR 4/6).	
-	Concretion (12.7 x 5.4 x 5.4 cm; 535.8 g)	Ore? 100 percent burned & split into 3 pieces. Unmodified irregular chunk.	659
-	Angular debris (15.9 g)	1145 (chalcedonic silicified wood). Bench.	659B
-	Abrader (8.0 x 7.0 x 1.0 cm; 90 g)	2000 (fine yellow sandstone). Ground flat on 1 surface. Bench.	659C
-	Bones (3)	Dog (2 *Canis* sp.; 1 burned and boiled); and Unknown mammal (1). On bench.	660
-	Wood (10.0 g)	Root fragments? Bench.	661
22	Projectile point (2.9 x 0.9 x 0.3 cm; 1.0 g)	1140 (chalcedonic silicified wood). Narrow stem for hafting without distinct notching. OP 1.	673
22	Mano fragment (11.4+ x 6.8+ x 3.8 cm; 410+ g)	2000 (sandstone). Finely ground on 2 surfaces. OP 1.	826
23	Beans (4; 0.2 g)	OP 4.	679

256 Windes et al.

Table I.3.22. Site 29SJ 628, Pithouse D Distribution of Floor 1 Materials, cont'd.[a]

Antechamber	Artifact Class	Lithic Material, Ceramic Ware, or Faunal Species	FS No.
-	Sherds (18)	Floor (see Volume II, Table II.2.30).	688
	Lino Gray (2)	Cibola Grayware.	
	Plain Gray (14)	Cibola Grayware.	
	Obelisk Gray (1)	Cibola Grayware.	
	Woodruff Smudged (1)	Mogollon Tradition.	
-	Sherds (23)	All Cibola Tradition. (See Volume II, Table II.2.30).	695
	Lino Gray and plain gray (11)		
	neckbanded (1)		
	unclassified indented corrugated (3)		
	White Mound B/w (1)		
	Chaco-McElmo B/w (2)		
	Unclassified PII-PIII whiteware (4)		
	Wingate B/r (1)		
-	Chipped stone (8)	Floor	689
	Angular debris (2)(total 3.5 g)	1053 (chalcedonic High Surface Chert).	
	Whole flakes (2)(total 2.6 g)	1072 (yellow-spotted Zuni chert).	
	Whole flake (0.3 g)	1113 (cherty silicified wood).	
	Fortuitous perforator (1.5 g)	1140 (chalcedonic silicified wood).	
	Angular debris (9.0 g)	1234 (translucent chalcedony with red & black inclusions).	
-	Blade (11.0 x 6.5 x 1.2 cm; 98.8 g)	2126 (Cliff House Sandstone). Bifacially flaked with some retouch. Flattish, triangular piece that resembles a crude tchamahia blade.	689B
-	Minerals (2; largest 1.7 x 1.5 x 0.5 cm; all = 3.2 g)	5041 (gypsum selenite). Natural, tabular, irregular pieces.	689C
-	Minerals (9; largest 5.5 x 1.9 x 1.6 cm; all = 29.1 g)	5040 (gypsum; burned selenite). Natural, tabular, irregular pieces.	689C
-	Bones (35)	Cottontail (17; 1 boiled), jackrabbit (11), prairie dog (2: 1 boiled), pocket gopher (1), kangaroo rat (1), mammal (3). Floor.	690
-	Charcoal (15.3 g)	Includes some *Juniperus* sp. (unburned & carbonized). Floor.	691
-	Corn cob fragment (0.6 g)	*Zea mays*. Carbonized. Floor.	692
-	Turquoise (3; largest 0.4 x 0.4 x 0.2 cm; 0.5 g)	5300 (turquoise). Rock Color 5G 7/4, 5G 6/6. Floor.	693
-	Awl (9.6 x 1.7 x 0.2 cm; 4.9 g)	Jackrabbit (*Lepus* sp.) tibia. Floor.	694A
-	Awl (7.2 x 1.7 x 0.2 cm; 3.4 g)	Jackrabbit (*Lepus* sp.) tibia. Floor.	694B

Chapter 3: Basketmaker III Excavation Reports   257

Table I.3.22. Site 29SJ 628, Pithouse D Distribution of Floor 1 Materials, cont'd.[a]

Antechamber	Artifact Class	Lithic Material, Ceramic Ware, or Faunal Species	FS No.
-	Bone	Pronghorn antelope (*Antilocapra americana*) phalanx. Floor.	696
-	Concretions (5) (13.7 x 5.5 cm; 854.8 g) (10.7 x 4.2 cm; 420 g) (5.7 x 3.8 x 2.9 cm; 39.9 g) (4.6 x 2.7 x 1.2 cm; 16.7 g) (4.5 x 3.5 x 1.2 cm; 19.5 g)	2000 (sandstone). Floor Bowl-shaped; natural broken sphere. Unmodified. Bowl-shaped; natural broken sphere. Unmodified. Crude bowl-shaped. Spot burn. Unmodified. Natural chunk; 100% burned. Unmodified. Natural; shallow, cup-shaped. Unmodified.	697
-	Cobble (20.1 x 10.5 x 4.3 cm; 1178.2 g)	3300 (andesite?; green with black specks). Natural, flattish cobble from San Juan River drainages? Axe blank? Floor? Catalogued as Level 1 fill.	698
-	Mano (18.6 x 11.2 x 3.5 cm; 1176.4 g)	2000 (sandstone). Burned. Floor? Catalogued as Level 1 fill.	698
24	Mano (13.4 x 10.4 x 2.1 cm; 729 g)	2000 (sandstone). Edge burned. Red paint (Munsell 10YR 5/6). Bench.	720
25	Palette (19.0 x 13.0 x 2.0 cm; 638 g)	2000 (sandstone). Tabular, irregular shape. Red paint (Munsell 10R 4/4) on 1 surface. Partly burned/blackened. Former firepit liner? Bench.	721
26	Polishing stone (7.0 x 7.0 x 3.0 cm; 93 g)	4000 (quartzite). Pebble. Location uncertain. Floor.	722
27	Sandstone slab (11.5 x 9.0 x 8.7 cm; 1401 g)	2000 (sandstone). Floor.	723
28	Concretion (7.2 x 2.7 x 1.8 cm; 61.8 g)	2000 (sandstone). Natural fossilized cylindrical shrimp burrow. Unmodified. Floor.	724
29	Manuport/polishing stone? (4.8 x 2.2 x 1.5 cm; 24.4 g)	4000 (quartzite). Natural pebble with minor pecking marks. Floor.	725
30	Manuport (6.1 x 5.7 x 2.4 cm; 121 g) Manuport fragment (4.9+ x 3.3+ x 2.1+ cm; 48.7 g) Manuport fragment (6.0+ x 5.0 x 2.1 cm; 90.3 g)	4000 (quartzite). Natural pebble. Floor. 4000 (quartzite). Natural pebble. 4000 (quartzite). Natural pebble; possible some polishing?	726
31	Palette (13.0 x 12.0 x 2.0 cm; 407 g)	2000 (sandstone). Tabular, irregular shape. Red paint (Munsell 10R 4/4) on both surfaces. Burned. Floor. See Akins 1997:Fig.5.36.	727
32	Lino Gray jar sherd	Cibola Grayware. Bottom of vessel. Floor.	728
-	Concretion bowl (13.0 diameter x 7.5 cm; 1113.6 g)	2000 (sandstone). Natural sphere fragment with some exterior grinding. Burned. Floor.	832
-	Biscuit mano (11.1 x 8.0 x 2.4 cm; 524 g)	2000 (sandstone). 2 surfaces ground. Floor.	836
-	Lino Smudged bowl sherd (1)	Cibola Grayware. Posthole 4??	-
33	Trough metate (55 x 38 x 14 cm)	2000 (sandstone). Placed upright in West Wing Wall construction. Left in situ.	-

[a] See distribution in Figure I.3.23. All bones noted for boiling stains or burning if present (Akins: analysis data base).

Table I.3.23. Site 29SJ 628, Pithouse G Distribution of Floor fill and Floor 1 Materials.[a]

Artifact Number	Artifact Class	Lithic Material, Ceramic Ware, or Faunal Species	FS No.
Pithouse Main Chamber floor fill			
-	Corn cob fragments (2; 0.6 g)	*Zea mays*. Carbonized. Floor fill.	758
-	Projectile point (5.1 x 1.9 x 0.5 cm; 4.1g)	1113 (cherty silicified wood), large corner-notched "Tularosa" point. Poor flake removal. Serrated edges. Floor fill.	759
-	Bones (15)	Cottontail (10), mammal (5). Floor fill.	760
-	Hematite (2) (4.7 x 2.4 2.4 cm; 4.1 g) (2.3 x 1.8 x 1.8 cm; 7.0 g)	5221 (red ocher). Natural irregular cylinder in 3 pieces. 10R 2.5/2. Natural irregular chunk. Munsell 2.5YR 5/6.	761
-	Awl (8.3 x 1.7 x 2.2 cm; 12.5 g)	Artiodactyl metapodial. Floor fill.	762
-	Chipped stone (9) Whole flakes (3) (total 4.6 g) Utilized flake (20.5 g) Angular debris (2) (total 4.6 g) Angular debris (2.6 g) Utilized flake (1.8 g)	Floor 1140 (chalcedonic silicified wood). 1140 (chalcedonic silicified wood). 1140 (chalcedonic silicified wood). 1142 (chalcedonic silicified wood). 1142 (chalcedonic silicified wood).	763
-	Polishing stone (13 x 9 x 5 cm; 319 g)	4000 (quartzite). Natural pebble.	763
-	Mineral (4.3 x 3.4 x 2.9 cm; 47.0 g)	5110? (limonite? concretion nodule). Natural; has attached calcite crystals.	
-	Sherds (16): Plain gray (14) Unclassified PII-III B/w (1) Lino B/g (1)	Mixed ceramic traditions. Floor fill.	764
-	Groundstone	2000 (sandstone). Floor fill. Missing.	765
-	Concretion (17.4 x 13.7 x 3.2 cm; 1249.5 g)	2000 (sandstone). Natural trough shape with ground exterior and pecked interior. Burned. Firedog? Top of FP 1 fill.	788
-	Bones	FP 1 fill. Missing.	842

Table I.3.23. Site 29SJ 628, Pithouse G Distribution of Floor fill and Floor 1 Materials, cont'd.[a]

Artifact Number	Artifact Class	Lithic Material, Ceramic Ware, or Faunal Species	FS No.
Ventilator Shaft floor			
–	Concretions (2) (12.7 x 11.1 cm; 1824 g) (11.3 x 8.3 cm; 853.4 g)	2000 (sandstone). Unmodified. Subspherical. 100 percent burned. 2 pieces. Unmodified. Spherical. 100 percent burned. Fragments.	774
–	Biscuit mano (8.8 x 7.7 x 3.4 cm; 379.5 g)	2000 (sandstone). Oval shape with 2 convex grinding surfaces.	775
–	Mano fragment?/abrader (8.7+ x 8.4 x 1.5 cm; 146 g)	2000 (sandstone). 1 finely ground surface.	776a
–	Mano (21.4 x 10.3 x 4.0 cm; 1680.7 g)	2000 (sandstone). Flat, rectangular block, ground & pecked on 2 opposite surfaces without end beveling. Brand new mano.	776b
–	Hammerstone (7.4 x 5.6 x 4.3 cm; 251 g)	4000 (quartzite). Natural pebble; sooted, burned & battered.	777
–	Chopper (17.7 x 11.0 x 5.6 cm; 608.5 g)	2000 (gray, well-indurated sandstone). Natural flake chipped at opposite ends to form 2 bits. Red (Munsell 2.5YR 6/6?) paint? residue.	778
–	Lapidary abrader/anvil? (17.5 x 11.5 x 5.0 cm; 1303 g)	2000 (sandstone). Tabular, triangular-shaped with 2 well-ground surfaces. Some edge burning.	779a
–	Groundstone	2000 (sandstone). Missing.	779b
–	Groundstone	2000 (sandstone). Missing.	779c
–	Abrader (30.0 x 12.0 x 4.0 cm; 2089 g)	2000 (sandstone). Shallow metate-like grinding basin 24 x 12 cm.	780
–	Concretion (11.5 x 8.0 x 4.7 cm; 236 g)	2000 (friable yellow sandstone). Scoop-shaped; slightly ground to shape.	781
–	Sherd (1): Lino Fugitive Red jar	Cibola Grayware. Ventilator floor.	782
–	Whole flake (1.7 g)	1140 (chalcedonic silicified wood).	783
–	Bones (12)	Cottontail (4), jackrabbit (2), Gunnison's prairie dog (1), artiodactyl (1), mammal (4).	784

[a] Floor materials not triangulated (see Pithouse G plan, Figure I.3.25). All bones examined for cooking brown and burning (Akins: analysis data base).

Table I.3.24. Site 29SJ 628, Pithouse E Distribution of Floor Fill and Floor 1 Materials.[a]

Artifact Number	Artifact Class	Lithic Material, Ceramic Ware, or Faunal Species	FS No.
1	Awl (18.1 x 1.2 x 0.6 cm; 14.9 g)	Indeterminate large mammal shaft. Bench.	367
2	Awl (8.3 x 1.1 x 1.6; 4.3 g)	Bobcat (*Lynx rufus*) ulna. Bench.	368
3	Awl (4.8 x 0.8 x 0.2 cm; 0.98 g)	Jackrabbit (*Lepus* sp.) tibia. Bench.	369
4	Awl (11.3 x 0.9 x 0.8 cm; 7.7 g) Bone scraper ?	Indeterminate large mammal shaft. Bench. Bench. Not analyzed (missing).	377
5	Projectile point (2.5 x 1.1 x 0.2 cm; 0.6 g)	1050 (white chert), corner-notched projectile point. Floor fill.	430
6	Polishing stone	Floor. Missing.	437
-	Sherds (133)	Floor fill (see Volume II, Table II.2.30).	441
-	Concretions (10) (17.5 x 9.4 cm; 749.4 g) (9.6 diameter x 5.7 cm; 387.7 g) (8.5 diameter x 5.3 cm; 287.8 g) (5.6 x 4.3 cm; 125.5 g) (7.5 x 4.1 x 3.6 cm; 137 g) (3.6 x 3.0 cm; 44.3 g) (2.9 x 2.1 cm; 15.1 g) (11.3 x 6.9 x 2.5 cm; 143.8 g) (6.0 x 4.7 x 1.0 cm; 37.2 g) (2.7 diameter x 1.3 cm; 8.3 g)	2000 (sandstone). Floor fill Natural, irregular shape. 100% burned, causing some spalling. Natural half sphere with internal cavity. Shows some bag ware. Natural rough half spheroid. Red (Munsell 2.5YR 6/8) paint spots. Natural sphere. Natural, peanut shape. Slightly burned. Natural sphere. Shows some bag ware. Natural nodule. 100% burned. Natural irregular tabular piece. Natural flattish, ovoid flake. Natural half sphere with cup-depression in center. Some grinding by cup.	442
-	Bones (67)	Jackrabbit (18; 5 burned, 5 boiled), Cottontail (17), Coyote (5), Dog (1), Bushy-tailed woodrat (1), Mule deer (1), Gunnison's prairie dog (6), Artiodactyl (6), mammal (12). Floor fill.	443
-	Anvil (13.0 x 11.0 x 3.0 cm; 627 g) Abrader-anvil (11.0 x 10.0 x 3.0 cm; 441 g)	2000 (sandstone). Floor fill. 2000 (sandstone), anvil on one face. Floor fill.	444
-	Chipped stone (14) Utilized flake (1.4 g) Utilized flakes (2) (total 31.0 g) Angular debris (3.7 g) Whole flake (1.1 g) Angular debris (2) (total 156.6 g) Angular debris (4) (total 10.3 g) Whole flakes (2) (total 5.7 g) Utilized flake (0.8 g)	Floor fill 1112 (cherty silicified wood). 1142 (chalcedonic silicified wood). 1112 (cherty silicified wood). 1044 (chert and silicified clasts of Morrison Formation). 1110 (splintery silicified wood). 1140 (chalcedonic silicified wood). 2202 (silicified concretion). 1113 (cherty silicified wood).	446

Table I.3.24. Site 29SJ 628, Pithouse E Distribution of Floor Fill and Floor 1 Materials, cont'd.[a]

Artifact Number	Artifact Class	Lithic Material, Ceramic Ware, or Faunal Species	FS No.
7	Awl (11.9 x 1.1 x 0.6 cm; 7.1 g)	Indeterminate large mammal shaft. Floor.	448
-	Corn cobs fragments (10; 2.8 g)	*Zea mays*. Carbonized. Floor fill.	449
-	Charcoal (25.8 g)	Floor fill.	450
-	Palette (17.6 x 11.6 x 4.7.0 cm; 942.7 g)	2000 (sandstone). Concretion fragment, half sphere. All surface ground with flat surface smeared with red paint (Munsell 2.5YR 5/6). Floor fill.	451
-	Shaft smoother (5.8 x 4.4 x 3.6 cm; 91.0 g)	2000 (coarse sandstone). Squarish block with 6 mm wide groove on opposite sides. Floor fill.	452
-	Bead fragment (4.2 x .6 mm)	2770 (calcite). White (Rock Color N9). 1.5 mm drill hole. Floor fill.	453
-	Malachite (10 x 8 x 4 mm; 0.6 g)	5320 (malachite). Natural nodule (Rock Color 10GY 5/2). Floor fill.	454
-	Groundstone (16.0 x 14.5 x 8.2 cm; 2385 g)	2000 (soft yellow sandstone). Natural block, slightly ground on top with 1 mm scratches & large (12 x 55 mm) groove in center. Slightly burned. Floor fill.	456a
-	Groundstone (19.0 x 17.0 x 7.8 cm; 3810 g)	2000 (hard gray sandstone). Irregular block, with sides pecked? Moderate grinding on top. Floor fill.	456b
-	Sherds (43)	Bench top (see Volume II, Table II.2.30).	471
-	Concretions (3) (5.5 x 5.4 x 4.7 cm; 157.7 g) (4.3 x 4.1 x 4.0 cm; 70.9 g) (5.2 x 2.9 x 1.6 cm; 20.0 g)	2000 (sandstone). Bench. Natural sphere. Natural sphere. Slightly burned. Natural irregular shape.	472
-	Stone	Bench. Missing.	473
-	Bones (8)	Jackrabbit (3), Cottontail (1), Pronghorn (2), mammal (2). Bench.	478
-	Core (85.5 g) Whole flake (8.5 g)	2221 (silicified sandstone). Bench. 1140 (chalcedonic silicified wood).	479
-	Retouched flake (18.7 g)	1112 (cherty silicified wood). Bench.	812
8	Turquoise (14 x 10 x 9 mm; 1.8 g)	5300 (turquoise). Nodule with 1 surface & 1 edge ground smooth. Rectangular, block shape. Some? matrix present. Rock Color 5G 7/4. Bench PH 16.	564
9	Manuport (5.5 x 2.6 x 1.4 cm; 24.3 g)	4000 (quartzite). Natural pebble. Bench PH 22.	563
10	Awl (9.7 x 1.6 x 0.3 cm; 4.0 g)	Jackrabbit (*Lepus* sp.) tibia. Bench PH 27.	475
11	Pipe (5.3 x 1.4-2.0 cm diameter; 19.2 g)	Light tan-gray unfired clay. Cracked & friable. Flared ridge (24 mm diameter) near cup end; 2mm hole through center. Bench PH 28.	474

Table I.3.24. Site 29SJ 628, Pithouse E Distribution of Floor Fill and Floor 1 Materials, cont'd.[a]

Artifact Number	Artifact Class	Lithic Material, Ceramic Ware, or Faunal Species	FS No.
12	Retouched flake (1.2 g)	3550 (Obsidian, Red Hill). Sourced by Shackley and Dillian (2000) to Mt. Taylor. Bench PH 29.	605
13	Bone	Cottontail (*Sylvilagus* sp.) tibia. Bench PH 33.	606
14	Pipe (5.7 x 2.3 cm diameter; 27.0 g)	Dark gray unfired clay. Cracked & friable. Cup end with 2-3 mm through center. Bench PH 40.	457
15	Whole flake (28.3 g)	1010 (fossiliferous chert). Bench PH 44.	482
16	Pendant (3.9 x 3.0 x 0.4 cm; 8.0 g)	5040 (gypsum). White (Rock Color N9). Both surfaces & all edges ground. Flat, rectangular shape, rounded on top where center hole (3 mm diameter) has worn through edge. Bench PH 49.	481
16	Utilized flake (3.8 g)	1142 (chalcedonic silicified wood). Bench PH 49.	483
17	Turquoise (9 x 6 x2 mm; 0.1 g)	5300 (turquoise). Both surfaces and all edges ground smooth. Some matrix present. Rock Color 10G 8/2 & 10GY 6/4. OP 1.	491
-	Sherds (93)	Floor (see Volume II, Table II.2.30).	480
-	Abrader (13.2 x 13.1 x 3.0 cm; 736 g)	2000 (sandstone). Tabular, triangular shape. 2 surfaces ground (1 fine). Floor.	484a
-	Abrader (8.0 x 7.0 x 3.0 cm; 272.0 g)	2000 (sandstone). Tabular, rectangular shape. 2 surfaces ground (1 fine). Floor.	484b
-	Chipped stones (7): Utilized flake (7.2 g) Utilized flake (2; total 113.3 g) Retouched flake (4.5 g) Angular debris (8.5 g) Utilized flake (0.4 g) Angular debris (4.4 g)	Floor 1072 (Zuni yellow-spotted chert). 1140 (chalcedonic silicified chert). 1140 (chalcedonic silicified chert). 1142 (chalcedonic silicified chert). 3520 (Jemez obsidian). OHL # 7689. Sourced to Valle Grande (Shackley and Dillian 2000). 5010 (colorless quartz).	485
-	Mineral (6.4 x 3.3 x 0.8 cm; 22.6 g)	5041 (gypsum selenite). Natural, flat piece.	485B
-	Hammerstone (5.3 x 5.3 x 3.3 cm; 93.3 g)	1112 (cherty silicified wood). Spherical, battered along edges. Reused tested core?	485C
-	Hammerstone (7.5 x 6.6 x 5.8 cm; 417.1 g)	4000 (gray quartzite). Spherical, battered along edges.	485C
-	Manuport (8.3 x 3.2 x 2.0 cm; 102.1 g)	4000 (brown quartzite). Broken natural pebble, split lengthwise.	485C
-	Pecking Stone (7.7 x 5.1 x 3.8 cm; 193.3 g)	4000 (quartzite). Broken natural pebble, battered on both ends.	485C
-	Mineral (6.6 x 3.4 x 1.2 cm; ? g)	5041 (gypsum selenite). Missing.	485
-	Abrader (9.2+ x 9.2 x 3.5 cm; 465 g)	2000 (sandstone). Tabular, rectangular fragment? 1 finely ground surface. Burned. orange (Munsell 5YR 5/8) paint smear. Floor.	486a
-	Mano fragment (7.0+ x 10.0 x 3.1 cm; 330.1 g)	2000 (sandstone). 100% burned; sooted. 1 ground surface. Floor.	486b

Table I.3.24. Site 29SJ 628, Pithouse E Distribution of Floor Fill and Floor 1 Materials, cont'd.[a]

Artifact Number	Artifact Class	Lithic Material, Ceramic Ware, or Faunal Species	FS No.
-	Bones (11)	Jackrabbit (2), Cottontail (4), Pronghorn (3), Mule deer (1), artiodacyl (1). Floor	487
-	Adobe chunks (5; largest 15 x 14.3 x 11 cm thick; 1033 g; total 2702 g)	Gray adobe. 2 with double beam impressions (estimated 6 & 11 cm diameters; estimated 5 & 7 cm diameters). Floor	488
-	Corncob fragment (1.2 g)	*Zea mays*. Carbonized. Floor	489
-	Charcoal (6.5 g)	Carbonized brush. Floor	490
18	Anvil-abrader (30.3 x 20.7 x 5.8 cm; 5.3 kg)	2000 (sandstone). Natural rectangular, tabular block. High spots on bottom worn. 1 surface finely ground with horseshoe-pecked pattern. Slightly burned. Ventilator tunnel	498
18	Sherds (15)	Ventilator tunnel (see Volume II, Table II.2.30)	499
18	Concretion (8.0 x 7.0 x 2.1 cm; 130 g)	2000 (sandstone). Natural tabular, rectangular shape with cup (31 mm diameter & 9 mm deep) in center. Slight grinding. Ventilator tunnel	500
18	Bones (3)	Jackrabbit (1), Cottontail (1), artiodactyl (1). Ventilator tunnel	501
18	Pot cover (5.7 x 5.6 x 1.1 cm; 61 g)	2000 (sandstone). Tabular; disc shape formed by edge chipping. Ventilator tunnel	502a
18	Firepit liner? (6.7+ x 4.4+ x 1.5 cm; 92.0+ g)	2000 (sandstone). Tabular, rectangular shape. 80% burned. Minor grinding on 1 edge. Ventilator tunnel	502b
18	Angular debris (28.0 g)	1110 (splintery silicified wood). Ventilator tunnel	503
18	Awl (13.8 x 1.4 x 0.5 cm; 9.1 g)	Indeterminate large mammal shaft. Ventilator tunnel	559
19	Hatch? cover fragment (21.5+ x 30.0 x 2.3 cm; 2016g)	2000 (sandstone). Thin, tabular slab, moderate grinding on 1 surface. Burned spot. Ventilator shaft floor	514
19	Mano fragment (11.2+ x 12.9 x 3.0 cm; 593+ g)	2000 (sandstone). 2 ground surfaces (1 fine). Ventilator shaft floor	515
19	Bead (5mm diameter, 1.4 mm thick)	5420 (serpentine). 2 mm hole straight through disc. Ground, all sides and edges. Ventilator shaft floor.	516
19	Concretions (7) (5.8 x 5.2 cm; 170.2 g) (4.7 x 5.1 cm; 126.9 g) (3.5 x 2.8 cm; 34.5 g) (3.3 x 2.7 cm; 29.2 g) (3.4 x 2.8 cm; 34.1 g) (5.7 x 2.4 cm; 54.2 g) (4.5 x 1.7 cm; 29.2 g)	2000 (sandstone). Ventilator shaft floor (see Volume II, Chapter 9) Slightly burned, natural sphere Natural sphere Natural spheroid Natural sphere with some light grinding/wear. 1 ground facet Natural sphere Partial sphere with cupped out center. Hollow shrimp burrow ring, 1 edge ground	516

Table I.3.24. Site 29SJ 628, Pithouse E Distribution of Floor Fill and Floor 1 Materials, cont'd.[a]

Artifact Number	Artifact Class	Lithic Material, Ceramic Ware, or Faunal Species	FS No.
19	Sherds (11)	Ventilator shaft floor (see Volume II, Table II.2.30).	517
19	Bones (16)	Jackrabbit (4), Cottontail (8), Coyote (1), Mountain sheep (1), mammal (2). Ventilator shaft floor.	518
19	Floor polisher fragment? (7.5+ x 5.8+ x 1.8++ cm; 103+ g)	4000 (quartzite). 100% burned cobble fragment. Ventilator shaft floor.	519
19	Chipped stones (3) Utilized flake (4.1 g) Utilized flake (6.8 g) Core (23.3 g)	Ventilator shaft floor 1150 (yellow-brown silicified wood). 1140 (light-colored to white chalcedonic silicified wood). 1145 (dark-colored chalcedonic silicified wood).	519
19	Charcoal (5.8 g)	Ventilator shaft floor.	520
-	Charcoal (7.6 g)	Floor.	555
20	Lino Smudged bowl sherd	Southwest PH.	537
21	Retouched flake (3.5 g)	1050 (white chert). Northeast PH.	556
21	Hammerstone (6.4 x 6.0 x 5.4 cm; 225.2 g)	1112 (cherty silicified wood). Northeast PH.	557
22	Awl (11.9 x 1.7 x 0.5 cm; 14.1 g)	Indeterminate large mammal shaft. Floor.	565
23	Polishing stone (9.5 x 5.7 x 1.6 cm; 151 g)	3000 (igneous rock). Natural pebble with 1 polished surface and yellow (Munsell 7.5YR 6/6) paint smear. Floor.	612
24	Stone	Red cobble? Floor. Missing.	613
25	Mano (15.0 x 12.0 x 2.6 cm; 800.8 g)	2000 (sandstone). 2 ground surfaces; 3 large flakes removed at edges. Edge burned. Floor.	614
26	Concretion fetish (14.9 x 8.3 x 6.8 cm; 900.2 g)	2000 (sandstone). Natural crude Venus-like (with swollen belly & no head). Floor.	615
27	Mano (18.2 x 9.5 x 2.6 cm; 661 g)	2000 (sandstone). 2 ground surfaces with white (Rock Color N9) splots and red (Munsell 2.5YR 4/6) paint smear on 1 surface. Floor.	616
28	Polishing stone (12.5 x 5.6 x 2.2 cm; 277 g)	4450 (green shist). Oblong, flattish shape. Natural pebble with 1 smoothed surface. Floor.	617
29	Mano (17.8 x 11.8 x 3.7 cm; 1402.2 g)	2000 (sandstone). 2 ground surfaces. Red (Munsell 10R 4/6) paint smear on 1 surface. Floor.	618
30	Mano (17.1 x 10.6 x 2.7 cm; 758.0 g)	2000 (sandstone). 2 ground surfaces. Floor.	619
31	Lapidary abrader (20 x 17.2 x 3.0 cm; 1828.7 g)	2000 (sandstone). Tabular, triangular shaped. 2 ground surfaces (1 fine). Floor.	620

Table I.3.24. Site 29SJ 628, Pithouse E Distribution of Floor Fill and Floor 1 Materials, cont'd.[a]

Artifact Number	Artifact Class	Lithic Material, Ceramic Ware, or Faunal Species	FS No.
32	Firepit liner? (15.3 x 13.8 x 3.3 cm; 756 g)	2000 (sandstone). Tabular, irregular shape. 100% burned; sooted. Small area ground on 1 surface. Floor.	621
33	Pot cover? fragment (10.5+ x 6.3+ x 2.3 cm; 305 g)	2000 (sandstone). Partial disc shape with 1 ground surface & edge. Ground surface covered in yellow paint (Munsell 10YR 6/8).	622
34	Manuport (5.8 x 5.7 x 3.3 cm; 155.7 g)	4000 (quartzite). Burned natural pebble fragment. Floor.	623
-	Sherds (3): Plain gray (1) Lino Fugitive Red (1) Unclassified PII-PIII whiteware jar (1)	Floor (see Volume II, Table II.3.20).	756
-	Bone	Floor. Missing.	757
-	Worked bone (awl/needle fragment?)(8.1+ x 0.7 x 0.3 cm; 2.6+ g)	Indeterminate medium-to-large mammal split shaft. Floor fill.	798
-	Worked bone	Jackrabbit (*Lepus californicus*) tibia. Floor fill.	799

[a] See distribution in Figure I.3.27. All bones examined for cooking brown and burning (Akins: analysis data base).

Table I.3.25. Site 29SJ 628, Pithouse A Distribution of Floor 1 Materials.[a]

Artifact Number	Artifact Class	Lithic Material, Ceramic Ware, or Faunal Species.	FS No.
-	Charcoal (56.4 g)	Piñon (*Pinus edulis*), Juniperus sp., greasewood (*Sarcobatus vermiculatus*), sagebrush (*Artemesia* sp.), misc. shrubs. Floor.	70
-	Radiocarbon sample (7.9 g)	Greasewood (*Sarcobatus vermiculatus*) & sagebrush (*Artemesia* sp.). Calibrated date A.D. 710±60 (see Table I.6.4). Floor.	70
1	Worked bone	Jackrabbit (*Lepus californicus*) radius. Edge rounded. Floor. Missing.	71
2	Awl (11.7 x 1.3 x 0.5 cm; 10.2 g)	Indeterminate large mammal shaft splinter. Floor.	72
-	Roofing adobe (19 x 12.5 x 7.9 cm; 1408 g)	Vegetal impressed on 1 side; opposite side impressed with 2 est 5 cm diameter parallel beams. Sooted. Floor.	73
3	Needle (6.3 x 0.8 x 0.1 cm; 0.9 g)	Indeterminate medium-to-large mammal shaft fragment. Floor 1.	74

Table I.3.25. Site 29SJ 628, Pithouse A Distribution of Floor 1 Materials, cont'd.[a]

Artifact Number	Artifact Class	Lithic Material, Ceramic Ware, or Faunal Species	FS No.
-	Sherds (13)	Floor	
	Lino Gray jar necks and rims (6)	Cibola Grayware.	
	Lino Gray jar w/ fugitive red (1)	Cibola Grayware.	
	Plain gray (2)	Cibola Grayware.	
	Obelisk Gray jar w/ fugitive red (1)	Cibola Grayware.	
	Lino B/g bowl (2)	Tusayan Whiteware.	
	Woodruff Smudged bowl (1)	Mogollon tradition.	76
4	Antler (18.5 g)	Mule deer (*Odocoileus hemionus*) skull polished. Slightly mislocated on map (<35 cm). Floor. Missing.	77
-	Corncob fragment (1.1 g)	Floor.	78
5	Charcoal (85.9 g)	Piñon (*Pinus edulis*), *Juniperus* sp., greasewood (*Sarcobatus vermiculatus*)/saltbrush (*Atriplex* sp.), sagebrush (*Artemesia* sp.), corn (*Zea mays*; 2 cob fragments), misc. shrubs. FP 1 fill.	79
5	Radiocarbon sample (9.9 g)	Greasewood (*Sarcobatus vermiculatus*)/saltbrush (*Atriplex* sp.) & sagebrush (*Artemesia* sp.). Calibrated date AD 700±50 (see Vol. I, Table I.6.4). FP 1 fill.	79
5	Bean fragments (4; 0.1 g)	*Phaseolus* sp. Carbonized. FP 1.	80
5	Sherd	FP 1 fill.	
	Lino Red (Tallahogan Red) bowl (1)	Cibola? Tradition.	83
5	Concretion (55 cm diameter; 122 g)	2000 (sandstone). Burned. FP 1 fill.	84
-	Chipped stones (5)	Floor	
	Core (251.1 g)	1053 (chalcedonic High Surface Chert).	
	Utilized flake (139.2 g)	1110 (splintery silicified wood).	
	Utilized flake (2.8 g)	1113 (cherty silicified wood).	
	Utilized flakes (2)(total 103. 5 g)	1140 (chalcedonic silicified wood).	87
-	Minerals (4.2 x 3.1 x 0.6, 7.5 g; 2.5 x 1.9 x 0.8, 4.3 g)	5041 (gypsum selenite). Natural, tabular, irregular pieces.	87C
-	Bones (22)	Jackrabbit (4; 1 burned); cottontail rabbit (8; 1 burned); prairie dog (2; 1 burned), pocket gopher (2), pronghorn antelope (2), wolf (1), unidentified mammal (3). Floor.	88
6	Awl (9.9 x 1.4 x 1.7 cm; 11.1 g)	Artiodactyl metapodial. SE PH fill.	90
6	Wood fragments (44.7 g)	SE PH fill.	91

Table I.3.25. Site 29SJ 628, Pithouse A Distribution of Floor 1 Materials, cont'd.[a]

Artifact Number	Artifact Class	Lithic Material, Ceramic Ware, or Faunal Species	FS No.
6	Concretion (13.1 x 3.9 x 2.4 cm; 197.2 g)	2000 (sandstone). Natural rib-shaped piece. SE PH shim.	92
7	Sherd (1): plain gray	NW Posthole.	93
8	Charcoal (5.5 g)	NW Posthole.	96
9	Charcoal (6.2 g)	SW Posthole.	94
-	Concretions (4) (13.0 x 9.7 x 4.8 cm; 580.1 g) (7.8 x 6.6 x 5.5 cm; 319.1 g) (5.5 cm diameter x 4.1 cm; 104.7 g) (2.9 cm diameter x 1.6 cm; 9.6 g)	2000 (sandstone). Floor.	
10	Retouched flake (blade)(9.6 g)	Burned.	95
-	Polishing stone? (5.0 x 4.3 x 2.9 cm; 89.6 g)	1054 (chalcedonic High Surface Chert). WN A fill. Missing.	89
11	Concretions (2) (5.7 cm diameter x 3.2 cm; 99.2 g) (11.2 x 4.3 x 3.8 cm; 278.2 g)	4000 (quartzite). Natural pebble. Floor.	97
11	Sherds (5): Lino Gray (1) Plain gray (2) Lino Smudged (2)	2000 (sandstone). WN 2(B) fill. Tool type #7.	101
11	Hammerstone? (8.7 x 8.3 x 4.2 cm; 477.6 g)	WN 2 (B) fill. Cibola Grayware. Cibola Grayware. Cibola Grayware.	102
12	Sherds (2): Lino Fugitive Red (1) La Plata B/w (1)	1111 (splintery silicified wood). Natural block-shape; minor pounding on 1 end. WN 2 (B) fill.	103
12	Worked clay (5; largest 7.3 x 5.3 x 1.5 cm; total 104.2 g)	WN 3 (C) fill. Cibola Grayware. Cibola Whiteware.	107
13	Corncob fragment (0.8 g)	Crude, tabular, slightly curved fragments (none fit together) of unfired clay; 1 rounded edge. 10YR 7/2 gray. WN 3 (C) floor.	235
13	Bones (2)	Zea mays (carbonized). WN 4 (D) fill.	114
13	Charcoal (5.8 g)	Jackrabbit (Lepus californicus) radius & unidentified medium-to-large mammal rib. WN 4 (D) fill.	115
		WN 4 (D) fill.	116

268 Windes et al.

Table I.3.25. Site 29SJ 628, Pithouse A Distribution of Floor 1 Materials, cont'd.[a]

Artifact Number	Artifact Class	Lithic Material, Ceramic Ware, or Faunal Species	FS No.
14	Selenite (6.5 x 4.2 x 1.2 cm; 35.9 g; 1.6 x 1.4 x 0.7 cm; 1.2 g)	5041 (selenite gypsum). Natural chunks. WN 5 (E).	108
14	Sherds (4): Plain gray (3) La Plata B/w (1)	WN 5 (E). Cibola Grayware. Cibola Whiteware.	109
14	Charcoal (7.2 g)	WN 5 (E).	110
14	Bones (2)	Cottontail (*Sylvilagus* sp.) mandible & metacarpel. WN 5 (E).	111
14	Knife (6.1 x 5.5 x 1.0 cm; 51.0 g)	4000 (quartzite). Discoid, flat natural pebble. Edge 65 percent bi- and unifacially flaked, plus rare hammering along edge. Wall Niche 5 (E) fill. Not a "pecking stone."	822
15	Blade (bifacially flaked, non-hafted) (3.2 x 2.3 x 0.6 cm; 4.1g)	3520 (Jemez Mt. obsidian). WN 6 (F) fill. Sourced to Valle Grande by Shackley and Dillian (2000).	117
16	Sherds (3) Lino Gray Fugitive red jar fragments (2) White Mound? B/w bowl rim with Fugitive red exterior	In ventilator tunnel. Each piece smashed during excavation. Cibola Graywar. Cibola Whiteware.	99
17	Metate fragment (26.8 x 16.8 x 6.3 cm; 3856 g)	2000 (sandstone). Floor.	134
-	Lino Gray jar sherd	Cibola Grayware (sooted). Renumbered from FS 99. Unlikely to be FS 134 from the floor.	134
18	Palette (18.5+ x 17.7+ x 4.5 cm; 1860.9 g)	2000 (sandstone). Metate fragment with red (2.5YR 4/4±) paint smear in trough. Rests on 2 flat slabs. Floor.	128
19	Floor polisher? (10.9 x 10.2 x 8.2 cm; 1308 g)	2000 (fine sandstone). Natural sphere ground on 2 opposite curving sides. Floor.	129
20	Mano fragment (10.5+ x 10.7 x 2.5 cm; 448.0 g)	2000 (sandstone). 1 end chipped during manufacture. Rested inside FS 126.	125
21	Lino Gray partial seed jar	Cibola Grayware. Heavily sooted. Has mano fragment (FS 125) inside. Floor?	126
22	Scraper? (16.6 x 3.1 x 0.4 cm; 23.5 g)	Large mammal mandible; edges rounded & smoothed. Floor.	130

[a] See distribution in Figure I.3.29. All bones examined for cooking brown and burning (Akins; analysis data base).

Table I.3.26. Site 29SJ 628, Pithouse F Distribution of Floor Fill and Floor 1 Materials.[a]

Artifact Number	Artifact Class	Lithic Material, Ceramic Ware, or Faunal Species	FS No.
Pithouse F			
1	Firepit liner? (33 x 28 x 3.1 cm; 2773.5 g)	2000 (sandstone). Tabular, sub-oval shape. Edge chipped & some edge grinding. 1 face is 70 percent burned. Broken into 3 pieces. Floor.	634
2	Groundstone (20+ x 38 x 7.1cm; 8.85 kg)	2000 (sandstone). Tabular, squarish shape. 2 ground surfaces (1 light, 1 moderate). Floor fill.	635
3	Firepit liner/lapidary? abrader (23.3 x 17.0 x 2.4 cm; 1443 g)	2000 (sandstone). Tabular, rectangular shape. 80 percent burned with narrow area ground though burned material. Embedded in floor.	636
3	Charcoal (3.0 g)	Under FS 636.	669
4	Charcoal (5.6 g)	HP 2, Pot rest fill?	670
5	Awl (8.6 x 1.4 x 0.4 cm; 1.1 g)	Indeterminate large mammal shaft splinter. Northwest PH.	678
6	Charcoal (11.2 g)	Juniper (*Juniperus* sp.), mountain mahogany (*Cercocarpus montanus*), greasewood (*Sarcobatus vermiculatus*). FP 1 fill.	683

[a] See distribution in Figure I.3.20. All bones examined for cooking brown and burning (Akins: analysis data base).

270 Windes et al.

Table I.3.27. Site 29SJ 628, Surface Storage Cists and Firepit 2, Distribution of Materials.[a]

Artifact Number	Artifact Class	Lithic Material, Ceramic Ware, or Faunal Species	FS No.
Cist 1			
-	Sherds (81)	In fill between floors (see Volume II, Table II.2.30)	118
1	Lino Gray seed jar (crushed)	43 cm below surface (lower floor contact). Contained yellow clay. Set in Floor 1, rested on Floor 2. See Table II.2.11a and Plate II.3.5.	119
1	Clay (3 bags)	Unusual yellow clay. Contents of FS 119.	120
-	Azurite (6; largest 6 x 5 x 4 mm; total 0.8 g)	5310 (azurite). Rock Color 5PB 3/2. Subfloor fill.	121
-	Bones (26)	Jack rabbit (7), cottontail rabbit (14), prairie dog (4), rock squirrel (1). Fill.	122
-	Concretions (3) (9.0 x 5.2 x 4.9 cm; 220 g) (5.0 x 4.5 x 2.7 cm; 64.0 g) (4.8 x 4.8 x 1.0 cm; 28.0 g)	2000 (sandstone). Fill. Natural lump with minor grinding? Discoidal/subspherical natural piece. Fragment.	123
-	Concretion (2.0 x 2.0 x 0.8 cm; 5.1 g)	Manganese?, natural piece.	123
-	Chipped stones (4) Angular flake (1.9 g) Utilized flake (2.7 g) Angular debris (2; total 4.3 g)	Fill (above upper floor) 1113 (cherty silicified wood). 1140 (chalcedonic silicified wood). 1140 (chalcedonic silicified wood).	124
2	Awl (7.8 x 1.3 x 1.8 cm; 7 g)	Artiodactyl metapodial tip. Floor 2 (location approximate).	135
-	Charcoal for species identification	Level 1 fill.	141
3	Pot polishing stone (4.7 x 3.7 x 1.1 cm; 34 g)	4000 (quartzite). Natural pebble. Floor 2.	147
4	Polishing stone? (9.3 x 7.1 x 4.2 cm; 419 g)	4000 (quartzite). Natural cobble. Floor 2.	148
5	Polishing stone (13 x 9.5 x 4.8 cm; 819 g)	3300 (andesite?, green with black specks). Igneous cobble from the San Juan River drainage? Floor 2 fill (9 cm above floor).	149
Cist 2			
-	Sherds (42)	Fill (see Volume II, Table 2.30).	136
-	Chipped stones (4) Utilized flake (5.0 g) Utilized flake (3; total 56.6 g)	Fill 1112 (cherty silicified wood). 1150 (jasper silicified wood).	137
-	Hammerstone? (6.5 x 4.0 x 3.9 cm; 142.5 g)	1142 (chalcedonic silicified wood). Slight pounding & smudge of red paint (Munsell 2.5YR 5/8).	137A

Table I.3.27. Site 29SJ 628, Surface Storage Cists and Firepit 2, Distribution of Materials, cont'd.[a]

Artifact Number	Artifact Class	Lithic Material, Ceramic Ware, or Faunal Species	FS No.
-	Bones (7)	Jack rabbit (4), cottontail rabbit (2), small/medium mammal (1) Fill.	138
6	Mano fragment	2000 (sandstone). Fill? Lost in field?	-
Cist 1 & 2			
-	Pot cover fragments (2; est. 20 diameter x 1.9 cm; 604+ g)	2000 (sandstone). Sooted on 1 surface & slightly ground on other. Concretion disc (see Volume II, Chapter 9).	748
Cist 3			
-	Bone	Artiodactyl long bone fragment.	181
Cist 4			
-	Sherds (6)	See Volume II, Table II.2.30,	244
-	Metate fragment? (16.5+ x 10.7+ x 2.4 cm; 532.2+ g)	2000 (sandstone). 3 pieces.	245
-	Mano fragment (8.2+ x 10.2+ x 2.4 cm; 291.5 g)	2000 (sandstone). 1 surface ground.	246a
-	Mano fragment (6.5+ x 8.8+ x 2.2 cm; 164.8+ g)	2000 (sandstone). 1 surface with some grinding.	246b
-	Pendant (3.1 x 3.1 x 0.4 cm; 11.7 g)	Manganese? concretion with 2 mm biconical hole near center of 1 edge. Squarish with all 4 edges & 1 surface ground. Rock Color 10R 2/2. Surface near Cist 4.	672
Cist 5			
-	Sherds (25)	See Volume II, Table II.2.30.	665
-	Mano (15.4 x 10.9 x 2.5 cm; 554 g)	2000 (sandstone). Ground on 2 surfaces. Worn out.	666
-	Bones (4)	Jack rabbit (1), cottontail rabbit (1), mid-to-large mammal (2).	667
-	Chipped stones (3) Core (38.4 g) Core (69.8 g) Utilized flake (0.9 g)	Fill? 1112 (cherty silicified wood). 1140 (chalcedonic silitificified wood). 3510 (Grants Ridge obsidian). Sourced to Mt. Taylor by Shackley and Dillian (2000). Formerly identified as Red Hill obsidian by Cameron and Sappington (1984).	668
-	Limonite (3.4 x 1.5 x 0.8 cm; 5.3 g)	5110 (yellow ocher). Ground on 1 surface of wedge-shaped natural piece. Used for paint? (Munsell 2.5Y 6/6).	674
Firepit 2			
-	Tallahogan Red sherd	In the fill.	738

[a] See distribution in Figures I.3.32-I.3.34. All bones examined for cooking brown and burning (Akins: analysis data base).

Chapter 4
Pueblo I Site Excavation Reports

This chapter summarizes the site reports for excavations and tests conducted by the Chaco Center between 1973 and 1975 at four sites in and outside of Chaco Canyon: 29Mc 184, 29SJ 299 (PI component), 29SJ 721, and 29SJ 724. Testing at 29Mc 184 in 1975 was done to determine if it was an early Pueblo II site. This site, however, is part of an unusually large Pueblo I community discussed in Chapter 8. The Pueblo I house at 29SJ 299 is reported here; other, mostly earlier components, were covered in Chapter 3. All the components at 29SJ 721, including a possible Basketmaker III pithouse and an unfinished late Pueblo II/early Pueblo III kiva, are reported here. 29SJ 724 consists of three Pueblo I houseblocks, of which only the middle one was excavated. Tests in the northern roomblock midden are also covered here.

Previously, few Pueblo I sites had been investigated in Chaco Canyon unless they were uncovered in the excavations at later sites or exposed in the banks of the Chaco Wash. The most notable exceptions are the masonry buildings marking the initial focal points of greathouse construction at a number of sites in the canyon and throughout the San Juan Basin (Judd 1964; Windes 2004, 2007; Windes and Ford 1996) by at least the mid-A.D. 800s. Early work in these canyon structures (e.g., Pepper 1920) failed to take note of floor features, so we are unable to decipher whether they represent typical early habitation units or the crucial shift to public architecture. The arc-shaped footprint of the buildings is typical of A.D. 800s Pueblo I house construction, and it is also characteristic of early greathouses.

Pithouses of Pueblo I age were also found under the sites and middens in the Casa Rinconada area (Senter 1939) and exposed in the wash bank near Chetro Ketl (Judd 1924). These houses are reported in Chapter 5. Tabulated data can be found at the end of the chapter, and figures and photos are interspersed throughout.

TESTING AT 29MC 184

Several sites were tested in the summer of 1975 to locate a site that had been occupied in the early A.D. 800s. Aside from the slab architecture denoting such a site, ceramics of Kana'a Banded-style grayware and Kiatuthlanna Black-on-white were assumed to be the temporal Pueblo I indicators—expectations that we now know are temporally wrong for the Chaco region and the greater San Juan Basin. One of the sites selected for testing was well advertised by a series of slab-lined surface structures (Plate I.4.1) just east of State Road 57, about 14 km south of the park.

This site was apparently visited and inventoried (as Site "4x") as early as the 1920s or 1930s by J. Edgar Hewett's staff on the Smith Ranch, where substantial survey and excavations were being carried out. The first known recorded collections were made by Joel Shiner for the National Park Service in 1957 (Table I.4.1), although he collected some surprisingly late sherds that are not matched by any found there today. Shiner provides the first observation that we know of for the "many single roomed structures on the mesa," which denotes the early community here.

Three separate houses are evident at 29Mc

Plate I.4.1. 29Mc 184, House C, single family habitation unit outlined by wall foundation slabs. a. Looking north; Peter McKenna behind backwall (CHCU neg. 12109B). b. Looking southwest (CHCU neg. 12110). Photographs by Tom Windes, 1974.

184, each marked by rows of upright slabs along a ridge at an elevation of 1,971 m (6,465 ft). A fourth house was later found along the same alignment as the other three but there was less surface evidence for it. All faced southeast with depressions marking buried pitstructures in front of the houses and with refuse areas beyond. The area around the southwestern house in the series (House C) was sufficiently deflated to reveal all four rooms (Figure I.4.1, Table I.4.2). The site is notable in that there were no subsequent occupations either overlying it or in close vicinity, unlike the majority of Pueblo I sites within the park. It is also notable that the two eastern houses (Houses A and B) formed prominent mounds in contrast to all other Pueblo I houses in the valley. The associated middens for these two, however, were not voluminous (a total of about 61 m^3).

Testing was conducted in each of the midden areas by use of 1.5-x-1.5-m pits excavated until sterile deposits were reached. A lack of specimens occurred after only 8-20-cm of soft, charcoal-flecked sand was removed. Overall, the average depth of the middens was probably no more than 12-cm. Refuse in front of the southwestern house rested on brownish gray clay in a slight depression, perhaps overlying a buried pithouse. All fill was screened through quarter-inch mesh and then replaced in the pits after placing beer cans at the bottom in each corner.

Surface ceramics were primarily plain gray, Lino Gray (i.e., necks and rims), and occasionally San Juan Redware, La Plata Black-on-white and White Mound Black-on-white, and two well-polished and slipped decorated sherds similar to White Mound Black-on-white. Two neckbanded sherds were also observed. Testing revealed no differences from the types and frequencies recovered in the surface samples (Table I.4.1).

It is instructive to compare the various ceramic tallies made at different times and by different sampling strategies (see Table I.4.1). Note the loading of decorated and rare ceramics from the 1957 and 1972 grab samples that skew the ceramic time into the A.D. 900s for the site occupation. Even more important is the loss of the late sherds from the surface caused by collection. While it is not as dramatic here, such loss at other sites can sometimes affect the temporal placement of the ceramic assemblage owing to the loss of the rare, temporally sensitive sherds from their original context. I suspect that the highly visible site location next to the road, which probably attracted Shiner, has also led to the loss of other rare ceramics that might have indicated subsequent (e.g., A.D. 900s) occupation at the site, or, as discussed later, postoccupational offerings deposited at the site.

From these ceramic remains, we can deduce that occupation was relatively short and occurred at about A.D. 750-850 or a little later, similar to 29SJ 724. In retrospect, the period was exactly what was being sought by Hayes but the overall lack of neckbanded sherds caused the search to shift elsewhere, eventually settling on the

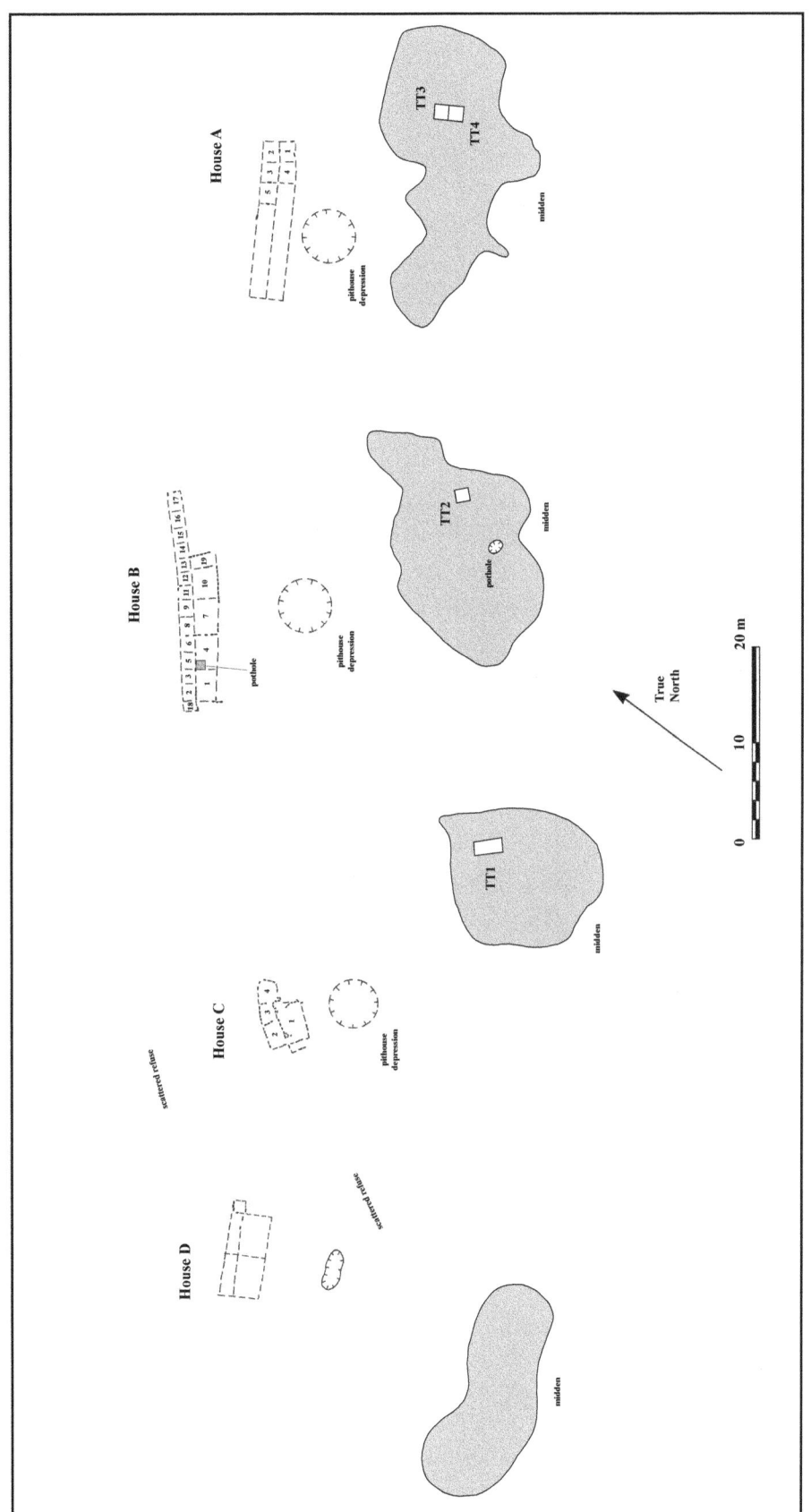

Figure I.4.1. 29Mc 184, plan of the four Pueblo I houses in the South Fork Valley, Fajada Wash (CHCU 6598I). Houses A and B are partly built with Type I masonry. Squares mark test pits. Modified from the 1975 original by Tom Windes and Johnny Martinez.

excavation of 29SJ 629 (Windes 1993), which was much too late.

In the 1990s, 29Mc 184 was reinvestigated to broaden our understanding of the site occupation within the larger area. The adjacent valley and ridges, covering about five square miles, were surveyed with the help of the Sierra Club to document the valley occupation. This research was enormously successful and led to the discovery of an associated large Pueblo I community and a probable great kiva adjacent to 29Mc 184, with a more widespread Pueblo II settlement scattered up and down the valley but spatially distinct from the Pueblo I settlement. The surface of each midden was examined (Table I.4.1) and a select number of sites was chosen for chipped stone in-field analysis (Moss, Volume II).

Despite the lack of further excavation at 29Mc 184, the occupation of this site and within the surrounding area provides an important perspective on the Pueblo I of the Chaco Canyon environs. It has been difficult to obtain a clear picture of the Chaco Pueblo I occupation because it was thought that the vast majority of the early occupations were buried beneath locations that saw sustained residential use and reuse. In the 29Mc 184 area, however, Pueblo I sites are widespread and unobscured by later occupations.

The long, shallow valley overlooked by 29Mc 184 and a host of other Pueblo I sites runs for over 30 km back into Chaco Canyon through Fajada Gap, adjacent to Fajada Butte. Runoff flows north and empties into the Fajada (Vicente) Wash, which empties into the Chaco Wash. The physical connection of the site and its environs to Chaco provides an opportunity to assess the cultural continuity between the two areas, particularly in light of the efforts expended in excavations at Fajada Gap and the examination of the Fajada Gap Community (Windes 1993).

Although South Fork Valley appears barren of cover and unappealing for habitation, it was the focus of widespread occupation during the Pueblo I period. Luckily, the proximity of a number of Pueblo I houses near 29Mc 184 appears to make the location one of the most important in the valley (see Chapter 8). Downslope from 29Mc 184 to the south is another large Pueblo I house, and several other smaller houses occur to the east and northeast. Close by is a partial arc of upright slabs (29Mc 620) that may mark an early great kiva. Pueblo I houses are found on a number of ridges and hills bordering the valley, while storage facilities in the form of large, oval, slab-lined cists occur adjacent to or within the primary drainage areas. This pattern seems to occur in other major drainages to the west that drain into the Kin Klizhin and Kin Bineola washes and eventually into the Chaco River. A number of large circles of upright slabs in these areas (e.g., two just north of Bee Burrow ruins and one near Upper Kin Klizhin) may also mark community centers.

Nevertheless, the valley clearly lacks resources that would seem paramount for sustained, intensive settlement. No trees exist to provide cover, building materials, or fuel for occupants today, and water could only be obtained, intermittently, from the valley bottom. In order to grow crops in the valley, it seems likely that a wetter climate would have been necessary. A rain gauge placed in the valley on 1 January 1995 enables comparison with the other gauges in the area (see Chapter 2). The South Fork Valley gauge almost always provides the least amount of precipitation during every season, particularly when compared with the nine gauges set along the length and breadth of nearby Chaco Canyon.

Although the readings may not reflect prehistoric conditions, given the recent placement of the gauge and the current environmental trends, nevertheless it is instructive. South Fork Valley provides an ideal laboratory for future research of Chacoan settlement during the Pueblo I and Pueblo II periods, especially during the transition from scattered hamlet occupation to the aggregated greathouse communities that took place in the late A.D. 800s/early 900s.

Further Investigations at 29SJ 299

In 1974, excavations by the author recommenced at 29SJ 299 with a focus on the Pueblo I occupation evident to the southwest of the Basketmaker pithouses (see Chapter 3; Figure I.3.2) in the form of four contiguous slab-lined surface storage rooms. The investigations began with the author, who cleared the ramada and surface rooms, but William Gillespie and Kelly Masterson excavated half of the pithouse in 1974 after the author left to investigate stone circles (Windes 1978). The assignment of structure and field specimen numbers continued from that of the previous year's excavations.

Pithouse E (Figures I.4.2 and I.4.3, Plate I.4.2)

Unlike the Basketmaker houses, Pithouse E was deeply buried by alluvial deposits. Its location was predicted on the basis of the room and ramada behind it. Time constraints allowed only about half of the pithouse to be excavated.

Fill

A semicircle of charcoal-flecked sand bordered by sterile yellow-tan sand first indicated the presence of Pithouse E. Seven arbitrary levels were required to remove the 220-cm of overburden. The uppermost 185-cm of fill (Levels 1 through 5) had accumulated naturally and was composed of sands flecked with charcoal and interspersed with thin, water-deposited layers of clay and occasional lenses of refuse and charcoal. Most of the pottery recovered from these units was Pueblo II and derived from activities associated with subsequent use of the location after the pithouse was abandoned.

A small, posthole-like pit, burned on the sides and filled with ash and charcoal, was found about a meter below the surface within the naturally deposited overburden. At 160-cm depth, three more small unlined pits were arranged in a row extending less than a meter, with a fourth one centered slightly more than a meter from the row. These pits ranged in diameter from 8 to 14-cm and were 7-cm deep. They pits resemble those found in the fill of Pithouse A at 29SJ 724 (this chapter), another Pueblo I pithouse located 3.6 km down canyon next to the mouth of Werito's Rincon. Associated with the pits was a natural layer of clay, designated Floor 1 (Figure I.4.3), and an adobe feature measuring 59 by 56 cm and 9-cm high.

Wall and roofing adobe was first encountered in Level 6 (185-210-cm depth), resting on the bench along the northern side of the pithouse. More was recovered from between the wing walls and the southern wall in scattered concentrations 3 to 27-cm thick. Fewer than 20 chunks of adobe with beam impressions were recovered, exhibiting casts of poles 36 to 75 mm in diameter. One chunk revealed reed impressions, 7-9 mm in diameter, set perpendicular to a 6-cm-diameter beam impression and separated from it by 37 mm of adobe. In places, adobe from the roofing continued to the floor fill. The floor was covered by a layer of sand four or more centimeters in thickness.

Floor 2

A whitish clayey material covered the sole flat, sandy pithouse floor (Floor 2), possibly derived from natural alluviated clay deposits and calcium carbonates.

Plate I.4.2. Site 29SJ 299, Pithouse E floor after clearing half the structure. Looking northwest. Photograph by Kellie Masterson, 1974 (CHCU neg. 9297).

278 Windes

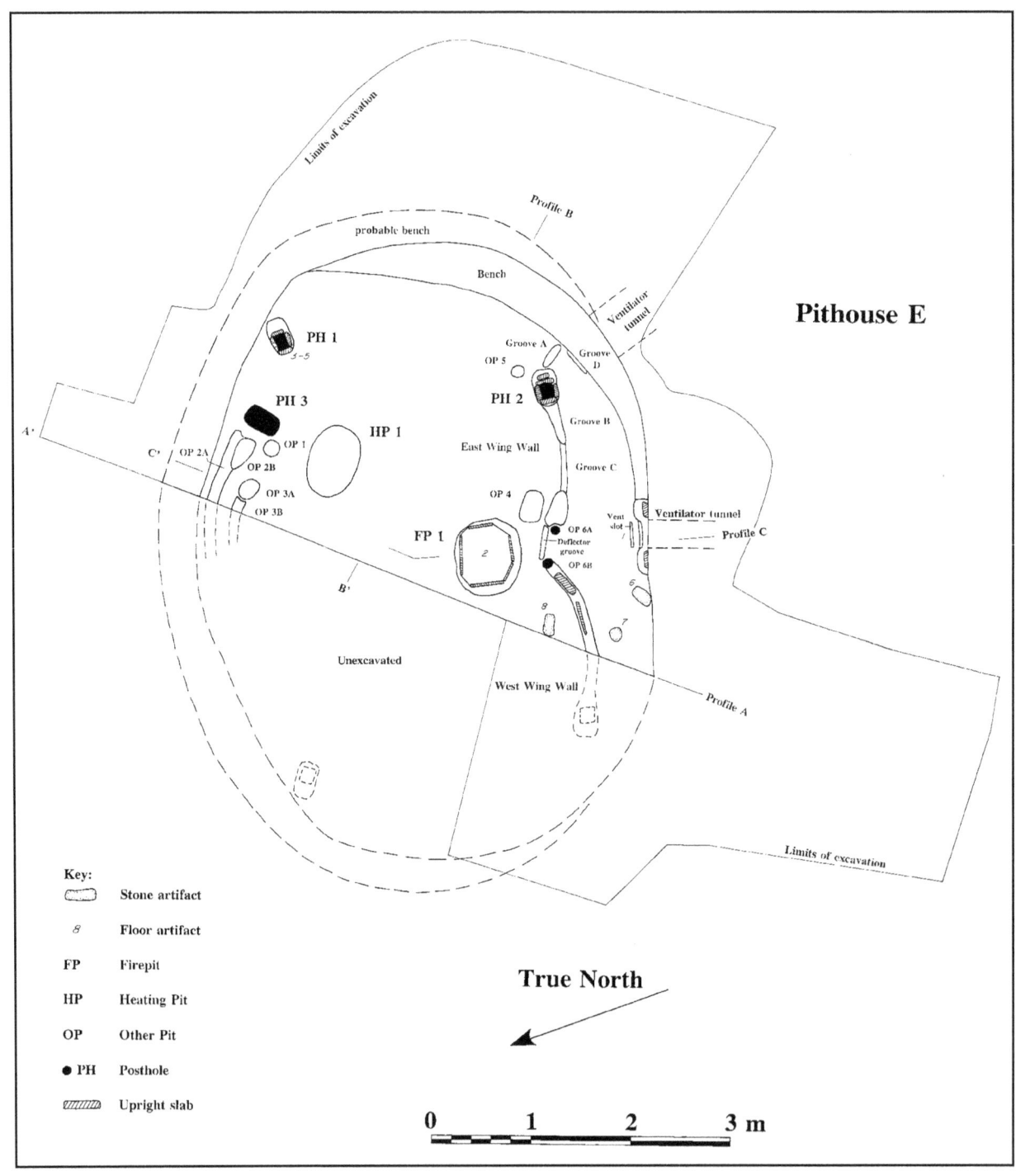

Figure I.4.2. Site 29SJ 299, Pithouse E plan (CHCU 95523). See Table I.4.3 for the list of specimens. Original by Kellie Masterson and Bill Gillespie, 1974.

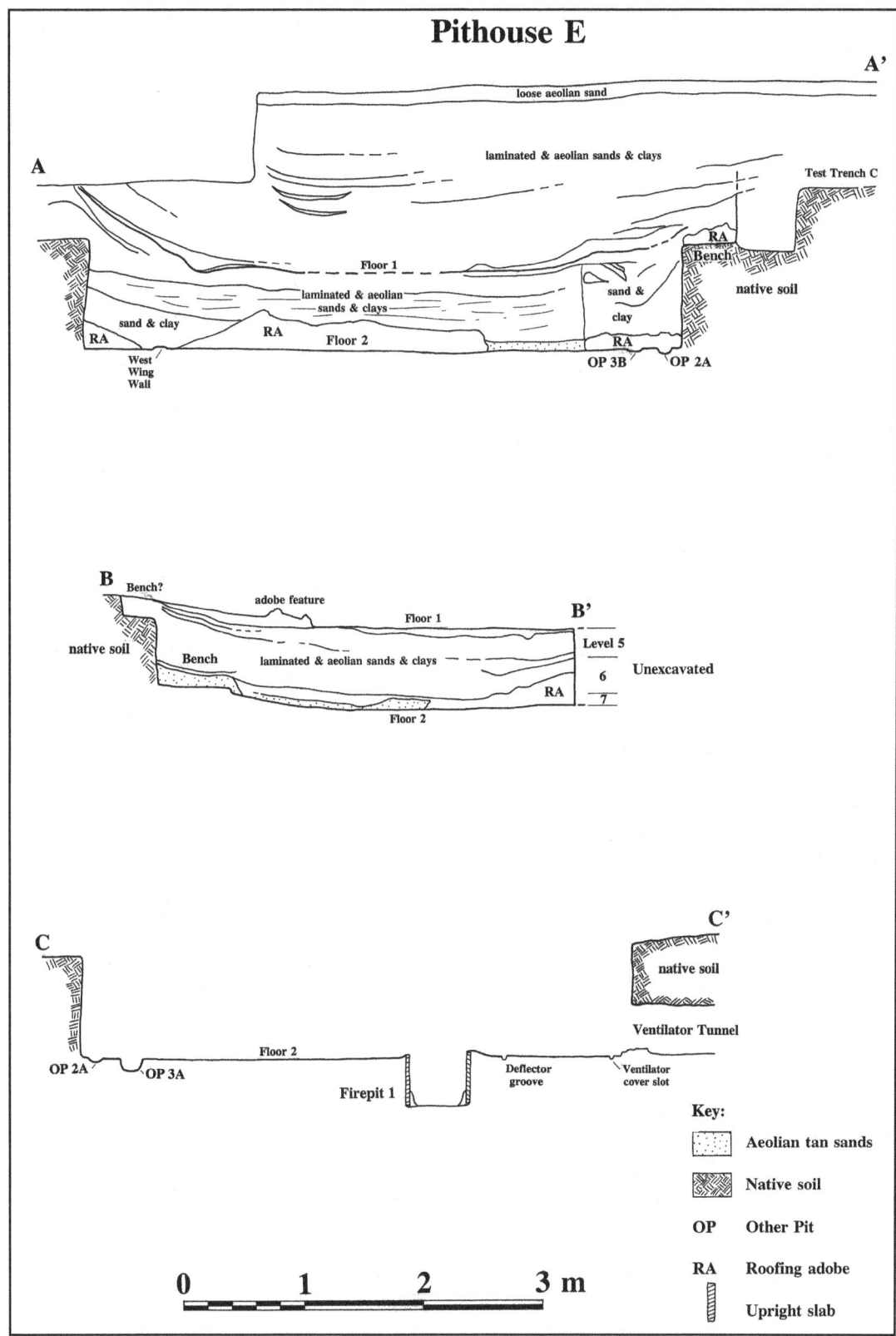

Figure I.4.3. Site 29SJ 299, Pithouse E profiles (CHCU 65968). Originals by Kellie Masterson and Bill Gillespie, 1974.

Floor Features (Tables I.3.1 and I.3.2)

Numerous features were encountered in the floor, despite the structure being only partially excavated. A hexagonal firepit was located 130-cm from the ventilator mouth. It was lined with four large slabs, one a cracked metate that projected slightly above the floor. A coping of adobe covered the slabs. A well-fired heating pit (OP 9) was located in the northeastern corner of the floor, and another may be located in the opposite corner under the unexcavated fill. OP 9 had vertical walls and a flat bottom and was filled with sand, 4 to 7-cm deep, oxidized in layers that indicated multiple uses. Under this was a 3-cm-thick deposit of charred seeds identified as amaranth (Alden Hayes, personal communication 1974). This was followed by an ash layer and 6-cm of clean sand. An archaeomagnetic sample yielded a DuBois revised date of A.D. 770 ± 23 (Figure I.6.8, Table I.6.6).

Next to the heating pit was a bell-shaped storage pit (OP 6), which contained a chalcedony flake and a mouse skeleton. Nearby OP 7 and OP 8 were pits associated with long, shallow grooves. These features are found in a number of Pueblo I pithouses, including one at 29SJ 724 (this chapter), but their function is unknown. OP 7 was filled with reddish brown sand, but the attached groove, with vertical sides and a convex bottom, had only yellow-tan sand. OP 8 and its attached groove, semicircular in cross-section, were both filled with the yellow-tan sand. The grooves were 15-cm apart and continued under the unexcavated part of the house; thus, their complete size and shape are unknown. OP 4, 5, and 8 were shallow with slightly sloping sides and flat or dish-shaped bottoms and filled with yellow-tan sand and little or no charcoal flecks. OP 4 through OP 9 were plastered with whitish clayey material and sealed with reddish brown plaster.

Placed against the northeastern bench and in the east wing wall were two of the four main roof supports, OP 1 and OP 2. Two others are presumed to exist in identical positions on the west side of the pithouse. Those uncovered were rectangular with rounded corners and filled with crushed lignite packing, with a stone footing at the bottom. Shims in each pit enclosed a space for a post about 15-cm in diameter. The postholes were unlined but had been fire-reddened to harden the sides or to kill micro-organisms that might damage the wood. No wood remains were found. About 57-cm from OP 1 was a lignite-filled pit, OP 3, constructed at an angle leaning toward the pithouse center. This must have had an auxiliary roof support post.

Two wing walls radiated out from two shallow postholes set south of the firepit. These holes were filled with sand and may have helped to hold a stone slab deflector (now missing) set in the groove between the two postholes. The wing walls were formed by upright slabs, 40-cm high, encased in mud and set in floor grooves. Most of the east wing wall was missing, although the grooves were evident.

Floor Specimens (Figure I.4.2, Table I.4.3)

Few artifacts were found on the floor. Within and just outside the area enclosed by the west wing wall were a mano blank, a mano fragment, a hammerstone, and several unmodified pieces of sandstone (fragments of the wing wall slabs?). The tools, at least, suggest a locus for mealing activities, which are often located within the wing wall areas (e.g., Gillespie 1976:111; Windes 1993:166, 168).

A few rodent bones, flakes, and sherds were scattered over the floor. Many of the sherds are of later types and are difficult to explain in terms of their association with the floor (Table I.4.3). It is a mixed assemblage of Pueblo I sherds from the A.D. 750-850 era along with Pueblo II sherds from the A.D. 1000s. Rodent activity and reuse/extensive long-term use of the pithouse are possibilities.

It is extremely unlikely that the pithouse

was used for more than a century, nor that an intact roof survived without constant upkeep. The fact that no roofing elements were evident suggests that the roof timbers were removed for use elsewhere shortly after abandonment. Rodent activity of such an extent that this many later sherds could have moved to the bottom of a filled pithouse is unlikely, and no such evidence of rodent burrowing was encountered. The archaeomagnetic date from the heating pit and the plaza and room ceramic samples support a date of about A.D. 800. We know that postoccupational activities took place about 60-cm above the pithouse floor, so it can only be assumed that the structure was cleared out and saw limited later use that is not indicated by any other lines of evidence.

Two turkey skeletons, 1-2-cm above the floor, were found above the deflector slot and among the stones behind the west wing wall. They probably were part of a ritual abandonment for the pithouse, because other instances of turkey and dog burials have been noted in similar circumstances (Emslie 1978; Gillespie 1976:152; Senter 1939; Vivian and Mathews 1965:17). However, the placement of the turkeys may have occurred after reoccupation in the A.D. 1000s rather than centuries earlier when the site was first abandoned. It is clear that usable materials had been removed upon the final abandonment.

Walls

There was little to distinguish the pithouse walls from the surrounding native sands except for the fine rootlets growing along the walls. At the time of excavation, the walls extended a mere 20-cm above the bench. No plaster was left on the walls.

Wall Features

The native deposits of sand had been cut back 48-cm to form a bench that probably encircled three-quarters of the house. In the excavated half, the bench terminated just above the point where the wingall met the house wall, leaving the ventilator area without a bench. The bench was not plastered, and no postholes were found in it to support poles that might have been leaned against the roof stringers. On the southeastern side of the house a lower shelf, 10-15-cm high and unplastered, ran between the ventilator collar and near the northeastern posthole.

An oval tunnel entered the chamber through the upper bench near the termination of the eastern wing wall. Whitish plaster sealed the sand-filled tunnel of unknown length. A thin wash of adobe covered the tunnel sides for a short distance where it entered the pithouse at a point 134° from true north. The tunnel floor continued across the 35-cm width of the lower bench shelf in a trench 3-4-cm deep. A long slot, evidently to support a slab cover, was set at the base of the shelf below where the tunnel floor terminated. This tunnel was either the original ventilator tunnel or a subsidiary one.

The ventilator used during the last occupation of the pithouse was located in the south wall opposite the firepit. It too was oval and sealed with 7-cm of whitish clayey plaster. The ventilator walls and floor did not appear to have been plastered, although most of the tunnel was not excavated and the shaft was not found. The mouth was buttressed on the sides by a slab partly covered with adobe and whitish plaster. The ventilator floor, 10-15-cm above the pithouse floor, had been repaired with a thin strip of reddish brown adobe, which was later covered when the mouth was sealed. Below and in front of the mouth was a small step with a slot in front of it for a slab to cover the ventilator mouth. Lying nearby was the chipped sandstone slab cover, 38 by 35 by 1 cm.

Discussion

The pithouse, located 8 m southeast of Rooms 12 to 15, was similar in construction to the contemporary pithouse excavated at 29SJ 724. Four main posts linked by stringers at the top supported the crossbeams, which were covered with reeds and mud. Side poles evidently were placed along the upper bench, although they left no trace. Entry probably was by ladder through the roof above the firepit. Removal of part of the upper bench and the elongated shape of the postholes suggest that the pithouse had been reroofed. This might have occurred when many of the floor pits were sealed and the ventilator repaired, perhaps as a result of a period of abandonment. It does seem unlikely, however, that OP 3, a postulated auxiliary roof support, would have been needed after a new roof was added. OP 3 was not sealed. At final abandonment, both tunnels were sealed and the slabs, roof timbers, and usable artifacts removed.

The tunnel at the southeast side of the house, large enough to accommodate entry, seems out of place if it had been a ventilator. It was probably built before the lower bench shelf; otherwise the slot in front of the mouth for the cover would have been unable to block off the mouth completely.

Grooves next to the north wall are similar to those in other Chaco Pueblo I pithouses (29SJ 724 and Bc 50). Bullard (1962:167-169) argues that such grooves might have anchored logs at the base of looms, but there is no evidence of logs in the Chaco examples and they seem too shallow for such a function. Pits at the end of the grooves, where posts holding looms would be expected, are unsuitable for holding posts. The pithouse at Bc 50 (Senter 1939) had one of the main roof supports set at the end of the groove. That groove was filled with fine yellow sand. Pithouse E had two grooves set parallel and close together and left unsealed, suggesting use for something other than looms. Whatever their purpose, they disappear in later Chacoan pitstructures. Similar grooves, however, show up in Pueblo III and Pueblo IV kivas in the Rio Grande area (Ellis and Dodge 1990), where a ritual use is proposed.

Natural filling of the pithouse must have taken a century or more (see Pithouse B in Chapter 3 for an example of natural filling). Pueblo II pottery occurred in the fill all the way to the floor, probably much of it washed down from the small house (29SJ 298) and Pithouse B on the ridge nearby. The burned spots and small postholes found in the fill indicate that the depression was also utilized in Pueblo II times for limited activities, similar to those noted for the fill of the 29SJ 724 pithouse. In addition, the secondary ventilator and late floor sherds indicate some reuse of the structure floor long after its original abandonment in Pueblo I times.

Rooms (Figures I.4.4 and I.4.5, Table I.3.1)

North of Pithouse E were four contiguous storage rooms. All had suffered from erosional degradation, and little remained of their architecture.

Room 12

The easternmost unit, Room 12, was enclosed by low walls of adobe turtleback construction laid in a rectangle, 126-x-220-cm and 24-cm deep. Each of the adobe courses was concave along the bottom from being forced over the patted, convex top of the course below (Plate I.4.3).

Plate I.4.3. Turtleback adobe wall construction. Example from Horse Collar Ruin (42SA 6819), Natural Bridges National Monument, Utah. Pen is 13.8-cm long, next to cobble. Photograph by Tom Windes, 2005.

Turtlebacks found in the fill suggest the average size was 12-14-cm long, 8-10-cm wide, and 5-6-cm high. The east wall was bracketed by upright slabs set 17-cm apart. Little remained of the floor except patches of gray plaster, 1-2-cm thick. No evidence of a roof was found except for a single piece of adobe impressed with a 5.5-cm-diameter beam. The fill consisted of adobe wall fall and windblown sand, which yielded little cultural material aside from some plain gray sherds and turkey bones.

Room 13

Next to Room 12 was an outline of a room, 134-x-279-cm and 9-cm deep, marked by a few upright slabs. A slab foundation had been set in a narrow trench and affixed with mortar, but the majority of slabs have long since disappeared. The floor was poorly preserved but exhibited a 1-cm-thick plaster coat in the eastern half of the room. The fill was marked by a granulated gray clay and charcoal flecks that contrasted with the clean yellow-tan sands surrounding the rooms. A single plain gray sherd came from the fill; several others were left on the well-preserved fragment of floor in the southeastern corner.

Room 14 (Plate I.4.4)

Next to Room 14 was a poorly delineated room, 118-x-265-cm and 10-15-cm deep. Wall foundations were marked only by a few upright slabs. A poorly preserved floor exhibited patches of gray clay plastering, 2-4-cm thick. The entire western end of the room had weathered away. Fill consisted of tan windblown sand. One plain gray sherd came from the fill.

Room 15

The westernmost room, unlike the others, was semisubterranean and shaped like a shallow bathtub, 80-95-cm wide and 182-cm long. The

Plate I.4.4. Site 29SJ 299, storage Room 14 after clearing. Contiguous Rooms 15 (left) and 13 (right) just visible. Looking southeast. Photograph by Tom Windes, 1974 (CHCU neg. 9154).

walls and floor were covered in thick gray clay, 10-cm for the walls and 2-3-cm for the floor. Three small slabs were embedded in the wall on the east side. The northern wall top revealed two plugs of clay, 7 and 9-cm in diameter set 80-cm apart, which mark former postholes and a possible back entry. The room was overlain with 5-cm of clean sand, with the remaining 15-cm of fill consisting of melted clay and adobe from the walls. Below that were 1-2-cm of clay fragments mixed with sand, possibly from roofing, followed by 17-cm of charcoal-flecked sand laminae and occasional pieces of clay and adobe. Overall, the fill ranged in depth from 15 to 31-cm. One piece of chipped stone and a few plain gray sherds came from the fill; the floor also yielded some plain gray sherds.

Ramada 2
(Figures I.4.4 and I.4.5, Plate I.4.5, Tables I.3.1 and I.3.6)

A second ramada (the first was Basketmaker III; see Chapter 3), or a series of contiguous ramadas, was found in front (south) of Rooms 12-15. The perimeter of the ramada was indicated by two parallel rows of 11 post supports that

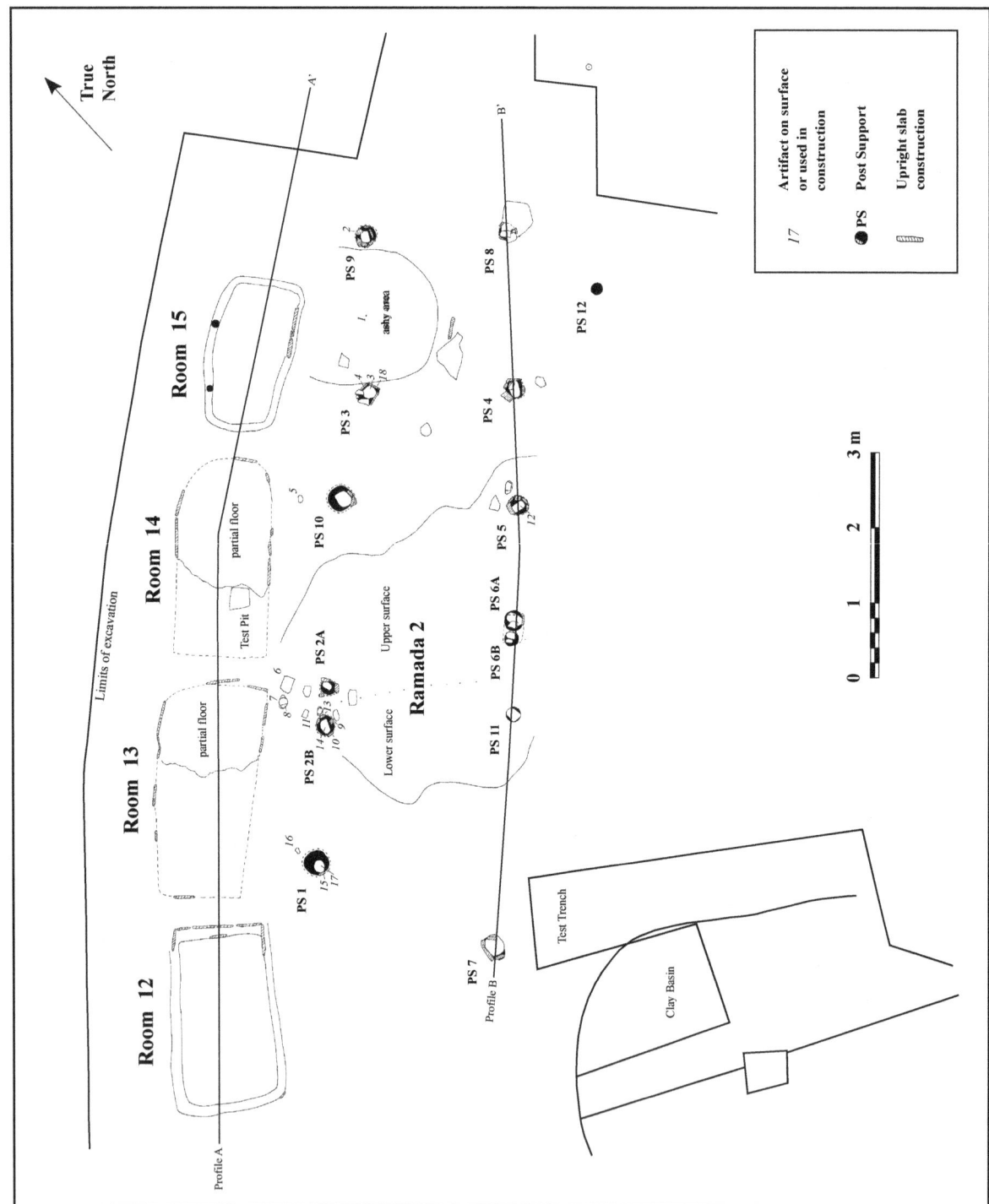

Figure 1.4.4. Site 29SJ 299, Rooms 12-15 and Ramada 2 plans (CHCU 55504). See Table 1.4.4 for the list of specimens. Originals by Tom Windes, 1974.

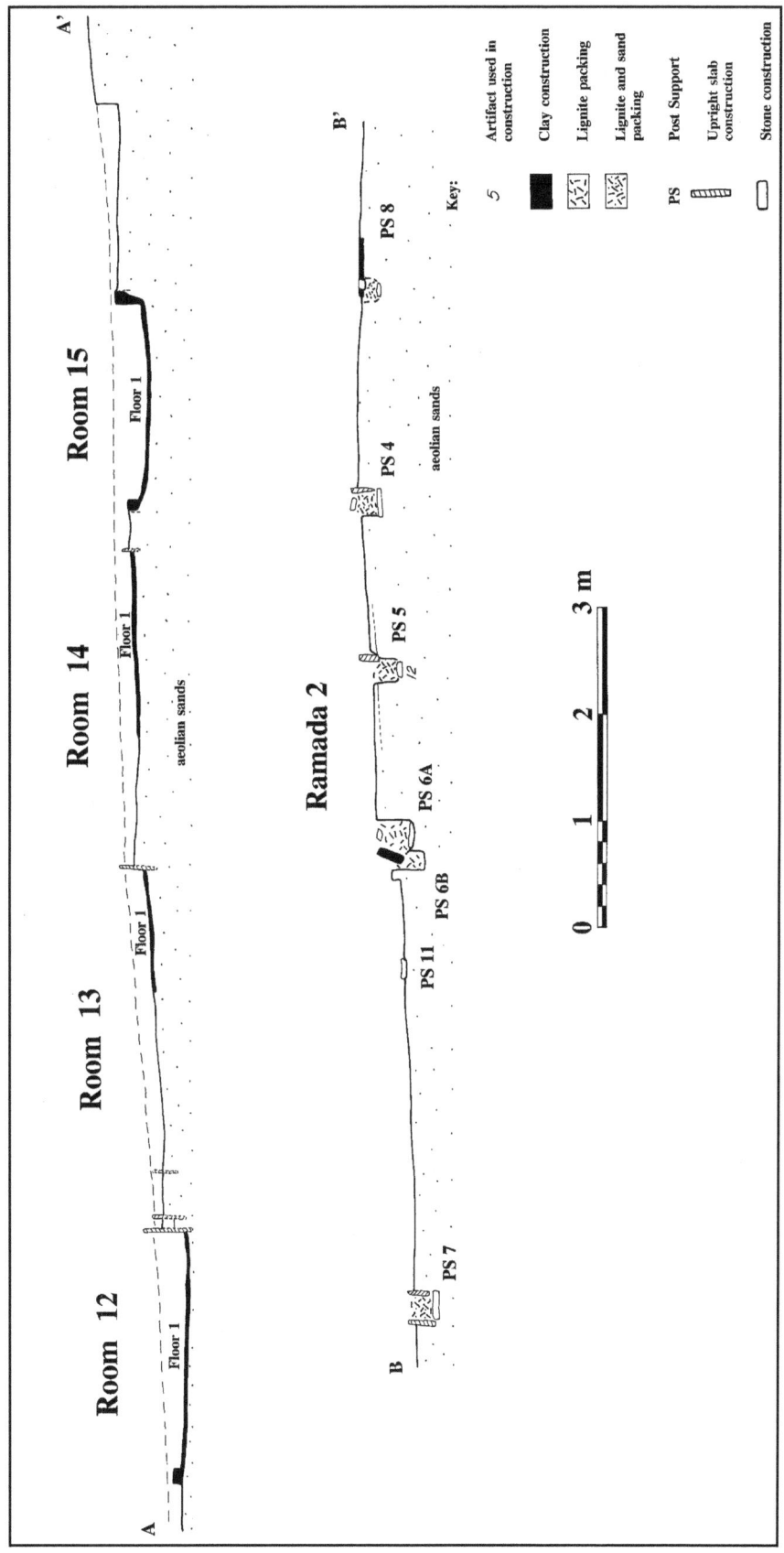

Figure I.4.5. Site 29SJ 299, Rooms 12-15 and Ramada 2 profiles (CHCU 55505). Originals by Tom Windes

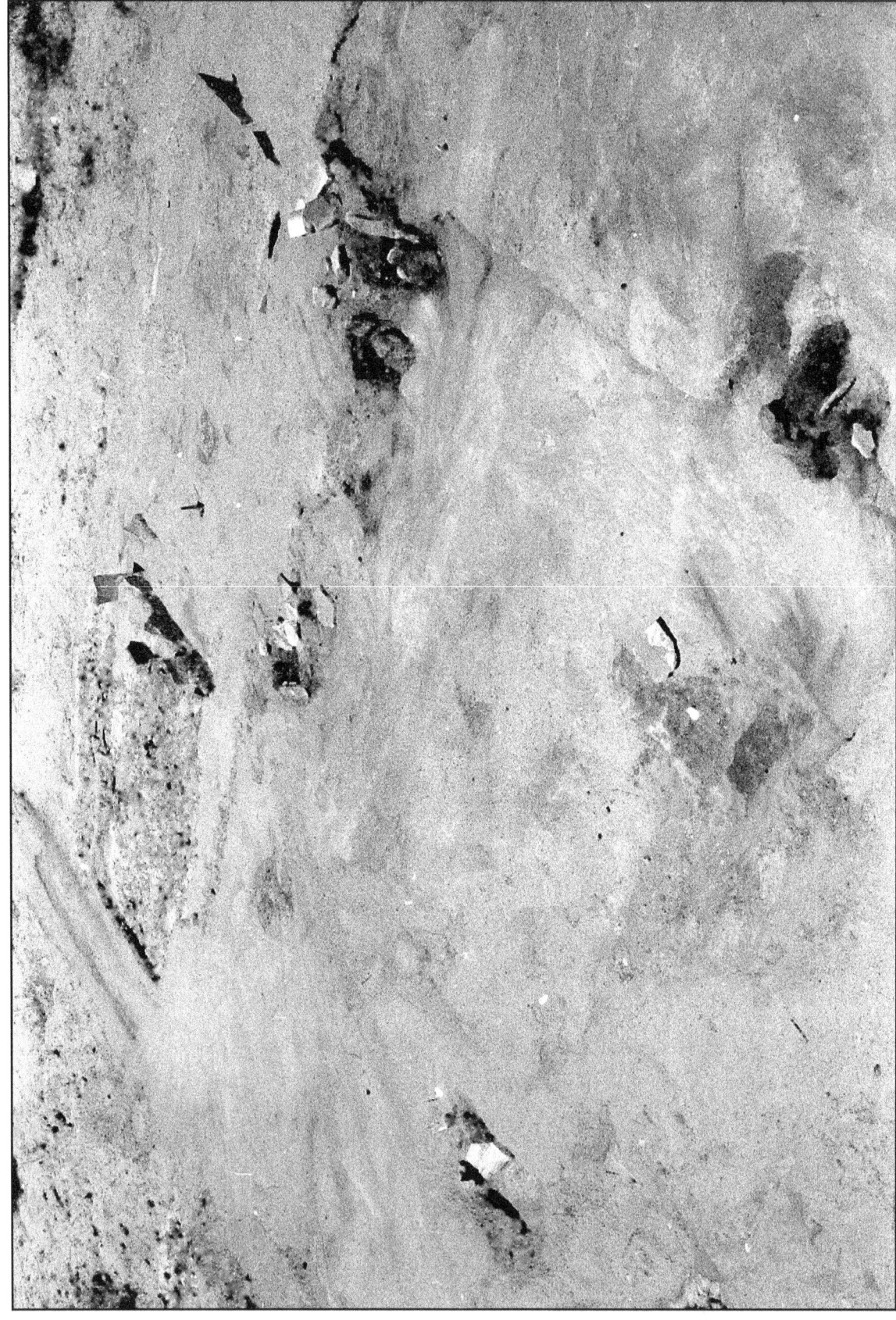

Plate I.4.5. Site 29SJ 299, Ramada 2 post supports and storage Rooms 12 (with mud cracks from rain) and 13 in background. Looking west-northwest. Photograph by Tom Windes, 1974 (CHCU neg. 9264).

outlined a trapezoidal area measuring 2.4-x-11-m. Postmolds ranged between 13 and 40-cm across (the distance between the shims), although posts were probably 15-20-cm in diameter. All post supports contained lignite packing or pieces of lignite mixed with sand; rotted wood fragments were found in Post Supports 1, 6A, and 10. Sandstone shims, employed in nine supports (Plate I.4.6), were reused materials—79 percent were burned stones or were reused ground stone tools (Table I.4.4). More possible shims were found on top or next to the support. Adobe bricks, 22-x-10-x-7-cm and 17-x-16-x-25-cm, served as shims in Support 6A. All but one of the supports contained stone footings. Gray-banded (probably Precambrian cross-bedding) quartzite cobbles were used in Supports 3 and 9—the closest known source of this material is the San Juan River, about 85 km to the northwest (Helene Warren, personal communication 1975).

The ramada surface exhibited patches of packed, discolored sand around the post supports and in the eastern half of the sheltered area. A distinct 15-cm dropoff separated the eastern supports in front of Rooms 14 and 15 from the western ones in Room 13. The western surface appeared to have continued under the eastern surface, which was 4-cm higher. The two surfaces were found near Support 5, where most of the shims rested on the lowermost surface. Aside from the supports, no other features were found in the ramada area.

It is clear that the supports were not contemporaneous. A 43-x-38-x-5-cm thick chunk of clay covered Support 8. A later support was superimposed over Support 6B. A double set of posts, 23-cm apart, formed Support 2. Burned shims were found in every eastern support but were absent in three of the five western ones. The western supports lack conformity and rectilinear arrangement, while the eastern ones appear similar as a group. In short, the western supports appear to have been the original construction and were replaced by a newer framework in the eastern half. These two events may correlate with the two phases of construction of the storage rooms.

Miscellaneous Site Features

Clay Basin (Figure I.4.4)

Six meters southeast of Room 12 was an ovoid deposit of compacted grayish brown clay, 5-6 m across, identical to that used in the storage rooms. The clay consisted of alternating charcoal-flecked layers of sand and clay, 5-8-cm thick, with the upper 27-cm entirely of sandy clay. Extensive trenching revealed that the clay had washed into an 80-cm-deep basin, underlain by at least 40-cm of lignite and charcoal-flecked sand devoid of cultural specimens. Test trenches next to the basin yielded moderate amounts of early pottery, but no evidence for a structure was found in the clay. It probably derived from erosion of the adobe storage rooms upslope.

Site Conclusions

Pithouse E, along with the other occupations discussed in Chapter 3, was part of a long-term use of the ridge. Site refuse was sparse and there was little evidence of extensive remodeling,

Plate I.4.6. Site 29SJ 299, Ramada 2 post supports (PS 2). Note shims. Photograph by Tom Windes, 1974 (CHCU neg. 9252).

suggesting a number of intermittent occupations at the site between approximately A.D. 615 and the early A.D. 1000s, with a later occupation evident by the unexcavated kiva or pit next to Pithouse A. The Pueblo I component, discussed here, appears to have been of very short duration at about A.D. 800 with almost no refuse accumulation. Abandonment of the house, perhaps for a new location on the nearby ridges to the east where later, prolific occupations took place a few decades later, was orderly with little of value left behind.

The Pueblo I occupation is similar to that of other hamlets in the area (see 29SJ 724, below), including those in the community setting in the South Fork of Fajada Wash (Chapter 9). It comprised one or two families and was short enough to leave little refuse. This residence seems typical of occupation in the Chaco area—one of many scattered small hamlets representing a relatively small population that had little investment in stability and permanence in the area.

Excavations at 29SJ 721

This site is located on a small, canyon-floor knoll (elevation 1,884 m; 6,180 ft) located a few meters south of the talus of South Mesa (Figure I.4.6, Plate I.4.7). Just to the west of the site is a long ridge on which a number of sites were located, including the excavated contemporary site of 29SJ 724 and, beyond that, the mouth of Werito's Rincon. Across the canyon from the site is the Chacoan greathouse of Hungo Pavi and the mouth of Mockingbird Canyon. When surveyed in 1972, a few upright slabs and a scattering of early sherds were all that marked 29SJ 721. The cultural evidence suggested one or two pithouses, one slab-lined surface room, one slab-lined hearth, and six slab-lined storage cists of Basketmaker III-Pueblo I age. In addition, a few late sherds suggested some Pueblo III activity. Excavations confirmed the presence of the predicted features, along with an unfinished

Plate I.4.7. Site 29SJ 721, initial excavations at Pithouse A. South Mesa talus slope in background. Looking southeast. Photograph by Tom Windes, 1973 (CHCU neg. 5826).

Pueblo III kiva.

The knoll is V-shaped and opens toward the north, extending approximately 44 m north-south and 56 m east-west. It is the remnant of the former mesa talus and is composed of Menefee Formation shales and clays topped by a thin mantle of tan, windblown sand and vegetation typical of the Upper Sonoran Life Zone. The highest point is in the southwest part where one pithouse was built. At one time the knoll consisted of a more sharply defined hill, but it has since been gently rounded by aeolian sands. Thus, when the pitstructure builders sank their chambers into the knoll, the majority of each was set down into subsurface gray clay deposits but with sections extending down through the blown sand that had covered the original slopes.

Excavations were conducted by the author and four Navajo laborers (Ken Augustine, Alvin Dennison, Ben Norberto, and Bruce Yazzie) for three weeks in August 1973. Surface collections were made around each feature and then the vegetation of grasses and brush was removed by hand. The surface was characterized by 10-cm of aeolian sand, which was removed with shovels, and the cultural materials bagged as surface materials. Depressions were trenched for suspected pitstructures, and then the trenches expanded until the pitstructure perimeter was cleared. Little stratigraphy was noted in the fill

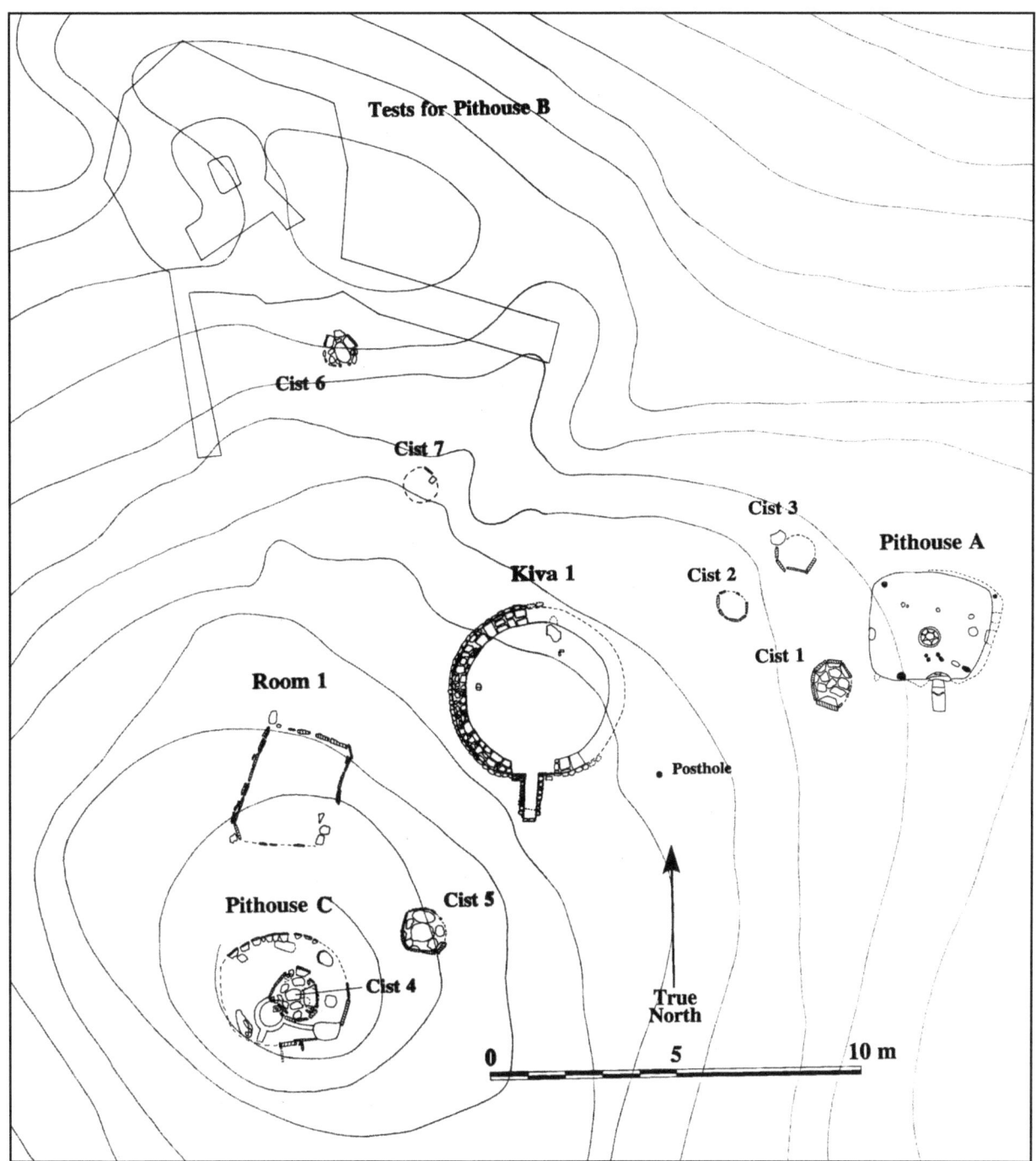

Figure I.4.6. Site 29SJ 721, site plan with contours (CHCU 65677). Contour interval is one foot (30.5-cm); absolute elevation is approximate. Original by Tom Windes, 1974.

of the pitstructures; fill was generally removed in arbitrary levels. New levels were started after a depth of 30 to 40-cm whenever distinct changes in the fill or its content were observed. Floor artifacts and the 5-cm of fill above the floor were designated as floor material. Random eighth-inch mesh screening was used to check on the presence and density of cultural material in the fill. Small samples were taken from all floors and some pits for eventual pollen analysis. Large samples for flotation were not collected, so the flotation analyses that were conducted 17 years later utilized these smaller samples instead. The site is particularly notable for its sparse cultural remains, especially faunal material (only 26 bones).

Pithouse A
(Figures I.4.7 and I.4.8, Plate I.4.8, Table I.4.5)

Investigations started on the east side of the knoll where a flattened area, a few artifacts, and charcoal-flecked sand suggested a buried pitstructure. After shovel stripping the loose sand off the area to a depth of about 10-cm, the dark outline of a small structure emerged. Initially its small size (8.3 m³) suggested the antechamber of a larger pithouse similar to those found earlier in the year at 29SJ 628 (Chapter 3). A ventilator tunnel extended to the south of the structure and its appearance suggested that floor contact was close to the surface. Both expectations were wrong.

Fill

Postoccupational fill in Pithouse A was removed in four arbitrary levels, totaling 90-95-cm in depth and encompassing 8.3 m³. The first 10-cm of sand removed after the loose surface material had been cleared constituted Level 1. Another 70-cm was removed as Levels 2 and 3, which were composed of aeolian and alluvial sands and trash. Occasional spalls, debitage, ceramics, rodent bones, and, rarely, dense concentrations of charcoal were

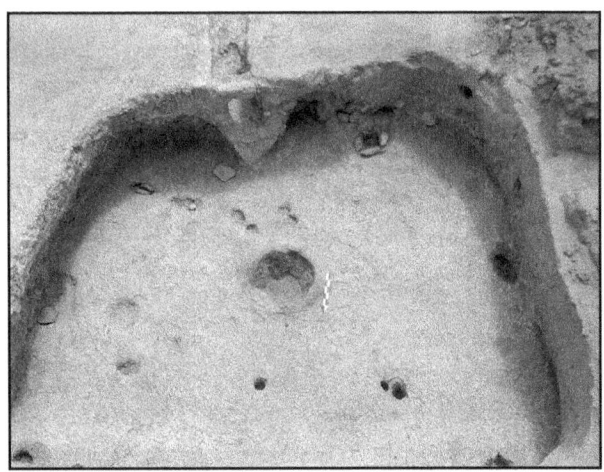

Plate I.4.8. Site 29SJ 721, Pithouse A after clearing. Note unusual above floor ventilating system. Looking south. Photograph by Tom Windes, 1973 (CHCU neg. 5831).

found, but cultural materials declined in density as the depth increased in the soft deposits. The charcoal probably came from the several roasting pits ("cists") located just upslope of the pithouse. Although late sherds were found in the initial clearing, only Basketmaker pottery was recovered once inside the pithouse.

Level 4, 10-15-cm deep, was similar to the overlying deposits except for the sudden increased density of tan adobe chunks and burned twigs that marked former roof materials. More than 40 chunks exhibited one or two sooted pole impressions. Estimated diameters of the 52 impressions ranged from 2.5 to 10-cm, with a mean of 5.5-cm; the pole impressions were concentrated along the east and south walls. In the southeast corner was a rotted 6-cm diameter pole, 37-cm long, that was unsuitable for dendrochronological dating. A 3-4.5-cm deposit of charcoal-flecked aeolian sand had accumulated between the floor and roof deposits, and the few artifacts recovered from this level were designated as floor materials.

Floor

Because the pithouse was dug into natural clays, the builders may have felt it unnecessary to plaster

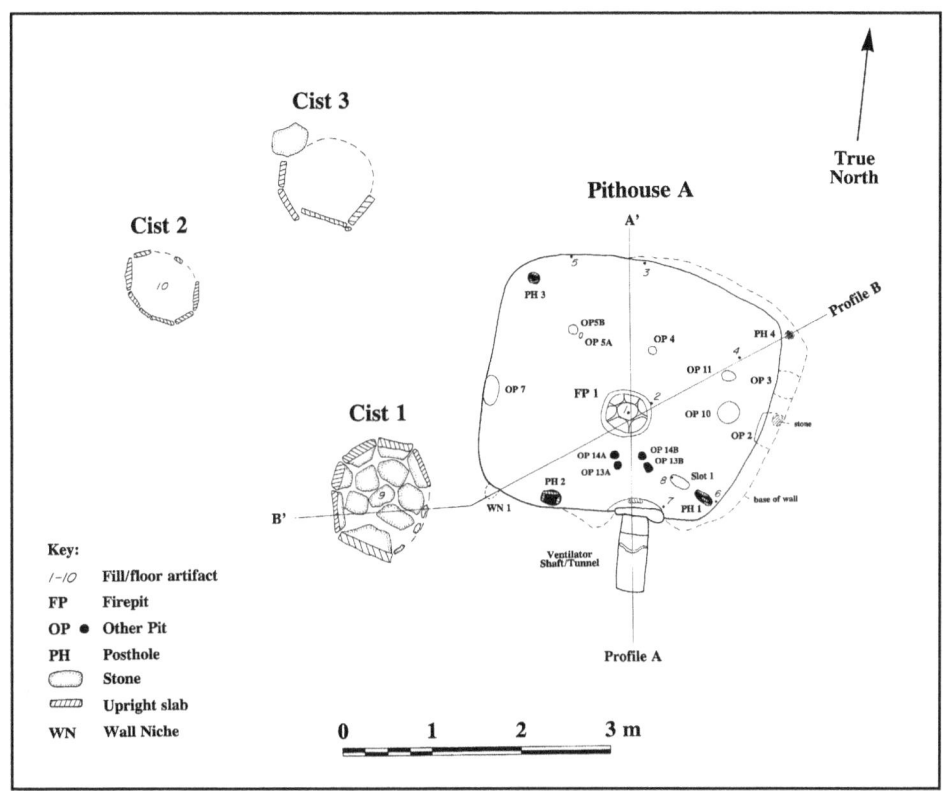

Figure I.4.7. Site 29SJ 721, plans of Pithouse A and Cists 1-3 (CHCU 65678). See Table I.4.5 for the list of specimens. Original by Tom Windes, 1974.

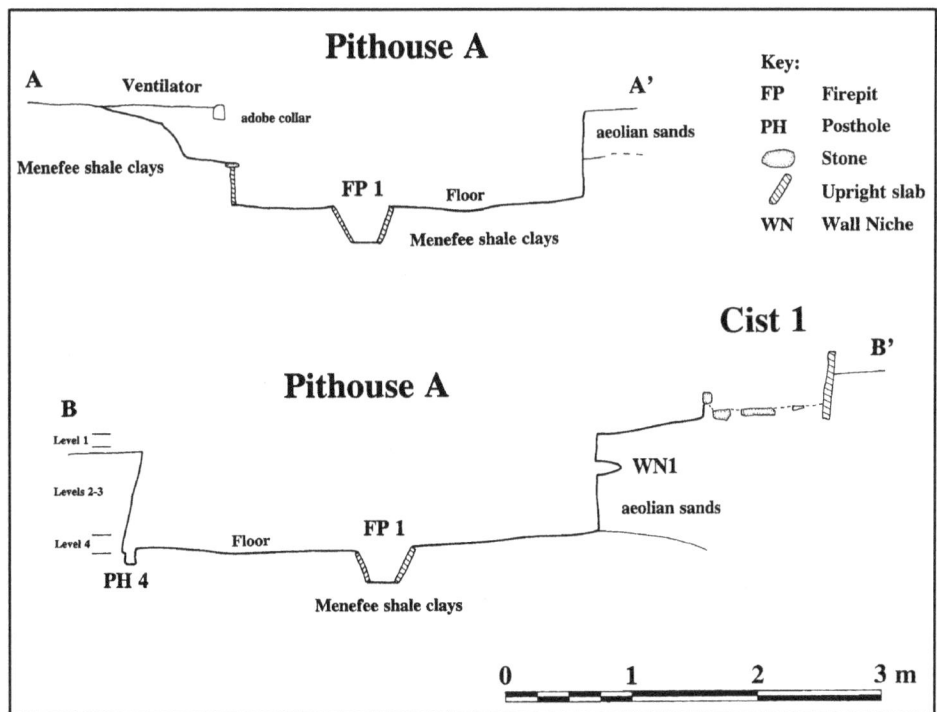

Figure I.4.8. Site 29SJ 721, profiles of Pithouse A and Cist 1 (CHCU 65997). See Table I.4.5 for the list of specimens. Original by Tom Windes, 1974.

the floor. Little was done to modify the surface other than smoothing it. Digging stick marks were not observed in the floor or walls and must have been intentionally removed. Although small, reddish brown concretions were found in the floor, several subfloor tests confirmed the natural state of the floor clay and concretions. Overall floor dimensions were 330-cm east-west by 290-cm north-south (9.2 m²), a very small pitstructure.

Floor Artifacts (Figure I.4.7, Table I.4.5)

Aside from a number of adobe roofing impressions on the floor, few materials remained (15 sherds, 15 pieces of chipped stone, and no bones). A large Lino Gray jar fragment, possibly used as a dish, was left leaning over the northeast rim of the firepit, and a lapstone was recovered from the floor just east of the vent. The only pipe at the site, a possible ritual artifact (e.g., Heitman 2011:187), was recovered against the north wall, 10-cm above the floor. In addition, the only bone awl also came from Pithouse A, 25-cm above the floor. Because both were in good condition and were nearly exclusive to pithouses in the other excavated sites described here, these two artifacts might be considered part of the Pithouse A tool inventory at the time of abandonment. Their placement can be explained by their being cached above the floor in the side wall or in roof materials (see Pithouse A at 29SJ 724 for a similar situation).

Floor Features (Tables I.4.6-I.4.7)

A number of pits had been constructed in the floor, further reducing the use area by 0.6 m². None were sealed and all contained the charcoal-flecked sand that filled the pithouse. No artifacts were found in the pits.

Firepit

A slab-lined firepit (Plate I.4.9) had been placed

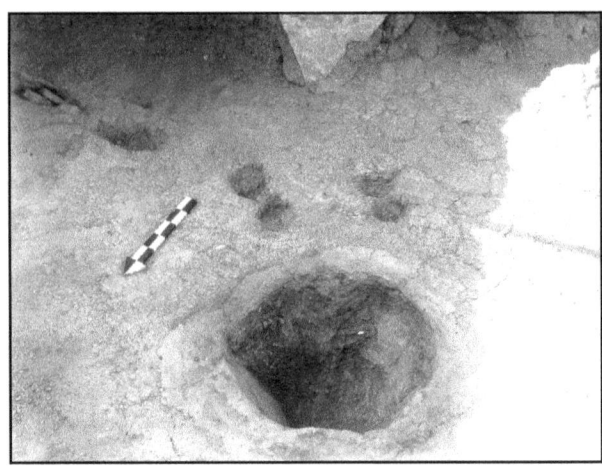

Plate I.4.9. Site 29SJ 721, Pithouse A floor and Firepit 1. Looking southeast. 30-cm north arrow. Photograph by Tom Windes, 1973 (CHCU neg. 5788).

about 75-cm from the ventilator opening. It contained 4 to 10-cm of sandy floor fill, followed by 18-23-cm of ash, charcoal, oxidized sand, and a few unburned rodent bones. The bottom of the pit and the six slanting wall slabs had been covered with adobe. The latter had been burned and were sampled for archaeomagnetic dating (DuBois: A.D. 765 ± 25, but later revised to A.D. 720 [DuBois 2008:98]), which should reflect the early use of the firepit. An alternative date would place its use at about A.D. 900 (Figure I.6.10, Table I.6.6). There was no evidence of a deflector or ancillary heating pits.

Other Pits

Aside from the firepit, 16 other pits had been dug into the floor (Table I.4.6). Three of them contained shims and must have supported either posts or slabs. Although there was no clear four-post arrangement to support a roof, four of these pits were probably postholes and are discussed below. A single pit on the approximate alignment of the ventilator and firepit was located in the traditional area reserved for a sipapu (OP 4), although its fill was postoccupational. Two slots set in a row in the southeastern corner probably held slabs for a small wingwall (or storage bin), although there was not a corresponding set to the southwest. Two pairs of small pits between the firepit and ventilator resemble historical examples of entry-ladder rests (Plate I.4.8), while the shallow basin east of the firepit was suitable to hold the rounded-bottom ceramic vessels of the day. Several pits (OP 2, 3, and 7) were set at the base of walls, and these were some of the largest in the structure. Their size suggests a storage function. The remainder was small pits but no function can be attributed to them.

Postholes (Table I.4.7)

Three pits contained shims and were located in or near corners, suggesting main roof support postholes. The southeastern one (OP 1) has been linked to a similar, adjacent pit as part of a wing wall; however, it could have also have held a main post as well as a slab or several smaller posts. A pit without shims in the northeast corner and shimmed pits in the remaining corners probably mark the positions for the primary roof posts despite their uneven placement and size. The western pits (OP 6, OP 8) both had three shims, which were highly burned. In addition, three more burned, small, tabular, shim-like stones were found on the floor next to OP 8.

Walls

Little was done to prepare the walls after excavation into the thick, gummy, gray clay deposits except for smoothing the clay when it was still damp. The east wall, half of the north wall, and most of the south wall were of natural clay deposits. These areas overhung the floor by as much as 30-cm, although this may have resulted from wall slumpage after abandonment. If the overhang were original, however, OP 12, the northeastern posthole, could not have held a vertical post, although the pit shape does allow for one with considerable slant. Deep, vertical undercuts at each side of the elevated ventilator attest to man-made modifications rather than natural processes.

The remaining walls were simply cut vertically into the natural, aeolian sands. White caliche stains often marked these walls, but, at times, the postoccupational fill was difficult to distinguish from the surrounding sands. No wall plaster was evident. In the west wall, composed entirely of sand, was an adobe footing with a large stone set flush in the center of the wall, directly behind OP 7, perhaps to strengthen the wall.

Wall Features

Ventilator

The primary wall modification allowed entrance for the above-floor ventilator (Plate I.4.10). An atypical ventilator construction produced a slanting trench that began 32-cm above the floor and ended at the present ground surface. As such, it was somewhere between a formal tunnel and an upward shaft. The vent had been dug through native clays and left unplastered, and the trench remained visible on the surface for its entire length of 109-cm. A rectangular adobe collar separated the trench from the pithouse interior. Typical for its time, the ventilator entry bulged into the pithouse with the adjacent pithouse walls cut back and away from the entry. A small tabular stone was set horizontally in the vent mouth at the bottom of the adobe collar, forming a protruding lip. This rested on a large vertical slab set into the floor and flush with the wall. Removal of the slab revealed no earlier signs of construction.

The ventilator opening was 25-cm wide, the same as the ventilator trench, and 37-cm high. Oddly, it was not centered in the south wall but was considerably offset to the east, disturbing the normal symmetry seen at contemporary sites. Thus, the traditional alignment of ventilator-firepit-sipapu was poorly arranged. Fill within the ventilator was similar to that in the main chamber, except no artifacts were recovered. There was no

Plate I.4.10. Site 29SJ 721, Pithouse A above-floor ventilator. Looking south. 30-cm scale. Photograph by Tom Windes, 1974 (CHCU neg. 5828).

evidence of a ventilator roof or of how it might have been covered during inclement weather. A flat stone could have suitably covered the vent entrance at the ground level, although there was nothing that would have prevented the flow of water into the main chamber through the ventilator during storms. The ventilator also would have allowed cold air into the structure during the winter.

Wall Niche

A small pocket niche was found in the southwestern corner (OP 9) of the house about 37-cm above the floor. It contained charcoal-flecked sand identical to that in the main chamber but otherwise was devoid of cultural materials.

Roof

The mass of roofing impressions in Level 4 clearly mark the destruction of the roof shortly after abandonment and the salvage of timbers. The 52 pole impressions revealed two size groupings, with means of 5.0 and 7.9-cm diameters, respectively. A larger number of smaller-diameter poles (which held less weight) would have been used for the side leaners and a smaller number of secondaries would have spanned the rectangular framework over the center of the house. The vast majority of the 52 impressions (81 percent) fell within the small-diameter group, from 2.5-6.5-cm, and are assumed to have been used as leaners around the sides of the house. The remaining casts, 7-10-cm in diameter, are presumed to have marked the small secondary beams which overlain the primaries or were from over the primary beams.

Pits in the four corners of the floor must mark placement of the traditional four-post roof supports, although the pits are not a homogenous group. The small house could have been easily spanned by logs without the necessity of post supports, but it was too shallow to live in without an elevated roof supported by posts. Entrance through the roof smoke hole by means of a two-pole ladder set between the firepit and ventilator is evident from the ladder rests.

Discussion

This small house could not have held more than a few residents, possibly only a couple. Although a shift in ladder location is evident by the two sets of ladder rests, there is no evidence of remodeling or repair of the floor that would suggest extensive use of the house and longevity of the occupation. In addition, a paucity of trash outside the house also indicates a short occupation. The above-floor ventilator design might suggest occupation of the house during the warmer months because of the difficulty of preventing cold-air drainage into the house unless the ventilator opening could be tightly sealed. It is clear that when the house was abandoned, everything of value was taken, probably including the structural wood. The lack of food preparation tools, particularly manos and fragments of metates, which are commonly discarded at abandonment, also suggest a short occupation in which there was little time to accumulate worn-out tools. Finally, the lack of trash in the postoccupational fill argues against subsequent occupation of the knoll.

Pithouse B

Behind Pithouse A, the ridge spur ran northward from the top of the knoll and hooked west a short distance. Within the hook, a noticeable depression appeared to mark another buried pithouse that we designated Pithouse B (Figure I.4.6). A few scattered spalls and the remains of a cist just upslope also seemed to justify testing the area. The surface was cleared of brush and artifacts, and a test trench was placed across the depression. Removal of the first 10-15-cm of soft, charcoal-flecked sand yielded only a few sherds. After an additional 50-60-cm of sterile aeolian sands was removed, a flat sheet of gray clay was encountered. The clay appeared to be a floor, but it ascended to the top of the ridge spur. A test pit sunk through the clay revealed it to be 5-30 mm thick, underlain by another 21-cm of sterile aeolian sand, 3-cm of sand with scarce flecks of lignite, and, finally, at least 20-cm more of sterile clays.

Obviously, no structure existed in the depression. The lowest layer of clay evidently was part of the natural deposits forming the ridge spur into which Pithouse A had been excavated. The floor-like clay layer, which seemed to extend indefinitely in all directions, connected with the ridge spur and was undoubtedly derived from it. The deposition was very similar to that found in the nearby kiva, and, perhaps, the events occurred simultaneously, influenced by cultural activities. If the clay layer spread naturally, it is puzzling that it only occurred once during the entire time since the knoll was occupied.

Pithouse C
(Figures I.4.6, I.4.9, and I.4.10; Plate I.4.11)

On the highest part of the knoll was a partial oval, 345-x-290-cm, of upright sandstone slabs. It appeared to mark either a very small pithouse or a large storage cist, and it was designated Pithouse C. In the center was an intrusive roasting pit (Cist

Plate I.4.11. Site 29SJ 721, Pithouse C with intrusive Cist 4 in the center. Photograph by Tom Windes, 1973 (CHCU neg. 5813).

4). A surface collection of artifacts revealed a few sherds spanning the Basketmaker III through the Pueblo III periods. After removal of the vegetation, the fill in and around the structure was investigated by shovel and trowel.

Fill

Two levels of fill were removed from the house. Tan windblown sand, 10-cm deep, containing small pieces of charcoal and little cultural debris, constituted Level 1. The remaining 5-22-cm of fill, Level 2, was similar except for the addition of adobe chunks and a few dislodged wall slabs. Some of the adobe came from the firepit, which had been partially destroyed by Cist 4; the remainder probably represented structural material.

Floor

The crest of the ridge had been removed by the builders to a depth of 25-cm, cutting into the natural clay deposits. The resulting clay pit was then smoothed to serve as the house floor except for a narrow strip along the north side that extended over aeolian sands. This strip was plastered over with 25- to 35-mm-thick clay to extend the area of the house floor. Overall, the

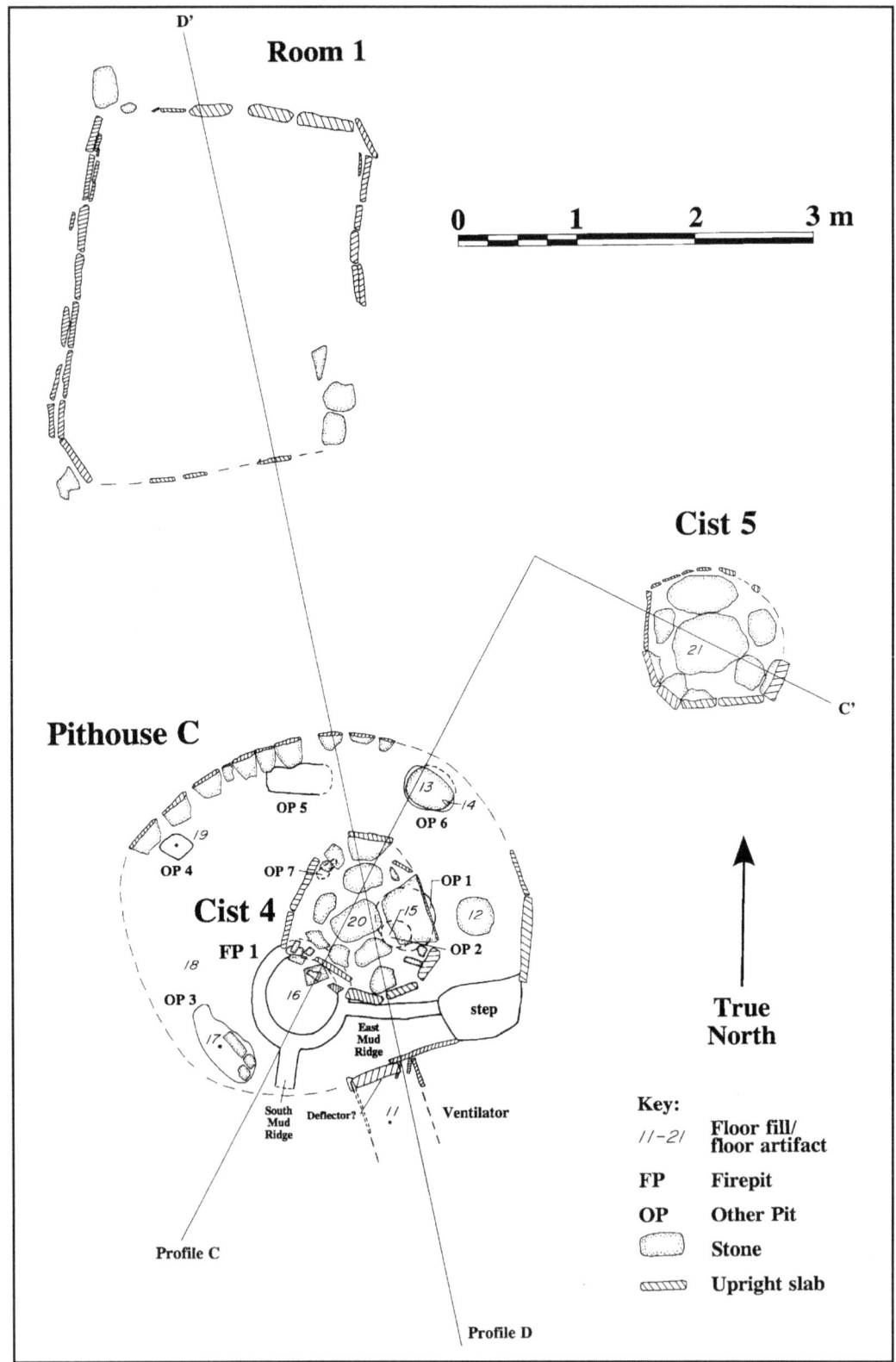

Figure I.4.9. Site 29SJ 721, plans of Pithouse C, Cists 4-5, and Room 1 (CHCU 65680). See Table I.4.5 for the list of specimens. Original by Tom Windes, 1973.

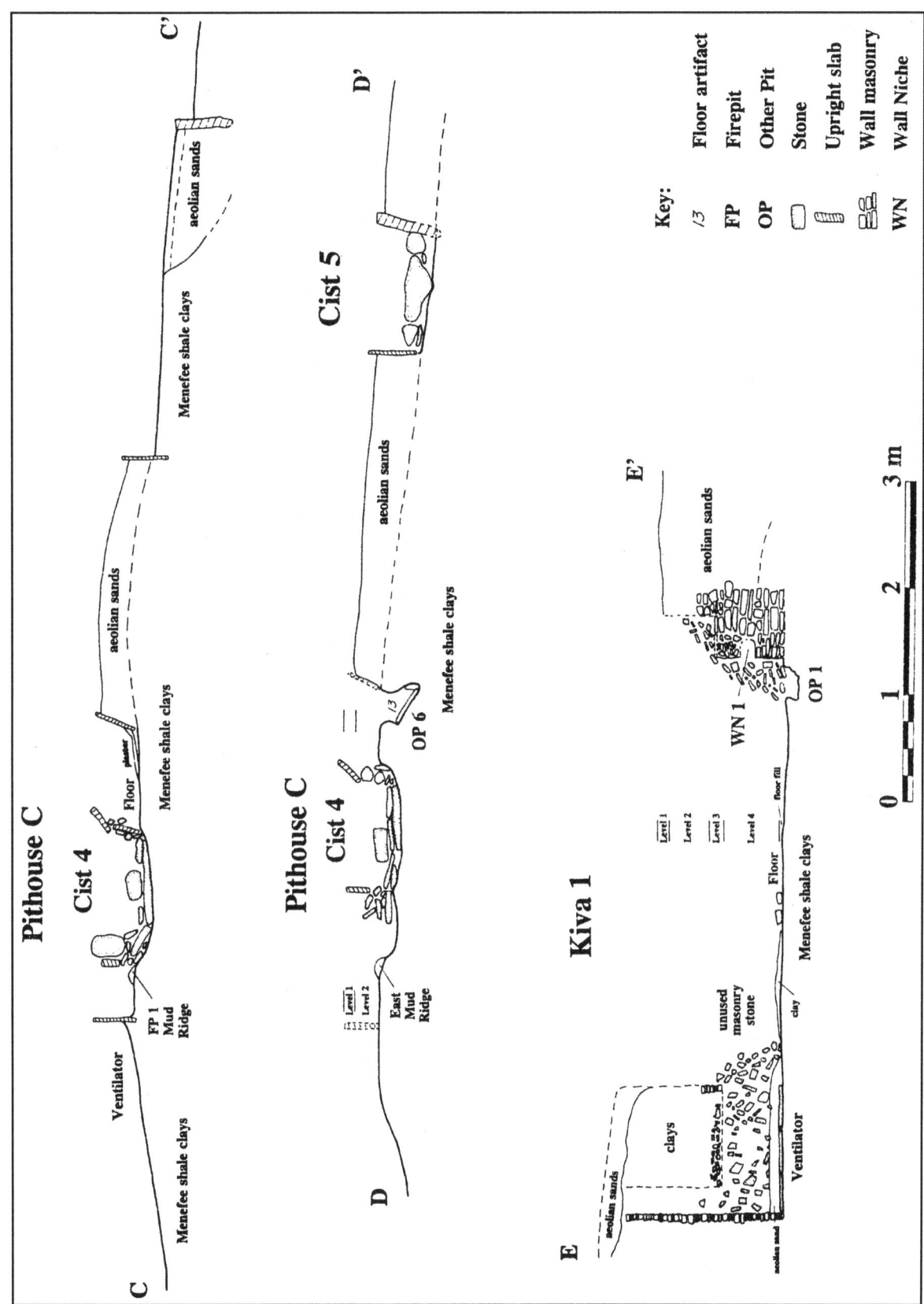

Figure I.4.10. Site 29SJ 1721, profiles of Pithouse C, Kiva 1, and Cists 4 and 5 (CHCU 65681). Original by Tom Windes, 1973.

floor covered 8.3 m², although features reduced it by 1.5 m².

Floor Artifacts (Figure I.4.9, Table I.4.5)

Only a few sherds and pieces of chipped stone debitage west of the firepit were recovered from the floor. A chipped-edge sandstone cover had been placed in the bottom of OP 6 in the northeastern corner, and a flaked bi-face knife was recovered from the fill 8-cm above it.

Floor Features (Tables I.4.6-I.4.7)

Firepit

A circular, adobe-collared firepit was located on the southwestern side of the house. About one-third of it had been destroyed by the intrusive roasting pit (Cist 4) that probably contributed the numerous clay chunks and pieces of stone, ash, and charcoal found in the upper 14-cm of the firepit. The lower 6-cm of firepit fill consisted of ash, charcoal, and fire-reddened sand from firepit use. The 13-cm-wide adobe collar had been remodeled once with the application of an additional adobe coat 15-mm thick. The second coat was fire-reddened from contact with the roasting pit. Otherwise, very little heat discoloration was evident within the firepit. An archaeomagnetic sample from the firepit initially suggested an A.D. 1300s/1400s use (Table I.6.6), which is normally an indication of A.D. 900s/1000s use (see Chapter 6). In this case, however, the plot more likely relates to the nearby A.D. 600s part of the archaeomagnetic curve (Figure I.6.10); a later revised analysis (DuBois 2008) provided a date of A.D. 620 ± 26.

Radiating to the south-southwest and east from the firepit were raised ridges of clay, 5-cm high and 18-cm wide. Termination of the south-southwest ridge, less than 40-cm from the firepit, marks the former wall perimeter. The east mud ridge abuts a 10-cm high, rectangular platform of clay covered with adobe plaster. If the opening in the wall behind the platform was an entryway, then the platform served as a low step into the chamber.

In addition to the firepit, six pits were found in the house floor. All contained charcoal-flecked, sandy fill identical to Level 2. Two pits were found under the roasting pit, the rest near the walls. OP 1, similar in size to the firepit, was located just east of the house center and included the smaller pit, OP 2, at one end but extending 4-cm deeper. Their temporal association is uncertain, and OP 2 contained organic matter not found in OP 1. OP 1 could have held a vessel, although that would have blocked the opening into OP 2. A pit similar to OP 1 east of the firepit in Pithouse A might also have been a pot rest.

Ten centimeters southwest of the firepit was a semi-oblong pit (OP 3) with three smooth sides and an unmodified, irregular east side. Inside were three burned tabular stones overlying charred brush. Ash, charcoal, clay chunks, and a Lino Gray-like sherd were recovered from the pit. OP 4, in the northwestern corner, also yielded chunks of clay and a tiny crystal. Next to the wall was OP 5, a U-shaped trough that contained a few spalls. Its bottom started at floor level on the east end and gradually deepened to 11.5-cm at the opposite end. In the northeastern corner was OP 6, with a slab purposely placed at a 45° angle to cover one side and the pit bottom—the pit edge had to be removed in order to recover it. At the foot of the slab, another slab had been set vertically against the north pit wall.

Three of the pits reflected the normal positions for a four-post roof support arrangement, but evidence for such use was lacking. Instead, OP 6 appears to have served as a storage pit; the function of the others (OP 3 and OP 4) is unclear. OP 5 might have been natural.

Walls

Large vertical slabs, set in mortar, were found along the east end and south sides of the house.

Thin slabs rested against the sloping bank that had been cut during the initial house construction, and which formed the north wall foundation. At one time the slab wall evidently encircled the chamber, but it had been partly removed after abandonment. Removal of fill from around the wall exterior failed to uncover any postmolds, and no bench was present.

Wall Features

Despite the lack of a deflector, the slab wall next to the firepit had been modified to serve as an above-ground ventilator. A large slab, 40-x-40-cm and 9-cm thick, had been set in the south wall, unmortared, with two others set in clay perpendicular to the first, forming a 50-cm-long tunnel—a practical design considering the slope of the knoll. One of the two parallel slabs was missing but its former position in the native clay was apparent. The purpose of the large slab was apparently to cover the ventilator opening when not in use.

Roof

The absence of the traditional framework marked by postholes and a bench suggests that the house roof consisted of poles set next to the wall slabs at an angle to meet over the center of the chamber, similar in form to a tipi. Then, the conical roof would have been covered by brush, bark, or other closing material and overlain with a thick application of mud.

Discussion

Similar in size to Pithouse A, this was a small Basketmaker III chamber with little floor space. Except for a single remodeling of the firepit, there are no signs of extensive use of the house. There was no catastrophic abandonment of the house, and important tools and the valuable major roof supports were salvaged. After abandonment, the location was reused for a large roasting pit.

Room 1
(Figure I.4.6, Plate I.4.12)

Downslope and 240-cm to the north from Pithouse C was a rectangular outline of vertical slabs. A surface collection of artifacts was made in conjunction with the clearing of Pithouse C (Table I.4.5). Removal of only 13-cm of charcoal-flecked, aeolian sand (Level 1) was sufficient to expose the room floor. Artifacts in the fill consisted of three Lino Gray sherds and a Puerco Black-on-red sherd.

Floor

Smoothed native gray clay, into which the floor had been cut, served as the floor at the south end of the room. The slope of the knoll left the northern two-fifths of floor underlain by charcoal-flecked aeolian sand that had been covered by a 15-cm thick application of gray clay. The floor was 330-cm long, north-to-south, 255-cm wide, and encompassed 8.4 m². No floor features were found.

Walls

Deeply set vertical sandstone slabs, one or two

Plate I.4.12. Site 29SJ 721, Room 1, a slab-lined storage room. Looking northwest. 30-cm north arrow. Photograph by Tom Windes, 1973 (CHCU neg. 5794).

rows wide, constituted the wall foundations. In at least one instance, a slab had been set 45-cm into the ground. Slabs ranged from up to 35-cm high, 40-cm long, and 10-cm thick. In places, especially on the north side, the wall consisted of short, elongated stones resting loosely on the ground. Spaces along the wall may reflect scavenging of the slabs for use elsewhere. A 50-70-cm space in the middle of the east wall may have marked the entry. Although the wall exterior was carefully cleared, no evidence for posts was found; however, a small, rotted piece of wood was recovered along the north wall. Walls were probably built primarily of mud.

Roof

Surprisingly, no evidence of roofing, not even roofing adobe, existed. Perhaps the room was unfinished, but it is impossible to be sure.

Cists and Isolated Features
(Figures I.4.6-I.4.10, Plates I.4.13-I.4.15)

Six or seven slab-lined cists were found across the site (Table I.4.6). Two types of pits were evident. Category 1 pits consisted of haphazardly arranged, large, unshaped burned slabs and other stones (Plates I.4.13 and I.4.15). This category of pits comprises Cists 1-2, and 4-6. They probably were used as cooking or roasting pits or kilns. The occupational fill consisted of abundant quantities of ash, charcoal, burned brush, and as many as 25-30 rough, fire-cracked stones covered by postoccupational aeolian sand. Little cultural material was recovered from these cists (Table I.4.5). This category of pits comprises Cists 1-2, and 4-6. They probably were used as cooking or roasting pits or kilns.

A layer of fire-reddened sand and adobe chunks overlay the other burned material in Cist 2. Larger, rough stones formed crude pit bottoms except in Cist 2. Often a thin layer of ash, 1-2-cm thick, was found under the flagstones. Cist 4 was the largest and most extensively burned of the pits.

A small pit underneath, OP 7 in Pithouse C, appears to have derived from the use of this feature. The approximate inside area of the pits ranged between 0.61 and 1.21 m^2 (mean = 0.85 m^2).

Only a few artifacts were associated with the cists. Cist 1 yielded a Lino Gray body sherd from under the flagstones. Debitage and additional plain gray body sherds came from the sandy fill covering Cists 4-6.

Category 2 cists, smaller than those in the first type, consisted of three pits with nearly vertical, thin slab sides (Plate I.4.14) and indeterminate bottoms of aeolian sand. Generally, there was little evidence of burning. Cist 2 was filled with burned material and stones but morphologically was dissimilar from the first category of cists. Perhaps it was originally a Category 2 cist but was later reused as a Category 1 feature. Cist 7 consisted of a single upright slab associated with a second slab fallen next to it. Several other slabs scattered in the sand nearby attest to the cist's former existence. Cist 3 was filled with charcoal-flecked postoccupational sands but was missing part of its north side. These cists range from 0.42 to 0.70 m^2 (mean = 0.56 m^2) in area.

The second category of cists resembles storage pits that are typical on early sites. These pits are widely scattered in Chaco on Chacra Mesa and at the heads of small rincons, often isolated from habitation areas. Their presence here suggests association with one or both pithouses, although they are much smaller than their counterparts at Shabik'eschee Village (mean = 2.5 m^2).

The only chronometric dates from the cists were obtained from a number of pieces of piñon, all deadwood, recovered from Cist 4; the latest piece postdated A.D. 621 (Table 6.2).

Kiva 1
(Figures I.4.10 and I.4.11, Plate I.4.16)

A few Pueblo II-III sherds were recovered from the site during the 1972 inventory survey and a

Plate I.4.13. Site 29SJ 721, Cist 1, a roasting pit. Looking northeast. 30-cm north arrow. Photograph by Tom Windes, 1973 (CHCU neg. 5791).

Plate I.4.14. Site 29SJ 721, Cist 2, a slab-lined storage cist reused as a firepit. Note layer of ash and charcoal in bottom fill wedge and near-vertical setting of slabs. Looking southeast. 30-cm north arrow. Photograph by Tom Windes, 1973 (CHCU neg. 5790).

Plate I.4.15. Site 29SJ 721, Cist 4, a roasting pit built in the center of Pithouse C. Note haphazard arrangement of slabs. Looking southwest. Photograph by Tom Windes, 1973 (CHCU neg. 5810).

Plate I.4.16. Site 29SJ 721, unfinished Kiva 1 after clearing. Photograph by Tom Windes, 1973 (CHCU neg. 5800).

few more came to light during excavation. The predominance of earlier pottery at the site, the presence of early structures, and the absence of masonry remains argued for the late ceramics to be intrusive, perhaps from nearby 29SJ 722, a Pueblo II-III site. Deep trenching at another depression between Pithouses A and C, however, revealed a Pueblo III kiva, showing how easily surface indicators and interpretations can be wrong.

Fill

Excavation began with removal of 10-cm of aeolian sand from a depression. Artifacts from this deposit were combined with those from the surface. Directly under the sand was a hard-compacted fill varying in depth from 30 to 50-cm. Because of the slope of the knoll, road picks were required to remove it. The matrix of this deposit, Level 1, was brown loam mixed with clay, charcoal, and sand, but artifacts were scarce.

Two curious holes, possibly postholes,

were found during surface stripping southeast of the kiva. The first was 170-cm from the kiva and the other, about 6 m further to the southeast, was buried under the backdirt and subsequently not measured. Both were similar in morphology and size. Subsequent stripping revealed no other features.

Level 2, about 35-40-cm deep, revealed the first clues of coming events. The eastern half continued as before (i.e., Level 1), but the western half became sandy with a few ash lenses. In this part, 70-85-cm below the surface, masonry was encountered and thoughts of a pithouse vanished. A few shovel strokes later, the remains of an adult female were found at the same level, 23-cm inside the southwestern arc of the kiva wall. No burial pit was discernable and, despite screening, only a single polished black bowl sherd was recovered 4-5-cm above the left knee. Another 20-cm beneath the skeleton the kiva bench top was reached and Level 2 was terminated.

Level 3, starting below the bench, consisted of soft, damp, aeolian sand speckled with charcoal flecks similar to the west half of Level 2. The northeastern quarter of the kiva, however, consisted of un-laminated sands with charcoal flecks sandwiched between thin layers of gray clay. Throughout Level 3 were large stones, probably from the collapsed wall or bench. Because of the differences in fill and the desire to control for cultural material in the two separate, underlying deposits, Level 3 was terminated after only 10-15-cm.

From just below the bench to 2-cm above the kiva floor, Level 4 fill (53-cm deep) continued exactly as the preceding level. The south half of unstratified aeolian sands yielded just three sherds; the west half was similar except for a slightly higher sherd frequency. In the northeastern quarter, however, unstratified sands gave way to laminae of sand and gray clay, yielding sherds from Basketmaker III to Pueblo III times. The thicknesses of the individual lamina were remarkably uniform: each gray clay layer was close to 2-cm in thickness while the intervening sand layers, from the floor up, were 8, 9, 7, 8, 8, 2, and 19-cm thick and extended into Level 3. This unusual deposition was also observed in "Pithouse B" and was similar to that in Pithouses D and G at 29SJ 628 and Kiva G at 29SJ 627 (Truell 1992). The last 2-cm of fill, although identical to Level 4, was arbitrarily considered floor fill.

Besides the fill described above, an additional deposit was noted. A homogenous mass of tightly packed hard gray clay and stone covered the bench and walls from the wall tops to the floor. The deposit ran counter-clockwise from the west side of the ventilator recess to the north side of the kiva. The same material filled the ventilator tunnel from 10-cm above the floor to 20-30-cm above the tunnel wall tops. Ten centimeters of aeolian sand covered the tunnel floor. Pockets of air and sand, trash, and other fill non-conformities generally expected in wall fall were absent. A comparable mass of clay and stone was lacking along the western side, although isolated stones from wall fall did occur in the fill and on the bench.

Floor

The floor consisted of smoothed native gray clay, identical to that used in the mortar and found mixed with rubble along the east side. Three subfloor tests (not on the map) up to 43-cm deep revealed that the floor clay was natural, but none of the tests reached the bottom of the deposit. Narrow strips of sand along the east and northeast sides revealed the natural clay slope 17-cm below the bench.

Floor Artifacts (Figure I.4.11, Table I.4.5)

A mere six sherds were recovered from the floor, but their type and placement were startling. At the mouth of the ventilator and continuing 56-cm into the tunnel were the pieces of a large polished

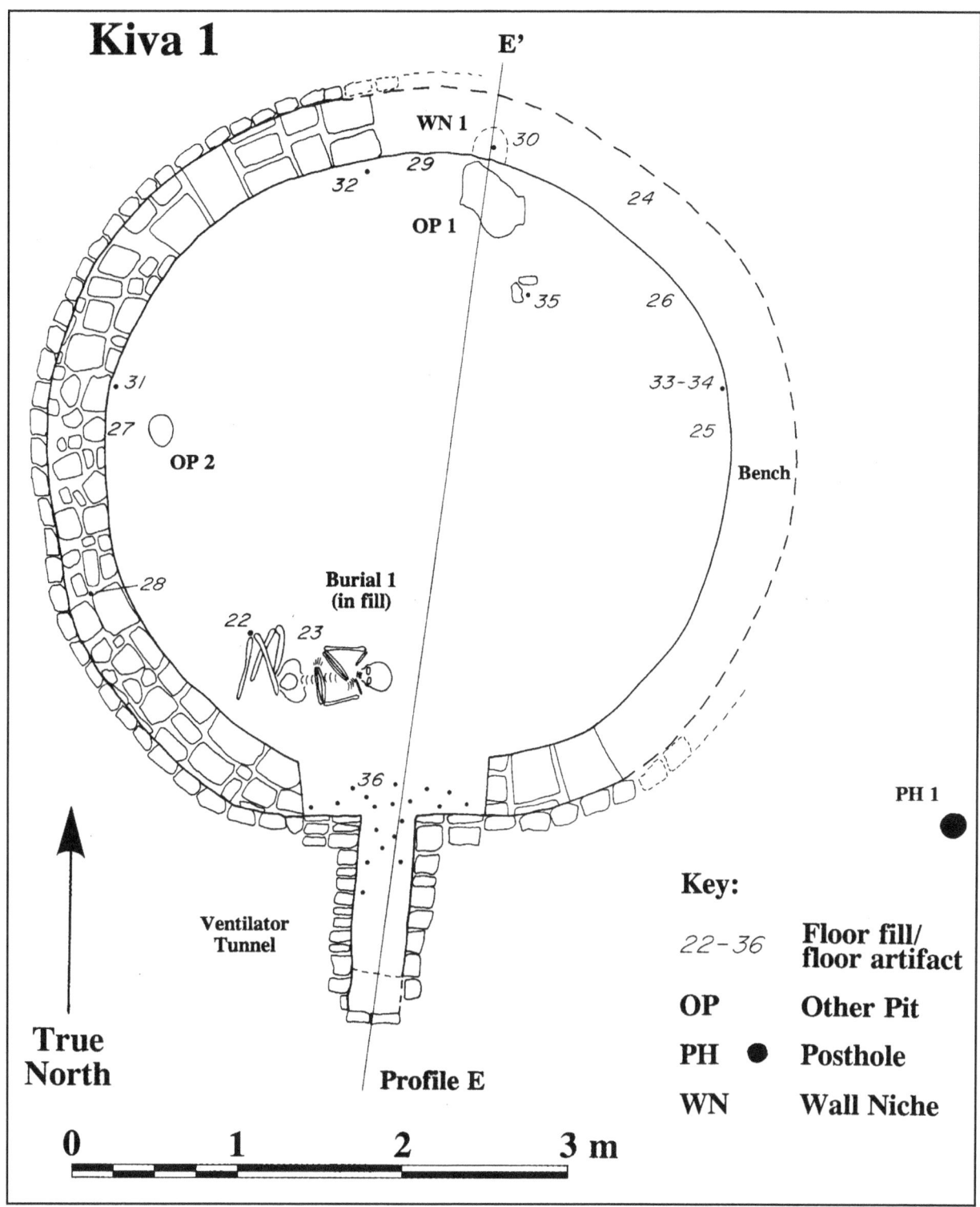

Figure I.4.11. Site 29SJ 721, plan of Kiva 1 (CHCU 65679). See Table I.4.6 for the list of specimens. Woodruff Smudged bowl sherds were deliberately placed in fill, and on and under the floor (FS 22, 31-33, 35-36) at the cession of construction. Original by Tom Windes, 1973.

black and orange bowl sherd of Woodruff Smudged. Opposite the tunnel and against the north bench face lay another Woodruff Smudged bowl sherd, on an alignment that bisected the tunnel at 178.5°/358.5° or nearly exactly true north-south. An indented corrugated sherd lay nearby. Likewise, Woodruff Smudged bowl sherds had been placed at the east and west sides of the floor along an alignment of 88.5°/268.5° or almost exactly true east-west. Just 10-15-cm above the western sherd was another that matched it. Under the eastern floor sherd, beneath the floor 15-cm, was a chalcedony flake. Finally, a sixth Woodruff Smudged bowl sherd came off the floor 69-cm in front of the bench face on the north-northeast side. Two flat, unshaped, rectangular pieces of sandstone rested directly north and west of the sherd. Similar stones lying to the east and south of the sherd may have been removed before their importance was recognized.

Floor Features (Table I.4.6)

Formal features associated with the floor were lacking. On the west side of the floor, 34-cm from the bench, was an irregular shallow pit (OP 2), possibly natural. A few concretion fragments occurred in the bottom but resembled those that occurred naturally in the floor clay. A second pit (OP 1), 3-cm from the bench and 28-cm below the niche in the bench face, was also irregular in shape but hand-smoothed around the edge of the mouth (Plate I.4.17). The bottom was rough because of numerous protruding reddish-brown concretion fragments. The fill in both pits was postoccupational and matched that in Level 4.

Walls

The masonry veneer above the bench was the last construction before work was terminated. It was built in a style similar to the bench, with masonry one or two courses wide starting at the top of the bench to cover the adjacent native earth.

Plate I.4.17. Site 29SJ 721, Kiva 1, pit and wall niche at north end of floor. Photograph by Tom Windes, 1973 (CHCU neg. 5805).

Its maximum height was 37-cm, possibly close to its original height. The eastern wall was not cleared but left under the mass of clay and stone that would have required a pick to remove. No plastering was evident, and pilasters were absent.

Wall Features

Bench

A masonry bench encircled the kiva, leaving a floor diameter of about 380-cm. The bench was 70-cm high, 50-60-cm wide, and rested on the natural clay floor. Scabbled stones were set in alternating bands of large blocks and multiple rows of smaller, tabular sandstones. Chinking often was used to fill gaps between bands and between stones of the same band (Plate I.4.18). Hawley (1934:14) referred to this style as Inferior Type III masonry, noting a "marked carelessness in workmanship" and bands of "uneven width, varying from the horizontal," and dated it to between A.D. 1062 and 1090 (1934:25-27). In contrast, the bench top was covered with large tabular stones, often spanning the bench width.

At the north end of the kiva, a sand-filled hole in the bench face (Plate I.4.17) appeared to have been formed from the removal of a stone. The hole exhibited tapered, smoothed sides and bottom (i.e., a niche) and contained a chacodonic flake, which had been placed intentionally.

Ventilator (Plate I.4.19)

At the south end of the kiva, a gap 108-110-cm wide and 37-40-cm deep had been left in the bench. Centered in the wall within this gap was the floor-level ventilator, built by cutting a trench down from the surface. The tunnel was 118-cm long and 33-cm wide, with walls extending upward 45-cm. Three rectangular flagstones, 40-x-35-cm and 5-cm thick, served as the ventilator floor. These were locked in place by the slightly overlapping ventilator wall stones, the same technique employed to anchor the bench top slabs under the walls. No tunnel ceiling had been built, and clearly the trench had been left open at the cessation of construction. The masonry lining the ventilator shaft rose 135-cm, stopping 45-cm below the present ground surface. It also was only partly intact on the south and part of the west sides. The upper 20-cm of fill in the shaft consisted of clayey loam and trash; the remainder was clay mortar and construction stone.

Plate I.4.18. Site 29SJ 721, Kiva 1, west wall bench masonry. Photograph by Tom Windes, 1973 (CHCU neg. 5806).

Plate I.4.19. Site 29SJ 721, Kiva 1 ventilator tunnel mouth where broken Woodruff Smudged bowl was found. Photograph by Tom Windes, 1973 (CHCU neg. 5807).

Roof

No evidence for roofing was recovered. The width of the bench suggests that pilasters were to have been added for a cribbed roof.

Discussion

It is clear that the kiva was abandoned before completion of construction for the following reasons. First, the following points:

1. Formal floor features were absent, particularly the important firepit, deflector, and sipapu.

2. No roofing remains or pilasters to support a roof were found.

3. The walls and bench were left unplastered, as was the sandy part of the floor.

4. The mass of gray clay and construction stone in the ventilator tunnel extended above the finished walls, indicates that this unused material had been dumped into an open and unfinished tunnel from above.

5. The same homogenous mass of clay and stone filling the tunnel covered the eastern wall and bench and must have been deposited simultaneously. The

composition of the material matches that used in the finished masonry and it therefore represents unused building materials. It was probably derived from the gray clay that was removed from the hole excavated for the kiva. Because of its composition, compactness, and context, there is virtually no possibility that the material represents wall fall.

Second, the arrangement of the Woodruff Smudged bowl sherds on the floor, to the exclusion of all others except a single corrugated sherd, indicates a deliberate act following structure abandonment. It is unlikely the sherds were placed in their existing locations during construction because of the high probability of disturbance. Their placement suggests that the recovered fill smudged sherds were also not randomly deposited. Most have been discussed above, but two others came from unknown locations within Level 2. Similar acts have not been reported in Chaco Canyon, although the behavior observed may be related to rare events, such as the incomplete construction of ceremonial structures, which are seldom identified archaeologically. Kivas 3 and 4 at Bc 51 were apparently unfinished but did not display a similar scheme of sherds (Kluckhohn 1939c:35, 37, Table 2), although polished black sherds were found in both.

Puebloan cosmology centers around six directions: north, south, east, west, up, and down, and each is associated with a color. Is it a coincidence that the polished black and orange-red sherds in the ventilator, the southern position, occurred in a direction commonly associated with the color red in Puebloan thinking (Parsons 1939:365)? Or that black is associated with "above" at Hopi (Parsons 1936:333, 744, 1191; 1939:365) and 'below' at Zuni (Parsons 1939:365)? On the basis of the kiva sherd placements, it can be argued that the findings here reflect a similar prehistoric cosmology or a ritual that, in this case, accompanies abandonment of kiva construction.

The builders of the kiva must have come from a house located somewhere else as there are no Pueblo III residential structures at 29SJ 721. Inhabitants living within 100 m of the site, at 29SJ 722 and 29SJ 646, appear to be logical candidates because of the temporal placement of the kiva in the late A.D. 1000s/early A.D. 1100s (based on ceramics and masonry style), which overlaps with the occupations of these locations. 29SJ 646 is large but appears to have had plenty of room for expansion. 29SJ 722, on the other hand, consists of about five rooms and a possible kiva perched on a small rock knoll less than 60 m north of 29SJ 721. The crowded conditions caused by a house built on a rocky knoll could have required construction of a new kiva on more suitable ground nearby. Another tantalizing bit of circumstance, a polished black-and-red sherd recovered from the surface of 29SJ 722, might indicate cultural ties if it came from the vessel recovered at 29SJ 721. Smudged sherds were not recovered from 29SJ 646; however, although that site was covered with numerous ceramics, perhaps their absence is merely due to sampling error.

Whatever prompted cessation of construction is not discernible in the archaeological record at this point. Five polished sherds were placed on the floor, four of them at the cardinal directions, when constructed ceased. A period of time elapsed, certainly less than a year, and, perhaps, only after a single windstorm accumulated 10-cm of sand over the ventilator floor. Then the remaining mortar and construction stone was dumped into the kiva, covering the masonry and the black sherd on the eastern side and filling the ventilator tunnel. The encapsulation of the stones in the mortar indicates the plasticity of the mortar when it was discarded, as if it had been discarded during the actual construction.

After abandonment of the kiva, sand drifted off the top of the knoll into the chamber and piled up along the western side. Sand built up more slowly along the eastern side, alternating with thin layers of gray clay derived from the discarded construction mortar. David Love (personal communication 1973), a geologist now with the New Mexico State Bureau of Mines, believed that the laminae derived from seasonal conditions of freezing and thawing of the clay mortar rather than from intermittent rainstorm erosion. It is also plausible that the unlaminated sands marked areas where the kiva was partly reexcavated, removing the natural stratigraphy of laminae that should have covered the entire chamber. If the number of clay layers is any indicator, the kiva may have refilled in less than 10 years, at which point the woman died and was interred with a black sherd over one knee high in the kiva fill.

The final deposition of a hard brown loam nearly obliterated the kiva depression. The same material can be found as part of the nearby Menefee Formation. The material might also have come from later buildings not evident on the surface or from the walls of Room 1 just upslope during a period wetter than when the sand was deposited in the kiva.

Discussion

The small size of the knoll may have prevented more extensive use of the site and limited it to the individual structures found. The inhabitants of 29SJ 722, however, favored a smaller, rocky knoll a few meters to the north, which suggests that habitation space was not the crucial factor for the limited use of the 29SJ 721 knoll. The latter's closeness to the mesa and the limitation of winter sunlight, may have been instrumental in discouraging substantial occupation of the knoll.

Establishing the temporal relationship of the various site structures and features is difficult. The paucity of ceramics, along with the long periods of time during which the recovered ceramic types were manufactured, prevent precise temporal placement of the structures. A few chronometric dates help place some limits on dates of the site occupation, but architectural style remains the primary source of temporal information.

The presence of two pithouses of different architectural styles could suggest functional or temporal differences or both. Both are smaller than the norm, and it could be argued that with one built on top of the ground and the other deep in the ground that they represent occupations by the same group during different seasons. The archaeomagnetic plots from the firepit samples, however, do not suggest contemporaneity. Pithouse C is unusual for its location on top of a knoll. The slab base walls and the two low ridges radiating from its circular clay firepit are common to late Basketmaker III and early Pueblo I pithouses. Its small ventilator is not only a practical adaptation to the pithouse placement on top of the ground but also indicative of ventilator architecture that postdates the late A.D. 600s.

Pithouse A architecturally resembles structures later than Pithouse C. The ventilator is similar, but the wing walls, ridges, and circular firepit have disappeared. Cooking and heating were done in a hexagonal slab-lined firepit, a type common in the Pueblo I and later periods (Gladwin 1945:44; McKenna 1986:13). Yet the bulging entrance of the ventilator into the main chamber and the rectangular house shape were attributes that usually failed to last beyond Pueblo I times. Architecture, ceramics, and archaeomagnetic dates suggest that Pithouse A was an A.D. 700s house and that Pithouse C was built in the A.D. 600s.

The common association of storage cists with pithouses makes it unlikely that the storage cists on the site are fortuitous. Two of these pits (Cists 2 and 3), situated just upslope and west of Pithouse A, suggest contemporaneous use with Pithouse A. Whether the cists and pithouse share the same ground surface could not be determined, although their depths were approximately the same. The remains of Cist 7 were not close to any structure, and, therefore, no association with other structures can be made.

The similarity and proximity of the roasting pits suggest use as a group or successive use over time. Lino Gray body sherds found under Cist 1 and in the sandy fill of Cists 4-6 suggest at least general temporal association. Cist 1, used as a roasting pit, was very close to Pithouse A but may be later than the pithouse. It seems too close to have been used simultaneously and may have been the source of the charcoal deposits found in the pithouse fill. The conversion of Cist 2 from storage to a roasting pit provided the best clue that baking or roasting activities postdate the storage cists and Pithouse A. Clearly, Cist 4 postdates Pithouse C. Nine tree-ring dates obtained from firepit fuel in Cist 4 merely place use of Cist 4 after A.D. 621. Tentatively, then, use of the pits is assigned to the A.D. 700s. Unfortunately, radiocarbon samples from Cists 2, 5, and 6 have not been processed.

Architecturally, Room 1 is associated with the Pueblo I (A.D. 800s) period when elongated, above-ground, slab-lined storage room foundations were common. The wall foundation slabs used in Room 1 and Pithouse C are similar, but the wall foundations are more complete in Room 1, appearing as if the slabs were robbed from Pithouse C. Slabs used for the roasting pits are not similar to those in Room 1 in size and shape. Storage rooms were typically aligned behind the pithouse, about where the Pueblo III kiva was located. Time did not permit a thorough investigation of the perimeter, but it would not be surprising if the kiva had been placed in earlier pithouse remains. The two postholes south of the kiva suggest that an additional structure is still to be located. On the other hand, the room's proximity and placement north of Pithouse C, a classic Pueblo I layout between pithouse and surface storage facility, suggest that these two structures may be related but the room's orientation is atypical.

To briefly reiterate, Pithouse C presumably was the earliest structure on the site, followed by Pithouse A, Cist 2, and Cist 3. It is unclear where Room 1 belongs. All, however, are probably seventh- or eighth-century structures. Later, but still in the eighth century, the knoll became a favored locale for baking or roasting, perhaps by inhabitants from one of the sites nearby. A lengthy hiatus then occurred until builders from a neighboring Pueblo III site started construction on the kiva. Although diagnostic sherds specifically dating to this period were not found on the floor of the kiva, the few in the upper fill probably relate to the brief period of construction of the kiva. The Toadlena B/w and Chaco-McElmo B/w sherds in the kiva fill, along with the architectural form and the masonry style, suggest the late A.D. 1000s or very early 1100s for the construction of the kiva.

No matter what the sequence of use at the site, it was always brief. Extensive trash and remodeling of the structures—indicators of extensive, lengthy occupations—were absent. The small size of the pithouses suggests that habitation was restricted to small nuclear families or that they were built for some special use.

PUEBLO I OCCUPATION AT 29SJ 724

At an elevation of 1,884 m (6,180 ft), the three separate roomblocks (Figure I.4.12) at 29SJ 724 are situated on a long, curving ridge of residual gravel that extends off the talus of South Mesa, east of the mouth of Weritos Rincon. These roomblocks were initially inventoried by Lloyd Pierson in 1960, who assigned the site number Bc 159 to the upper southern house, Bc 161 to the middle house, and Bc 162 to the lowest northern one on the ridge. The site complex was later reported as an extensive Basketmaker III community (Vivian and Mathews 1965:28). In 1972, the roomblocks were resurveyed by the author and designated 29SJ 724.

Each roomblock revealed a double or triple arc of upright slabs along the crest of the sand-covered ridge. The higher southern roomblock

(House III) contained about five or six rooms. To the east was a light scattering of trash, mixed with intrusive Pueblo II ceramics, and a probable pithouse. The middle house (House I), 30 m downslope, appeared to have about six rooms with a large scattering of trash to the east. This house (Figures I.4.12 and I.4.13) was excavated and forms the basis for this report (Plate I.4.20). Sixty-two meters further down the ridge to the north was another roomblock (Houseblock II or the North House), which was midden tested in 1975 (Figure I.4.12) and a sample of chipped stone field analyzed in 1999 (see Moss, Volume II). It contained about 10 Pueblo I rooms with an early Pueblo II room built over the southwestern end. Trash was scattered downslope to the south, over one or more pitstructures. Finally, at the junction of the ridge and talus is a late Basketmaker III site (29SJ 648), and on a knoll at the toe of the ridge is a two-room Pueblo II site (29SJ 723). Another small Pueblo II site (29SJ 725) was located on a low mound just below the main ridge in the flats to the west (Figure I.4.12).

Hungo Pavi, a large Bonito phase ruin, is located across the canyon and provides a central locus for the later small houses clustered in the vicinity of the two major side drainages, Mockingbird Canyon and Weritos Rincon. The location is ideal with arable land supplied with water from the Chaco Wash and runoff from Weritos Rincon and Mockingbird. In Pueblo III times, a large masonry dam retained much of the water collected from the cliff tops above Weritos Rincon (Lagasse et al. 1984). Water can also be obtained from bedrock potholes, with a capacity of between 4 and 200 liters, that border the cliff tops directly behind the site. Probably as a result of runoff and the particular orientation of the nearby cliffs, enhancing passive solar heating (Windes 1993), Pueblo II and Pueblo III sites abound at the mouth of the rincon. Stone for building also was readily available from the nearby cliffs.

Plants were plentiful on the site, some

Plate I.4.20. Site 29SJ 724. Excavations at a classic Pueblo I house located at the mouth of Werito's Rincon. Note the deep pithouse and the contiguous arc of storage rooms. Looking southwest. Photograph by Tom Windes, 1974 (CHCU neg. 9380).

historically intrusive. Galleta, blue grama grass, and sand dropseed are dominant, followed by lesser numbers of winterfat, saltbrush, snakeweed, hedgehog cactus, prickly pear cactus, narrow-leaf yucca, Russian thistle, and asters. After a period of abundant moisture, large quantities of purslane, a nutritious plant, sprout on the site. Sacaton grass was common in the drainage areas bordering the ridge.

Excavation at the Central House started 12 August 1974 and finished on 18 September 1974. We returned to the site in 1975 to examine the pithouse further and to search for additional floor features in Rooms 1 and 9 and in the plaza. Finally, in 1976, the plaza surface was systematically cleared in its entirety, which revealed more pits and postholes. More archaeomagnetic sampling was also done. The site was backfilled except for the pithouse, which was left half filled. Finally, a search for clays and lithic sources was done nearby. The source of many of the chipped stone materials at the site is only a short distance away in the talus slope, where lag gravels, including fragments of petrified wood, were exposed.

Most of the excavation work was done by

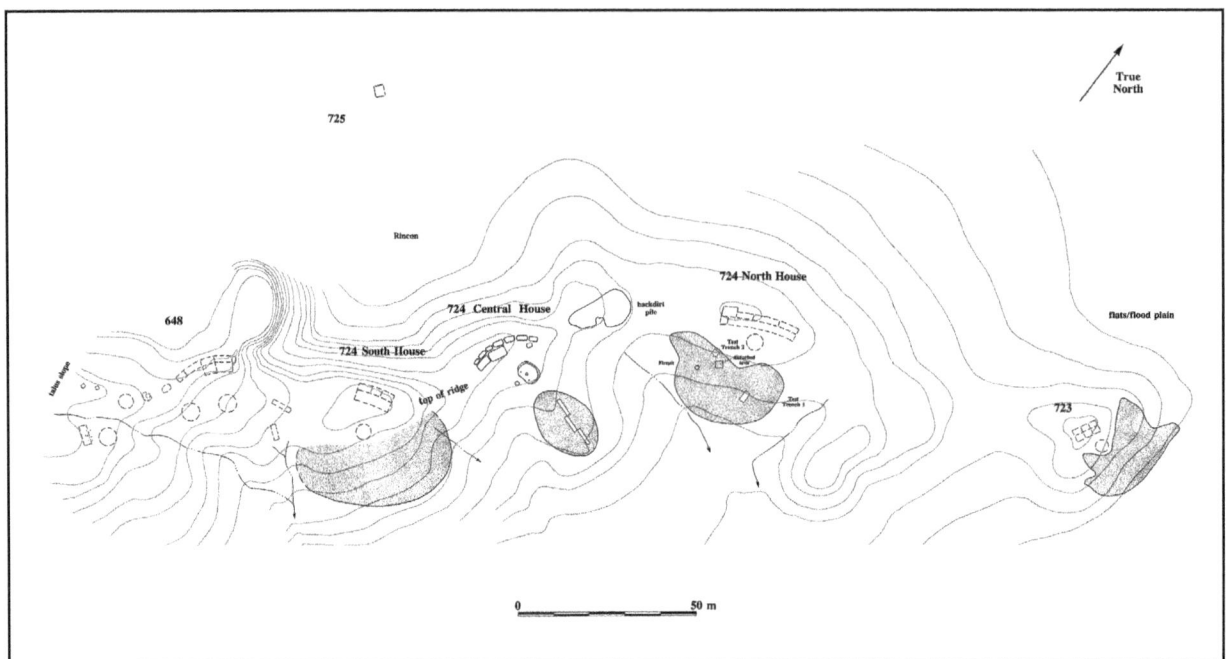

Figure I.4.12. Site occupation of the 29SJ 724 ridge and its adjacent flood plain and mesa talus (CHCU 65987-65988). Contour interval is one foot (30.5-cm); absolute elevations are approximate. Original by Tom Windes, 2003.

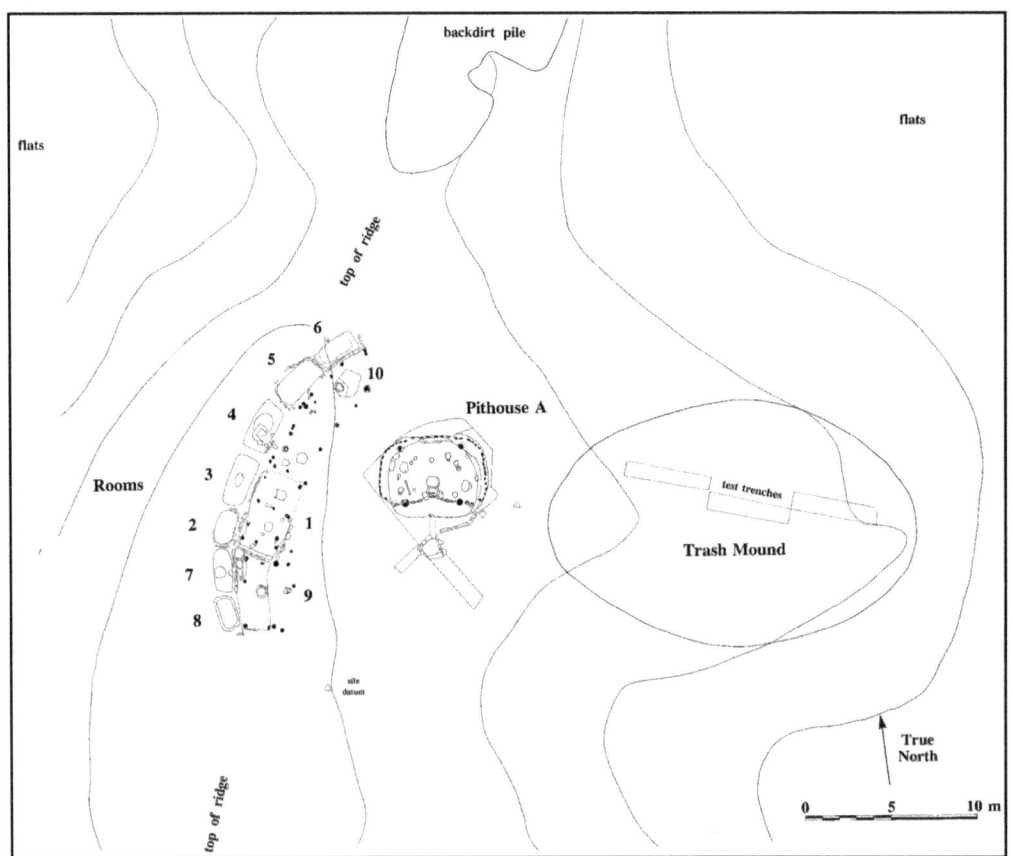

Figure I.4.13. Site 29SJ 724, site overview of Roomblock I and associated pithouse (CHCU 65697). Contour interval is one meter; absolute elevations are approximate. Original by Tom Windes, 1974.

Navajos living in the vicinity, most of whom were veterans of the previous field season: Ken Augustine, Chee Beyale, Alvin Dennison, James Kee, Junior Lopez, Nelson Trujillo, John Wero, and Bruce Yazzie (Plate I.4.21). Junior Lopez and Bruce Yazzie mapped much of the site and also took room notes. Several volunteers worked at the site: the Curtis Family—Ty, Greg, Bob, Curt, Kathy, and Bonnie—from Lake Havasu City, Arizona, and their friend Cindy Davis; Frank and Linda Creelman; Pam Freund of Taos, New Mexico; and Paul and Dorothy Etavard, photographers from St. Louis. Members of the National Park Service who worked at the site were Mac Formen of Chaco Canyon National Monument and W. James Judge, Peter McKenna, Robert Powers, and John Schelberg of the Chaco Center.

Since the site was only a short distance from the road, the excavation crew walked in from the road to lessen impacts on the fragile environment. Two trips were made to the site with a pickup truck to unload and retrieve the large lock-box in which the tools were stored. Excavation was accomplished solely with hand tools.

Light trash was stripped off the saddle separating House I from House II and the backdirt was deposited there. Rooms not evident from the surface were located after the entire roomblock area was stripped of loose sand. This also exposed the ventilator shaft opening of the pithouse. Rooms were excavated in 10 or 20-cm levels, which have been combined for analysis and reporting. The south half of the pithouse was excavated in 20-cm-deep levels, the remainder in natural layers. A grid was superimposed over the trash area and three relatively unproductive grids were excavated. Screening with quarter-inch screen was limited to the fill of floor features. Pollen, flotation, and other samples were collected but not with a preplanned research design. All mapping was done with a plane table and alidade.

Rooms

(Figures I.4.14 and I.4.15, Plates I.4.22 and I.4.23, Tables I.4.8-I.4.10)

Nine rectangular or oval rooms were aligned in an arc facing southeast (Figure I.4.14). Seven rooms forming the back part of the arc were fronted by two larger rooms at the south end and a ramada. A tenth room, isolated from the others, was located at the north end of the ramada. Except for the unit of three rooms at the south end of the roomblock and the isolated room, room positions were clearly marked on the surface by rows of upright slabs.

All rooms were semisubterranean, dug into hard residual gravelly earth (see Lekson 2004). The smaller rooms were sunk 30 to 80-cm below the surface. Four of them (Rooms 2, 7, 8, and 10) resembled sunken bathtubs that gave rise to the term "tub rooms." Backed into the ridge slope were the two larger rooms, varying in depth from 15 to 20-cm deep. Specimens from the loose sand and the surface were collectively designated as surface material for each room. Generally, once the loose sand had been removed, room outlines became evident. The grayish brown mixture of

Plate I.4.21. Overview of the Pithouse A, 29SJ 724, excavations in 1974. Floor is partly cleared. Note secondary slab wall in fill just above the floor next to the author. Looking east. L to R: Junior Lopez, James Kee (in hat), Ken Augustine (with scarf), Tom Windes, and John Wero (hat). Photograph by Paul Etavard, 1974 (CHCU neg. 79364).

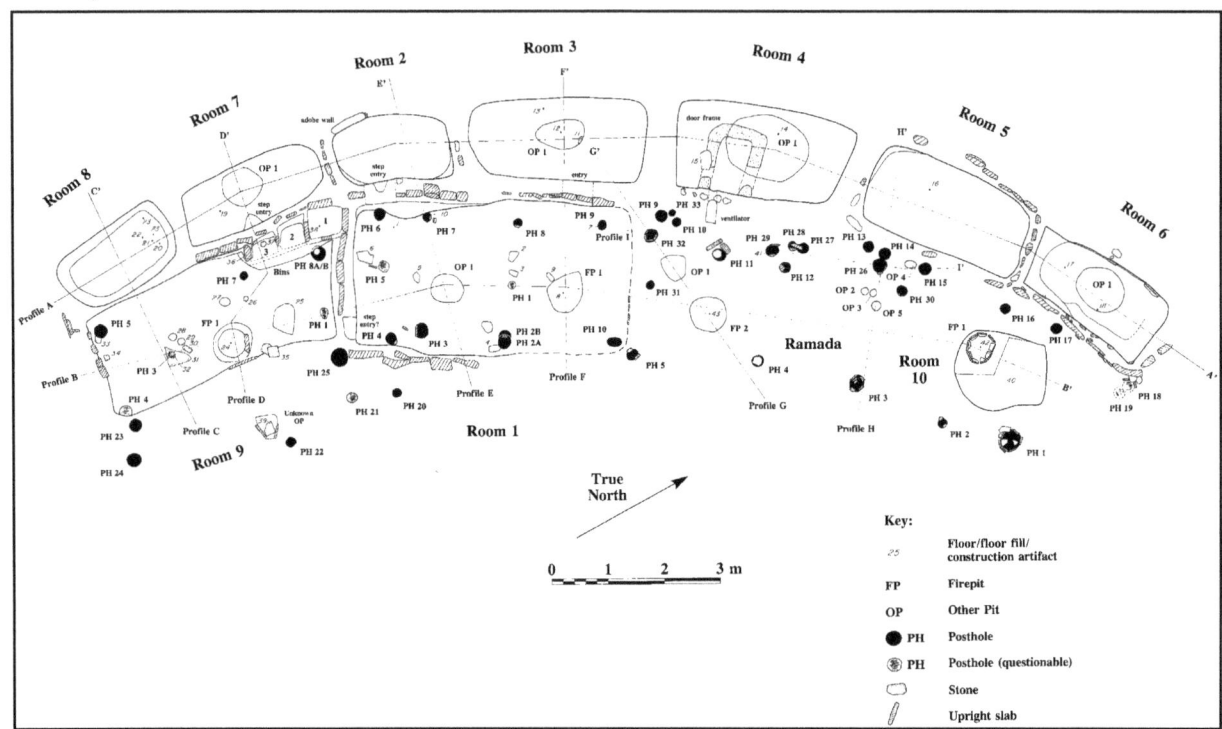

Figure I.4.14. Site 29SJ 724, Plan view of ramada and rooms showing profile lines and the floor fill and floor artifacts listed in Table I.4.9 (CHCU 65698). Originals by W. James Judge, Tom Windes, and Bruce Yazzie, 1974.

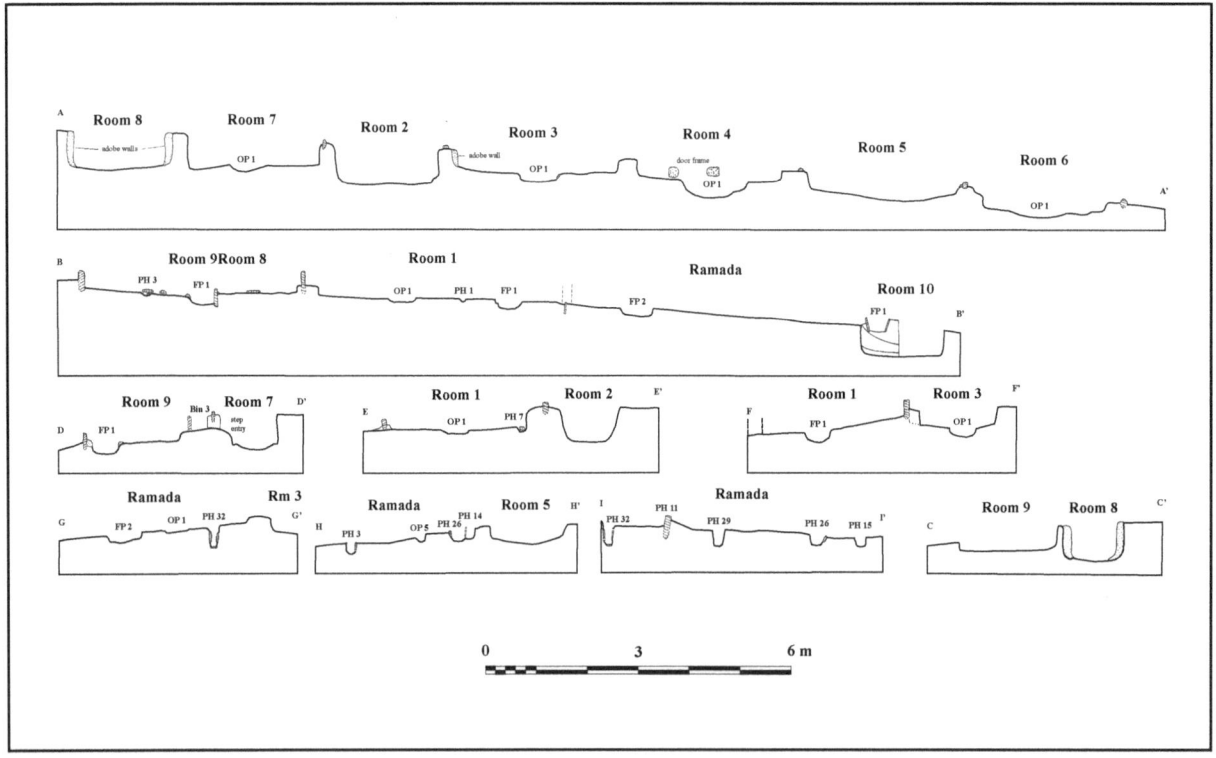

Figure I.4.15. Site 29SJ 724, profiles of surface rooms and ramada (CHCU 65699). Originals by Tom Windes 1974, 1975, and 1976.

Plate I.4.22. Site 29SJ 724. Excavations in the surface storage rooms. The stacks of stone reflect the amount of stone used in the primarily adobe room walls. Note the selection of the storage room placement along the highest spine of the ridge-a common practice. Living Room 9 in foreground backed by storage Rooms 7 and 8. Looking north. Photograph by Tom Windes, 1974 (CHCU neg. 9237).

Plate I.4.23. Site 29SJ 724. Excavations in the surface storage rooms. The stacks of stone reflect the amount of stone used in the primarily adobe room walls. Note the selection of the storage room placement along the highest spine of the ridge-a common practice. Excavators are Ben Norberto, Alvin Dennison, Junior Lopez, and Ken Augustine. Looking south. Photograph by Paul Etavard, 1974 (CHCU neg. 31615).

clay and adobe containing numerous stones in each room easily contrasted with the surrounding native gravel and yellowish sand. This was removed in 10 or 20-cm levels, although for analytical and descriptive purposes these strata have been condensed as "fill." A control block was left in one corner until the room was finished. Specimens from the fill occurred in nominal numbers and charcoal was almost nonexistent.

Besides the exceptions noted for individual rooms, all rooms were filled mostly with building materials. The upper part consisted of above-surface wall fall, which in two cases was sufficiently intact to reveal the style of construction: courses of puddled mud were interspersed with occasional rows of small stones laid horizontally. These stones averaged from 10 to 20-cm long, 10 to 15-cm wide, and 4 to 7-cm thick. They were readily available along the cliff tops behind the site, although many were burned or discarded artifacts evidently obtained from other ruins nearby. The use of stone increased near the wall top, occurring in rows every 10 or 20-cm of elevation.

The walls were sometimes strengthened by a row of foundation slabs set along the edge of the room. This was not a universal practice; it tended to be employed where little remained of the original ground surface; for example, between rooms, where ground support was the weakest. Some of the walls appeared to have been shared by adjoining rooms. In the small rooms, walls without slab foundations apparently were of turtleback construction Turtlebacks are of short sections of semi-plastic mud about the thickness of a man's arm that are placed in rows over the patted convex brick below (Plate I.4.3; see Morris 1959:170; Vivian 1965:14, Figure 3).

Under the wall fall and extending to the floor, the fill became softer with fewer stones and chunks of adobe and clay, more gravel, sand, and, rarely, pieces of roofing. Recognizable roofing consisted of twigs and adobe casts of beams. This layer was generally 15 to 25-cm thick. Although some of the gravel derived from erosion, much of it apparently was incorporated into the building mud. Sand was more prevalent in this lower layer, indicating the slow rate at which the roofing collapsed. Once the roof was gone, walls were subject to greater erosion, resulting in quicker demise. Little aeolian sand was found on the floors. In the shallow rooms, roof and wall fall blended together preventing differentiation.

Rooms generally exhibited rough, slightly bulging walls that sloped inward to merge with the floor. Corners were rounded, with each wall blending into the next. The dish-shaped floors were rough and uneven. Occasionally, adobe plaster partially covered the gravelly floors and walls.

Room 1

Fill

The fill in Room 1 was typical of the site, consisting mostly of adobe and stone. Just below the surface the remains of an entire fallen wall were evident. The breadth of the wall fall matched the length of the east wall foundation slabs, revealing the east wall as the source of the fall. Rows of small stones were laid horizontally in the mud wall (Plate I.4.24) identical in style to the wall in Room 5. Nearly 140-cm separated the top row of stones from the base of the east wall, although single stones had fallen in position up to 164-cm away. Adding the 18-cm height of the east wall foundation to these measurements reveals a former wall height of at least 158-182-cm. Altogether, about 110 wall stones, some sherds, debitage, a hammerstone, a door cover, and two groundstones were recovered from the fill.

Floor

Packed, gravelly native earth with remnants of a thin clay plaster covered the floor in the southern third of the room.

Plate I.4.24. Site 29SJ 724, Room 1 wall fall. Note the linear series of upright slabs in the middle of the room that mark former horizontal stone placement in primarily adobe room walls. Bipod photograph by Randy Morrison, 1974 (CHCU neg. 9278).

Floor Features (Tables I.4.10 and I.4.11)

Firepit

Opposite the floor pit, at the north end of the room, was an oblong firepit lined with adobe and barely fire-reddened on one side. A small fire, leaving 2-3-cm of ash and charcoal, had been built over 1-3-cm of yellowish tan sand covering the bottom. This, in turn, was buried by 10-14-cm of aeolian, charcoal-flecked sand. Several flakes were found in the fill. A hammerstone, door cover, and two groundstones also came from the room surface.

Postholes

A number of postholes with varying amounts of lignite (a poor grade of local coal) fill were placed around the room perimeter. The six largest (PH 2-4, 6, 8-9) ranged from 10 to 42-cm deep and 14 to 26-cm across. One or two stone shims in each were common. Posthole 2 revealed two overlapping holes of similar size. A posthole for the northeastern corner could not be found but perhaps was supplemented by a nearby ramada Posthole 5. Four chunks of adobe, including one with about a 6-cm-diameter beam impression, were found in Posthole 6. A hammerstone came from the bottom of Posthole 9, which was filled with sand, clay, and a few pieces of lignite.

Three circular postholes (PH 1, 5, 7), less than 18-cm in diameter and 14-cm deep, were placed about midway between the six main postholes. Lignite and shims were absent; they probably held auxiliary roof posts. Posthole 7 yielded a hammerstone in the fill.

Floorpit

In the center of the south part of the room was an unlined and unburned basin similar in shape to a firepit. It was filled with charcoal-flecked, clayey material.

Floor Specimens (Figure I.4.14, Table I.4.10)

Sherds and debitage were scattered about in small numbers, plus a piece of limonite, two manos, and four groundstones were recovered.

Walls

Below the surface, walls were simply unlined, gravelly native earth. On the surface, large, unshaped slabs set in adobe composed the wall foundations along the south and part of the east and west walls. A wall on the north side could not be located and probably the adobe wall had melted away over time.

Doorways

Breaks between wall foundation slabs along the south and west walls suggest access points into adjoining Rooms 9 and 2, respectively. The break in the south wall, east end, is marked by a slanted indentation which may have served as a small step, but little notice of this feature was taken during excavation so additional supporting evidence for doorway access is unavailable. At the south end of the west wall, the break leads directly onto another indentation that seems certain to have been a step for access into and out of Room 2, which was quite deep.

Room 8 also appears to have had door into the living room in front of it, and a nearly intact, adobe door frame fell into Room 4.

Discussion

Similar to Room 9, this room appears to have been built as a partially enclosed ramada living area. The large wall foundation slabs next to the room probably mark walls built solely for Room 1 except for sharing the south wall with Room 9. The north perimeter presumably aligned with the wall between Rooms 3 and 4. Three small, upright stones set in a row, of little use for wall support, were found along the expected perimeter. Nevertheless, if the north and half of the east sides were left open, as it appears, then a formal perimeter might not have existed.

All wood apparently was salvaged from the room after abandonment. The arrangement of postholes indicates that the roof was shifted or rebuilt. The post seated in Posthole 2 was shifted slightly to form a new alignment just inside the initial one.

Room 2 (Plate I.4.25)

Fill

Collapsed and melted wall adobe along with 46 small stones constituted the entire fill. Artifacts were absent except for three trough metate fragments undoubtedly used for wall construction.

Floor

The floor was unlined, gravelly native earth. No floor features and specimens were found.

Walls

Gravelly native earth with small patches of plaster, 1-2-cm thick, was applied to the walls below the original ground surface. A 4-cm-thick clay

Plate I.4.25. Site 29SJ 724, Room 2 after clearing. Note the deep, tub-like excavation. 30-cm north arrow. Bipod photograph by Randy Morrison, 1974 (CHCU neg. 9366).

liner covered the south side. At the surface, small, upright stones were set about 11-cm back from the edge on the south and north sides. Along the east side, the row was set back 23-cm and consisted of stones almost double in size. At the south end of the row a 55-cm-wide gap was found opposite an alteration in the room side, a probable entry. Only a strip of clay 12-cm wide and 4-cm high bordered part of the west side.

Discussion

Wall foundation slabs at the south and north ends probably supported walls common to the adjoining rooms. There is a 55-cm-wide gap near the north end of the east row of foundation slabs. The position and size of the eastern slabs suggest use as a separate foundation for the west wall of Room 1. This gap could have marked an entryway between the two rooms. Although a Room 1 posthole is directly in front of the passage, it may have held a post step rather than a roof support.

Room 3 (Plate I.4.26)

Fill

Room 3 contained the typical fill but yielded an unusually high number of stones (N = 180), which presumably were inserted throughout the above ground adobe walls. A 10-cm-diameter ball of burned and charred adobe was found in the southwestern corner, 10-cm below the wall. Less than 10-cm above the floor at the south end were chunks of roofing. One wedge-shaped piece of gravel and adobe was patted smooth on both sides, while another exhibited two parallel beam impressions; the measurable one was for an 8-cm diameter beam. Sherds, debitage, two manos, one mano fragment, three metate fragments, and five groundstones were in the fill, probably utilized in the walls.

Floor

The floor was unlined, gravelly native earth.

Plate I.4.26. Site 29SJ 724, Room 3 after clearing. Note the shallow subfloor pit feature. 30-cm north arrow. Bipod photograph by Randy Morrison, 1974 (CHCU neg. 9364).

Floor Features (Table I.4.8)

Near the room center was an unlined, basin-shaped pit filled with sand and chunks of roofing. One chunk of gravel and adobe was patted smooth and another revealed twig impressions, 2-4 mm in diameter. Two plain gray sherds and a metate fragment also came from the pit but nothing to suggest its initial use.

Floor Specimens (Figure I.4.14, Table I.4.10)

Sherds and debitage, one bone, and one bead were recovered from the floor.

Walls

The below-ground walls were unlined, gravelly native earth exhibiting occasional patches of adobe, 1-cm thick. In the east wall, 80-cm from the northeast corner, was a passage filled with clay that continued eastward to a row of wall foundation slabs. This passage extended from the floor to the surface and was 61-cm wide. No slab wall foundations were evident, although a row of stones near the top of the fill and parallel to the south wall was evidently the slab foundation, which had been pulled into the room when the south wall fell. The slabs along the east side, 25-cm from the room edge, probably are foundation stones for Room 1's west wall. Two of these slabs blocked the passageway into Room 3 from Room 1. Thus, either Room 3 was abandoned when Room 1 was built or another entryway existed, which was not evident.

Room 4 (Plate I.4.27)

Fill

Sand with some gravel, clay, and 60-100 stones constituted the fill of this storage room. Numerous turtleback pieces, many of them 15-cm wide and exhibiting fingerprints, were scattered near the top of the fill along the south wall. Just to the north was a U-shaped adobe block, 80-x-63-cm and 19-cm thick, resting on 2-cm of clean sand on the floor. This was a fallen door frame, 58-cm wide on the inside and 90-cm from the inside top to the east wall sill. The inner surface of the frame was rounded smooth but the outside was rough and irregular. Centered within the door frame was a coyote coprolite full of cactus spines (Mollie Toll, personal communication 1976), the only one found at the site, which mark a post abandonment intrusion. A shaped sandstone slab, 37 by 28 cm, was found between the frame and the east wall, which may have been the sill stone. A few sherds, a piece of selenite, a concretion, a shell bead, and a sandstone cover were the only cultural remains from the fill.

Plate I.4.27. Site 29SJ 724, Room 4 before and after clearing. (a) Rectangular-shaped adobe mass in fill is a fallen east door frame (CHCU neg. 9359). (b) After clearing, note the shallow central sub-floor pit. 30-cm north arrow. Bipod photographs by Randy Morrison, 1974 (CHCU neg. 9363).

Floor

The floor consisted of unlined, gravelly native earth.

Floor Features (Table I.4.8)

Floorpit. A huge, unlined basin-shaped pit, extending under the door frame, took up nearly a third of the floor. Soft brown sand, gravel, three stones, and bits of charcoal filled the pit, which also yielded three gray sherds, possible turkey dung, a groundstone, and three rodent bones.

Floor Specimens (Figure I.4.14, Table I.4.10)

Two decorated and six plain gray sherds, debitage, a worked piece of sandstone, a hammerstone, and a rodent bone came from the floor.

Walls

Room 4 was dug into unlined, gravelly native earth. Against the east wall, directly opposite the door frame, were two 20-x-20-cm adobe projections to which the frame had been attached. Just above the floor between the projections was a circular air tunnel, 18-cm in diameter, extending horizontally through the wall 60-cm and then opening out on the sloping plaza surface. Slab wall foundations were not evident. A short row of unattached stones bordered the east wall side by the tunnel and might have been dislocated foundation stones.

Remarks

The nature of the fill suggests one or more walls did not fall into the room. Stones were fewer than expected and the mass of hard packed wall fall absent. The door frame was separated from the main wall. Given the distance the frame fell into the room, the doorway must have been approximately 70 to 80-cm high. The south wall was probably built of turtlebacks without supporting slabs. The tunnel under the east wall might have served as a fresh air duct.

Room 5 (Plate I.4.28)

Fill

The adobe fill, which was typical within the rooms, yielded 259 stones, indicative of much stone use within the Room 5 walls. In the top of the fill were parallel rows of small upright stones between 8 and 22-cm apart (Plate I.4.28a). These covered most of the north half of the room with the uppermost row of stones leaning westward, pinpointing their origin to the collapse of the east wall, 123-cm away. In the southern half, upright stones were distributed in an arc, with the top of the arc located 76-cm from the east wall. Vertical spacing between the stones (9 to 25-cm) approximates that for the rows in the north half, suggesting the same origin. Between the stones and filling the rest of the room was a hard, grayish brown mud, 17-cm thick. When this layer was removed, no other stones were evident. The remaining 15 to 20-cm of fill was soft brown sand full of rootlets, a little gravel, and laminated gray clay. A piece of groundstone was the sole artifact found in the fill, a probable wall stone.

Floor

The floor was unlined, gravelly native earth.

Floor Features (Table I.4.8)

The center of the floor was scooped out 13-cm deeper than the rest and covered with gray clay that still showed hand, and possibly foot, impressions. It is uncertain whether the shallow, poorly defined 110-x-170-cm basin represents a floor pit or an effort to level the floor during construction.

Floor Specimens (Figure I.4.14, Table I.4.10)

Four plain gray sherds (one with fugitive red

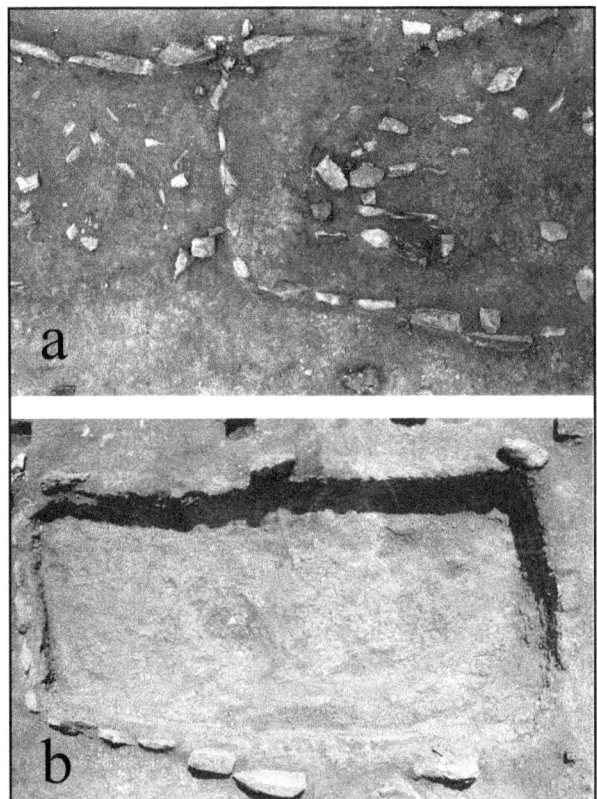

Plate I.4.28. Site 29SJ 724. (a). Rooms 4 and 5 after clearing showing the stone and adobe wall fall (CHCU neg. 9275). (b) Room 5 after excavation; east is at the top (CHCU neg. 9362). Bipod photographs by Randy Morrison, 1974.

paint) were clustered at the south end.

Walls

Subterranean walls were unlined, gravelly native earth. Along the north edge of the room and continuing west and south were small, upright stones affixed in a strip of mortar. Other stones, loosened from the mortar, continued along the surface to the south corner. A single stone set in mortar on the east side suggests that a slab wall foundation once encircled the room to support above-ground walls.

Discussion

Although only the east wall was evident, the 259 stones from the fill probably represent other adobe and stone walls. Adding the height of the fallen wall to the depth of the room results in a minimum inside room height of 155-cm. The stones set in the north wall follow the room contour, indicating that they were added specifically for Room 5's walls.

Room 6 (Plate I.4.29)

Fill

About 154 wall stones and wall abobe filled the room. Otherwise, little cultural material came from the fill—a few sherds, two metate fragments, and two other groundstones used within the walls or left at abandonment.

Floor

Puddled adobe, 15 mm thick, covered the floor. Along the south and east sides the floor was elevated 10 to 30-cm, creating a ledge that partially encircled the room.

Floor Features (Table I.4.8)

In the room center was a 5-to-10-cm-deep basin (OP 1). It appeared to fit the pattern of the irregular, rough floor rather than being an intentionally made pit similar to the better-defined

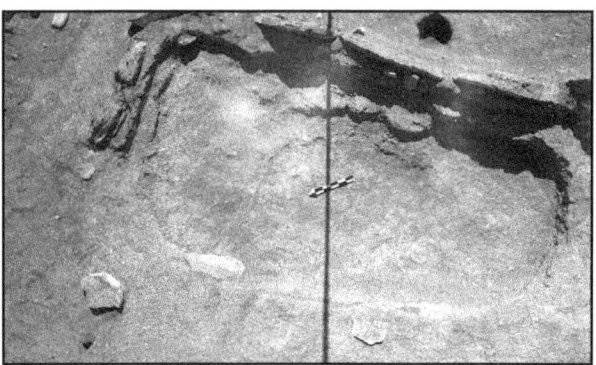

Plate I.4.29. Site 29SJ 724, Room 6 after clearing. Bipod photograph by Randy Morrison, 1974 (CHCU neg. 9360).

shallow basins found in a number of rooms.

Floor Specimens (Figure I.4.14, Table I.4.10)

A small piece of ground hematite came from the shallow basin area. A flotation sample from the south end of the floor yielded two tiny pieces of lithic angular debris.

Walls

Except for the west side, which had been plastered with 6-cm of adobe, the subterranean walls were left unlined after excavation into the ridge gravels. Occasionally, along the lip of the room, stones were placed flush with the sides. On the east side, a row of these stones were paralleled by foundation slabs more than three times larger, set back from the edge 5-20-cm.

Discussion

The shape of the floor and walls suggests that originally Room 6 was a smaller, bathtub-shaped structure similar to storage Rooms 2, 7, 8, and 10. Room 6 was added to Room 5 and apparently shared Room 5's northeast wall. Although the floor basin appears natural, its location in the center of the room is suspect. Perhaps it was originally a deeper pit used in conjunction with the bathtub-shaped room.

Room 7 (Plates I.4.30-I.4.31)

Fill

Melted adobe from the walls and 110 wall stones filled the room. Pieces of turtlebacks, up to 15-cm thick, clustered at the south end of the room, where stones were scarce, and probably mark the fallen south wall. A beam impression 6-cm in diameter was found in the southwestern corner, 10-cm above the floor. About 1-cm of aeolian sand covered the floor. Sherds and debitage (those from the lower part of the fill were lost, including a polished black sherd), a squash seed, charred corncob fragments, a metate fragment, four other groundstones, and a piece of hematite came from the fill. The squash seeds may mark some storage of gourds or squash within the room.

Floors

Unlined, gravelly native earth with tiny patches of adobe marked the floor.

Plate I.4.30. Site 29SJ 724, Room 7 after clearing. Note the deep, tub-like excavation, and the fill of wall adobe and stone. 30-cm north arrow. Photograph by Randy Morrison, 1974 (CHCU neg. 9351).

Plate I.4.31. Site 29SJ 724, Rooms 7 (left) and 8 (right) after clearing. Note the deep, tub-like excavation for both rooms. The large back living area with a firepit is Room 9. Looking east. 30-cm north arrow. Photograph by Tom Windes, 1974 (CHCU neg. 9236).

Floor Features (Table I.4.8)

Floor pit.

Near the room center was an unlined, basin-shaped pit filled with building material. Opposite the pit was the protruding part of the east wall, undoubtedly the cause for positioning the pit off center next to the west wall.

Floor Specimens (Figure I.4.14, Table I.4.10)

A plain gray sherd was the only floor artifact.

Walls

A thin, 1-cm-thick coating of mud covered the gravelly subterreanean walls. When the room was constructed, a large, protruding mound of native earth covered with a thin mud plaster was left along the east wall. It was 35-cm wide, extended into the room 22-cm, and continued above the floor 30-cm. The top was gently rounded and curved down to the floor. Puddled adobe raised the lower east and north walls to the surface to secure the wall foundation slabs. Stones were not set along the south and west sides, which apparently employed adobe turtleback construction for the above-ground walls.

Discussion

The bulge in the east wall aligns with a "bin" in Room 9 and might have served as a step. Access to the floor pit would have required use of the step from the side and pivoting on its slanting top to enter or exit—an odd and difficult maneuver that might negate the entry interpretation.

Room 8 (Plate I.4.31)

Fill

The fill in Room 8 was the same as in the others and yielded 59 wall stones. A mass of roofing material was located 13-cm above the floor against the east wall. This consisted of adobe and twigs, 2-5 mm in diameter. Some twigs were charred and retained the bark. Otherwise, cultural material was scarce; only a plain gray sherd and a lapstone were recovered.

Floor

A 3-mm-thick layer of gravelly adobe covered the floor except at the north end, which was of native earth. There were no floor features.

Floor Specimens (Figure I.4.14, Table I.4.10)

Sherds, debitage, rodent bones, and pieces of hematite and limonite were found on the floor.

Walls

An adobe liner, averaging 10-cm thick, covered the native earth sides below the ground surface. Slab wall foundations were not used; instead, adobe walls were probably added to the top of the adobe lining.

Discussion

The south and west walls of stone and mud fell into the room after considerable deposits of clay and gravel had accumulated along the west side of the floor. Remains of the east and north walls were not evident; perhaps they were only of mud, or they fell into adjoining rooms. Estimated wall height above the surface was about one meter; therefore, the inside room height was approximately 170-cm. An entryway probably existed on the east side, allowing access from Room 9 by stepping over the partition or wall into the depths of Room 8.

Apparently Room 8 was built prior to Room 9, although they were built as a unit. The thin residual gravel wall separating the two rooms would have collapsed if Room 9 had been built first. The adobe liner served to strengthen the Room 8 wall so it did not collapse when Room 9 was built.

Room 9 (Plate I.4.31)

Fill

Postoccupational deposits constituting the fill yielded 50-100 wall stones and wall adobe in the habitation room. An 8-cm-thick layer of nearly sterile, tan sand covered the floor. A mano fragment and several pebbles were found on the surface. Sherds, debitage, seeds from an ant nest, a charred corncob fragment, a concretion, a piece of limonite, a broken awl, a sandstone cover, and a piece of groundstone came from the fill—a prolific amount compared with the finds in the back storage rooms.

Floor

Unlined, gravelly native earth constituted the floor.

Floor Specimens (Figure I.4.14, Table I.4.10)

Sherds and debitage were scattered about in small numbers. Close to the firepit were three burned sandstone jar covers, a mano, a piece of groundstone, a stone cover, and a hammerstone (in Posthole 3). Another stone cover lay just north of the firepit and a groundstone was on top of the east wall, nearby. Next to the south wall were a mano and another groundstone, more evidence for food preparation and tool maintenance activities within the room.

Floor Features (Tables I.4.8-I.4.9)

Firepit

Built against the east wall was an oval firepit nearly encircled by an adobe collar, 8 to 10-cm wide and 5-cm high. A slab, projecting slightly above the floor, formed the northeast side. Fire-reddened clay formed the other, nearly vertical sides. The flat bottom was of native earth. Gravelly sand filled the upper 15-cm of the firepit and sand, charcoal, and burned twigs the lower 10-cm. A large fugitive red Lino Gray sherd was found in the fill. An archaeomagnetic sample did not reliably date due to its poor clustering (A.D. 830 ± 72; see its plot in Figure I.6.8, Table I.6.6), nevertheless the plot and resulting mean date is reasonable given the archaeological evidence.

Postholes (Table I.4.9)

Four deep postholes (PH 2, 5, 8, 24), set quadrilaterally, supported a roof that extended beyond the east wall in portico style. Single, lignite-filled postholes, about 50-cm deep, were located in both the southwest and northwest corners. Just outside the corners of the east wall were a matching pair of lignite-filled postholes, 35 and 60-cm deep, with a horizontal stone in the bottom of each. Only one contained a shim. Posthole 8, in the northwestern corner, revealed two lignite-filled holes of similar size, one cut partially away by the other.

A number of shallower, possibly auxiliary roofing postholes or supports for platforms were were scattered about the floor. None contained lignite or shims, and only the deepest, Posthole 7, seemed suitable for supporting a post. A hammerstone was found in Posthole 3.

Bins

A large shelf of native earth had been left against the north end of the west wall. Several large, upright slabs, including a trough metate set on end, divided the shelf top into three unplastered "bins." Each was filled with post-occupational wall or roofing adobe and mud and sand. Two flakes came from the northern bin fill, and a hammerstone from the floor of the southern bin.

Against the inside of the low east wall, behind the firepit, a tabular slab had been positioned like a deflector. Directly in line with this slab and the firepit were two other slabs of uncertain use anchored in the ground 120-cm to the east. One was unifacially ground.

Construction of the firepit had destroyed an earlier hearth 15-cm below the floor. Little was left of the hearth beyond a semicircle of fire-reddened earth and soft, charcoal-flecked sand.

Walls

Below the surface, the room walls were unlined, gravelly native earth. Upright slab foundations for walls occur along the south, north, and the northern half of the west sides at the surface of the room.

Discussion

Room 9 appears to have been built as a partially enclosed ramada, with mud and stone walls at each end. Walls of the two storage rooms behind Room 9 probably provided the only shelter along the west side—the direction of the prevailing winds. The row of slabs on the western side correspond to the length of Room 7 and, therefore, are surmised to belong solely to that room. No wood remains were found, indicating that it was salvaged. Posthole sizes reveal the main roof supports were about 15 to 20-cm in diameter.

Possibly the three jar covers were used on jars stored in the three bins. Bin 3, however, might have been an entry into Room 7 rather than a storage feature. The association of artifacts next to the firepit suggests a food-processing area with jars being set over the fire, blackening the covers. The chipped sandstone covers (40-x-28-x-5-cm and 47-x-42-x-5-cm) on each side of the firepit might have been used to cover the fire or as covers for the bins.

Room 10 (Plate I.4.32)

Fill

The fill in this room was atypical, yielding a mere 10 stones. The fill consisted primarily of sand mixed with bits of charcoal, gravel, and clay chunks. Nearly clean sand, 6-7-cm deep,

Plate I.4.32. Site 29SJ 724, Room 10, partly excavated leaving the post-occupational Firepit 1 in situ. Note the deep, tub-like excavation. Photograph by Paul Etavard, 1974 (CHCU neg. 9370).

covered the floor. A slab-lined firepit (FP 1) had been placed in the fill on the southwest side (Plate I.4.32); it was later collected. Consequently, a large bulk of fill under the firepit was left unexcavated. Beneath the firepit, an ashy pit was visible in profile.

Floor

A layer of 2-3-cm of ash-stained abobe, with sterile native earth underneath, covered the floor. There were no floor features within the excavated area.

Fill and Floor Specimens

Surface

Any cultural material was removed during the initial clearing of the site.

Plate I.4.33. Site 29SJ 724, closeup of Firepit 1 in the plaza built in the post-occupational fill of Room 10. Photograph by Tom Windes, 1974 (CHCU neg. 9209).

Fill

Sherds, debitage, a rodent bone, and a pecking stone came from the room fill.

Floor (Figure I.4.14, Table I.4.10)

Five plain gray sherds, a rodent bone, a hammerstone, a piece of petrified wood, and a charred corncob fragment were found on the floor—probably de facto trash.

Walls

Unlined, gravelly native earth formed the room walls, but there was no evidence for walls or slab foundations at the ground level.

Discussion

The room appears to have been dismantled and then, after a period of time, intentionally filled. It is unlikely that nearby Room 6 would have been constructed until Room 10 was no longer in use. Room 10 probably represents one of the earliest activity areas on the site; the firepit and its fill, one of the latest. The positioning of Room 10 among ramada Postholes 1-2, and 16-17 suggest that the room might have been sheltered by the ramada roofing during at least part of its use.

Discussion of Rooms

Two types of surface rooms are evident. One type, Rooms 1 and 9, exhibits firepits and a number of tools scattered over a large floor area. Posts once supported a ramada-like framework, and the rooms appear to have been only partially enclosed by high mud walls. These two rooms served as work areas and loci for domestic activities. Their light framework indicates temporary occupation during the warmer months of the year.

The remaining rooms are smaller, deeper, and practically devoid of artifacts. The few artifacts found were probably left on the roof at abandonment. These rooms evidently were used for storage. Groundstone fragments found in them probably came exclusively from wall fall. Room construction is more substantial, exhibiting two styles of walls, often in the same room. Slab foundations supported mud walls incorporating occasional courses of small stones. Where slabs are absent, the walls seem to be built entirely of turtlebacks without use of stone. A covering of small poles overlain with brush and adobe provided roofing. Walls in the largest of the small rooms reached a height of about 120 to 150-cm, while those around the smaller, tub-shaped rooms probably did not exceed 100-cm in height.

Differential storage use is attributed to the eight rooms. There are two classes of storage rooms: small, tub-shaped rooms and larger, shallow rooms. The smaller rooms are associated with the two habitation rooms, except for isolated Room 10. The other rooms are associated with the ramada. These associations suggest seasonal use of the storage rooms. If the semi-protected habitation rooms were used during the fall and spring and the ramada during the summer, then the storage rooms might also reflect the same seasonal distinctions.

Different requirements for food storage might be indicated in the room architecture. Some foods require humidity to prevent shriveling (e.g., root crops), whereas others must be kept in a dry place (e.g., beans and corn). Temperatures are also important; some foods require cooler storage temperatures than others. For instance, squashes stored at temperatures below 50° F are subject to damage whereas while beans and peas are better stored between 32° and 40° F (USDA 1970). Corn and squash were evident at the site, while beans are also a common puebloan food although they do not preserve well in archaeological sites

The smaller, deeper rooms would be useful for maintaining cooler temperatures in the warmer months and warmer temperatures in the colder months. The reverse is true for the shallower, larger rooms. Perhaps the ventilator into Room 4 was used to regulate temperatures or to provide fresh air to stored foods. Burned Pueblo I rooms in the La Plata District have yielded quantities of fine seeds, grass seeds, shelled corn, beans, and tubers stored in jars, revealing the kinds of foodstuffs that some storage rooms contained (Morris 1939:68, 78).

Many of the rooms exhibit a shallow floor basin which is perfect for supporting the large, round-bottomed culinary jars of the time. It seems unlikely, however, that only a single basin would always be constructed in the center of the floor to support a storage jar. Perhaps these basins denote rooms where jars full of water were kept to increase the humidity. It might be significant that only one of the four deep, tub-shaped rooms contains a floor pit. On the other hand, all four of the shallow storage rooms exhibit a floor pit or shallow, scooped-out basin in the center.

Ramada and Plaza Areas
(Figures I.4.14 and I.4.15)

The outdoor work area (plaza) was marked by features between the rooms and pithouse. Most of the area was sheltered from the elements by a post-and-brush ramada that fronted Rooms 4 through 6. Postholes in front of Room 9 were also in the plaza area, but their position close to the room indicates that they supported a short extension of the Room 9 roof, which provided shade over the east wall. The north end of Room 1 was indistinct from the ramada and they may have shared a common roof. A similar architectural arrangement was built at 29SJ 629, a nearby Pueblo II house (Windes 1993).

Fill

Deposits under the ramada and in the plaza east of Rooms 1 and 9 consisted of adobe washed from the room walls, sand, and isolated wall? stones.

Floor

Packed native earth distinguished the plaza surface from the fill above. Only a single surface was evident, and it contained all the features.

Floor Features (Figure I.4.14, Table I.4.8)

Postholes
(Plates I.4.34 and I.4.35, Table I.4.11)

Twenty-two to twenty-four postholes were aligned in two rows parallel and southeast of Rooms 4, 5, and 6. They ranged in diameter from 14 to 46-cm and were less than 23-cm deep. The estimated size of the posts used in the postholes averaged 14.6-cm. Like the post sizes estimated for Rooms 1 and 9, all were less than 21-cm in diameter. Three ramada posthole numbers (6-8) were discarded because they were located in Room 1. Postholes 18 and 19 probably are not real and were dropped from the list.

Several clusters of postholes suggest realignment of the ramada or post replacement. The shape and close proximity of Other Pits 2, 3, and 5 next to a cluster of postholes suggest that they might have been ramada postholes.

The predominant fill in the postholes was

Plate I.4.34. Site 29SJ 724, Ramada Posthole 1, showing several shims. 30-cm north arrow. Photograph by Peter McKenna, 1975 (CHCU neg. 9344).

Plate I.4.35. Site 29SJ 724, Plaza/Ramada area, Other Pits 2-5 and Postholes 13-14 and 25-26. 10-cm north arrow. Photograph by Tom Windes, 1975 (CHCU neg. 12145).

tan sand. Most, however, exhibited evidence of lignite, but only Postholes 4, 5, 9, and 12 contained lignite packing. Wood was absent. One to five sandstone shims were employed in six postholes; Posthole 1 yielded 12 shims (Plate I.4.34). Three postholes (4, 5, and 11) in front of Room 4 had a stone placed horizontally in the bottom, as did Posthole 1.

The remaining six postholes were recorded in front of Room 9, and they may have supported a roof that extended slightly over the plaza to shade the short, east wall of Room 9. If the room was open, the extended roof would have also shaded the room interior by mid-morning from the hot, summer sun.

Firepits

At the north end of the ramada was Firepit 1 (Plates I.4.32-I.4.33), 96-cm east of where Rooms 5 and 6 join. Ten slightly burned slabs set in mortar formed the oval firepit. The sides extended 6 to 12-cm below the base of the slabs; the bottom was flat. A mixture of fine sand and ash filled the pit, charcoal was absent. On top was a gray sherd. Clearing around the firepit revealed Room 10 underneath. Firepit 2 (Plate I.4.36) was found in 1976 during the clearing of the plaza. It was a burned pit, partly plaster lined, from which an archaeomagnetic sample was collected (A.D. 700 ± 42; Figure I.6.8, Table I.6.6). It resembled a heating pit and contained gray ashy sand and charcoal.

Other Pits

Few features other than postholes were discovered in the ramada outdoor work area. Those that were unburned and generally did not fit the profile of a posthole were designated "Other Pits" in keeping with the later Chaco Center designation for floor features not otherwise classifiable. Although Other Pits 2, 3, and 5 may have been postholes (see above), they were shallower than the posthole norm, lacked lignite, and may represent some sort of activity areas, perhaps for

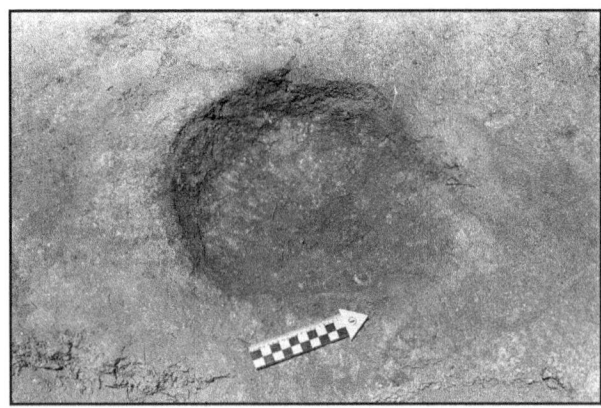

Plate I.4.36. Site 29SJ 724, Plaza Firepit 2. 10-cm north arrow. Photograph by Tom Windes, 1975 (CHCU neg. 12106).

food production (e.g., a grinding locus).

Other Pit 1 was a shallow, storage-like pit near Firepit 1. An oval basin (Other Pit 4), within the same cluster as Other Pits 2, 3, and 5, has the appearance of a mealing-bin basin for capturing cornmeal but lacks adequate work room for processing food on a metate. All the other pits were poorly lined, if at all, with a thin mixture of plaster and native gravels and sands.

Floor Specimens (Table I.4.10)

Sherds and debitage, a piece of groundstone, and a metate fragment were found on the surface but just a few sherds and chipped stone were found in the fill. No distinct cluster of cultural material was found that might have marked work loci.

Pithouse A
(Figures I.4.16 and I.4.17,
Plates I.4.37 and I.4.38)

The pithouse was discovered when the ventilator shaft opening was identified on the surface. Running east from the ventilator were four large slabs set in a row just below the surface. A test trench (TT1) across the ventilator was expanded to include the south half of the pithouse, leaving the north half temporarily unexcavated. Twelve levels were removed in 20-cm depths, except for the last which was 5 to 15-cm above the floor. The slope was such that the surface on the west side of the pithouse was 40 to 50-cm higher than the east side.

Fill

Through Level 5 (80-100-cm deep), when the first signs of a superstructure were uncovered, the fill consisted of hard, water-deposited sand, clay, and gravel (Plate I.4.39). In Level 5, the darkened outline of the pithouse became definite, marked by a mass of large stones which continued until about Level 8 (Plate I.4.40). More than

Plate I.4.37. Site 29SJ 724, Pithouse A, showing stone artifacts, mostly groundstone and posthole shims, left on floor. Looking south. 30-cm north arrow. Photograph by Jim Judge, 1974 (CHCU neg. 9389).

Plate I.4.38. Site 29SJ 724, overview of Pithouse A. Looking south. 30-cm north arrow. Photograph by Tom Windes, 1974 (CHCU neg. 10681).

136 of these stones slanted toward the center of the floor in an arc from the southeast around to the east and north. All were unshaped, with 74 percent exceeding 30-x-25-x-10-cm in size. I suspect that these were used in the same manner as similarly positioned stones found in the 29SJ 423 great kiva—as a protective stone liner built around the exterior base of the walls to retard erosion. A hawk skull (*Buteo regalis*; FS 559) was found among the stones. Below Level 5, the fill was characterized by clean sand and gravel on the west side and large stones and adobe on the east side.

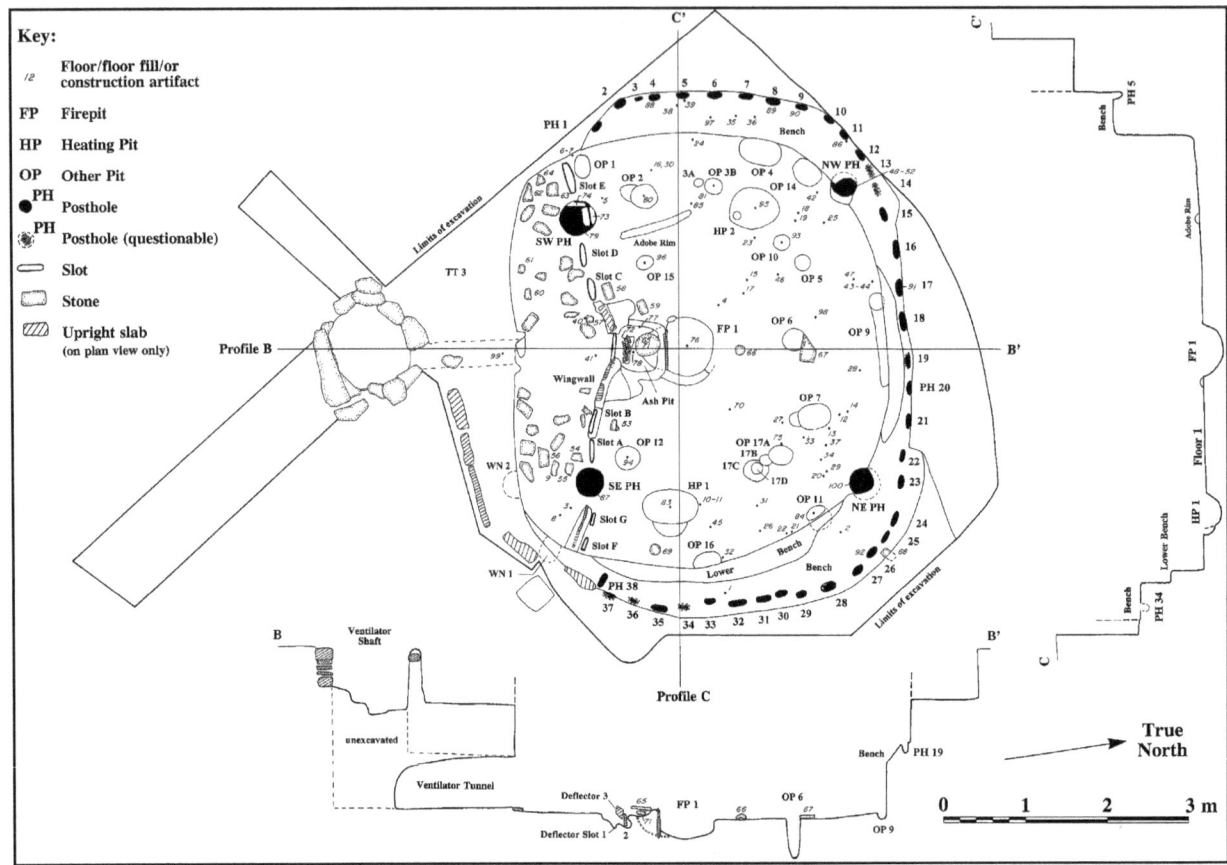

Figure I.4.16. Site 29SJ 724, Pithouse A, plan view and profiles and the distribution of floor fill and floor artifacts listed in Tables I.4.12, I.4.15 (CHCU 65700). Original by Bruce Yazzie, Junior Lopez, and Tom Windes, 1974.

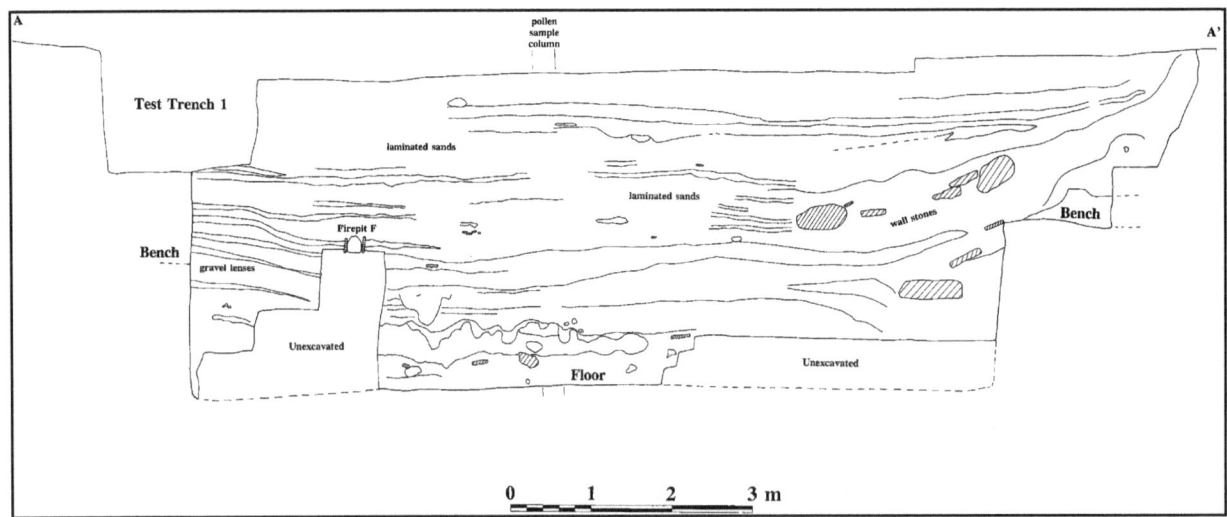

Figure I.4.17. Site 29SJ 724, Pithouse A, profile of fill (CHCU 65701). See Figure I.4.18 for profile location. Original by Tom Windes, 1974.

Plate I.4.39. Site 29SJ 724, Pithouse A, post-occupational fill of alluvial sands and clays, west side. Looking north. 30-cm north arrow and vertical metric scale (10-cm increments). Photograph by Ken Augustine, 1974 (CHCU neg. 9233).

Plate I.4.40. Site 29SJ 724, Pithouse A, showing numerous large slabs in fill that presumably covered the former above-ground exterior wall. Note slab wall around surface periphery of pithouse. Looking south-southeast. Photograph by Tom Windes, 1974 (CHCU neg. 9316).

Plate I.4.41. Site 29SJ 724, tiny, slab-lined firepits (A and C) in the Pithouse A fill. Note other tiny firepits in background. 30-cm north arrow. Photograph by Tom Windes, 1974 (CHCU neg. 9229).

Plate I.4.42. Site 29SJ 724, tiny, slab-lined firepits (A and C) in the Pithouse A fill. 30-cm north arrow. Photograph by Tom Windes, 1974 (CHCU neg. 9317).

Nine curious features were uncovered in Level 7 on the west side of the pithouse (Figure I.4.18, Plates I.4.41 and I.4.42). All were miniature slab-lined firepits filled with burned brush and occurring at the same depth within a 150-x-200-cm area (Table I.4.8). Most were barely 10-cm across with six to ten tabular smoked and fire reddened stones (typically 10-x-10-x-1-cm) placed at a slight angle around the sides, without mortar. Sterile, laminated sand and gravel surrounded the firepits above and below—a floor or use surface could not be distinguished. The sand in contact with the firepits was oxidized. Four to eight more firepits, many of them destroyed during excavation, were represented by the 40 thin, burned stones and two burned spots found in association.

The only cultural material recovered from the firepits was a Bennett Gray sherd (Lino Gray with trachyte temper) from Feature A. Within

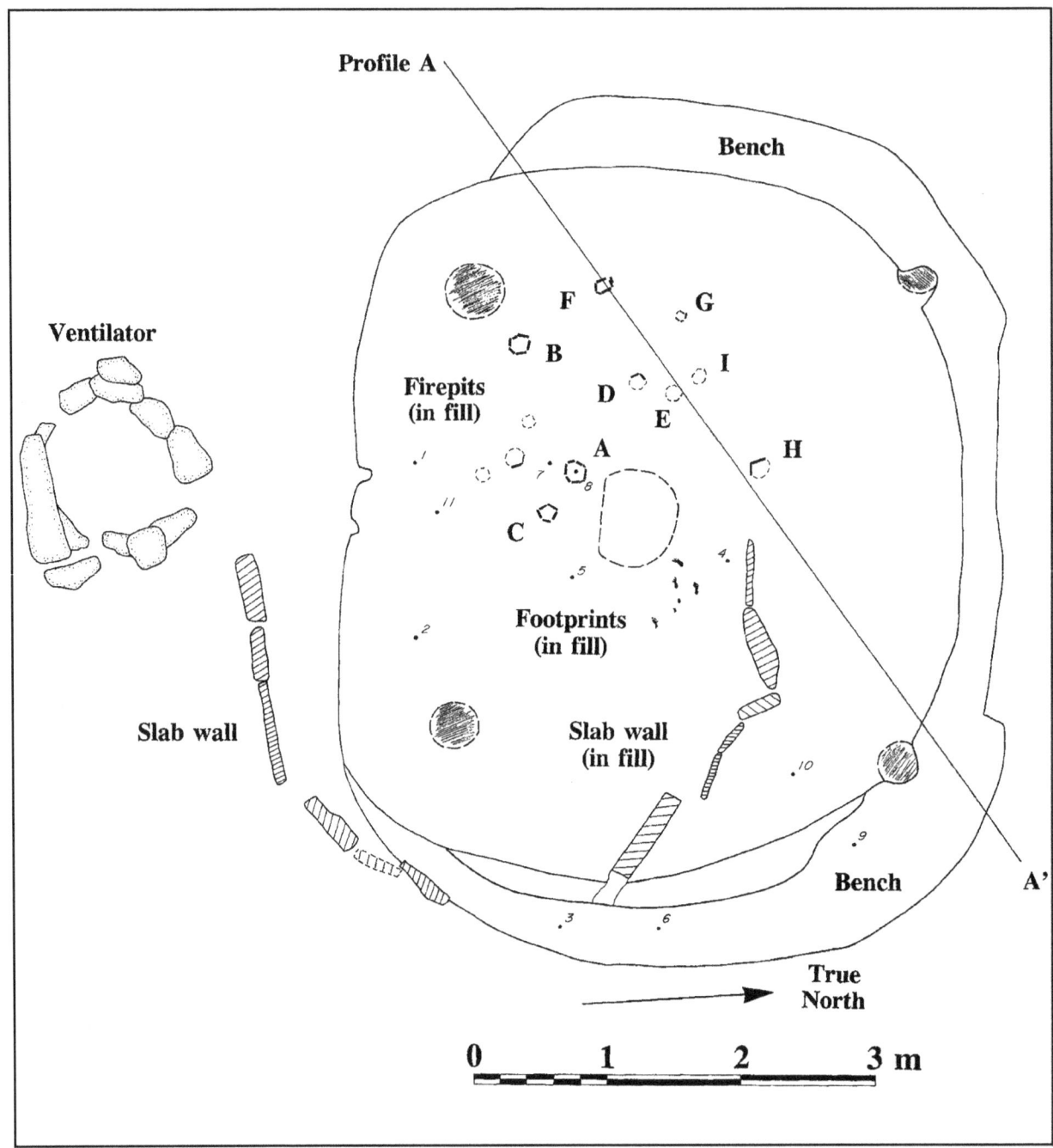

Figure I.4.18. Site 29SJ 724, Pithouse A reoccupation showing secondary slab walls, tiny firepits (A-I), and footprints on use surface (CHCU 65701). Numbers mark artifacts at same level with firepits (see list in Table I.4.12). See Figure I.4.17 for Profile A - A'. Original by Tom Windes, 1974.

Features A, B, and C, two stones, one slightly above the other, rested upright against identical stones in the sides. Feature G yielded one upright stone inside. As a group, the stones within the four firepits did not appear fortuitous and probably served as some aspect of the firepit use.

Little cultural material was recovered from the sandy deposits in association with the firepits. Thus, the small number of intact artifacts recovered from this level (Level 7) may be tools used during the firepit activities. Two artifacts, a biscuit mano and a polishing stone, were found among the firepits at the same level (Table I.4.12). Several others, including a pot cover found on the bench, two mauls, and four fragments of groundstone, were recovered from the same general depth along with a scattering of sherds, bones, and chipped stone.

The top of the main pithouse bench was on the same level as the firepits but artifacts from the bench were included with the pithouse floor items. Near the center of the fill several bare heel and footprints were impressed into the clay (Plate I.4.43). A drawing of the best preserved footprint was examined in about 1976 by Dr. Donald Saye, an Albuquerque podiatrist, who believed that it was made by a female about 12 years of age or a little older. This footprint was 20-cm long and showed a stride of 49-cm.

Finally, two crude, slab-lined walls may have been part of this postoccupational use of the pithouse (Plate I.4.38). One segment on the surface followed the general outline of the pithouse; the other was sunk in the fill and attached to the eastern pithouse bench. Whether these two walls served to distinguish space, acted as windbreaks, or formed some other function, could not be determined.

Remains of the pithouse superstructure were concentrated in Levels 10 through 12 (180-225-cm depth). A well-compacted, yellow clayey sand layer, 5 to 18-cm thick, formed the upper part of this material. Underneath were concentrations, extending to within 5-cm of the floor, of adobe

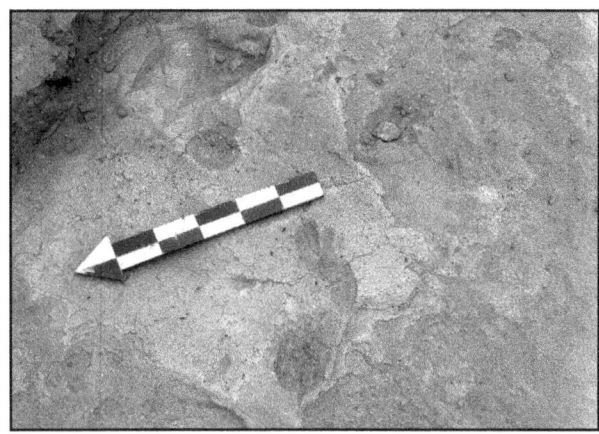

Plate I.4.43. Site 29SJ 724, human footprints in the Pithouse A fill at the same level as the tiny firepits and slab wall. 30-cm north arrow. Photograph by Tom Windes, 1974 (CHCU neg. 9247).

chunks with wood impressions. Eighteen of 24 chunks exhibited multiple impressions, indicating that poles, 3 to 6-cm in diameter, were placed parallel to and touching one another, with larger timbers, 7 to 9-cm placed perpendicular to and 2-cm underneath the smaller poles, and all were encased in adobe. The sections of adobe exposed to the pithouse interior exhibited a charred, gummy resin. Twig impressions, 4.5 - 9 mm in diameter, were associated with a few chunks. The only wood pieces recovered from roofing material were four fragments of undatable juniper (Table I.6.2).

A 16-cm-thick layer of organic material (Feature I) underlay the yellow sand and adobe chunks, although in one place the reverse was true. This material coincided with the existence of the bench above it and was not found along the ventilator side. A large section, 130-cm long, fell relatively intact on the west side, stretching down from the bench face toward the center of the floor. It was constructed of three layers of reeds or corn stalks alternated with two layers of fibers (pine needles and Mormon tea?) placed at right angles (Plate I.4.44). In and under this, in the first 10-cm above the floor was a thick deposit of trash, the richest in the site. Sherds, debitage, bone tools, and so on, were found in what was

Plate I.4.44. Site 29SJ 724, Pithouse A fill, Feature I, matting and reeds that were part of the former wainscotting around the top of the bench. 30-cm north arrow. Photograph by Tom Windes, 1974 (CHCU neg. 9330).

part of Feature I (Table I.4.13). Also a surprising amount of minerals used for paints and ornaments (see Fretwell, Volume II) was associated with Feature I and the bench top, including worked and unmodified pieces of malachite, hematite, limonite, and selenite.

The impression is that the Feature I material served as backing or part of the wainscoting fabric encircling the bench. This fabric may have been used as a pegboard for caching small tools and other items, and it collapsed onto the bench top and floor after pithouse abandonment. The density and variety of materials from Feature I (Table I.4.13) reflect the probable tools and refuse of everyday use. The amount of squash seeds is particularly notable given their fragile nature—it represents one of the highest numbers of squash seeds recovered during the entire Chaco project. Under much of Feature 1 material was 3-6-cm of aeolian sand covering the floor, which may have been intentionally placed during pithouse use.

Upper Bench

Native earth was cut back 40 to 80-cm to form a bench that encircled three quarters of the pithouse. This terminated at each end above where the wing walls attached, leaving the ventilator side without a bench. A 10-mm-thick layer of ash and smoke-stained clay covered the bench top. Except on part of the east side, the bench face was covered with plaster 5 to 25 mm thick. Small amounts of trash and tools were recovered from the bench top on the east and west sides.

The north side of the bench narrows to 10 to 12-cm. Instead of the bench face dropping vertically to the floor here, it descends at a sharp angle for 35-cm and then drops vertically 63-cm to the floor and floor Pit 9.

Upper bench features (Table I.4.14)

A series of 36 slots filled with sand or lignite, but no wood, was placed along the back side of the bench top. Large gaps in the series suggested that three other postholes once existed. One slot contained shims and five others included as floor-related materials on the north and west sides yielded chipped stones, squash seeds, and a plain gray sherd (Table I.4.15).

Lower bench

When the bench was uncovered on the east side, its dark surface terminated well behind the edge of the floor. Removal of the light trash and sand fill from its gravelly, unplastered face revealed a lower bench, 42-cm above the floor, covered with a brownish gray clay 9-cm thick. A 200-cm-long test trench through the benches revealed the top of the lower bench was a stratum of natural clay resting upon and overlain by strata of native gravel and sand.

Lower bench slab wall

Attached to the lower bench and the face of the upper bench was a crude wall of upright slabs extending 300-cm across the pithouse fill. The slabs resembled, in both material and size, those recovered from the east half of the pithouse fill and the row near the surface, east of the ventilator. Under the wall was 30 to 40-cm of Feature I material and sand covering the floor. The top of the slab wall was 15 to 30-cm below the level of the firepits scattered in the fill on the west side.

Floor

A single ash-stained layer of clay, 12 to 32 mm thick, covered the flat, gravelly floor. The wing walls separated the southern part of the floor (19 percent of the total floor area) from the rest. This part was elevated 5 to 10-cm above the main pithouse floor. A color photograph of the floor during excavation can be found in *American Archaeology* (Stewart 2003:14).

Floor Features
(Plate I.4.37, Tables I.4.8-I.4.9)

Floor pits
A multitude of circular, oval, and irregular-shaped pits covered the floor in an arc around the firepit. Fifteen of the 21 pits were lined with clay, the rest with gravelly, native earth. In cross-section, the pits were generally basin shaped with flat or dished bottoms. OP 6 (a sipapu), north of the firepit, however, was conical and more than twice as deep as any other pit. An expanding groove in the shape of a baseball bat (Plate I.4.45) formed OP 9, next to the north wall. One storage pit, OP 11, expanded into a bell-shape under the bench (Plate I.4.46), and OP 17, 65-cm long, comprised three or four overlapping pits.

All 21 pits were open at the time of abandonment and later filled with charcoal-flecked, aeolian tan sand. Fire-reddened pits on each side of the chamber were the only ones with use contents. One, HP 1, contained a dark, 6-cm-thick layer of sand and charcoal under the tan sand. The other, HP 2 (Plate I.4.47), was more heavily burned and yielded a lower, 9-cm-thick layer of purplish sand and pieces of burned brush. A secondary pit in the bottom was filled with aeolian sand. Nine pits yielded a scattering of trash in the aeolian sand. Most common were rodent bones in five pits and a chipped stone in three others.

Postholes
Four postholes were positioned in a square on the floor. Two were set within the wing walls, less than a meter from the pithouse sides. The others were placed partially within the bench at an angle (Plate I.4.46). Crushed lignite filled the lower part of each hole, with the remaining space filled with sand, abundant charcoal, and trash. Three massive shims, blackened from contact with the lignite, enclosed a space 28-x-35-cm for stabilizing the former southwestern roof support post. Two of the shims were trough metate fragments. Undatable juniper fragments also came from this hole. The northwest posthole (Plate I.4.48) yielded a cache of offerings placed in the trashy sandy fill after structure abandonment. In the cache were shell pendants, an *Olivella* bead, a pendant, talc, malachite, a bone awl, and a projectile point (Table I.4.15, see Volume II, Plate II.10.2). The projectile point was unique for the park collections, an obsidian Archaic reworked late Paleo-Indian Jimmy Allen point (see Plate II.6.15) with parallel-oblique flaking (Huckell 2011). It can also be seen at *http://www.nps.gov/museum/exhibits/chcu/obj/projectile point chcu29928a.html.*

Floor ridge (Plate I.4.49)
In the southwestern part of the pithouse, perpendicular to the wingwall, was a ridge of adobe set over the floor with the south end broken off. It curved slightly at the north end as if to enclose Other Pit 2 next to it but its function is unclear.

Wing walls

Little remained of the wing walls except for a thin slab, 40-cm high and covered with mud, between

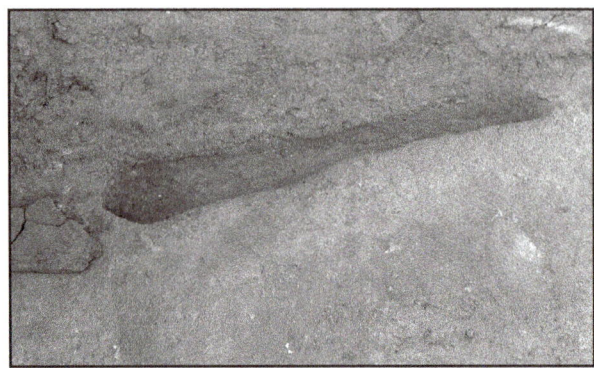

Plate I.4.45. Site 29SJ 724, Pithouse A floor, Other Pit 9, a long floor groove near the north wall. Looking north. Photograph by Tom Windes, 1974 (CHCU neg. 9392).

Plate I.4.46. Site 29SJ 724, Pithouse A floor, Other Pit 11 (right) and the Northeast Roof Support Posthole. Note that OP 11 goes under the bench wall. 30-cm north arrow. Photograph by Tom Windes, 1974 (CHCU color neg. 9401).

Plate I.4.47. Site 29SJ 724, Pithouse A floor, Other Pit 13 (Heating Pit 2). 24-cm-long trowel. Photograph by Tom Windes, 1974 (CHCU neg. 9397-color, 9282).

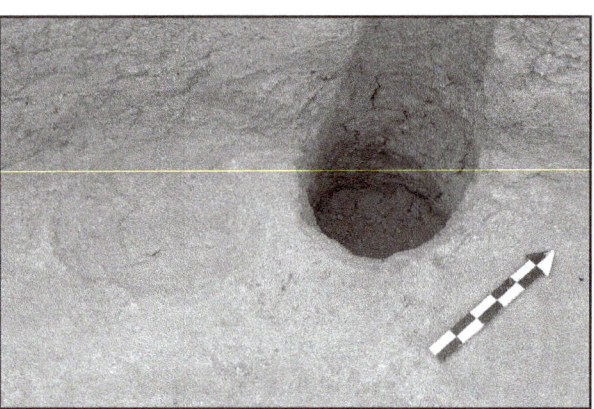

Plate I.4.48. Site 29SJ 724, Pithouse A floor, Other Pit 14 (left) and the Northwest Roof Support Posthole. 30-cm north arrow. Photograph by Tom Windes, 1974 (CHCU color neg. 9399).

Plate I.4.49. Site 29SJ 724, Pithouse A floor, Other Pit 2 (foreground) and the Floor Ridge. 30-cm north arrow. Photograph by Tom Windes, 1974 (CHCU color neg. 9404).

the southeast posthole and the upper bench wall. Next to the slab, on one side, were two slots similar to those in the upper bench top. The former wing walls were marked by five grooves. Four of the five were clay-lined and cut into the floor. The fifth was placed in a raised adobe strip, 10-cm high, that slants upward 35-cm above the floor to encase two vertical stones next to the deflector complex. A similar mass of adobe and stone, 51-cm high, begins the wing wall on the other side of the deflector complex. Slabs to fit the grooves were not found on the floor or in the fill.

Ash pit

Directly south of the firepit was a shallow, unburned, clay-lined basin containing ash, charcoal, tan sand, and trash. Fragments of rodent bones, corncobs, eggshells, wood, stone, and a single plain gray sherd in the trash were overlain by four stones, including an unusually shaped concretion and a sandstone cover. The fill did not appear to be discarded firepit contents. A semicircle of fire-reddened clay on the bottom disclosed an earlier, sealed firepit, estimated at 50-cm in diameter. This was 155-cm from the ventilator mouth. An adobe collar resting on the floor partially enclosed the ash pit, terminating at the mass of adobe and stone.

Deflector complex

Between the wing walls and within the ash pit were two slots and a row of small stones. The slot at the south end of the ash pit might have held a slab. Flanking and partially overhanging this slot were two large masses of adobe and stone marking the beginnings of the wing walls. Although vandalized, it appears that a 15-cm-thick adobe arch once connected the two masses. Impressions on the north side, at each end of the arch, might represent vertical posts, 10 to 12-cm in diameter. Ten to 15-cm north of the slot was a second slot, slightly bulging at each end. Between the two slots and overlapping part of the second slot were eight small stones stacked in a row, but the stone use is uncertain.

Firepit

The firepit was a plastered, D-shaped basin with a thin, vertical slab set along the south side, 185-cm from the ventilator mouth. Bordering the east side was an unburned adobe collar, broken off at the north end. The edge of the floor under the collar was fire-reddened from firepit use. Two years after excavations, the firepit was re-investigated for archaeomagnetic sampling. It was discovered that the initial firepit had been remodeled four times, with a progression of remodelings starting from the southern end in the ash-pit depression (Figure I.4.19). Samples were collected from four of them (Figures I.6.8, Table I.6.6), including the last use. Firepit 1 was the latest and Firepit 5 was the earliest. All were adobe lined except for Firepit 4, which was lined with small upright stones. Dates of A.D. 785 ± 17 (Firepit 5), A.D. 790 ± 37 (Firepit 4), A.D. 885 ± 31 (Firepit 3) and A.D. 900 ± 39 (Firepit 1) suggest two eras of use, in the late 700s and in the late 800s (but see DuBois 2008 for slightly revised dates of 770, 740, 830, and 840, respectively).

The last firepit fill comprised three distinct strata. The upper 12 to 16-cm was purplish sand and ash speckled with pieces of burnt brush. One large piece was of undatable juniper. Underneath were 7-8-cm of nearly sterile yellow sand, like that associated with Feature I but foreign to the immediate vicinity except in the Chaco Wash. It does not resemble the sand in the floor pits. The firepit bottom was covered with 3-4-cm fill identical to the upper purplish layer but with streaks of yellow sand. A small pink pebble came from the top stratum and a large plain gray sherd from the west edge of the firepit.

Ventilator

Aligned with the firepit, 162.5° from true north, was an unlined horizontal tunnel with an adobe collar lining its mouth. Several turtlebacks found in the fill nearby evidently were part of the broken

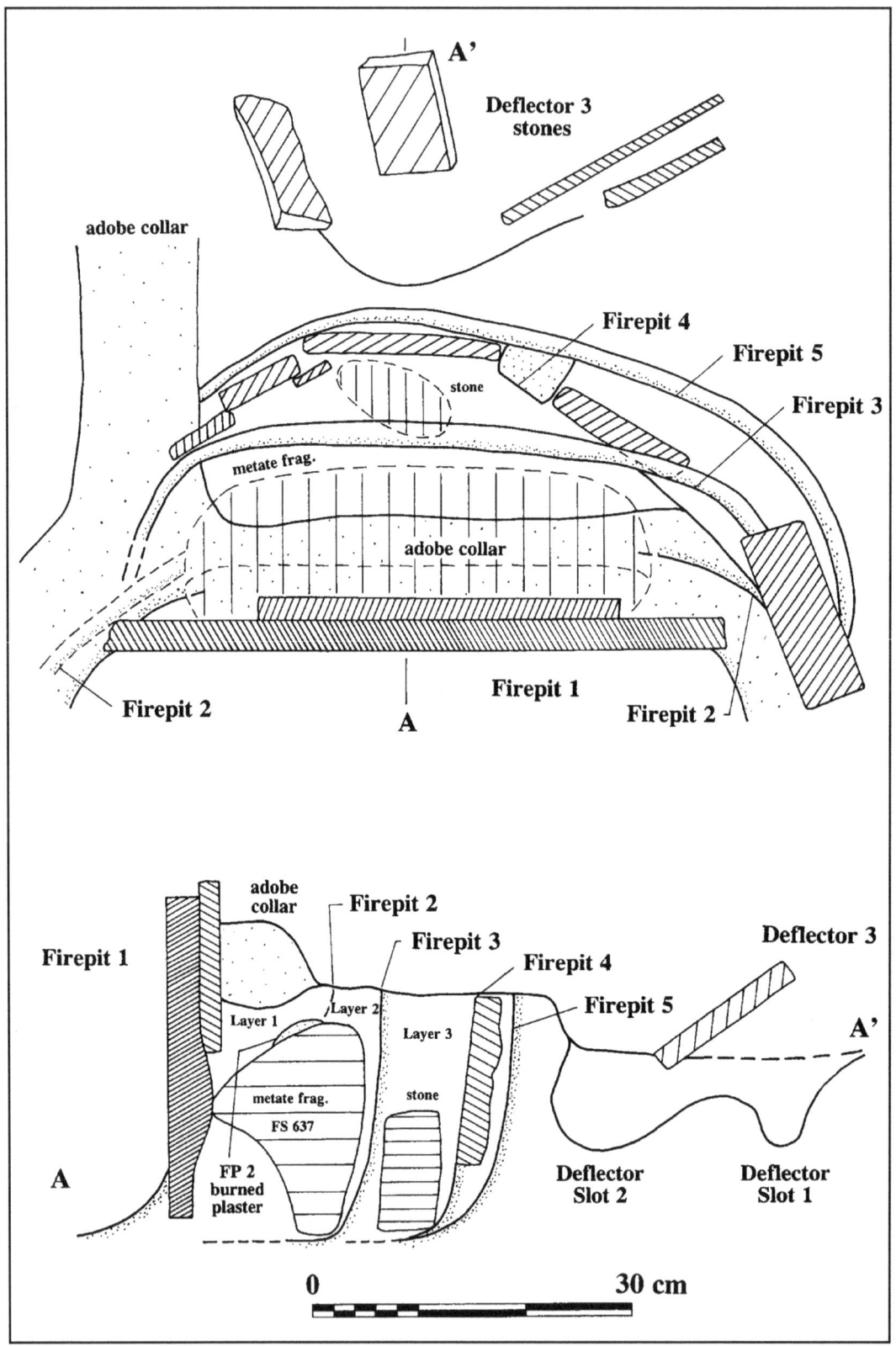

Figure I.4.19. Site 29SJ 724, Pithouse A firepit complex remodelings (CHCU 65979). Original by Tom Windes, 1974.

collar top. A small stone was set flush in the floor at the mouth.

Inside the mouth 13-cm was the articulated skeleton of an adult cottontail rabbit (species identification by Tom Mathews, personal communication 1975) with a few squash seeds. Laminated sand and light trash filled the tunnel and part of the shaft above. Next to the rabbit was a 3-cm-diameter, 20-cm-long, piece of wood that probably was once part of the tunnel roof.

The top of the trash-filled ventilator shaft was oval and partly lined with large, unmodified stones. A huge vertical stone, 92-x-30-x-12-cm, was placed across the south side, underlain by four more stone courses. Stones were intermittent elsewhere and nonexistent below 59-cm in depth. Walls were primarily of trash fill. Although the shaft is large, the narrow tunnel would prohibit entry into the main chamber via the ventilator.

Floor specimens (Figure I.4.16, Table I.4.15)
Numerous specimens occurred on or near the floor, clustering on the northeast and northwest sides of the pithouse. Tools of chipped stone and bone were common and often associated with Feature I material. Few artifacts came from the south half other than groundstone. Thirty pieces of sandstone were scattered next to and behind the wing walls. Most were close to the two postholes in aeolian sand 2-3-cm above the floor. Many were blackened from contact with lignite and not from smoke. Six others, clustered around and under the crude slab wall near the northeast posthole, were 0-8-cm above the floor and associated with lignite and Feature I material. Those stained with lignite must have been posthole shims removed when the roof supports were taken.

The groundstone found on and near the floor (Plate I.4.50) may have derived from several activities. Much of it could have been part of the roof entrance liner that was dismantled and tossed onto the floor (a common practice at 29SJ 627 [Truell 1992] and at 29SJ 629 [Windes 1993]) during the scavenging of the roof superstructure.

Plate I.4.50. Site 29SJ 724, Pithouse A floor fill, showing artifacts and other stone clustered south of the firepit. Note post-occupational slab wall in foreground. 30-cm north arrow. Photograph by Jim Judge, 1974 (CHCU neg. 9311).

This is probably particularly true of the several metate fragments, which are prized construction stones after the metate is worn out or broken. The several whole manos probably mark food reduction activities in the south half of the pithouse. Several pot covers found around the northern floor periphery of the pithouse, generally next to floor pits, may mark loci for ceramic storage containers.

The many bone tools on and above the floor indicate that basketry, clothing, and other activites associated with bone tools, particularly awls, were commonplace. The many tinklers (see Stratton, Volume II), however, have an uncertain function. The unworked bones commonly revealed no evidence of boiling or burning and probably represent post-occupational use of the pithouse by rabbits and other rodents. The rabbit skeleton on the ventilator floor certainly represents post-occupational deposition—probably the remains of a rabbit trapped in the structure.

Walls
Above the bench and on the south side, the pithouse walls were unplastered, gravelly native earth that extended to the surface.

Wall Cavities

In the wall 74-cm south of where the east wing wall was attached was an opening, tightly packed with gravel. It was 13-cm above the floor and 34-cm across at its widest. Native clay formed the lower 33-cm and no top was found. The deposition within and surrounding the cavity matches that of the lower bench, suggesting that the cavity is natural.

An unplastered, conical cavity occurred almost directly above the termination of the east wing wall, 51-cm above the floor. It was 20-x-23-cm and 28-cm deep with sand, a plain gray sherd, and a rodent bone as contents.

Discussion

The style of the superstructure is consistent with other Pueblo I pithouses. Four posts about 30-cm in diameter or less, linked by four stringers, supported the frame. Two layers or more of poles were laid across the stingers and covered with brush and mud. Along the sides, boards or groups of poles were set in the bench slots to lean against the stringers. All of this wood was robbed after abandonment.

Wainscoting of reeds and fibers (Feature I) was added behind the side poles or boards. The ease with which articles and trash could accumulate or be stored in the reed layer probably accounts for the mass of specimens in association. Ash and burned material indicate that part of Feature I burned, possibly after abandonment. After the wainscoting was in place, a thick layer of yellow clayey sand was applied on top. A final coat of adobe might have been added after that. This type of wall lining apparently is common in Chaco pitstructures. Kivas at Chetro Ketl (Senter 1939:21) and Pueblo Bonito (Pepper 1920:76, 81; Judd 1964:187) often exhibited boards or poles set along the bench with grass packed behind. Three boards and wainscoting were found associated in a Pueblo I pithouse at Bc 50 (Senter 1939:20, 23). Width (23-cm) and thickness (2.5-cm) of these three boards would allow easy placement in many of the bench slots of Pithouse A. The use of boards in pitstructures leaves little doubt that the bench slots could have supported boards in Pithouse A if not multiple sets of leaner poles.

The area above and behind the wing walls was roofed differently. Wainscoting was absent below, as it was in the Bc 50 pithouse (Senter 1939:23). Most likely poles were laid from the ground surface to the southern stringer and covered with mud. If entry was through the roof, as it appears, then this would also create a relatively level ramp for access to the roof. The two small floor slots next to the southeast wing wall might have held a board and wainscoting partition that extended to the roof.

Remodeling is evident within the firepit-ashpit-deflector complex. The earlier firepit was 30-cm closer to the ventilator and probably used in conjunction with the southern deflector slot 26-cm away. The second slot probably is for a two-pole ladder. Later the firepit was moved to its present position and a new deflector built in the form of an arch flanked by two posts. The row of small stones in front of the arch might represent deflector remains. Sometime after the initial use of the firepit, adobe collars were added to the firepit and the new "ashpit."

The many floor pits represent diverse functions. OP 6, located 128-cm north of the firepit and covered by a groundstone, probably represents the sipapu. Heating pits are common pithouse features (Bullard 1962:163-166), and two occur in Pithouse A. Coals and ashes from the firepit could have been placed in the pits for radiant heating in the colder months. HP 1 is sufficiently oxidized for a fire to have been built in it, and its fill is identical to that of the firepit. On the other hand, fires do not appear to have been built in the poorly oxidized HP 2 (see Plate I.4.47).

Many of the pits were undoubtedly used for storage. None of the pits are located along the alignment of the four roof stringers and, therefore, auxiliary postholes appear absent. OP 2 and OP 12 are of sufficient size to have held jars but both are smaller than room pits that might have served a similar purpose. The small shelves at the sides of three pits are unexplained. Although grooves similar to OP 9 have been suggested as loom supports (Bullard 1962:168), its shallowness, plastering, and proximity to the wall suggest otherwise. Pueblo I pithouses at 29SJ 299, Bc 50 (Senter 1939:Map 2) and possibly 29SJ 721 (Pithouse C) also reveal these unusual grooves on the north side along the ventilator, firepit, and sipapu (if present) alignment. Pitstructures from other periods in Chaco Canyon do not exhibit these grooves. Perhaps they served as an altar area for holding religious paraphernalia. Similar troughs are located next to walls in Pueblo III and Pueblo IV rooms (Barnett 1969:83; 1974:12). Ellis and Dodge (1990) suspect a ritual use for similar features found in Pueblo III and Pueblo IV kivas in the Rio Grande area.

After a short period of abandonment, the timbers and wing wall and deflector slabs were removed. The clusters of blackened and burned stones found near the postholes probably represent shims removed during salvage. The other stones might represent previous activities that took place behind the wing walls, although it is obvious that tools of value, such as metates, were taken at abandonment. Bone tools are the exception, with vast numbers of them left, as in the Bc 50 pithouse (Senter 1939:20) and others recently excavated in Chaco. Seven bone awls, needles, and tinklers came from the wainscoting on the northeast side, and 19 from the west side.

Shortly after the roof was dismantled, the lower bench was constructed and the large slab wall attached. Large stones of similar morphology in the fill and in a row near the surface east of the ventilator suggest contemporaneity with the slab wall. Although it is evident that the roof supports had been removed previously, there is little doubt that the mass of stone in the fill came from a collapsed superstructure. Possibly a shelter of some sort had been built within the east half of the abandoned pithouse and covered with adobe and stones.

On the west side of the pithouse, the several tiny firepits and the footprints appear to relate to a later activity. Despite the differences in depth between the features on each side, however, their relative distribution hints of concurrent activities. The size of the firepits would have been unsuitable for heating or cooking. Perhaps the abandoned pithouse provided a place of recreation for children. Construction of a shelter would also indicate adult, presumably male, participation.

No deep trenching was done to look for additional pithouses. But the nature of the ridge and the symmetry of the central roomblock dictates that another pithouse is not present. Other pithouses certainly exist in association with the houses along the ridge higher and lower than the central house, however.

Trash Mound (Figure I.4.13)

The slope in front of the room block and pithouse was relatively flat and narrow, forming a short lateral ridge. This was a favorite location of the local inhabitants for dumping trash. A baseline was run across the center of this ridge (110°/290°) and a grid established. In order to prevent future erosion of the trash area, alternating sections of the grid were selected for excavation. This allowed a continuous profile to be drawn along the baseline. The remaining surface trash was subsequently stripped of all chipped stone and most of the ceramics, the only specimens evident.

Although refuse was common on the surface and the soil was stained a promising light gray, excavation revealed only 20-cm of soft, trashy fill. Patches of sterile, gravelly sand were encountered just under the surface, although rodent burrows often carried refuse deeper. After the first 10-cm, the amount of refuse decreased considerably, and by a depth of 20-cm almost nothing was recovered. The trash consisted primarily of ash and sherds with a scattering of debitage. No sandstone artifacts were recovered. Fewer than 10 bones were collected, all from rodents. Fifteen cubic meters of fill were removed, of which nine were predominately trash.

Conclusions

Six archaeomagnetic samples from the central roomblock (Chapter 6) indicate a primary occupation in the late 700s with perhaps some use into the early A.D. 800s. The sparse amount of refuse, however, does not support lengthy continual occupation. Except for a neckbanded and an indented corrugated sherd on the surface, utility ware sherds were plain gray with occasional fugitive red wash, undoubtedly all from Lino Gray vessels. Decorated types included La Plata Black-on-white, Lino Black-on-white, Piedra Black-on-white, and White Mound Black-on-white or their equivalents, and redware types of Abajo, Bluff, and Sanostee. Polished black ceramics were also present. The ceramic assemblage was strictly late Basketmaker III or early Pueblo I. Room layout is characteristic of the Pueblo I period but the temporary nature of the surface habitation rooms indicates the early transition to surface living but for seasonal use.

Houses of similar layout and ceramics include House 3 and Protokiva C on Wetherill Mesa (Hayes and Lancaster 1975), Section 1 at White Mound (Gladwin 1945), Site 23 in the La Plata District (Morris 1939), and 29SJ 299 and 29Mc 184 (this volume) in Chaco Canyon.

The building techniques of two individuals, presumably men, are reflected in the construction of the central roomblock and the associated ramada and pithouse. If the pithouse was built by and housed a nuclear family (but see Lightfoot 1994), the presence of dual activity loci would be unexpected. Presumably, an experienced male would be responsible for house construction, and help by others would be directed or guided by him. If the builders were from the same nuclear family, then similar building techniques would be expected.

If matrilocal residence was common, however, males from different residence groups with different construction skills learned elsewhere would likely be involved in the site construction. Thus, we might expect that different aspects of building, representing two or more kin groups, might be evident in the archaeological record. On the other hand, construction by the participants who were to live in the structure and were helped by a neighbor could also account for the differences.

Examination of the many pits and postholes in the pithouse reveals some non-random differences when the pithouse is split along the ventilator-firepit axis, the logical division if occupied by two families. Three building traits were selected to test the possibility that two non-related builders were present: the depth of similar pits and the presence or absence of stone footings under posts (Table I.4.14).

The four roof support holes are located in two areas, in the wing walls and backed into the northern face of the bench. Each set supports a different roof weight and, superficially, resembles one another, as expected. But, the western two postholes exhibit the same depth, a stone footing, and a thick lignite packing. In contrast, more variability is seen in the eastern two postholes, which are of unequal but deeper depths than the western two, contain less lignite, and lack the stone footing.

The contrast is more marked when the 36 bench slots are examined (Table I.4.14). Again, the western holes are significantly shallower (corrected $x^2 = 5.49$, d.f. $= 1, p = .02$) and contain more lignite (corrected $= 21.8$, d.f. $= 1, p = .0005$). Spacing of the slots also does not appear random (corrected $x^2 = 6.2$, d.f.$=1, p = .02$). The sample of wing wall grooves does not present meaningful differences.

Floor pits are difficult to compare because

of their varied, and often unknown, functions. Their numbers are about equal on each side, if the sipapu and OP 9 along the axis of division are disregarded. Nevertheless, the trend continues with the western pits being shallower than the eastern pits (mean 8.9 versus 14.1-cm), but not significantly (corrected $x^2 = 1.55$, d.f. = 1, $p = .25$). Both heating pits are the same depth, but one occurs on each side.

Artifacts within the pithouse might also reflect the dichotomy. A cluster of bone tools on each side may mark two separate but identical work areas. Nearly equal numbers of groundstone and blackened shims occur on each side behind the wing walls.

The same trends in posthole construction are evident in the habitation rooms (Table I.4.9). A more consistent use and deeper packing of lignite, as well as the presence of stone footings, associates Room 9 with the builder of the west side of the pithouse. Room 9 postholes are on average deeper than those in Room 1, but their depths are similar to those on the pithouse's west side. Likewise, the variable use of lignite and depths of holes, and the absence of stone footings in the Room 1 postholes, are duplicated on the eastern side of the pithouse.

Despite the presence of 14 ramada postholes (Table I.4.11), there is no clear dichotomy in construction. Six postholes in a trapezoid alignment front Room 4. Four of the six contained lignite packing of unknown depth, and three had stone footings. These six on average were shallower than the remaining eight postholes (14.0 versus 18.6-cm). Eight postholes fronted Room 5 and part of Room 6. None contained packing, but one had a stone footing. Four of those at the north end, fronting Room 6, yielded only sand fill. It appears that the two methods of posthole construction observed in the pithouse continued at the ramada, but less stringently. Those in front of Room 4 reflect the habits of the builder of the west half of the pithouse, and the others, the builder of the eastern half.

In summary, it appears that builders with different experiences on posthole construction built the different units of architecture. The two builders or groups of builders are assumed to be related, with each constructing and then occupying about half the site. This hypothesis is supported by the presence of just two surface habitation rooms, each normally considered to reflect a separate residential unit.

The total area of the habitation rooms nearly matches that of the pithouse, 20.5 versus 22.1 m^2. Space under the ramada, difficult to measure accurately, totals about 18.3 m^2. Storage rooms yield 22.8 m^2 of floor space. Thus, space among the different architectural units is fairly constant. Overall, Wilshusen (1989a:Table 2) shows that the amount of dirt removed for the construction of Pithouse A was more than enough to build the surface rooms.

Space allocated to the two residential units is relatively constant but not equal, except in the pithouse, where it is difficult to allocate space other than equally. Habitation Room 9 is only 63.0 percent the size of Room 1, and its associated storage room space is 64.4 percent of Room 1's. Assuming that the ramada postholes reflect "apartments" belonging to the same two residential units, then Room 4 and the ramada in front appear to go with the Room 9 complex. Rooms 5 and 6 and the remaining ramada space should go with the Room 1 complex. Despite adding the storage capacity (e.g., floor space) of Room 4 to the Room 9 complex and Rooms 5 and 6 to the other complex, the storage proportion remains unchanged at 64.1 percent.

The ramada space of the two complexes also is of similar proportion, 70.2 percent, even though the ramada does not front the entire three-room span. This all suggests that the residential group utilizing Rooms 1, 2, 3, 5, and 6 and part of the ramada required slightly more floor space for various activities. Perhaps this was necessary because this area housed a larger family than the rooms belonging to the smaller residential group.

Room 10 probably relates to the earliest occupation of the pithouse, with the other rooms added later. Architecturally, the tub-shaped rooms behind the habitation rooms appear the earliest in the row. It could be argued, however, that the ramada and its associated rooms are earlier. The ramada fits an intermediary stage before more permanent above-ground occupation takes place. Also, the ramada is positioned directly behind the pithouse as if it were built before the habitation rooms. Instead, it is likely that the row of rooms and ramada were built nearly contemporaneously. Trash was absent in all rooms except from Room 10, suggesting that Rooms 1 through 9 were used until the site was abandoned.

Materials removed from the pithouse, particularly the boards or side poles, indicate construction of a new pithouse nearby. The large size of the north roomblock downslope and its slightly later age, revealed perhaps by sparse numbers of neckbanded sherds, suggests the inhabitants did not go far. Possibly, the entire ridge reflects the movement of a family through time, starting with Basketmaker III at the top and culminating with the Pueblo II house at the bottom. If this were true, a similar posthole dichotomy would be expected, at least in the north roomblock.

NORTH ROOMBLOCK (BC 162, 29SJ 724)
(Figure I.4.12)

In the summer of 1976, two test trenches were placed in the trash on the south slope of the north roomblock in hopes of finding a Pueblo I house occupied in the early 800s. A double row of vertical slabs, six meters long or more, marked the Pueblo I rooms. A small Red Mesa phase house of spalls, mud, and stones situated at the west end was the source of limited Pueblo II trash. The few neckbanded sherds on the surface could have belonged to either house, so a closer examination of the trash area was deemed necessary.

The test trenches were oriented north-south and the northwest corners were 11.33 m at 167° (true) and 22.72 m at 134° (true) from the site stake (rebar). One trench was 1.5-x-3-m and located in abundant refuse; the western one was 1.5-x-1.5-m in relatively scarce trash. Pueblo I and Pueblo II sherds were mixed with chipped stone debitage, charcoal, ash, and broken rock on the surface and in the first 10-cm. All fill was screened through quarter-inch mesh. Level 2 (10-20-cm) was dominated by Pueblo I artifacts and encompassed the bottom of the trash. A third 10-cm level in Test Trench 2 (the western one) was primarily sterile yellowish sand and gravel, and thus the testing was terminated. Cans were placed at the corners of the test trenches and then the trenches were refilled.

Examination of the ceramics (Table I.4.16) indicates that the Pueblo I house was occupied at about the same time as the central roomblock or a little later. Some of the neckbanded sherds might have come from the Pueblo I house but most were concentrated below the Pueblo II house and none were found in the lower levels of trash.

In 2001, a chipped stone sample was field analyzed in the midden at the north roomblock to compare with the excavated material from the central roomblock and to increase the overall Pueblo I sample (see Moss, Volume II).

Table I.4.1. Ceramic Samples from 29Mc 184: Grab Sample (1957), Midden Testing (1975), and Midden Transects (1998).[a]

Ceramic Type	House A Midden							
	TT 3-4, Surface		TT 3-4, Level 1		Surface Transect		Midden Totals	
	No.	Percent	No.	Percent	No.	Percent	No.	Percent
CIBOLA CULINARY		[92]		[80]		[96]	24	[93]
Lino Gray	2	6	6	5	16	3	638	3
Plain gray	30	83	96	73	512	93	2	89
Plain gray w/ Fugitive red	-	-	2	2	-	-	4	T
Wide neckbanded	1[b]	3	2	2	1	T		1
CHUSKA CULINARY		[3]		[2]		[T]		[1]
Plain gray	-	-	1	1	1	T	2	T
Sheep Springs Gray	-	-	2	2	-	-	2	T
Capt. Tom Corrugated	1	3	-	-	-	-	1	T
CIBOLA WHITEWARE		[3]		[15]		[3]		[6]
La Plata B/w	-	-	-	-	2	T	2	T
White Mound B/w	-	-	2	2	5	1	7	1
Kiatuthlanna B/w	-	-	-	-	1	T	1	T
Unclassified BMIII-PI B/w	1	3	2	2	5	1	8	1
Unclassified BMIII-PI W/w	-	-	16	12	5	1	21	3
Unclassified PII-III W/w	-	-	-	-	1	T	1	T
CHUSKA WHITEWARE				[1]				[T]
Crozier B/w	-	-	1	1	-	-		T
TUSAYAN WHITEWARE				[1]				[T]
Lino B/g	-	-	1	1	-	-		T
CHUSKA REDWARE								
Sanostee B/r	-	-	-	-	-	-	-	-
Totals	36	101	132	10	551	99	719	100
Sherd Density[c]	-		210		3.0			
Midden percentage		2		3		66		

[a] T = trace (less than 0.5 percent). Ware percentages = [ ]; combined ware and type percentages = ( ).
[b] Wide neck coils are slightly indented.
[c] Density is m³ for test trench samples and m² for surface transect samples.
[d] Samples collected in 1957 by Joel Shiner, US National Park Service (C92590-92591). The site visibility and Shiner's notes place the collection as from 29Mc 184.
[e] This rim sherd is indented corrugated on the exterior; an odd piece (Mesa Verde Whiteware?).

344 Windes

Table I.4.1. Ceramic Samples from 29Mc 184: Grab Sample (1957), Midden Testing (1975), and Midden Transects (1998), cont'd.[a]

Ceramic Type	House B Midden							
	TT 2, Surface		TT 2, Level 1		Surface Transect		Midden Totals	
	No.	Percent	No.	Percent	No.	Percent	No.	Percent
CIBOLA CULINARY		[79]		[88]		[97]		[95]
Lino Gray	1	7	2	1	11	2	14	291
Plain gray	9	64	88	45	484	93	581	T
Plain gray w/ Fugitive red	-	-	-	-	2	T	2	1
Wide neckbanded	1	7	2	1	4	1	7	
CHUSKA CULINARY				[2]				[T]
Plain gray	-	-	3	2	-	-	3	T
Sheep Springs Gray	-	-	-	-	-	-	-	-
Capt. Tom Corrugated	-	-	-	-	-	-	-	-
CIBOLA WHITEWARE		[21]		[9]		[3]		[4]
La Plata B/w	-	-	-	-	2	T	2	T
White Mound B/w	1	7	-	-	5	1	6	1
Kiatuthlanna B/w	-	-	1	1	-	-	1	T
Unclassified BMIII-PI B/w	1	7	4	2	4	1	9	1
Unclassified BMIII-PI W/w	1	7	4	2	4	1	9	1
Unclassified PII-III W/w	-	-	-	-	-	-	-	-
CHUSKA WHITEWARE								
Crozier B/w	-	-	-	-	-	-	-	-
TUSAYAN WHITEWARE								
Lino B/g	-	-	-	-	-	-	-	-
CHUSKA REDWARE						[T]		[T]
Sanostee B/r	-	-	1	-	2	T	3	T
Totals	14	100	105	99	518	99	637	99
Sherd Density[c]	-		233		4.5			
Midden percentage		1		2		45		

--for notes, see box at bottom of table on p. 343

Table I.4.1. Ceramic Samples from 29Mc 184: Grab Sample (1957), Midden Testing (1975), and Midden Transects (1998), cont'd.[a]

Ceramic Type	House C							
	TT 1, Surface		TT 1, Level 1		Surface Transect		Midden Totals	
	No.	Percent	No.	Percent	No.	Percent	No.	Percent
CIBOLA CULINARY		[93]		[77]		[93]		[92]
Lino Gray	4	4	4	5	44	4	52	4
Plain gray	78	85	59	69	959	88	1096	87
Plain gray w/ Fugitive red	3	3	-	-	-	-	3	T
Wide neckbanded	1	1	-	-	5	T	6	T
Narrow neckbanded	-	-	1	1	-	1	-	T
Neckbanded-unk. type[d]	-	-	2	2	-	-	2	T
CHUSKA CULINARY				[6]		[2]		[2]
Bennett Gray	-	-	2	2	1	T	3	T
Plain gray	-	-	3	3	18	2	21	2
Sheep Springs Gray	-	-	-	-	-	-	-	-
Capt. Tom Corrugated	-	-	-	-	-	-	-	-
CIBOLA WHITEWARE		[7]		[14]		[5]		[6]
La Plata B/w	-	-	-	-	1	T	1	T
White Mound B/w	1	1	6	7	16	1	23	2
Kiatuthlanna B/w	-	-	-	-	2	T	2	T
Unclassified BMIII-PI B/w	4	4	2	2	22	2	28	2
Unclassified BMIII-PI W/w	1	1	4	5	14	1	19	2
Unclassified PII-III W/w	-	-	-	-	-	-	-	-
UNCLASSIFIED PI-PII C/W	-	-	-	-	-	-	—	-
CHUSKA WHITEWARE				[1]		[T]		[T]
Crozier B/w	-	-	-	-	-	-	-	-
Tunicha B/w	-	-	1	1	-	-	1	T
Unclassified Whiteware	-	-	-	-	1	T	1	T
TUSAYAN WHITEWARE								
Lino B/g	-	-	-	-	-	-	-	-
LINO SMUDGED	-	-	-	-	1	[T]	1	[T]
WHITE MT. REDWARE	-	-	-	-	-	-	-	-
SAN JUAN REDWARE				[1]		[T]		[T]
Abajo R/o	-	-	1	1	-	-	1	T
Unclassified Redware	-	-	-	-	1	T	1	T
TALLAHOGAN RED	-	-	-	-	1	T	1	[T]
CHUSKA REDWARE				[1]		[T]		[T]
Sanostee B/r	-	-	1	1	2	T	3	T
Totals	92	100	86	100	1088	100	1266	98
Sherd Density[c]	-		478		15.9		-	
Midden percentage		1		1		32		

--for notes, see box at bottom of table on p. 343

Table I.4.1. Ceramic Samples from 29Mc 184: Grab Sample (1957), Midden Testing (1975), and Midden Transects (1998), cont'd.[a]

Ceramic Type	House D midden Midden Transect		Site Grab Sample[d]		Site Totals	
	No.	*Percent*	No.	*Percent*	No.	*Percent*
CIBOLA CULINARY				*[42]*		*[92]*
Lino Gray	19	*5*	3	*16*	112	*4*
Plain gray	365	*88*	5	*26*	2685	*88*
Plain gray w/ Fugitive red	-	-	-	-	7	*T*
Wide neckbanded	-	-	-	-	17	*1*
Narrow neckbanded	-	-	-	-	1	*T*
Neckbanded-unk. type	-	-	-	-	2	*T*
CHUSKA CULINARY				*[5]*		*[1]*
Bennett Gray	-	-	-	-	3	*T*
Plain gray	-	-	1	*5*	27	*1*
Sheep Springs Gray	-	-	-	-	2	*T*
Capt. Tom Corrugated	-	-	-	-	1	*T*
CIBOLA WHITEWARE		*[6]*		*[42]*		*[6]*
La Plata B/w	1	*T*	1	*5*	7	*T*
White Mound B/w	8	*2*	5	*26*	49	*2*
Kiatuthlanna B/w	-	-	-	-	4	*T*
Unclassified BMIII-PI B/w	9	*2*	2	*11*	56	*2*
Unclassified BMIII-PI W/w	5	*1*	-	-	54	*2*
Unclassified PII-III W/w	-	-	-	-	1	*T*
UNCLASSIFIED PI-PII C/W	-	-	1[e]	*(5)*	1	*(T)*
CHUSKA WHITEWARE						*[T]*
Crozier B/w	-	-	-	-	1	*T*
Tunicha B/w	-	-	-	-	1	*T*
Unclassified Whiteware	-	-	-	-	1	*T*
TUSAYAN WHITEWARE						*[T]*
Lino B/g	-	-	-	-	1	*T*
LINO SMUDGED	3	*(1)*	1	*(5)*	8	*(T)*
WHITE MT. REDWARE	-	-	-	-	1	*(T)*
SAN JUAN REDWARE		*[1]*				*[T]*
Abajo R/o	1	*T*	-	-	2	*T*
Unclassified Redware	2	*T*	-	-	3	*T*
TALLAHOGAN RED	-	-	-	-	1	*(T)*
CHUSKA REDWARE						*[T]*
Sanostee B/r	-	-	-	-	6	*T*
Totals	413	*101*	19	*99*	3054	*99*
Sherd Density[c]	4.0		-			
Midden percentage		*69*		-		

--for notes, see box at bottom of table on p. 343

Table I.4.2. Metrics for Surface Rooms Exposed at 29Mc 184.

Provenience	Length (cm)	Width (cm)	Height/Depth (cm)	Floor Area (m^2)	Lining[a]
West House (House C)[b]					
Room 1	440	304	–	11.14	L-S
Room 2	272	173	–	4.66	L-S
Room 3	224	144	–	3.14	L-S
Room 4	234	184	–	4.28	L-S
Central House (House B; east end is tentative, especially from Room 10 on)[c]					
Room 1	690⁻	260±		17.9±	L-S
Rooms 2-3				5.4?	L-S
Room 4 (pothole in W corner)	695	260±		18.1±	L-S, Type I
Rooms 5-6				5.8?	L-S, Type I
Room 7	600±	260±		15.6±	L-S
Rooms 8-9				5.8?	
Room 10	832±?	260±		21.6±	L-S
Rooms 11-13				5.7?	
Room 14				3.8?	
Rooms 15-17				9.7?	
Room 18				?	
Room 19	260±	140		3.6±	L-S
East House (House A; much spall rubble on surface)[c]					
Room 1				7.0±	
Rooms 2-3				8.7±	
Room 4				4.8±	
Room 5+[c]				unknown	

[a] L-S: Wall foundations lined with upright slabs. Several appear to be a mixture of Type I masonry, spalls, and adobe.
[b] The West House (House D) rooms are too indeterminate to warrant sizing as are parts of the East and Central Houses.
[c] Measurements for House A & B are uncertain and the houses appear not exactly as mapped when revisited in 2013.

Table I.4.3. Site 29SJ 299, Pithouse E, Distribution of Floor 2 Materials[a].

Artifact Number	Artifact Class	Lithic Material, Ceramic Ware, or Faunal Species	FS No.
–	Awl (15.2-x-1.8-x-2.7-cm; 22.8 g)	Mule deer tibia (*Odocoileus hemionus*)	500
–	Polishing stone (6.7-x-5.2-x-3.3-cm; 5.6 g)	4000 (quartzite). Natural manuport?	503
–	Pot lid (14.4-x-13.8-x-0.5-cm; 155.7 g)	2000 (sandstone). Burned. Shaped irregular round by edge chipping	507
–	Bead (1.1-x-0.5-cm diameter; 0.3 g)	Shell (*Olivella dama*)	508
–	Cooking slab? (23-x-20-x-2.2-cm; 1841.8 g)	2000 (sandstone). 2 edges and 2 faces ground. Irregular shape. Burned firepit liner stone?	519
–	Hammerstone (5.8-x-5.5-x-4.4-cm; 188.8 g)	1112 (cherty silicified wood). Spheroid	529.1
–	Hammerstone (6.3-x-6.2-x-5.5-cm; 236.2 g)	1051 (High Surface Chert). Spheroid	529.2
–	Pot lid (6.5-x-6.4-x-0.6-cm; 39 g)	2000 (sandstone). Lightly burned. Shaped round by edge chipping	530
–	Active abrader (8.2-x-6-x-2.2-cm; 110 g)	2000 (coarse yellow sandstone). Mano-like fragment	533

Table I.4.3. Site 29SJ 299, Pithouse E, Distribution of Floor 2 Materials, cont'd.[a]

Artifact Number	Artifact Class	Lithic Material, Ceramic Ware, or Faunal Species	FS No.
1	Turkey skeletons (2)	*Meleagris gallopavo*. Found 1-cm above deflector slot	534
2	Corn cobs (2+; 1.5⁻ g)	*Zea mays* (carbonized). In Firepit 1	536
3	Lapidary abrader (13.8-x-9.4-x-3-cm; 800 g)	2000 (sandstone). Shim used in SE roof support hole (PH 2). Rectangular block shape; finely ground on 2 sides	540.1
4	Metate fragment (23-x-19.9-x-8.6-cm; 59 kg)	2000 (sandstone). Shim used in SE roof support hole (PH 2). Finely ground on bottom: possible lapstone?	540.2
5	Metate fragment (15.5-x-11.5-x-3.3-cm; 548 g)	2000 (sandstone). Shim used in SE roof support hole (PH 2). Piece of the metate trough.	540.4
–	Plain gray jar sherd	Cibola Grayware. In fill of SE roof support hole (PH 2).	541A
–	Bones (2)	Bushy-tailed woodrat femur and turkey coracoid. In PH 2	542
6	Mano blank (28-x-13-x-8-cm; 5200 g)	2000 (sandstone). Loaf-shaped. Pecked to shape with some grinding. Lightly burned.	543
7	Hammerstone (17-x-13-x-8-cm; 2317.2 g)	4000 (quartzite). Massive river cobble with slight hammering on 1 end	544
8	Mano (15-x-12-x-3.5-cm; 3596 g)	2000 (sandstone).	545
9	Bones	Articulated kangaroo rat skeleton (*Dipodomys ordii*). In heating pit	504
–	Bone	Jackrabbit (*Lepus californicus*) humerus. North half of floor.	501
–	Bones (43)	Cottontail (21), jackrabbit (17), Gunnison's prairie dog (4), and a coyote radius (1). Test Trench E area of floor	516
–	Bones (20)	Cottontail (10), jackrabbit (7), Gunnison's prairie dog (1), and unclass. small/medium mammal (1). South half of floor.	527
–	Bones (5)	Cottontail (1), jackrabbit (1), prairie dog (2), Ord's kangaroo rat (1)	538
–	Bone tinkler (11.5-x-2.0-x-1.3-cm; 4.7 g)	*Lepus sp.* (jackrabbit; epiphyses ground off). Level 7 (floor fill/floor). Under the roofing adobe.	550
–	Sherds (200)	Level 7 (floor fill/floor; roof fall). See Table II.2.27, Volume II	518
–	Sherds (42)	Level 7 (floor contact, North half). See Table II.2.27, Volume II	499
–	Sherds (31)	Level 7 (floor contact, South half). See Table II.2.27, Volume II.	526
–	Core (max. dimension, 5.1-cm; 38.6 g)	1112 (cherty silicified wood) with 4 platforms. South half of floor	528

[a] See distribution in Figure I.4.2. Unnumbered floor artifacts did not have specific locations: FS 500 & 503 = north half of pithouse. FS 507–508 = north half of pithouse on bench top. FS 519 = Test Trench E. FS 529-530 & 533 = south half of pithouse.

Table I.4.4. Site 29SJ 299, Ramada 2, Distribution of Artifacts Used in Post Support Construction.[a]

Artifact Number	Artifact Class	Lithic Material, Ceramic Ware, or Faunal Species	FS No.
1	Active abrader (12.2-x-8.4-x-2.4-cm; 438 g)	2000 (sandstone). Reworked mano fragment.	427
2	Floor polisher (17-x-11-x-8-cm; 2155 g)	4000 (quartzite). Used as a shim in Post Support 9. River cobble.	444
3	Anvil (20-x-17-x-4-cm; 2381 g)	4000 (quartzite). Used as a base stone in Post Support 3. Partly burned river cobble. Concentrated peck marks on both faces.	445
4	Mano (21.3-x-13.2-x-3.7-cm; 1551 g)	2000 (sandstone). Used as a shim in Post Support 3	446
5	Mano (16.5-x-11.4-x-3.2-cm; 1073 g)	2000 (sandstone). Possible shim. Next to Post Support 10.	447
6	Anvil/lapstone (21.8-x-16.6-x-4.4-cm; 2863 g)	2000 (sandstone). Rectangular block. Finely ground on one side. Pecking concentrated in one corner.	448
7	Abrader? (14-x-11-x-5-cm; 1588 g)	2000 (sandstone). Reworked rectangular metate fragment.	449
8	Lapstone (19.3-x-13.5-x-1.7-cm; 608 g)	2000 (sandstone). Concretion disc. One side partly finely ground.	450
9	Reworked metate fragment (20-x-11-x-10-cm; 3345 g)	2000 (sandstone). Used as a shim in Post Support 2B	451
10	Mano (23.2-x-10.2-x-3.0-cm; 935 g)	2000 (sandstone). Used as a shim in Post Support 2B. Burned? Worn out mano?	452
11	Anvil (21-x-13-x-6-cm; 2438 g)	2000 (sandstone). Used as a shim in Post Support 2B. Reworked metate fragment. Partly burned.	453
12	Passive abrader (20.5-x-12.3-x-4.3; 1873 g)	2000 (sandstone). Used as a base stone in Post Support 5	454
13	Groundstone (marginal; 10.5-x-9.3-x-3.2-cm; 483 g)	2000 (sandstone). Used as a shim in Post Support 2B. Spot grinding.	455
14	Lapstone (20-x-13.8-x-5.7-cm; 2667 g)	2000 (sandstone). Used as a base stone in Post Support 2B. One side finely ground.	456
15	Mano (18.6-x-9.8-x-2.6-cm; 851 g)	2000 (sandstone). Used as a shim in Post Support 1. In pieces.	457
16	Lapidary? abrader (14.1-x-9.1-x-2.2-cm; 453 g)	2000 (sandstone). Possible shim. On surface near Post Support 1. Burned.	458
17	Passive abrader (21-x-13.8-x-7.6-cm; 3220 g)	2000 (sandstone). Used as a base stone in Post Support 1. Ovoid with face partly ground. Burned spot.	459
18	Hatch or jar cover fragment (17.3+-x-13.4+-x-2.3-cm; 362 g)	2000 (sandstone). Used as a shim in Post Support 3. Chipped edge. Estimated original size: 28-cm diameter.	470

[a] See distribution in **Figure** I.4.4.

Table I.4.5. Site 29SJ 721, Distribution of Floor Fill and Floor Materials.[a]

Artifact Number	Artifact Class	Lithic Material, Ceramic Ware, or Faunal Species	FS No.
Pithouse A			
-	Dendrochronological specimens	Non-coniferous (carbonized). Discarded by laboratory. Floor.	2
1	Fuel (dendrochronological specimen)	Non-coniferous (carbonized). Discarded by laboratory. Firepit 1 fill.	3
1	Bones (9)	Cottontail (6), jackrabbit (1), & unidentified small mammal (probably rabbit; 2). Firepit 1 fill.	13
2	Sherds (2) Plain gray jar La Plata/White Mound B/w	Floor, NE edge of Firepit 1.	21
3	Dendrochronological specimens (roofing?)	Non-coniferous (not-carbonized). Discarded by laboratory. Contact with center of west wall; 8cm above floor.	4
4	Awl (9.4-x-7.4-x-1.2-cm; 2.5 g)	Jackrabbit (*Lepus* sp.) ulna. Lev. 4 (25 cm above floor).	14
-	Sherds (4) Plain gray jar Lino Gray jar Obelisk Gray jar La Plata/White Mound bowl B/w	Level 4 (floor fill).	19
-	Sherds (11) Plain gray jars (6) Plain gray jar (large) with Fugitive red paint Lino Gray jar with Fugitive red paint Obelisk Gray jar Woodruff Smudged bowl	Floor.	20
5	Pipe (5.2-x-3.7-x-2.7-cm; 29.0 g)	Unfired gray clay. Cup end is flared. No hole. Level 4 (10cm above floor) against north wall.	24
6	Corn cob fragment	*Zea mays*. Carbonized. Level 4 (7cm above floor).	25
-	Chipped stones (4) Whole flake (6.0 g) Whole flake (1.9 g) Utilized flake fragment (0.6 g) Angular debris (4.3 g)	Level 4 (floor fill). 1052 (clear chalcedony, High Surface Chert). 1113 (cherty silicified wood). 1113 (cherty silicified wood). 1120 (red silicified wood).	32

Table I.4.5. Site 29SJ 721, Distribution of Floor Fill and Floor Materials, cont'd.[a]

Artifact Number	Artifact Class	Lithic Material, Ceramic Ware, or Faunal Species	FS No.
-	Chipped stones (12)	Floor	
	Angular debris (6.6 g)	1052 (clear chalcedony, High Surface Chert).	
	Utilized flake (3) (total 62.6 g)	1112 (cherty silicified wood).	
	Whole flake (4.4 g)	1112 (cherty silicified wood).	
	Angular debris (1.0 g)	1112 (cherty silicified wood).	
	Core (40.0 g)	1112 (cherty silicified wood).	
	Core (6.5 g)	1140 (chalcedonic silicified wood).	
	Utilized flake (2) (total 12.3 g)	1150 (yellow-brown silicified wood).	
	Angular debris (2) (total 2.0 g)	1230 (chalcedony with red inclusions).	33
7	Anvil (17-x-13-x-2-cm; 1043 g)	2000 (sandstone). Secondary use mortar.	37
8	Concretion (5.3-x-5.3-x-4.7-cm; 149.5 g)	2000 (sandstone). Natural sphere. In west end of slot.	38
Cist 1			
9	Plain gray jar sherd	Under flagstone floor.	68
Cist 2			
10	Dendrochronological specimen fragments	*Populus* sp. (carbonized). Discarded by laboratory. Fill.	1
Pithouse C			
-	Chipped stone (6)	Level 2	
	Utilized flake (3.7 g)	1080 (Washington Pass chert).	
	Utilized flake (2) (total 6.5 g)	1113 (cherty silicified wood).	
	Whole flake (4.1 g)	1113 (cherty silicified wood).	
	Angular debris (0.3 g)	1140 (chalcedonic silicified wood).	
	Utilized flake (2.6 g)	1140 (chalcedonic silicified wood).	
	Utilized flake (3.1 g)	1661 (mottled light brown Zuni chert pebble).	
-	Sherds (10)	Level 2	9
	Plain gray jars (7)		
	Lino Gray jar		
	White Mound? B/w bowl with Fugitive red exterior		
	Unclassified PI whiteware bowl with Fugitive red exterior		
-	Bone	Unknown small mammal (rabbit size). Level 2.	104
-	Bone	Unknown small mammal (rabbit size). Upper 10cm of fill.	112
11	Hammerstone (5.2-x-5.1-x-3.9-cm; 136.5 g)	1053 (High Surface Chert). Ventilator floor/surface.	113
12	Hatch cover (32-x-33-x-1.9-cm; 3.6 kg)	2000 (sandstone). Chipped oval-shape. Ground on one surface. Hematite (10YR 4/6) on both sides. Light sooting. Floor.	91
			93

Table I.4.5. Site 29SJ 721, Distribution of Floor Fill and Floor Materials, cont'd.[a]

Artifact Number	Artifact Class	Lithic Material, Ceramic Ware, or Faunal Species	FS No.
13	Hatch cover (35.5-x-39.7-x-2.2-cm; 5.5 kg)	2000 (sandstone). Chipped square to oval. Ground flat on one surface. In OP 6.	94
14	Knife (4.8-x-3.1-x-0.6-cm; 7.5 g)	1040 (tan Brushy Basin chert) All edges retouched. Triangular shaped. In bottom of OP 6.	92
15	Vegetal Material (19.6 g)	OP 2 fill.	119
16	Whole flake (0.3 g)	1113 (cherty silicified wood). Firepit 1 fill.	101
16	Obelisk Gray jar sherd	Firepit 1 fill.	106
17	Obelisk Gray jar sherd	OP 3 fill.	107
18	Chipped stone (2) Angular debris (4.6 g) Angular debris (0.5 g)	Floor (west side of FP 1). 1112 (cherty silicified wood) 3510 (Mt. Taylor obsidian). Sourced by Shackley and Dillian (2000).	100
18	Sherds (16) Plain gray jars (11) Plain gray jars with Fugitive red paint (2) ino Gray jar Obelisk Gray jars (2) with Fugitive red	Floor (west side of Firepit 1).	105
19	Crystal (1.1-x-0.6-x-0.6-cm; 0.7 g)	5020 (quartz crystal). 4 cm deep in OP 4.	115
Cist 4 (roasting pit)			
20	Fuel (dendrochronoloical specimens; 9)(5.0-8.2-cm estimated diameter)	*Pinus edulis* (piñon). Eight dated. Probably deadwood. Latest: A.D. 434fp-561vv (CNM 179-187). Fill above rock bottom.	80
20	Plain gray jar sherds (2)	Fill.	85
20	Utilized flake (1.8 g)	1113 (cherty silicified wood) Fill.	86
20	Fuel (dendrochronological specimen) (estimated 5.2+ cm diameter)	Floor (earlier firing than FS 80 material). Deadwood. A.D. 492fp-621++vv (CNM-188).	95
20	Sherds (5) Plain gray jar (4) Obelisk Gray jar	Assoc. with slab wall of cist.	108
Cist 5			
21	Plain gray jar sherd	Fill above rock bottom.	76

Table I.4.5. Site 29SJ 721, Distribution of Floor Fill and Floor Materials, cont'd.[a]

Artifact Number	Artifact Class	Lithic Material, Ceramic Ware, or Faunal Species	FS No.
21	Dendrochronological specimen (estimated diameter 4.0+ cm)	*Pinus edulis* (piñon). Carbonized. Not dated. Fill above rock bottom.	79
21	Non-hafted bifacially flaked blade (1.5+-x-2.1-x-0.5-cm; 2.1 g)	1053 (High Surface Chert). End missing.	87
Room 1			
-	Chipped stones (10)	Surface	
	Whole flakes (4) (total 7.1 g)	1052 (clear chalcedony, High Surface Chert).	
	Angular debris (5.7 g)	1053 (High Surface Chert).	
	Angular debris (2.9 g)	1054 (High Surface Chert).	
	Utlized flake (5.7 g)	1113 (cherty silicified wood).	
	Core (57.0 g)	1140 (chalcedonic silicified wood).	
	Utilized flake (5.2 g)	4000 (quartzite).	
	Whole flake (1.6 g)	4000 (quartzite).	61
Kiva			
22	Woodruff Smudged bowl sherd	4-5-cm above Burial 1 left knee cap.	39
23	Burial 1 (adult female)	70-cm below surface; about 85-cm above the floor. Placed on back with knees flexed & arms nearly crossed. Map placement approximate.	40
-	Eggshell (15 pieces; restored egg: 45-x-43-mm; 2.7 g)	*Meleagris gallopavo*. Munsell 2.5Y 8/2. Level 4, 30-cm above floor in NE corner.	52
24	Utilized flake (0.8 g)	1145 (chalcedonic silicified wood). Under wall fall NE side.	102
24	Plain gray jar sherds (7)	Just above NE bench top, under wall fall.	109
25	Sherds (7)	Level 4 (floor fill), east side near bench.	57
	Plain gray jars(6)	Cibola Grayware.	
	Red Mesa B/w bowl	Cibola Whiteware.	
26	Chipped stones (3)	Level 4 (floor fill), NE side near bench.	58
	Angular debris (0.1 g)	1145 (chalcedonic silicified wood).	
	Angular debris (1.5 g)	1235 (chalcedony with reddish-purple inclusions).	
	Angular debris (0.3 g)	4000 (quartzite).	
26	Sherds (25)	Level 4 (floor fill), NE side near bench.	66
	Plain gray jars (17)	Cibola Grayware (2 sooted).	
	Lino Gray bowl (1)	Cibola Grayware.	
	Lino Gray jar with Fugitive red exterior (3)	Cibola Grayware.	
	Chaco Corrugated (2)	Cibola Grayware (sooted).	
	White Mound B/w bowl	Cibola Whiteware.	
	Mancos B/w bowl	Mesa Verde Whiteware.	

Table I.4.5. Site 29SJ 721, Distribution of Floor Fill and Floor Materials, cont'd.[a]

Artifact Number	Artifact Class	Lithic Material, Ceramic Ware, or Faunal Species	FS No.
27	Sherds (3)	Level 4 (floor fill), west side next to bench.	
	Plain gray jars (2)	Cibola Grayware.	
	Plain gray jar with Fugitive red exterior	Cibola Grayware.	67
28	Maul/axe fragment (11.7+-x-10.4-x-5.3-cm; 860.6+ g)	3241 (diorite; San Juan River cobble). Broken across 2 notches; bit missing. Poll shows some hammering? 10-cm below top of wall, 20-cm in from wall.	50
29	Chipped stones (2)	Floor, north side next to bench.	
	Retouched flake (1.9 g)	1235 (translucent chalcedony with red-purple inclusions).	59
	Angular debris (0.1 g)	1140 (chalcedonic silicified wood).	
30	Angular debris (1.5 g)	1052 (clear chalcedony, High Surface Chert). Wall Niche 1 fill.	60
31	Woodruff Smudged bowl sherd	Floor, west side within 10-cm of bench.	71
32	Sherds (2)	Floor, north side within 10-cm of bench.	72
	Chaco Corrugated jar		
	Woodruff Smudged bowl		
33	Woodruff Smudged bowl sherd	Floor, east side within 10-cm of bench.	73
34	Angular debris (5.1 g)	1140 (chalcedonic silicified wood). 15-cm under floor and FS 73.	89
35	Woodruff Smudged bowl sherd	Floor, NNE/NE side, 69-cm from bench.	74
36	Woodruff Smudged bowl (partial; 26 pieces)	Polished red-orange on exterior. Floor, south side: vent recess & into vent tunnel.	75
Cist 6 (roasting pit)			
—	Plain gray jar sherds (9)	Fill above rock bottom.	78
—	Whole flake (0.3 g)	1052 (clear chalcedony, High Surface Chert) Fill.	88

[a] See distributions in Figures I.4.7, I.4.9, and I.4.11. All bones examined for cooking brown and burning (Akins: analysis data base).

Table I.4.6. List of Features at 29SJ 721 Except for Postholes.

Feature	Length (cm)	Width (cm)	Height/ Depth (cm)	Volume[b] (liters)	Fill Type	Fill Period	Lining	Open/ Sealed	Comments
Pithouse A									
Firepit 1	47	42	28	33.2	25, 28	Occ	L-SP	O	Mouth = 1649 cm². Rim adobe lined.
Other Pit 1									See PH 1.
Other Pit 2	39	21	12	4.9±	11	PO	U	O	Nearly rectangular.
Other Pit 3	39	20	6	2.3±	11	PO	U	O	
Other Pit 4	8	7.5	14	0.9	11	PO	U	O	Sipapu? 51 cm N. of FP 1.
Other Pit 5A	6	6	15	0.3	11	PO	U	O	Posthole?
Other Pit 5B	10	10	21	1.8	11	PO	U	O	Posthole?
Other Pit 6									See PH 3.
Other Pit 7	25	16	16	6.4	11	PO	U	O	
Other Pit 8									See PH 2
Other Pit 9									See Wall Niche 1.
Other Pit 10	25	22	7.5	2.2	11	PO	U	O	Pot Rest.
Other Pit 11	17	10.5	8	1.1	11	PO	U	O	
Other Pit 12									See PH 4.
Other Pit 13A	13	10	7	0.6	11	PO	U	O	South ladder rests, 26 cm apart.
13B	9	9	4	0.3	11	PO	U	O	
Other Pit 14A	8	9	5	0.3	11	PO	U	O	North ladder rests, 22 cm apart.
14B	10	9	4	0.3	11	PO	U	O	
Slot 1	24	12	6	1.3	11	PO	U	O	Wing wall slab support hole.
Wall Niche 1	11	11	17	0.8	10	PO	U	O	43 cm above floor.
Ventilator shaft	109	37	25	-	11	PO	U	O	32 cm above floor.
Pithouse C									
Firepit 1	60	60	20	61.0	25,28	PO	L-P	O	Remodeled. Little oxidation.
Other Pit 1	52	52	22	31.1	11	PO	U	O	Potrest? Basin-shaped.
Other Pit 2	26	26	4	1.4±	34	PO	U	O	In OP 1. Rodent nest?
Other Pit 3	74	36	20	38.3	30,42	PO	U	O	3 stones in bottom
Other Pit 4	24	21	9	3.6	11,42	PO	L-P	O	

Table I.4.6. List of Features at 29SJ 721 Except for Postholes, cont'd.

Feature	Length (cm)	Width (cm)	Height/ Depth (cm)	Volume[b] (liters)	Fill Type	Fill Period	Lining	Open/ Sealed	Comments
Other Pit 5	58	24-31	0-11.5	5±	10	PO	U	O	Trough. Not a feature?
Other Pit 6	44	36	17-33	36.8	11	PO	U	O	Proj. point & cover inside
Other Pit 7	18	10	5	0.8	11	PO	U	O	Slot (part of Cist 4?).
East Mud Ridge	78	18	5	-	44	-	L-P	-	
South Mud Ridge	35	18	6	-	44	-	L-P	-	
Step	68	48	10	-	44	-	L-P	-	In SE corner: clay covered platform
Deflector	42	9	55±	-	56	-	-	-	Ventilator cover?
Ventilator	50+	53	?	-	?	PO	L-S	O	On the surface
Kiva									
Other Pit 1	50	27	11	10.5±	11	PO	L-P	O	Irregular shape.
Other Pit 2	20	13	7	0.5±	11	PO	U	O	
Wall Niche 1	20	19	18	5.4±	11	PO	L-P	O	30 cm above floor.
Vent tunnel	118	33	45+	-	41	PO	L-M	O	Fragments of Woodruff Smudged bowl on floor.
Vent shaft	33	25	135	-	41	PO	L-M	O	
Outside Features									
Posthole 1	14	13	7	1.4	11,14	PO	?	O	Posthole? 170 cm SE of Kiva.
Room 1	330	255	30	-	11,14	PO	L-S	O	Slab-lined wall foundations. E. wall entry?
Cist 1	130	125	45-53	581.8	21,29	Occ	L-S	O	Roasting pit with slanted slab walls. 25-30 stones in fill. Stone-lined bottom.
Cist 2	96	79	48	203.3	27,29	Occ	L-S	O	Storage cist reused for roasting pit. Vertical slab walls, unlined bottom.
Cist 3	104	104?	25?	166.6±	11	PO	L-S	O	Storage cist with vertical slab walls, unlined bottom.
Cist 4	94	83	40	553.3	24,29	Occ	L-S	O	Roasting pit with slanted slab walls in Pithouse C. Stone-lined bottom. Tree-ring dates.
Cist 5	127	116	33	516.8	11,29	Occ	L-S	O	Roasting pit with slanted slab walls. Stone-lined bottom.
Cist 6	92	85	18	103.0	25,29	Occ	L-S	O	Roasting pit with slanted slab walls. Stone-lined bottom.
Cist 7	?	?	?	-	10	PO	L-S?	O	One slab left. Storage cist?

[a] See Tables I.7.4–I.7.5 for an explanation of the feature and attribute codes.
[b] Volumes for features are approximate.

Table I.4.7. List of Postholes at 29SJ 721.[a]

Posthole No.	Length (cm)	Width (cm)	Depth (cm)	Volume[b] (liters)	Fill Type	Fill Period	Shims	Base Stone	Est. post size (cm)	Lining	Comments
Pithouse A											
Posthole 1	21	11	7	1.4	11	PO	4	0	-	L-S	Slab support? Sealed over. Formerly OP 1.
Posthole 2	24	19	10	3.2	11	PO	3	0	-	L-S	Shims burned. Formerly OP 8
Posthole 3	17	17	8	1.8	11	PO	3	0	-	L-PS	Shims burned. Sealed over? Formerly OP 6
Posthole 4	11	11	14	1.3	11	PO	0	0	-	U	Formerly OP 12

[a] See Tables I.7.4-I.7.5 for an explanation of the feature and attribute codes.
[b] Volumes for features are approximate.

Table I.4.8. List of Features at 29SJ 724, Except for Roofing Postholes.[a]

Feature	Length (cm)	Width (cm)	Height/Depth (cm)	Volume[b] (liters)	Fill Type	Fill Period	Lining	Open/Sealed	Comments
Room 1									
Firepit 1	60	56	18	41.5	27,30	Occ	L-P	O	Mouth = 2714 cm². No collar. Heating Pit?
Other Pit 1	54	54	7	13.4	11,12	PO	U	O	Mouth = 2271 cm².
Room 3									
Other Pit 1	74	57	18	49.8	14	PO	U	O	Mouth = 3488 cm².
Room 4									
Other Pit 1	140	112	36	325.3	11,15?	PO	U	O	Mouth = 13264 cm².
Room 6									
Other Pit 1	84	73	8	37.5	14,45	PO	U	O	Mouth = 6114 cm².
Room 7									
Other Pit 1	68	61	11	28.6	42	PO	U	O	Mouth = 3600 cm².
Room 9									
Firepit 1	48	47	25	37.4	14,20	Occ/PO	L-SP	O	Mouth = 1940 cm². Adobe rim, 5 cm wide, 8-10 cm high.
Bin 1	60	60	20-30	84.9	14,42	PO	L-S	O	Mouth = 3047 cm².
Bin 2	49	44	20-30	61.9	14,42	PO	L-S	O	Mouth = 2224 cm².
Bin 3	45	35	20-30	46.0	14,42	PO	L-S	O	Mouth = 1652 cm².
Pithouse A fill									
Firepit A	19.5	11.5	13	1.3-2.0	20	Occ	L-S	O	9 tiny slabs.
Firepit B	11	11	9	0.7	20	Occ	L-S	O	6 tiny slabs.
Firepit C	20±	10±	15+?	2-3?	20	Occ	L-S	O	5 tiny slabs.
Firepit D	10?	10?	7	0.7	20	Occ	L-S	O	2+ tiny slabs.
Firepit E	10?	10?	10±	1.0	20	Occ	L-S	O	timy slabs
Firepit F	10	10	10	0.7	20	Occ	L-S	O	6 tiny slabs.
Firepit G	6.5	6.5	6	0.3	25	Occ	L-S	O	5 tiny slabs.
Firepit H	14-16	14-16	10	1.5±	20	Occ	L-S	O	5-6 tiny slabs.
Slab wall	320	6-14.5	19-41	-	-	Occ	L-S	-	6 large slabs.
Pithouse A									
Firepit 1	70	58	26	74.7	10,27,28	PO/Occ	L-SP	O	D-shaped.
Firepit 2	50±	50±	32±	39.4e	?	PO	L-P	O	
Ash Pit	50	45±	5	?	11	Occ?	L-P	O	

Table I.4.8. List of Features at 29SJ 724, Except for Roofing Postholes,[a] cont'd.[a]

Feature	Length (cm)	Width (cm)	Height/ Depth (cm)	Volume[b] (liters)	Fill Type	Fill Period	Lining	Open/ Sealed	Comments
Heating Pit 1	64	36	15	38.3	20,27	Occ	L-P	O	Mouth = 2249 cm². See OP 8. Shelf = 40 x 24 x 11 cm.
Heating Pit 2	68	32	15-18	30.0	27,28	Occ	L-P	O	Mouth = 2398 cm². See OP 13. Cut by HP 2. Posthole?
pit in bottom	11	10	9+	1.4	11	PO?	L-P	O	
Other Pit 1	38	20	6	2.2	11	PO?	L-P	O	Bowl-shaped.
Other Pit 2	53	23-30	7-11	7.1	11	PO?	L-P	O	
Other Pit 3A	10	10	11	0.6	11	PO	U	O	
Other Pit 3B	23	19	7	2.2	11	PO	L-P	O	
Other Pit 4	53	35	12	15.9	11	PO	L-P	O	
Other Pit 5	24	23	10	3.1	11	PO	U	O	Posthole?
Other Pit 6	30	30	54	26.7	11	PO	U	O	Sipapu.
Other Pit 7	41	35	20	15.4	11	PO	L-P	O	Shelf = 15 x 12 x 3 cm (0.5 l)
Other Pit 8									See Heating Pit 1.
Other Pit 9	120	11-18	8	10.5	11	PO	L-P	O	Bowl-shaped.
Other Pit 10	24.5	19.5		2.0	11	PO	U	O	Bowl-shaped.
Other Pit 11 top	25	14	15	7.0	11	PO	U/L-P$_{lip}$	O	Bell-shaped pit.
bottom	30	23							
Other Pit 12	34	32	11.3	7.8	11	PO	U	O	Pot Rest.
Other Pit 13									See Heating Pit 2.
Other Pit 14	40	28	4	3.1	11	PO	L-P	O	Basin-shaped.
Other Pit 15	23	16	5	1.4	30/32	PO	L-P	O	
Other Pit 16	36	21	7	3.0	11	PO	L-P	O	Basin-shaped.
Other Pit 17A	30	25	12	5.4	11	PO	L-P	O	Basin-shaped. Cuts OP 17B.
Other Pit 17B	15	15	12	1.7	11	PO	L-P	O	Basin-shaped. Cuts OP 17C.
Other Pit 17C	30	28	11	5.1	11	PO	L-P	O	Basin-shaped.
Other Pit 17D	12	12	24	2.7	11	PO	U	O	Posthole? Cuts OP 17C.
Adobe rim (floor)	89	9	5	-	-	-	L-P	-	Assoc. with OP 2.
Wall Niche 1	20	28	23	10.2-13.1	10	PO	U	O	51 cm above floor.
Wall Niche 2	34	33	8+	6.0+	14,20	PO	L-P	O	13 cm above floor. Unexcavated.

Chapter 4: Pueblo I Excavation Reports 359

Table I.4.8. List of Features at 29SJ 724, Except for Roofing Postholes, cont'd.[a]

Feature	Length (cm)	Width (cm)	Height/Depth (cm)	Volume[b] (liters)	Fill Type	Fill Period	Lining	Open/Sealed	Comments
Ventilator tunnel	230	65	50		10,12 14,31	PO	U	O	Adobe collar at mouth. Wood lintels (rotted away) for roof.
Ventilator shaft	100	90	197		10,31	PO	U/L-M	O	
Deflector 1 slot	43	4-6	5-6	1.2	11	PO	?	O	Slab missing. Assoc. with FP 2.
Deflector 2 slot	38	?	10-13	-	11	PO	?	O	Slab missing. Assoc. with FP 1.
Deflector 3									
East Wing Wall	245	10	40+	-	-	-	L-PS	-	Mostly removed.
Slot A	34	7	8	1.2	11	PO	L-P	O	Slab support hole.
Slot B	32	4	4	0.5	11	PO	L-P	O	Slab support hole.
Slot F	14	8.5	7	0.5	11	PO	?	O	Slab support hole.
Slot G	13	7	10	0.7	11	PO	?	O	Slab support hole.
West Wing Wall	255	?	?	-	-	-	L-PS	-	Mostly removed.
Slot C	23	4	5	1.0	11	PO	L-P	O	Slab support hole.
Slot D	31	7	6	1.2	11	PO	L-P	O	Slab support hole.
Slot E	42	7	17	6.4	11	PO	L-P	O	Slab support hole.
Plaza/Ramada:									
Firepit 1	51	47	28	40.4	27	Occ	L-PS	O	Mouth = 1856 cm². In Room 10
Firepit 2	63	60	20	41.1	20,22	Occ	U/L-P	O	Top of fill. Formerly FP "A". Mouth = 3286 cm².
Other Pit 1	66	50	6	8.3	11	PO	L-P	S	
Other Pit 2	14	14	10	1.5	11,14	PO	L-P	O	
Other Pit 3	14	13	13	1.9	11	PO	L-P	O	
Other Pit 4	21	12	10	1.5	11	PO	U	O	
Other Pit 5	17	17	14	1.9	11,14	PO	U/L-P	O	

[a] See Tables I.7.4–7.5 for an explanation of the feature and attribute codes.
[b] Volumes for features are approximate.

Table I.4.9. List of Postholes in Rooms 1 and 9 at 29SJ 724.[a]

Posthole No.	Length (cm)	Width (cm)	Depth (cm)	Volume[b] (liters)	Fill Type	Fill Period	Shims	Base Stone	Est. postsize (cm)	Lining	Comments
Room 1:											
Posthole 1	12	12	5	0.6	?	PO	0	0		U?	Not a Feature?
Posthole 2A	23	21	42	16.0	13,15	Occ	2	0		U	Main support.
Posthole 2B	19	19	42	11.9	52	Occ	1	0		U	Earlier PH. Cut by PH 2A.
Posthole 3	25	20	31	13.7	15,52	Occ	1	0		U	Main support.
Posthole 4	23	20	36	10.6	13,1522	PO/Occ	1	0		U	Main support.
Posthole 5	16	16	10	2.0	14	PO	0	0		U	Not a PH?
Posthole 6	18	18	31	7.9	13,1415	PO	1	0		U	Roof support or post step.
Posthole 7	18	18	14	2.3	13,14	PO	0	0		U	Auxiliary PH?
Posthole 8	27	22	20	9.4	14	PO	1	1?		U	Auxiliary PH? Sealed.
Posthole 9	18	15	16/19	4.1	13,52	PO	1	0		U	Formerly plaza. PH 8–redug. Adobe collar. Hammerstone in bottom.
Posthole 10	25	18	37	13.4	13,15	Occ	1	0		U	Main support.
Posthole 20	16	14	13	2.4	13	PO	0	0	10	U	Exterior to rm.
Room 9:											
Posthole 1	16	11	3	0.3	?	PO	0	0		U?	Not a feature?
Posthole 2											Not a feature.
Posthole 3	15	15	5	0.5	?	PO	0	0		U	Not a PH?
Posthole 4	18	18	?	?	?	?	0	0		U?	Not a feature?
Posthole 5	27	27	46	26.3	52	Occ	1	0		U?	Main support.
Posthole 6											Not a feature.
Posthole 7	12	12	19	3.0	14	PO	0	0		U?	
Posthole 8A	21	20	53	18.4	52	Occ	0	0		U	Main support.
Posthole 8B	21	20	48	16.6	52	Occ	0	0	12 x 10 (mold)	L-P	Earlier PH. Cut by PH 8A.
Posthole 21	18	16	12	2.7	14	PO	0	0	10	U	Adobe bottom; PH? Exterior to rm.
Posthole 22	17	16	20	4.3	14	PO	0	0	9	L-P	Exterior to rm.
Posthole 23	19	19	11	3.3	13	PO/Occ?	0	0	15	U	Exterior to rm.
Posthole 24	25	25	60	29.5	15?,52	Occ	0	1	13	U?	Main support. Exterior to rm.
Posthole 25	33	31	35	28.1	11,15?	Occ	0	1		U	Adobe plug. Main support. Exterior to rm.

[a] See Tables I.7.4-7.5 for an explanation of the feature and attribute codes.
[b] Volumes for features are approximate.
Note: Postholes 21-23 were not included within the statistical database.

Table I.4.10. Site 29SJ 724, Room and Plaza Distribution of Floor 1 Materials.[a]

Artifact Number	Artifact Class	Lithic Material, Ceramic Ware, or Faunal Species	FS No.
Room 1			
1	Door cover fragment (52 x 27 x 3.5 cm; 7.3 kg)	2000 (sandstone). Ellipsoid. Mortar attached. Natural?	99
-	Plain gray jar sherds (6) White Mound B/w (1)	Cibola Grayware. Cibola Whiteware.	131
-	Utilized flake (12. 7 g)	1141 (chalcedonic silicified wood).	132
-	Hematite (3.4 x 1.1 x 1.1 cm; 4.0 g)	5221 (red ocher). Squarish curved cylinder. Highly polished over caliche patination but natural? No evidence of grinding. Munsell 2.5YR 5/8.	133
2	Lapidary abrader (17.8 x 15.9 x 3.1 cm; 1307 g)	2000 (sandstone). Highly ground on 1 surface. Trapezoidal shape. Next to north wall.	316
3	Groundstone (16 x 14 x 3 cm)	2000 (sandstone). Next to north wall. Missing.	317
4	Mano (17.4 x 11.1 x 4.5 cm; 1224 g)	2000 (sandstone). Next to east wall in NE corner.	318
5	Groundstone (20.2 x 15.3 x 2.8 cm; 925.7 g)	2000 (sandstone). Burned. Lightly ground on 2 surfaces. Irregular shape. FP 1 liner stone? Center of room.	319
6	Trough metate fragment (30+ x 23 x 4 cm; 3629 g)	2000 (sandstone). Next to south wall.	320
7	Hammerstone (9.4 x 8.7 x 8.1 cm; 814 g)	4000 (quartzite). Edge battering; burned. Spherical shape. In PH 9.	544
8	Whole flake (0.4 g) Angular debris (0.3 g)	1140 (chalcedonic silicified wood). In FP 1 fill. 1140 (chalcedonic silicified wood).	552
9	Mano (21.7 x 12.4 x 3.1 cm; 1382 g)	2000 (sandstone).	564
10	Hammerstone (7 x 5 x ? cm)	Unknown material. In PH 7 top fill.	--
Room 3			
11	Trough metate fragment (14+ x 12+ x 4 cm; 797 g)	2000 (sandstone).	189
-	Lino Gray jar sherd Plain gray jar sherds (2)	Cibola Grayware. Cibola Grayware 1 sooted.	195
-	Bone	Unidentified rabbit humerus.	196
-	Utilized flake (2.9 g) Angular debris (9.0 g) Whole flake (0.5 g)	1053 (chalcedonic High Surface Chert). 1110 (splintery silicified wood). 1141 (chalcedonic silicified wood).	197
12	Plain gray jar sherds (2)	Cibola Grayware. In OP 1 fill.	198

Table I.4.10. Site 29SJ 724, Room and Plaza Distribution of Floor 1 Materials, cont'd.[a]

Artifact Number	Artifact Class	Lithic Material, Ceramic Ware, or Faunal Species	FS No.
13	Bead (5 dia x 1 mm)	5053 (calcite). Discoid shape. 2 mm dia. uni-conical drill hole.	211
-	Fossilized shark tooth (2.3-g)	In floor flotation sample. Missing.	243
-	Whole flake (0.1 g)	1113 (cherty silicified chert). In floor flotation sample. Not in chipped stone analysis.	243
Room 4			
14	Cover? fragment (16.7+ x 12.6+ x 1.7 cm; 687+ g)	2000 (sandstone). Edge-chipped to shape. Burned. 2 pieces. Fill of OP 1.	202
-	Plain gray jar sherds (4) Lino Fugitive Red jar sherd White Mound B/w sherd (3) Lino B/g bowl sherd	Cibola Grayware (1 sooted). Cibola Grayware. Cibola Whiteware. Tusayan Whiteware.	207
-	Hammerstone (5.7 x 5.2 x 4.4 cm; 145 g)	1051 (chalcedonic High Surface Chert). Nodule; minimal battering. Spherical shape.	208
-	Utilized flake (1.6 g)	1140 (chalcedonic silicified wood).	209
-	Bone	Prairie dog (*Cynomys gunnisoni*) middle rib.	210
15	Vent cover (39 x 27 x 4.0 cm; 6000 g)	2000 (sandstone). Ellipsoid. Natural? On top of door frame.	300
-	Plain gray jar sherds (3)	Cibola Grayware.	301
-	Turkey dung?	*Meleagris gallopavo*?	302
-	Bone	Cottontail skull (*Sylvilagus* sp.).	303
Room 5			
16	Plain gray jar sherds (2) Lino Fugitive Red jar sherd	Cibola Grayware. (1 sooted). Cibola Grayware.	333
-	Lino Gray jar sherd	Cibola Grayware stuck in floor.	592
Room 6			
17	Angular debris (0.9 g) Angular debris (0.2 g)	1110 (splintery silicified wood). From floation sample. 1140 (chalcedonic silicified wood).	2 47
18	Hematite (2.7 x 2.3 x 1.5 cm; 9.5 g)	5221 (red ocher). Ground flat on 1 surface. Munsell red 10R 4/6.	252
Room 7			
19	White Mound B/w sherd	Cibola Whiteware.	478

364 Windes

Table I.4.10. Site 29SJ 724, Room and Plaza Distribution of Floor 1 Materials, cont'd.[a]

Artifact Number	Artifact Class	Lithic Material, Ceramic Ware, or Faunal Species	FS No.
Room 8			
20	Plain gray jar sherds (2)	Cibola Grayware (2 sooted).	329
21	Bones (2)	Cottontail scapula (1) and jackrabbit tibia (1).	330
22	Utilized flake (4.7 g)	1142 (chalcedonic silicified wood).	331
23	Limonite nodule (1.4 x 0.8 x 0.8 cm; 0.6 g) Hematite nodule (1.6 x 1.2 x 0.8 cm; 1.6 g)	5110 (yellow ocher). Natural. Munsell 7.5YR 6/6. 5221 (red ocher). Some grinding (bag ware?). Munsell 10R 4/8.	332
Room 9			
24	Bead fragment (3.5 mm diameter x 0.5 mm)	2770 (calcite). Discoid shape. 2 mm dia. bi-conical drill hole. ½ bead. Recovered from FP 1 flotation sample.	348
24	Bone	Unidentified rodent tooth. In FP 1 flotation sample.	348
24	Flotation sample	*Atriplex*/*Sarcobatus* and *Artemesia*. In FP 1 flotation sample.	348
24	Corncob fragments (3+; 0.6 g)	*Zea mays* (carbonized). In FP 1 flotation sample.	348
24	Seeds	Indian rice grass? In FP 1 fill.	388
25	Cover fragment	2000 (sandstone). Chipped edges. Between east wall and Bin 3. Left on site.	455
26	Abrader fragment (9.8+ x 8.8+ x 3.5 cm; 355 g)	2000 (sandstone). 1 surface ground.	456
27	Pot cover	2000 (sandstone). Associated with FS 458-459. Missing.	457
28	Pot cover (14.5 x 14 x 1.5 cm; 500 g)	2000 (sandstone). Associated with FS 457, 459. Burned. Discoid shape formed by edge chipping & light grinding.	458
29	Pot cover (14.8 x 13.45 x 1.0 cm; 368 g)	2000 (sandstone). Associated with FS 457-458. Burned. Irregular shape formed by edge chipping.	459
30	Mano (18.1 x 10.5 x 3.4 cm; 1399 g)	2000 (sandstone).	460
31	Cover fragment	2000 (sandstone). South of FP 1. Left on site.	461
32	Hammerstone (6.3 x 4.8 x 3.8 cm; 179 g)	4000 (quartzite). Edge battered; some flake removal on natural cobble. Irregular/spherical shape. In PH 3.	462
33	Mano fragment (9.3+ x 10.4 x 2.4 cm; 4001 g)	2000 (sandstone).	463
34	Lapstone abrader/anvil fragment (9.8+ x 9+ x 2.6 cm; 339 g)	2000 (sandstone). 1 surface highly ground with minor pecking. Opposite surface with high spots ground off. Edge grinding.	464
35	Lapidary abrader (19 x 18.6 x 5 cm; 3515 g)	2000 (sandstone). 1 surface highly burned and ground. 1 end edge chipped to shape. No pecking.	466

Table I.4.10. Site 29SJ 724, Room and Plaza Distribution of Floor 1 Materials, cont'd.[a]

Artifact Number	Artifact Class	Lithic Material, Ceramic Ware, or Faunal Species	FS No.
36	Trough metate fragment	2000 (sandstone). Slab liner of Bin 3. Not analyzed. Left in situ.	467
37	Hammerstone (8.7 x 8.3 x 3.5 cm; 381 g)	1110 (splintery silicified wood). Pecking created sharp edges. Ovoid shape. In Bin 3.	468
38	Angular debris (2)(total 2.9 g)	1680 (misc. pink chert). In fill of Bin 1.	477
39	Groundstone (cover fragment?)	2000 (sandstone). In Unknown OP in front of Room 9. Left on site.	469
Room 10			
40	Bone	Prairie dog (*Cynomys gunnisoni*) middle rib.	309
40	Natural stone nodule	1110 (Splintery silicified wood).	310
40	Corncob fragment (1; 0.8 g)	*Zia mays*. Carbonized.	311
40	Hammerstone/Core (7.2 x 5.5 x 5.0 cm; 206 g)	1130 (silicified palm wood with vascular rays). Edges battered. Test core–several flakes removed. Irregular/spherical shape.	312
40	Plain gray jar sherds (12) White Mound B/w (3) Woodruff Smudged bowl sherd	Cibola Grayware. 6 sooted. Cibola Whiteware. Mogollon Brownware	313
Plaza			
–	Plain gray jar sherds (12)	Cibola Grayware. Scattered in front of Rooms 4 and 5	626
–	Chipped stones (3) Angular debris (1.5 g) Whole flake (15.1 g) Whole flake (29.0 g)	Scattered in front of Rooms 4 and 5. Not in chipped stone analysis 1020 (misc. chert grading to quartzite) 1053 (chalcedonic High Surface Chert) 1112 (cherty silicified wood).	627
41	Chipped stones (3) Angular debris (0.0 g) Angular debris (0.1 g) Whole flake? (0.1 g)	1112 (cherty silicified wood). 1140 (chalcedonic silicified wood). 1140 (chalcedonic silicified wood).	635
41	Hammerstone fragment (6.6+ x 3.9 x 3.3 cm; 103.4+ g)	1112 (cherty silicified wood). 1 end battered; opposite end missing. In Posthole 29.	635
42	Bone	Unidentified small/medium mammal long bone. In FP 1 (over Rm 10).	79
42	Plain gray jar sherd	In plaza FP 1 (over Rm 10). Sooted?	80

366 Windes

Table I.4.10. Site 29SJ 724, Room and Plaza Distribution of Floor 1 Materials, cont'd.[a]

Artifact Number	Artifact Class	Lithic Material, Ceramic Ware, or Faunal Species	FS No.
43	Plain gray jar sherds (2)	Cibola Grayware. In FP 2 fill. Sooted.	
	Lino Gray bowl sherd (1)	Cibola Grayware.	
	White Mound B/w bowl sherd	Cibola Whiteware.	628
-	Chipped stone (1):	Not in analysis	
	Whole flake (5.1 g)	1052 (chalcedonic High Surface Chert).	
	Manuports (4; 13.2 g)	Natural gravel terrace material (concretions, sandstone, petrified wood).	629
43	Hammerstone (7.6 x 6.1 x 4.8 cm; 299 g)	4000 (quartzite) River cobble with ends & 1 edge battered. In FP 2.	630
43	Wood (10.5 g)	Unidentified vegetal material.	631
43	Turquoise nodule (2 x 1 x 1 mm)	5300 (turquoise). Natural. Rock Color 10G 8/2. In FP 2.	632
43	Corncobs (3; 0.7 g)	*Zea mays*. Carbonized. In FP 2 fill.	633
43	Bone (1)	Unidentified small/medium mammal long bone shaft fragment. Not catalogued. Missing.	634
-	Core (5.1 x 4.5 x 3.2 cm; 108.8 g)	1112 (cherty silicified wood). Near PH 24 and Datum A.	553

[a] See distribution in Figure I.4.14. All bones examined for cooking brown ("boiled?") and burning (Akins: analysis data base).

Chapter 4: Pueblo I Excavation Reports   367

Table I.4.11. List of Ramada Postholes in the 29SJ 724 Plaza.[a]

Posthole No.	Length (cm)	Width (cm)	Depth (cm)	Volume[b] (liters)	Fill Type	Fill Period	Shims	Base Stone	Est. post size (cm)	Lining	Comments
Posthole 1	21	21	21-38	27.8	11	PO	12	1	22-x-18	L-SP	
Posthole 2	19	17	18	2.8	14	PO	2	0	16-x-15	U?	
Posthole 3	32	24	21	12.6	22,4552	PO/Occ	6	0	22-x-18	L-SP	Partly burned.
Posthole 4	22	22	16	5.4	11,52	PO/Occ	0	1	17-x-17	L-P	
Posthole 5	15	15	18	4.2	11,52	PO/Occ	3	1	10-x-13	U	
Posthole 6											Not a feature. In Room 1.
Posthole 7											Not a feature. In Room 1.
Posthole 8											Renumbered as PH 9, Room 1.
Posthole 9	19	19	16	4.3	14,52	PO/Occ	1	0	13-x-13	L-P	
Posthole 10	15	14	6	1.0	14,52	PO/Occ	0	0	13-x-13	L-P	
Posthole 11	23	23	6	2.5	12	PO	2?	1	13-x-13	L-P	
Posthole 12	20	17	12	2.8	11,52	PO/Occ	1?	0	12-x-12	L-P	Same as PH 27?
Posthole 13	20	18	16	4.3	13	PO/Occ	0	0	16-x-16	L-P	
Posthole 14	23	18	23	6.8	13	PO/Occ	0	0	10-x-18	L-P	
Posthole 15	21	20	17	5.1	13	PO/Occ	0	0	14-x-10	L-P	
Posthole 16	20	16	14	3.4	11	PO	0	0	14-x-13	L-P	
Posthole 17	20	19	21	5.7	11	PO	0	0	12-x-12	L-P	
Posthole 18	23	20	16	5.1	10	PO	0	0	-	U	Not a feature?
Posthole 19	18	17	15	3.8	10	PO	0	0	-	U	Not a feature?
Posthole 20											See Room 1.
Posthole 21											See Room 9.
Posthole 22											See Room 9.
Posthole 23											See Room 9.

Table I.4.11. List of Ramada Postholes in the 29SJ 724 Plaza, cont'd.[a]

Posthole No.	Length (cm)	Width (cm)	Depth (cm)	Volume[b] (liters)	Fill Type	Fill Period	Shims	Base Stone	Est. post size (cm)	Lining	Comments
Posthole 24											See Room 9.
Posthole 25											See Room 9. Renumbered as PH 30.
Posthole 26	24	24	23	10.4	13	PO/Occ	2	0			Sealed with plaster.
Posthole 27	17	16	20	4.6	13,52	Occ	0	0		L-P	Same as PH 12?
Posthole 28	13	13	10	2.0	52	Occ	2	1		L-P	Metate fragment shim.
Posthole 29	26	24	36	13.9	13,15	PO/Occ	2	0	15-x-9	L-SP	Contains post mold. Sealed.
Posthole 30	18	17	18	4.3	11,17	PO/Occ?	2	0		U	Formerly plaza PH 25.
Posthole 31	15	15	30	5.3	12	PO	0	0		L-P	
Posthole 32	21	21	40	14.2	52	Occ	5	1	14-x-10	U	Contains post mold.
Posthole 33	11	9	15	1.2	13,14	PO/Occ	0	0		U	

[a] See Tables I.7.4-7.5 for an explanation of the feature and attribute codes.
[b] Volumes for features are approximate.

Table I.4.12. Site 29SJ 724, Pithouse A, Distribution of Materials at the Same Level (Bottom of Level 7) as the Fill Firepits.[a]

Artifact Number	Artifact Class	Lithic Material, Ceramic Ware, or Faunal Species	FS No.
1	Mano fragment (13.2+ x 9.4 x 2.3 cm; 491+ g)	2000 (sandstone).	95
2	Groundstone	2000 (sandstone). Left in field?	96
3	Axe (21.7 x 12.7 x 7.8 cm; 2287 g)	2200 (quartzitic sandstone). Flaked to shape with 2 notches. Sharp bit and poll slightly pounded.	97
4	Maul? (16.4 x 9.1 x 7.0 g; 1048 g)	2000 (sandstone). Natural concretion with notch? Burned. Excavation damage from mattock/shovel.	98
5	Metate fragment (18+ x 17+ x 9 cm; 3629+ g)	2000 (sandstone).	101
6[b]	Pot cover (12.8 x 10.7 x 1.2 cm; 221 g)	2000 (sandstone). Crude disc: edge chipped + slight grinding on 1 surface. Burned. On East Bench top.	102
7	Selenite (3.6 x 0.8 x 0.5 cm; 1.9 g)	5041 (gypsum). Natural, rectangular cylinder. Next to Firepit A.	105
8	Bennett Gray jar sherd	Chuska Grayware. In top of Firepit A.	109
8	Corn cob fragment (0.0 g)	*Zea mays*. Carbonized. In charcoal fill of Firepit A, from C-14 sample of carbonized brush (22.1 g).	113
-	Bones (2)	Jackrabbit (*Lepus californicus*) humerus & gray fox (*Urocyon cineroargentes*) scapula. General Level 7 fill.	118
-	Angular debris (2.5 g) Angular debris (2.4 g)	1110 (splintery silicified wood). General Level 7 fill. 5010 (colorless quartz).	119
-	Plain gray jar sherds (19) Lino Fugitive Red jar sherd	Cibola Grayware. General Level 7 fill. Cibola Grayware.	120
9[b]	Awl (8.4 x 1.5 x 0.2 cm; 2.7 g)	Jackrabbit (*Lepus* sp.) tibia. On top of bench.	121
10	Awl? (5.4 x 0.7 x 0.3 cm; 0.4 g)	Wood splinter smoothed to a taper at each end.	126
11	Polishing stone (9.0 x 4.9 x 2.0 cm; 123 g)	4000 (quartzite). Natural pebble. Flake off 1 edge–excavation damage? Touching FS 104.	103
11	Biscuit mano (9.3 x 7.3 x 3.3 cm; 364 g)	2000 (sandstone). Touching FS103.	104

[a] See distribution in Figure I.4.18. Bench artifacts not listed (see Table I.4.14) except for Floor Artifacts. All bones examined for cooking brown and burning (Akins: analysis data base).
[b] Artifacts also listed as pithouse floor material.

Table I.4.13. Site 29SJ 724, Pithouse A List and Distribution of Feature 1 (Wall Wainscotting) Materials.[a]

Artifact Number	Artifact Class	Lithic Material, Ceramic Ware, or Faunal Species	FS No.
-	Bones (6)	Jack rabbit (4; 2 boiled), prairie dog (1), small/medium mammal (1). Level 11.	213
-	Roofing impressions (4; largest 6.3-x-3.9-x-3.7-cm; total 183.6 g)	Adobe. Parallel beam (3-4-cm dia.?), finger, & vegetal (juniper?) impressions. Sooted on 1 side. Level 11.	214
-	Roofing impression (9.3-x-4.0-x-3.9-cm; 116.7 g)	Adobe. Parallel beam impressions. Caked with soot on 1 side. Level 11.	215
-	Sherds (11) Plain gray jar (8) Plain gray jar (1) Plain gray jar with fugitive red (2)	Level 11 Cibola Grayware (3 sooted). Chuska Grayware (sooted). Cibola Grayware.	216
-	Chipped stones (5) Angular debris (2.7 g) Angular denris (1.6 g) Whole flake (5.7 g) Angular debris (2.8 g) Whole flake (2.9 g)	Level 11 1113 (cherty silicified wood). 1140 (chalcedonic silicified wood). 1145 (chalcedonic silicified wood). 1145 (chalcedonic silicified wood). 1150 (jasperized silicified wood).	217
-	Squash seeds (2 seeds & 3 fragments; 0.1 g)	Cucurbita sp. Level 11.	218
-	Sanostee B/r bowl sherd	Chuskan Redware. Level 11.	219
12	Awl (11.4-x-1.1-x-0.5-cm; 6.7 g)	Large mammal, indeterminate element splinter. Level 11.	220
13	Awl (9.5-x-1.7-x-1.4-cm; 5.1 g)	Jackrabbit (Lepus sp.) tibia. Level 11.	221
14	Awl (13.7-x-0.6-x-0.8-cm; 8.9 g)	Large mammal, indeterminate element splinter. Level 11.	222
-	Matting/roofing material	Juniperus sp. (shredded bark). Level 11. Near FS 224 and 289.	225
-	Corn cobs (16 fragments; 7.5 g)	Zea mays. Carbonized.	226
-	Plant materials (flotation)	Juniperus, Atriplex/Sarcobatus (saltbush/greasewood), Chrysothamnus (rabbitbrush), Artemesia (sagebrush), Populus/salix (cottonwood/willow), Zea mays (corn), Chenopodium (goosefoot). See Toll report (this report).	245
-	Chipped stones (2) Retouched flake (5.7 g) Retouched flake (3.2 g)	1140 (chalcedonic silicified wood). 1142 (chalcedonic silicified wood).	267
-	Selenite (6.5-x-2.2-x-1.9-cm; 13.9 g)	5041 (gypsum). Burned white. Ground spatulate-shaped.	268
-	Plain gray jar sherds (6)	Cibola Grayware Tradition (4 sooted).	269
-	Corn cobs (2 fragments; 0.8 g)	Zea mays. Carbonized.	270

Table I.4.13. Site 29SJ 724, Pithouse A List and Distribution of Feature I (Wall Wainscotting) Materials, cont'd.[a]

Artifact Number	Artifact Class	Lithic Material, Ceramic Ware, or Faunal Species	FS No.
-	Bones (25)	Cottontail (10; 1 burned, 1 boiled), jack rabbit (14; 9 boiled), small/medium mammal (1; boiled).	271
-	Squash seeds (9 seeds, 19 fragments; 0.3 g)	*Cucurbita* sp.	272
-	Dendrochronological samples (5)	*Juniperus* sp. (3), non-coniferous (2). No dates (CNM 221-225).	337
-	Unidentified seed fragment	From flotation sample.	349
-	Chipped stones (6)	From flotation sample	
	Angular debris (2; total 2.0 g)	1040 (chalcedonic silicified wood).	
	Whole flake (1.5 g)	1112 (cherty silicified wood).	
	Angular debris (0.3 g)	1112 (cherty silicified wood).	
	Whole flake (1.6 g)	4000 (quartzite).	
	Angular debris (0.6 g)	4000 (quartzite).	349
43	Drill (3.3-x-1.6-x-1.0-cm; 3.3 g)	1120 (red-colored silicified wood). Retouched projecting spur.	381
44	Selenite (3.3-x-1.5-x-0.4-cm; 3.5 g)	5041 (gypsum selenite). Ground on 2 surfaces & 1 edge. Roundish rectangular shape.	382
-	Selenite (2.9-x-2.7-x-0.6-cm; 4.3 g)	5041 (gypsum). Unmodified natural flattish irregualr piece.	383
45	Awl (5.9-x-1.7-x-1.4-cm; 3.5 g)	Jackrabbit (*Lepus* sp.) tibia. Level 12 ash (floor fill).	384
46	Awl (4-sided implement)(14.3-x-0.8-x-0.6-cm; 8.3 g)	Large mammal, indeterminate shaft splinter.	385
47	Awl (4-sided implement)(11.8-x-1.0-x-0.7-cm; 9.0 g)	Large mammal, indeterminate. Shows weaving grooves.	386
-	Roofing impressions (14; largest 13-x-11-x-4.7; 23.5-x-10.4-x-5.0-cm thick; total 4382.1 g)	Adobe. Parallel beam (8-10-cm dia.±), finger, & vegetal impressions. Loaf-shaped & sooted on top of loaf.	402
-	Vegetal (modern root?)	*Rumex* sp. (canaigre/dock/sorrel).	425
-	Limonite (3.9-x-2.5-x-1.4-cm; 12.4 g)	5110 (yellow limonite). Natural nodule with 1 narrow edge ground? Burned. Munsell 7.5Y 6/6.	426
-	Squash seeds (18+ fragments; 0.5 g)	*Cucurbita mixta*.	427
-	Calcite (1.7-x-1.4-x-0.6-cm; 0.9 g)	5052 (calcite, crystal). Natural tabular chunk. Rock color pinkish 5YR 8/1.	428
-	Corn cobs (3 fragments; 0.6 g)	*Zea mays*. Carbonized.	429
-	Manuport (3.1-x-2.4-x-1.0-cm; 10.8 g)	4000 (banded quartzite). Natural flattish pebble.	430
-	Corn stalks (12+ fragments; 0.8 g)	*Zea mays*.	431
-	Plain gray jar sherds (3)	Cibola Grayware (1 sooted).	432
-	Chipped stones (3)		
	Retouched flake (8.3 g)	1050 (High Surface Chert).	
	Whole flake (1.4 g)	1142 (chalcedonic silicified wood).	
	Utilized flake (8.8 g)	1150 (jasperized silicified wood).	433

Table I.4.13. Site 29SJ 724, Pithouse A List and Distribution of Feature I (Wall Wainscotting) Materials, cont'd.[a]

Artifact Number	Artifact Class	Lithic Material, Ceramic Ware, or Faunal Species	FS No.
-	Selenite (5; largest 4.9-x-2.4-x-0.9-cm; total 29.9 g)	5041 (gypsum). Natural chunks. 1 surface ground? flat.	434
-	Selenite (2.6-x-1.4-x-0.9-cm; 4.1 g)	5041 (gypsum). Tabular but ground on all edges to a boat shape. Looks like a crystal. No drill hole.	435
-	Roofing impressions (6; largest 10.7-x-4.9-x-4.0-cm; total 646.6 g)	Adobe. Parallel beam (8-10cm dia.?) impressions. Sooted on 1 side.	436
-	Bones (12)	Cottontail (2), jack rabbit (10; 3 boiled).	437
-	Roofing impressions (2; largest 5.0-x-4.3-x-3.5-cm; total 94.4 g)	Adobe. 4 = parallel beam (5-7-cm dia.?) & finger impressions. Sooted on 1 side. Under postoccupational slab wall.	520
-	Plain gray jar sherds (3)	Cibola Grayware (2 sooted). Under postoccupational slab wall.	521
-	Corn cob (fragment; 0.6 g)	*Zea mays*. Carbonized. Under postoccupational slab wall.	522
	Minerals (6) Selenite (3; largest 3.1-x-1.1-x-0.3-cm; total 2.1 g) Calcite (3; largest 2.5-x-1.7-x-0.8-cm; total 7.4 g)	Under postoccupational slab wall. 5041 (gypsum). Natural flakes. 5050 (soft calcite). Natural, irregular chunks. 1 edge ground round. Rock color white N9.	523
97	Waddled disc of clay (3.1-x-3.1-x-1.1-cm; 12.4 g)	Unfired gray clay.	535
98	Tinkler (13.4-x-1.6-x-0.2-cm; 7.5 g)	Jackrabbit (*Lepus* sp.) tibia. Drilled hole in 1 end.	539-1[b]
98	Tinkler (11.4-x-1.3-x-0.2-cm; 5.0 g)	Jackrabbit (*Lepus* sp.) tibia. Drilled hole in 1 end.	539-2
98	Tinkler (11.6-x-1.5-x-0.3-cm; 5.1 g)	Jackrabbit (*Lepus* sp.) tibia. Drilled hole in 1 end.	539-3
98	Tinkler (11.3-x-1.3-x-0.3-cm; 4.5 g)	Jackrabbit (*Lepus* sp.) tibia. Drilled hole in 1 end.	539-4
98	Tinkler (9.3-x-1.4-x-0.4-cm; 4.7 g)	Jackrabbit (*Lepus* sp.) tibia. Drilled hole in 1 end.	539-5

[a] See distribution in Figure I.4.16. All bones examined for cooking brown and burning (Akins: analysis data base).
[b] FS 539 artifacts are approximate location.

Table I.4.14. List of Postholes in the 29SJ 724 Pithouse.[a]

Posthole No.	Length (cm)	Width (cm)	Depth (cm)	Volume[b] (liters)	Fill Type	Fill Period	Shims	Base Stone	Est. post size (cm)	Lining	Comments
NE posthole	41	41	74	97.7	32,52	PO/Occ	1	0		U	Main support.
SE Posthole	38	34	63	62.8	32,52	PO/Occ	0	0		U	Main support.
NW Posthole	40	32	55	±48.0	32,52	PO/Occ	0	1		L-P	Main support.
SW Posthole	43	43	55	81.9	30,52	PO/Occ	3	1		L-P	Main support. 2 shims metate frags.
Bench Pole Support Holes:											
Posthole 1	14	9	6.5	0.6	52	Occ	0	0		U	SW corner.
Posthole 2	16	11	8	1.0	52	Occ	0	0		U	
Posthole 3	11	5	4.5	0.1	52	Occ	0	0		U	
Posthole 4	16	8	7	0.5	52	Occ	0	0		U	
Posthole 5	20	8	9	0.8	52	Occ	0	0		U	
Posthole 6	19	8	7	0.8	52	Occ	0	0		U	
Posthole 7	18	7	7.5	0.6	52	Occ	0	0		U	
Posthole 8	17	9	9	1.1	52	Occ	0	0		U	
Posthole 9	17	8	7	0.6	52	Occ	0	0		U	
Posthole 10	15	8	8	0.7	52	Occ	0	0		U	
Posthole 11	13	7	8	0.6	52	Occ	0	0		U	
Posthole 12	16	7	7.5	0.7	52	Occ	0	0		U	
Posthole 13	?	?	?	?	10	PO	0	0		U	
Posthole 14	?	?	?	?	10	PO	0	0		U	
Posthole 15	17	9	7	0.9	52	Occ	0	0		U	
Posthole 16	19.5	7.5	6	0.9	52	Occ	0	0		U	
Posthole 17	22	9	9.5	1.4	13	Occ?	0	0		U	
Posthole 18	24	8	9	1.4	10	PO	0	0		U	
Posthole 19	21	6	7	0.7	10	PO	0	0		U	
Posthole 20	16	7.5	4	0.3	10	PO	0	0		U	
Posthole 21	18	6	6	0.6	11	PO	0	0		U	

Table I.4.14. List of Postholes in the 29SJ 724 Pithouse, cont'd.[a]

Posthole No.	Length (cm)	Width (cm)	Depth (cm)	Volume[b] (liters)	Fill Type	Fill Period	Shims	Base Stone	Est. post size (cm)	Lining	Comments
Posthole 22	15	5	3	0.2	11	PO	0	0	0	U	
Posthole 23	16	8	6	0.6	10	PO	0	0	0	U	
Posthole 24	20	7	5	0.6	10	PO	0	0	0	U	
Posthole 25	15	7	9	0.8	13	Occ	0	0	0	U	
Posthole 26	17	10	18	2.2	13	Occ	0	0	0	U	
Posthole 27	16	10	17	2.1	13	Occ	0	0	0	U	
Posthole 28	19	12	13	2.2	13	Occ	2	0	0	U	
Posthole 29	14	8	19	1.7	52	Occ	0	0	0	U	
Posthole 30	15	9	9	0.9	52	Occ	0	0	0	U	
Posthole 31	21	8	8	1.0	52	Occ	0	0	0	U	
Posthole 32	23	7	7	1.0	13	Occ	0	0	0	U	
Posthole 33	14	8	6	0.5	13	Occ	0	0	0	U	
Posthole 34	17	5	9?	0.8	10	PO	0	0	0	U	
Posthole 35	19	8	10	1.3	11,13	Occ	0	0	0	U	
Posthole 36	?	?	?	?	?	?	?	?	?	?	
Posthole 37	15	8	11	1.0	52	Occ	0	0	0	U	
Posthole 38	15	5.5	10	1.2	13	Occ	0	0	0	U	SE corner.

[a] See Tables I.7.4-I.7.5 for an explanation of the feature and attribute codes.
[b] Volumes for features are approximate.

Table I.4.15. Site 29SJ 724, Pithouse A distribution of floor fill and Floor 1 materials.[a]

Artifact Number	Artifact class	Lithic Material, Ceramic Ware or Faunal Species	FS No.
1	Pot cover (12.8 x 10.7 x 1.2 cm; 221 g)	2000 (sandstone). Crude disc: edge chipped + slight grinding on 1 surface. Burned. On East Bench top.	102
2	Awl (8.4 x 1.5 x 0.2 cm; 2.7 g)	Jackrabbit (*Lepus* sp.) tibia. On top of bench.	121
3	Trough metate frag. (13 x 12 x 5 cm; 9.6 kg)	2000 (sandstone). Level 12 (15 cm above the floor).	141
4	Wood fragment (root?) (5.2 x 2.3 x 0.6 cm; 1.8 g)	Level 12 (3 cm above floor).	171
5	Awl (13.7 x 0.6 x 0.8 cm; 8.9 g)	Large mammal, indeterminate element splinter. 27 cm above floor.	172
6	Awl (17.7 x 2.3 x 1.6 cm; 25.5 g)	Artiodactyl metapodial. 26 cm above floor.	173
7	Awl (12.1 x 0.6 x 0.5 cm; 5.3 g)	Large mammal, indeterminate element splinter. 26 cm above floor next to wall.	174
8	Malachite nodule (4 x 4 x 2 mm; 0.05 g)	5320 (malachite). Unmodified. Rock Color 10GY 7/2. Level 12 (5 cm above floor).	175
9	Groundstone (2.9 x 1.9 x 1.9 cm; 13.3 g)	1013 (fossiliferous chert). 1 surface ground flat. Level 12 (5-6 cm above floor).	176
10	Limonite (4.1 x 2.3 x 1.2 cm; 10.7 g)	5110 (yellow limonite). Tabular, triangular shaped. 1 edge ground flat. Munsell 7.5YR 6/6. Level 12 (9 cm above floor). Approximate location.	177
11	Concretion (3.7 x 3.2 x 2.8 cm; 34.1 g) Concretion (3.2 x 2.7 x 2.3 cm; 18.9 g)	2000 (sandstone). Oval-shaped balls, both burned. Level 12 (12 cm above floor). Approximate location.	178
12-14	See Table I.4.12		
15	Awl (6.8 x 2.4 x 1.6 cm; 11.9 g)	Artiodactyl metapodial. Level 11. Location approximate.	223
16	Spatula (14.2 x 2.0 x 0.6 cm; 11.7 g)	Dog/coyote/wolf (*Canis* sp.) radius. Level 11.	224
-	Sandstone nodule (21. x 1.3 x 1.2 cm; 4.5 g)	2000 (sandstone). Burned red. Slightly ground. Top of upper bench.	227
-	Plain gray jar sherd	Cibola Grayware. Top of upper bench.	228
-	Beads (2; 5mm dia x 4; 4.5mm dia x 4; total 0.1 g)	2650 (black shale). 2 mm holes. Recovered from flotation sample. Level 11 ash.	246
-	Vegetal material	*Atriplex/Sarcobatus*, *Juniperus* sp., *Populus/salix*, *Gutierrezia*, *Artemisia*, *Zea mays* cob fragments & kernels. Level 11 ash. Recovered from flotation sample.	246
-	Radiocarbon date from corn kernels (10)	*Zea mays*. Date (CAMS-8184) = calibrated 2δ A.D. 713±111 (Stuiver & Pearson 1987). Recovered from flotation sample.	246
-	Bone (1)	Small/medium-size mammal (boiled).	246
-	Hematite (6.1 x 5.2 x 4.0 cm; 156.6 g)	5200 (hematite). Natural chunk ground on 1 side and parts of 1 end. Munsell red 10R 4/8. Level 11.	253

Table I.4.15. Site 29SJ 724, Pithouse A distribution of floor fill and Floor 1 materials, cont'd.[a]

Artifact Number	Artifact class	Lithic Material, Ceramic Ware or Faunal Species	FS No.
-	Chipped stones (6)	Level 11	
	Core (4.8 x 3.6 x 2.5 cm; 48.7 g)	1112 (cherty silicified wood).	
	Utilized flakes (2; 11.7 g)	1140 (chalcedonic silicified wood).	
	Fortuitous perforator (2.3 x 2.2 x 0.8 cm; 5.3 g)	1140 (chalcedonic silicified wood). Small projection retouched.	
	Whole flake (3.9 g)	1145 (chalcedonic silicified wood).	
	Whole flake (12.6 g)	1150 (jasperized silicified wood).	
	Core (3.7 x 3.3 x 2.4 cm; 30.9 g)	1150 (jasperized silicified wood).	254
-	Hammerstone (4.6 x 4.5 x 3.5 cm; 136.0 g)	1112 (cherty silicified wood). Natural cubic-like shape with very minor battering at a few edges.	254B
-	Pebble	Probably quartzite manuport. Level 11. Missing.	255
-	Minerals (2)		
	Selenite (2.2 x 2.2 x 0.5 cm; 2.8 g)	5041 (gypsum). Level 11. Natural, irregular tabular piece.	256
	Selenite (4.2 x 2.4 x 1.3 cm; 8.5 g)	Natural, irregular piece.	257
-	Corncob fragments (4; 1.2 g)	*Zea mays*. Carbonized. Level 11.	
-	Sherds (ca. 50)	Level 11	
	Lino/plain gray (ca. 43)	Cibola Grayware.	
	Unclassified BMIII-PI white ware (5)	Cibloa Whiteware.	
	Woodruff Smudged bowl sherd (1)	Puerco Valley Brownware.	
	Abajo R/o bowl sherd (1)	San Juan Redware.	258
-	Bones (27)	Cottontail (8; 1 burned, 1 boiled), jackrabbit (12: 5 boiled), prairie dog (1), unknown bird (1), red-tailed hawk (3), ferruginous hawk (1), unclassified medium/large mammal (1). Level 11.	259
17	Bones (2)	Jackrabbit (*Lepus californicus*) metatarsal & unidentified rabbit humerus. 1 cooked. Level 11.	260
18	Bone (1)	Jackrabbit (*Lepus californicus*) femur. Level 11.	261
19	Bones (6)	Cottontail vertebrates, mandible, & scapulas. All boiled. Level 11 ash.	262
20	Worked bone (4-sided implement)(19.4 x 1.2 x 1.0 cm; 14.5 g)	Sandhill crane (*Grus canadensis*) tarsometatarsus. Level 11 ash.	273
21	Tinkler (14.0 x 1.6 x 0.4 cm; 8.0 g)	Jackrabbit (*Lepus* sp.) tibia. Drilled hole in 1 end. Level 11 ash.	274
22	Angular debris chipped stone (1); (2.2 g)	1140 (chalcedonic silicified wood). Level 11 ash.	275
23	Awl (15.5 x 2.2 x 0.8 cm; 24.2 g)	Artiodactyl metapodial. Level 11/12 ash.	276
24	Tinkler (14.0 x 1.6 x 0.4 cm; 8.2 g)	Jackrabbit (*Lepus* sp.) tibia. Drilled hole in 1 end. Level 10 ash.	277

Table I.4.15. Site 29SJ 724, Pithouse A distribution of floor fill and Floor 1 materials, cont'd.[a]

Artifact Number	Artifact class	Lithic Material, Ceramic Ware or Faunal Species	FS No.
25	Awl (11.8 x 9.0 x 0.6 cm; 6.4 g)	Medium/large mammal, indeterminate element splinter. Level 11/12 ash.	278
26	Flaker (16.1 x 1.8 x 0.7 cm; 18.4 g)	Large mammal tibia?/radius? Level 9.	279
27	Awl (16.5 x 1.5 x 0.7 cm; 13.7 g)	Artiodactyl, indeterminate element split. Level 12 ash (floor fill).	280
28	Paleo-Indian projectile point (4.8 x 2.0 x 0.6 cm; 5.3 g)	3520 (Jemez obsidian). Valle Grande source (Shackley and Dillian 2000). Jimmy Allen Late-Paleo point with Archaic reworking. Level 12 ash (floor fill). See the Chaco WEB site, image P23 or Western National Parks Association 2004:47 for color photograph.	281
29	Knife (5.7 x 2.1 x 1.2 cm; 14.0 g)	1140 (chalcedonic silicified wood). Massive, drill-shaped tool. Level 12 ash (floor fill).	282
30	Selenite (5.7 x 2.2 x 0.8 cm; 7.3 g)	5041 (gypsum). Unmodified natural, flat, splintery irregular piece.	287
31	Malachite nodule (10 x 6 x 4 mm; 0.7 g)	5320 (malachite). Unmodified. Rock Color 5G 6/6. Level 11 ash.	289
32	Groundstone (9.5 x 3.8 x 1.2 cm; 72.6 g)	2000 (sandstone). Small natural rectangular tablet. Very slight grinding on surface & edges. Limonite smeared? Munsell 10YR 6/6. Level 12 ash (floor fill).	290
33	Polishing stone	Probably quartzite (4000). Level 12 ash (floor fill). Missing.	291
34	Polished pebble	Probably quartzite (4000). Level 12 (4 cm above floor). Missing.	292
35	Roof impressions (8)(largest 15.1 x 7.0 x 5.6 cm; total 1352 g)	Adobe closing material w/ finger prints and small (5-10 cm dia) beam impressions. Sooted and unsooted. Level 12 (4 cm above floor).	293
36	Shell bead (1.1+ x 0.5 dia cm; 0.2 g)	0008 (*Olivella dama*). Top broken off. 9 cm above bench. See Vol. II, Plate II.10.2.	295
37	Pendant (4.2 x 3.0 x 0.4 cm; 7.5 g)	2551 (Red dog shale). Both surfaces & all edges ground. Biconical hole (2 mm dia.) at 1 end. 9 cm above bench. Munsell 2.5YR 6/6.	296
38	Chipped stones (8) Utilized flakes (2)(24.9 g total) Utilized flake (7.0 g) Retouched flake (2.8 g) Whole flake (2) (11.6 g total) Utilized flake (3.3 g) Utilized flake (6.8 g)	Approximate location. Level 12 (floor fill). 1112 (cherty silicified wood). 1140 (chalcedonic silicified wood). 1140 (chalcedonic silicified wood). 1140 (chalcedonic silicified wood). 1142 (chalcedonic silicified wood). 1150 (jasperized silicified wood).	283
39	Awl tip (5.0+ x 0.6 x 0.4 cm; 1.4 g)	Medium/large mammal, indeterminate shaft fragment. Top of upper bench on west side.	335
	Worked mineral (2.4 x 1.3 x 0.5 cm; 1.6 g)	2551 (Red dog shale). Irregular, tabular shape; 2 surfaces and 2 edges ground. Munsell red 2.5YR 5.5/8. Top of bench.	336

Table I.4.15. Site 29SJ 724, Pithouse A distribution of floor fill and Floor 1 materials, cont'd.[a]

Artifact Number	Artifact class	Lithic Material, Ceramic Ware or Faunal Species	FS No.
-	Roof impressions (3)(largest 9.5 x 5.2 x 5.0 cm; total 430 g)	Adobe closing material. smoked with carbon deposits and small (7-10 cm dia.) beam impressions. West wingwall area.	353
-	Misc. bone (35)	Cottontail (9: 6 boiled), jackrabbit (20: 6 boiled), unidentified small/medium mammal (5; 1 boiled), & unidentified medium/large mammal (1). On bench.	357
-	Sherds (27) Plain gray jar (21) Plain gray jar with Fugitive red (1) Unclassified BMIII-early PI mineral B/w bowl (2) White Mound B/w bowl (2) Pena B/w bowl sherd	On bench, west side Cibola Grayware (16 sooted). Cibola Grayware. Cibola Whiteware. Cibola Whiteware. Chuska Whiteware.	358
-	Chipped stones (6) Utilized flake (72.1 g) Angular debris chipped stone (4.3 g) Whole flake (29.1 g) Angular debris chipped stone (7.2 g) Utilized flake (24.0 g) Utilized flake (3. 6 g)	All on bench, west side 1053 (chalcedonic High Surface Chert). 1053 (chalcedonic High Surface Chert). 1112 (cherty silicified wood). 1112 (cherty silicified wood). 1140 (chalcedonic silicified wood). 1150 (jasperized silicified wood).	359
-	Selenite (2.4 x 1.3 x 0.7 cm; 1.8 g)	5041 (gypsum) Unmodified. On bench, west side.	359B
-	Corncob frags.(10; 2.2 g)	*Zea mays*. Carbonized. On bench, west side.	360
-	Misc. bone (8)	Cottontail (4), jackrabbit (3), and prairie dog (1). On SW side of floor.	364
-	Sherds (8): Lino gray & plain gray	Cibola Grayware. On SW side of floor.	365
-	Angular debris chipped stone (14.1 g)	1142 (chalcedonic silicified wood). On SW side of floor.	366
-	Chipped stones (12) Angular debris chipped stone (4.2 g) Retouched flake (3.6 g) Utilized flake (6.0 g) Utilized flake (2)(19.5 g total) Utilized flake (2.1 g) Core (6.2 x 5.3 x 4.4 cm; 142.5 g) Core (5.1 x 3.9 x 3.1 cm; 75.9 g) Core (4.0 x 3.3 x 3.1 cm; 30.7 g) Core (5.2 x 4.4 x 3.3 cm; 88.2 g) Core (5.0 x 4.0 x 2.1 cm; 42.8 g)	All in area of FS 378-379, on SE side of floor. 1112 (cherty silicified chert). 1113 (cherty silicified wood). 1130 (silicified palm wood). 1140 (chalcedonic silicified wood). 4000 (quartzite). 1011 (fossiliferous chert). 1053 (chalcedonic High Surface Chert). 1140 (chalcedonic silicified wood). 1140 (chalcedonic silicified wood). 2221 (silicified quartzose sandstone).	367
-	Hammerstone (6.1 x 5.1 x 3.6 cm; 136.2 g)	4000 (quartzite). Minor battering on ends. On SE floor between vent & postoccupation slab wall.	368

Table I.4.15. Site 29SJ 724, Pithouse A distribution of floor fill and Floor 1 materials, cont'd.[a]

Artifact Number	Artifact class	Lithic Material, Ceramic Ware or Faunal Species	FS No.
–	Polishing stones/manuports (2)	On SE floor between vent & postoccupation slab wall. In collections missing.	369
–	Sherds (23) Lino Gray jar (1) Lino Gray ladle bowl (1) Bennett Gray jar (1) Plain gray jar (14) Plain gray jar with Fugitive red (2) Unclassified Cibola Whiteware bowl (1) White Mound B/w bowl (1) Lino B/g bowl (2)	On SE floor between vent & postoccupation slab wall. Cibola Grayware. Cibola Grayware/Whiteware. Chuska Grayware. Cibola Grayware (10 sooted). Cibola Grayware. Cibola Whiteware (sooted). Cibola Whiteware (sooted). Tusayan Whiteware.	370
–	Bones (22)	Cottontail (7), jackrabbit (13; 2 boiled), coyote (2). On SE floor between vent & postoccupation slab wall.	371
–	Corncob fragments (2)(1.6 g)	*Zea mays*. Carbonized. In area of FS 378-379, SE side of floor.	372
–	Sherds (8): Plain gray jar sherds (7) Redware (1)	In area of FS 378-379, SE side of floor. Cibola Grayware (3 sooted). Unclassified; not re-found.	373
–	Eggshell fragments (18; 0.63 g)	Turkey (*Meleagris gallopavo*)? Top of FP 1.	377
–	Eggshell fragments (3; 0.1 g)	Turkey (*Meleagris gallopavo*)? Top of FP 1.	436
40	Eggshell fragments (58; 1.07 g)	Turkey (*Meleagris gallopavo*)? Between vent & FP, 1-3 cm above floor.	378
41	Squash seeds (5; 0.5 g)	*Cucurbita* sp. Between vent & FP, 7-10cm above floor.	379
42	Pot cover (5.8 x 5.7 x 0.6 cm; 33.2 g)	2000 (sandstone) Disc: 2 faces & entire edge ground. Edge also beveled. 0-10 cm above floor.	380
43-47	See Table I.4.12		
–	Corn cob fragments (3; 0.1 g)	Carbonized. In C-14 sample of carbonized brush (ca. 150 g) from FP 1.	412
48	Misc. bone (44 pieces)	Cottontail (19; 5 boiled), jackrabbit (10; 4 boiled), pocket gopher (1), kangaroo rat (1), prairie dog (6), unidentified small/medium mammal (6; 2 boiled), unidentified rodent (1; boiled), hawk claw (1). In NW Posthole fill. See Volume II, Plate II.10.3c.	413
49	Awl (18.8 x 1.5 x 1.6 cm; 29.1 g)	Mule deer (*Odocoileus hemionus*) metapodial. Shows weaving grooves. In NW Posthole fill. See Volume II, Plate II.10.3i.	414

Table I.4.15. Site 29SJ 724, Pithouse A distribution of floor fill and Floor 1 materials, cont'd.[a]

Artifact Number	Artifact class	Lithic Material, Ceramic Ware or Faunal Species	FS No.
50	Chipped stones (18)	NW Posthole fill.	
	Whole flake (2.6 g)	1052 (chalcedonic High Surface Chert).	
	Utilized flake (4.0 g)	1105 (silicified wood w/ quartz crystals).	
	Utilized flakes (2)(total 11.8 g)	1112 (cherty silicified wood).	
	Angular debris (3.0 g)	1112 (cherty silicified wood).	
	Utilized flake (3.1 g)	1113 (cherty silicified wood).	
	Utilized flakes (5)(total 41.2 g)	1140 (chalcedonic silicified wood).	
	Whole flake (0.3 g)	1140 (chalcedonic silicified wood).	
	Angular debris (0.4 g)	1140 (chalcedonic silicified wood).	
	Whole flakes (2)(total 1.4 g)	1142 (chalcedonic silicified wood).	
	Core (8.1 x 5.7 x 5.0 cm; 249.2 g)	2202 (silicified fine grained brown chert); similar to Pintado chert (2221).	
	Utilized flake (1.6 g)	2551 (claystone/baked clays).	
	Utilized flake (0.7)	3510 (Grants Ridge obsidian). Sourced to Mt. Taylor by Shackley and Dillian (2000).	415
50	Sherds (3):	NW Posthole fill.	
	Lino Gray seed jar	Cibola Grayware.	
	Plain gray jar	Cibola Grayware.	
	Unclassified BMIII-PI whiteware jar	Cibola Whiteware.	415B
50	Minerals (8)	NW Posthole fill.	
	Gypsum (2; largest 1.9 x 1.0 x 0.6 cm; total 1.4 g)	5040 (gypsum) Natural powdery white nodules. Rock Color 5YR 8/1, Munsell 10YR 8/2. 5041 (gypsum). Natural pieces.	
	Selenite (4; largest 3.8 3.8 x 1.9 cm; total 50 g)	5110 (yellow limonite). Ground on 2 surfaces & 1 edge. Munsell 7.5YR 7/6.	
	Limonite (3.5 x 1.6 x 0.9 cm; 5.0 g)	1112 (cherty silicified wood)? Cylinder shape. Natural.	
	Manuport (1.9 x 0.6 x 0.5 cm; 0.9 g)		415
50	Mineral (2.4 x 1.7 x 0.5 cm)	2551 (Red dog shale). Trapezoid shape. Unmodified. Loaned out, then lost.	415
50	Concretion (4.8 x 4.7 x 1.8 cm; 39.5 g)	2000 (sandstone). Doughnut-shaped with 15 mm hole thru center. Minor grinding on edges. NW Posthole fill. See Volume II, Plate II.10.3a.	415E
50	Squash seed fragment (0.1 g)	*Cucurbita* sp. In NW Posthole fill.	415
52	Malachite (6)(largest 12 x 10 x 8 mm; total 2.5 g)	5320 (malachite). Natural nodules. Rock Color green 10G 6/2. NW Posthole fill. See Volume II, Plate II.10.3d.	416A
52	Projectile point (est. 4.4 x 1.8 x 0.4 cm; 1.7 g)	1080 (Washington Pass chert). Classic PI corner-notched point. Base missing. In NW Posthole fill. See Volume II, Plate II.10.3b.	416B
52	Misc. chipped stone (0.8 g)	1080 (Washington Pass chert).	416B
52	Shell artifact (2.5 x 1.0 x 0.3 cm; 1.2 g)	0008 or 1080 (Munsell red 2.5YR 4/8: flat & claw-shaped; highly ground and polished on all surfaces). Could this be Washington Pass chert, instead? NW Posthole fill. See Volume II, Plate II.10.2f.	416C

Chapter 4: Pueblo I Excavation Reports   381

Table I.4.15. Site 29SJ 724, Pithouse A distribution of floor fill and Floor 1 materials, cont'd.[a]

Artifact Number	Artifact class	Lithic Material, Ceramic Ware or Faunal Species	FS No.
52	Shell bead (1.2 x 0.5 dia. cm; 0.2 g)	0008 (*Olivella dama*). Top ground off for string hole. NW Posthole fill. See Volume II, Plate II.10.3e.	416D
52	Pendant (3.1 x 1.9 x 0.4 cm; 4.6 g)	2770 (calcite). Both surfaces & all edges ground. Biconical hole (2 mm dia.) at 1 end. Rectangular shape. NW Posthole fill. See Volume II, Plate II.10.3h.	416E
52	Pendant (3.5 x 0.7 x 0.5 cm; 2.1 g)	2770 (calcite). All sides ground; notched at 1 end, grooves at other. Biconical hole (1 mm dia.) at notched end. Tapered cylindrical shape. NW Posthole fill. See Volume II, Plate II.10.3g.	416F
53	Trough metate fragment (12.1+ x 10.4+ x 9 cm; 13.9+ kg)	2000 (sandstone). 100% burned and blackened. Reused as a fire dog? Trough = 6+ cm deep.	439
54	Trough metate fragment (14.1+ x 16.1+ x 4.6 cm; 15.5+ kg)	2000 (sandstone). Trough = 1.1 cm deep.	440
55	Mano fragment (13.8+ x 9.8 x 3.5 cm; 638+ g)	2000 (sandstone). 3/5 mano; airfoil shape, well ground on 2 surfaces. Trailing edge has been flaked. 15 cm south of PH.	441
56	Cover fragment (28+ x 14.6+ x 2.1 cm; 1431 g)	2000 (sandstone). Ground flat on 1 surface; lightly ground on opposite surface.	442
57	Groundstone (12.2 x 9.1 x 8.9 cm; 1401 g)	2000 (sandstone). Burned black. Irregular shape. Ground smooth on 1 surface. Firept liner? Metate fragment?	443
58	Mano blank? (22x 14.5 x 8 cm; 4500 g)	2000 (sandstone). Burned. Loaf-shaped, formed by pecking. Ground on 2 surfaces.	444
59	Mano (18.5 x 12.0 x 4.4 cm; 2000 g)	2000 (sandstone). Blockish, with 1 ground surface.	445
60	Groundstone (14.8 x 10.1 x 4.0 cm; 821g)	2000 (sandstone). Burned 100%. Irregular shape; lightly ground on opposite surfaces. Firepit liner fragment?	446
61	Mano (17.1 x 10.8 x 4.5 cm; 1029 g)	2000 (sandstone).	447
62	Trough metate fragment (29.5+ x 17.0+ x 7.5 cm; 44.5+ kg)	2000 (sandstone). Trough = 5.3 cm deep.	448
63	Lapidary abrader (19.7 x 16.5 x 6.3 cm; 4280 g)	2000 (sandstone). Rectangular block. 2 opposite surfaces well ground creating slight troughs.	449
64	Trough metate fragment (11.7+ x 14+ x 8.3 cm; 17.6+ kg)	2000 (sandstone). 50% burned. Trough = 3.9 cm deep.	450
65	Pot or pit cover (31 x 30.6 x 2 cm; 4000 g)	2000 (sandstone). Chipped oval; opposing surfaces ground, plus pecked on 1 surface. Burned in center on 1 side. Over ash pit.	451
66	Concretion	2000 (sandstone). Missing.	452

Table I.4.15. Site 29SJ 724, Pithouse A distribution of floor fill and Floor 1 materials, cont'd.[a]

Artifact Number	Artifact class	Lithic Material, Ceramic Ware or Faunal Species	FS No.
67	Lapidary abrader/anvil (36.5 x 20.8 x 1.4-3.4 cm; 3175 g)	2000 (sandstone). Trapozidal/triangular shape. 1 highly-ground surface with light grinding on opposite side. 1 edge chipped to shape; rest natural. Found over OP 6.	453
68	Mano (22.0 x 12.2 x 5.2 cm; 3000 g)	2000 (sandstone).	454
69	Pot cover (12.3 x 12.2 x 1.1 cm; 260 g)	2000 (sandstone). Discoid shape formed by edge chipping. Burned.	470
70	Unifacially ground slab (14.5 x 11.5 x 7.5cm; 1545.3 g)	2000 (sandstone). Highly burned blocky shape. Slightly ground on edges from bag ware? Firepit liner? Approximate location.	471
71	Firedog? (14.3 x 11.7 x 5.7 cm; 1082 g)	2000 (sandstone). Burned natural concretion. Some grinding. 2-3 cm above ash pit.	472
72	Mano fragment (11.6+ x 12.3+ x 2.9 cm; 551 g)	2000 (sandstone). Part of deflector complex.	473
73	Trough metate fragment	2000 (sandstone). Shim in SW Posthole. Left on site?	474
74	Trough metate fragment	2000 (sandstone). Shim in SW Posthole. Left on site?	475
75	Hammerstone (7.5 x 5.7 x 5.4 cm; 254 g)	4000 (quartzite). Natural cobble with some battering. 11cm above floor.	476
76	Bones (11)	Cottontail (1), jackrabbit (5), unidentified small/medium mammal (4; 1 boiled), & unknown (1). In FP 1 ash layer.	479
76	Plain gray sherds (2)	Cibola Grayware. In FP 1 ash layer.	480
76	Selenite (3.4 x 2.4 x 0.8 cm; 6.2 g)	5041 (gypsum). Natural piece. In FP 1 ash layer.	481
76	Corncobs (14; total 6.2 g)	*Zea mays*. Carbonized. In FP 1 ash layer.	482
76	Charcoal fragment	Piñon (*Pinus edulis*). In FP 1 ash layer.	507
77	Lino Gray sherd	Cibola Grayware. On edge of FP 1.	483
78	Eggshells (15; 0.37 g)	Turkey (*Meleagris gallopavo*)? In ash pit fill.	484
78	Bones (21)	Cottontail (11; 1 boiled), jackrabbit (3), prairie dog (2), unidentified small/medium mammal (5). In ash pit fill.	485
78	Corncobs (14+; 2.4 g)	*Zea mays*. Carbonized. In ash pit fill.	486

Table I.4.15. Site 29SJ 724, Pithouse A distribution of floor fill and Floor 1 materials, cont'd.[a]

Artifact Number	Artifact class	Lithic Material, Ceramic Ware or Faunal Species	FS No.
78	Chipped stones (18)	Ash pit fill.	
	Retouched flake (2.0 g)	1053 (chalcedonic High Surface Chert).	
	Utilized flake (19.4 g)	1110 (splintery silicified wood).	
	Angular debris (0.7 g)	1110 (splintery silicified wood).	
	Utilized flakes (2)(total 8.3 g)	1112 (cherty silicified wood).	
	Whole flakes (2)(total 3.3 g)	1112 (cherty silicified wood).	
	Utilized flakes (2)(total 21.4 g)	1140 (chalcedonic silicified wood).	
	Whole flake (0.9 g)	1140 (chalcedonic silicified wood).	
	Angular debris (2)(total 5.2 g)	1140 (chalcedonic silicified wood).	
	Angular debris (0.8 g)	1142 (chalcedonic silicified wood).	
	Utilized flake (5.5 g)	1150 (jasperized silicified wood).	
	Angular debris (2.0 g)	1610 (dark gray chert).	
	Utilized flake (2.1 g)	2202 (silicified fine-grained brown concretion).	
	Angular flakes (2)(total 10.0 g)	4000 (quartzite).	487
78	Selenite (4.4 x 2.7 x 0.6 cm; 9.8 g)	5041 (gypsum). Unmodified, trapezoid shape. Ash pit fill.	
	Limonite (5 nodules; 0.8 g)	5110 (yellow limonite). Unmodified. Munsell 5YR 6/8.	488A
79	Wood fragments (ca. 8 & 15 tree rings)	*Juniperus* sp. Post fragments? SW Posthole fill.	506
80	Woodruff Smudged bowl sherd	OP 2 fill.	508
81	Utilized flake (9.4 g)	1142 (chalcedonic silicified wood). OP 3 fill.	509
82	Bones (4)	Cottontail (2), jackrabbit (1), unidentified small/medium mammal (1). OP 6 fill.	510
82	Corncob fragment (1; 0.1 g)	*Zea mays*. Carbonized. OP 6 fill.	510
83	Utilized flake (6.5 g)	1053 (chalcedonic High Surface Chert). HP 1 fill.	511
84	Utilized flake (6.0 g)	1112 (cherty silicified wood). OP 11 fill.	593
85	Pot cover fragments (16.8 x 12+ x 0.5 cm; 154.2 g)	2000 (sandstone). Burned around edges from use on pot over fire? Natural discoid shape.	512
86	Clay pipe? (3.7 x 3.6 x 2.8 cm; 15.9 g)	Unfired gray clay. Flared-cup shape end. No hole. Similar to pipe from 29SJ 721 (FS 24). West upper bench.	513
87	Corn cob (1; 1g)	*Zea mays*. Carbonized. SE Posthole.	421
87	Plain gray jar sherds (3)	Cibola Grayware. SE Posthole.	422
	Sanostee R/o (1)	Chuska Redware.	
87	Utilized flake (7.8 g)	1140 (chalcedonic silicified wood). SE Posthole.	423

Table I.4.15. Site 29SJ 724, Pithouse A distribution of floor fill and Floor 1 materials, cont'd.[a]

Artifact Number	Artifact class	Lithic Material, Ceramic Ware or Faunal Species	FS No.
--	Plain gray sherds (4)	Cibola Grayware. SE Posthole fill.	514
87	Bone (1)	Jackrabbit (*Lepus californicus*) tibia. SE Posthole fill.	514
87	Utilized flake (2.8 g)	1140 (chalcedonic silicified wood). SE Posthole fill.	514
88	Squash seeds (tiny fragments)	*Cucurbita* sp. In Bench PH 4.	515
89	Angular debris (5.7 g)	1140 (chalcedonica silicified wood). In Bench PH 8.	516
90	Whole flake (4.0 g)	1112 (cherty silicified wood). In Bench PH 9.	517
90	Bone (1)	Cottontail tibia. In Bench PH 9.	517
91	Whole flakes (2)(total 2.8 g) Angular debris (0.1 g)	1142 (chalcedonica silicified wood). 1140 (chalcedonica silicified wood). In Bench PH 17.	518
92	Plain gray jar sherd	Cibola Grayware. In Bench PH 26.	519
93	Bone	Cottontail rib. In OP 10.	524
94	Bones (2)	Unidentified small/medium mammal long bones. 1 burned. In OP 12.	525
95	Bones (2)	Jackrabbit astragalus & unidentified rabbit rib. In HP 2.	526
95	Lino Gray jar sherd	Cibola Grayware. In HP 2.	528
96	Bones (3)	Cottontail skull, and unidentified small/medium mammal (long bone & unknown). In OP 15.	527A
96	Selenite (2 fragments; 0.3 g)	5041 (gypsum). Burned white. Unmodified. In OP 15.	527B
96	Squash seeds (fragments of 4-8 seeds?)	*Cucurbita mixta*. In OP 15.	529
97-98	See Feature 1, Table II.4.12		535, 539
99	Mammal skeleton	Cottontail rabbit (*Sylvilagus* sp.). Complete skeleton in vent (postoccupational).	314
99	Eggshells (2; 0.1 g)	Turkey (*Meleagris gallopavo*)? In ventilator with rabbit.	314
100	Bones (3)	Cottontail femurs. In NE Posthole.	417
100	Bones (8)	Cottontail (3; 2 boiled), jackrabbit (3), woodrat (1), & pocket gopher (1). In NE Posthole.	418
100	Utilized flake (14.8 g)	1150 (jasperized silicified wood). In NE Posthole.	419
100	Whole flake (11.5 g) Utilized flake (13.5 g)	1054 (chalcedonic High Surface Chert). In NE Posthole. 1141 (chalcedonic silicified wood).	420

Table I.4.15. Site 29SJ 724, Pithouse A distribution of floor fill and Floor 1 materials, cont'd.[a]

Artifact Number	Artifact class	Lithic Material, Ceramic Ware or Faunal Species	FS No.
100	Plain gray jar sherd	Cibola Grayware. In NE Posthole.	424
100	Plain gray jar sherd (1) Woodruff Smudged bowl sherd (1)	Cibola Grayware. In NE Posthole. Puerco Valley Brownware.	424
-	Bead (9 x 8 x 2 mm; 0.2 g)	2551 (Red dog shale). Munsell 10R 5/8. Biconical hole (2 mm diameter). On backdirt pile.	641[b]
-	Metate fragment (20.1+ x 16.5+ x 8.8 cm; 3345±g)	2000 (sandstone). 100% burned and sooted; possible firepit liner or firedog. Trough = 6.5 cm deep. On backdirt pile.	648[b]
-	Anvil/abrader (23.5 x 16.7 x 4.0 cm; 2375 g)	2000 (sandstone). Tabular block, chipped to shape. One surface finely ground flat, with isolated peck marks. On backdirt pile.	649[b]
-	Mano fragment (6.5+ x 11.5 x 2.5 cm; 159.4+ g)	2000 (sandstone). Burned & sooted. On backdirt pile.	650[b]
-	Concretion sphere (2.5 cm diameter; 17.1 g)	2000 (sandstone). Ground round. On backdirt pile.	651[b]
-	Mineral (6; 28.7g; largest: 5.6 x 2.1 x 1.8 cm; 13.9; 5.0 x 1.7 x 1.0 cm; 9.1 g)	5041 (gypsum selenite). Natural pieces. On backdirt pile.	652[b]
-	Bracelet fragment (4.8 x 0.4 x 0.5 cm; 2.6 g)	0008 (*Glycymeris gigantea*). Biconical hole (2 mm dia.) & ground grooves across bracelet. On backdirt pile. See Vol.II, Plate II.10.2.	653[b]
-	Bone	On backdirt pile. Missing.	654[b]
-	Malachite nodule (10 x 5 x 4 mm; 0.2 g)	5320 (malachite). Rock Color 5G 7/2-10G 6/2. On backdirt pile.	655[b]
-	Core (3.5 x 2.9 x 2.4 cm; 32.6 gm)	1112 (cherty silicified wood). On backdirt pile.	656[b]
-	Sherds (26)	Plain grayware (1 with fugitive red paint). On backdirt pile.	657[b]
-	Corn cob fragments (3; 10.8· gm)	*Zea mays* (carbonized). On backdirt pile.	658[b]

[a] See distribution in Figure I.4.16. All bones examined for cooking brown ("boiled"), and burning (Akins: analysis data base). Most C-14 samples not listed. Materials from the Northwest Posthole may have been placed at abandonment for ritual closing of the structure.

[b] Given the profusion of cultural material on the floor and associated fill in Pithouse A, the find of rare artifacts and groundstone on top of the pithouse backdirt pile suggests their original proximity to the last fill removed from the pithouse (floor fill/floor). These materials were recovered in the fall of 1976.

Table I.4.16. Rough Sort Ceramic Frequencies from Midden Testing at 29SJ 724, Houseblock II (North House).[a]

	Test Trench 1			Test Trench 2		Totals	
	Surface	Level 1	Level 2	Level 1	Level 2		
Ceramic Type	No.	No.	No.	No.	No.	No.	*Percent*
CIBOLA CULINARY							*[82]*
Lino Gray	-	4	10	1	1	16	*3*
Plain gray	21	173	112	29	26	361	*76*
Plain gray with Fugitive red	-	4	7	2	1	14	*3*
Wide neckbanded	-	1	-	-	-	1	*T*
Narrow neckbanded	1	1	-	-	-	2	*T*
CHUSKA CULINARY							
Narrow neckbanded	2	4	-	-	-	6	*[2]*
Neck indented corrugated	2	1	1	-	-	4	*11*
CIBOLA WHITEWARE							*[5]*
La Plata B/w	-	1	-	1	-	2	*T*
White Mound B/w	-	4	2	-	1	7	*1*
Unclassified BMIII-PI M/w	-	-	2	1	-	3	*1*
Red Mesa B/w	-	-	1	-	1	2	*T*
Gallup B/w	-	1	-	-	1	2	*T*
Unclassified PI-PII B/w	-	-	-	1	-	1	*T*
Unclassified PII-PIII B/w	-	6	-	-	-	6	*1*
UNCLASSIFIED WHITEWARE		1					*[5]*
Unclassified PI-II Whiteware	-	5	2	3	-	21	*4*
Unclassified PII-III Whiteware	-	1	1	-	1	3	*1*
TUSAYAN WHITEWARE							
Lino B/g	2	1	-	-	-	3	*[1] 1*
WOODRUFF SMUDGED WARE	2	6	5	-	-	13	*(3)*
SAN JUAN REDWARE							*[2]*
Abajo R/o	1	2	-	-	-	3	*1*
Bluff B/o	-	1	-	-	-	1	*T*
Unclassified redware	-	5	-	1	-	6	*1*
LINO RED (Tallahogan Red)	-	-	-	1	-	1	*(T)*
Totals	32	231	143	40	32	478	*100*

[a] T = trace (less than 0.5 percent). Ware percentages = [ ]; combined ware and type percentages = ( ).

Chapter 5

Other Excavations and Data Recovery at Early Puebloan Sites In and Around Chaco

Although archaeological investigations in Chaco Canyon over the past century have focused primarily on the greathouses and Pueblo II-III small houses, a number of early puebloan sites were excavated or tested prior to the work of the Chaco Center. Several were reported in published works (e.g., Judd 1924, 1927); other findings remain only in archive notes or were never reported. This chapter summarizes those investigations and reports.

For the most part, early investigations of early puebloan sites involved pithouses discovered underneath later houses or exposed in the Chaco Wash after the sides of the banks had collapsed. Two areas were prominent in these early findings. One was among the small houses and the great kiva, Casa Rinconada, in a rincon across from Pueblo Bonito where relic hunting and subsequent university field schools concentrated work between the 1890s and the 1940s (Figure I.5.1, Plates I.5.1 and I.5.2).

The other was next to the bend in the Chaco Wash that sweeps around the bluff where Shabik'eschee Village (Roberts 1929) is located. As an extension of occupation off the bluffs into the flats of Chaco Canyon, the area must contain numerous Basketmaker III and Pueblo I pithouses judging from the number of structures that have been exposed in the sides of the Chaco Wash.

Pithouses and Rooms in the Vicinity of Casa Rinconada and Pueblo Bonito

The Casa Rinconada area is particularly relevant for understanding the rise of Pueblo Bonito and the associated community of small house sites that cluster within the Rinconada rincon area and, separately, within nearby South Gap and for a short distance to the west along the south side of the canyon. The break between the two habitation areas suggests that the rincon area was occupied by people who knew one another, but who probably had separate social and political status from the larger small house settlement in and around South Gap, but both were still part of a larger community that included Pueblo Bonito.

At least eight Basketmaker III-Pueblo I pithouses were excavated over the years, mostly by students from the University of New Mexico (UNM) Field Schools and the School of American Research (SAR). Two pithouses were associated with the late Pueblo I structure underneath Bc 50, but the others occurred in isolation and lacked discernible surface structures. The level of reporting varies considerably; for at least two pithouses there are little or no notes of the fieldwork which left us with confusing identifications. Nevertheless, the incidental discovery of early structures in

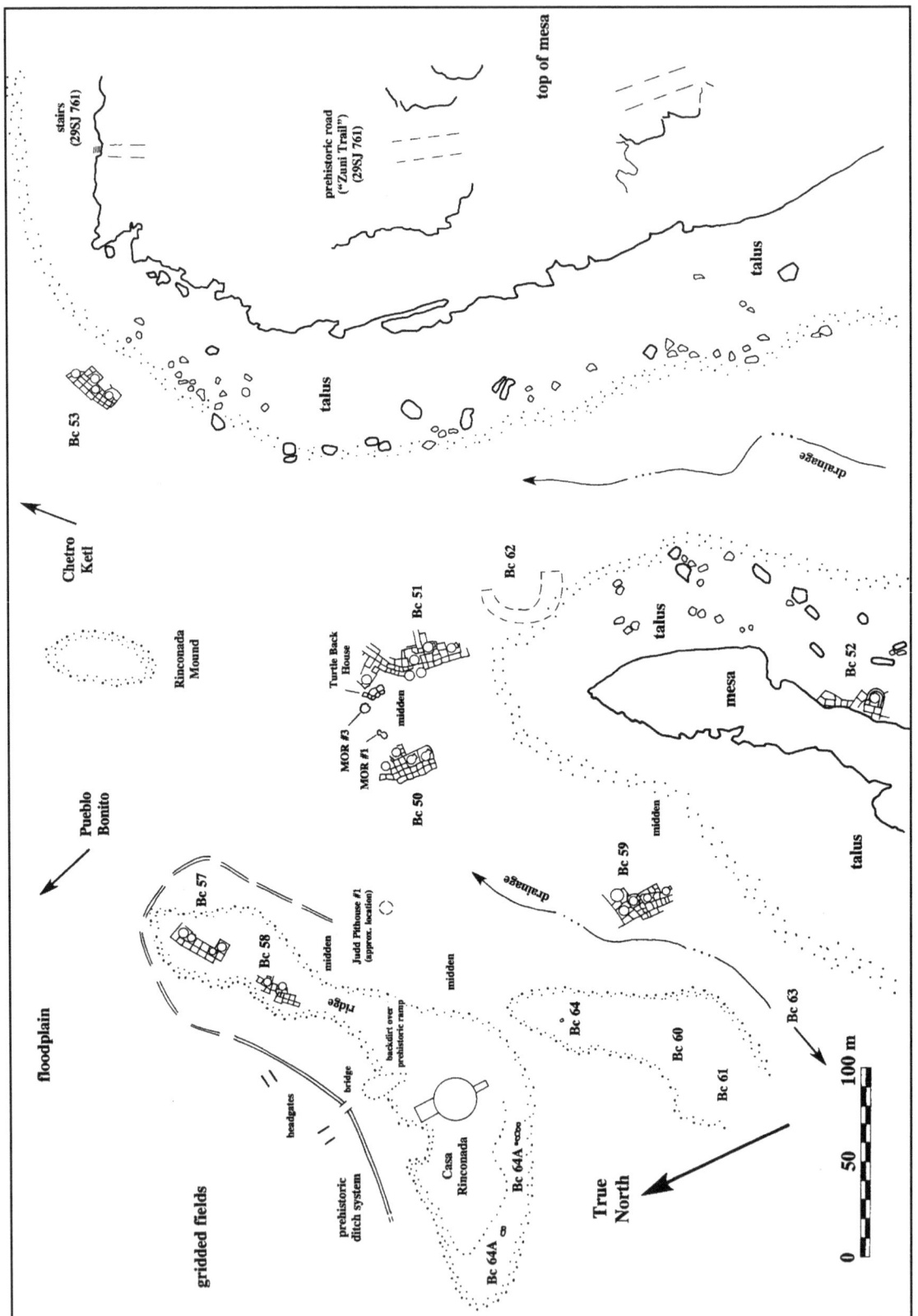

Figure I.5.1. Sites in the Casa Rinconada rincon area (CHCU 65989). Thanks to Gwinn Vivian for information regarding the ditch system. Original by Tom Windes, 2004.

Plate I.5.1. Overview looking north-northwest of the deep rincon extending south behind Bc 51 (29SJ 395). Note the excavations at Bc 52, against the cliff face about midway along the cliff, and the small projection on the horizon marking New Alto. Photograph by William Mulloy in 1940 or 1941 (CHCU neg. 31030).

Plate I.5.2. Overview of the 1940-1941 excavations at Bc 52 (29SJ 400) just south of Bc 51 (29SJ 395). Bc 52 may have been constructed partly to support a staircase or ramp for a prehistoric road connecting Tsin Kletzin and Casa Rinconada. Photograph by William Mulloy (CHCU neg. 31024).

the rincon does provide some insights into the early occupation there.

Bc 50 Substructure House

At the most famous small house site in the rincon, Bc 50 (e.g., Brand et al. 1937), seven early rooms were found underneath the masonry roomblock (Figure I.5.2) along with two pitstructures that probably were first constructed in the mid to late A.D. 800s. A large house clearly was present but was not traced out under the later house. The early rooms were lined with massive upright slabs, encased in adobe, and topped with a crude masonry of adobe; small, horizontal, tabular stones; and spalls (Glenn 1939; Hibben 1937b). The latter might be considered similar to the Type I masonry described for the initial above-ground constructions at early greathouses (e.g., Judd 1964; Lekson 1984), such as at Pueblo Bonito. Part of the early construction used adobe turtlebacks (see Plate I.4.3). The mix of adobe and slab foundation uprights was also encountered in the earliest structures at 29SJ 627 (Truell 1992), which were cross-dated with ceramics to between the late A.D. 700s and the late A.D. 900s. In retrospect, and with a better grasp of the ceramics, the 29SJ 627 initial construction could easily have been started in the mid to late A.D. 800s.

Little material was noted in direct contact with the early room floors at Bc 50. Room 7 yielded a mano and six hammerstones in the fill, and a rare ax head on the floor. There was also a possible bear skeleton on the floor, unusual among Chacoan faunal remains, along with part of a human skull (Senter 1939).

There were few notes for most of the remaining rooms, although Glenn (1937) describes the architecture in detail and lists artifacts from Rooms 4 and 5 (Table I.5.1). Both rooms yielded manos, bone awls, and polishing stones. Room 5 also contained a firepit and several postholes, suggesting that it served as a large living room (305-x-582-cm). Room 6, only partly excavated, contained two slab bins and may also have functioned as a front living room. Inhabitants of these two front rooms may have first built the Feature 2 pithouse and then, later, the Feature 5 pithouse. Both pithouses are directly in front of the two front rooms and probably represent a social unit of two families or a large extended family. Presumably, additional living rooms, backed by storage rooms, extended south under the main Bc 50 superstructure.

At Bc 50, Feature 5 (Figure I.5.3), a deep pithouse, was encountered in front of the northern-most early room, Room 7 (Senter 1939; Truell 1986:Figure A.39). This pithouse exhibited a sipapu, five roof support holes, a trough-like pit along the back wall (see 29SJ 299 and 724 in Chapter 4 for similar features), numerous other floor pits (Table I.5.2), an enclosing bench, a narrow ventilator tunnel, and a wall that partitioned off a 3.5 m² work area in the southern part of the pithouse, with masonry bins at each end. The partition wall was built of adobe, including one turtleback, and jacal poles.

This structure is similar to Pithouse C at 29SJ 627 (Truell 1992) and Pithouse B at 29SJ 1360 (McKenna 1984) near Fajada Butte, which were used primarily during the A.D. 900s but might have been first built in the A.D. 800s. The lengthy use of the structure is evident in the six floor replasterings, as well as its intensive use. In all three cases, the partitioning of the southern work area by a high masonry wall is a prominent feature. As late as A.D. 800, this style of partition was commonly built of upright slabs covered over with adobe.

There were also five heating pits aligned in a semi-circle around the slab-lined firepit. The arrangement of the heating pits is interesting, particularly if Senter's assessment of the large, deep, north heating pit as a "secondary firepit" is considered, or possibly a burned vaulted sipapu (Wilshusen 1989b). This deep oxidized pit is flanked by shallow, smaller heating pits, as is the nearby, central, slab-lined firepit. Thus, two separate areas for heating, cooking, and meal preparation could be present, similar to the dichotomy of floor features in Pithouse A at 29SJ 724 (Chapter 4) and even later in Pueblo Alto, Room 110 (Windes 1987b). Perhaps two different families or social groups (i.e., households) occupied the pithouse.

Feature 5 was not trash-filled, suggesting a hiatus in site occupation. Little cultural material came from the structure, but a cache of nine polished river pebbles (pottery and floor polishers?) and a white stone pipe were found in the north wall niche (Heitman 2011:187, Figure 6.13; Senter 1939). A shell bracelet was recovered from one of the wall recesses. A stone maul, a palette, two turquoise and one gray stone pendant, 15 bone awls, and two worked concretions also came from the fill. The bone awls appear to have come from the collapsed wainscotting, mirroring the finds in Pithouse A at 29SJ 724 (Chapter 4). A stone ball 12 cm in diameter covered the sipapu. Finally, four turkey and two dog skeletons, plus a dog skull, were found just above the floor. Although some may have been trapped in the structure and died, one dog was interred in a slab box.

A surface ramada (Figure I.5.3) was found between Feature 5 and the northernmost room, a feature also found at 29SJ 299 and 29SJ 724. A hearth was centered among four slab-lined ramada postholes. A large shallow basin (Feature 4) had been dug into the native earth just beyond the early house (Senter 1939:7) that may have served as an adobe mixing pit. It was oval, measuring, 213-x-254-cm and 25 cm deep, and contained a trough metate just above the floor. Similar mixing basins were associated with 29SJ 628 (Chapter 3) and 29SJ 299 (Chapter 4). Ceramics suggest use of the pit in the late A.D. 800s or early 900s.

Directly south of Feature 5 was another pithouse, Feature 2 (Kelley 1939a, 1939b), a deep chamber that exhibited plastered walls of native earth (with one section built of turtlebacks), the usual four roof support holes, numerous floor pits and wall niches, a sipapu (8 cm in diameter and 13 cm deep and filled with yellow sand), a slab-lined firepit with an adobe collar, an adobe-covered slab deflector, an adobe-and-slab-lined bin built against the north wall, and a narrow ventilating tunnel lined with slabs and upright poles (Figure I.5.2, Plate I.5.3). The mouth of the ventilator bulged into the main chamber and was elevated slightly above the main floor.

Slab walls leading from the deflector to the house walls partitioned off the typical work area. The walls slightly overhung the floor and there was no bench, although high shelves were cut into the walls on the north and south sides. Two basin-shaped pits to the sides of the firepit in photographs appear to be heating pits, a paired-pit dichotomy common to many Pueblo I pithouses, including that at 29SJ 724 and probably in Pithouse E at 29SJ 299 (see Chapter 4). Interestingly, a fine yellow sand had been deliberately spread across the floor and into numerous pits during the last occupation, a behavior also noted during the Chaco Project excavations and in Feature 5 (above). Unfortunately, no detailed map of Feature 2 could be found, although notes indicate that one was made. The size of Feature 2 is unknown, but the sketched outline suggests that it is similar in size to Feature 5.

Three pottery vessels were recovered from the Feature 2 floor: an Abajo Red-on-orange bowl (Mogollón 2004:40), a Lino Gray jar, and a "Lino" Black-on-gray bowl that has been re-identified by the author as White Mound Black-on-white. This vessel assemblage is nearly identical to the floor assemblage recovered from nearby Pithouse A at Bc 51 (see below). Two trough metates rested against the wall near the ventilator opening in the work area enclosed by the slab wing walls. A possible hatch cover had been set against the west wall, and a few other large stones, some set in the floor, were found. An unworked "core" of red dog shale was also recovered from the floor. A possible broken stone pot cover was recovered next to the firepit.

In addition, the presence of La Plata Black-on-white, Red Mesa Black-on-white (Kiatuthlanna Black-on-white?; Jernigan 1981), and Abajo Red-on-orange, as defined by Hawley (1936), plus many "Lino" Gray sherds suggest last use of the structure in the late A.D. 800s or early A.D. 900s. The lack of neck-decorated culinary ware, however, suggests that a late A.D. 800s closure is more reasonable. After abandonment, the structure filled with trash generated by activities associated with the early occupation of the subsequent "small house" at Bc 50. The adjacent Feature 5 pithouse continued to be occupied into the A.D. 900s.

The early rooms associated with Features 2 and 5 were similar to those excavated at 29SJ 627 (Truell 1992: Figure 5.1) near Fajada Butte, where basal slabs were used in construction of the semi-subterranean storage room in the A.D. 800s and 900s. Sherds and vessels (e.g., Red Mesa Black-on-white and Exuberant Corrugated) recovered from above and below the floors of the early Bc 50 rooms and Feature 5 indicate that those structures use was in the A.D. 900s rather than the Pueblo I period assigned to it by the excavators.

During the UNM excavations, Red Mesa Black-on-white was considered the type ceramic for Pueblo I (Hibben 1937b:84; Senter 1939:6) rather than for early Pueblo II, as it is used now. Lino Gray was classified as Basketmaker III pottery. Hawley (1939:15) argues that "Lino" Gray pottery (which includes plain gray body sherds from neck-decorated culinary vessels)

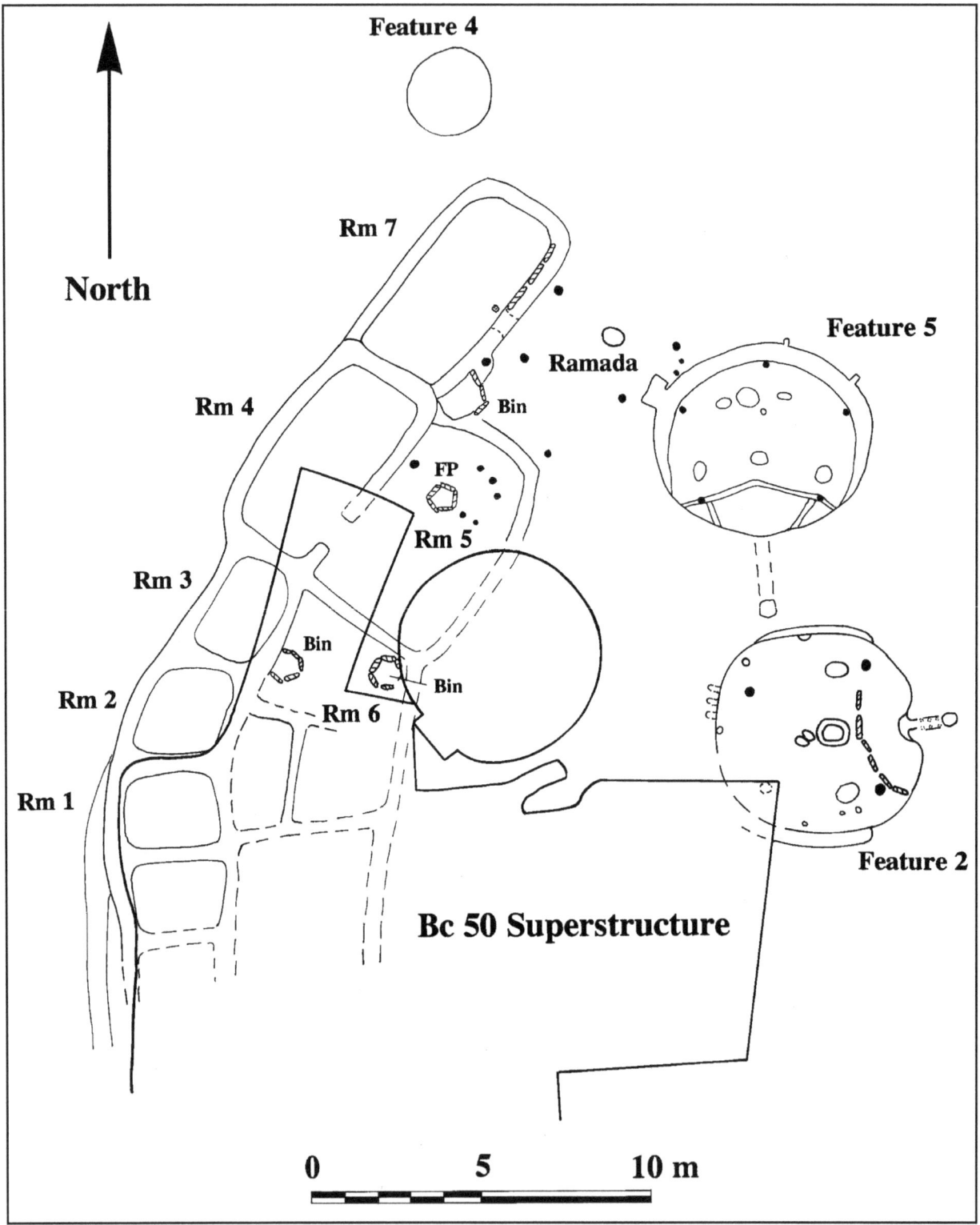

Figure I.5.2. Part of the late Pueblo I-early Pueblo II occupation beneath Bc 50 (29Sj 394). Revised map after Senter (1939) and Truell (1992). Scale, plan, and floor features in Feature 2 are approximate (CHCU 65990).

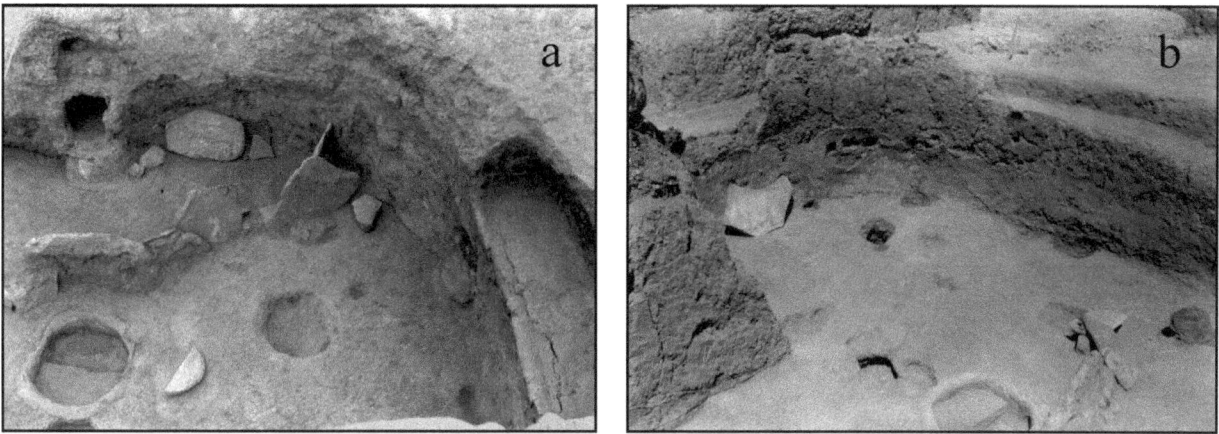

Plate I.5.3. Feature 2 (pithouse) floor at Bc 50 (29SJ 394). (a) Looking east at the southeast corner. Note shelf in top of wall at right. (b) Looking northwest. Note unexcavated balk to the left. Courtesy of the Maxwell Museum, University of New Mexico. Photographer unknown.

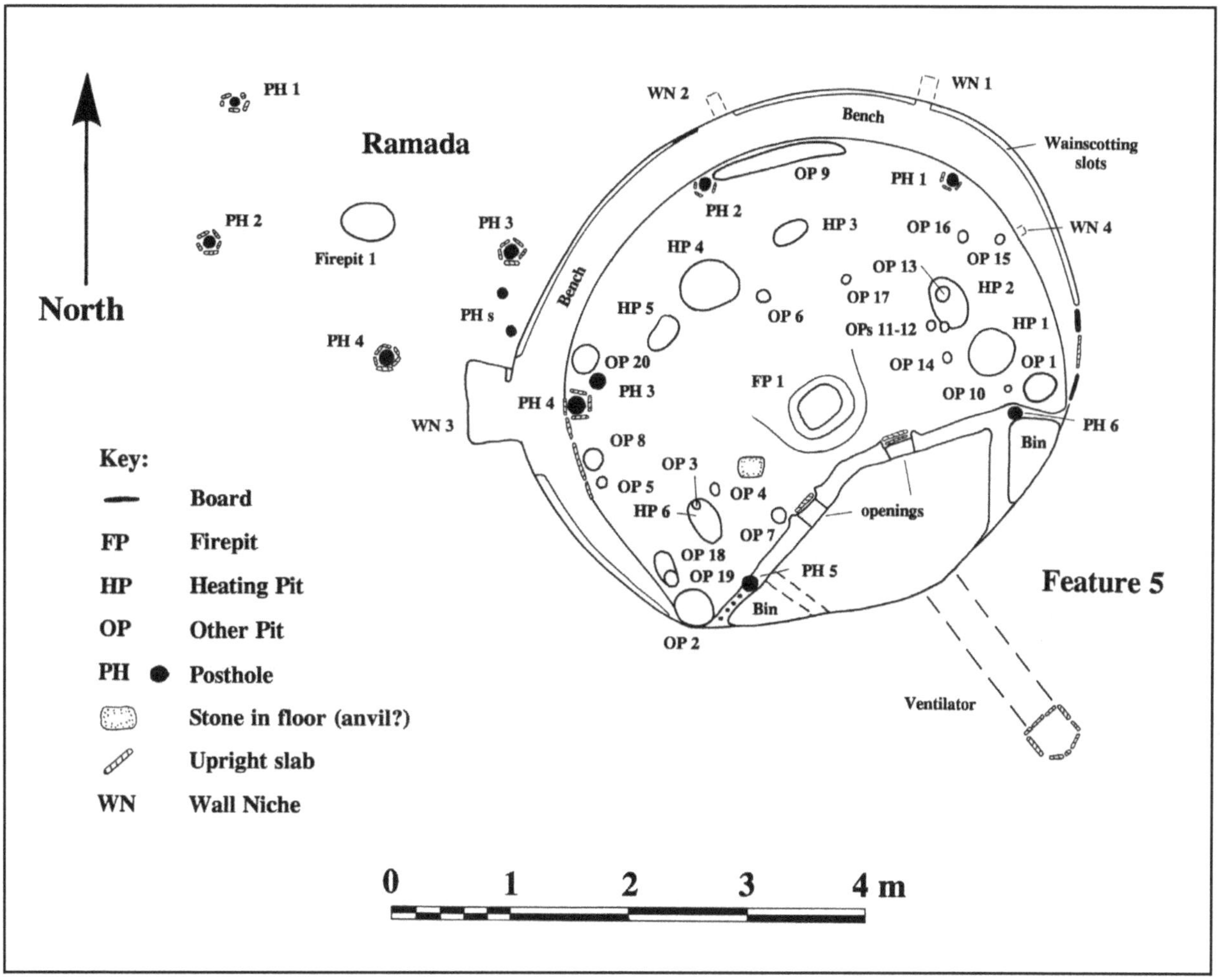

Figure I.5.3. Plan of the Feature 5 pithouse and ramada at Bc 50 (CHCU 65991). See Table I.5.2 for feature data. Plan and scale are approximate. Original by Donovan Senter (1939).

could represent either Lino Gray or neckbanded vessels but was generally recovered during the UNM excavations from contexts without associated banded or corrugated sherds. Thus, Hawley believes that "Lino" Gray is the proper designation for all the plain gray body sherds found at the UNM sites. In contexts with a notable lack of banded or corrugated sherds, this assumption is probably correct. Therefore, pre-A.D. 875 deposits certainly existed in some quantity at Bc 50 and 51. However, whether these deposits can be classified as Basketmaker III rather than A.D. 800s Pueblo I is not known given the information we have on these early collections. Most likely, the UNM excavators encountered both Basketmaker III and Pueblo I deposits, which are dominated by culinary vessels of Lino Gray and are difficult to separate without additional data. Use of this typology continued during the 1970s surveys in the early years of the Chaco Project when Lino Gray was considered solely Basketmaker III pottery. Subsequent excavations revealed that Lino Gray was common to both Basketmaker III and Pueblo I periods (see Volume II, Chapter 2).

Bc 50-51 Midden

Under the midden between Bc 50 and Bc 51, three shallow pithouses and several storage cists were exposed during excavations. Three of these features were designated with MOR numbers; presumably the "M" refers to a midden structure. MOR #3 (Figure I.5.4), in the northeast section of the midden, was about 50 cm deep and 500-x-524-cm (Kluckhohn 1939a: Figure 4; Truell 1986: Figure A.40); Red Mesa Black-on-white and Exuberant Corrugated sherds were found on the floor. The neck of a Lino Gray Fugitive Red jar on the floor, however, suggests an earlier use than the A.D. 900s indicated by other ceramics unless the earlier vessel was an heirloom. Hawley (1937a; 1937b: Figure 7) indicates that part of the nearby site midden contained Basketmaker III (overlain by Pueblo I) ceramics. The Lino Gray jar and the shallow house depth suggest a Basketmaker vintage for the structure.

MOR #3 contained a number of slab-lined bins and was overlaid by several others, one of which contained an extended burial. The latter cist, however, appears to have been a burial crypt rather than a storage cist reused for an inhumation (see photo in Kluckhohn and Reiter 1939: Plate 4). The slab-lined cists in the fill, 76 cm above the pithouse floor, were built after the pithouse was abandoned.

MOR #3 was found in 1936 and excavated by UNM students, mostly during a weekend in 1937, under Wesley Bliss's supervision (Clark 1938). The pit was unlined except for a thin layer of plaster over the surrounding deposits. A flexed burial was found at the flagstone entrance to the structure. The pithouse had few floor features aside from several storage bins: a central firepit, roof support postholes, a subfloor storage? pit, a possible sipapu, and possible ladder support holes. An unusual series of contiguous bins was built against the southwestern wall, but there was no evidence of the openings ever having been enclosed. No notes are available for these bins, but the map suggests that stone slabs once formed the side walls of each bin (leaving the troughs depicted in the map) with a possible small post at one end of each side wall adjacent to the opening. Floor artifacts (Figure I.5.4) are listed as a Lino Gray jar neck (#1) in a corner bin and a mano (#2) and trough metate (#3) on the floor.

Excavation at a second pithouse, MOR #1, was started in 1937 by Robert Lister, later Chief of the Chaco Center, and finished the following year by UNM students Anne Wyman (1938), Norma? Jones, and Majorie Flinn (1938). This odd structure (Figure I.5.4) was found in midden sections Di and Do but these designations do not relate to the published versions of the midden grids. Overall, the bi-lobed structure was about 175-x-500-cm, although no scale is given on the

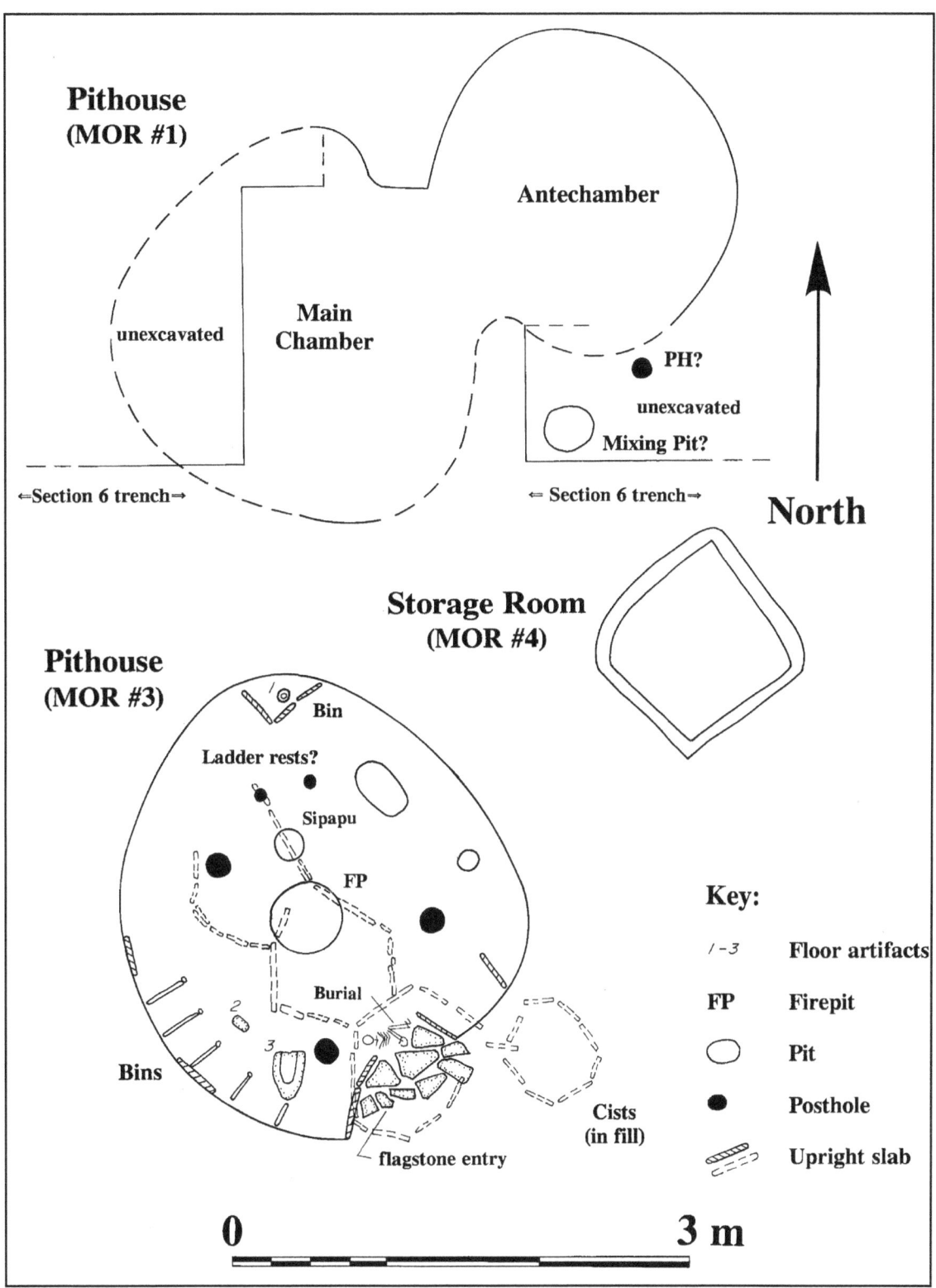

Figure I.5.4. Basketmaker III-Pueblo I structures (MOR#1, MOR #3, and MOR #4) uncovered in the midden between Bc 50 and Bc 51 in 1937–1938 by the University of New Mexico Field Schools (CHCU 65992). Floor artifacts in MOR #3 = 1 - Lino Gray jar neck, 2 - mano, 3 - metate. Maps/sketches by Donald Hastie, Wesley Bliss, and Anne Wyman. Scale and north arrow are approximate.

map. The measurements for the two lobes are 168-x-175-cm and 132-x-224-cm. The overall size was determined by reference to the six-foot-wide grid units, however, these grids were subdivided in 1937 into three-foot units (Hawley 1939:10), but the grid numbers could not be correlated with the notes. The two connected, circular chambers were filled with early Pueblo II trash.

The excavators believed that the structure consisted of an antechamber with a floor 15 cm above the level of the main chamber floor. That plan and the shallow 30-cm-depth indicate that the structure was probably a Basketmaker III house. About one-third of the main chamber was supposed to be excavated during the following season but no additional notes exist. Wyman (1938) describes a fireplace and suggests that it was in the main chamber but provides no additional details. No other floor features are mentioned. A small bone awl was found 13 cm above the floor; the floor yielded only "Lino" Gray sherds.

The small structure was apparently unlined or lined with a thin adobe plaster as no wall slabs were shown in the field drawing. Nevertheless, Kluckhohn and Reiter (1939: Map 1) show a structure, possibly slab-lined judging from the map symbols, at the west end of the long, east-west "coordinating" Trench 6 that connected Bc 50 and Bc 51. This position matches the pithouse grids (Wyman 1938) for MOR #1.

Finally, MOR #4 (Figure I.5.4), found somewhere in the midden, was briefly described by Donald Hastie (1938) as an adobe-lined room. The overall internal size of the room appears to have been about one meter square. The room yielded mostly "Lino Gray" sherds, but little additional information is known for the structure. The estimated location, although approximate, places MOR #4 directly over the storage cists at Turtle Back House (Pithouse A, see below), excavated a decade later. The adobe construction as well as the shape and size of MOR #4 suggest that Bin D at Turtle Back House was initially excavated as MOR #4 in 1938, but the poor notes makes the match uncertain. Gordon Vivian's notes on Turtle Back House, however, mention that the structure apparently had been cut by the 1938 trenching, which strongly indicates that MOR #4 was, indeed, one of the cists associated with the pithouse.

Kluckhohn (1939a:28) mentions two more structures with circular walls of slabs and small stones set in abundant mortar that were discovered late in the 1937 field season in Trench 6, almost under Kiva 4 at Bc 50. These features were exposed one and two meters below the surface, on and dug into the native gray clays that underlay the sites. Presumably they are part of the structure, perhaps Feature 2 or another unreported feature, found under Bc 50 (Hibben 1937b), which may date to late Pueblo I times (see above). The map shows them immediately over or next to Features 2 and 5, both pitstructures, which were completely excavated in 1939. Kelley (1939b) implies that the features were found along the Section 6 Trench, and that the northeastern quadrant of one was excavated by Helen Stevenson in 1938 that he later completed as Feature 2.

Turtle Back House (Pithouse A) - Bc 51

Another unusually shaped pithouse, Turtle Back House (Pithouse A; Figure I.5.5, Plates I.5.4-I.5.5), was uncovered near Bc 51 in 1949 just outside the house and west and southwest of Bc 51's Kiva 6 and Room 27. This odd, semisubterranean structure was about 76 cm deep. Its shallowness suggests Basketmaker origins, but few notes describe its setting or contents. Six large, slab-lined storage cists were attached to its outer slab-and-adobe-turtleback wall. These cists, also of slab and adobe construction, provided considerable storage space for the pithouse inhabitants. After excavation the pithouse was slathered in cement for stabilization and remained as a tourist exhibit until it was backfilled in about 1978 (Jim Trott, personal communication

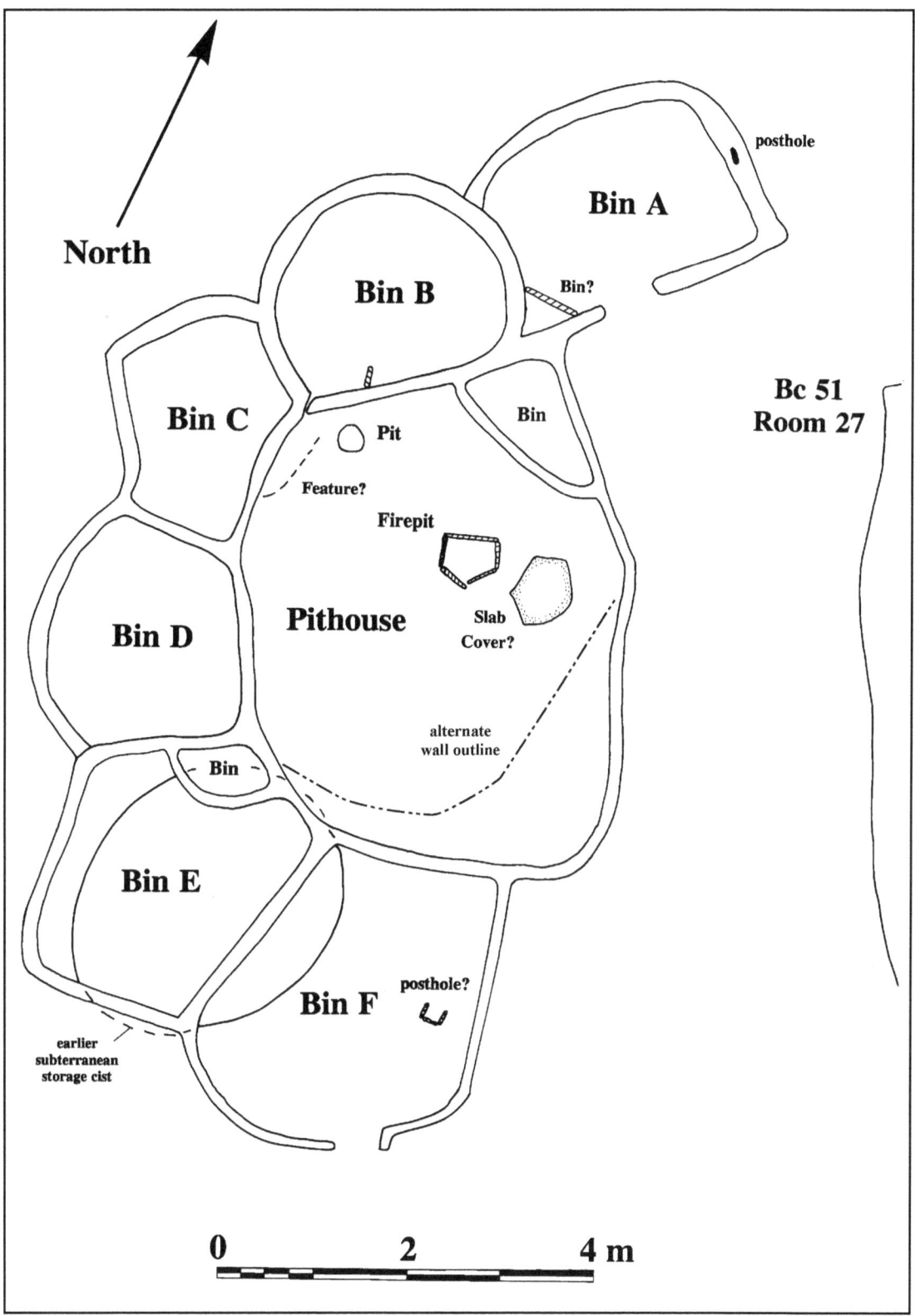

Figure I.5.5. Turtle Back House (Pithouse A) excavated in 1949 next to Bc 51 by the University of New Mexico Field School and exhibited as a tourist attraction until it was backfilled in 1978 (CHCU 65993). Composite of sketches by Raymond Rixey (see CHCU 85112). Scale is approximate.

Plate I.5.4. Excavations next to Bc 51 (29SJ 395) at Turtle Back House, a Pueblo I pithouse, in 1949 by the National Park Service. Looking south.

Plate I.5.5. Turtle Back House. (a) A Pueblo I pithouse with attached storage cists next to Bc 51 (upper left). Looking southeast. (b) Note firepit in the living room. Walls are of upright slabs and adobe, capped by Park Service cement turtlebacks. Photographs by R. Gordon Vivian (?) in 1949 (CCNHP collections, slides 19.1.01 and 19.1.11).

2003). Although scaled individual sketches of the pithouses and cists were drawn by Raymond Rixey in 1949, they do not fit together and must be considered only approximate renderings. Rixey made two drawings of the pithouse, which vary somewhat in general outline. Figure I.5.5 brings these disparate drawings together. This map compares favorably with Gordon Vivian's 1952 map (Vivian Archives 1033; CHCU 55199) except for the bin location of Cist E, which Vivian shows among Bins D-F and the pithouse.

Overall, the pithouse was 396 cm east-west by 488 cm north-south (Rixey 1949) and contained a slab-lined firepit and one other unidentified floor feature, probably a floor pit, and an odd feature in the corner not identified in the original drawing. A large slab, perhaps used to cover the firepit, was found on the floor next to the firepit. Two small pantries (bins) were also built into the pithouse wall and one of the cists.

Ceramics from the pithouse and bins were mostly "Basketmaker" (meaning "Lino" Gray), with "much Fugitive Red and Abajo Black-on-red." There is some confusion regarding the three vessels recovered from the pithouse. Vivian (1950) reports them as having been collected from the pithouse floor proper, whereas Rixey (1949) places them in the corner of Bin B. They are now in the NPS Chaco Collections and are listed from the northwestern corner of Bin A: a Lino Gray duck pot, an Abajo Red-on-orange bowl, and a partial bowl of White Mound Black-on-white with a fugitive red exterior (Plate I.5.6). This assemblage suggests last use of the structure in the late A.D. 700s or 800s. The bins were large (Table I.5.3) and probably served as storage facilities-the fact that they are contiguous suggests a Pueblo I architectural style despite the shallow, early Basketmaker III-like pithouse depth. A dog burial was recovered from Bin C. Under Bins E and F was another shallow structure, which appears to have been a circular, unlined storage cist similar to some of the Basketmaker ones reported at 29SJ 299 (Chapter 3).

Structures Adjacent to Casa Rinconada Bc 64A (29SJ 1200)

On the south slope of the ridge extending west from Casa Rinconada, another small, shallow pithouse with an antechamber and five nearly contiguous cists (Bc 64a; 29SJ 1200) to the east were excavated by Joe Maloney, an SAR student, in 1936 (Plate I.5.7; Vivian and Reiter 1960:9). There is no report for this work. All structures were lined with upright slabs. The pithouse was about 3 m across and 9 m long (including the antechamber). A second, unexcavated pithouse might exist just to the west near the toe of the ridge but there is no evidence for use of the ridge top, which extends west from the great kiva.

When the pithouse was examined during the 1972 survey, upright slabs still marked parts of the walls. By 2003, however, little was left of the structure and only a few wall slabs were evident on the west and south sides. The house is marked by two depressions in the sides of the slope along with a pile of sandstone blocks just downslope that appear to have been thrown out of the structure during the archaeological work. The blocks, which are comparable in size to late wall-building material, seem unlikely architectural remains for the pithouse, however.

The five cists (Figure I.5.6; Plate I.5.8) were located 47 m east of the pithouse and were about 1.2, 1.5, 1.6, 2.0, and 2.3 m in diameter; all five are located along the same contour just above the flats and across from the former UNM Research Station student hogans. The single architectural unit formed by the contiguous cists suggests early Pueblo I construction, before storage facilities became more formalized with the advent of surface rooms at about A.D. 800. A few upright slabs downhill from the cists indicate the presence of a buried living room. The amount of refuse at the site suggests habitation use, which would suggest that a pithouse might be found further downslope to the south.

The architectural style of the room basal-

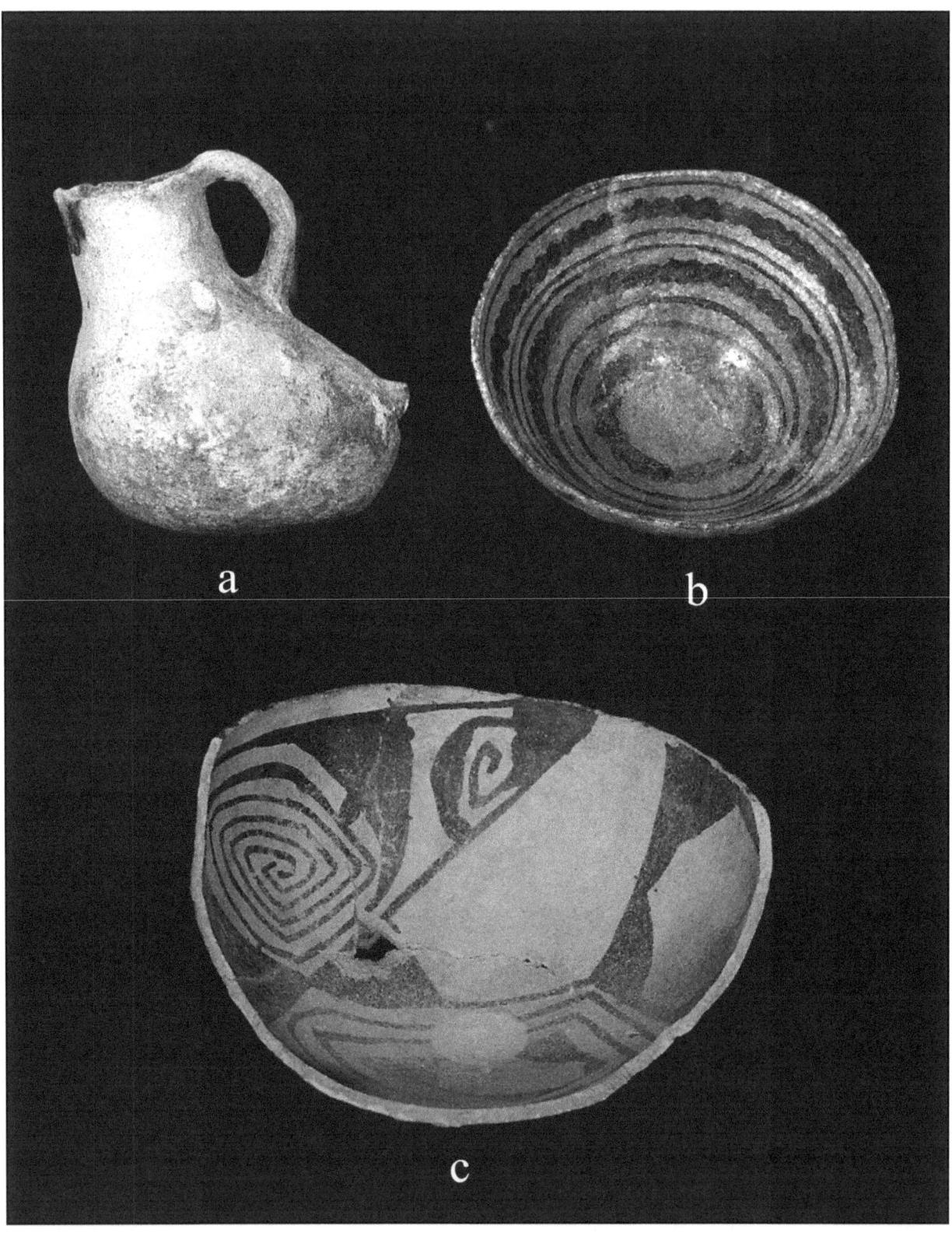

Plate I.5.6. Pottery from the floor of Turtle Back House (Pithouse A), Bin A. (a) Lino Gray duckpot, (b) Abajo Red-on-orange bowl, (c) White Mound Black-on-white bowl fragment with fugitive red exterior (CHCU neg. 2612–2614).

Chapter 5: Other Excavations and Data Recovery   401

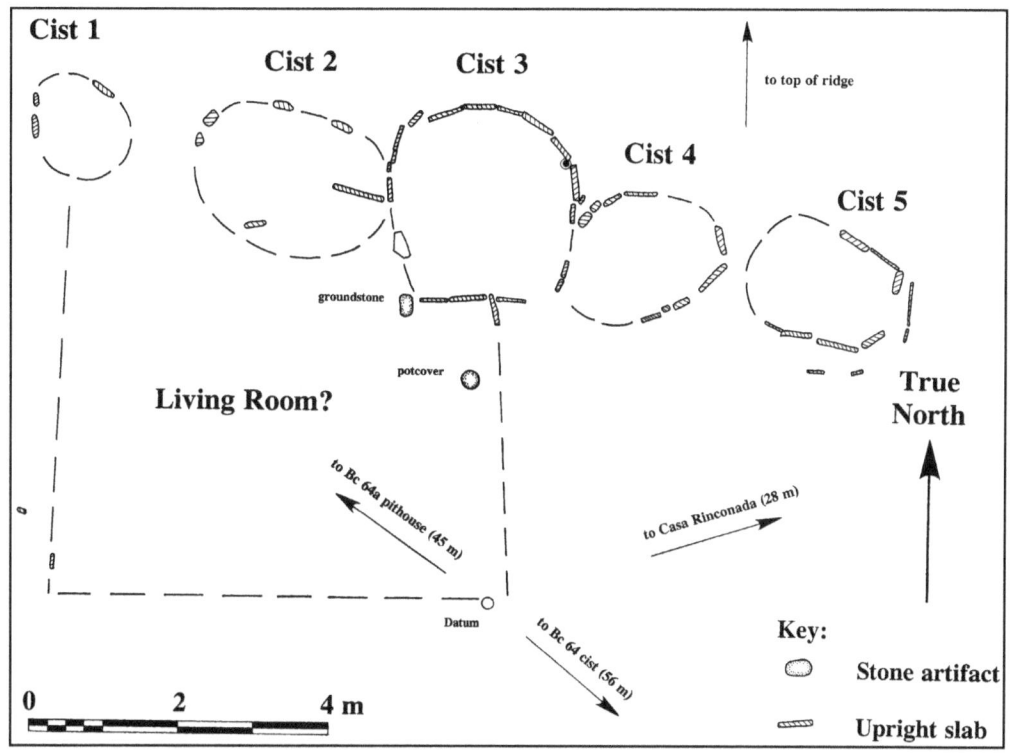

Figure I.5.6. 29SJ 1200, a Pueblo I component of five storage cists and probable living room (CHCU 65994). Mapped in 2003 by Tom Windes, Beth Bagwell, and G. B. Cornucopia. Cist numbers were assigned in 2004 by author and do not correspond to the "pithouse" labels for these same features in Table I.5.5.

Plate I.5.7. Joe Maloney excavates a slab-lined pithouse at Bc 64A (29SJ 1200) in 1936 near Casa Rinconada (CHCU neg. 78060).

Plate I.5.8. One of five slab-lined storage cists (Cist 3?) excavated by Joe Maloney in 1936 at Bc 64A (29SJ 1200) below Casa Rinconada. Note firepit in cist. (CCNHP collections, slide 19.1.03).

wall slabs is associated with the surprisingly tightly-dated associated ceramic assemblage (Table I.5.4). There are few late ceramics despite the close proximity of the A.D. 1000s Casa Rinconada on the ridge above and the plethora of student activities nearby in the 1930s and 1940s at the UNM Research Station, including sherd sorting and washing from the Bc-house excavations at Bc 50, 51, 57, 58, and 59.

Archive catalog sheets list several artifacts from the "Rinconada Pit Houses" (Anonymous 1936?), although caution must be exercised as all six features with artifacts (presumably the single pithouse and five cists mapped in Figure I.5.6) were designated as "pithouses." I assume that the excavated cists were simply given a pithouse label for convenience and slides in the park's collections taken in the 1950s or 1960s also listed the storage cists as pithouses. Oddly, the catalogued items (Table I.5.5) were limited to groundstone (manos and fragments [15], metate fragments [3], and "rubbing stones" [2]-presumably groundstone), bone awls (4), projectile point fragments (2), and a hammerstone (1). Manos were recovered from all six features and on the surface nearby, suggesting food preparation was a major activity in and around the features. When the five cists were mapped in December 2003, a complete sandstone pot cover (28-x-24-x-1-cm) was found in front of the largest cist along with a sandstone anvil (28-x-17-x-4-cm). There is no mention of other bulk materials, such as ceramics and chipped stone, although surely they were recovered in some numbers because both materials are common in the site area today.

Another slab lined cist (1-2 m in diameter, Bc 64), also excavated in 1936 by Maloney, was located 62 m east of the others in the saddle between two north-south ridges immediately south of Casa Rinconada just off the tourist trail. Overall, the ridge complex may contain both late Basketmaker III and early Pueblo I occupations.

Given the prominence of the ridge on which Casa Rinconada was placed, there could have been more pithouses and other evidence of early occupations on the ridge top before they were removed when Casa Rinconada was built in the late A.D. 1000s. An examination of the refuse covering the ridge slope directly east of the great kiva contains ceramics that are temporally linked with the construction and use of the kiva in the late A.D. 1000s and early 1100s: Gallup Black-on-white and Chaco-McElmo Black-on-white, White Mountain Redwares, and indented corrugated sherds (Table I.5.4). Half of the sherd sample (N = 302), however, indicates a much earlier use of the ridge before the great kiva was built: plain gray, Lino Gray, wide neckbanded, and a very few decorated sherds suggest use of the ridge in the A.D. 800s and, perhaps, into the 900s.

Recent cataloguing of the 1941-1942 field school materials from Bc 57, located on the ridge extending northeast from Casa Rinconada, identified a number of La Plata Black-on-white sherds from room fill and subfloor deposits that suggest Basketmaker III or Pueblo I occupation underneath the Pueblo II-III houses (Bc 57 and Bc 58). However, of the 5,014 ceramics from the excavations at Bc 59 in the rincon bottom nearby (McKenna 1981a), a mere 47 might date early, perhaps from the late A.D. 800s or more probably the early 900s. The paucity of evidence suggests that no Basketmaker or Pueblo I occupation occurred under the later houseblock at Bc 59 but that some early ceramics might be expected for the known A.D. 900s occupation buried within the site.

Judd's Pithouse No. 1

In 1920, Neil Judd excavated a shallow unburned pithouse "100 yards east of Casa Rinconada" (Judd 1924:400) in the midden of a small house. The direction and distance place this structure in the midden area below and southeast of Bc 58 or near Bc 50 and Bc 51, a prominent pair of small houses that must have seen much looting for burial plunder prior to being excavated by Judd's crew. Truell (1986:249), however, suggests its location was under Bc 53 (Roberts 1940), considerably farther to the east (380 m) from Casa Rinconada, but that site lacks the prominent midden mentioned by Judd.

Overall, the unlined circular structure was nearly a meter deep and 5.2 m in diameter (Judd 1924:401; Truell 1986: Figure A.41). Floor features were minimal, with a circular, adobe-lined firepit offset to the southeast (filled with greasewood fuel), three slab-lined bins built against the southeastern wall, and two niches carved into the southwestern wall slightly below floor level. No ventilator or entry was noted. Three shallow trough metates had been left on the floor along with a single mano. In addition, the bins yielded a La Plata Black-on-white bowl and "a number of small objects probably utilized in pottery making"—kaolin, red ocher, yellow clay, and a ball of sandstone (Judd 1924:402, 407). A clay pipe was also found on the floor between the firepit and bins.

Oddly, this structure does not seem to have been encountered during the field school sessions by the University of New Mexico, when all of the potential sites in the Rincon where this pithouse might have been located were excavated. From the architectural attributes of the pithouse (circular and shallow), it is surmised that the structure was probably of early Basketmaker III in age.

Although our knowledge of the early Puebloan occupation of the Casa Rinconada area is limited, the available evidence suggests that at least a scattering of early dwellings existed. They were probably not contemporary, but given the dearth of information, it is impossible to estimate the settlement density. The lack of architectural similarity among the various pithouses suggests a lack of cultural unity and that the houses were constructed by unrelated families or at different times. From what we know of early architecture in Chaco (see Chapters 3 and 4, this volume), the diversity in house types in the Rincon is quite surprising.

Surface evidence of pitstructures is lacking in areas where no later houses were built. We might presume that early occupations were limited primarily to the areas used later; there is little evidence for Basketmaker or early Pueblo occupations elsewhere in the rincon. The buried structures indicate that the rincon was a favored location for occupation in the earliest of puebloan times. Excavation data from the Bc sites in the rincon suggest, however, that a large influx of people arrived in the rincon by the late A.D. 800s, when several above-ground houses were built that endured in remodeled form, with some intermittently occupied into the A.D. 1200s.

Under Pueblo Bonito

In 1925, during exploratory trenching across Pueblo Bonito's West Court, two slab-lined pithouses were discovered 3.6 m below the west plaza surface, or about 2 m below the level of the 1925 canyon flats south of the site (Judd 1964:22, Figure 7). Considering their architecture and placement deep within the site, they must be either Basketmaker or early Pueblo I in age. In addition, a stone-topped, 41-cm-high, curving adobe room wall remnant was discovered 1.9 m below the floor in Bonito's Room 241 in the southeastern roomblock (Judd 1964:22, 288). This may have marked an early (Pueblo I?) roomblock not associated with the pithouses across the plazas to the west. Otherwise, the extent of early, pre-A.D. 860 occupations at Pueblo Bonito is unknown.

Judd's Pithouse 2 near Chetro Ketl

In 1922, during the excavations at Pueblo Bonito, Neil Judd (1924) discovered another pithouse buried in the alluvial flats of Chaco Canyon southeast about 670 m from Chetro Ketl. Much of this pithouse had collapsed into an arroyo channel, but the remainder was excavated (Plate I.5.9) and the resultant collections and

Plate I.5.9. Neil Judd's excavations at Pithouse 2 (29SJ 1678), in an arroyo bank east of Chetro Ketl Photograph by Neil M. Judd, 1922. (a) Before excavation; note posthole under floor at right. (b) Post excavation. Courtesy of the National Geographic Society (CHCU neg.15862).

notes housed at the Smithsonian Institution (see Glenn 1982). Remnants of this structure are still visible and were re-recorded in 1972 as 29SJ 1678, although little remains. More of the site is exposed in gully banks just to the west at 29SJ 1679.

Heavy rains during the summer of 1922 collapsed the Chaco Wash north bank, leaving half of Pithouse 2 exposed 3.7 m below the surface. Overall, the pithouse was about 1.9 m deep and 3.9 m in diameter with an encircling adobe bench 89 cm high and 66 cm wide (Judd 1924:403; Truell 1986: Figure A.38). The remaining bench revealed two roof support holes (for 17- and 21-cm-diameter posts) carved into the bench face and a series of smaller, 5-cm-diameter posts on top next to the wall as side supports (see Chapter 4). A mass of burned roofing had collapsed into the structure below the bench level.

Several slab-lined bins had been built against the southern wall (bench?) of the pithouse, and one contained charred corncobs and kernels. A rectangular depression, 38-x-56-x-9-cm deep, was found on the eastern side, while a slab-lined firepit (56 cm in diameter and 23 cm deep) had been built in the floor center. An undescribed posthole-like pit is shown next to the rectangular depression.

This pithouse provided the most abundant collection of pottery vessels of any Basketmaker or Pueblo I site excavated in Chaco Canyon. Many, if not all, the vessels were stored along the south wall but were crushed by the fallen roof deposits; 11 jars and 8 bowls were restored and are illustrated by Judd (1924: Plates 4-7) but eight others were restored later. The 27 vessels were reexamined by the author in 1999 and could be classified as an assemblage dominated by Kiatuthlanna Black-on-white (Judd 1924: Plate 4) and Kana'a (wide neck) Banded (clapboard style) pottery (Table I.5.6; Plate I.5.10). Two of the Kiatuthlanna vessels were large ollas (Judd 1924: Plate 4), while four other vessels were brought from the Chuska Mountains region (see King 2003, 2004).

This assemblage is exceedingly rare (see Volume II, Chapter 2), probably as a result of the lack of excavation in sites of this time period. Architecture and ceramics mark pithouse use in the A.D. 875-900 period (late Pueblo I) or later, although tree-ring samples from the burned roofing yielded one tentative date of A.D. 777r from a 5-cm-diameter pole (Table I.6.2). This was thought to be much too early for a construction date (Gordon Vivian in Bannister 1965:168), a conclusion with which I concur. A previously

Plate I.5.10. Chuskan neckbanded culinary jars recovered from Pithouse 2 (29SJ 1678) excavated by Neil Judd in 1922. (a) Gray Hills Banded (National Museum of Natural History [NMNH] 324814), (b) Tocito Gray (NMNH 324817), (c) Capt. Tom Corrugated (NMNH 324819), and d. Gray Hills Banded (NMNH 324837). Vessels now housed at the Smithsonian Institution. Photographs by Valerie King, 2004.

tree-ring dated sample of A.D. 720+x was deemed undatable upon reevaluation in 1968 by the tree-ring laboratory.

Other objects recovered from the pithouse include a pipe or two, basket fragments, a charred pair of sandals, two bone awls, a reworked shell bracelet fragment, two knives or scrapers, and several hammerstones, manos, and grinding stones along with three thin (presumably trough) metates. A skeleton of a young female lying on the floor suggests that the structure was ritually abandoned and burned (see Schlanger and Wilshusen 1993), one of very few such sites excavated thus far in Chaco Canyon.

Near Peñasco Blanco

In 1971, R. Gwinn Vivian (1970a, 1972, 1974) investigated water control systems in Chaco Canyon. This work included testing some features associated with canals that ran along the north and south sides of Chaco Canyon. In the floodplain below and to the east of Peñasco Blanco, several tests of floodgates and other small structures were conducted (see Vivian 1972, Feature A-23). The unpublished data from this research are curated in the Chaco Archives (CHCU 661). Adjacent to water control feature A-3, a shallow pithouse (A-23) was excavated by Robert Buettner and Jonathan Haas in May 1971.

According to Haas's field notes, the site was located on the top of the southernmost rise of a series of three hills of yellow gravel near the lowest benches of North Mesa. It is closest to 29SJ 1761 but has never been given a site number. The structure (Figure I.5.7) was a shallow, 50-cm-deep, partially slab-lined, oval pithouse, 250-x-290-cm in the same size category as those investigated at the nearby Basketmaker settlement of 29SJ 423 (Chapter 3) on top of the mesa south of Peñasco Blanco.

The pithouse was filled with natural deposits of sand and gravel, with occasional concentrations of large chunks of charcoal. The presence of charcoal suggested that the structure might have burned, although only a few burned spots were found on the floor. On the surface on the northern side of the house fill was a small, slab-lined hearth without cultural fill, obviously postdating use of the house.

The house was partially lined with slabs on the western and east-southeastern sides, which extended from the floor to the surface and were set at a slight outward angle. The remaining walls were apparently native earth embedded with some small stones. A possible entry was noted at the southeastern side of the house, where the house fill extended beyond a break in the house walls. The floor was plastered but had been broken through in places, making its definition difficult. Against the southeastern wall slabs was a circular, clay-lined firepit, 60-x-50-cm and 12 cm deep. No description of the firepit contents was provided. Next to the firepit and extending in front of the proposed entryway was a plastered, oval pit depression measuring 120-x-100-cm and reaching a maximum depth of 17 cm. A third pit near the center of the room was circular, 30-x-30-cm and 30 cm deep but no observations were made of its contents, presumably similar to the house fill. No other floor features were evident.

Few artifacts from the site were present. The remains of a partial grayware jar, probably Lino Gray, were recovered in the fill in the northwestern corner, and nine other sherds, two pieces of chipped stone, and a core came from the fill. Two late sherds were recovered from the fill: a Red Mesa or Gallup Black-on-white jar sherd and an indented corrugated sherd. Both are assumed to have been intrusive from later activities, perhaps during use of the surface hearth. No cultural material was found on the floor. Overall, the occupation of the house appears to have been a very short one in Basketmaker III times. Perhaps it served as a fieldhouse rather than for primary habitation.

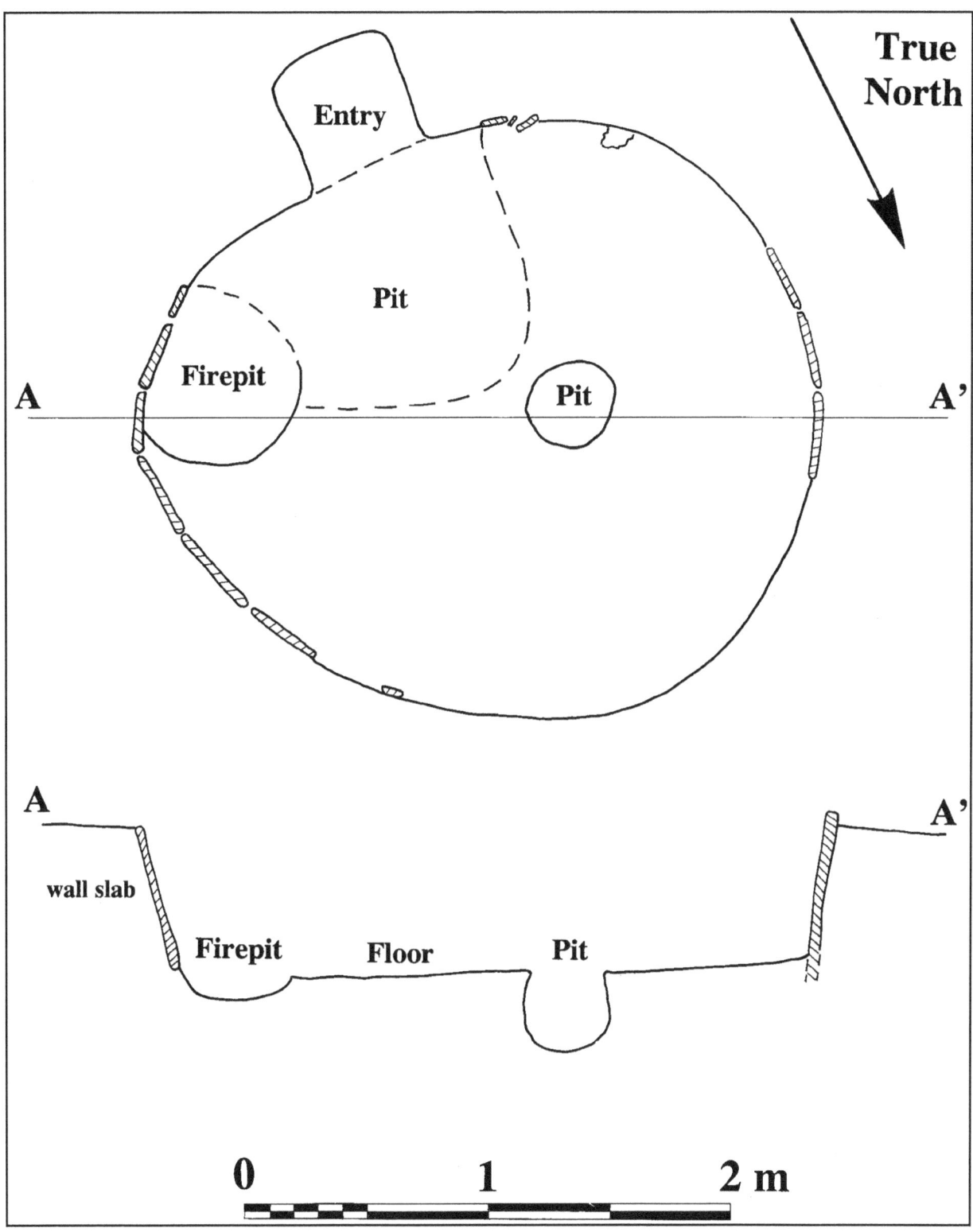

Figure I.5.7. Plan view of a small pithouse excavated by Robert Buettner in 1971 below Peñasco Blanco during water control research (CHCU 65995). Another unnumbered site is located on the north side of the Chaco Wash just above the floodplain next to Canal A-23 near 29SJ 1761 and the NPS west boundary fence.

Near Fajada Butte

Between the Visitors' Center and the park campground, a small, late pueblo site, Bc 236 (Bradley 1971), was excavated to salvage the remains before they pitched into the Chaco Wash. Under this Pueblo III structure, a solitary half pithouse was found (Bradley 1971: Figure 6; Truell 1986: Figure A.42) 120 cm below the surface; the rest had collapsed into the wash. This structure was slab-lined and 2 m in diameter. A narrow bench, encircling the house 74 cm above the floor and 10 cm wide, once held side poles that helped to support the upper roof framework. A 25-cm-diameter firepit, 8 cm deep, was found under the thick adobe floor plaster east of center. The only other floor feature was a small posthole-like hole, 10 cm in diameter and 15 cm deep, just east of the firepit.

The little cultural material found in the structure included a hand-full of sherds and bones (including dog or coyote and antelope), a turquoise bead fragment, and a mano. The sherds were dominated by Red Mesa Black-on-white and neckbanded utility ware, indicative of an A.D. 900s age, although the small amount of La Plata and Kana'a Black-on-white suggests that it might be as early as Pueblo I. An initial late Pueblo I occupancy appears common to many sites in the area.

In 2010, during the renovation of the campground sewage pump house and pipe system in the park maintenance area, a small Basketmaker III habitation site was discovered (Stewart 2010:11). It was assigned number 29SJ 519 to associate it with a nearby unrelated site from the 1972 inventory survey. In the early 1970s, the site was badly damaged during initial construction of the pump station and its pipelines but cultural resource personnel were not alerted that cultural material had been discovered at the time. Recent radiocarbon and archaeomagnetic samples place the occupation in the early A.D. 600s, and at least two pitstructures and other pits were located but more of the site remains under the concrete pad and the maintenance area asphalt pavement. Excavation notes and material from this site, including some evidence for on-site pottery production, is currently being analyzed and written up by Dabney Ford and Roger Moore (n.d.).

Shabik'eschee Village

Although Shabike'schee Village is noted primarily as a Basketmaker III settlement, Roberts (1929) excavated three pithouses that were architecturally Pueblo I in style (Houses C, X, and the protokiva). House C revealed the distinctive bench common to Pueblo I pithouses, which supported 24 leaner wall poles. The row of contiguous cists behind the pithouse probably represents associated storage facilities, typical of A.D. 700s storage-facility alignments. Roberts (1929:21) described this house as atypical and as a "protokiva," like his nearby "Protokiva" (Roberts 1929: Plate 7a), excavated across the draw to the west. The west protokiva reveals the early use of stone masonry around the ventilator tunnel, which eventually became prevalent in Chaco pitstructure construction.

Pithouses in the Exposed Chaco Wash Below Shabik'eschee Village

Below Shabik'eschee Village in the sides of the Chaco Wash are numerous indications of Basketmaker and Pueblo I occupations in the form of pithouses, cists, artifacts, and fallen house walls (Figure I.5.8). Some of these were noted by Amsden and Roberts (n.d.:39-42) 2 m deep during their reconnaissance of the Chaco area as well as by Judd (1927) and Roberts (1926-1927, 1929). Over the years, structures and other evidence of the early occupations have fallen into the wash during major periods of flooding when the banks were undercut and then collapsed. Right after one such collapse in the spring of 2000, the

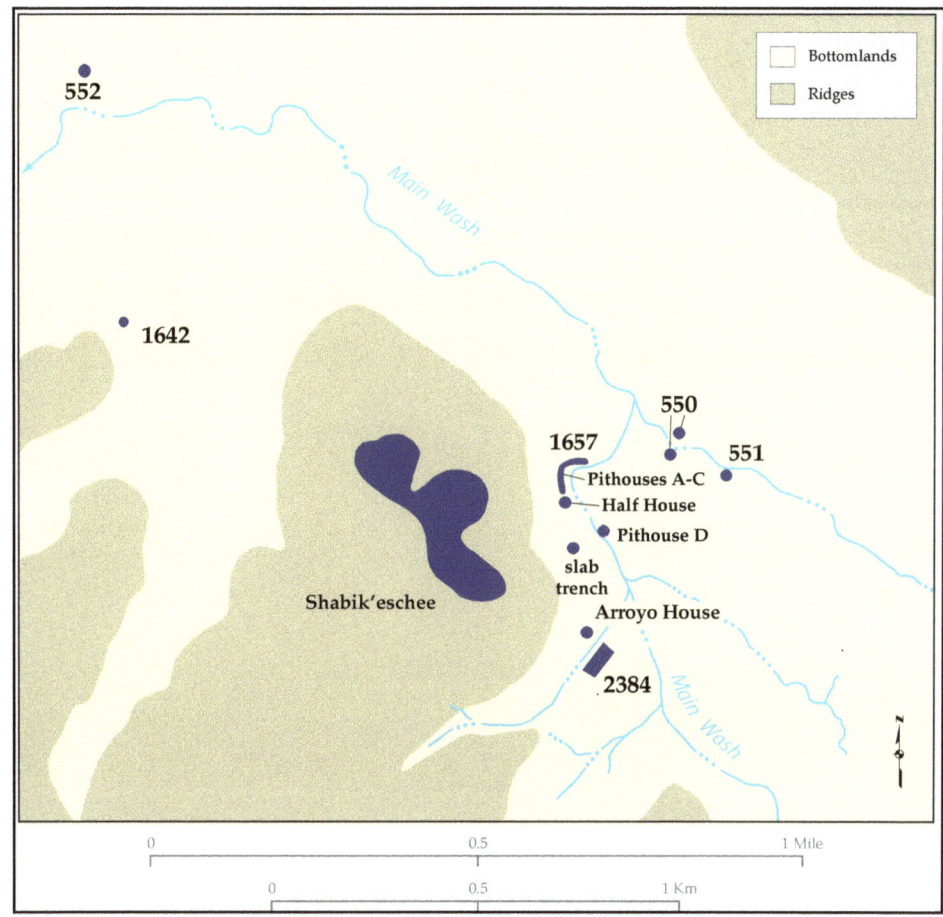

Figure I.5.8. Location of exposed pitstructures and other features in the banks of the Chaco Wash and its tributaries below the mesatop Shabik'eschee Village (dotted area). All site numbers are 29SJ. Original by Jamie Schubert and Tom Windes (CHUC 98331).

entire area was reexamined for structures (the last time it had been previously examined thoroughly was by the author's 1972 survey crew) and a map made of the visible remains (Figure I.5.9). Between 1972 and 2003, at least eight pithouses were evident in the sides of the main wash and its adjacent tributaries, which indicate that a large pithouse village once existed in the Chaco floodplain as well as at Shabik'eschee on the mesa above. This area was reinvestigated by Wills in about 2009 (Wills et al. 2012).

Structures exposed in the wash were found at various elevations (Table I.5.7), with the deepest, Half House, extending about 4.9 m below the top of the banks and of Pueblo I derivation. Another, Pithouse A, was 4.5 m below the flood plain and of Basketmaker III age. The shallowest (Pithouse C) was 3 m deep but probably of Pueblo I age. Of the exposed houses, only two were excavated and just one was reported: Half House (Adams 1951). Continual bank erosion further exposes houses of this settlement. Flooding of the wash during the 2000 to 2003 drought, for instance, has resulted in extensive loss of such features from bank collapse.

Half House

This little known pitstructure was excavated in 1947 by Adams (1951), eleven years after it was discovered exposed in the collapsed bank of the Chaco Wash directly below Shabik'eschee

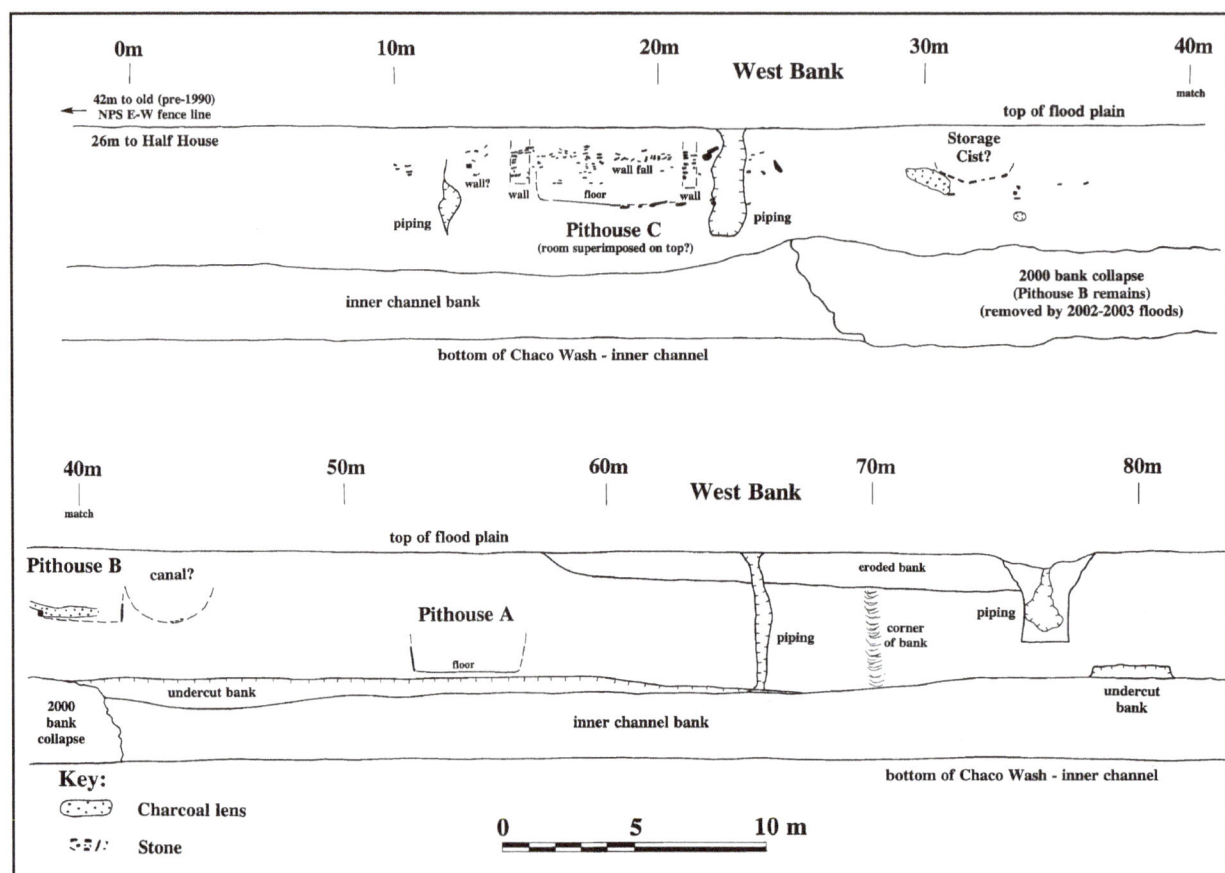

Figure I.5.9. Elevation views of Basketmaker III and Pueblo I structures (29SJ 1657) in the Chaco Wash west bank below Shabik'eschee Village (CHCU 98331). Mapped in June 2000 by Tom Windes, Eileen Bacha, Peg Kaiser, Cheryl Srnka, and Jamie Schubert.

Plate I.5.11. Excavations at Half House (part of 29SJ 1657), a Pueblo I pithouse buried in the canyon bottomlands below Shabik'eschee Village, in 1947. Photographs by Myrtle Vivian (Courtesy of R. Gwinn Vivian). The photo on the left is looking west and the photo on the right is looking south-southwest.

Village (Plate I.5.11). The structure floor was 4.9 m (16 feet; Adams 1951:275) below the present floodplain surface. The location of the pithouse was identified from photos in 2003 in a cut 10 m north of the old NPS boundary fence. Spalls and sherds are still embedded in the bank adjacent to the excavation site.

Half House was about 4 m in diameter, excavated less than 2.5 m into the original ground, and had filled naturally. One-third of the structure had fallen into the wash. There was no bench but a number of floor features were found, including a central slab-lined firepit and a post deflector. The latter was placed between the two slab-and-post wing walls that extended to two pits partly lined with small slab, the latter along with a third pit on the northern side, most certainly were for seating the main roof supports (a fourth had undoubtedly fallen into the wash). These were filled with crushed lignite, a commonly used material for seating posts in Chaco. A low clay ridge connected the firepit with the wing wall. The alignment of the firepit and deflector indicates that an entry or ventilator once existed just west of south, although it was not reported. A probable heating pit was located east of the firepit and a few other pits were scattered about the floor.

Ceramics (Table I.5.8) on and just above the floor indicate a Pueblo I assemblage of Lino Black-on-gray, La Plata Black-on-white, White Mound Black-on-white, and Kiatuthlanna Black-on-white, and Sanostee Black-on-orange. Three trough metates rested on the floor, two leaning against the north wall. In addition, three manos and a hammerstone, a core, four flakes, a polishing stone, and a hammerstone concretion were recovered from the floor. Evidently, the abandonment of the structure had been a leisurely one; someone had re-entered the structure at or after abandonment, leaving footprints (see a similar situation at 29SJ 724; Chapter 4).

A number of tree-ring specimens were obtained from the postoccupational fill of Half House (and one from the floor) and several were dated to between A.D. 644 and 748 (Bannister 1965:164). Reexamination in 1968 (Robinson et al. 1974) revealed that none could be redated (Table I.6.2). Architecture and ceramics indicate that the structure was of late Pueblo I origin. A firepit 67 cm below the pithouse floor is probably Basketmaker in origin.

Arroyo House

Near the mouth of a side arroyo, another pithouse was discovered by Roberts (1926-1927, 1929: Plate 8a, 70-71; Judd 1927:168, Figure 169) just upstream from Half House past the old 1970s east-west monument boundary. Judd (1964:21) later confused this pithouse with Half House. This trash-filled pithouse, about 7.9 m in diameter, was exposed in the arroyo bank, with the pithouse floor at 4.1 m below the modern surface (Plate I.5.12). It contained a central slab-lined firepit, 55 cm in diameter, with a deflector (a discarded metate) positioned south of the firepit. Two deep (> 50 cm) roof support postholes packed with lignite remained, but most of the dwelling had collapsed into the arroyo. Roberts identified it as a Basketmaker III house based on ceramics, although its slanting walls and depth suggest a late Basketmaker III or Pueblo I house. Roberts also recovered a bone needle from the floor.

Just across the wash from this pithouse, Roberts (1926-1927) discovered and tested a partially built greathouse (29SJ 2384; Figure I.5.10, Plate I.5.13; Roberts 1929: Plate 8a background), which shared an identical floor plan with the partially built greathouse recorded by Gordon Vivian (Vivian and Mathews 1965:81) in the park housing area and later remapped by the author. Gallup and Chaco-McElmo Black-on-white ceramics recovered by Roberts indicated that his "Small Pueblo" was built in the early A.D. 1100s. In 1983, during the Chaco Additions survey, Peter McKenna and Lisa Wills noted a pithouse under the north bank of the greathouse (south bank of the Chaco Wash) and an "earlier

Plate I.5.12. Arroyo House (right) and Roberts's Small House (left) in a side arroyo below Shabik'eschee Village. Arrows mark the exposed walls of Small House (29SJ 2384), an uncompleted late greathouse. Photograph by Neil M. Judd, 1926. Courtesy of the National Geographic Society (CHCU neg.38993).

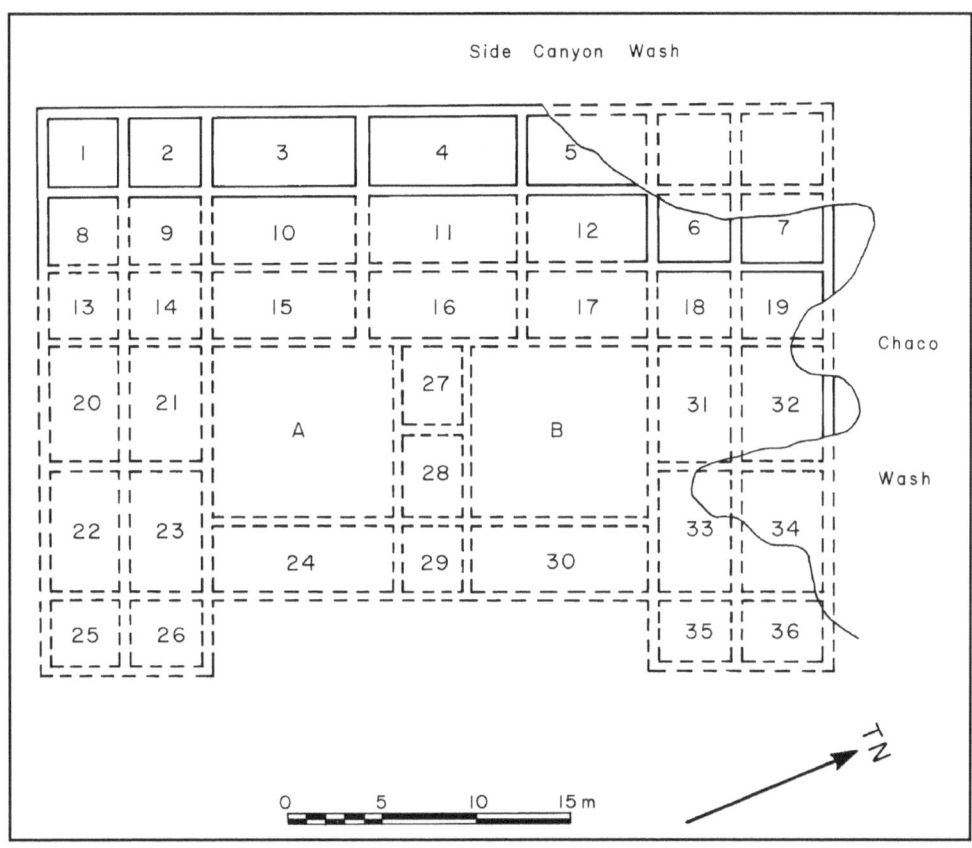

Figure I.5.10. Plan of a late unfinished greathouse (29SJ 2384) below Shabik'eschee Village cleared and tested by Frank H. H. Roberts, Jr., in 1926 (CHCU 98332). Original by Frank Roberts, Jr.

Plate I.5.13. Roberts's Small House site (29SJ 2384), an unfinished Chacoan greathouse, looking east at the exposed collapsed room walls in a side arroyo below Robert's Shabik'eschee Village. Photograph by Art Ireland, 1979.

site eroding out of arroyo bank at the south end of pueblo." In 2000, I noted another pithouse under the greathouse in the side arroyo and possibly a second one a bit further south. These may mark former pitstructures of Pueblo I or early Pueblo II age, but they have not been thoroughly documented and are difficult to relocate. Finally, a block masonry wall of early A.D. 1100s style was observed just to the south of 29SJ 2384 in the east arroyo bank, marking yet another architectural feature in the crowded flood plain.

When Amsden and Roberts excavated nearby Turkey House (29SJ 2385) in the side rincon immediately east of Shabik'eschee and south of 29SJ 2384, they discovered a slab-lined pitstructure underneath Room 4 (Amsden and Roberts n.d.). From their descriptions and the pottery recovered from it, the pitstructure probably dates to the late A.D. 800s but little more is known of this feature.

Houses Noted During the 1972 Survey and Later

During the 1972 inventory survey, John Schelberg, Earl Neller, Roger Huckins, and the author recorded a number of structures in the Chaco Wash exposed in the west bank between Arroyo House and 90 m past Half House, designating them as 29SJ 1657 (Figure I.5.8). Just downstream from Half House was an upright slab and adobe floor marking another pithouse (Figures I.5.9 and I.5.11). This structure (Pithouse A) fell into the wash after flooding in March or April 2003, leaving a pile of small, tabular stones; several large thin slabs (largest: 62-x-51-x-3-cm); numerous sherds, chipped stones, bones, and a few groundstone; and a large chunk of natural petrified wood. Much of this material was probably from the pithouse fill judging from the amount of cultural material protruding from the fill before the collapse. Although the ceramic assemblage in the fill is Pueblo I, the depth of the floor below the floodplain and the shallow, slab-lined pit may mark the pithouse as Basketmaker III in origin.

Just upstream from Pithouse A, a deep, U-shaped, alluvium-filled ditch or man-made canal about 2 m below the bank top, was beautifully exposed when the bank collapsed in 2003. This ditch was about 3.5 m across and about 2 m deep and filled with fine-grained, layered sandy sediments; it later was investigated by Wills et al. (2012:335).

Further upstream toward Half House, two concentrations of spalls and slabs marked at least two other structures (Pithouses B and C), both several meters below the top of the bank. A collapsed spall-and-adobe wall, of possible Pueblo I construction, had fallen into Pithouse C. Pithouse B collapsed into the wash in 2000. Just downstream from Half House, in about the Pithouse B-C location, Gwinn Vivian (personal communication 2004) in 1947 found a bone awl and many Lino Fugitive Red sherds, evidence of additional pithouse material in the arroyo channel walls.

Just 44 m beyond the old park boundary fence (a new boundary fence was built in 1998), the remains of a slab-lined trench (Figure I.5.12) were found across from Pithouse D in the south bank. Soil piping has exposed a feature lined with thin, upright, sandstone slabs about 2.2 m below the modern floodplain. This trench is at least 2.8 m long and a mere 20 cm wide. Although it might be a pitstructure ventilator trench, it seems much too narrow and angles downward. Its depth suggests a Pueblo I feature, but Gwinn Vivian (personal communication 2004) believes that it might be a later water control gate (see Wills et al. 2012:335, 337). Vivian found a similar slab-lined ditch near Kin Kletso that was 160 cm long and 24-27 cm wide.

In 1972, the author noted "cist" remains in this same locale, probably this very feature. In addition, a burned upright post, 8.3 cm in diameter, was noted in the same erosion pipe or very close, evidence of additional features. This

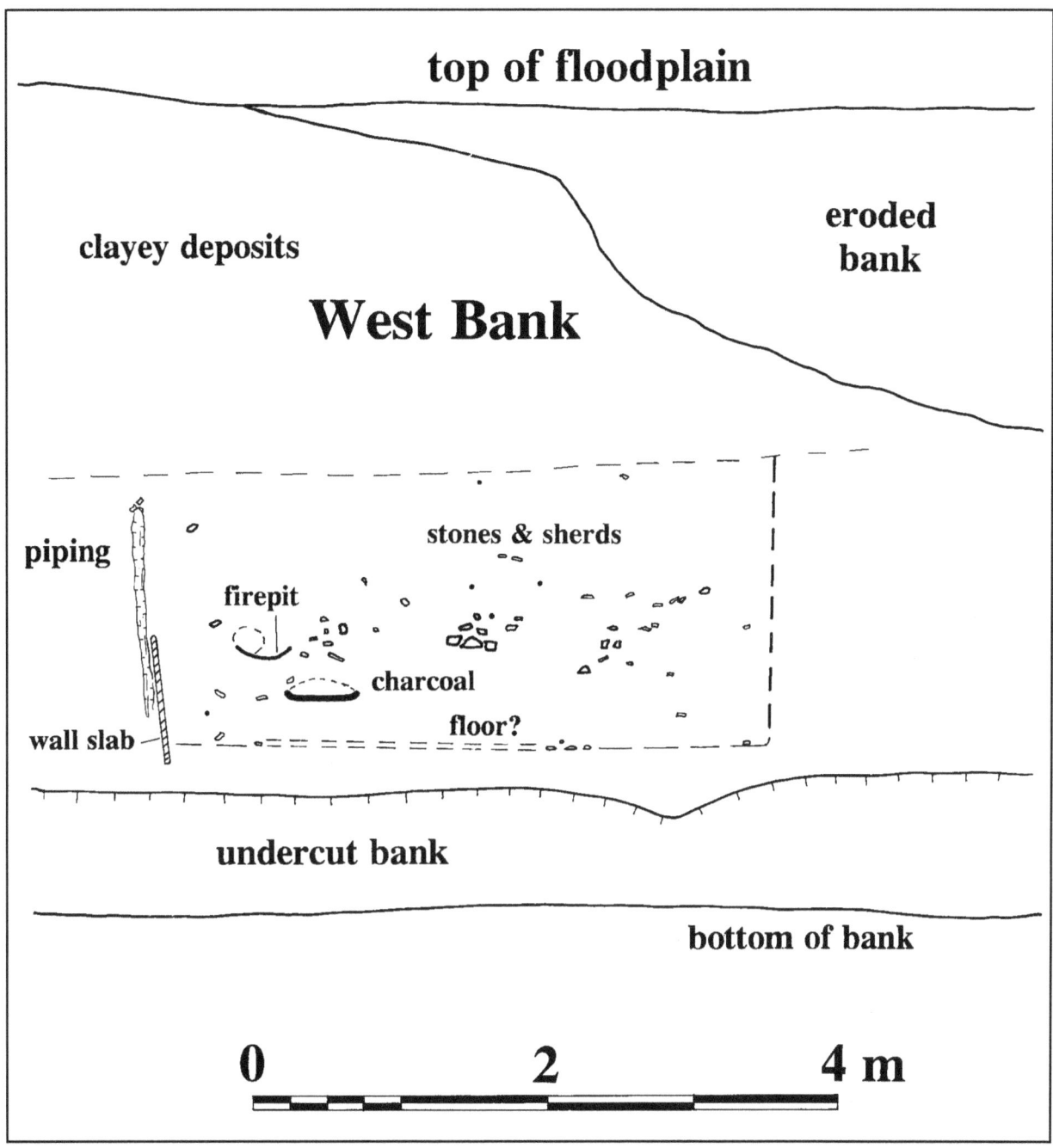

Figure I.5.11. Elevation view of Pithouse A (29SJ 1657) in the west bank of Chaco Wash below Shabik'eschee Village (CHCU 98333). This Basketmaker III pithouse collapsed into the wash in 2003. Mapped in June 2000 by Jamie Schubert and Peg Kaiser.

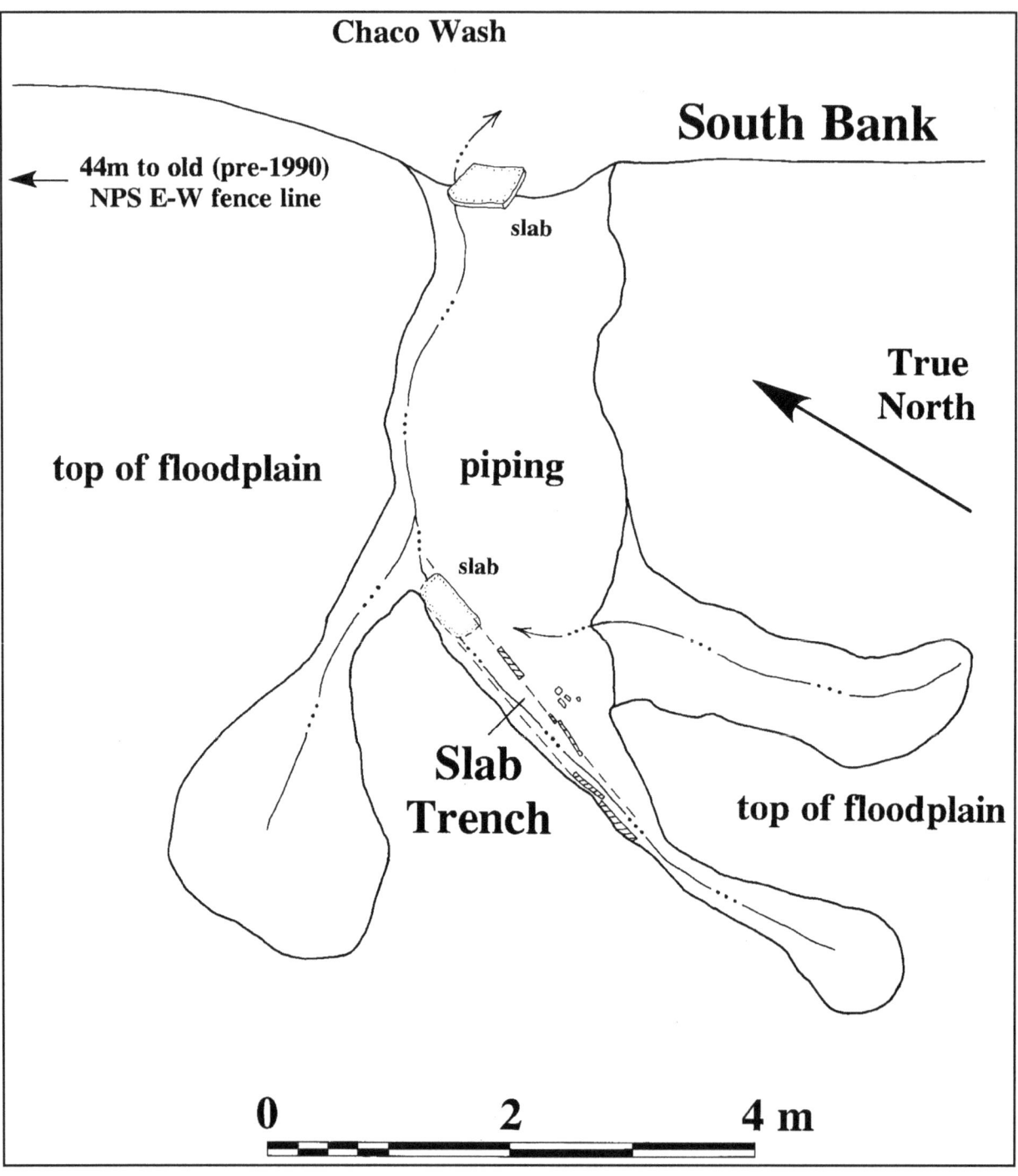

Figure I.5.12. Plan view (looking down) of a slab-lined trench (29SJ 1657) in the south bank of the Chaco Wash below Shabik'eschee Village (CHCU 98334). The trench is 220 cm below the present top of the floodplain. Extensive soil piping has dislodged some slabs. Structure is possibly associated with a buried pithouse. Mapped in June 2000 by Tom Windes.

piece was collected (CHCU 91427) but could not be dated by the tree-ring laboratory. It was ponderosa pine and was estimated to have been originally between 12 and 15 cm in diameter, possibly a pithouse roof support.

Also just outside the original park boundary (still fenced), in the north bank of Chaco Wash nearly across from Half House, Lynn Robbins first recorded Bc 373 in 1964, the pithouse documented here as Pithouse D (Figure I.5.13), and then collected artifacts found associated with it. Robbins noted two pithouse floors, one 4.7 m below the floodplain (7.6 m across with a firepit) and the other at about 3.5 m (4.3 m across and no firepit). The structure floor, still evident in 2000, is about 4.2 m below the top of the floodplain evidently the lower floor noted by Robbins. This structure was recorded again during the 1972 survey and again in about 1995, when the pithouse floor firepit and a number of floor artifacts fell into the wash when the bank collapsed.

Ceramics and parts of a Lino Gray Fugitive Red olla (Table I.5.8) were collected by various park archaeologists over several decades before the final collapse of the remaining pithouse. Because it was outside the park boundary at the time, Park Service salvage attempts could not be carried out. These collections were at times confused with those from nearby Half House, which was apparently used as a locational marker for the area when topographic quadrangle maps were lacking. A subsequent flood carried off these artifacts, including much of a Lino Gray Fugitive Red olla. Little remains of this structure now, although the firepit remains were still evident on the outer wash channel bank in 2000.

Nearly across from Pithouse A lies the mouth of a tributary that drains Sheep Camp Canyon 2.4 km upstream. This deeply incised arroyo also reveals early cultural material and structures. Gwinn Vivian (personal communication 2004) predicts that later water control features will be found along this drainage near Sheep Camp Canyon. The 1972 survey crew of Dave Barde, Milo McLeod, John Thrift, and Jack Bertram recorded several concentrations of spalls and slabs in the arroyo banks about 3 m below the surface at 29SJ 550 and 551 (Figure I.5.8). Neither site rebar stake has been relocated, so the location of these features is uncertain. One feature consisted of a horizontal 2.5-m-long row of large stones, initially thought to have been a water-control feature, exposed in the bank 20-30 m southwest of the 550 site rebar stake. A partially restorable Lino Gray Fugitive Red jar was recovered from 29SJ 551, where two possible pithouses and a hearth were noted in the south bank. In 1973, the newly collapsed north bank revealed a floor along with burned reeds, roofing material, and other artifacts.

A slab-lined cist (Figure I.5.14) was found in 2000 at 29SJ 550 in the north bank of Sheep Camp Canyon tributary near where it empties into the Chaco Wash. A scatter of burned and unburned stones aligned horizontally adjacent to the cist slabs marks the former use surface 3.3 m below the present-day floodplain. Directly across from this cist in the south bank, cultural material (burned spalls, a whiteware sherd, and a mano) was noted along a horizontal, linear, erosional non-conformity that lies 3.9 m below the surface.

Downstream from Pithouse A about 1 km, the Chaco Wash formerly meandered in a big loop close to the service road. In 1973, fresh bank collapse revealed a masonry room or two exposed in the north bank wall. By 2000, it was clear that the features indicated a compound Type I slab masonry-lined pitstructure (29SJ 552) that has lost about one-third to one-half of its architecture (Figures I.5.8 and I.5.15). A pile of slabs below the bank reveals where the outer part of Pitstructure A has collapsed into the wash. An erosion pipe just to the west exposes the stone from the outer walls. Since it was first noted in 1972, little deterioration has occurred up through 2000. The recent erosional pipe exposed an 87-cm-deep, 26-cm-diameter posthole filled with

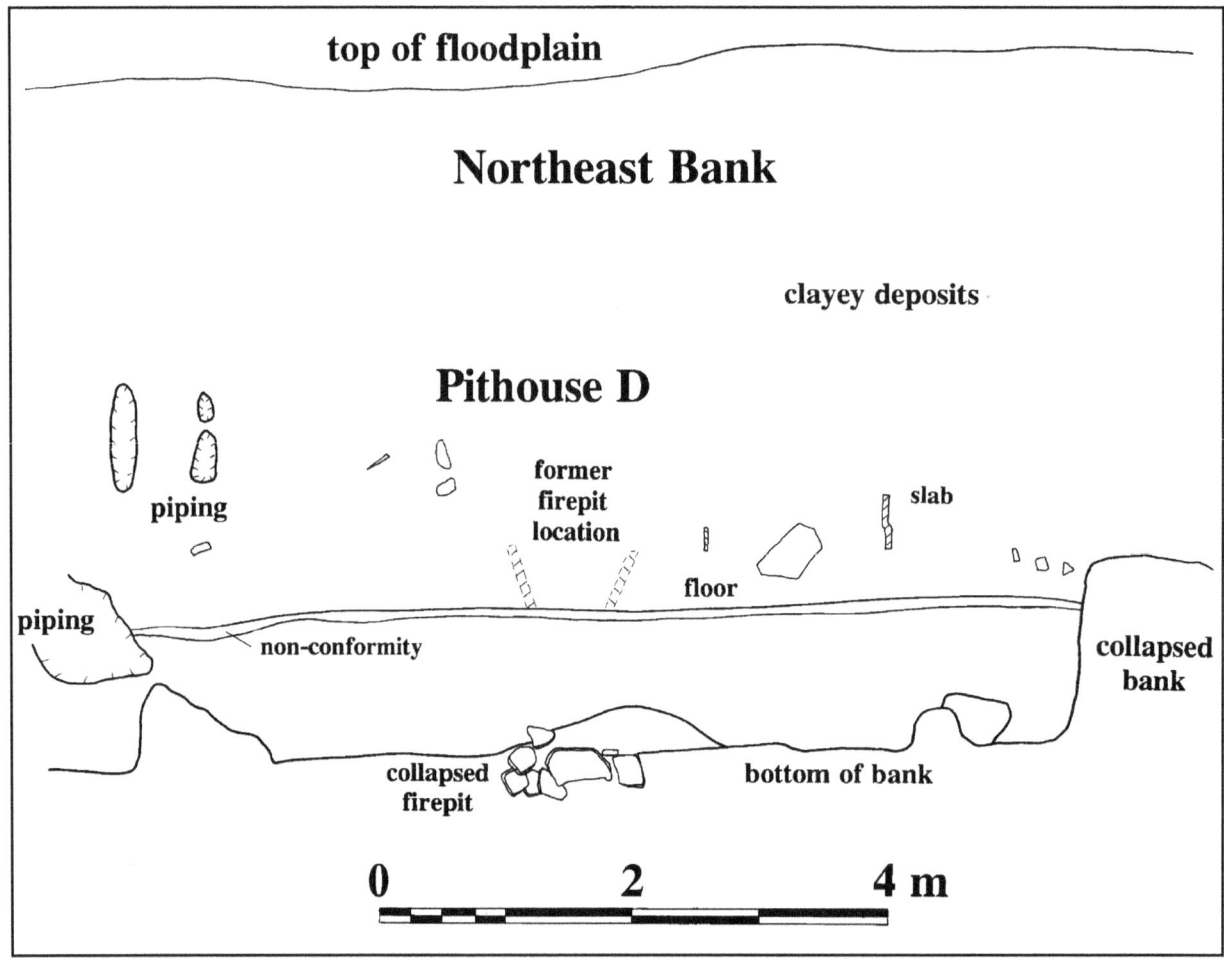

Figure I.5.13. Elevation view of Pithouse D remains (29SJ 1657) in the Chaco Wash north bank below Shabik'eschee Village (CHCU 98335). Most of the pithouse has collapsed into the wash during the past 40 years. Mapped in June 2000 by Cheryl Srnka and Eileen Bacha.

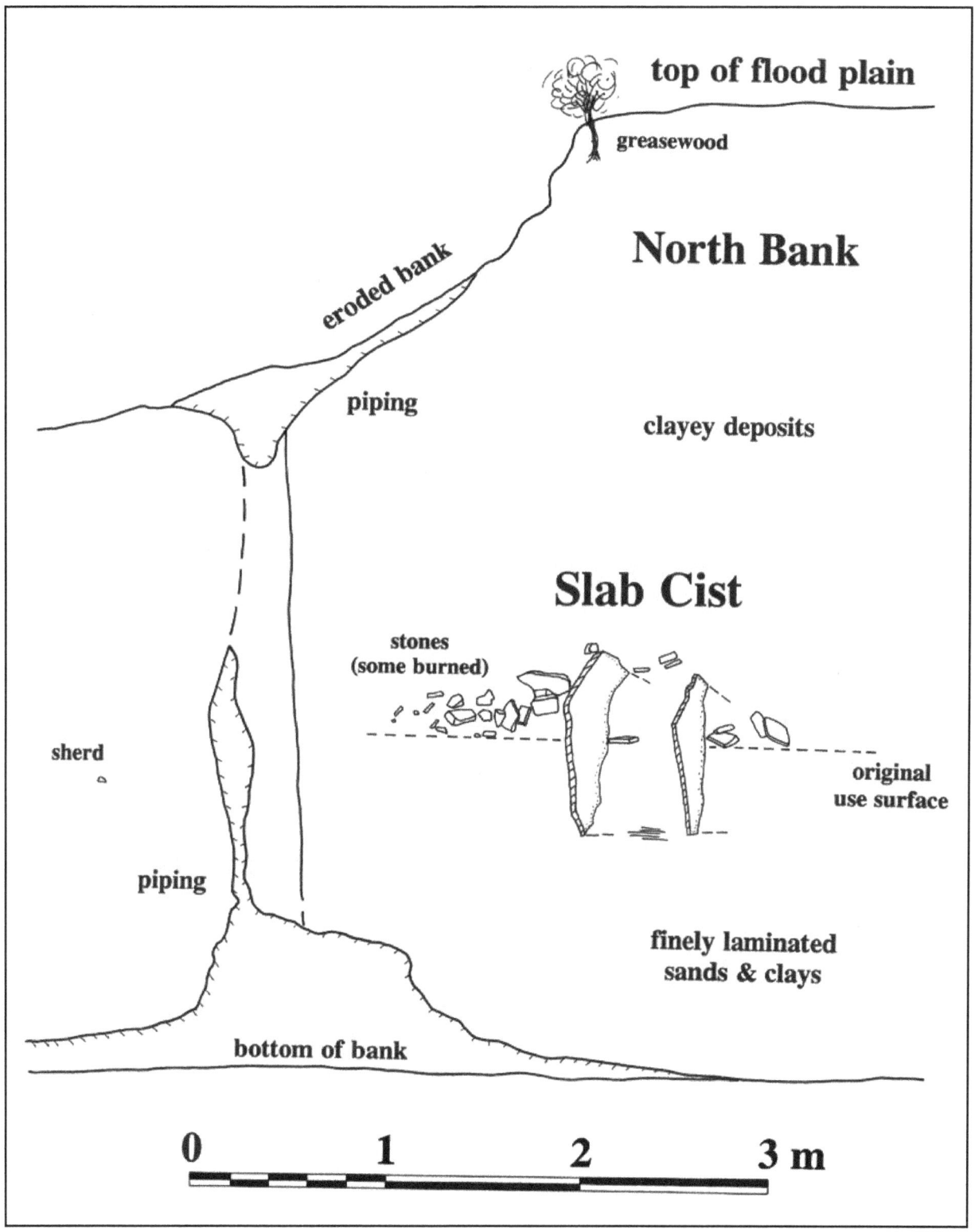

Figure I.5.14. Elevation view of a deeply buried Basketmaker III? slab-lined cist (29SJ 550) in the bank of Sheep Camp Canyon tributary near its confluence with the Chaco Wash below Shabik'eschee Village (CHCU 98336). Note probable original ground surface. Mapped in June 2000 by Tom Windes.

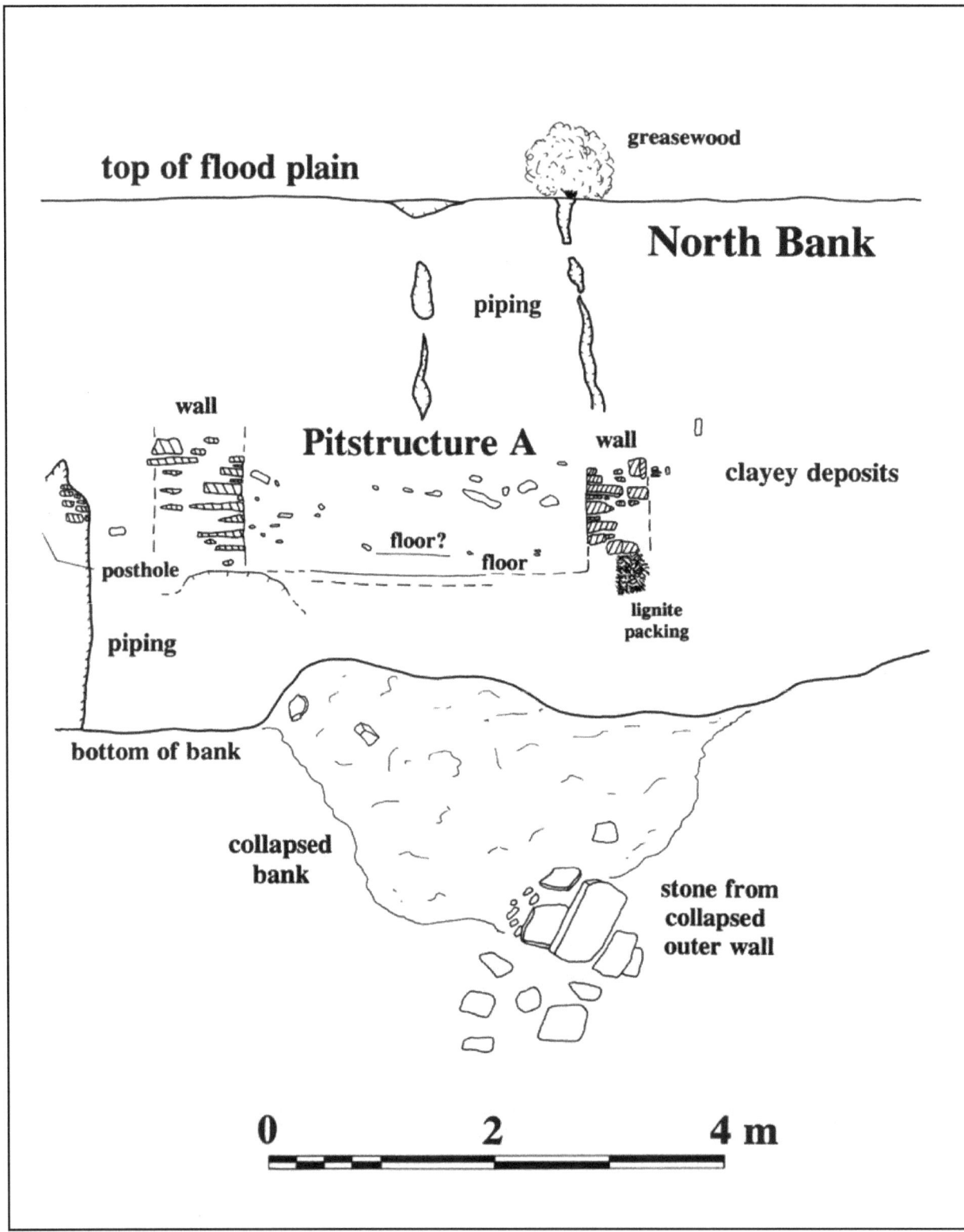

Figure I.5.15. Elevation view of a deeply buried pitstructure (29SJ 552) in the north bank of the Chaco Wash below and west of Shabik'eschee Village (CHCU 98337). Masonry structure is probable of late Pueblo I-early Pueblo II age. Mapped in June 2000 by Tom Windes.

crushed lignite under the masonry wall. This must mark one of the main roof supports, which was set next to the wall and angled down under the masonry. More crushed lignite was noted under the east wall foundation. The architecture of this structure resembles the Pueblo I architecture of the Protokiva at nearby Shabik'eschee (Roberts 1929:62-68). These architectural details suggest either Pueblo I or early Pueblo II construction. The depth of the floor (3.4 m) and the wall tops between 2.4 and 2.5 m below the floodplain suggest its construction is earlier than early Pueblo II times. The only artifacts recovered from the site were two plain gray body sherds.

About 8 m west in the same bank is a tall, vertical erosion pipe that contains evidence of another pitstructure: burned sandy flooring, stacked stones, and a lignite-filled pit, which is a probable posthole. Two pieces of burned piñon were obtained from about 10 cm above the burned floor, but neither could be tree-ring dated. Chip Wills (personal communication 2000) remembers several other pitstructures exposed in this area but none are now evident.

Steve Hall (1977) dated a hearth exposed in the Chaco Wash banks about 500 m upstream from the old boundary fence. This hearth was 4.5 m below the floodplain and radiocarbon dated to about 1300 B.C. (I-7170; not calibrated), considerably earlier than the nearby structures at the same depth.

Summary of Shabik'eschee Area Features

Over the years a substantial number of pithouses (nine or more; Table I.5.7) and other features have been exposed in the Chaco Wash and its tributaries directly below Shabik'eschee Village. Regular monitoring of this area has not been conducted since the 1972 survey, and undoubtedly other structures have fallen into the wash or arroyos in the intervening years. Clearly a substantial Basketmaker III pithouse village lies buried in the Chaco flats that complemented the well-known village on the mesa above. In addition, some Pueblo I and early Pueblo II settlement is also apparent.

The 3-4 m depth of these early structures provides some clues to the wash setting. A tremendous amount of in-filling has occurred since these structures were inhabited. For these houses to have been built in the Chaco flood plain, the wash must have been incised or the inhabitants would have been at the mercy of potentially destructive yearly flooding. In addition, the water table must have been well below the pithouse floors, otherwise the inhabitants would have been faced with constant dampness on the floors and calving of the bases of the pithouse walls-conditions unsuitable for habitation. Because Pueblo I structures are evident higher in the banks, flooding and subsequent massive aggradation must have taken place here between the Basketmaker and Pueblo I occupations (see Dean 1996: Figure 3; Gumerman 1988).

In summary a deep water table was probably common during the Basketmaker occupation of the floodplain, making the floodplain unsuitable for farming (cf. Wills et al. 2012:335, 338). Judd's Pithouse 2 was also deeply buried near Chetro Ketl, suggesting that much of the canyon experienced considerable in-filling by the time of the late Pueblo II-Pueblo III period.

During the late Puebloan occupation, however, a few houses were built on top of the floodplain within the lower canyon, where they remain to this day. The Shabik'eschee area clearly was an important one, as two late great kivas were built nearby. One, 29SJ 1642, was built in the A.D. 900s or 1000s at the top of a small knoll in the flats just to the west of Shabik'eschee Village (Figure I.5.8). A small part of exposed masonry of small, tabular stone indicates construction occurred in the late 1000s. In addition to the A.D. 1000s ceramics, those from the late 800s and 900s are also common on the knoll's slopes. Without excavation, it is not possible to determine when the first kiva was built, but elsewhere great kivas commonly replaced earlier habitation structures. This may be the case here, too. The 1642 kiva depression was tested in 1970 by Gwinn Vivian (personal communication 2001), who exposed wall masonry in four test pits and calculated a kiva diameter of 17 m. One late sherd of Mesa Verde Black-on-white on the site suggests that a very late use or reuse of the site might have occurred.

Interestingly, the other great kiva (29SJ 2557) is located in the rincon south-southwest of 29SJ 2384 about 300 m to the south of Shabik'eschee (just off the Figure I.5.8 map), and is covered with late ceramics of Mesa Verde Black-on-white, indicative of very late construction and use. Few small house sites are in the vicinity, which indicates that the great kivas probably served a considerable stretch of the canyon beyond Shabik'eschee.

Lake Valley

In about 1979, the dirt road (State Road 371) connecting Crownpoint and Farmington was paved. The preparation for this work resulted in the excavation of several puebloan sites along the highway right-of-way. Because they are the closest excavations to Chaco Canyon and the work uncovered Basketmaker III and Pueblo I houses, this work is pertinent to the findings in Chaco Canyon.

Two reports were eventually published (Doleman 1979; Wiseman 1982b). These early sites provided supplementary data for archaeomagnetic studies (Chapter 6) and feature analyses (Chapter 7). None of the sites revealed extensive refuse and all must be considered of short occupation, perhaps even seasonal. In some cases, sites revealed discontinuous, multicomponent occupations. There was little or no evidence of burning in any of the early structures at these sites.

Doleman (1979) excavated two unburned Pueblo I house sites (LA 14704 and 14705) on the north bank overlooking the Chaco River adjacent to where the new highway bridge now crosses. A third unburned house (LA 14695) was excavated several miles to the south along the highway right-of-way near the Becenti Chapter House; this Basketmaker III house had a shallow, 70-cm-deep, rectangular main chamber with a three-quarters bench, and an attached antechamber. It was similar to those excavated at 29SJ 299 (Chapter 3) and produced a single tree-ring date of 464np - 625++vv (Tree-ring lab# CHA-15). An adult and a juvenile male had been placed in the corner bins in the pithouse at abandonment but neither burial was marked by violence.

Three noncontiguous storage cists were clustered nearby. Although the pithouses at the bridge site conform to the general Pueblo I hamlet architecture, dating to the A.D. 800s, there was a paucity of surface architecture. Scattered pitrooms and ramadas were found on the surface but not the classic contiguous arc of storage rooms seen in the Chaco Canyon examples at 29SJ 299 and 724 (Chapter 4) and in the Fajada Wash, South Fork areas.

Besides architectural data, one site, LA 14704, yielded a large vessel collection that helps to correlate ceramic time with architectural traits. This assemblage (N = 43 vessels) came predominantly from a surface room and the pithouse (Table I.5.6). The collection was mostly Lino Gray jars but included one Kana'a Neck Banded jar, one La Plata Black-on-white bowl, two White Mound Black-on-white bowls, a Crozier Black-on-white bowl, and one early Kiatuthlanna Black-on-white bowl. Of the collection, only two vessels were made in the Chuska tradition utilizing trachyte temper. Sherds from the same vessel types listed above were collected across the site together with Peña Black-on-white and a few redwares. Notably, of the 2,580 sherds recovered, only one was neck coiled of Kana'a Banded.

The collection is indicative of the A.D. 875-

900 period and is similar to Judd's Pithouse 2 vessel assemblage shown above in Table I.5.6. There is a large difference, however, in the ratio of service wares versus culinary wares. At LA 14704, the assemblage is overwhelmingly culinary jars, mostly sooted, whereas the Judd pithouse yielded a collection more balanced between service and culinary vessels. Although the difference may reflect permanent versus seasonal occupations, it may also be linked to the numbers or composition of the inhabitants as well as the type of abandonment. It is common for large numbers of culinary vessels to be left behind in pitstructures (e.g., McKenna 1984; Windes 1993; for those at 29SJ 299, see Chapter 3), as their replacement value must have been low. The discrepancy in service ware numbers, however, is perhaps indicative of different modes of abandonment (see Schlanger and Wilshusen 1993).

In 1978, Wiseman (1982b) excavated two early pithouse sites (LA 15844 and 15845) at Lake Valley on the lower bluffs adjacent to where the new bridge was constructed across the Chaco River. The Feature 10 pithouse at LA 15845 was 2 m deep and had a ventilator tunnel, marking it as an early Pueblo I structure. Three associated semisubterranean storage facilities were built as two units, which also suggest an A.D. 700s architectural style. There was no formal midden but refuse was scattered lightly around the site. An adult male skeleton found in the pithouse fill shows evidence of death from blunt-force trauma to the skull and penetration of the body by five arrows. This find suggests ritual closure of the pithouse upon its abandonment (e.g., Schlanger and Wilshusen 1993).

LA 15844 was a multicomponent site, including an early shallow pitstructure and an attached antechamber, characteristics of Basketmaker III construction. The main chamber was small, 2.3-x-2.4-m, which is typical of many Basketmaker III pithouses. Two nearby slab-lined storage features may be Pueblo I in age. Surface hearths were common.

The Lake Valley sample offers some contrasts with the sites excavated in Chaco Canyon, but overall they share similar architecture, artifact inventories, and discard behaviors common to the region in the A.D. 600s and 700s. It is noteworthy that all of the A.D. 600s and 700s/early A.D. 800s sites in both areas reflect short occupations by one or two families with little refuse discard, suggesting the transitory nature of settlement during this early period.

What contrasts sharply with the overall sample in Chaco Canyon and Lake Valley is the cluster of shallow pithouses in the Casa Rinconada area. They fail to follow the general architectural plans and sizes seen elsewhere in Chaco and among pithouses in the greater San Juan Basin. Unfortunately, it is difficult to understand these unusual structures in the greater context given the paucity and poor excavation notes.

Table I.5.1. Floor fill and Floor 1 materials from substructure Rooms 4 and 5 at Bc 50 (29SJ 394).

No.	Artifact Type	Lithic Material, Ceramic Ware, or Faunal Species	FS No.
Room 4			
1	Awl (7.0 x 1.9 cm)	Unknown species. Leg bone. In fill	-
2	Polishing stone (5.7 x 5.4 x 0.6 cm)	4000? (quartzite?). Circular, flat pebble? In fill	-
4	Polishing stone (2.5 x 2.2 x 0.3 cm)	4000? (quartzite?). Red stone. In fill	-
5	Polishing stone (7.6 x 4.5 x 3.2 cm)	4000? (quartzite?). 5 cm above floor	-
6	Polishing stone (5.7 x 4.5 x 0.6 cm)	4000? (quartzite?). Triangular shaped. Floor	-
7	Polishing stone (5.7 x 4.5 x 0.6 cm)	4000? (quartzite?). Chip broken off 1 end. Floor	-
8	Polishing stone (7.7 x 3.2 x 1.0 cm)	4000? (quartzite?). Chip broken off 1 end. Floor	-
9	Biscuit mano (8.9 x 3.8 x 5.1 cm)	2000 (sandstone). 23 cm above floor	-
10	Mano (19.1 x 11.4 x 0.7 cm)	2000 (sandstone). Edge flaking. Floor	-
Room 5			
1	Polishing stone (5.1 x 4.5 x 0.6 cm)	4000? (quartzite?). Thin, oval pebble. 8 cm above Floor 2	-
-	Polishing stone (5.1 x 3.8 x 1.3 cm)	4000? (quartzite?). Thin, oval white pebble. Fill	-
-	Mano (10.2 x 9.5 x 2.5 cm)	2000 (sandstone). Fill, 15 cm above Floor 1	-
-	Awl (10.2 x 2.5 x 1.0 cm)	Unknown species. Mammal rib. Spatula-shaped at one end. Fill	-
-	Awl (7.6 x 2.5 x 0.6 cm)	Unknown species. Spatula shaped. Fill	-
-	Projectile point (1.9 x 3.8 x 0.4 cm)	White chert? Side-notched. Fill	-
-	Awl (12.7 x 0.6 x 0.6 cm)	Unknown species. End missing. Fill	-
-	Bone tool (6.4 x 1.9 x 0.6 cm)	Unknown species. Hole through 1 end; opposite end missing. Fill	-
-	Burial (extended)	On lower floor (Floor 2)	-
-	Ceramic vessel (pitcher?)	Unclassified. Found with burial on Floor 2	-

Table I.5.2. List of features at Bc 50 (29SJ 394) in the substructure Feature 5 pithouse, the associated surface ramada, and of the adobe mixing basin.[a]

Feature	Length (cm)	Width (cm)	Height/ Depth (cm)	Est. Volume (liters)	Fill Type	Fill Period	Lining	Open/ Sealed	Comments
Pithouse (Feature 5)									
Firepit 1	58	43	?	?	?	?	L-S	?	Mouth = 2,003 cm^2. Base stone; adobe rim collar 18 cm wide
Heating Pit 1	53	53	10	17.6	20	Occ	U	?	Mouth = 2,206 cm^2
Heating Pit 2	36	36	10	8.1	20	Occ	U	?	Mouth = 1,018 cm^2
Heating Pit 3	41	25	5	3.4	?	?	?	?	Mouth = 855 cm^2
Heating Pit 4/FP	56	53	20	46.7	10, 25	Int?/Occ	U	?	Mouth = 2,333 cm^2
Heating Pit 5	41	25	5	3.4	?	?	?	?	Mouth = 855 cm^2
Heating Pit 6	48	33	10	12.9	10, 25	Int?/Occ	U	?	Mouth = 1,288 cm^2. Cut by OP 3
Other Pit 1	30	30	8	5.7	10	Int	?	?	
Other Pit 2	46	38	15	ca. 12.9	10	Int	L-P	?	
Other Pit 3	10	10	15	1.8	?	?	?	?	
Other Pit 4	15	15	?	?	10	Int	?	?	
Other Pit 5	17	17	5	1.1	?	?	?	?	
Other Pit 6 (sipapu)	12	12	?	?	?	?	?	?	
Other Pit 7	23	23	18	7.5	10	Int	?	?	
Other Pit 8	36	30	13	ca. 6.3	10	Int	?	?	
Other Pit 9	122	10	5	?	10	Int	L-P	?	
Other Pit 10	10	10	20?	1.6?	?	?	?	?	
Other Pit 11	10	10	25.4	2.0	?	?	?	?	Ladder rest?
Other Pit 12	10	10	10–25?	?	?	?	?	?	Ladder rest?
Other Pit 13	25	25	25	ca. 4.5	?	?	U	?	
Other Pit 14	13	13	10–25?	?	?	?	?	?	Ladder rest?
Other Pit 15	10	10	15	1.2	?	?	?	?	
Other Pit 16	18	18	10	1.1	?	?	?	?	
Other Pit 17	10	10	10	0.8	?	?	?	?	
Other Pit 18	38	18	13	?	10	Int	?	?	
Other Pit 19	15	15	20	3.5	10	Int	?	?	
Posthole 1	13	13	41	5.4	?	?	L-S	?	3 shims
Posthole 2	13	13	36	4.8	?	?	L-S	?	1 shim
Posthole 3	12	12	20	2.3	16	Occ	?	?	Auxiliary roof post (juniper)
Posthole 4	20	20	71?	22.3	16	Occ	L-S	?	3 shims. Juniper main roof post
Posthole 5	18	18	?	?	?	?	?	?	
Niche 1	10	10	20	1.6	?	?	?	O	Contained cache of 9 smooth pebbles and white stone pipe
Niche 2	10	10	20	1.6	?	?	?	O	
Niche 3	76–89	?	51	?	10	Int?	L-M?	?	Shell bracelet on floor
Niche 4	8±	8±	?	?	?	?	?	?	
Vent Shaft	38	38	152	2195	?	PO	L-M	?	
Vent Tunnel	183	30	30	?	?	PO	U	?	
Ramada									
Firepit	58	46	?	?	?	?	?	?	

Table I.5.2. List of features at Bc 50 (29SJ 394) in the substructure Feature 5 pithouse, the associated surface ramada, and of the adobe mixing basin.[a]

Feature	Length (cm)	Width (cm)	Height/ Depth (cm)	Est. Volume (liters)	Fill Type	Fill Period	Lining	Open/ Sealed	Comments
Posthole 1	30	25	?	?	19	Occ	L-S	O	Shims = 5?
Posthole 2	30	30	?	?	19?	Occ?	L-S	O	Shims = 5? Built into Bin wall
Posthole 3	30	30	61	431	19	Occ	L-S	O	Shims = 5? Populus sp (ablus?) post, 15 cm in diameter. Base stone
Posthole 5[b]	25	25	46	35.9	13	Occ	L-A/S	O	Shims = 6? Partly lined with turtlebacks
Posthole 6	18	18	?	?	?	?	?	?	
Adobe Mixing Basin	254	149	25	?	?	?	L-M	O	Whole trough metate 2 cm above bottom

[a] See Tables I.7.4 and I.7.5 for an explanation of the feature and attribute codes.
[b] There is no Posthole 4.

Table I.5.3. Features at Turtleback House (Pithouse A), Bc 51 (29SJ 395).

Feature	Length (cm)	Width (cm)	Height/ Depth (cm)	Area[a] (m²)	Est. Volume (liters)	Fill Type	Fill Period	Lining	Comments
Main Chamber	603	396	?	13.7, 17.0†	?	?	?	L-PS	
Corner bin	151±	89±	?	0.96±	?	?	?	L-PS	
Firepit 1	89	76	?	?	?	?	?	L-S	
Pit	28±	28±	?	0.06±	?	?	?	U?	
Bin A	244±	152	88	4.7	4136	?	?	L-PS	
Corner bin	51±	42±	?	0.11±	?	?	?	L-PS	
Bin B	216	195	82	4.2	3444	?	?	L-PS	4 vessels on floors
Bin C	195	168	61	3.4	2074	?	?	L-PS	
Bin D	241	183	58	4.2	2436	?	?	L-PS	
Bin E	229	183	70	5.3	3710	?	?	L-PS	
Corner bin	75±	53±	?	?	?	?	?	L-PS	
Subfloor cist	305±	251±	?	6.4±	?	?	?	U?/L-P?	
Bin F	305	274	76	7.4	5624	?	?	L-PS	

[a] Areas and volumes for features are approximate. Many features had very little information, and all original map scales were approximate. Estimated dimensions taken from map(s). Lining: L-PS = lined with plaster and upright slabs. U = unlined.
† Different floor areas reflect the two different map sizes for the main chamber.

Table I.5.4. Ceramics recovered during the 1947 excavations at Half House (29SJ 1657), the 2003/2004 surface tallies at Bc 64a (29SJ 1200), and from the Casa Rinconada (29SJ 386) refuse.

	Half House Provenience														
	Unknown		Layer 3		Layer 4-5a		Layer 5R1[a]				Layer 5R3		Layer 5b		Layer 5d[b]
Ceramic Type	N	Percent	N	Percent	N	Percent	N	Percent	N	Percent	N	Percent	N	Percent	N	Percent
CIBOLA CULINARY		[100]		[63]		[61]		[92]				[81]		[91]		[78]
Lino Gray	-	-	-	-	-	-	22	6			17[c]	11	17	11	5[d]	7
Plain gray	42	100	4	50	36	47	320$_{34}$	84			112$_{44}$	70	116$_{11}$	78	40	59
Wide neckbanded	-	-	1	13	7	9	6	2			-	-	-	-	8	12
Narrow neckbanded	-	-	-	-	3	4	1	T			-	-	2	1	-	-
CHUSKA CULINARY						[3]						[1]		[1]		
Bennett Gray	-	-	-	-	-	-	1	-			1	-	-	-	-	-
Plain gray	-	-	2	-	2	3	-	-			-	-	1	1	-	-
CIBOLA WHITEWARE				[13]		[14]		[3]				[18]		[7]		[16]
La Plata B/w	-	-	-	-	-	-	2	T			7[e]	4	2	1	6	9
Whitemound B/w	-	-	-	-	-	-	5	1			20	13	7	5	2	3
Kiatuthlanna B/w	-	-	1	13	2	3	2	T			1	1	2	1	-	-
Unclassified BMIII-PI B/w	-	-	-	-	3	4	-	-			-	-	-	-	-	-
Red Mesa B/w	-	-	-	-	5	7	2	T			-	-	-	-	-	-
Unclassified PI-PII B/w	-	-	-	-	1	1	-	-			-	-	-	-	3	4
Unclassified Whiteware	-	-	2	25	12	(16)	3	(1)			-	-	1	(1)	-	-
CHUSKA WHITEWARE																
Tunicha B/w	-	-	-	-	-	-	-	-			-	-	-	-	-	-
Tusayan Whiteware	-	-	-	-	-	-	-	-			-	-	-	-	-	-
Smudged Ware	-	-	-	-	-	-	11	(3)			-	-	-	-	-	-
SAN JUAN REDWARE						[4]		[2]				[1]		[1]		[4]
Bluff R/o / Abajo R/o	-	-	-	-	1	1	2	T			2	1	/1	1	3	4
Unclassified redware	-	-	-	-	2	3	4	1			-	-	-	-	-	-
CHUSKA REDWARE						[1]										[1]
Sanostee B/r	-	-	-	-	1	1	-	-			-	-	-	-	1	-
Totals	42	100	8	100	76	100	381	101			160	102	149	101	68	99

T = trace (less than 0.5 percent). [Ware percentages]; (Combined ware and type percentages). Subscripts denote numbers of Fugitive Red sherds.
[a] Excludes 2 fired coils of clay.
[b] Layer 5d is floor fill of wall and roofing adobe one foot above floor.
[c] Several rim and body fragments comprise a partially restorable Lino Fugitive red pitcher.
[d] 1 unfired punctate effigy fragment.
[e] 1 restorable La Plata B/w bowl.
[f] One partially restorable Lino Gray olla (56 pieces).
[g] Majority of rim and body sherds are from one or two partially restorable Fugitive Red Lino Gray ollas.

Table I.5.4. Ceramics recovered during the 1947 excavations at Half House (29SJ 1657), the 2003/2004 surface tallies at Bc 64a (29SJ 1200), and from the Casa Rinconada (29SJ 386) refuse, cont'd.

Ceramic Type	Half House Provenience									29SJ 1200				Casa Rinconada	
	Floor level		Floor Pit 1		Floor Pit 2		Totals		Cist Transect		East Transect	
	N	Percent	N	Percent	N	Percent	N	Percent	N	Percent	N	Percent
CIBOLA CULINARY		[35]		[100]		-		[86]		[88]		[61]
Lino Gray	-	-	9[f]	9	-	-	70	7	16	6	11	4
Plain gray	6[g]	35	88[9]	91	-	-	764	76	213	80	125	41
Wide neckbanded	-	-	-	-	-	-	22	2	4	1	4	1
Narrow neckbanded	-	-	-	-	-	-	6	1	2	1	5	2
Unclassified indented corrugated	-	-	-	-	-	-	-	-	4	2	39	13
CHUSKA CULINARY		-		-		-		[T]		[3]		[5]
Bennett Gray	-	-	-	-	-	-	2	T	4	2	-	-
Plain gray	-	-	-	-	-	-	3	T	-	-	8	3
Unclassified indented corrugated	-	-	-	-	-	-	-	-	4	2	8	3
CIBOLA WHITEWARE		[53]		-		-		[8]		[5]		[12]
La Plata B/w	2	12	-	-	-	-	19	2	3	1	-	-
White Mound B/w	4	24	-	-	-	-	38	4	2	1	-	-
Kiatuthlanna B/w	3	18	-	-	-	-	11	1	-	-	2	1
Unclassified BMIII-PI B/w	-	-	-	-	-	-	3	T	2	1	7	2
Red Mesa B/w	-	-	-	-	-	-	7	1	-	-	-	-
Unclassified PI-PII B/w	-	-	-	-	-	-	4	T	6	2	2	1
Puerco B/w	-	-	-	-	-	-	-	-	-	-	8	3
Gallup and Chaco B/w	-	-	-	-	-	-	-	-	-	-	6	2
Chaco-McElmo B/w	-	-	-	-	-	-	-	-	-	-	12	4
Unclassified PII-PIII B/w	-	-	-	-	-	-	-	-	-	-	-	-
UNCLASSIFIED WHITEWARE	1	(6)	-	-	-	-	19	(2)	9	(3)	55	(18)
CHUSKA WHITEWARE		-		-		-		[T]		-		[1]
Tunicha B/w	-	-	-	-	-	-	1	T	-	-	-	T
Unclassified BMIII-PI C/w	-	-	-	-	-	-	-	-	-	-	1	T
Unclassified M/w	-	-	-	-	-	-	-	-	-	-	2	1
Unclassified whiteware	-	-	-	-	-	-	-	-	-	-	1	T
TUSAYAN WHITEWARE		-		-		-		-		[T]		-
Lino B/g	-	-	-	-	-	-	-	-	1	T	-	-
SMUDGED WARE	1	(6)	-	-	-	-	12	(1)	-	-	-	-
San Juan Redware		-		-		[89]		[2]		-		[T]
Bluff B/o / Abajo R/o	-	-	-	-	-	-	6	1	-	-	-	-
Unclassified redware	-	-	-	-	8	89	17	2	-	-	1	T
WHITE MOUNTAIN REDWARE		-		-		[11]		[T]		-		(1)
Chuska Redware	-	-	-	-	1	11	3	T	-	-	2	-
Sanostee B/r	-	-	-	-	-	-	-	-	-	-	-	-
Totals	17	100	97	100	9	100	1007	99	266	99	302	98

Table I.5.5. Materials From Floor Fill and Floor in Pithouses and Cists, Bc 64a (29SJ 1200).[a]

No.[†]	Artifact Type	Lithic Material, Ceramic Ware, or Faunal Species	UNM FS No.
P 1			
	Projectile point (2.3-x-2.9-cm)	4000? (white quartz). 15 cm from north wall. Broken? A blade?	P-1-1
	Mano (11.4-x-8.2-x-3.8-cm)	2000 (sandstone). Biscuit mano? On floor, 15 cm from west wall and 46 cm from south wall	P-1-A
	Mano (21-x-12.7-x-3.5-cm)	2000 (sandstone). On floor near center	P-1-B
P 2			
	Awl (11.1-x-1.3-cm)	unknown mammal. On floor, northwest corner; 7.6 cm from north wall and 15.2 cm from west wall	P-2-1
	Projectile point (1.9+-x-1.3-cm)	chalcedony (gray to brown). 20 cm above floor	P-2-2
	Awl (9.5-x-1.2-cm)	unknown mammal. On floor, northeast of firepit	P-2-3
	Abrader (14.0-x-7.3-x-1.0-cm)	2000 (sandstone). In northeast corner near surface	P-2-C
	Mano (18.3-x-11.5-x-2.5-cm)	2000 (sandstone). 10 cm above floor; 7 cm from north wall and 25 cm from west wall	P-2-D
	Metate fragment (23.5+-x-7.8+-x 6.1-cm)	2000 (sandstone). 20 cm above floor, near door? in southeast corner	P-2-E
	Metate fragment (19.7+-x-19+-x-7-cm)	2000 (sandstone). On floor, north side of firepit	P-2-F
	Mano fragment (8.6+-x-10.8-x-2.9-cm)	2000 (sandstone). In backdirt	P-2-V
P 3			
	Mano (22.2-x-10.5-x-4.8-cm)	2000 (sandstone). 5 cm "down" (?); 91 cm from north wall and 122 cm from east wall	P-2-I
P 4			
	Hammerstone (8.9 x 8.3 x 5.7 cm)	Igneous. 91 cm "down" (?); 46 cm from south bench and 122 cm from west wall	P-4-J
	Mano fragment (10.5+ x 12.7 x 2.9 cm)	2000 (sandstone). 30 cm "down" (?); 30 cm from south wall and 91 cm from west wall	P-4-K
	Mano (20.6 x 10.4 x 2.5 cm)	2000 (sandstone). 30 cm "down" (?); in northwest corner: 10 cm from west wall and 8 cm from north wall. Coated in "fugitive" red paint	P-4-L
	Mano (16.4 x 11.4 x 3.2 cm)	2000 (sandstone). 45.5 cm "down" (?); 61 cm from north wall and 30 cm from east wall	P-4-M
	Mano fragment (8.5+ x 11.4 x 2.7 cm)	2000 (sandstone). On surface	P-4-N
	Mano (13 x 6 x 2.5 cm)	2000 (sandstone). On floor, leaning against north wall, 91 cm from west wall	P-4-O
	Mano fragment (20.9+? x 13.3 x 2.5 cm)	2000 (sandstone). On floor, 91 cm from west wall and 91 cm from north wall	P-4-P
	Metate (45.7 x 33 x 3.8 cm)	2000 (sandstone). 20 cm above floor. 61 cm from west wall and 30 cm from south bench	P-4-Q
P 5			
	Abrader (9.2 x 6.7 x 4.4 cm)	2000 (sandstone). 15 cm "down" (?); in south half	P-5-G
	Mano (19.6 x 12.1 x 3.2 cm)	2000 (sandstone). 8 cm above floor, 13 cm from north wall and 20 cm from south wall (error in wall measurements)	P-5-H
P 6			
	Awl (30 x 1.9 cm)	Unknown mammal. On floor, 15 cm from west wall and 46 cm from south wall	P-6-1
	Awl (6.0 x 1.0 cm)	Unknown animal. On floor, near center	P-6-2
	Mano (17.5 x 12.7 x 3.8 cm)	2000 (sandstone). On floor, near center	P-6-R
	Mano (12.1 x 10.8 x 3.5 cm)	2000 (sandstone). 3 cm below floor (between floors); in northeast corner	P-6-S
	Mano (17.1 x 7.3 x 2.9 cm)	2000 (sandstone). 3 cm below floor (between floors); in northeast corner	P-6-T
	Abrader (8.2 x 5.4 x 1.6 cm)	2000 (sandstone). 3 cm below floor (between floors); in northeast corner	P-6-U
Surface			
	Mano fragment (10.4+ x 10.1 x 2.2 cm)	2000 (sandstone). 91 cm west of P 4	S-A
	Mano fragment (15.2+ x 10.7 x 3.8 cm)	2000 (sandstone). 1097 cm east of P 3	S-B
	Metate fragment (36.8+? x 15.2+ x 5.1 cm)	2000 (sandstone). West of hollow, on hilltop	S-C
	Abrader (12.7 x 7.6 x 3.2 cm)	2000 (sandstone). 30 cm west of P 2	S-D
	Abrader (7.6 x 7.0 x 2.2 cm)	2000 (sandstone). 152 cm south of P 1	S-E

[a] Materials recovered by the University of New Mexico Field School, 1936. All measurements listed in catalog forms but converted from inches (Vivian Archives 2125 [Folder 2], Chaco Archives, National Park Service, Albuquerque, New Mexico).
[†] All proveniences listed as "P"; perhaps an abbreviation for "pit" or "pithouse," although most are undoubtedly storage cists. Because of reference to a bench and a firepit, P 2 and P 4 may be part of the sole pithouse excavated. Apparently bulk materials such as chipped stone, bones, and sherds were excluded from the catalog list.

Table I.5.6. Vessels Recovered from Judd's Pithouse No. 2 near Chetro Ketl in 1922 and Doleman's Lake Valley Site at LA 14704 in 1976.[a]

Type	Pithouse 2					LA 14704				
	Bowl	Jar	Ladle	Total	Percent	Bowl	Jar	Ladle	Total	Percent
Lino Gray	1	2		3	11.1		30		30	69.8
Lino Smudged							1		1	2.3
Bennett Gray							4		4	9.3
Chapin Gray							1		1	2.3
Kana'a Banded		1		1	3.7		1		1	2.3
Kana'a Banded (clapboard style)		5		5	18.3					
Tocito Gray (banded)		1		1	3.7					
Narrow neckbanded		1		1	3.7					
La Plata B/w	1			1	3.7	1			1	2.3
White Mound B/w	2	1		3	11.1	2			2	4.7
Crozier B/w			1	1	3.7	1			1	2.3
Kiatuthlanna B/w	2	3	2	7	25.9		1		1	2.3
Kiatuthlanna/early Red Mesa B/w		1		1	3.7					
early Red Mesa B/w		1		1	3.7					
BMIII-PI mineral painted	1			1	3.7					
brownware (painted)	1			1	3.7		1		1	2.3
Total	8	16	3	27	99.9	4	39	-	43	99.9
Percent	29.6	59.3	11.1	100.0		9.3	90.7	-	100.0	

[a] Pithouse 2 vessels housed at the National Museum of Natural History (Smithsonian Institution) under catalog numbers 324801–324811, 324814–324821, 324837. All appear to have been sand- or sherd-tempered except for six Chuskan ceramic-tradition vessels (Bennett, Tocito, and Crozier). Data on LA 14704 vessels from Doleman 1979:Table 19.

Table I.5.7. Structures Exposed Between 1972 and 2003 in the Chaco and the Sheep Camp Canyon Washes Below the Mesa-Top Part of Shabik'eschee Village (29SJ 1657).

Site (29SJ)	Structure	Depth of floor below flood-plain (cm)	Architectural Time	Ceramic Time[a]	Stratigraphic Time
550	cist and associated surface	335	BMIII-PII	unknown	late BMIII/PI
550	pithouse	ca. 400	unknown	PI/PII	BMIII?
551	pithouses (2?)	ca. 300	unknown	PI	PI
552	Pitstructure A	340	late PI/early PII	PI?	PI
1657	Arroyo House pithouse	410	unknown	BMIII (Roberts)	BMIII
1657	Half House pithouse	488	PI	PI	late BMIII/PI
1657	Pithouse A	450	BMIII	PI (fill)	BMIII
1657	Pithouse B	280	BMIII?	PII (fill)	PI
1657	room above Pithouse C	100	late PI/early PII	none	early PII
1657	Pithouse C	150	unknown	none	PI
1657	Pithouse D, upper floor	423	BMIII?	PI (fill)	BMIII
1657	Pithouse D, lower floor	489	BMIII?	PI (fill)	BMIII
1657	slab ditch	220	PI?	none	PI

[a] Ceramics from Pithouses A, B, and D are from bank collapse and are assumed to be primarily from fill above the pithouse floor.

Table I.5.8. Collapsed Bank Ceramics Retrieved from Pithouses (29SJ 1657) Exposed in the Chaco Wash Below the Mesa-Top Part of Shabik'eschee Village.

	Pithouse A fill		Pithouse B bank					Pithouse D	
	N	Percent	N	Percent	Fallen bank	Fill	Fl. 1 + 6"	N	Percent
Plain gray (coarse sand)	28	67	178[a]	62	41[b]	378[c]	7	426	53
Plain gray (trachyte)			2	1					
Plain gray/Fugitive Red			17	6	74[R1]	79[R1]	26[R1]	179	22
Lino Gray (rim/neck)	2	5	12	4	4	27	42[R1]	73	9
Lino Gray (Fugitive Red)							27[R1]	27	3
Kana'a Neckbanded	2	5	16	6					
Sheep Springs Neckbanded			3	1					
Tohatchi Neckbanded			4	1					
Rim fillet			1	T					
La Plata B/w			2	1	2			2	T
White Mound B/w	5	12	5	2	11[R1]	9	1	21	3
White Mound B/w with Fugitive Red exterior					1			1	T
Kiatuthlanna B/w			12	4			1	1	T
Kiatuthlanna B/w with Fugitive Red exterior					1	11[R1]		12	1
unclass. BMIII-PI B/w	2	5	2	1		3		3	T
Red Mesa B/w	1	2	6	2	1			1	T
Gallup B/w			1	T					
PII-PIII M/w			5	2					
Cibola Whiteware	1	2	19	7		10		10	1
Unclassified smudged			3	1	1	31[R2]		32	4
San Juan Redware	1	2				11		11	1
Abajo R/O						4		4	T
Totals	42	100	289	101	136	563	104	803	97
Approx. Date (A.D.):		850-875		875-925			875-925		

[a] 20 were sooted
[b] 28 were sooted
[c] 185 were sooted.
[R] Majority of sherds part of a partly restorable vessel. Number = number of restorable vessels. Probably all Fugitive Red vessels represent one or two ollas.
Pithouse A and B material catalogued as Accession 691; collected by Jeremy Moss and Tom Windes, 2000-2001.
Pithouse B material recovered from wash channel in April 2001.
Some Pithouse D material catalogued as C90181 under Bc373 (Accession 478) collected by Lynn Robbins in the 1960s. Matin Mayer collected the bulk of material from Pithouse D in May 1966 and 1967 (Catalog # 44163–44173).
Counts do not include small fragments and T = trace amounts (<0.5 percent).